2학기 전과정

적중100 plus

영어 **기출문제집**

중**3**

천재 | 이재영

Best Collection

구성과 특징

교과서의 주요 학습 내용을 중심으로 학습 영역별 특성에 맞춰 단계별로 다양한 학습 기회를 제공하여
단원별 학습능력 평가는 물론 중간 및 기말고사 시험 등에 완벽하게 대비할 수 있도록 내용을 구성

Words & Expressions

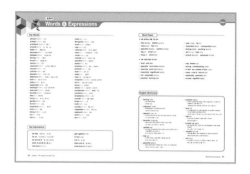

Step1	Key Words 단원별 핵심 단어 설명 및 풀이
	Key Expression 단원별 핵심 숙어 및 관용어 설명
	Word Power 반대 또는 비슷한 뜻 단어 배우기
	English Dictionary 영어로 배우는 영어 단어
Step2	실력평가 단원별 수시평가 대비 주관식, 객관식 문제풀이
Step3	서술형 대비 학업성취도 및 수행능력평가 대비 서술형 문제풀이

Conversation

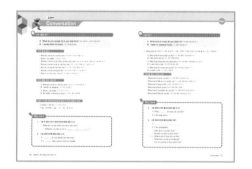

Step1	핵심 의사소통 소통에 필요한 주요 표현 방법 요약
	핵심 Check 기본적인 표현 방법 및 활용능력 확인
Step2	대화문 익히기 교과서 대화문 심층 분석 및 확인
Step3	교과서 확인학습 빈칸 채우기를 통한 문장 완성 능력 확인
Step4	기본평가 시험대비 기초 학습 능력 평가
Step5	실력평가 단원별 수시평가 대비 주관식, 객관식 문제풀이
Step6	서술형 대비 학업성취도 및 수행능력평가 대비 서술형 문제풀이

Grammar

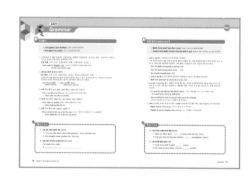

Step1	주요 문법 단원별 주요 문법 사항과 예문을 알기 쉽게 설명
	핵심 Check 기본 문법사항에 대한 이해 여부 확인
Step2	기본평가 시험대비 기초 학습 능력 평가
Step3	실력평가 단원별 수시평가 대비 주관식, 객관식 문제풀이
Step4	서술형 대비 학업성취도 및 수행능력평가 대비 서술형 문제풀이

Reading

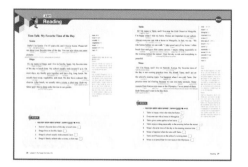

Step1	구문 분석 단원별로 제시된 문장에 대한 구문별 분석과 내용 설명
	확인문제 문장에 대한 기본적인 이해와 인지능력 확인
Step2	확인학습A 빈칸 채우기를 통한 문장 완성 능력 확인
Step3	확인학습B 제시된 우리말을 영어로 완성하여 작문 능력 키우기
Step4	실력평가 단원별 수시평가 대비 주관식, 객관식 문제풀이
Step5	서술형 대비 학업성취도 및 수행능력평가 대비 서술형 문제풀이
	교과서 구석구석 교과서에 나오는 기타 문장까지 완벽 학습

Composition

|영역별 핵심문제|
단어 및 어휘, 대화문, 문법, 독해 등 각 영역별 기출문제의 출제 유형을 분석하여 실전에 대비하고 연습할 수 있도록 문제를 배열

|단원별 예상문제|
기출문제를 분석한 후 새로운 시험 출제 경향을 더하여 새롭게 출제될 수 있는 문제를 포함하여 시험에 완벽하게 대비할 수 있도록 준비

|서술형 실전 및 창의사고력 문제|
학교 시험에서 점차 늘어나는 서술형 시험에 집중 대비하고 고득점을 취득하는데 만전을 기하기 위한 학습 코너

|단원별 모의고사|
영역별, 단계별 학습을 모두 마친 후 실전 연습을 위한 모의고사

on the textbook

교과서 파헤치기

- **단어Test1~3** 영어 단어 우리말 쓰기, 우리말을 영어 단어로 쓰기, 영영풀이에 해당하는 단어와 우리말 쓰기
- **대화문Test1~2** 대화문 빈칸 완성 및 전체 대화문 쓰기
- **본문Test1~5** 빈칸 완성, 우리말 쓰기, 문장 배열연습, 영어 작문하기 복습 등 단계별 반복 학습을 통해 교과서 지문에 대한 완벽한 습득
- **구석구석지문Test1~2** 지문 빈칸 완성 및 전문 영어로 쓰기

Lesson 5

Are You into Books?

교과서

Words & Expressions

Key Words

- **achieve**[ətʃíːv] 동 이루다, 얻다
- **arrest**[ərést] 동 체포하다
- **arrival**[əráivəl] 명 도착
- **author**[ɔ́ːθər] 명 저자
- **borrow**[bárou] 동 빌리다
- **celebrate**[séləbrèit] 동 기념하다, 축하하다
- **charge**[tʃɑːrdʒ] 명 기소, 혐의
- **childhood**[tʃáildhùd] 명 어린 시절
- **choose**[tʃuːz] 동 고르다
- **copy**[kápi] 명 (책) 한 부 동 베끼다, 복사하다
- **decide**[disáid] 동 결심하다
- **editor**[édətər] 명 편집자
- **elementary school** 초등학교
- **express**[iksprés] 동 표현하다
- **freedom**[fríːdəm] 명 자유
- **further**[fɔ́ːrðər] 부 더, 더 멀리
- **government**[gávərnmənt] 명 정부, 정권
- **graduation**[grædʒuéiʃən] 명 졸업
- **harsh**[hɑːrʃ] 형 가혹한, 혹독한
- **hometown**[hóumtaun] 명 고향
- **independence**[ìndipéndəns] 명 독립
- **library**[láibrèri] 명 도서관
- **literary**[lítərèri] 형 문학의, 문학적인

- **literature**[lítərətʃər] 명 문학
- **loneliness**[lóunlinis] 명 외로움
- **longing**[lɔ́ːŋiŋ] 명 동경, 갈망
- **movement**[múːvmənt] 명 운동
- **novel**[návəl] 명 소설
- **particular**[pərtíkjulər] 형 특별한, 특정한
- **poem**[póuəm] 명 (한 편의) 시
- **poet**[póuit] 명 시인
- **poetry**[póuitri] 명 (문학 장르) 시
- **present**[prizént] 동 선사하다, 주다
- **publication**[pʌbləkéiʃən] 명 출판, 발행
- **publish**[pʌ́bliʃ] 동 출판하다
- **rare**[rɛər] 형 희귀한
- **recommend**[rèkəménd] 동 추천하다
- **remain**[riméin] 동 남아 있다, 계속 ~하다
- **sew**[sou] 동 바느질하다
- **shine**[ʃain] 동 빛나다
- **thus**[ðʌs] 부 그러므로
- **treatment**[tríːtmənt] 명 대우, 처리
- **wallet**[wálit] 명 지갑
- **whole**[houl] 형 전체의, 모든
- **yearbook**[jiərbuk] 명 졸업 앨범

Key Expressions

- **a surprise ending** 뜻밖의 결말
- **advise against** 반대하는 충고를 하다
- **be well known for** ~로 유명하다
- **by hand** 손으로
- **check out** (도서관에서) 대출하다
- **come out** 나오다
- **give it a try** 시도하다
- **give up** 포기하다
- **hang out with** ~와 시간을 보내다
- **have ~ in mind** ~을 염두에 두다
- **How about ~?** ~하는 것이 어때?
- **How would you like ~?** ~을 어떻게 하기를 원하니?
- **I can't wait!** 무척 기대됩니다!

- **Let me see.** 글쎄, 어디 보자.
- **Long time no see.** 오랜만이다.
- **look forward to** ~을 기대하다
- **look good on** ~에 잘 어울리다
- **in a hurry** 서둘러
- **new arrival** 신착 도서, 새로 도착한 것
- **put up** 세우다, 내걸다
- **take a seat** 자리에 앉다
- **take part in** ~에 참가하다
- **turn on** ~을 켜다
- **What brings you here?** 무엇 때문에 여기 왔니?
- **What's up?** 무슨 일 있니?
- **You can say that again.** 정말 그래.. 동의한다.

Word Power

※ 서로 비슷한 뜻을 가진 어휘

□ **achieve** 이루다 : **accomplish** 성취하다

□ **choose** 고르다 : **select** 선택하다

□ **freedom** 자유 : **liberty** 자유

□ **longing** 동경, 갈망 : **aspiration** 열망

□ **thus** 그러므로 : **hence** 그래서

□ **author** 저자 : **writer** 작가

□ **decide** 결심하다 : **determine** 결정하다

□ **loneliness** 외로움 : **solitude** 외로움

□ **rare** 희귀한 : **scarce** 희소한

□ **wallet** 지갑 : **purse** 지갑

※ 서로 반대의 뜻을 가진 어휘

□ **arrival** 도착 ↔ **departure** 출발

□ **dependence** 의존 ↔ **independence** 독립

□ **borrow** 빌리다 ↔ **lend** 빌려주다

□ **rare** 희귀한 ↔ **common** 흔한

※ 동사 → 명사

□ **achieve** 이루다, 얻다 → **achievement** 성취

□ **celebrate** 기념하다 → **celebration** 축하

□ **decide** 결심하다 → **decision** 결심

□ **govern** 지배하다 → **government** 정부, 정권

□ **depend** 의존하다 → **dependence** 의존

□ **arrive** 도착하다 → **arrival** 도착

□ **choose** 고르다 → **choice** 선택

□ **express** 표현하다 → **expression** 표현

□ **graduate** 졸업하다 → **graduation** 졸업

□ **recommend** 추천하다 → **recommendation** 추천

English Dictionary

□ **harsh** 가혹한, 혹독한
→ unpleasant and causing pain to the body or senses
불쾌하고 신체나 감각에 고통을 야기하는

□ **hometown** 고향
→ the town where someone was born and grew up
누군가가 태어나서 자란 마을

□ **independence** 독립
→ the state of not being governed by another country
다른 나라의 지배를 받지 않는 상태

□ **literature** 문학
→ written works which are of artistic value
예술적 가치가 있는 글로 된 작품

□ **loneliness** 외로움
→ a feeling of being unhappy because you are away from other people
다른 사람들로부터 떨어져 있어서 불행한 느낌

□ **longing** 동경, 갈망
→ a strong feeling of wanting something
무언가를 원하는 강한 감정

□ **poem** (한 편의) 시
→ a piece of writing, arranged in patterns of lines and of sounds 행과 운율의 패턴에 따라 배열된 문학 작품

□ **poet** 시인
→ a person who writes poems 시를 쓰는 사람

□ **publication** 출판, 발행
→ the action of making something known to the public
대중들에게 알려지도록 하는 행위

□ **rare** 희귀한
→ not common; unusual 흔치 않은, 진기한

□ **recommend** 추천하다
→ to suggest as being good or worthy
좋거나 가치있는 것으로 제안하다

□ **sew** 바느질하다
→ to make or mend with a needle and thread
바늘과 실로 만들거나 수리하다

□ **whole** 전체의, 모든
→ not divided; all 나누어지지 않은, 전부의

서답형

01 다음 짝지어진 단어의 관계가 같도록 빈칸에 알맞은 말을 쓰시오.

> possible : impossible
> = dependence : _____

02 다음 짝지어진 단어의 관계가 나머지와 <u>다른</u> 것은?

① achieve – achievement
② decide – decision
③ publish – publication
④ depend – dependent
⑤ arrive – arrival

03 다음 영영풀이가 가리키는 것을 고르시오.

> a strong feeling of wanting something

① happiness   ② longing
③ loneliness   ④ satisfaction
⑤ harshness

중요

04 다음 중 밑줄 친 부분의 뜻풀이가 바르지 <u>않은</u> 것은?

① I stopped by the library to <u>check out</u> some books. (대출하다)
② What are you <u>looking forward to</u>? (앞으로 나아가다)
③ Why don't you <u>take a seat</u> here? (자리에 앉다)
④ These red pants don't <u>look good on</u> you. (~에게 잘 어울리다)
⑤ Do you <u>have something in mind</u>? (~을 염두에 두다)

서답형

05 다음 우리말에 맞게 빈칸에 알맞은 말을 쓰시오.

(1) William Shakespeare는 훌륭한 시인이자 극작가였다.
   ➡ William Shakespeare was a great _____ and playwriter.

(2) 당신이 가장 좋아하는 작가는 누구인가요?
   ➡ Who is your favorite _____?

(3) 그녀의 첫 번째 소설의 출판이 취소되었다.
   ➡ The _____ of her first novel was canceled.

(4) 나의 할아버지는 항상 그의 고향을 그리워하신다.
   ➡ My grandfather always misses his _____.

(5) 불을 켜줄래? 여기 너무 어둡구나.
   ➡ Will you _____ on the light? It's too dark here.

06 다음 주어진 문장의 밑줄 친 express와 <u>다른</u> 의미로 쓰인 것은?

> In class, we learned how to <u>express</u> our opinions clearly.

① I <u>expressed</u> concern about the changes.
② Teenagers often have difficulty <u>expressing</u> themselves.
③ My twins <u>express</u> their feelings in the paintings.
④ I'm going to travel by <u>express</u>.
⑤ Words cannot <u>express</u> how happy I am now.

 01 다음 짝지어진 단어의 관계가 같도록 빈칸에 알맞은 말을 쓰시오.

> sell : buy = _____ : lend

02 다음 영영풀이가 가리키는 것을 영어로 쓰시오.

> the town where someone was born and grew up

➡ _____

03 다음 우리말에 맞게 빈칸에 알맞은 어구를 쓰시오.

(1) 그는 한 마디도 없이 서둘러 나갔다. (3 words)
➡ He went out _____ without saying a word.

(2) 그는 손으로 의자를 만들었다. (2 words)
➡ He made a chair _____.

(3) 내 딸은 그녀의 친구들과 시간을 보내는 것을 좋아한다. (3 words)
➡ My daughter likes to _____ her friends.

 04 다음 문장의 빈칸에 들어갈 말을 〈보기〉에서 골라 쓰시오.

┌─ 보기 ─────────────┐
│ further / independence / charge / │
│ graduation / shine │
└───────────────────┘

(1) August 15 is the day when Koreans celebrate their _____ from Japan.

(2) He was arrested on the _____ of robbery.

(3) Stay inside until _____ notice.

(4) The sun will _____ brightly after the rain.

(5) She plans to study abroad after _____.

05 다음 우리말을 주어진 단어를 이용하여 영작하시오.

(1) 홍콩은 1997년에 영국으로부터 독립을 얻어냈다. (gained, the UK)

➡ _____
_____

(2) 나는 나의 소설을 출판하기 전에 나의 사진들을 확인할 필요가 있다. (check, novel)

➡ _____

(3) 숲은 몇몇 희귀한 곤충들과 식물들의 서식지이다. (forest, home)

➡ _____
_____

06 다음 주어진 우리말과 일치하도록 주어진 단어를 모두 배열하여 영작하시오.

(1) 지금 체육관에서 졸업식이 열리고 있다.
(ceremony / being / the graduation / the / gym / now / in / held / is)

➡ _____
_____

(2) 처벌은 가혹하고 불평등했다.
(punishment / harsh / the / was / and / unfair)

➡ _____
_____

(3) 나는 법의 이름으로 당신을 체포합니다.
(you / of / in / I / name / the / the / arrest / law)

➡ _____
_____

Conversation

① 추천 요청하기

> **A** Can you recommend some good music? 좋은 음악 좀 추천해 줄 수 있니?
> **B** I recommend you listen to *Happy*. 나는 *Happy*를 들어보라고 추천해.

- 상대방에게 추천을 요청하는 표현은 'recommend(추천하다)'를 사용하여 나타낸다. 상대방에게 요청을 나타낼 때는 can, could, would 등의 조동사를 사용하여 'Can you recommend ~?'(~을 추천해 주실 수 있나요?), 'Could you recommend ~?'(~ 좀 추천해 주시겠습니까?) 등으로 나타낸다.

- 구체적인 내용을 몰라서 상대에게 무엇을 추천할지 물어볼 때는 'What would you recommend?'(무엇을 추천하시겠습니까?), 'Which one would you recommend?'(어느 것을 추천하시겠습니까?) 등으로 나타낸다.

- 상대로부터 추천 요청을 받고 추천을 해 줄 때는 'I recommend ~.'(나는 ~을 추천한다.)라고 한다. recommend는 'recommend+명사', 'recommend -ing', 'recommend (that) 주어(+should)+동사원형 ~'의 형태로 문장을 구성한다.

추천 요청하기

- Can you recommend ~?　　　　　　　~을 추천해 주시겠어요?
- Could / Would you recommend ~?　~을 추천해 주시겠습니까?
- What would you recommend?　　　무엇을 추천하시겠습니까?
- Which one would you recommend?　어느 것을 추천하시겠습니까?

추천하기

- I recommend+명사[동명사] / (that) 주어+(should+)동사원형 ~ 나는 ~을 추천한다.
- How about ~? ~는 어떠니?

핵심 Check

1. 다음 대화의 흐름으로 보아 빈칸에 들어가기에 적절한 것은?

B: Hello, Ms. Seo.

W: Hi, Minjun. Long time no see. What brings you here?

B: I have to write a book report. Can you recommend a good novel to read?

W: _____ There's a new Ken Kuller book, *22nd Street*.

① What do you like?　　　　② How about a mystery?
③ Why do you read novels?　④ Which one do you like better?
⑤ Can I check it out?

2 기대 표현하기

A You look excited. 너 흥분된 것처럼 보인다.

B Yeah. I'm looking forward to a big curling match this Tuesday.
응. 나는 이번 목요일 큰 컬링 시합을 기대하고 있어.

■ 앞으로 일어날 일이나 하고 싶은 일에 대한 기대를 표현할 때 '~을 기대한다.'라는 의미로 'I'm looking forward to ~.'나 'I look forward to ~.'의 표현을 사용한다. '~을 기대하다'라는 의미의 'look forward to'에서는 to가 전치사이기 때문에 그 뒤에 명사나 동명사가 오는 점에 주의한다. '빨리 ~하고 싶다, ~을 너무 하고 싶다.'라는 뜻으로 'I can't wait for ~.' 'I am dying to ~.' 'I'm expecting to ~.'라고 하기도 한다.

■ 'I can't wait!'(너무 기대된다!/빨리 보고 싶어!)는 원하던 일이 다가오고 있어 빨리하고 싶은 기대감을 나타내는 표현이며, 직역의 의미는 '~하는 것을 기다릴 수 없다'이고, 보통 '당장 ~하고 싶다, 빨리 ~했으면 좋겠다'로 해석한다. to 뒤에는 동사원형을 쓰지만, 뒤에 명사구가 올 경우에는 'I can't wait for+명사(명사구)'의 형태로 쓰기도 한다.

■ '기대하다'라는 의미의 expect를 써서 'I'm expecting to 동사원형 ~'이라고 하거나 '열망하다'라는 의미의 동사 'long'을 사용하여 'I'm longing to+동사원형, I'm longing for+명사'라고 하거나, 형용사 'eager(열망하는)'를 써서 'I'm eager to+동사원형', 'I'm eager for+명사'의 형태로 나타내기도 한다.

기대 표현하기

• I'm looking forward to+명사(구)	~하기를 기대한다.
• I can't wait for+명사 / to+동사원형	빨리 ~했으면 좋겠다.
• I am expecting to+동사원형	~하기를 기대한다.
• I am longing for+명사 / to+동사원형	~하기를 열망한다.
• I am eager for+명사 / to+동사원형	~하기를 기대한다.

핵심 Check

2. 다음 우리말과 일치하도록 빈칸에 알맞은 말을 고르시오.

A: Hi, Sora. You look excited.

B: Yeah. I'm really looking forward to this Tuesday.

A: This Tuesday? What's on Tuesday?

B: There's a big curling match. _____

① How about you?
② I can't wait!
③ Will you recommend one?
④ But I don't watch it.
⑤ There're lots of things to see.

Listen – Listen & Answer Dialog 1

Minjun: Hello, Ms. Seo.

Ms. Seo: Hi, Minjun. ❶Long time no see. What brings you here?

Minjun: I have to write a book report. ❷Can you recommend a good novel to read?

Ms. Seo: ❸How about a mystery? There's a new Ken Kuller book, *22nd Street*.

Minjun: Oh, I've heard of ❹him. Can you show me the book?

Ms. Seo: It's in the "❺New Arrivals" area. It's really popular among teens in Great Britain.

Minjun: Thank you for your help. Can I ❻check it out?

Ms. Seo: Sure. You can borrow new books for seven days.

Minjun: Okay.

민준: 안녕하세요, 서 선생님.

서 선생님: 안녕, 민준아. 오랜만이구나. 무슨 일로 여기에 온 거니?

민준: 독후감을 써야 해서요. 읽기에 좋은 소설을 추천해 주시겠어요?

서 선생님: 추리 소설은 어떠니? Ken Kuller의 신간, '22번가'가 있단다.

민준: 아, 그에 관해 들어 본 적이 있어요. 책을 보여 주실 수 있나요?

서 선생님: '신착 도서' 서가에 있단다. 그 책은 영국의 십 대들 사이에서 많은 인기를 끌고 있단다.

민준: 도와주셔서 감사합니다. 그 책을 대출할 수 있을까요?

서 선생님: 물론이지. 신간은 7일간 빌릴 수 있어.

민준: 알겠습니다.

❶ Long time no see.: 오랜만이다.　❷ 상대방에게 추천을 요청하는 표현은 'recommend(추천하다)'를 사용하여 나타낸다.
❸ 상대로부터 추천 요청을 받고 추천을 해 줄 때 사용할 수 있는 표현으로 'How about a mystery?' 등을 쓴다.
❹ him은 Ken Kuller를 가리킨다　❺ new arrival: 신착 도서, 새로 도착한 것　❻ check out: (도서관에서) 대출하다

Check(√) True or False

(1) Minjun has to write a book report.　　　　　　T ☐ F ☐

(2) Minjun can borrow new books for a week.　　　T ☐ F ☐

 Listen – Listen & Answer Dialog 2

Sora: Hey, Minjun. What are you doing?

Minjun: I'm reading a novel for a book report.

Sora: Let me see. Oh, is this a new book by Ken Kuller?

Minjun: Yeah, I borrowed ❶it this morning. Do you know Ken Kuller?

Sora: Of course. I'm a big fan of his. I've read all of his mystery books.

Minjun: I think he's a great writer. I can't ❷stop reading this book.

Sora: You know what? His novel *Four Eyes* has been made into a movie.

Minjun: Yeah. I saw the movie poster. It ❸looks interesting.

Sora: It'll come out next Thursday. I'm ❹looking forward to seeing it!

Minjun: Maybe we can see the movie together.

소라: 안녕, 민준아. 뭐 하고 있니?

민준: 나는 독후감을 쓰려고 소설을 읽고 있어.

소라: 어디 봐. 아, 이거 Ken Kuller의 신간이지?

민준: 맞아, 오늘 아침에 이걸 대출했어. 너는 Ken Kuller를 알고 있니?

소라: 물론이지. 난 그의 열렬한 팬이야. 그의 추리 소설은 모두 읽었어.

민준: 내 생각에 그는 위대한 작가야. 이 책을 손에서 놓을 수가 없어.

소라: 그거 알아? 그의 소설 '네 개의 눈'이 영화로 만들어졌어.

민준: 맞아. 나도 영화 포스터를 봤어. 재미있어 보이더라.

소라: 영화는 다음 주 목요일에 개봉한대. 그걸 보는 게 기대돼!

민준: 아마 우리 영화를 같이 볼 수 있겠다.

❶ it은 Ken Kuller의 신간을 가리킨다　❷ stop+~ing: ~하는 것을 멈추다, stop+to부정사: ~하기 위해 멈추다
❸ look+형용사: ~하게 보이다　❹ look forward to ~ing: ~을 기대하다 = I can't wait to ~

Check(√) True or False

(3) The movie *Four Eyes* will come out next Thursday.　　　T ☐ F ☐

(4) Minjun is going to see the movie with Sora this Thursday.　T ☐ F ☐

Listen More – Listen and complete

Mike: Good morning, Jiho.

Jiho: Good morning.

Mike: Take a seat, please. ❶How would you like your hair done?

Jiho: Well, I'm taking my pictures for the ❷ yearbook. So I want to look cool.

Mike: When do you take the pictures?

Jiho: This Friday at Dream & Joy Park.

Mike: Sounds good. Do you have a ❸particular style in mind?

Jiho: No. Can you recommend one for me?

Mike: Look at this. ❹How about this style? It'll look good on you.

Jiho: Wow, I like it. ❺I can't wait to see how I'll look in the pictures.

Mike: I'm sure you'll look cool.

❶ How would you like ~?: ~을 어떻게 하기를 원하니?

❷ yearbook: 졸업 앨범

❸ particular: 특정한, 특별한

❹ 추천 요청에 제안하는 표현으로 'I recommend this style.' 또는 'Why don't you try this style?' 등으로 바꾸어 표현할 수 있다.

❺ 기대감을 표현하는 말로 'I'm looking forward to seeing how I'll look in the pictures.'로 바꾸어 표현할 수 있다.

 My Speaking Portfolio

Jane: Nice to meet you, Mr. Henry. Is O. Henry your real name?

Mr. Henry: No. My real name is William Sydney Porter.

Jane: Can you tell me ❶where you're from?

Mr. Henry: I'm from the U.S.

Jane: What do you usually write?

Mr. Henry: I'm a short story writer. I have written about 300 short stories.

Jane: Wow! You're great! What is special about your short stories?

Mr. Henry: ❷They're well known for their ❸ surprise endings.

Jane: Can you recommend a popular story with a surprise ending?

Mr. Henry: Sure. I recommend *The Last Leaf*.

Jane: What is ❹it about?

Mr. Henry: ❹It's about a sick girl and an old artist who saves her life.

Jane: Oh, I want to read ❹it. ❺I can't wait.

❶ 간접의의문의 어순으로 '의문사+주어+동사' 순서로 이어진다.

❷ be well known for: ~로 유명하다

❸ a surprise ending: 뜻밖의 결말

❹ it은 *The Last Leaf*를 가리킨다.

❺ 기대감을 나타내며 'I'm looking forward to reading it.'으로 바꾸어 표현할 수 있다.

 Wrap Up 1

Tony: ❶May I take your order?

Suji: There're so many ❷kinds of hot dogs here. Can you recommend one?

Tony: How about the potato hot dog? It's very popular.

Suji: Okay, I'll have one.

Tony: Try our milkshake, too. It ❸goes well with the potato hot dog.

❶ '주문하시겠어요?'를 뜻하며 'Are you ready to order?' 등으로 바꾸어 쓸 수 있다.

❷ kind: 종류

❸ go well with: ~와 잘 어울리다

 Wrap Up 2

Emily: You look ❶excited.

James: Yeah. I'm going to the Thunder concert this Friday. I can't wait!

Emily: Who are you going to the concert with?

James: With my mom.

Emily: Does your mother like hip-hop?

James: Yes, ❷she's into hip-hop. ❸She's really looking forward to the concert.

❶ excited: 신이 난

❷ be into ~: ~을 좋아하다

❸ 기대감을 나타내며 'She's longing for the concert.' 등으로 바꾸어 쓸 수 있다.

● 다음 우리말과 일치하도록 빈칸에 알맞은 말을 쓰시오.

Listen – Listen & Answer Dialog 1

Minjun: Hello, Ms. Seo.

Ms. Seo: Hi, Minjun. _____ time _____ see. What _____ you here?

Minjun: I have to write _____ _____ _____. Can you _____ a good novel to read?

Ms. Seo: How _____ a mystery? There's a new Ken Kuller book, *22nd Street*.

Minjun: Oh, I've heard of him. Can you _____ _____ the book?

Ms. Seo: It's in the "_____ _____" area. It's really _____ among teens in Great Britain.

Minjun: Thank you for your help. Can I _____ it _____?

Ms. Seo: Sure. You can _____ new books for seven days.

Minjun: Okay.

해석

민준: 안녕하세요, 서 선생님.
서 선생님: 안녕, 민준아. 오랜만이구나. 무슨 일로 여기에 온 거니?
민준: 독후감을 써야 해서요. 읽기에 좋은 소설을 추천해 주시겠어요?
서 선생님: 추리 소설은 어떠니? Ken Kuller의 신간, '22번가'가 있단다.
민준: 아, 그에 관해 들어 본 적이 있어요. 책을 보여 주실 수 있나요?
서 선생님: '신착 도서' 서가에 있단다. 그 책은 영국의 십 대들 사이에서 많은 인기를 끌고 있어.
민준: 도와주셔서 감사합니다. 그 책을 대출할 수 있을까요?
서 선생님: 물론이지. 신간은 7일간 빌릴 수 있어.
민준: 알겠습니다.

Listen – Listen & Answer Dialog 2

Sora: Hey, Minjun. What are you doing?

Minjun: I'm reading a _____ for a _____ _____.

Sora: Let _____ _____. Oh, is this a new book by Ken Kuller?

Minjun: Yeah, I _____ it this morning. Do you know Ken Kuller?

Sora: Of course. I'm a _____ _____ of his. I've read _____ of his mystery books.

Minjun: I think he's a great writer. I can't _____ _____ this book.

Sora: You know _____? His novel *Four Eyes* _____ _____ _____ into a movie.

Minjun: Yeah. I saw the movie poster. It looks _____.

Sora: It'll _____ _____ next Thursday. I'm _____ _____ _____ _____ it!

Minjun: Maybe we can see the movie _____.

소라: 안녕, 민준아. 뭐 하고 있니?
민준: 나는 독후감을 쓰려고 소설을 읽고 있어.
소라: 어디 봐. 아, 이거 Ken Kuller의 신간이지?
민준: 맞아, 오늘 아침에 이걸 대출했어. 너는 Ken Kuller를 알고 있니?
소라: 물론이지. 난 그의 열렬한 팬이야. 그의 추리 소설은 모두 읽었어.
민준: 내 생각에 그는 위대한 작가야. 이 책을 손에서 놓을 수가 없어.
소라: 그거 알아? 그의 소설 '네 개의 눈'이 영화로 만들어졌어.
민준: 맞아. 나도 영화 포스터를 봤어. 재미있어 보이더라.
소라: 영화는 다음 주 목요일에 개봉한대. 그걸 보는 게 기대돼!
민준: 아마 우리 영화를 같이 볼 수 있겠다.

Listen More – Listen and complete

Mike: Good morning, Jiho.

Jiho: Good morning.

Mike: _____ _____ _____ , p l e a s e . _____ _____ _____ _____ your hair done?

Jiho: Well, I'm taking my pictures for the _____. So I want to look _____.

Mike: When do you _____ the pictures?

Jiho: This Friday at Dream & Joy Park.

Mike: Sounds good. Do you have a _____ style in _____?

Jiho: No. Can you _____ one for me?

Mike: Look at this. How about this style? It'll _____ _____ _____ you.

Jiho: Wow, I like it. I _____ _____ _____ _____ how I'll look in the pictures.

Mike: I'm _____ you'll look cool.

My Speaking Portfolio

Jane: Nice to meet you, Mr. Henry. Is O. Henry your _____ _____?

Mr. Henry: No. My real name is William Sydney Porter.

Jane: Can you tell me _____ _____ _____?

Mr. Henry: I'm from the U.S.

Jane: What do you _____ write?

Mr. Henry: I'm a _____ _____ _____. I have written about 300 short stories.

Jane: Wow! You're great! What is _____ about your short stories?

Mr. Henry: They're _____ _____ _____ their surprise endings.

Jane: Can you _____ a popular story with a _____ _____?

Mr. Henry: Sure. I _____ *The Last Leaf.*

Jane: What is it about?

Mr. Henry: It's about a sick girl and an old artist _____ _____ _____ _____.

Jane: Oh, I want to read it. I _____ _____.

Mike: 안녕, 지호야.
지호: 안녕하세요.
Mike: 자리에 앉으렴. 머리를 어떻게 해 줄까?
지호: 음, 저는 졸업 앨범에 들어갈 사진을 찍을 거예요. 그래서 멋져 보이고 싶어요.
Mike: 언제 사진을 찍니?
지호: 이번 금요일에 Dream & Joy Park에서요.
Mike: 멋지구나. 마음에 둔 특별한 스타일이 있니?
지호: 아니요. 저를 위해 하나 추천해 주시겠어요?
Mike: 이걸 보렴. 이 스타일은 어떠니? 너에게 잘 어울릴 거야.
지호: 와, 마음에 들어요. 제가 사진에서 어떻게 보일지 빨리 보고 싶어요.
Mike: 틀림없이 멋져 보일 거야.

Jane: 만나서 반갑습니다, Henry 씨. O. Henry가 당신의 본명인가요?
Mr. Henry: 아니요. 제 본명은 William Sydney Porter입니다.
Jane: 어디 출신이신지 말씀해 주시겠어요?
Mr. Henry: 저는 미국 출신입니다.
Jane: 주로 무엇을 쓰시나요?
Mr. Henry: 저는 단편 소설 작가입니다. 300여 편의 단편 소설을 썼죠.
Jane: 와! 대단하시네요! 당신의 단편 소설은 무엇이 특별한가요?
Mr. Henry: 그것들은 뜻밖의 결말로 유명합니다.
Jane: 뜻밖의 결말이 있는 유명한 이야기를 하나 추천해 주실 수 있나요?
Mr. Henry: 물론이죠. 저는 '마지막 잎새'를 추천합니다.
Jane: 그것은 무엇에 관한 이야기인가요?
Mr. Henry: 아픈 소녀와 그녀의 목숨을 구하는 늙은 화가의 이야기예요.
Jane: 아, 그것을 읽고 싶네요. 무척 기대됩니다.

[01~02] 다음 대화를 읽고 물음에 답하시오.

Tony: (A)May I take your order?

Suji: There're so many kinds of hot dogs here. Can you recommend one?

Tony: _____ It's very popular.

Suji: Okay, I'll have one.

Tony: Try our milkshake, too. It goes well with the potato hot dog.

01 위 대화의 밑줄 친 (A)와 바꾸어 쓸 수 없는 것은?

① Are you ready to order now? ② Would you like to order?

③ Shall I take your order? ④ Can I get your order?

⑤ Let me confirm your order.

02 위 대화의 빈칸에 들어갈 말로 어색한 것은?

① You don't have to try potato hot dog.

② How about the potato hot dog?

③ I recommend the potato hot dog.

④ Why don't you try the potato hot dog?

⑤ If I were you, I'd try the potato hot dog.

[03~04] 다음 대화를 읽고 물음에 답하시오.

Emily: You look excited.

James: Yeah. I'm going to the Thunder concert this Friday. I can't wait!

Emily: Who are you going to the concert with?

James: With my mom.

Emily: Does your mother like hip-hop?

James: Yes, she's into hip-hop. (A)She's really looking forward to the concert. (wait)

03 위 대화의 밑줄 친 (A)를 같은 의미가 되도록 주어진 단어를 사용하여 다시 쓰시오.

➡ _____

04 Where will James and his mom go this Friday?

➡ _____

[01~03] 다음 대화를 읽고 물음에 답하시오.

Minjun: Hello, Ms. Seo.

Ms. Seo: Hi, Minjun. Long time no see. What brings you here?

Minjun: I have to write a book report. (A)읽기에 좋은 소설을 추천해 주시겠어요?

Ms. Seo: How about a mystery? There's a new Ken Kuller book, *22nd Street*.

Minjun: Oh, I've heard of ⓐhim. Can you show me the book?

Ms. Seo: It's in the "New Arrivals" area. It's really popular among teens in Great Britain.

Minjun: Thank you for your help. Can I check ⓑit out?

Ms. Seo: Sure. You can borrow new books for seven days.

Minjun: Okay.

서답형

01 위 대화의 밑줄 친 (A)의 우리말을 주어진 단어를 모두 배열하여 완성하시오.

(to / you / recommend / good / a / can / read / novel)

➡ _____

서답형

02 위 대화의 밑줄 친 ⓐ와 ⓑ가 각각 가리키는 것을 찾아 쓰시오.

➡ ⓐ _____ ⓑ _____

03 위 대화의 두 사람의 관계로 적절한 것은?

① interview – interviewee
② traveller – flight attendant
③ patient – doctor
④ tourist – guide
⑤ student – librarian

[04~06] 다음 대화를 읽고 물음에 답하시오.

Sora: Hey, Minjun. What are you doing?

Minjun: I'm reading a novel for a book report.

Sora: Let me see. Oh, is this a new book by Ken Kuller?

Minjun: (A) Yeah, I borrowed it this morning. Do you know Ken Kuller?

Sora: (B) I've read all of his mystery books.

Minjun: (C) I think he's a great writer. I can't stop reading this book.

Sora: (D) You know what? His novel Four Eyes has been made into a movie.

Minjun: (E) Yeah. I saw the movie poster. It looks interesting.

Sora: ⓐ그것은 다음 주 목요일에 개봉할 거야. ⓑI'm looking forward to seeing it!

Minjun: Maybe we can see the movie together.

04 위 대화의 (A)~(E) 중 주어진 문장이 들어가기에 적절한 곳은?

Of course. I'm a big fan of his.

① (A) ② (B) ③ (C) ④ (D) ⑤ (E)

서답형

05 위 대화의 밑줄 친 ⓐ의 우리말을 주어진 단어를 써서 영작하시오. (come)

➡ _____

06 위 대화의 밑줄 친 ⓑ와 바꾸어 쓰기에 어색한 것은?

① I can't wait to see it!
② I'm expecting to see it.
③ I'm longing to see it.
④ I'm eager to see it.
⑤ I'm going to see it.

[07~08] 다음 대화를 읽고 물음에 답하시오.

Mike: Good morning, Jiho.

Jiho: Good morning.

Mike: Take a seat, please. How would you ⓐ like your hair done?

Jiho: Well, I'm taking my pictures for the yearbook. So I want to look ⓑcool.

Mike: When do you take the pictures?

Jiho: This Friday at Dream & Joy Park.

Mike: ⓒSounds good. Do you have a particular style in mind?

Jiho: No. Can you recommend one for me?

Mike: Look at this. How about this style? It'll look good ⓓon you.

Jiho: Wow, I like it. I can't wait ⓔseeing how I'll look in the pictures.

Mike: I'm sure you'll look cool.

서답형

07 위 대화의 밑줄 친 ⓐ~ⓔ 중 어법상 틀린 것을 찾아 바르게 고치시오.

_____ ➡ _____

중요

08 위 대화를 읽고 대답할 수 없는 것은?

① What will Jiho take his pictures for?

② What does Jiho want to do?

③ When is Jiho going to take pictures?

④ Where is Jiho going to take pictures?

⑤ How long should Jiho wait to see his new style?

[09~10] 다음 대화를 읽고 물음에 답하시오.

Jane: Nice to meet you, Mr. Henry. Is O. Henry your real name?

Mr. Henry: No. My real name is William Sydney Porter.

Jane: Can you tell me where (A)[you are / are you] from?

Mr. Henry: I'm from the U.S.

Jane: What do you usually write?

Mr. Henry: I'm a short story writer. I have written about 300 short stories.

Jane: Wow! You're great! What is special about your short stories?

Mr. Henry: They're well (B)[knowing / known] for their surprise endings.

Jane: Can you recommend a popular story with a surprise ending?

Mr. Henry: Sure. I recommend *The Last Leaf*.

Jane: What is it about?

Mr. Henry: It's about a sick girl and an old artist who (C)[save / saves] her life.

Jane: Oh, I want to read it. I can't wait.

09 위 대화의 (A)~(C)에서 알맞은 것을 골라 쓰시오.

➡ (A) _____ (B) _____ (C) _____

10 위 대화의 내용과 일치하지 않는 것은?

① O. Henry의 본명은 William Sydney Porter 이다.

② O. Henry는 미국 출신이다.

③ O. Henry는 단편 소설 작가로 300여 편의 단편 소설을 썼다.

④ O. Henry의 단편 소설은 뜻밖의 결말로 유명하다.

⑤ O. Henry의 '마지막 잎새'를 추천한 이유는 슬픈 결말 때문이다.

Conversation 서술형 시험대비

[01~02] 다음 대화를 읽고 물음에 답하시오.

Minjun: Hello, Ms. Seo.

Ms. Seo: Hi, Minjun. Long time no see. What brings you here?

Minjun: I have to write a book report. Can you recommend a good novel to read?

Ms. Seo: How about a mystery? There's a new Ken Kuller book, *22nd Street*.

Minjun: Oh, I've heard of him. Can you show me the book?

Ms. Seo: It's in the "New Arrivals" area. It's really popular among teens in Great Britain.

Minjun: Thank you for your help. Can I check it out?

Ms. Seo: Sure. You can borrow new books for seven days.

Minjun: Okay.

01 What does Ms. Seo recommend to Minjun?

➡ _____

02 Where can Minjun find out the book that Ms. Seo recommended?

➡ _____

03 다음 대화를 읽고 대화의 내용과 일치하도록 빈칸을 완성하시오.

Mike: Good morning, Jiho.

Jiho: Good morning.

Mike: Take a seat, please. How would you like your hair done?

Jiho: Well, I'm taking my pictures for the yearbook. So I want to look cool.

Mike: When do you take the pictures?

Jiho: This Friday at Dream & Joy Park.

Mike: Sounds good. Do you have a particular style in mind?

Jiho: No. Can you recommend one for me?

Mike: Look at this. How about this style? It'll look good on you.

Jiho: Wow, I like it. I can't wait to see how I'll look in the pictures.

Mike: I'm sure you'll look cool.

Jiho went to a hairdresser, Mike. Jiho is taking his pictures for (A)_____ this Friday at (B)_____. Jiho didn't have a particular style in mind, so he asked Mike (C)_____. Mike suggested one for him. Jiho was looking forward to (D)_____. Mike was sure that (E)_____.

04 다음 대화가 자연스럽게 이어지도록 순서대로 배열하시오.

Minjun: Do you know Ken Kuller?

Sora: Of course. I'm a big fan of his. I've read all of his mystery books.

(A) You know what? His novel *Four Eyes* has been made into a movie.

(B) Maybe we can see the movie together.

(C) Yeah. I saw the movie poster. It looks interesting.

(D) I think he's a great writer. I can't stop reading this book.

(E) It'll come out next Thursday. I'm looking forward to seeing it!

➡ _____

Grammar

① 과거완료

> • Jake was late for school because he **had missed** the bus.
>
>   Jake는 버스를 놓쳐서 학교에 지각했다.
>
> • He **had been** wounded in the arm. 그는 팔에 부상을 당했었다.

■ 과거완료는 과거 이전에 일어난 일이 과거의 어느 시점까지 영향을 미칠 때 쓰며, 'had+과거분사'의 형태로 쓴다. 과거완료도 현재완료처럼 완료, 경험, 계속, 결과의 용법이 있다. 또한 과거의 어느 시점에서 그보다 먼저 일어난 일을 나타낼 때도 쓰이며 이것을 보통 '대과거'라고 한다.

- She **had** just **woken** from a deep sleep. 그녀는 막 깊은 잠에서 깨어난 참이었다. 〈완료〉
- She **had** never **ridden** a horse before. 그녀는 전에 말을 타 본 적이 한 번도 없었다. 〈경험〉
- He **had worked** for the family for long. 그는 그 가족들을 위해 오랫동안 일을 했었다. 〈계속〉
- He **had gone** abroad to study more. 그는 공부를 더 하기 위해 유학을 갔다. 〈결과〉
- She remembered everything that **had happened** long before. 그녀는 오래 전에 일어난 일을 모두 기억하고 있었다. 〈대과거〉

■ 한 문장에 두 가지 과거의 일이 나올 때, 두 동작이 거의 동시에 일어났거나 시간차가 거의 없이 연속적으로 일어났을 경우에는 단순과거로 표현한다. 또, 접속사 after나 before는 전후 관계를 분명히 나타내는 표현이므로 과거완료 대신 과거시제를 많이 쓴다.

- The door **opened** and Jo **walked** in. 문이 열리더니 Jo가 걸어 들어왔다. 〈시간차가 거의 없는 연속 동작〉
- I **left** before he **arrived**. 나는 그가 도착하기 전에 떠났다. 〈전후 관계가 명백함〉

핵심 Check

1. 다음 괄호 안에서 알맞은 말을 고르시오.

   (1) They believed the accident (has just occurred / had just occurred).

   (2) Kirk knew that water (had got / got) in and rusted the engine.

   (3) He returned home after he (has met / met) Juliet.

2 'It ~ that ...' 강조 구문

- **It was** Judy **that** lost her wallet on the bus. 버스에서 지갑을 잃어버린 것은 바로 Judy였다.
- **It was** her wallet **that** Judy lost on the bus. 버스에서 Judy가 잃어버린 것은 바로 지갑이었다.

■ 'It + is/was + 강조어(구) + that ...'의 형태로 특정 부분을 강조하여 나타낼 때 사용한다. 강조하고자 하는 부분을 'it is/was'와 'that' 사이에 쓰고, 나머지 부분을 that 뒤에 써서 주어, 목적어인 명사, 부사 (구/절) 등을 강조한다. 'be'동사는 문장의 시제에 맞춰 'is'나 'was'를 사용한다.

- I received a phone call from your mother.
  - → **It was** I **that** received a phone call from your mother. (주어 강조)
  - → **It was** a phone call **that** I received from your mother. (목적어인 명사 강조)
  - → **It was** from your mother **that** I received a phone call. (부사구 강조)

■ 'It ~ that ...' 강조 구문에서 강조하는 대상이 명사일 경우, that 대신에 관계대명사 who[whom](사람일 경우) 또는 which(사물이나 동물일 경우)로 바꿔 쓸 수 있으며, 시간 또는 장소의 부사(구/절)일 경우, when(시간) 또는 where(장소)로 바꿔 쓸 수 있다.

- She bought some bread at the bakery yesterday. 그녀는 어제 그 제과점에서 약간의 빵을 샀다.
  - → **It was** she **that**[**who**] bought some bread at the bakery yesterday.
  - → **It was** some bread **that**[**which**] she bought at the bakery yesterday.
  - → **It was** yesterday **that**[**when**] she bought some bread at the bakery.
  - → **It was** at the bakery **that**[**where**] she bought some bread yesterday.

■ 'It ~ that ...' 강조 구문에서 강조하는 대상이 부사(구/절)일 경우 that 다음에 완전한 절이 나오지만 그 외의 경우에는 불완전한 절이 나오는 것에 유의한다. 또한 강조되는 부분에 보어(형용사)나 동사는 올 수 없다.

- **It was** at the restaurant **that**[**where**] I had dinner with her. 내가 그녀와 저녁을 먹은 곳은 바로 그 식당이었다. (that 다음에 완전한 절)
- It was pretty that she was at that time. (보어(형용사) 강조 ×)
- It was did that I the dishes last night. (동사 강조 ×)

핵심 Check

2. 다음 괄호 안에서 알맞은 말을 고르시오.

(1) (It / That) was in the afternoon that I met Joseph.

(2) It is Molly (that / what) is talking on the phone.

(3) It was Raymond (whom / which) he taught English.

01 다음 빈칸에 들어갈 말로 알맞은 것은?

> John said that he _____ his friend on his way home.

① meet   ② meets   ③ met

④ has met   ⑤ had met

02 다음 괄호 안에서 알맞은 말을 고르시오.

(1) He (already left / had already left) when I returned home.

(2) He told me gloomily that he (was called / had been called) up for army service.

(3) (It / That) was Jane Austen that wrote *Pride and Prejudice* in 1813.

(4) It is you (which / who) are to blame.

03 다음 빈칸에 알맞은 것은?

> However, it was literature _____ he loved most.

① where   ② when   ③ who

④ that   ⑤ what

04 다음 우리말에 맞게 주어진 어휘를 바르게 배열하시오.

(1) 나는 2주 전에 산 배낭을 잃어버렸다.

(two weeks, the backpack, I, I, bought, lost, had, before, that)

  ➡ _____

(2) 그는 열쇠를 잃어버렸다는 것을 알았다.

(he, had, the keys, he, realized, lost, that)

  ➡ _____

(3) 모든 사람이 말하고 있는 바로 그 영화이다.

(everybody, talking, the movie, is, is, it, that, about)

  ➡ _____

01 다음 중 어법상 <u>어색한</u> 것은?

① Ted said that he had never missed a day's work because of illness.

② She strongly insisted that she was not there.

③ Jessica came to the meeting late because she had missed the bus.

④ Ann said her grandmother had lived on the farm.

⑤ When I came back home, I found somebody had broken a cup.

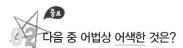

02 다음 중 어법상 <u>어색한</u> 것은?

① It was in 1945 that World War Ⅱ ended.

② It was Ben who sang on the stage.

③ It was told that Mirae me a lie the other day.

④ It was Betty whom he met in the library.

⑤ It was dinner which we had together last Saturday.

03 다음 빈칸에 알맞은 말이 바르게 짝지어진 것은?

> • It was the red shirt _____ she bought online.
> • He said that he _____ his homework the night before.

① that – had finished

② which – has finished

③ that – has finished

④ which – finished

⑤ what – have finished

서답형

04 다음 괄호 안에서 알맞은 말을 고르시오.

(1) It was by far the worst speech that he (has ever made / had ever made).

(2) Linda wore the necklace which her boyfriend (had presented / presented) to her.

(3) Pamela died in 1992 in Detroit, where she (lived / had lived) since 1957.

(4) It was Kate (which / who) lost her wallet in the museum.

(5) It was yesterday (which / when) she lost her smartphone.

(6) It was in the library (which / where) we studied math with Jane.

05 주어진 문장의 <u>틀린</u> 부분을 찾아 올바르게 고친 것을 고르시오.

> He had said that he lived in Korea for 10 years.

① He had said that he lives in Korea for 10 years.

② He had said that he lived in Korea for 10 years.

③ He had said that he had lived in Korea for 10 years.

④ He said that he had lived in Korea for 10 years.

⑤ He said that he has lived in Korea for 10 years.

06 다음 문장의 밑줄 친 부분 중 어법상 어색한 것은?

> He ①wasn't exactly ②a stranger. I ③ have met him ④once ⑤before.

①   ②   ③   ④   ⑤

07 빈칸 (A)와 (B)에 알맞은 말이 바르게 짝지어진 것은?

> It is a number of books on the subject ___(A)___ he ___(B)___ up to now.

	(A)	(B)
①	what	has written
②	if	had written
③	if	wrote
④	that	wrote
⑤	that	has written

08 다음 〈보기〉의 밑줄 친 that과 쓰임이 같은 것은?

> ┌─ 보기 ─┐
> It was in 1813 that Jane Austen wrote *Pride and Prejudice.*

① I can't walk that far.
② The entire population of one city in China is more than that of three cities in Korea.
③ It was Chaucer that really turned English into a literary language.
④ I heard that you've been abroad.
⑤ Look at that man over there.

[09~10] 다음 문장의 빈칸에 알맞은 말은?

09

> When I came back home, I found somebody _____ the room.

① cleans   ② cleaned
③ had cleaning   ④ had cleaned
⑤ has cleaned

10 중요

> It was my grandfather _____ named me Jongsu.

① that   ② what   ③ when
④ which   ⑤ where

11 다음 우리말을 바르게 영작한 것을 고르시오.

> The Statue of Liberty를 건축한 사람은 바로 Gustave Eiffel이었다.

① It was the Statue of Liberty that Gustave Eiffel built.
② It was Gustave Eiffel that built the Statue of Liberty.
③ It was Gustave Eiffel what built the Statue of Liberty.
④ It was Gustave Eiffel when built the Statue of Liberty.
⑤ It was Gustave Eiffel which built the Statue of Liberty.

서답형

12 다음 문장에서 어법상 어색한 것을 바르게 고쳐 다시 쓰시오.

> Sherill found the box that Adam hid a week before.

➡ _____

_____

서답형

13 다음 두 문장을 한 문장으로 바꿔 쓰고자 한다. 빈칸에 들어갈 알맞은 말을 쓰시오.

> • Son started to play soccer when he was 8 years old.
> • Son played soccer wonderfully at the stadium yesterday.
> = Son played soccer wonderfully at the stadium yesterday as he _____ it since he was 8 years old.

➡ _____

14 다음 중 It ~ that 쓰임이 나머지와 다른 하나는?

① It is in July that we go camping together.
② It is important that Koreans remember the true meaning of the traditional holiday.
③ It was in the restaurant that I had *samgyupsal* with Anne yesterday.
④ It was her umbrella that she lost after enjoying dinner at the restaurant.
⑤ It was yesterday that she asked me to go for a walk.

15 다음 밑줄 친 과거완료의 용법이 〈보기〉와 같은 것은?

> ┤ 보기 ├
> Linda <u>had been</u> sick in bed for a week.

① The child <u>had</u> just <u>wakened</u>.
② I thought she <u>had</u> never <u>ridden</u> a horse before.
③ How long <u>had</u> you <u>had</u> the symptoms?
④ Mary didn't know he <u>had gone</u> to America.
⑤ She realized that everybody <u>had been</u> listening to the song.

서답형

16 다음 문장에서 어법상 <u>어색한</u> 것을 바르게 고쳐 다시 쓰시오.

(1) I looked at something I had never seen ago.

➡ _____
_____

(2) He had remembered what he read.

➡ _____
_____

(3) It was the lamp who someone broke in the room.

➡ _____
_____

(4) It was when Mike told his wife something which she realized her mistake.

➡ _____
_____

(5) It is the school gym that we play basketball every Saturday.

➡ _____
_____

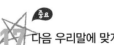
17 다음 우리말에 맞게 영작한 것을 고르시오.

> 그것은 세상 사람 누구도 본 적이 없는 것이었다.

① It had been something that the world never saw before.
② It had been something that the world had never seen before.
③ It was something that the world has never seen before.
④ It was something that the world had never seen before.
⑤ It was something that the world had never seen ago.

01 시간 흐름에 따른 사건 전개에 맞게 빈칸을 채워 문장을 완성하시오.

> My mom bought a new smartphone for me last month.
> → I lost the smartphone yesterday.
> → I don't have the smartphone now.

➡ I lost the smartphone that my mom
_____ last month.

02 다음 우리말에 맞게 주어진 어구를 바르게 배열하시오.

(1) Joanne이 점심으로 먹은 것은 바로 김밥이었다. (Joanne, was, ate, that, *gimbap*, lunch, it, for)

➡ _____
_____

(2) 내가 수영 수업을 받는 날은 바로 토요일이다. (swimming, I, that, it, take, is, a, Saturdays, lesson, on)

➡ _____
_____

(3) 그 경찰관은 Green 씨가 빨간 신호등을 무시하고 운전했다고 말했다. (Mr. Green, the police officer, light, driven, said, had, red, a, through)

➡ _____
_____

(4) 우리는 그 차가 고장 나기 전까지 15년 동안 소유했다. (it, we, car, 15 years, had, broke, had, that, before, for, down)

➡ _____
_____

03 다음 문장에서 어법상 어색한 것을 바르게 고쳐 다시 쓰시오.

(1) He has never studied English before he went to London.

➡ _____

(2) Daniel was never to London until he met Jane.

➡ _____
_____

(3) He took items that he has given to Carolyn and gave them to Dora.

➡ _____
_____

(4) It was her wallet who Judy lost on the bus.

➡ _____
_____

(5) It was a small island that I was born.

➡ _____
_____

(6) It was carefully that he drove his car.

➡ _____
_____

04 그림을 보고, 주어진 어휘를 이용하여 빈칸을 알맞게 채우시오.

(1) Jessica noticed that her brother _____ Plum's toy. (break, already)

(2) _____ that the spider wanted to catch. (it, a ladybug)

05 다음을 when을 이용하여 한 문장으로 연결할 때 빈칸을 알맞게 채우시오. (시제에 유의할 것.)

(1) I came back home. I found one thing. Somebody opened the window.
　➡ When I came back home, I found that somebody _____ the window.

(2) Mariel promised to meet Charlotte at the cafe. She went there very late. Charlotte already left the cafe. So, she couldn't meet her.
　➡ When Mariel got to the cafe to meet Charlotte, she _____ the cafe.

06 다음 문장을 주어진 단어를 강조하는 문장으로 고쳐 쓰시오. that은 사용하지 말 것.

> My brother bought the cake at the store last night.

(1) My brother
　➡ _____

(2) bought
　➡ _____

(3) the cake
　➡ _____

(4) at the store
　➡ _____

(5) last night
　➡ _____

07 다음 문장의 밑줄 친 부분을 강조하는 문장으로 바꿔 쓰시오.

(1) I learned how to read and write <u>at the age of six</u>.
　➡ _____

(2) <u>My dad</u> gets up earliest in my family.
　➡ _____

(3) I eat <u>an egg sandwich</u> when I feel blue.
　➡ _____

(4) Did I see <u>Nick</u> at the bookstore?
　➡ _____

Reading

A Poet Who Loved Stars

In the sky where seasons pass in a hurry
관계부사 where가 이끄는 절이 선행사 the sky를 수식한다.
Autumn fills the air.
And ready I stand, without a worry,
To count all the stars there.

......

Memory for one star,
Love for another star,
Loneliness for another star,
Longing for another star,
Poetry for another star,
And, oh, mother, mother for another star.

......

Have you read these lines before? They are part of the poem
현재완료 경험 용법   = these lines
"Counting Stars at Night" by Yoon Dong-ju. The poem was written a
long time ago but still remains one of Korea's favorite poems.
                                one of+복수 명사: ~ 중의 하나
Dong-ju was born in 1917 near Yanbin, China. As a young boy, he
                                              as 다음에 he was 생략
loved sports, and he was a soccer player for his school. He also loved
sewing so much that he sewed the numbers on all his friends' soccer
        so+형용사/부사+that ~: 너무 …해서 ~하다
uniforms. However, it was literature that he loved most. In elementary
                     it is ~ that … 강조 구문: …한 것은 ~이다
school he wrote a lot of poems. He even made a literary magazine with
                                        심지어
his cousin, Song Mong-gyu. In middle school he once borrowed a poetry
book by a famous poet of the time, Baek Seok, and copied the whole
        a famous poet of the time과 Baek Seok은 동격 관계
book by hand. He really wanted to have his own copy of the rare book.
                                                            희귀한(not common: unusual)

poet 시인

in a hurry 서둘러

loneliness 외로움

longing 동경, 갈망

poetry (문학 장르) 시

poem (한 편의) 시

remain 남아 있다, 계속 ~하다

sew 바느질하다

literature 문학

literary 문학의, 문학적인

copy 베끼다, 복사하다; 복사본, (책) 한 부

whole 전체의, 모든

by hand 손으로, 직접

rare 희귀한

확인문제

● 다음 문장이 본문의 내용과 일치하면 T, 일치하지 <u>않으면</u> F를 쓰시오.

1 "Counting Stars at Night" was written a long time ago by Yoon Dong-ju. ☐

2 When he was a young boy, he loved sports, and he was a soccer player for his village. ☐

3 In elementary school he wrote many poems. ☐

4 In middle school he even made a literary magazine with his cousin. ☐

His parents wanted him to be a doctor, but Dong-ju chose to study literature at a college in Seoul. During his college years, he often hung out with other young poets and wrote poetry where he expressed feelings about his hometown and lost country. To celebrate his graduation, he wished to publish 19 of his poems under the title, *Heaven, Wind, Stars, and Poetry*. He made three copies of the book by hand. One was given to his close friend, Jeong Byeong-uk, another was presented to his favorite professor, and the last one was kept for himself. However, his professor advised against his plan because he thought the Japanese government would not allow the publication. Dong-ju followed his advice and gave up the idea.

Dong-ju decided to study further in the country where his father had studied before. So, in 1942, Dong-ju and his cousin began to study in Japan. On July 10 the following year, his cousin was arrested by the Japanese police for taking part in an independence movement. Four days later, Dong-ju was also arrested on the same charges. In 1945, Dong-ju and his cousin died in prison after harsh treatment by the police. It was just a few months later that Korea achieved independence from Japan.

In 1948, Jeong Byeong-uk brought Dong-ju's poems to the poet's brother, and they were finally published. The book was given the title the poet had thought of many years before. His poems are loved by people of all ages, and thus they still shine brightly in our hearts like the stars in the autumn night sky.

hang out with ~와 시간을 보내다
hometown 고향
celebrate 기념하다
graduation 졸업
publish 출판하다
government 정부
publication 출판, 발행
further 더, 더 멀리
arrest 체포하다
take part in ~에 참가하다
independence 독립
charge 기소, 혐의
harsh 가혹한, 혹독한
treatment 대우, 처리
achieve 이루다, 얻다
shine 빛나다

 확인문제

• 다음 문장이 본문의 내용과 일치하면 T, 일치하지 않으면 F를 쓰시오.

1 Dong-ju wrote poetry where he expressed feelings about his hometown and lost country. ☐

2 To celebrate his graduation, Dong-ju published 19 of his poems under the title, *Heaven, Wind, Stars, and Poetry*. ☐

3 In 1943, Dong-ju's cousin was arrested by the Japanese police for taking part in an independence movement. ☐

4 In 1948, Jeong Byeong-uk brought Dong-ju's poems to Dong-ju's parents, and they were finally published. ☐

● 우리말을 참고하여 빈칸에 알맞은 말을 쓰시오.

1 A Poet _____ Loved Stars

2 In the sky _____ seasons pass _____ _____ _____

3 Autumn _____ the air.

4 And ready I stand, _____ _____ _____ ,

5 To _____ all the stars there.

6 _____ for one star,

7 Love for _____ star,

8 _____ for another star,

9 _____ for another star,

10 Poetry _____ another star,

11 And, oh, mother, mother _____ _____ _____ .

12 Have you read _____ _____ before?

13 They are _____ _____ the poem "Counting Stars at Night" _____ Yoon Dong-ju.

14 The poem was written a long time ago but _____ _____ one of Korea's favorite _____ .

15 Dong-ju _____ _____ in 1917 near Yanbin, China.

16 As a young boy, he loved sports, and he was a soccer player _____ _____ _____ .

17 He also loved sewing _____ much _____ he sewed the numbers on all his friends' soccer uniforms.

---

1 별을 사랑한 시인

2 계절이 지나가는 하늘에는

3 가을로 가득 차 있습니다.

4 나는 아무 걱정도 없이

5 가을 속의 별들을 다 헤일 듯합니다.

6 별 하나에 추억과

7 별 하나에 사랑과

8 별 하나에 쓸쓸함과

9 별 하나에 동경과

10 별 하나에 시와

11 별 하나에 어머니, 어머니.

12 당신은 이 시 구절을 읽어 본 적이 있는가?

13 이것은 윤동주의 시 '별 헤는 밤'의 일부이다.

14 시는 오래 전에 쓰였지만 여전히 한국이 가장 좋아하는 시 중의 하나로 남아 있다.

15 동주는 중국 연변 근처에서 1917년에 태어났다.

16 어린 소년이었을 때 그는 운동을 좋아했고, 학교의 축구 선수였다.

17 그는 또한 바느질하는 것을 무척 좋아해서 친구들의 축구 유니폼에 번호를 바느질해 주기도 했다.

18 However, _____ _____ literature _____ he loved most.

19 In elementary school he wrote _____ _____ _____ _____.

20 He even made _____ _____ _____ with his cousin, Song Mong-gyu.

21 In middle school he once borrowed a poetry book by a famous poet of the time, Baek Seok, and _____ the whole book _____ _____.

22 He really wanted _____ _____ _____ _____ of the rare book.

23 His parents wanted him _____ _____ _____ _____, but Dong-ju chose to study literature at a college in Seoul.

24 During his college years, he often _____ _____ _____ other young poets and wrote poetry _____ he expressed feelings about his hometown and _____ _____.

25 _____ _____ _____ _____, he wished to publish 19 of his poems _____ _____ _____, *Heaven, Wind, Stars, and Poetry*.

26 He made _____ _____ of the book _____ _____.

27 One _____ _____ _____ his close friend, Jeong Byeong-uk, _____ was presented to his favorite professor, and _____ _____ _____ was kept for himself.

28 However, his professor _____ _____ his plan because he thought the Japanese government would not allow the publication.

18 그러나 그가 가장 사랑한 것은 문학이었다.

19 초등학교에 다닐 때 그는 많은 시를 썼다.

20 심지어 사촌 송몽규와 문학잡지를 만들기도 했다.

21 그가 중학교에 다니던 때 한번은 당대의 유명한 시인 백석의 시집을 빌려 와서 책 전체를 필사하기도 했다.

22 그는 정말로 그 희귀한 책을 한 부 갖고 싶었던 것이다.

23 그의 부모는 그가 의사가 되기를 바랐지만 동주는 서울에 있는 대학에서 문학 공부를 하기로 했다.

24 대학 시절에 그는 종종 다른 젊은 시인들과 어울려 다녔고, 고향과 잃어버린 조국에 대한 심정을 표현하는 시를 썼다.

25 졸업을 기념하여 그는 '하늘과 바람과 별과 시'라는 제목으로 자신의 시 19편을 출판하고 싶어 했다.

26 그는 책 세 부를 손으로 만들었다.

27 한 부는 가까운 친구인 정병욱에게 주었고, 또 하나는 그가 가장 좋아하는 교수에게 선물했으며, 마지막 하나는 자신이 보관했다.

28 그러나 그의 교수는 일본 정부가 출판을 허가하지 않으리라 여겨, 그의 계획에 반대하는 충고를 했다.

29 Dong-ju _____ his advice and _____ _____ the idea.

30 Dong-ju decided _____ _____ _____ in the country where his father _____ _____ before.

31 So, in 1942, Dong-ju and his cousin _____ _____ _____ in Japan.

32 On July 10 the following year, his cousin was arrested by the Japanese police _____ _____ _____ _____ an independence movement.

33 Four days later, Dong-ju was also arrested _____ _____ _____ _____.

34 In 1945, Dong-ju and his cousin died in prison _____ _____ by the police.

35 _____ _____ just a few months later _____ Korea achieved independence from Japan.

36 In 1948, Jeong Byeong-uk brought Dong-ju's poems to the poet's brother, and _____ _____ _____ _____.

37 The book _____ _____ the title the poet _____ _____ _____ many years before.

38 His poems _____ _____ _____ people of all ages, and thus they still shine brightly in our hearts _____ the stars in the autumn night sky.

29 동주는 그의 충고를 따랐고 그 생각을 포기했다.

30 동주는 그의 아버지가 예전에 공부했던 나라에서 학업을 이어 가기로 했다.

31 그리하여 1942년에 동주와 그의 사촌은 일본에서 공부를 시작했다.

32 다음 해 7월 10일에 그의 사촌은 독립운동에 가담했다는 이유로 일본 경찰에게 체포되었다.

33 나흘 뒤 동주 역시 같은 혐의로 체포되었다.

34 1945년에 동주와 그의 사촌은 경찰의 가혹 행위를 당한 후 감옥에서 사망했다.

35 한국이 일본으로부터 독립을 이룬 것은 그로부터 불과 몇 달 후의 일이었다.

36 1948년에 정병욱이 동주의 시를 시인의 동생에게 가져다주었고, 마침내 그것들은 출판되었다.

37 그 책에는 시인이 수년 전에 생각해 두었던 제목이 붙었다.

38 그의 시는 모든 세대의 사랑을 받고 있고, 따라서 그것들은 가을밤 하늘의 별처럼 우리 가슴 속에 여전히 밝게 빛나고 있다.

우리말을 참고하여 본문을 영작하시오.

1 별을 사랑한 시인

➡ _____

2 계절이 지나가는 하늘에는

➡ _____

3 가을로 가득 차 있습니다.

➡ _____

4 나는 아무 걱정도 없이

➡ _____

5 가을 속의 별들을 다 헤일 듯합니다.

➡ _____

6 별 하나에 추억과

➡ _____

7 별 하나에 사랑과

➡ _____

8 별 하나에 쓸쓸함과

➡ _____

9 별 하나에 동경과

➡ _____

10 별 하나에 시와

➡ _____

11 별 하나에 어머니, 어머니,

➡ _____

12 당신은 이 시 구절을 읽어 본 적이 있는가?

➡ _____

13 이것은 윤동주의 시 '별 헤는 밤'의 일부이다.

➡ _____

14 시는 오래 전에 쓰였지만 여전히 한국이 가장 좋아하는 시 중의 하나로 남아 있다.

➡ _____

15 동주는 중국 연변 근처에서 1917년에 태어났다.

➡ _____

16 어린 소년이었을 때 그는 운동을 좋아했고, 학교의 축구 선수였다.

➡ _____

17 그는 또한 바느질하는 것을 무척 좋아해서 친구들의 축구 유니폼에 번호를 바느질해 주기도 했다.

➡ _____

18 그러나 그가 가장 사랑한 것은 문학이었다.

➡ _____

19 초등학교에 다닐 때 그는 많은 시를 썼다.

➡ _____

20 심지어 사촌 송몽규와 문학잡지를 만들기도 했다.

➡ _____

21 그가 중학교에 다니던 때 한번은 당대의 유명한 시인 백석의 시집을 빌려 와서 책 전체를 필사
하기도 했다.

➡ _____

_____

22 그는 정말로 그 희귀한 책을 한 부 갖고 싶었던 것이다.

➡ _____

23 그의 부모는 그가 의사가 되기를 바랐지만 동주는 서울에 있는 대학에서 문학 공부를 하기로 했다.

➡ _____

_____

24 대학 시절에 그는 종종 다른 젊은 시인들과 어울려 다녔고, 고향과 잃어버린 조국에 대한 심정을
표현하는 시를 썼다.

➡ _____

_____

25 졸업을 기념하여 그는 '하늘과 바람과 별과 시'라는 제목으로 자신의 시 19편을 출판하고 싶어
했다.

➡ _____

_____

26 그는 책 세 부를 손으로 만들었다.

➡ _____

27 한 부는 가까운 친구인 정병욱에게 주었고, 또 하나는 그가 가장 좋아하는 교수에게 선물했으며,
마지막 하나는 자신이 보관했다.

➡ _____

_____

28 그러나 그의 교수는 일본 정부가 출판을 허가하지 않으리라 여겨, 그의 계획에 반대하는 충고를 했다.

➡ _____

_____

29 동주는 그의 충고를 따랐고 그 생각을 포기했다.

➡ _____

30 동주는 그의 아버지가 예전에 공부했던 나라에서 학업을 이어 가기로 했다.

➡ _____

31 그리하여 1942년에 동주와 그의 사촌은 일본에서 공부를 시작했다.

➡ _____

32 다음 해 7월 10일에 그의 사촌은 독립운동에 가담했다는 이유로 일본 경찰에게 체포되었다.

➡ _____

_____

33 나흘 뒤 동주 역시 같은 혐의로 체포되었다.

➡ _____

34 1945년에 동주와 그의 사촌은 경찰의 가혹 행위를 당한 후 감옥에서 사망했다.

➡ _____

35 한국이 일본으로부터 독립을 이룬 것은 그로부터 불과 몇 달 후의 일이었다.

➡ _____

36 1948년에 정병욱이 동주의 시를 시인의 동생에게 가져다주었고, 마침내 그것들은 출판되었다.

➡ _____

_____

37 그 책에는 시인이 수년 전에 생각해 두었던 제목이 붙었다.

➡ _____

38 그의 시는 모든 세대의 사랑을 받고 있고, 따라서 그것들은 가을밤 하늘의 별처럼 우리 가슴 속에 여전히 밝게 빛나고 있다.

➡ _____

_____

[01~03] 다음 글을 읽고 물음에 답하시오.

In the sky where seasons pass ___ⓐ___ a hurry
Autumn fills the air.

And ready I stand, without a worry,
To count all the stars there.
......
Memory for one star,
Love for another star,
Loneliness for another star,
Longing for another star,
Poetry for another star,
And, oh, mother, mother for another star.
......

(A)Have you read these lines before? They are part of the poem "Counting Stars at Night" ___ⓑ___ Yoon Dong-ju. (B)The poem was written a long time ago but still remains one of Korea's favorite poem.

01 위 글의 빈칸 ⓐ와 ⓑ에 들어갈 전치사가 바르게 짝지어진 것은?

	ⓐ	ⓑ		ⓐ	ⓑ
①	on	from	②	in	by
③	in	from	④	on	to
⑤	for	by			

중요

02 위 글의 밑줄 친 (A)의 현재완료 용법과 같은 것을 모두 고르시오.

① We have done it several times.
② He hasn't seen her since last night.
③ John hasn't eaten his hamburger yet.
④ He has seen my sister once.
⑤ I have known him for the past 5 years.

서답형

03 위 글의 밑줄 친 (B)에서 어법상 틀린 부분을 찾아 고치시오.

_____ ➡ _____

[04~06] 다음 글을 읽고 물음에 답하시오.

His parents wanted him to be a doctor, but Dong-ju chose to study literature at a college in Seoul. (A)[During / While] his college years, he often hung out with (B)[another / other] young poets and wrote poetry where he expressed feelings about his hometown and lost country. To celebrate his graduation, he wished to publish 19 of his poems (a)'하늘과 바람과 별과 시'라는 제목으로. He made three copies of the book by hand. One was given to his close friend, Jeong Byeong-uk, (C)[another / the other] was presented to his favorite professor, and the last one was kept for himself. However, his professor advised against his plan because he thought the Japanese government would not allow the publication. Dong-ju followed his advice and ___ⓐ___ the idea.

04 위 글의 빈칸 ⓐ에 들어갈 알맞은 말을 두 개 고르시오.

① abandoned   ② offered
③ gave up   ④ explained
⑤ suggested

서답형

05 위 글의 괄호 (A)~(C)에서 어법상 알맞은 낱말을 골라 쓰시오.

➡ (A) _____ (B) _____ (C) _____

서답형

06 위 글의 밑줄 친 (a)의 우리말에 맞게 주어진 어휘를 이용하여 8 단어로 영작하시오.

> title, *Heaven, Wind, Stars, and Poetry*

➡ _____

_____

[07~09] 다음 글을 읽고 물음에 답하시오.

Dong-ju was born in 1917 near Yanbin, China. ⓐAs a young boy, he loved sports, and he was a soccer player for his school. He also loved sewing so much that he sewed the numbers on all his friends' soccer uniforms. However, it was literature that he loved most. In elementary school he wrote a lot of poems. He even made a literary magazine with his cousin, Song Mong-gyu. In middle school he once borrowed a poetry book by a famous poet of the time, Baek Seok, and copied the whole book by hand. He really wanted to have his own copy of the rare book.

07 위 글의 밑줄 친 ⓐAs와 같은 의미로 쓰인 것을 고르시오.

① They did as I had asked.
② She may need some help as she's new.
③ As you know, Julia is leaving soon.
④ She sang as she walked.
⑤ She was as beautiful as I had imagined.

서답형

08 본문의 내용과 일치하도록 다음 빈칸 (A)와 (B)에 알맞은 단어를 쓰시오.

> Dong-ju wrote many (A)_____ in elementary school, and even made (B)_____ _____ _____ with his cousin, Song Mong-gyu.

중요

09 Which question CANNOT be answered after reading the passage?

① When was Dong-ju born?
② What sport did Dong-ju love as a young boy?
③ Why did Dong-ju sew the numbers on all his friends' soccer uniforms?
④ When did Dong-ju make a literary magazine with his cousin, Song Mong-gyu?
⑤ What was the title of the poetry book that Dong-ju copied by hand?

[10~12] 다음 글을 읽고 물음에 답하시오.

Dong-ju decided to study further in the country ⓐwhere his father had studied before. So, in 1942, Dong-ju and his cousin began to study in Japan. On July 10 the following year, his cousin was arrested by the Japanese police for taking part in an independence movement. Four days later, Dong-ju was also arrested on the same ⓑcharges. In 1945, Dong-ju and his cousin died in prison after harsh treatment by the police. It was just a few months later that Korea achieved independence from Japan.

서답형

10 위 글의 밑줄 친 ⓐwhere를 두 단어로 바꿔 쓰시오.

➡ _____

11 위 글의 밑줄 친 ⓑcharges와 같은 의미로 쓰인 것을 고르시오.

① The admission charges are free.
② She always charges the battery before use.
③ He denied all charges in court.
④ A prosecutor charges a person with a crime.
⑤ He charges 100 dollars for the repairs.

서답형

12 In July 1943, why were Dong-ju and his cousin arrested by the Japanese police? Fill in the blanks with suitable words. (2 words)

> They were arrested by the Japanese police for _____ _____ an independence movement.

[13~15] 다음 글을 읽고 물음에 답하시오.

Dong-ju was born in 1917 near Yanbin, China. (①) As a young boy, he loved sports, and he was a soccer player for his school. (②) He also loved ____ⓐ____ so much that he sewed the numbers on all his friends' soccer uniforms. (③) In elementary school he wrote a lot of poems. (④) He even made a literary magazine with his cousin, Song Mong-gyu. (⑤) In middle school he once borrowed a poetry book by a famous poet of the time, Baek Seok, and copied the whole book by hand. He really wanted to have his own copy of the rare book.

서답형

13 위 글의 빈칸 ⓐ에 sew를 알맞은 형태로 쓰시오.

➡ _____ 또는 _____

14 위 글의 흐름으로 보아, 주어진 문장이 들어가기에 가장 적절한 곳은?

> However, it was literature that he loved most.

① ② ③ ④ ⑤

중요

15 According to the passage, which is NOT true?

① As a young boy, Dong-ju was a soccer player for his school.
② Dong-ju sewed the numbers on all his friends' soccer uniforms.
③ Dong-ju loved literature more than sewing.
④ In middle school Dong-ju made a literary magazine with his cousin, Song Mong-gyu.
⑤ Dong-ju really wanted to have his own copy of a poetry book by Baek Seok.

[16~18] 다음 글을 읽고 물음에 답하시오.

(A)His parents wanted him to be a doctor, but Dong-ju chose studying literature at a college in Seoul. During his college years, he often hung out with other young poets and wrote poetry where he expressed feelings about his hometown and lost country. To celebrate ①his graduation, he wished to publish 19 of ②his poems under the title, *Heaven, Wind, Stars, and Poetry*. He made three copies of the book by hand. One was given to ③his close friend, Jeong Byeong-uk, another was presented to his favorite professor, and the last one was kept for himself. However, ④his professor advised ____ⓐ____ his plan because he thought the Japanese government would not allow the publication. Dong-ju followed ⑤his advice and gave up the idea.

16 위 글의 빈칸 ⓐ에 들어갈 알맞은 전치사를 고르시오.

① on   ② against   ③ for
④ to   ⑤ over

17 밑줄 친 ①~⑤ 중에서 가리키는 대상이 나머지 넷과 **다른** 것은?

① ② ③ ④ ⑤

서답형
18 위 글의 밑줄 친 (A)에서 어법상 **틀린** 부분을 찾아 고치시오.

_____ ➡ _____

[19~21] 다음 글을 읽고 물음에 답하시오.

Dong-ju decided to study further in the country where his father had studied before. (①) So, ⓐin 1942, Dong-ju and his cousin began to study in Japan. (②) ⓑIn July 10 the following year, his cousin was arrested by the Japanese police ⓒfor taking part in an independence movement. (③) In 1945, Dong-ju and his cousin died in prison after harsh treatment ⓓby the police. (④) It was just a few months later that Korea achieved independence ⓔfrom Japan. (⑤)

19 위 글의 흐름으로 보아, ①~⑤ 중 주어진 문장이 들어가기에 가장 적절한 곳은?

Four days later, Dong-ju was also arrested on the same charges.

① ② ③ ④ ⑤

서답형
20 위 글의 밑줄 친 ⓐ~ⓔ에서 전치사의 쓰임이 적절하지 않은 것을 찾아 알맞게 고치시오.

_____ 번 ➡ _____

21 위 글의 주제로 알맞은 것을 고르시오.

① Dong-ju and his father's decision about his studying abroad
② Dong-ju's cousin who also began to study in Japan
③ Dong-ju's cousin's arrest by the Japanese police
④ the harsh treatment by the police in prison
⑤ Dong-ju and his cousin's independence movement and unfortunate death

22 다음 글의 밑줄 친 ⓐ를 'it is ~ that ...강조 구문'으로 고친 것 중 옳지 **않은** 것을 고르시오.

ⓐIn 1948, Jeong Byeong-uk brought Dong-ju's poems to the poet's brother, and they were finally published. The book was given the title the poet had thought of many years before. His poems are loved by people of all ages, and thus they still shine brightly in our hearts like the stars in the autumn night sky.

① It was in 1948 that Jeong Byeong-uk brought Dong-ju's poems to the poet's brother.
② It was Jeong Byeong-uk that brought Dong-ju's poems to the poet's brother in 1948.
③ It was brought that Jeong Byeong-uk Dong-ju's poems to the poet's brother in 1948.
④ It was Dong-ju's poems that Jeong Byeong-uk brought to the poet's brother in 1948.
⑤ It was to the poet's brother that Jeong Byeong-uk brought Dong-ju's poems in 1948.

[01~03] 다음 글을 읽고 물음에 답하시오.

In the sky ___ⓐ___ seasons pass ⓑin a hurry
Autumn fills the air.

And ready I stand, without a worry,
To count all the stars there.
......

Have you read these lines before? ⓒThey are part of the poem "Counting Stars at Night" by Yoon Dong-ju. The poem was written a long time ago but still remains one of Korea's favorite poems.

01 위 글의 빈칸 ⓐ에 들어갈 알맞은 단어를 쓰시오.

➡ _____

02 위 글의 밑줄 친 ⓑin a hurry와 바꿔 쓸 수 있는 두 단어를 쓰시오.

➡ _____

03 위 글의 밑줄 친 ⓒThey가 가리키는 것을 본문에서 찾아 쓰시오.

➡ _____

[04~06] 다음 글을 읽고 물음에 답하시오.

Dong-ju was born in 1917 near Yanbin, China. As a young boy, he loved sports, and he was a soccer player for his school. He also loved sewing so much that he sewed the numbers on all his friends' soccer uniforms. However, ⓐ그가 가장 사랑한 것은 문학이었다. In elementary school he wrote a lot of (A)[poems / poets]. He even made a (B)[literally / literary] magazine with his cousin, Song Mong-gyu. In middle school he once borrowed a poetry book by a famous poet of the time, Baek Seok, and copied the whole book by hand. He really wanted to have his own copy of the (C)[common / rare] book.

04 위 글의 괄호 (A)~(C)에서 문맥이나 어법상 알맞은 낱말을 골라 쓰시오.

➡ (A) _____ (B) _____ (C) _____

05 위 글의 밑줄 친 ⓐ의 우리말에 맞게 주어진 어휘를 이용하여 7 단어로 영작하시오.

that, most

➡ _____

06 다음 문장에서 위 글의 내용과 <u>다른</u> 부분을 찾아서 고치시오.

In middle school Dong-ju once copied by hand a whole poetry book he had bought, and it was written by Baek Seok, a famous poet of the time. He really wanted to have his own copy of the rare book.

_____ ➡ _____

[07~09] 다음 글을 읽고 물음에 답하시오.

In (A)1948, Jeong Byeong-uk brought Dong-ju's poems to the poet's brother, and they were finally published. The book ___ⓐ___ the title the poet had thought of many years before. His poems are loved by people of all ages, and thus (B)they still shine brightly in our hearts like the stars in the autumn night sky.

07 위 글의 빈칸 ⓐ에 give를 알맞은 형태로 쓰시오.

➡ _____

08 위 글의 밑줄 친 (A)1948을 영어로 읽는 법을 쓰시오.

➡ _____

09 위 글의 밑줄 친 (B)they가 가리키는 것을 본문에서 찾아 쓰시오.

➡ _____

[10~11] 다음 글을 읽고 물음에 답하시오.

Dong-ju decided to study ____ⓐ____ in the country where his father had studied before. So, in 1942, Dong-ju and his cousin began to study in Japan. On July 10 the following year, his cousin was arrested by the Japanese police for taking part in an independence movement. Four days later, Dong-ju was also arrested on the same charges. In 1945, Dong-ju and his cousin died in prison after harsh treatment by the police. It was just a few months later that Korea achieved independence from Japan.

10 위 글의 빈칸 ⓐ에 far의 비교급을 쓰시오.

➡ _____

11 Why did Dong-ju and his cousin die in prison in 1945? Fill in the blanks with suitable words.

Because there was _____ _____ by the Japanese police.

[12~14] 다음 글을 읽고 물음에 답하시오.

His parents wanted him to be a doctor, but Dong-ju chose to study literature at a college in Seoul. During his college years, he often hung out with other young poets and wrote poetry where he expressed feelings about his hometown and lost country. To celebrate his graduation, he wished to publish 19 of his poems under the title, *Heaven, Wind, Stars, and Poetry*. He made three copies of the book by hand. ⓐOne was given to his close friend, Jeong Byeong-uk, another was presented to his favorite professor, and the last one was kept for himself. However, his professor advised against ⓑhis plan because he thought the Japanese government would not allow the publication. Dong-ju followed his advice and gave up the idea.

12 위 글의 밑줄 친 ⓐ를 능동태로 고치시오.

➡ _____

_____

13 위 글의 밑줄 친 ⓑhis plan이 가리키는 것을 우리말로 쓰시오.

➡ _____

_____

14 본문의 내용과 일치하도록 다음 빈칸 (A)와 (B)에 알맞은 단어를 쓰시오.

Dong-ju majored in (A)_____ at a college in Seoul, though his parents wanted him to be (B)_____ _____.

해석

Communicate: Speak

Tom: Hi, Sora. You look excited.
look+형용사: ~하게 보이다

Sora: Yeah. I'm really looking forward to this Tuesday.
look forward to+명사: ~을 기대한다

Tom: This Tuesday? What's on Tuesday?

Sora: There's a big curling match. I can't wait!

구문해설 · look forward to+명사 = can't wait for+명사 = long for+명사 = be eager for+명사: ~을 기대하다

Tom: 안녕, 소라. 너 신나 보여.

Sora: 응. 나는 정말로 이번 주 화요일이 기대돼.

Tom: 이번 주 화요일? 화요일에 무슨 일이 있니?

Sora: 큰 컬링 게임이 있어. 나는 너무 기대돼!

Before You Read

Last week we celebrated August 15 in our class. We put up pictures of people

who had lived through harsh times and tried to achieve independence. Also,
과거보다 앞선 시점(대과거)이므로 과거완료   부정사의 명사적 용법(목적어)

there was a talk on writers who had expressed their longing for freedom in
= about   과거보다 앞선 시점(대과거)이므로 과거완료

literary works.

구문해설 · celebrate: 기념하다 · put up: 내걸다, 게시하다 · harsh: 가혹한, 혹독한 · independence: 독립 · longing: 동경, 갈망 · literary: 문학의, 문학적인

지난주에 우리는 반에서 8월 15일을 기념했습니다. 우리는 가혹한 시대를 살면서 독립을 쟁취하려고 노력한 사람들의 사진을 전시했습니다. 또한, 자유를 향한 동경을 문학 작품에 표현한 작가들에 관한 강연도 있었습니다.

Wrap Up READING

Do you enjoy plays, poems, novels, or cartoons? They are different kinds of

literature, and people differ in which kind they prefer. However, all of them
differ in: ~에 대해 다르다   which kind 이하는 간접의문문으로 전치사 in의 목적어

allow us to go beyond our own small world where we live. When we read
allow+목적어+to부정사: (목적어)가 ~하게 허락하다   where가 이끄는 관계부사절이 앞의 our own small world를 수식

literature, we come across the ideas of great writers who lived long ago. We

can even imagine being someone else or living in a completely different place.
동사 imagine의 목적어로 쓰인 동명사

In short, literature opens up for us new worlds that we have never visited
현재완료 경험 용법

before.

구문해설 · cartoon: 만화 · literature: 문학 · beyond: ~ 저편에[너머] · come across: ~을 우연히 만나다 · in short: 요컨대

당신은 희곡, 시, 소설 또는 만화를 즐기는가? 그것들은 다양한 종류의 문학으로, 어떤 종류를 선호하는지는 사람에 따라 다르다. 그러나 그것들은 모두 우리를 우리가 사는 작은 세계 너머로 가게 해 준다. 문학을 읽을 때, 우리는 오래 전에 살았던 위대한 작가들의 생각과 마주치게 된다. 심지어 우리는 다른 누군가가 되거나 완전히 다른 장소에서 사는 상상을 할 수도 있다. 요컨대, 문학은 이전에 가 본 적이 없는 새로운 세계를 우리 앞에 펼쳐 준다.

영역별 핵심문제

Words & Expressions

01 다음 영영풀이가 가리키는 것을 쓰시오.

> the state of not being governed by another country

➡ _____

02 다음 중 밑줄 친 부분의 뜻풀이가 바르지 <u>않은</u> 것은?

① My friends saw my picture in the <u>yearbook</u>. (졸업 앨범)
② I have nothing <u>particular</u> to do this afternoon. (특별한, 특정한)
③ The <u>poet</u> was in deep thought by the river. (시)
④ My grandfather <u>remained</u> a farmer for the rest of his life. (여전히 ~이었다)
⑤ Did you know how to <u>sew</u>? (바느질하다)

03 다음 문장의 빈칸에 들어갈 말을 〈보기〉에서 골라 쓰시오.

> ┤ 보기 ├
> rare / loneliness / poem / whole / literature

(1) He showed me the _____ he had written himself.
(2) The _____ wall was painted white.
(3) His hobby is collecting _____ stones.
(4) The greedy man lived in _____.
(5) I liked soccer and sewing, but I loved _____ the most.

04 다음 문장의 빈칸에 공통으로 들어갈 말을 고르시오.

> • Where do I need to check _____ the new arrivals?
> • Several animals come _____ only at night.
> • When I was hanging _____ with my boyfriend, my mother called me.

① out   ② on   ③ of   ④ in   ⑤ for

05 다음 주어진 문장의 밑줄 친 present(ed)와 같은 의미로 쓰인 것은?

> The waiter <u>presented</u> the bill to me.

① They wrote the letter after receiving the <u>present</u>.
② What can I get him for a birthday <u>present</u>?
③ The <u>present</u> situation is safe and peaceful.
④ Do you know who the <u>present</u> owner of this house is?
⑤ Last week Mike <u>presented</u> the documents to us.

06 다음 우리말을 주어진 단어를 이용하여 영작하시오.

(1) 강도가 은행 근처에서 체포되었다. (robber)
➡ _____

(2) 우리 팀은 혹독한 훈련을 겪었다. (through)
➡ _____

(3) 그는 그의 목표를 이루기 위해 최선을 다했다. (tried)
➡ _____

(4) 나는 공정한 대우를 원합니다. (fair)
➡ _____

07 다음 우리말과 일치하도록 주어진 단어를 모두 배열하여 영작하시오.

(1) 교수님은 설탕 사용에 반대하는 충고를 했다.
(advised / the / of / use / against / sugar / the / professor)

➡ _____

_____

(2) 우리의 졸업을 축하하고 파티를 하자!
(have / and / our / a / party / let's / graduation / celebrate)

➡ _____

_____

(3) 디자이너들과 편집자들은 좋은 책을 만들기 위해 최선을 다한다.
(to / their / make / a / book / editors / designers / good / try / best / and)

➡ _____

_____

Conversation

[08~09] 다음 대화를 읽고 물음에 답하시오.

Sora: Hey, Minjun. What are you doing?

Minjun: I'm reading a novel for a book report.

Sora: Let me see. Oh, is this a new book by Ken Kuller?

Minjun: Yeah, I borrowed it this morning. Do you know Ken Kuller?

Sora: Of course. I'm ⓐa big fan of his. I've read all of his mystery books.

Minjun: I think he's a great writer. I can't stop ⓑreading this book.

Sora: You know what? His novel *Four Eyes* ⓒhas been made into a movie.

Minjun: Yeah. I saw the movie poster. It looks interesting.

Sora: It'll ⓓcome out next Thursday. I'm looking forward ⓔto see it!

Minjun: Maybe we can see the movie together.

08 위 대화의 밑줄 친 ⓐ~ⓔ 중 어법상 틀린 것을 찾아 바르게 고치시오.

➡ _____

09 위 대화의 내용과 일치하지 않는 것은?

① 민준이는 독후감을 위해 소설을 읽고 있다.
② 소라는 Ken Kuller의 열렬한 팬이다.
③ 민준이는 Ken Kuller가 위대한 작가라고 생각한다.
④ Ken Kuller의 신간 소설이 영화로 만들어졌다.
⑤ Ken Kuller의 소설을 바탕으로 만들어진 영화가 다음 주 목요일에 개봉한다.

[10~12] 다음 대화를 읽고 물음에 답하시오.

Minjun: Hello, Ms. Seo.

Ms. Seo: Hi, Minjun. Long time no see. ⓐ무엇 때문에 여기에 왔니?

Minjun: (A) I have to write a book report. Can you recommend a good novel to read?

Ms. Seo: (B) There's a new Ken Kuller book, *22nd Street*.

Minjun: (C) Oh, I've heard of him. Can you show me the book?

Ms. Seo: (D) It's in the "New Arrivals" area. It's really popular among teens in Great Britain.

Minjun: (E) Thank you for your help. Can I check it out?

Ms. Seo: Sure. You can borrow new books for seven days.

Minjun: Okay.

10 위 대화의 (A)~(E) 중 주어진 문장이 들어가기에 적절한 곳은?

How about a mystery?

① (A) ② (B) ③ (C) ④ (D) ⑤ (E)

11 위 대화의 밑줄 친 ⓐ의 우리말을 4 단어로 영작하시오.

➡ _____

12 위 대화의 내용과 일치하지 <u>않는</u> 것은?

① 민준이는 독후감을 써야 한다.
② 민준이는 읽기 좋은 소설을 추천 받고 싶다.
③ 서 선생님은 민준이에게 추리소설을 추천하였다.
④ 신착 도서 서가에 Ken Kuller의 책이 있다.
⑤ '22nd Street'은 인기가 많아 지금 대여할 수 없다.

13 다음 대화가 자연스럽게 이어지도록 순서대로 배열하시오.

> Mike: Good morning, Jiho.
>
> Jiho: Good morning.
>
> Mike: Take a seat, please. How would you like your hair done?
>
> Jiho: Well, I'm taking my pictures for the yearbook. So I want to look cool.
>
> Mike: When do you take the pictures?
>
> (A) Look at this. How about this style? It'll look good on you.
>
> (B) This Friday at Dream & Joy Park.
>
> (C) No. Can you recommend one for me?
>
> (D) Wow, I like it. I can't wait to see how I'll look in the pictures.
>
> (E) Sounds good. Do you have a particular style in mind?
>
> Mike: I'm sure you'll look cool.

➡ _____

14 다음 짝지어진 대화가 <u>어색한</u> 것은?

① A: Can you recommend a gift shop nearby?
   B: Go to Anne's Gifts. There're lots of things to buy.

② A: Will you recommend a fun TV program?
   B: *Pam and Sam* is really fun.

③ A: I'm looking forward to visiting the restaurant by the river.
   B: Me, too. There we can have a nice dinner.

④ A: You look happy. What's up?
   B: I'm looking forward to seeing Ken Kuller's new movie.

⑤ A: I feel a little bored. Can you recommend a good movie?
   B: You can say that again. It's a good movie.

Grammar

15 다음 밑줄 친 부분과 바꿔 쓸 수 있는 것은?

> It was in a small village near Mokpo <u>that</u> I was born.

① what   ② which
③ who   ④ when
⑤ where

16 다음 문장 중에서 어법상 <u>어색한</u> 문장을 고르시오.

① I was very hungry because I had not eaten anything since then.
② When I came back home, I found somebody had done the dishes.
③ No one told me that the supermarket had closed.
④ He already left when I had returned home.
⑤ Before I came home, my brother washed our dog.

17 다음 ⓐ~ⓖ 중 어법상 옳은 것을 모두 고르시오.

ⓐ Dong-ju decided to study further in the country where his father had studied before.

ⓑ When he had got to school, the class already began.

ⓒ When Ms. Bae came back home, she found somebody has taken her corn.

ⓓ She could not go into her house because she had lost her key.

ⓔ I think it was on the bus that I lost it.

ⓕ It was Junsu which called me last night.

ⓖ That was Spanish which he learned when he was five.

➡ _____

18 다음 중 어법상 어색한 것을 고르시오. (2개)

① Because she did not have studied hard, she failed the test.

② It was 2014 that my family moved to this city.

③ Sora had never been to Busan before she was 16.

④ It was William Shakespeare who wrote *Romeo and Juliet*.

⑤ It was in 1885 that Vincent van Gogh painted *The Potato Eaters*.

Reading

[19~21] 다음 글을 읽고 물음에 답하시오.

Dong-ju was born in 1917 near Yanbin, China. As a young boy, he loved sports, and he was a soccer player for his school. He also loved sewing so much that he sewed the numbers ___ⓐ___ all his friends' soccer uniforms. However, it was literature that he loved most. In elementary school he wrote a lot of poems. He even made a literary magazine with his cousin, Song Mong-gyu. In middle school he once borrowed a poetry book by a famous poet of the time, Baek Seok, and copied the whole book ___ⓑ___ hand. He really wanted to have his own copy of the rare book.

19 위 글의 빈칸 ⓐ와 ⓑ에 들어갈 전치사가 바르게 짝지어진 것은?

ⓐ ⓑ	ⓐ ⓑ
① for – in	② on – at
③ in – by	④ for – at
⑤ on – by	

20 위 글의 주제로 알맞은 것을 고르시오.

① Dong-ju was a poet during the period of Japanese colonial rule.

② Dong-ju loved both sports and sewing.

③ What Dong-ju loved most of all was literature.

④ Copying the whole book by hand was a difficult way to have a poetry book.

⑤ Dong-ju liked Baek Seok's poems, so he copied the whole book by hand.

21 위 글을 읽고 알 수 없는 것을 고르시오.

① Where was Dong-ju born?

② Why did Dong-ju love sports as a young boy?

③ What did Dong-ju sew for his friends?

④ With whom did Dong-ju make a literary magazine in elementary school?

⑤ Whose poetry book did Dong-ju copy by hand in middle school?

[22~24] 다음 글을 읽고 물음에 답하시오.

His parents wanted him to be a doctor, but Dong-ju chose to study literature at a college in Seoul. During his college years, he often hung out with other young poets and wrote poetry ⓐ____ he expressed feelings about his hometown and lost country. ⓑTo celebrate his graduation, he wished to publish 19 of his poems under the title, *Heaven, Wind, Stars, and Poetry*. He made three copies of the book by hand. One was given to his close friend, Jeong Byeong-uk, another was presented to his favorite professor, and the last one was kept for himself. However, his professor advised against his plan because he thought the Japanese government would not allow the publication. Dong-ju followed his advice and gave up the idea.

22 위 글의 빈칸 ⓐ에 들어갈 알맞은 말을 고르시오.

① when   ② where
③ how   ④ which
⑤ why

23 위 글의 밑줄 친 ⓑTo celebrate와 to부정사의 용법이 <u>다른</u> 것을 <u>모두</u> 고르시오.

① It is time to celebrate the start of spring.
② Where did you meet to celebrate his graduation?
③ The purpose of the festival was to celebrate the harvest.
④ A first-birthday party is an event to celebrate the first birthday of a child.
⑤ On Chuseok, they gathered together to celebrate the harvest of the year.

24 According to the passage, which is NOT true?

① Dong-ju's parents hoped that Dong-ju would become a doctor.
② Dong-ju determined to study literature at a college in Seoul.
③ During his college years, Dong-ju often hung around with other young poets.
④ In his poems, Dong-ju expressed feelings about his hometown and lost country.
⑤ To celebrate his graduation, Dong-ju published 19 of his poems under the title, *Heaven, Wind, Stars, and Poetry*.

[25~26] 다음 글을 읽고 물음에 답하시오.

In 1948, Jeong Byeong-uk brought Dong-ju's poems to the poet's brother, and they were (A)finally published. The book was given the title the poet ⓐ____ of many years before. His poems are loved by people of all ages, and thus they still shine brightly in our hearts like the stars in the autumn night sky.

25 위 글의 빈칸 ⓐ에 think를 알맞은 형태로 쓰시오.

➡ _____

26 위 글의 밑줄 친 (A)finally와 바꿔 쓸 수 <u>없는</u> 말을 고르시오.

① lastly   ② at last
③ in the end   ④ eventually
⑤ in the long run

01 다음 문장의 빈칸에 들어갈 말을 〈보기〉에서 골라 적절한 형태로 쓰시오.

> ┤ 보기 ├
>
> be well known for / take part in / look forward to / give it a try

(1) Many people _____ the Polar Bear Swim in Busan every winter.

(2) I'm really _____ my favorite singer's concert.

(3) He _____ cooking skills.

(4) Don't give up! _____ again.

[02~04] 다음 대화를 읽고 물음에 답하시오.

Sora: Hey, Minjun. What are you doing?

Minjun: I'm reading a novel for a book report.

Sora: Let me see. Oh, is this a new book by Ken Kuller?

Minjun: Yeah, I borrowed @it this morning. Do you know Ken Kuller?

Sora: Of course. I'm a big fan of his. I've read all of his mystery books.

Minjun: I think he's a great writer. I can't stop (A)[to read / reading] this book.

Sora: You know what? His novel *Four Eyes* has been (B)[making / made] into a movie.

Minjun: Yeah. I saw the movie poster. ⓑIt looks interesting.

Sora: ⓒIt'll come out next Thursday. I'm looking forward to (C)[see / seeing] ⓓit!

Minjun: Maybe we can see the movie together.

02 위 대화의 (A)~(C)에 들어갈 말로 바르게 짝지어진 것은?

	(A)	(B)	(C)
①	to read	making	see
②	to read	made	seeing
③	reading	made	see
④	reading	made	seeing
⑤	reading	making	see

03 위 대화의 밑줄 친 @~ⓓ 중 나머지 셋과 가리키는 것이 다른 것을 찾아 무엇을 가리키는지 쓰시오.

➡ _____

04 위 대화를 읽고 대답할 수 없는 것은?

① What is Minjun doing?

② Has Sora read Ken Kuller's books?

③ When did Minjun borrow a new book by Ken Kuller?

④ Who wrote the novel *Four Eyes*?

⑤ When are Minjun and Sora going to see the movie?

[05~07] 다음 대화를 읽고 물음에 답하시오.

Mike: Good morning, Jiho.

Jiho: Good morning.

Mike: Take a seat, please. How would you like your hair done?

Jiho: Well, I'm taking my pictures for the yearbook. So I want to look cool.

Mike: When do you take the pictures?

Jiho: This Friday at Dream & Joy Park.

Mike: Sounds good. Do you have a particular style in mind?

Jiho: No. _____ (A)

Mike: Look at this. How about this style? It'll look good on you.

Jiho: Wow, I like it. I can't wait to see how I'll look in the pictures.

Mike: I'm sure you'll look cool.

출제율 90%

5 위 대화의 빈칸 (A)에 들어갈 말을 주어진 단어를 모두 배열하여 영작하시오.

> (you / one / can / me / recommend / for)

➡ _____

출제율 100%

6 위 대화에서 지호와 Mike의 관계로 적절한 것은?

① student – teacher
② customer – hairdresser
③ patient – doctor
④ tourist – guide
⑤ employer – employee

출제율 95%

7 위 대화의 내용과 일치하지 <u>않는</u> 것은?

① 지호는 졸업 앨범에 들어갈 사진을 찍을 것이다.
② 지호는 이번 금요일에 Dream & Joy Park에서 사진 촬영을 할 것이다.
③ 지호는 졸업 앨범을 위해 마음에 둔 특별한 헤어 스타일이 있다.
④ Mike는 지호에게 헤어 스타일 하나를 추천해 주었다.
⑤ 지호는 Mike가 추천한 스타일이 마음에 든다.

[08~11] 다음 대화를 읽고 물음에 답하시오.

Jane: Nice to meet you, Mr. Henry. Is O. Henry your real name?

Mr. Henry: No. My real name is William Sydney Porter.

Jane: Can you tell me where you're from?

Mr. Henry: I'm from the U.S.

Jane: What do you usually write?

Mr. Henry: I'm a short story writer. I have written about 300 short stories.

Jane: Wow! You're great! What is special about your short stories?

Mr. Henry: They're well known for their surprise endings.

Jane: (A)뜻밖의 결말이 있는 인기 있는 이야기를 하나 추천해 주실 수 있나요?

Mr. Henry: Sure. I recommend *The Last Leaf*.

Jane: What is it about?

Mr. Henry: It's about a sick girl and an old artist who saves her life.

Jane: Oh, I want to read it. I can't wait.

출제율 95%

8 위 대화의 밑줄 친 (A)의 우리말을 주어진 단어를 모두 배열하여 영작하시오.

> (you / with / a surprise / a popular / ending / story / recommend / can)

➡ _____
_____

출제율 90%

9 Why are Mr. Henry's short stories famous?

➡ _____
_____

출제율 90%

10 What is *The Last Leaf* about?

➡ _____
_____

출제율 95%

11 위 대화를 읽고 다음의 표를 완성하시오.

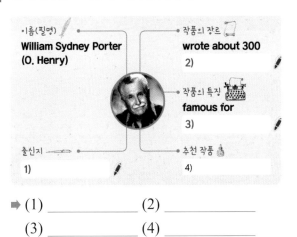

이름(필명)
William Sydney Porter (O. Henry)

작품의 갯수
wrote about 300
2)

작품의 특징
famous for
3)

출신지
1)

추천 작품
4)

➡ (1) _____ (2) _____
(3) _____ (4) _____

12 다음 두 문장을 because를 사용하여 두 사건의 시간차가 드러나도록 한 문장으로 연결하시오. 출제율 90%

- She was not upset.
- She bought some extra balloons.

➡ _____

_____

13 다음 중 어법상 어색한 문장은? 출제율 100%

① When I got home, the pizza party had already finished.
② It was my mother that named me Boram.
③ I had never seen a kangaroo before I went to Australia.
④ It is the park that Patricia plays badminton every weekend.
⑤ It was a storybook that he bought for his sister.

14 다음 밑줄 친 부분을 바르게 고쳐 문장을 다시 쓰시오. 출제율 95%

(1) He showed me some poems he wrote himself.

➡ _____

_____

(2) When I came back home, I found somebody turned on the TV.

➡ _____

(3) It was the bus which Judy lost her wallet.

➡ _____

_____

(4) It was 1776 what the U.S. gained independence from Great Britain.

➡ _____

_____

15 다음 빈칸에 들어갈 말을 순서대로 묶은 것은? 출제율 100%

- I'm sorry I lost the book you _____ me.
- It was at the age of five _____ I learned how to ride a bike.

① had lent – where
② had lent – when
③ lent – where
④ lent – what
⑤ lend – that

[16~17] 다음 글을 읽고 물음에 답하시오.

Dong-ju was born in 1917 near Yanbin, China. As a young boy, he loved sports, and he was a soccer player for his school. He also loved sewing so much that he sewed the numbers on all his friends' soccer uniforms. _____ⓐ_____, it was literature ⓑthat he loved most. In elementary school he wrote a lot of poems. He even made a literary magazine with his cousin, Song Mong-gyu. In middle school he once borrowed a poetry book by a famous poet of the time, Baek Seok, and copied the whole book by hand. He really wanted to have his own copy of the rare book.

16 위 글의 빈칸 ⓐ에 들어갈 알맞은 말을 고르시오. 출제율 90%

① However
② Therefore
③ That is
④ For example
⑤ As a result

17 위 글의 밑줄 친 ⓑthat과 문법적 쓰임이 같은 것을 고르시오. 출제율 95%

① The trouble is that we are short of money.
② Have you listened to that tape I gave you?
③ I'm glad that you like it.
④ It is you that are to blame.
⑤ The actress hid the fact that she was married.

[18~20] 다음 글을 읽고 물음에 답하시오.

His parents wanted him to be a doctor, but Dong-ju chose to study literature at a college in Seoul. (①) During his college years, he often hung out with other young poets and wrote poetry where he expressed feelings about his hometown and lost country. (②) He made three copies of the book by hand. (③) One was given to his close friend, Jeong Byeong-uk, another was presented to his favorite professor, and the last one was kept ____ⓐ____ himself. (④) However, his professor advised ____ⓑ____ his plan because he thought the Japanese government would not allow the publication. (⑤) Dong-ju followed his advice and gave up the idea.

18 위 글의 빈칸 ⓐ와 ⓑ에 들어갈 전치사가 바르게 짝지어진 것은?

ⓐ	ⓑ		ⓐ	ⓑ
① for – against		② by – for
③ in – against		④ for – for
⑤ to – on		

19 위 글의 흐름으로 보아, 주어진 문장이 들어가기에 가장 적절한 곳은?

> To celebrate his graduation, he wished to publish 19 of his poems under the title, *Heaven, Wind, Stars, and Poetry*.

① ② ③ ④ ⑤

20 위 글의 제목으로 알맞은 것을 고르시오.

① His Parents' Desire to Make Dong-ju a Doctor
② A Poet Who Expressed Feelings about Lost Country
③ Dong-ju Made Three Copies of the Book by Hand!
④ Dong-ju and His Close Friend Jeong Byeong-uk
⑤ The Unfulfilled Wish of the Publication of a Poetry Book

[21~22] 다음 글을 읽고 물음에 답하시오.

ⓐDong-ju decided to study further in the country where his father has studied before. So, in 1942, Dong-ju and his cousin began to study in Japan. On July 10 the following year, his cousin was arrested by the Japanese police for ⓑtaking part in an independence movement. Four days later, Dong-ju was also arrested on the same charges. In 1945, Dong-ju and his cousin died in prison after harsh treatment by the police. It was just a few months later that Korea achieved independence from Japan.

21 위 글의 밑줄 친 ⓐ에서 어법상 틀린 부분을 찾아 고치시오.

_____ ➡ _____

22 위 글의 밑줄 친 ⓑtaking part in과 바꿔 쓸 수 있는 말을 모두 고르시오.

① attending to
② participating in
③ dealing in
④ joining
⑤ taking into account

서술형 실전문제

[01~03] 다음 대화를 읽고 물음에 답하시오.

> Mike: Good morning, Jiho.
>
> Jiho: Good morning.
>
> Mike: Take a seat, please. How would you like your hair done?
>
> Jiho: Well, I'm taking my pictures for the yearbook. So I want to look cool.
>
> Mike: When do you take the pictures?
>
> Jiho: This Friday at Dream & Joy Park.
>
> Mike: Sounds good. Do you have a particular style in mind?
>
> Jiho: No. Can you recommend one for me?
>
> Mike: Look at this. How about this style? It'll look good on you.
>
> Jiho: Wow, I like it. I can't wait to see how I'll look in the pictures.
>
> Mike: I'm sure you'll look cool.

01 Where is Jiho going this Friday?

➡ _____

02 What does Jiho ask Mike to do?

➡ _____

03 For what is Jiho going to take pictures this Friday?

➡ _____

04 다음 문장에서 틀린 것을 고쳐 다시 쓰시오.

(1) The witness admitted that he did not tell the complete truth.

➡ _____

_____

(2) I learned that he was sick since last week.

➡ _____

(3) It was my parents got married in a small restaurant.

➡ _____

(4) It was his endless efforts who moved all the animals' hearts.

➡ _____

_____

05 다음 우리말을 주어진 어휘를 이용하여 영작하시오.

(1) 우리 이모는 London을 여러 번 방문했었기 때문에 그 도시를 아주 잘 알았다. (because, my aunt, so well, visit, 14 단어)

➡ _____

_____

(2) Vincent van Gogh가 1885년에 그린 것은 바로 The Potato Eaters였다. (paint, that, 12 단어)

➡ _____

_____

Dong-ju was born in 1917 near Yanbin, China. As a young boy, he loved sports, and he was a soccer player for his school. He also loved sewing so much that he (A)[sawed / sewed] the numbers on all his friends' soccer uniforms. However, it was literature (B)[that / what] he loved most. In elementary school he wrote a lot of poems. He even made a literary magazine with his cousin, Song Mong-gyu. In middle school he once (C) [borrowed / lent] a poetry book by a famous poet of the time, Baek Seok, and copied the whole book by hand. He really wanted to have his own copy of ⓐthe rare book.

06 위 글의 괄호 (A)~(C)에서 문맥이나 어법상 알맞은 낱말을 골라 쓰시오.

➡ (A) _____ (B) _____ (C) _____

07 위 글의 밑줄 친 ⓐthe rare book이 가리키는 것을 본문에서 찾아 쓰시오.

➡ _____

_____

08 What was the reason why Dong-ju copied Baek Seok's poetry book by hand? Answer in English beginning with "Because".

➡ _____

_____

[09~11] 다음 글을 읽고 물음에 답하시오.

His parents wanted him to be a doctor, but Dong-ju chose to study literature at a college in Seoul. During his college years,

he often (A)[hanged / hung] out with other young poets and wrote poetry where he expressed feelings about his hometown and lost country. To celebrate his graduation, he wished to publish 19 of his poems under the title, *Heaven, Wind, Stars, and Poetry*. He made three copies of the book by hand. One was given to his close friend, Jeong Byeong-uk, another was presented to his favorite professor, and the (B)[last / latest] one was kept for himself. However, ⓐ그의 교수는 일본 정부가 출판을 허가하지 않으리라 여겨, 그의 계획에 반대하는 충고를 했다. Dong-ju (C)[followed / refused] his advice and gave up the idea.

09 위 글의 괄호 (A)~(C)에서 문맥상 알맞은 낱말을 골라 쓰시오.

➡ (A) _____ (B) _____ (C) _____

10 위 글의 밑줄 친 ⓐ의 우리말에 맞게 한 단어를 보충하여, 주어진 어휘를 알맞게 배열하시오.

the publication / he thought / his plan / because / his professor / would not allow / advised / the Japanese government

➡ _____

_____

_____

11 What did Dong-ju express in his poetry? Answer in English in a full sentence. (9 words)

➡ _____

_____

01 다음 대화를 읽고 대화의 내용과 일치하도록 민준이의 일기를 완성하시오.

Sora: Hey, Minjun. What are you doing?

Minjun: I'm reading a novel for a book report.

Sora: Let me see. Oh, is this a new book by Ken Kuller?

Minjun: Yeah, I borrowed it this morning. Do you know Ken Kuller?

Sora: Of course. I'm a big fan of his. I've read all of his mystery books.

Minjun: I think he's a great writer. I can't stop reading this book.

Sora: You know what? His novel *Four Eyes* has been made into a movie.

Minjun: Yeah. I saw the movie poster. It looks interesting.

Sora: It'll come out next Thursday. I'm looking forward to seeing it!

Minjun: Maybe we can see the movie together.

Mon, Sep 7th, 2020

While reading the new book of Ken Kuller for (A)_____, Sora came to me and talked about Ken Kuller. I found that Sora already knew Ken Kuller and read (B)_____. She told me that his novel *Four Eyes* (C)_____. When I saw the movie poster, it looked (D)_____. Sora was looking forward to seeing it.

---

02 다음 내용을 바탕으로 시를 쓰시오.

소재 / 주제: animal

아이디어: What do you want to write?

> A cat whose name is Tommy lives with my family.

> Tommy washes his face every morning.

> Tommy has beautiful black eyes and little ears.

> Tommy jumps high to catch a butterfly.

> Tommy likes me very much.

> Tommy always sleeps in my bed.

형식: Which type of poem do you want to write?

A cat lives with my family. His name is (A)_____.

He is clean. He (B)_____ every morning.

He is cute. He has beautiful (C)_____ and little ears.

He is fast. He (D)_____ to catch a butterfly.

Tommy likes me very much. He always sleeps (E)_____.

단원별 모의고사

01 다음 우리말에 맞게 빈칸에 알맞은 말을 쓰시오.

(1) 사람들은 정부 정책에 따라야 한다.

➡ People should follow the _____ policy.

(2) Ms. Gray는 출판 전에 원고를 점검하고 있다.

➡ Ms. Gray is checking her draft before _____.

(3) 나의 언니는 영문학을 전공했다.

➡ My big sister majored in English _____.

(4) 그의 시는 문학잡지에 출판되었다.

➡ His poem was published in a _____ magazine.

[02~04] 다음 대화를 읽고 물음에 답하시오.

Minjun: Hello, Ms. Seo.

Ms. Seo: Hi, Minjun. Long time no see. ⓐ<u>What brings you here?</u>

Minjun: I have to write a book report. Can you recommend a good novel to read?

Ms. Seo: ⓑ<u>How about a mystery?</u> There's a new Ken Kuller book, *22nd Street*.

Minjun: Oh, ⓒ<u>I've heard of him.</u> Can you show me the book?

Ms. Seo: It's in the "New Arrivals" area. ⓓ<u>It's really popular among teens in Great Britain.</u>

Minjun: Thank you for your help. ⓔ<u>Can I check out it?</u>

Ms. Seo: Sure. You can borrow new books for seven days.

Minjun: Okay.

02 위 대화의 밑줄 친 ⓐ~ⓔ 중 어법상 틀린 것을 찾아 바르게 고치시오.

➡ _____

03 위 대화를 읽고 대답할 수 <u>없는</u> 것은?

① Why does Minjun come to Ms. Seo?

② What should Minjun write?

③ In which area is *22nd Street*?

④ How long can Minjun borrow new books?

⑤ Why is *22nd Street* popular among teens in Great Britain?

04 위 대화의 내용과 일치하도록 민준이의 일기를 완성하시오.

Mon, August 31st, 2020

Today, I went to the library to borrow a book. I had to write a book report but I didn't know what to read. I asked Ms. Seo to recommend (A)_____. She introduced (B)_____ _____. I heard that it's really popular (C)_____ in Great Britain. I found it in the (D)_____. I'm looking forward to reading this book.

[05~07] 다음 대화를 읽고 물음에 답하시오.

Sora: Hey, Minjun. What are you doing?

Minjun: I'm reading a novel for a book report.

Sora: Let me see. Oh, is this a new book by Ken Kuller?

Minjun: Yeah, I borrowed it this morning. Do you know Ken Kuller?

Sora: Of course. I'm a big fan of his. I've read all of his mystery books.

Minjun: I think he's a great writer. I can't stop reading this book.

Sora: You know what? His novel *Four Eyes* has been made into a movie.

Minjun: Yeah. I saw the movie poster. It looks interesting.

Sora: It'll come out next Thursday. I'm looking forward to seeing it!

Minjun: Maybe we can see the movie together.

05 When did Minjun borrow the new book by Ken Kuller?

➡ _____

06 Among Ken Kuller's novels, which one has been made into a movie?

➡ _____

07 What does Minjun think about Ken Kuller?

➡ _____

[08~10] 다음 대화를 읽고 물음에 답하시오.

Mike: Good morning, Jiho.

Jiho: Good morning.

Mike: Take a seat, please. How would you like your hair done?

Jiho: Well, I'm taking my pictures for the yearbook. So I want to look cool. ⓐ

Mike: When do you take the pictures?

Jiho: This Friday at Dream & Joy Park. ⓑ

Mike: Sounds good. ⓒ

Jiho: No. Can you recommend one for me?

Mike: Look at this. How about this style? It'll look good on you. ⓓ

Jiho: Wow, I like it. (A)I can't wait to see how I'll look in the pictures. (forward)

Mike: I'm sure you'll look cool. ⓔ

08 위 대화의 ⓐ~ⓔ 중 주어진 문장이 들어가기에 적절한 곳은?

| Do you have a particular style in mind? |

① ⓐ   ② ⓑ   ③ ⓒ   ④ ⓓ   ⑤ ⓔ

09 위 대화의 밑줄 친 (A)와 바꾸어 쓸 수 있는 말을 주어진 단어를 이용하여 다시 쓰시오.

➡ _____

10 위 대화가 이루어지는 곳으로 적절한 곳은?

① Post office   ② Airport
③ Hospital   ④ Library
⑤ Hair salon

[11~12] 다음 대화를 읽고 물음에 답하시오.

Jane: Nice to meet you, Mr. Henry. Is O. Henry your real name?

Mr. Henry: No. My real name is William Sydney Porter.

Jane: Can you tell me where you're from?

Mr. Henry: (A) I'm from the U.S.

Jane: What do you usually write?

Mr. Henry: (B) I have written about 300 short stories.

Jane: Wow! You're great! What is special about your short stories?

Mr. Henry: (C) They're well known for their surprise endings.

Jane: Can you recommend a popular story with a surprise ending?

Mr. Henry: (D) Sure. I recommend *The Last Leaf*.

Jane: What is it about?

Mr. Henry: (E) It's about a sick girl and an old artist who saves her life.

Jane: Oh, I want to read it. I can't wait.

11 위 대화의 (A)~(E) 중 주어진 문장이 들어가기에 적절한 곳은?

> I'm a short story writer.

① (A)　② (B)　③ (C)　④ (D)　⑤ (E)

12 위 대화를 읽고 대답할 수 <u>없는</u> 것은?

① What does Mr. Henry do?
② Where is Mr. Henry from?
③ How many short stories has Mr. Henry written?
④ What story does Mr. Henry recommend?
⑤ In *The Last Leaf*, how does an old artist save a sick girl?

13 다음을 같은 뜻이 되도록 빈칸에 알맞은 말을 쓰시오.

(1) I went to the cafe. Alicia went back home and I couldn't meet her.
= When I went to the cafe, Alicia _____ back home.

(2) Mr. Han said. He fixed the bike the day before. But it was a lie.
= Mr. Han said he _____ the bike the day before, but it was a lie.

14 Which is grammatically WRONG?

① It was not until yesterday that I noticed it.
② It was last Saturday when we threw a surprise party for Ms. Song.
③ It is the car who James Bond drove in the famous films called 007.
④ It was under the lemon tree where the concert was held.
⑤ It is my father who gets up earliest in my family.

15 다음 주어진 문장의 밑줄 친 부분과 용법이 같은 것은?

> My father regretted that he <u>had washed</u> his car.

① Tricia was not at home. She <u>had gone</u> shopping.
② Melina <u>had played</u> the piano since she was 6.
③ He <u>had failed</u> twice, but he decided to start again
④ I <u>had saved</u> my document before the computer crashed.
⑤ Unknown to me, he <u>had</u> already <u>signed</u> the agreement.

16 다음 문장에서 어법상 <u>어색한</u> 것을 바르게 고쳐 다시 쓰시오.

(1) It was fried chicken that I eat when I feel good.
➡ _____

(2) It was Mr. Brown saved the child in the river.
➡ _____

(3) She insisted that she was not there the previous night.
➡ _____

(4) When the children arrived at the camp, their parents has already started cooking.
➡ _____

17 다음 중 어법상 옳은 문장을 <u>모두</u> 고르시오.

① Jake was late for school because he had missed the bus.

② The train left when I had arrived at the station.

③ When Ms. Bae came back home, she found somebody had opened the kitchen door.

④ He was an engineer before he became an architect.

⑤ It was Uncle Ben which broke Plum's toy.

⑥ It was just a few months later that Korea achieved independence from Japan.

⑦ It was the drums when he played this year.

[18~20] 다음 글을 읽고 물음에 답하시오.

Dong-ju was born in 1917 near Yanbin, China. As a young boy, he loved sports, and he was a soccer player for his school. (A) <u>그는 또한 바느질하는 것을 무척 좋아해서 친구들의 축구 유니폼에 번호를 바느질해 주기도 했다.</u> However, it was literature that he loved most. In elementary school he wrote a lot of poems. He even made a ___ⓐ___ magazine with his cousin, Song Mong-gyu. In middle school he once borrowed a poetry book by a famous poet of the time, Baek Seok, and copied the whole book by hand. He really wanted to have his own copy of the rare book.

18 주어진 영영풀이를 참고하여 빈칸 ⓐ에 철자 l로 시작하는 단어를 쓰시오.

concerned with or connected with the writing, study, or appreciation of literature

➡ _____

19 위 글의 밑줄 친 (A)의 우리말에 맞게 한 단어를 보충하여, 주어진 어휘를 알맞게 배열하시오.

on all his friends' soccer uniforms / sewing / he / that / also / sewed / much / the numbers / loved / he

➡ _____

_____

20 본문의 내용과 일치하도록 다음 빈칸에 알맞은 단어를 쓰시오.

Among other things, what Dong-ju loved most was _____.

[21~23] 다음 글을 읽고 물음에 답하시오.

His parents wanted him to be a doctor, but Dong-ju chose to study literature at a college in Seoul. During his college years, he often hung out with other young poets and wrote poetry where he expressed feelings about his hometown and lost country. To celebrate his graduation, he wished to publish 19 of his poems under the title, *Heaven, Wind, Stars, and Poetry*. He made three copies of the book by hand. One was given to his close friend, Jeong Byeong-uk, another was presented to his favorite professor, and the last (A)one was kept for himself. ___ⓐ___, his professor advised against his plan because he thought the Japanese government would not allow the publication. Dong-ju followed his advice and gave up the idea.

21 위 글의 빈칸 ⓐ에 들어갈 알맞은 말을 고르시오.

① In addition ② In other words
③ Similarly ④ Thus
⑤ However

22 위 글의 밑줄 친 (A)one이 가리키는 것을 영어로 쓰시오.

➡ _____

23 Why did Dong-ju's professor advise against Dong-ju's plan? Answer in English beginning with "Because".

➡ _____
_____

[24~25] 다음 글을 읽고 물음에 답하시오.

Dong-ju decided to study further in the country where his father had studied before. So, in 1942, Dong-ju and his cousin began to study in Japan. On July 10 the following year, his cousin was arrested by the Japanese police for ⓐtaking part in an independence movement. Four days later, Dong-ju was also arrested on the same charges. In 1945, Dong-ju and his cousin died in prison after harsh treatment by the police. It was just a few months later that Korea achieved independence from Japan.

24 아래 〈보기〉에서 위 글의 밑줄 친 ⓐtaking과 문법적 쓰임이 같은 것의 개수를 고르시오.

┌─── 보기 ───┐

① The man standing over there is my father.
② He is good at speaking English.
③ He is taking part in an independence movement.
④ I watched him playing baseball.
⑤ His hobby is collecting stamps.

└────────────┘

① 1개   ② 2개   ③ 3개   ④ 4개   ⑤ 5개

25 According to the passage, which is NOT true?

① Dong-ju studied further in the country where his father had studied before.
② It was in 1942 that Dong-ju and his cousin began to study in Japan.
③ In 1942, Dong-ju's cousin was arrested by the Japanese police for taking part in an independence movement.
④ Dong-ju was also arrested in 1943.
⑤ Dong-ju and his cousin had died in prison before Korea was liberated from Japan's colonial rule.

[26~27] 다음 글을 읽고 물음에 답하시오.

Do you enjoy plays, poems, novels, or cartoons? They are different kinds of literature, and people differ in which kind they prefer. However, all of (A)them allow us to go beyond our own small world where we live. When we read literature, we come across the ideas of great writers who lived long ago. We can even imagine being someone else or ____ⓐ____ in a completely different place. In short, literature opens up for us new worlds that we have never visited before.

26 위 글의 빈칸 ⓐ에 live를 알맞은 형태로 쓰시오.

➡ _____

27 위 글의 밑줄 친 (A)them이 가리키는 것을 본문에서 찾아 쓰시오.

➡ _____

MEMO

Lesson 6

Together in Our Community

 의사소통 기능

- 충고하기
  I didn't bring my science homework. – If I were you, I'd do it during breaks.

- 허락 구하기
  Do you mind if I eat your sausage? – Not at all. Go ahead.

 언어 형식

- It ~ for ... + to부정사
  It is important **for kids to learn** to swim.

- 가정법 과거
  If she **had** a car, she **would drive** everywhere.

교과서
Words & Expressions

Key Words

- **additional** [ədíʃənl] 형 추가적인
- **borrow** [bárou] 동 빌리다
- **carry** [kǽri] 동 나르다
- **cause** [kɔːz] 동 초래하다
- **charger** [tʃáːrdʒər] 명 충전기
- **common** [kámən] 명 공유지, 공원
- **company** [kámpəni] 명 함께함, 동행
- **decide** [disáid] 동 결정하다
- **directly** [diréktli] 부 직접적으로
- **disappear** [dìsəpíər] 동 사라지다
- **disappoint** [dìsəpɔ́int] 동 실망하게 하다
- **either** [íːðər] 부 (부정문에서) 역시
- **fairly** [fέərli] 부 꽤
- **fill** [fil] 동 채우다
- **gladly** [glǽdli] 부 즐겁게
- **grassland** [grǽslænd] 명 초지, 풀밭
- **graze** [greiz] 동 풀을 뜯다
- **growl** [graul] 동 꼬르륵 소리가 나다
- **harsh** [hɑːrʃ] 형 가혹한, 냉혹한
- **lay** [lei] 동 두다, 놓다
- **lesson** [lésn] 명 교훈
- **lie** [lai] 동 놓여 있다
- **local** [lóukəl] 형 지역의

- **messy** [mési] 형 지저분한
- **mind** [maind] 동 신경을 쓰다, 싫어하다
- **notice** [nóutis] 동 알아채다
- **patient** [péiʃənt] 형 인내심이 있는 명 환자
- **per** [pər] 전 ~당, ~마다
- **pleasure** [pléʒər] 명 기쁨
- **pollute** [pəlúːt] 동 오염시키다
- **pollution** [pəlúːʃən] 명 오염
- **population** [pàpjuléiʃən] 명 개체 수, 인구
- **proud** [praud] 형 자랑스러운
- **raise** [reiz] 동 기르다, 올리다
- **resource** [ríːsɔːrs] 명 자원
- **seasick** [síːsik] 형 뱃멀미가 나는
- **secret** [síːkrit] 명 비밀
- **senior** [síːnjər] 형 나이가 많은
- **serious** [síəriəs] 형 진지한
- **share** [ʃɛər] 동 공유하다
- **sleepy** [slíːpi] 형 졸리는
- **support** [səpɔ́ːrt] 동 지지하다, 부양하다
- **talent** [tǽlənt] 명 재능
- **value** [vǽljuː] 동 소중히 여기다
- **view** [vjuː] 명 전망, 경관
- **volunteer** [vàləntíər] 동 자원봉사하다 명 자원봉사자

Key Expressions

- **ask a favor** 부탁하다
- **be allowed to** ~하는 것이 허용되다
- **be full of** ~으로 가득 차다
- **break a rule** 규칙을 어기다
- **by the way** 그런데
- **by tradition** 전통에 따라
- **community center** 지역 센터
- **give support to** ~을 후원하다
- **Go right ahead.** 계속하세요.
- **in harmony** 조화롭게
- **in secret** 몰래, 비밀리에
- **It's my pleasure.** 별말씀을요.

- **keep ~ in mind** ~을 명심하다
- **not ~ anymore** 더 이상 ~가 아닌
- **once upon a time** 옛날에
- **runny nose** 콧물
- **senior citizen** 어르신, 노인
- **sore throat** 인후염
- **stop -ing** ~하기를 중단하다
- **take care of** ~을 돌보다
- **take photos** 사진을 찍다
- **the number of** ~의 수
- **to make matters worse** 엎친 데 덮친 격으로
- **window seat** 창가 자리

Word Power

※ 서로 비슷한 뜻을 가진 어휘

□ **decide** 결정하다 : **determine** 결정하다
□ **gladly** 즐겁게 : **joyfully** 기쁘게
□ **messy** 지저분한 : **untidy** 지저분한
□ **patient** 인내심이 있는 : **tolerant** 참을성 있는

□ **fairly** 꽤 : **quite** 제법, 꽤
□ **harsh** 가혹한, 냉혹한 : **severe** 심한
□ **notice** 알아채다 : **detect** 탐지하다
□ **pleasure** 기쁨 : **amusement** 즐거움

※ 서로 반대의 뜻을 가진 어휘

□ **borrow** 빌리다 ↔ **lend** 빌려주다
□ **appear** 나타나다 ↔ **disappear** 사라지다
□ **harsh** 가혹한 ↔ **mild** 온화한
□ **notice** 알아채다 ↔ **ignore** 무시하다
□ **pleasure** 기쁨 ↔ **displeasure** 불쾌감

□ **directly** 직접적으로 ↔ **indirectly** 간접적으로
□ **fill** 채우다 ↔ **empty** 비우다
□ **messy** 지저분한 ↔ **tidy** 깨끗한
□ **patient** 인내심이 있는 ↔ **impatient** 조바심을 내는

※ 동사 → 명사

□ **decide** 결정하다 → **decision** 결정
□ **disappoint** 실망하게 하다 → **disappointment** 실망

□ **disappear** 사라지다 → **disappearance** 소멸
□ **pollute** 오염시키다 → **pollution** 오염

※ 명사 → 형용사

□ **addition** 추가 → **additional** 추가적인
□ **mess** 엉망인 상황 → **messy** 지저분한
□ **pleasure** 기쁨 → **pleasurable** 즐거운

□ **disappointment** 실망 → **disappointed** 실망한
□ **patience** 인내심 → **patient** 인내심이 있는
□ **pride** 자랑 → **proud** 자랑스러운

English Dictionary

□ **additional** 추가의
 → added; more 더해진, 더 이상의
□ **common** 공유지, 공원
 → a piece of land used jointly 공동으로 사용되는 땅
□ **grassland** 초지, 풀밭
 → land with grass 풀이 있는 땅
□ **graze** 풀을 뜯다
 → to feed on grass 풀을 뜯어먹다
□ **harsh** 가혹한, 냉혹한
 → unpleasantly severe 불쾌할 정도로 심한
□ **lesson** 교훈
 → something to be learned 배워져야 할 어떤 것
□ **notice** 알아채다
 → to become aware of 인식하게 되다

□ **per** ~당, ~마다
 → for each 각각에 대하여
□ **population** 개체 수, 인구
 → the total number of persons or animals 사람이나 동물의 전체 수
□ **resource** 자원
 → a source of supply, support, or aid 공급, 지원, 후원의 근원
□ **support** 지지하다, 부양하다
 → to supply things that are needed 필요한 것들을 제공해 주다
□ **value** 소중히 여기다
 → to think that someone or something is important 누군가나 어떤 것이 중요하다고 생각하다

서답형

01 다음 짝지어진 단어의 관계가 같도록 빈칸에 알맞은 말을 쓰시오.

> glad : sad = m_____ : tidy

02 다음 영영풀이가 가리키는 것을 고르시오.

> to eat grass in a field

① graze   ② carry
③ growl   ④ notice
⑤ raise

 중요

03 다음 중 밑줄 친 부분의 뜻풀이가 바르지 <u>않은</u> 것은?

① Some young people are not interested in following <u>tradition</u>. (전통)
② There are <u>additional</u> problems on the next page. (추가적인)
③ All around the world is suffering from water <u>pollution</u>. (오염)
④ Mr. Park is <u>proud</u> of his children. (자랑스러운)
⑤ Do you <u>mind</u> if I eat your sandwiches? (마음)

서답형

04 다음 우리말에 맞게 빈칸에 알맞은 말을 쓰시오. (처음 철자가 주어진 것도 있음.)

(1) 사람이 많아서 Chris는 나를 알아채지 못한 것처럼 보였다.
➡ There were many people, so Chris didn't seem to n_____ me.

(2) 그는 미래에 전망이 좋은 집에서 살기를 원한다.
➡ He wants to live in a house with a nice v_____ in the future.

(3) 중국은 세계에서 인구수가 가장 많다.
➡ China has the largest _____ in the world.

중요

05 다음 주어진 문장의 밑줄 친 common과 같은 의미로 쓰인 것은?

> Tom and Emma usually play tennis on a village <u>common</u>.

① This decision was taken for the <u>common</u> good.
② Jackson is a <u>common</u> English name.
③ A fever and a runny nose are <u>common</u> symptoms.
④ The grass on the <u>common</u> was green all summer long.
⑤ We are working together for a <u>common</u> purpose.

서답형

06 다음 우리말을 주어진 단어를 이용하여 영작하시오.

(1) Jane은 작년에 소아 병원에서 자원봉사를 했다. (children's, at)
➡ _____

(2) 나는 보통 공유지로 산책하러 간다. (go, on)
➡ _____

(3) 풀밭에 많은 말들이 있다. (on, there)
➡ _____

01 다음 짝지어진 단어의 관계가 같도록 빈칸에 알맞은 말을 쓰시오.

> directly : indirectly = patient : _____

02 다음 그림을 참고하여 동사의 과거형과 과거분사형을 쓰시오.

 vs

➡ sit – _____ – _____ ,
  seat – _____ – _____

 vs vs

➡ lie – _____ – _____ ,
  lie – _____ – _____ ,
  lay – _____ – _____

03 다음 문장의 빈칸에 들어갈 말을 〈보기〉에서 골라 쓰시오.

> ┤ 보기 ├
> values / harsh / lesson / support /
> resources

(1) The coach was _____ to the players.

(2) Mr. Jones has three children to _____ .

(3) Tim learned a valuable _____ from the book.

(4) The country is rich in natural _____ .

(5) Chris _____ trust most in a friendship.

04 다음 우리말에 맞게 빈칸에 알맞은 말을 쓰시오. (철자가 주어진 것은 주어진 철자로 시작하여 쓰고 빈칸 하나에 한 단어씩 쓸 것.)

(1) 나는 무척 배가 고파서 내 방에 숨어 몰래 초콜릿을 먹었다.
  ➡ I was very hungry, so I hid in my room and ate chocolate _____ s_____ .

(2) 너는 규칙을 어기면 경고를 받을 것이다.
  ➡ You will get a warning if you _____ _____ _____ .

(3) 그 수학 문제는 어려웠지만, 나는 마침내 풀었다.
  ➡ Though the math problems were tough, I solved them _____ _____ .

(4) 그는 당시에 돈이 없었다. 엎친 데 덮친 격으로 그는 신용카드를 갖고 있지 않았다.
  ➡ He had no money at that time. _____ m_____ m_____ _____ , he did not have his credit card with him.

05 다음 우리말을 주어진 단어를 이용하여 영작하시오.

(1) 여행 동안 내 충고를 명심해라. (during, keep, trip)
  ➡ _____

(2) 학생들은 도서관에서 크게 말하는 것이 허용되지 않는다. (loudly, allow)
  ➡ _____

(3) 한국인들은 전통에 따라 설날에 친척들을 방문한다. (relatives, New Year's Day, by)
  ➡ _____

Conversation

1 충고하기

> **A** I didn't bring my science homework. 나 과학 숙제를 가져 오지 않았어.
>
> **B** If I were you, I'd do it during breaks. 내가 너라면 휴식 시간에 그것을 할 거야.

■ 곤란한 일을 만난 사람에게 적절한 방법을 알려주거나 도움이 되는 충고를 할 때는 'If I were you, I'd ~.(내가 너라면 ~할 텐데.)'의 표현을 사용한다. '~하는 편이 더 낫다'의 의미로 'You had better ~'도 충고하는 의미로 쓰인다. 'You had better ~'는 주로 부모님이나 선생님처럼 더 권위가 있는 사람이 긴급한 상황이나 충고가 필요한 상황에서 쓴다. 친구 사이에 충고를 하는 경우에는 'You should ~.'를 더 많이 쓴다.

■ 그 외에 상대방에게 충고나 조언을 할 때는 'Why don't you ~?(~하는 것이 어떠니?)', 'I think you should ~.(나는 네가 ~해야 한다고 생각해.)', 'I advise you to ~.(나는 너에게 ~하라고 충고한다.)', 'I recommend that ~.(나는 ~를 추천한다.)', 'You really ought to ~.(너는 정말이지 ~해야 해.)', 'Have you thought about ~?(~을 생각해 봤니?)', 'In your position, I would ~.(네 입장이라면 나는 ~할 거야.)' 등으로 말한다.

충고하기

- If I were you, I'd ~.   만약 내가 너라면 ~할 텐데.
- If I were in your shoes, I'd ~.   만약 내가 네 입장이라면, 나는 ~할 텐데.
- You had better ~.   너는 ~하는 편이 더 낫다.
- Why don't you ~?   ~하는 것이 어떠니?
- I think you should ~.   나는 네가 ~해야 한다고 생각해.

충고에 답할 때

- Thank you for your advice.
- Okay. That's a good idea, too.
- Those are good ideas. Thank you.

핵심 Check

1. 다음 대화의 밑줄 친 우리말에 맞게 영작하시오.

B: Jimin, have you decided where to volunteer?

G: Not yet. Do you know a good place to volunteer?

B: <u>내가 너라면, 지역 주민 센터로 갈 거야.</u>

G: The community center? What can I do there?

B: There's a smartphone class for senior citizens, and they're looking for volunteers.

G: That sounds interesting, but I've never taught anyone.

➡ _____

2 허락 구하기

A Do you mind if I eat your sausage? 네 소시지 먹어도 되니?

B Not at all. Go ahead. 물론이지. 어서 먹어.

■ 다른 사람이 같이 있는 상황에서 어떤 일을 하기 전에 상대방에게 허락을 요청할 때는 허락을 요청하는 조동사를 사용하여 'May I ~?', 'Can I ~?', 또는 'Is it okay if I ~?' 등을 사용할 수 있다. 이런 표현 이외에도 좀 더 공손하게 나타내는 표현으로는 'Do you mind if ~?'를 사용할 수 있다.

■ 그 외에 상대방의 허락을 구하는 말은 'Would you mind if ~?', 'I'm wondering if I could ~.', 'Is it okay (with you) if I ~?', 'Would it be all right if I ~?' 등으로 표현할 수도 있다.

■ 'Do you mind if ~?'에서 'mind'는 '꺼리다, 신경 쓰다, 싫어하다'라는 의미이기 때문에 'Yes'라고 답변하면 '꺼린다, 신경 쓴다, 싫어한다'라는 의미로 허락하지 않는 것을 나타낸다. 상대방에게 괜찮다고 허락할 때는 '신경 쓰지 않으니까 하고 싶은 대로 하세요.'라는 의미로 'Not at all.', 'Of course not.', 'Certainly not.', 'No problem.', 'Sure. Go ahead.' 등을 사용한다. 상대방에게 허락해 주지 않을 경우에는 'I'm afraid I do.(죄송하지만, 안됩니다.)'라고 대답한다.

허락 구하기

• Do you mind if I ~? ~해도 되겠습니까?

허락할 때　No, not at all. / Certainly not. / Of course not.
　　　　　　No, I don't. / No problem. / Sure. Go ahead. 네, 괜찮습니다.

금지할 때　Yes, I do. / Sorry, but ~. / I'm afraid I ~. 미안하지만 안 됩니다.

• May I ~? ~해도 됩니까?

허락할 때　Yes, you may. 네, 괜찮습니다.

핵심 Check

2. 다음 대화의 빈칸에 들어가기에 가장 적절한 것은?

> **W:** Today's lesson is about taking photos with smartphones. Why don't you help the slow learners?
>
> **G:** Okay. Is there anything I should know?
>
> **W:** Yes. Please be patient and kind to the learners.
>
> **G:** I'll keep that in mind. By the way, ＿＿＿＿＿＿＿ if I use your charger?
>
> **W:** Of course not. Go right ahead.

① do you know　　　　　② do you mind
③ can I ask　　　　　　 ④ are you wondering
⑤ are you afraid

Listen – Listen & Answer Dialog 1

B: Jimin, have you ❶decided ❷where to volunteer?

G: Not yet. Do you know a good place ❸to volunteer?

B: ❹If I were you, I'd go to the community center.

G: The community center? What can I do there?

B: There's a smartphone class for ❺senior citizens, and they're looking for volunteers.

G: That sounds interesting, but I've never taught anyone.

B: Don't worry. All you need to do is help the teacher there.

G: Okay. Thanks for your advice.

소년: 지민아, 어디에서 봉사 활동 할지 결정했니?
소녀: 아직. 봉사 활동을 하기에 좋은 장소를 알고 있어?
소년: 내가 너라면, 지역 주민 센터에서 봉사 활동을 할 거야.
소녀: 지역 주민 센터? 거기에서 무엇을 할 수 있는데?
소년: 어르신들을 위한 스마트폰 수업이 있는데 거기에서 자원봉사자를 찾고 있어.
소녀: 그거 좋겠다. 하지만 난 누군가를 가르쳐 본 적이 없어.
소년: 걱정하지 마. 너는 그곳에서 선생님을 돕기만 하면 돼.
소녀: 알겠어. 조언해 줘서 고마워.

❶ decide: 결정하다　❷ '의문사+to부정사' 구문으로 '~할지'를 의미한다.　❸ a good place를 꾸며주는 to부정사의 형용사적 용법으로 사용되었다.
❹ 가정법 과거 구문으로 충고를 할 때 '내가 너라면, ~할 텐데.'의 표현이다. 'Why don't you go to the community center?' 또는 'I think you should go to the community center.' 등으로 바꾸어 충고를 할 수 있다.
❺ senior citizen: 어르신, 노인

Check(√) True or False

(1) Jimin takes the smartphone class with senior citizens. 　T ☐ F ☐

(2) Jimin has taught how to use the smartphone to someone. 　T ☐ F ☐

Listen – Listen & Answer Dialog 2

G: Thanks for letting me ❶volunteer here, Ms. Yun.

W: It's my pleasure, Jimin. I'm glad you decided to help.

G: Well, what should I do?

W: Today's lesson is about taking photos with smartphones. ❷Why don't you help the slow learners?

G: Okay. Is there anything I should know?

W: Yes. Please be ❸patient and kind to the learners.

G: I'll ❹keep that in mind. ❺By the way, ❻do you mind if I use your charger? My battery is a little low.

W: Of course not. Go right ahead.

소녀: 윤 선생님, 이곳에서 봉사 활동을 하게 해 주셔서 감사해요.
선생님: 천만에, 지민아. 네가 돕겠다고 해 줘서 나는 기쁘단다.
소녀: 음, 제가 무엇을 해야 하나요?
선생님: 오늘 수업은 스마트폰으로 사진을 찍는 것에 관한 거란다. 학습 속도가 느린 사람들을 도와주는 게 어떨까?
소녀: 네. 제가 알아 두어야 할 것이 있나요?
선생님: 그래. 인내심을 갖고 학습자들에게 친절히 대해 주렴.
소녀: 명심할게요. 그런데, 제가 선생님의 충전기를 사용해도 될까요? 제 배터리가 별로 남지 않아서요.
선생님: 물론이지. 사용하렴.

❶ 사역동사 let에 원형부정사 volunteer가 이어진다.
❷ 제안을 하는 표현으로 'What about helping the slow learners?' 등으로 바꾸어 표현할 수 있다.
❸ patient: 인내심 있는　❹ keep in mind: 명심하다　❺ by the way: 그런데
❻ 어떤 일을 하기 전에 상대방에게 허락을 요청하는 표현으로 'do you mind if ~?'를 사용할 수 있다.

Check(√) True or False

(3) Jimin is going to learn how to take photos with smartphone. 　T ☐ F ☐

(4) Ms. Yun wants Jimin to be patient and kind to the slow learners. 　T ☐ F ☐

Listen – Listen More

G: Wow, it feels great to be on this ship, Dad.

M: I feel the same, Sora. Here are our seats, 20A and 20B.

G: Yeah. ❶Do you mind if I take the ❷window seat? I like to see the view outside.

M: No problem.

G: ❸By the way, I want to eat something like noodles or sandwiches.

M: If I were you, I would't eat anything like that.

G: Why is that?

M: They may make you ❹seasick.

G: Oh, I see. Then, I'll have some ice cream.

M: That's not a good idea, ❺either. Let's eat after we arrive.

❶ 허락을 구하는 표현으로 'May I take the window seat?' 또는 'Can I take the window seat?' 등으로 바꾸어 표현할 수 있다.
❷ window seat: 창가 자리
❸ by the way: 그런데
❹ seasick: 뱃멀미를 하는
❺ either는 '또한'을 나타내며 부정문과 함께 쓰인다.

Speak – Talk in groups

A: I didn't bring my science homework.

B: ❶If I were you, I'd do it during breaks.

A: ❷Thanks for your advice.

❶ If I were you, I'd ~.는 충고하는 표현으로 Why don't you ~? 또는 I think you should ~. 등으로 바꿔 쓸 수 있다.
❷ 충고하는 말에 답하는 표현으로 That's a good idea. 등으로 바꿔 쓸 수 있다.

Speak – Talk in pairs.

A: ❶Do you mind if I eat your sausage?

B: ❷Not at all. Go ahead.

A: Thank you.

❶ 허락을 구할 때 쓰는 표현으로 Can[May] I ~?, Is it okay ~? 등으로 바꿔 쓸 수 있다.
❷ 허락하는 표현으로 No problem., Of course not. 등으로 바꿔 쓸 수 있다.

Wrap Up 5

(The phone rings.)

W: Hi, Kevin. What's up?

B: Hi, Aunt Victoria. I called to ❶ask you a favor.

W: What is it?

B: I need a ❷sleeping bag for my science camp. ❸Do you mind if I borrow yours?

W: ❹No, not at all.

❶ ask A a favor: A에게 부탁하다
❷ sleeping bag: 침낭, sleeping은 동명사
❸ 허락을 구하는 표현으로 'May I borrow yours?' 또는 'Is it okay if I borrow yours?' 등으로 바꾸어 표현할 수 있다.
❹ 허락하는 표현으로 "Of course not.", "Certainly not.", "No problem.", "Sure. Go ahead." 등을 사용한다.

Wrap Up 6

G: My stomach ❶growls every morning. What should I do?

B: Ha ha. Do you usually have breakfast?

G: No, I have no time to eat anything at home.

B: ❷If I were you, I'd bring some snacks.

G: That's a good idea.

❶ growl: 으르렁거리다, 꼬르륵 소리가 나다
❷ 가정법 과거 구문을 사용하여 충고하는 표현으로 'How about bringing some snacks?' 또는 'I recommend you to bring some snacks.' 등으로 바꾸어 표현할 수 있다.

● 다음 우리말과 일치하도록 빈칸에 알맞은 말을 쓰시오.

Listen – Listen & Answer Dialog 1

B: Jimin, have you decided _____ _____ _____?

G: Not yet. Do you know a good place _____ _____?

B: If I _____ you, I'd go to the _____ _____.

G: The _____ _____? What can I do there?

B: There's a smartphone class for _____ _____, and they're looking for volunteers.

G: That _____ interesting, but I've _____ _____ anyone.

B: Don't worry. All you need _____ _____ _____ _____ the teacher there.

G: Okay. Thanks for your _____.

Listen – Listen & Answer Dialog 2

G: Thanks for _____ _____ _____ here, Ms. Yun.

W: It's my _____, Jimin. I'm glad you decided to help.

G: Well, what should I do?

W: Today's lesson is about _____ _____ with smartphones. _____ _____ _____ help the _____ _____?

G: Okay. Is _____ _____ I should know?

W: Yes. Please be _____ and _____ to the learners.

G: I'll _____ _____ _____ _____ _____. _____ _____ _____, _____ _____ _____ _____ _____ I use your _____? My battery is _____ _____.

W: Of course _____. Go right ahead.

Listen – Listen More

G: Wow, it feels great to be _____ _____ _____, Dad.

M: I feel _____ _____, Sora. Here are our _____, 20A and 20B.

G: Yeah. _____ _____ _____ _____ _____ I take the _____ _____? I like to see the _____ _____.

M: No problem.

G: By the way, I want to eat something _____ _____ or _____.

해석

소년: 지민아, 어디에서 봉사 활동 할지 결정했니?

소녀: 아직. 봉사 활동을 하기에 좋은 장소를 알고 있어?

소년: 내가 너라면, 지역 주민 센터에서 봉사 활동을 할 거야.

소녀: 지역 주민 센터? 거기에서 무엇을 할 수 있는데?

소년: 어르신들을 위한 스마트폰 수업이 있는데 거기에서 자원봉사자를 찾고 있어.

소녀: 그거 좋겠다. 하지만 난 누군가를 가르쳐 본 적이 없어.

소년: 걱정하지 마. 너는 그곳에서 선생님을 돕기만 하면 돼.

소녀: 알겠어. 조언해 줘서 고마워.

소녀: 윤 선생님, 이곳에서 봉사 활동을 하게 해 주셔서 감사해요.

선생님: 천만에, 지민아. 네가 돕겠다고 해 줘서 나는 기쁘단다.

소녀: 음, 제가 무엇을 해야 하나요?

선생님: 오늘 수업은 스마트폰으로 사진을 찍는 것에 관한 거란다. 학습 속도가 느린 사람들을 도와주는 게 어떨까?

소녀: 네. 제가 알아 두어야 할 것이 있나요?

선생님: 그래. 인내심을 갖고 학습자들에게 친절히 대해 주렴.

소녀: 명심할게요. 그런데, 제가 선생님의 충전기를 사용해도 될까요? 제 배터리가 별로 남지 않아서요.

선생님: 물론이지. 사용하렴.

소녀: 와! 배에 타니 정말 좋아요, 아빠.

남: 나도 그렇단다, 소라야. 20A와 20B, 여기가 우리 자리야.

소녀: 네. 제가 창가 자리에 앉아도 괜찮을까요? 바깥 풍경을 보고 싶어요.

남: 그렇게 하렴.

소녀: 그런데, 국수나 샌드위치 같은 걸 먹고 싶어요.

M: _____ _____ _____ _____, I wouldn't eat anything _____ that.

G: Why is that?

M: They may _____ you _____.

G: Oh, I see. Then, I'll have _____ ice cream.

M: That's not a good idea, _____. Let's eat _____ _____ _____.

Speak – Talk in groups

A: I didn't _____ my science homework.

B: _____ I _____ you, I'd do it _____ _____.

A: Thanks _____ your advice.

Speak – Talk in pairs.

A: Do you _____ if I eat your sausage?

B: Not _____ _____. Go _____.

A: Thank you.

Wrap Up 5

(The phone rings.)

W: Hi, Kevin. _____ _____?

B: Hi, Aunt Victoria. I called to _____ _____ _____ _____.

W: What is it?

B: I need a _____ _____ for my science camp. _____ _____ _____ _____ I borrow yours?

W: _____, not at all.

Wrap Up 6

G: My _____ _____ every morning. What should I do?

B: Ha ha. Do you usually _____ _____?

G: No, I have _____ _____ to eat anything at home.

B: _____ _____ _____ _____, I'd bring some snacks.

G: That's a good idea.

해석

남: 나라면, 그런 것들을 먹지 않을 거야.
소녀: 왜 그럴죠?
남: 그런 음식들이 뱃멀미하게 할 수 있단다.
소녀: 오, 알겠어요. 그렇다면, 아이스크림을 먹을래요.
남: 그것도 좋은 생각이 아니야. 우리 도착한 뒤에 먹자.

A: 과학 숙제를 가져오지 않았어.
B: 내가 너라면, 쉬는 시간에 할 거야.
A: 조언 고마워.

A: 내가 네 소시지를 먹어도 될까?
B: 물론이지, 그러렴.
A: 고마워.

(전화벨이 울린다.)
여: Kevin, 안녕. 무슨 일이니?
소년: Victoria 이모, 안녕하세요. 부탁 좀 드리려고 전화했어요.
여: 그게 뭔데?
소년: 과학 캠프에 침낭이 필요해요. 제가 이모 것을 빌려도 될까요?
여: 물론이지.

소녀: 아침마다 나는 배가 꼬르륵거려. 어떻게 해야 할까?
소년: 하하. 너는 보통 아침을 먹니?
소녀: 아니, 집에서 뭘 먹을 시간이 없어.
소년: 내가 너라면, 간식을 좀 가져오겠다.
소녀: 그거 좋은 생각이야.

[01~02] 다음 대화를 읽고 물음에 답하시오.

Gina: My stomach ⓐgrowls every morning. What should I do?
Tom: Ha ha. Do you ⓑusually have breakfast?
Gina: No, I have ⓒno time to eat anything at home.
Tom: If I ⓓam you, I'd bring some snacks.
Gina: That's a ⓔgood idea.

01 위 대화의 밑줄 친 ⓐ~ⓔ 중 어법상 틀린 것을 찾아 바르게 고치시오.

➡ _____

02 위 대화의 내용과 일치하지 <u>않는</u> 것은?

① Gina는 매일 아침 배가 꼬르륵 거린다.
② Gina는 보통 아침을 먹지 않는다.
③ Gina는 아침에 집에서 무언가를 먹을 시간이 없다.
④ Tom은 Gina에게 간식을 가져올 것을 충고했다.
⑤ Gina는 Tom의 조언에 따라 아침을 먹고 올 것이다.

[03~04] 다음 대화를 읽고 물음에 답하시오.

(The phone rings.)
Victoria: Hi, Kevin. What's up?
Kevin: Hi, Aunt Victoria. I called to _____(A)_____.
Victoria: What is it?
Kevin: I need a sleeping bag for my science camp. (B)제가 이모 것을 빌려도 될까요? (yours / if / mind)
Victoria: No, not at all.

03 위 대화의 빈칸 (A)에 '부탁하다'를 의미하는 표현을 4 단어로 완성하시오.

➡ _____

04 위 대화의 밑줄 친 (B)의 우리말을 주어진 단어를 사용하여 영작하시오.

➡ _____

[01~03] 다음 대화를 읽고 물음에 답하시오.

> Brian: Jimin, have you decided where to volunteer?
>
> Jimin: Not yet. Do you know a good place to volunteer?
>
> Brian: _____(A)_____
>
> Jimin: The community center? What can I do there?
>
> Brian: There's a smartphone class for senior citizens, and they're looking for volunteers.
>
> Jimin: That sounds interesting, but I've never taught anyone.
>
> Brian: Don't worry. All you need to do is help the teacher there.
>
> Jimin: Okay. Thanks for your advice.

서답형

01 위 대화에서 다음 영영풀이가 나타내는 말을 찾아 쓰시오.

> to offer to do something without being forced to do it or without getting paid for it

➡ _____

02 위 대화의 빈칸에 들어갈 말로 <u>어색한</u> 것은?

① Do you mind if I go to the community center?

② If I were you, I'd go to the community center.

③ Why don't you go to the community center?

④ How about going to the community center?

⑤ If I were in your shoes, I'd go to the community center.

03 위 대화의 내용과 일치하지 <u>않는</u> 것은?

① 지민이는 어디에서 봉사활동을 할지 결정하지 못했다.

② Brian은 지민이에게 지역 주민 센터에서 봉사활동을 할 것을 제안했다.

③ 지역 주민 센터에 어르신들을 위한 스마트폰 수업이 있다.

④ 어르신들을 위한 스마트폰 수업에서 자원봉사자를 찾고 있다.

⑤ Brian은 어르신들을 위한 스마트폰 수업에서 어르신들을 도울 것이다.

[04~05] 다음 대화를 읽고 물음에 답하시오.

> Jimin: Thanks for letting me volunteer here, Ms. Yun.
>
> Ms. Yun: It's my pleasure, Jimin. I'm glad you decided to help.
>
> Jimin: Well, what should I do?
>
> Ms. Yun: Today's lesson is about taking photos with smartphones. _____(A)_____
>
> Jimin: Okay. Is there anything I should know?
>
> Ms. Yun: Yes. Please be patient and kind to the learners.
>
> Jimin: I'll keep that in mind. By the way, do you mind if I use your charger? My battery is a little low.
>
> Ms. Yun: Of course not. Go right ahead.

04 위 대화의 빈칸 (A)에 들어갈 말로 나머지와 의도가 <u>다른</u> 것은?

① I'm doubtful if you can help the slow learners.

② Why don't you help the slow learners?

③ How about helping the slow learners?

④ I want you to help the slow learners.

⑤ I think you need to help the slow learners.

중요

05 위 대화를 읽고 대답할 수 <u>없는</u> 것은?

① What does Ms. Yun get Jimin to do?

② What is Ms. Yun's today's lesson about?

③ What should Jimin keep in mind?

④ Why does Jimin need Ms. Yun's charger?

⑤ What kind of charger does Jimin need?

[06~08] 다음 대화를 읽고 물음에 답하시오.

> Sora: Wow, it feels great to be on this ship, Dad.
>
> Dad: I feel the same, Sora. Here are our seats, 20A and 20B.
>
> Sora: Yeah. _____(A)_____? I like to see the view outside.
>
> Dad: No problem.
>
> Sora: By the way, I want to eat something like noodles or sandwiches.
>
> Dad: If I were you, I wouldn't eat anything like that.
>
> Sora: Why is that?
>
> Dad: They may make you seasick.
>
> Sora: Oh, I see. Then, I'll have some ice cream.
>
> Dad: That's not a good idea, either. Let's eat after we arrive.

서답형

06 위 대화의 빈칸에 들어갈 말을 〈보기〉에 주어진 단어를 배열하여 완성하시오.

> ┌─ 보기 ─┐
>
> if / take / mind / seat / the / do / window / you / I

➡ _____

서답형

07 Why does Sora want to take the window seat?

➡ _____

서답형

08 Why doesn't Sora's dad want her to eat something like noodles or sandwiches?

➡ _____

_____

09 다음 대화가 자연스럽게 이어지도록 순서대로 배열하시오.

> Thanks for letting me volunteer here, Ms. Yun.

> (A) Okay. Is there anything I should know?
>
> (B) Well, what should I do?
>
> (C) Yes. Please be patient and kind to the learners.
>
> (D) It's my pleasure, Jimin. I'm glad you decided to help.
>
> (E) Today's lesson is about taking photos with smartphones. Why don't you help the slow learners?

➡ _____

중요

10 다음 중 짝지어진 대화가 <u>어색한</u> 것은?

① A: Do you mind if I sit here?
   B: Not at all.

② A: What should I do about the contest?
   B: If I were you, I'd just do my best.

③ A: I have a runny nose and a sore throat.
   B: How about wearing a warm coat?

④ A: I didn't bring my science homework.
   B: If I were you, I'd do it during breaks.

⑤ A: Do you mind if I borrow your pencil?
   B: Of course. You can use mine.

[01~03] 다음 대화를 읽고 물음에 답하시오.

(The phone rings.)
Victoria: Hi, Kevin. What's up?
Kevin: Hi, Aunt Victoria. I called to ask you a favor.
Victoria: What is it?
Kevin: I need a sleeping bag for my science camp. Do you mind if I borrow yours?
Victoria: No, not at all.

01 What does Kevin need for his science camp?

➡ _____

02 Does Victoria allow Kevin to borrow hers?

➡ _____

03 위 대화의 내용과 일치하도록 빈칸을 완성하시오.

> Kevin called Victoria to ask her a (A)_____. He needed (B)_____ for his science camp. When he asked if he could (C)_____ hers, she allowed him to use it.

04 다음 대화의 내용과 일치하도록 빈칸을 완성하시오.

> Brian: Jimin, have you decided where to volunteer?
> Jimin: Not yet. Do you know a good place to volunteer?
> Brian: If I were you, I'd go to the community center.

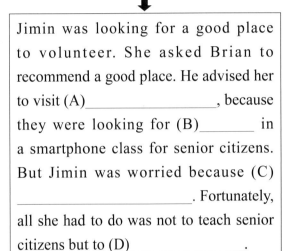

Jimin: The community center? What can I do there?
Brian: There's a smartphone class for senior citizens, and they're looking for volunteers.
Jimin: That sounds interesting, but I've never taught anyone.
Brian: Don't worry. All you need to do is help the teacher there.
Jimin: Okay. Thanks for your advice.

⬇

> Jimin was looking for a good place to volunteer. She asked Brian to recommend a good place. He advised her to visit (A)_____, because they were looking for (B)_____ in a smartphone class for senior citizens. But Jimin was worried because (C)_____. Fortunately, all she had to do was not to teach senior citizens but to (D)_____.

05 다음 대화가 자연스럽게 이어지도록 순서대로 배열하시오.

> (A) That's a good idea.
> (B) Ha ha. Do you usually have breakfast?
> (C) If I were you, I'd bring some snacks.
> (D) No, I have no time to eat anything at home.
> (E) My stomach growls every morning. What should I do?

➡ _____

Grammar

① It ~ for ... + to부정사

> • **It** is important **for kids to learn** to swim. 어린아이들이 수영을 배우는 것은 중요하다.
> • **It** is hard **for me to stay** in one place. 나는 한 장소에 머무는 것이 어렵다.

■ 쓰임과 의미 및 형태

쓰임: to부정사가 주어 역할을 할 때, 보통 주어 자리에 It을 쓰고 to부정사는 뒤에 쓴다. to부정사의 의미상 주어는 to부정사 앞에 'for+목적격'으로 쓴다.

의미: A가 …하는 것은 ~하다

형태: It is+형용사+for A+to부정사

■ to부정사의 의미상의 주어

to부정사의 동작을 실제로 하는 주체를 to부정사의 의미상의 주어라고 하며 그 행위의 주체가 문장의 주어나 목적어와 다를 때 to부정사 바로 앞에 'for+목적격'으로 나타낸다.

• **It** is impossible **for him to do** that. 그가 그것을 하기는 불가능하다. (him이 to do의 의미상의 주어임)

• **It** is necessary **for us to drink** enough water. 우리가 충분한 물을 마시는 것이 필요하다. (us가 to drink의 의미상의 주어임)

■ 이때 사람의 성격이나 성품을 나타내는 형용사(kind, nice, polite, rude, smart, stupid, wise 등)가 보어로 쓰일 때는 'of+목적격'의 형태로 나타낸다.

• **It** is kind **of you to say** so. 그렇게 말씀해 주시니 고맙습니다.

• **It** is rude **of you to talk** like that to your elders. 어른들에게 그렇게 말하는 것은 무례한 짓이다.

■ to부정사의 의미상의 주어가 일반적인 사람일 경우는 보통 생략한다. 또한 to부정사의 부정은 to부정사 앞에 not이나 never를 써서 'not[never]+to부정사'로 나타낸다.

• Oxygen is necessary (**for** us) **to survive**. 산소는 (우리가) 생존하는 데 필수적이다.

• This place is too cold (**for** people) **to live**. 이곳은 너무 추워서 (사람이) 살기에 부적당하다.

• It was hard **not to laugh**. 웃음을 참기가 힘들었다.

핵심 Check

1. 다음 빈칸에 알맞은 말을 어법에 맞게 쓰시오.

　(1) It is important _____ us to win the tennis match.

　(2) It was necessary _____ her to quit the stage.

　(3) It was wise _____ you to say so.

② 가정법 과거

> • **If** she **had** a car, she **would drive** everywhere.
> 만약 그녀가 차를 가지고 있다면, 어디든지 운전하며 다닐 텐데.

■ **쓰임과 의미 및 형태**

쓰임: 현재 이루어질 수 없는 상황을 가정하여 표현한다.

의미: 만약 ~한다면 …할 텐데

형태: If+주어+동사의 과거형 ~, 주어+would/could+동사원형 …

■ '만약 ~한다면 …할 텐데'라는 뜻으로, 현재 사실을 반대로 가정하거나 실현 가능성이 없는 일에 대해서 가정할 때 쓰며, 'If+주어+동사의 과거형 ~, 주어+조동사의 과거형(would/should/could/might)+동사원형 …'의 형태로 나타낸다. 가정법 문장이라는 표시로 if절에 과거 동사를 사용하는 것이며, 의미상 과거를 나타내지 않는다.

■ 가정법 과거 문장은 현재시제의 직설법으로 바꿔 쓸 수 있다.

• If I **had** enough money, I **could buy** you a present. 만약 내가 돈이 충분하다면, 너에게 선물을 사 줄 수 있을 텐데. (가정법 과거, 현재 사실의 반대 가정)

= As I don't have enough money, I can't buy you a present.

cf. If I have enough money, I can buy you a present. (조건문, 현재의 사실)

■ if가 이끄는 절의 동사가 be동사인 경우 주어의 인칭, 수에 상관없이 were를 쓰는 것이 원칙이지만 주어가 1, 3인칭 단수일 때는 was를 쓰기도 한다.

• If I **were**[was] a bird, I**'d fly** to you. 내가 새라면 너한테 날아가련만.

■ **가정법의 다양한 표현**

• As she is brave, she can try it. 그녀는 용감하기 때문에, 그것을 시도할 수 있다. (직설법)

= If she **were** not brave, she **could** not **try** it. 그녀가 용감하지 않다면, 그것을 시도할 수 없을 텐데. (가정법)

= **Were** she not brave, she **could** not **try** it. (If 생략 후 도치)

= **If it were not for** her bravery, she could not try it.

= **Were it not for** her bravery, she could not try it. (If 생략 후 도치)

= **Without** her bravery, she could not try it. (without = if it were not for)

※ if절의 동사가 'were' 또는 'had'일 때 생략하여 쓸 수 있으며, 이때 주어와 동사가 도치된다.

핵심 Check

2. 다음 우리말에 맞게 괄호 안의 단어를 바르게 배열하시오..

만약 그가 휴가 중이라면, 지금 부산에 있을 텐데. (he, he, vacation, in Busan now, were, be, would, if, on)

➡ _____

01 다음 각 가정법 과거 문장에서 어법상 어색한 단어를 한 개씩만 찾아 고치시오.

(1) If I am a popular singer, I would hold a free concert every month.

_____ ➡ _____

(2) If I had enough time, I can finish the project.

_____ ➡ _____

(3) If I have a younger sister, I would take good care of her.

_____ ➡ _____

(4) What will he say if he were here?

_____ ➡ _____

02 다음 중 어법상 바르지 <u>않은</u> 것은?

① It is necessary for us to prepare for the winter.
② It is easy for him to read the book.
③ It is important of you to study your English diligently every day.
④ It is impossible for her to do the work.
⑤ Air is necessary to live.

03 다음 빈칸에 들어갈 말로 알맞은 것은?

> If I _____ the CEO of a company, I would praise employees for making good decisions.

① be   ② will be   ③ am
④ were   ⑤ had

04 다음 빈칸에 알맞은 것을 고르시오.

> It is impossible _____.

① to escape   ② they escape
③ they to escape   ④ for them to escape
⑤ of them to escape

01 다음 중 어법상 어색한 문장은?

① If I had two cows, I would be richer.
② If the weather were nice, I would go to the beach.
③ If it were not for your help, I should not try it.
④ If I knew how to drive, I will drive to the sea.
⑤ If it rained, what would you do all day long?

02 다음 중 빈칸에 알맞은 것은?

> It was necessary _____ the driver to remove the tree to pass.

① for ② of ③ at
④ with ⑤ on

03 다음 문장의 밑줄 친 단어들 중 어법상 어색한 단어는?

> ①If I ②have ③enough money, I could ④buy ⑤it.

04 다음 중 어법상 바르지 않은 것은?

① It is easy for Sarah to play the piano.
② It is dangerous for kids to swim in this lake.
③ It is difficult for some parents to communicate with their children.
④ Is it possible for us to visit Saturn someday?
⑤ It is quite silly for you to try to force him to consent.

05 다음 중 같은 뜻을 가진 문장끼리 짝지어진 것은?

① If there were a cleaning robot, we would not have to clean the classroom.
= There is a cleaning robot, so we do not have to clean the classroom.
② If I were you, I would raise another cow.
= Though I am you, I will raise another cow.
③ If I had the choice, I could be a drummer.
= I don't have the choice, so I can't be a drummer.
④ I could send you an e-mail if I knew your address.
= I can't send you an e-mail, so I don't know your address.
⑤ Donald would want a camera if he didn't have a nice one.
= Donald doesn't have a camera, so he doesn't want to buy one.

서답형

06 다음 괄호 안에서 어법상 바른 것을 고르시오.

(1) If I (am / were) the boss, I could do whatever I want.
(2) If I (have / had) a time machine, I would go back to the past and study hard!
(3) It is impossible (for / of) me to carry the box.
(4) It is very kind (for / of) you to take care of the old people.

[07~08] 다음 우리말을 바르게 영작한 것을 고르시오.

07

만약 그녀가 차를 가지고 있다면, 어디든지 운전하며 다닐 텐데.

① If she has a car, she will drive everywhere.
② If she has a car, she would drive everywhere.
③ If she had a car, she would drive everywhere.
④ If she had a car, she will drive everywhere.
⑤ If she had had a car, she would have driven everywhere.

08

그가 답을 찾는 것은 어렵지 않았다.

① It was not difficult he to find the answer.
② It was not difficult for him to find the answer.
③ It was not difficult to find for him the answer.
④ It was not difficult to find the answer for him.
⑤ It was not difficult the answer for him to find.

09 주어진 문장의 밑줄 친 부분과 용법이 <u>다른</u> 것은?

I'd say sorry and buy an umbrella for her, if I were you.

① I am not sure if we are allowed to recommend that.
② If I were you, I would just do my best.

③ I don't like my black hair. If I had brown hair, I would look cool.
④ The men would put a machine there if they had one.
⑤ If my father were here and saw this, he would punish us.

10 다음 문장의 빈칸 (A)~(C)에 들어갈 말로 가장 적절한 것은?

• If there ____(A)____ no tests, I would always be playing.
• Were it not for your help, I ____(B)____ not succeed.
• If they ____(C)____ a car, they could give me a ride.

(A)	(B)	(C)
① was	can	have
② was	would	have
③ will be	could	had had
④ were	could	had
⑤ were	can	had

서답형

11 두 문장의 의미가 같도록 빈칸에 알맞은 말을 쓰시오.

(1) My dad can easily cook spaghetti.
= It is easy _____ _____ _____ _____ _____ spaghetti.

(2) He doesn't know how to solve the problem.
= It is impossible _____ _____ _____ _____ the problem.

(3) She kindly helped the poor children.
= It was kind _____ _____ _____ _____ the poor children.

12 다음 문장과 같은 의미의 문장을 고르시오.

> If there were no water, no living things could survive.

① Living things can survive so there is water.
② There is no water, so living things can't survive.
③ Though there is water, living things can survive.
④ As there is no water, living things can't survive.
⑤ As there is water, living things can survive.

13 다음 문장에서 생략할 수 있는 것을 고르시오.

> It is important for people to understand each other.

① It   ② is   ③ for people
④ to   ⑤ understand

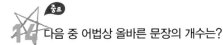

14 다음 중 어법상 올바른 문장의 개수는?

> ⓐ If I am you, I would spend more time outdoors.
> ⓑ If I had free time now, I can go inline skating.
> ⓒ If the weather were fine, we could go out for basketball.
> ⓓ It was a little difficult for I to explain everything in English.
> ⓔ It is hard for senior citizens knowing what teens like.
> ⓕ It was easy for her to find a creative solution.
> ⓖ It is hard for Dobin sings.

① 1개   ② 2개   ③ 3개   ④ 4개   ⑤ 5개

15 다음 우리말을 영작할 때, 바르지 <u>않은</u> 문장을 고르시오.

> 만약 무기가 없다면, 사람들은 조화를 이루며 살 수 있을 텐데.

① But for weapons, people could live in harmony.
② If it were not for weapons, people could live in harmony.
③ If there are no weapons, people could live in harmony.
④ Were it not for weapons, people could live in harmony.
⑤ Without weapons, people could live in harmony.

서답형

16 다음 문장에서 <u>틀린</u> 것을 고쳐 다시 쓰시오.

(1) If you are me, would you talk to the teacher?
　➡ _____
　_____

(2) It was wise for them to call the police directly.
　➡ _____
　_____

서답형

17 다음 문장에서 어법상 <u>어색한</u> 부분을 찾아서 한 단어만 고치시오.

(1) If I were you, I'll sit up straight.
　_____ ➡ _____

(2) It is dangerous of you to climb up the ladder.
　_____ ➡ _____

[01~02] 다음 우리말과 일치하도록 괄호 안에 주어진 단어들을 바르게 배열하시오.

01 중요

> 만약 그녀가 독일에 산다면, 독일어를 말할 수 있을 텐데.
> (she, she, Germany, German, lived, speak, could, if, in)

➡ _____

_____

02

> 너의 실수를 인정하다니 너는 현명하다.
> (mistake, you, your, it, admit, is, wise, of, to)

➡ _____

_____

03 중요

다음 문장과 같은 뜻이 되도록 괄호 안에 주어진 어휘를 활용하여 단어 수에 맞게 빈칸을 채우시오.

> Without tests, I would be happy.

(1) _____ tests, I would be happy. (it, be, 5 단어)

(2) _____ tests, I would be happy. (it, be, 4 단어)

(3) _____ tests, I would be happy. (there, no, 4 단어)

(4) _____ tests, I would be happy. (but, 2 단어)

(5) _____ tests, I won't be happy. (as, 3 단어, 직설법으로 쓸 것.)

04 다음 그림을 보고, 주어진 어휘를 이용하여 대화의 빈칸을 알맞게 채우시오.

> B: What did you do at the community center?
> A: I helped senior citizens to take pictures with their smartphone.
> B: It is very _____ them there. (you, kind, help, 5 단어)

05 다음 그림을 보고, 주어진 어휘를 이용하여 대화의 빈칸을 알맞게 채우시오.

> How can you lie in the place where I lay eggs? If I _____(be) you, I would not lie there.

06 다음 직설법 문장을 가정법 문장으로 고쳐 쓰시오.

(1) As my mother is busy now, we cannot go to the movies.

➡ _____

_____

(2) I am not a teacher, so I will not be the students' best friend.

➡ _____

_____

(3) Since there are tests, I won't be happy.

➡ _____

_____

(4) Because Chris doesn't finish his homework every day, he can't play baseball with us.

➡ _____

_____

07 다음 문장을 바꿔 쓸 때, 빈칸에 알맞은 말을 쓰시오.

(1) He was generous to give us the money to pay for the eggs.

= It was generous _____ us the money to pay for the eggs.

(2) He was considerate enough to keep his voice down.

= It was very considerate _____ his voice down.

(3) The street is dangerous, so she does not walk on at night.

= It is dangerous _____ on the street at night.

08 다음 주어진 문장과 뜻이 같도록 빈칸을 알맞게 채우시오.

As Mary doesn't know his name, she won't let me know it.

→ If Mary _____ his name, she _____ let me know it.

09 다음 우리말을 괄호 안에 주어진 단어들을 활용하여 영작하시오.

(1) Ryan이 바쁘지 않다면, 우리가 그의 집에 방문할 텐데. (be, busy, visit his house)

➡ _____

(2) 네가 이 드레스를 입으면, 더 예뻐 보일 텐데. (wear, look, this dress, pretty)

➡ _____

(3) 내가 영어로 말하는 것은 쉽지 않다. (easy, to, it, speak in English)

➡ _____

(4) 그들이 그 문을 수리하는 것은 가능하다. (possible, to, it, repair)

➡ _____

10 다음 글에서 어법상 잘못 쓰인 것을 찾아 알맞게 고치시오. (2곳)

The mothers were not good at Korean, so they could not read Korean books to their children. It was a little difficult of me to read the books aloud because of my throat got quite sore.

➡ (1) _____

(2) _____

The Story of the Commons

Once upon a time there was a small village in a forest. The villagers
옛날에
were farmers and raised cows. Luckily, some good grassland lay in the
raise–raised–raised: 기르다   lie–lay–lain: 놓여 있다
middle of the village.

The Commons: Space for Everyone

Head of a village: Let's share the commons.

Villager 1: My cow can get enough grass.

Villager 2: Yeah, there's plenty for every cow.

Everyone was allowed to use the grassland. Therefore, it was called
everyone은 단수 취급: was 사용. 'allow+목적어+to부정사'를 수동태로 전환한 것임.
"the commons." By tradition, each family only had one cow, so it was
                                                              가주어
easy for each cow in the village to find enough grass to eat. The grass
       to find의 의미상 주어   진주어   to eat: 형용사적 용법
on the commons was green all summer long.

Farmer 1: If I had two cows, I would be richer.

Farmer 1: No one will notice it.

But one day a villager broke the rule. He brought another cow and
let it graze on the commons. He thought that nobody would notice it. A
let(사역동사): 목적보어로 원형부정사인 graze를 취함.
happy feeling filled his heart when he thought of the milk and cheese
that the second cow would bring to his family.
목적격 관계대명사

common 공유지, 공원

grassland 초지, 풀밭

be allowed to ~하는 것이 허용되다

by tradition 전통에 따라

break a rule 규칙을 어기다

graze 풀을 뜯다

notice 알아채다

확인문제

● 다음 문장이 본문의 내용과 일치하면 T, 일치하지 않으면 F를 쓰시오.

1 In the middle of the village, there was some good grassland. ☐

2 The grassland was called "the commons" because cows can get enough grass. ☐

3 By tradition, each family only had one cow. ☐

4 It was difficult for each cow in the village to find enough grass to eat. ☐

5 One day a villager brought another cow and let it graze on the commons. ☐

6 The villager felt guilty after he broke the rule. ☐

Farmer 1: He has four children.

Farmer 1: If I were you, I would raise another cow.

Farmer 2: Thanks for the tip!

A few days later, the farmer visited a close friend who had four
children. He wanted to help his friend, so he told him in secret, "If I
were you, I would bring in one more cow and raise it on the commons."
The friend thanked him and did as he was told the next day.

Cow 1: Who are you?

Cow 2: I'm new.

Cow 3: Who is lying there?

Cow 4: I don't know.

Farmer 3: I can be the richest farmer in this village.

Soon, other villagers did the same. Some secretly brought one more
cow to the commons, while others brought even more to the grassland
without telling anyone. They thought that there would be enough grass
for the additional cows. Soon the village was full of happy-looking
farmers!

Cow 1: Hey, stop pushing me!

Cow 2: Move over!

Cow 3: This is my spot!

Cow 1: We need rain!

Cow 2: I'm hungry.

Cow 3: Me, too.

in secret 몰래, 비밀리에

additional 추가의

be full of ~으로 가득 차다

확인문제

● 다음 문장이 본문의 내용과 일치하면 T, 일치하지 <u>않으면</u> F를 쓰시오.

1 The farmer wanted to help his friend. ☐

2 The farmer told his friend that he should not raise one more cow on the commons. ☐

3 The friend thanked the farmer and brought in one more cow to the commons the next day. ☐

4 Some villagers brought one more cow to the commons openly. ☐

5 Other villagers brought even more to the grassland without telling anyone. ☐

6 The villagers worried that there would be no grass for the additional cows. ☐

The number of cows rose slowly at first. Then the cow population grew more quickly. The grass on the commons began to disappear, and it became harder for the cows to find grass to eat. To make matters worse, it did not rain for a long time.

Farmer 1: I don't have any cows left!

Cow 1: Good bye.

Head of a village: What happened to the commons?

In the past, when a dry year came, the small number of cows on the commons always found something to eat. However, no grass was left now because there were too many cows. Things were harsh for the villagers; many of the cows died.

Enjoy, but remember the rule: ONLY ONE COW PER FAMILY.

At last, the grass came back. Now it was able to support only one cow per family. The village went back to the one-family-one-cow rule. The villagers all learned an important lesson: when resources are shared, it is important for everyone to value the resources and use them fairly. The villagers now tell this story to their children. They call it "The Story of the Commons."

the number of ~의 수

population 개체 수, 인구

to make matters worse 엎친 데 덮친 격으로

harsh 가혹한, 냉혹한

per ~당, ~마다

support 지지하다, 부양하다

lesson 교훈

resource 자원

value 소중히 여기다

확인문제

● 다음 문장이 본문의 내용과 일치하면 T, 일치하지 않으면 F를 쓰시오.

1 The number of cows didn't rise quickly at first. ☐

2 What is worse, it rained heavily for a long time. ☐

3 In the past, when a dry year came, it was not difficult for the small number of cows on the commons to find something to eat. ☐

4 There was enough grass on the commons now though there were too many cows. ☐

5 All the villagers learned an important lesson: when resources are shared, everyone should value the resources and use them fairly. ☐

6 The villagers tell their children the story that is called "The Story of the Commons." ☐

● 우리말을 참고하여 빈칸에 알맞은 말을 쓰시오.

1 The Story of the _____

2 _____ _____ _____ _____ there was a small village in a forest.

3 The villagers were farmers and _____ cows.

4 Luckily, some good grassland _____ in the middle of the village.

5 The Commons: _____ _____ _____

6 Head of a village: _____ _____ the commons.

7 Villager 1: My cow can get _____ _____ .

8 Villager 2: Yeah, _____ _____ for every cow.

9 Everyone _____ _____ _____ _____ the grassland.

10 Therefore, it _____ _____ "the commons."

11 _____ _____ , each family only had one cow, so it was easy for each cow in the village to find _____ _____ _____ _____ .

12 The grass on the commons was green _____ _____ _____ .

13 Farmer 1: If I _____ two cows, I _____ _____ richer.

14 Farmer 1: No one will _____ it.

15 But one day a villager _____ _____ _____ .

16 He brought another cow and _____ _____ _____ on the commons.

17 He thought that _____ _____ _____ it.

18 A happy feeling filled his heart when he _____ _____ the milk and cheese that the second cow _____ _____ to his family.

1	공유지 이야기
2	옛날, 숲속에 작은 마을이 있었다.
3	마을 주민들은 농부였고 소를 길렀다.
4	다행히도, 마을 한 가운데에 좋은 목초지가 있었다.
5	공유지: 모두를 위한 장소
6	이장: 공유지를 함께 나누어 씁시다.
7	마을 사람 1: 내 소가 풀을 충분히 뜯을 수 있겠어.
8	마을 사람 2: 맞아, 모든 소에게 충분한 양이야.
9	모든 사람들이 목초지를 사용하도록 허락되었다.
10	그러므로 목초지는 '공유지'라고 불렸다.
11	전통에 따라 각 가정은 소가 한 마리만 있었고, 그래서 마을에 있는 소들이 충분히 먹을 풀을 찾는 것은 쉬운 일이었다.
12	공유지의 풀은 여름 내내 푸르렀다.
13	농부 1: 만약 소가 두 마리 있다면, 내가 더 부유할 텐데.
14	농부 1: 아무도 눈치 채지 못할 거야.
15	그러나 어느 날 마을 사람 하나가 규칙을 깨뜨렸다.
16	그는 또 다른 소를 가져와 공유지에서 풀을 뜯게 했다.
17	그는 아무도 그것을 눈치 채지 못할 거라고 생각했다.
18	두 번째 소가 가족에게 가져다 줄 우유와 치즈를 생각하자 그의 마음은 행복감으로 충만했다.

19 Farmer 1: He _____ four children.

20 Farmer 1: If I _____ you, I _____ _____ another cow.

21 Farmer 2: Thanks _____ the tip!

22 A few days later, the farmer visited a close friend _____ had four children.

23 He wanted to help his friend, so he told him _____ _____, "If I were you, I would _____ _____ one more cow and _____ _____ on the commons."

24 The friend thanked him and did _____ _____ _____ _____ the next day.

25 Cow 1: _____ are you?

26 Cow 2: I'm _____.

27 Cow 3: Who is _____ there?

28 Cow 4: I _____ _____.

29 Farmer 3: I can be _____ _____ farmer in this village.

30 Soon, other villagers _____ _____ _____.

31 Some _____ brought one more cow to the commons, while others brought _____ _____ to the grassland _____ _____ _____.

32 They thought that there would be enough grass for the _____ cows.

33 Soon the village was full of _____ farmers!

34 Cow 1: Hey, stop _____ me!

35 Cow 2: Move _____!

36 Cow 3: This is my _____!

37 Cow 1: We need _____!

38 Cow 2: I'm _____.

---

19 농부 1: 그는 아이가 네 명이나 있어.

20 농부 1: 내가 당신이라면, 소를 한 마리 더 기르겠어요.

21 농부 2: 조언 고마워요!

22 며칠 후, 그 농부는 아이가 네 명 있는 친한 친구 집을 방문했다.

23 그는 친구를 도와주고 싶어서 몰래 그에게 말했다. "내가 당신이라면, 소를 한 마리 더 데려와 공유지에서 키우겠어요."

24 친구는 그에게 고마워했고 그다음 날 자신이 들은 대로 했다.

25 소 1: 넌 누구니?

26 소 2: 난 새로 왔어.

27 소 3: 누가 저기 누워 있는 거야?

28 소 4: 몰라.

29 농부 3: 내가 마을에서 가장 부유한 농부가 될 수 있어.

30 곧, 다른 사람들도 그렇게 했다.

31 어떤 사람들은 은밀하게 소를 한 마리 더 공유지에 데려왔고, 또 어떤 사람들은 아무에게도 말하지 않고 훨씬 많은 소를 목초지에 데려왔다.

32 그들은 추가된 소에게도 충분한 풀이 있을 것이라고 생각했다.

33 곧 마을은 행복해 보이는 농부들로 가득 찼다!

34 소 1: 이봐, 밀지 마!

35 소 2: 저기로 가!

36 소 3: 여긴 내 자리야!

37 소 1: 비가 필요해!

38 소 2: 배고파.

39 Cow 3: _____, _____.

40 The number of cows _____ slowly at first.

41 Then the _____ _____ grew more quickly.

42 The grass on the commons began _____ _____, and it became _____ for the cows to find grass to eat.

43 _____ _____ _____ _____, it did not rain for a long time.

44 Farmer 1: I don't have any cows _____!

45 Cow 1: Good bye.

46 Head of a village: What _____ _____ the commons?

47 In the past, when a dry year came, the small number of cows on the commons always found _____ _____ _____.

48 However, no grass was left now because _____ _____ _____ _____ cows.

49 Things were _____ for the villagers; many of the cows died.

50 **Enjoy, but remember the rule: ONLY ONE COW _____ _____.**

51 _____ _____, the grass came back.

52 Now it was able to _____ _____ _____ _____ per family.

53 The village went back to the _____ rule.

54 The villagers all learned an important _____: when resources _____ _____, it is important for everyone _____ _____ the resources and use them _____.

55 The villagers now tell this story _____ their children.

56 They _____ _____ "The Story of the Commons."

39 소 3: 나도.

40 처음에는 소의 수가 천천히 늘어났다.

41 그러더니 소의 개체 수는 더 빨리 증가했다.

42 공유지의 풀은 사라지기 시작했고, 소들이 먹을 풀을 찾기가 더 힘들어졌다.

43 엎친 데 덮친 격으로, 오랫동안 비가 내리지 않았다.

44 농부 1: 이제 나는 남은 소가 없어!

45 소 1: 안녕.

46 이장: 공유지에 무슨 일이 일어난 거지?

47 과거에는 비가 오지 않는 해에도 공유지에 있는 적은 수의 소들이 먹을 것을 항상 찾을 수 있었다.

48 하지만, 지금은 소가 너무 많아서 풀이 남지 않았다.

49 상황은 마을 사람들에게 가혹했다; 많은 소들이 죽었다.

50 즐겨라. 그러나 규칙을 기억해라: 가구당 오직 소 한 마리.

51 마침내 목초지가 회복되었다.

52 이제는 가구당 한 마리의 소만 감당할 수 있게 되었다.

53 마을은 '한 가구, 한 마리 소' 규칙으로 돌아갔다.

54 마을 사람들 모두는 중요한 교훈을 배웠다. 즉, 자원이 공유될 때는 모두가 그 자원을 소중히 여기고 공평하게 사용하는 것이 중요하다는 것이다.

55 이제 마을 사람들은 이 이야기를 자신들의 후손에게 들려준다.

56 그들은 이 이야기를 '공유지 이야기'라고 부른다.

● 우리말을 참고하여 본문을 영작하시오.

1 공유지 이야기
➡ _____

2 옛날, 숲속에 작은 마을이 있었다.
➡ _____

3 마을 주민들은 농부였고 소를 길렀다.
➡ _____

4 다행히도, 마을 한 가운데에 좋은 목초지가 있었다.
➡ _____

5 공유지: 모두를 위한 장소
➡ _____

6 이장: 공유지를 함께 나누어 씁시다.
➡ _____

7 마을 사람 1: 내 소가 풀을 충분히 뜯을 수 있겠어.
➡ _____

8 마을 사람 2: 맞아, 모든 소에게 충분한 양이야.
➡ _____

9 모든 사람들이 목초지를 사용하도록 허락되었다.
➡ _____

10 그러므로 목초지는 '공유지'라고 불렸다.
➡ _____

11 전통에 따라 각 가정은 소가 한 마리만 있었고, 그래서 마을에 있는 소들이 충분히 먹을 풀을 찾는 것은 쉬운 일이었다.
➡ _____
_____

12 공유지의 풀은 여름 내내 푸르렀다.
➡ _____

13 농부 1: 만약 소가 두 마리 있다면, 내가 더 부유할 텐데.
➡ _____

14 농부 1: 아무도 눈치 채지 못할 거야.
➡ _____

15 그러나 어느 날 마을 사람 하나가 규칙을 깨뜨렸다.
➡ _____

16 그는 또 다른 소를 가져와 공유지에서 풀을 뜯게 했다.
➡ _____

17 그는 아무도 그것을 눈치 채지 못할 거라고 생각했다.
➡ _____

18 두 번째 소가 가족에게 가져다줄 우유와 치즈를 생각하자 그의 마음은 행복감으로 충만했다.
➡ _____
_____

19 농부 1: 그는 아이가 네 명이나 있어.

➡ _____

20 농부 1: 내가 당신이라면, 소를 한 마리 더 기르겠어요.

➡ _____

21 농부 2: 조언 고마워요!

➡ _____

22 며칠 후, 그 농부는 아이가 네 명 있는 친한 친구 집을 방문했다.

➡ _____

23 그는 친구를 도와주고 싶어서 몰래 그에게 말했다. "내가 당신이라면, 소를 한 마리 더 데려와 공유지에서 키우겠어요."

➡ _____
_____

24 친구는 그에게 고마워했고 그다음 날 자신이 들은 대로 했다.

➡ _____

25 소 1: 넌 누구니?

➡ _____

26 소 2: 난 새로 왔어.

➡ _____

27 소 3: 누가 저기 누워 있는 거야?

➡ _____

28 소 4: 몰라.

➡ _____

29 농부 3: 내가 마을에서 가장 부유한 농부가 될 수 있어.

➡ _____

30 곧, 다른 사람들도 그렇게 했다.

➡ _____

31 어떤 사람들은 은밀하게 소를 한 마리 더 공유지에 데려왔고, 또 어떤 사람들은 아무에게도 말하지 않고 훨씬 많은 소를 목초지에 데려왔다.

➡ _____
_____

32 그들은 추가된 소에게도 충분한 풀이 있을 것이라고 생각했다.

➡ _____

33 곧 마을은 행복해 보이는 농부들로 가득 찼다!

➡ _____

34 소 1: 이봐, 밀지 마!

➡ _____

35 소 2: 저기로 가!

➡ _____

36 소 3: 여긴 내 자리야!

➡ _____

37 소 1: 비가 필요해!

➡ _____

38 소 2: 배고파.

➡ _____

39 소 3: 나도.

➡ _____

40 처음에는 소의 수가 천천히 늘어났다.

➡ _____

41 그러더니 소의 개체 수는 더 빨리 증가했다.

➡ _____

42 공유지의 풀은 사라지기 시작했고, 소들이 먹을 풀을 찾기가 더 힘들어졌다.

➡ _____

43 엎친 데 덮친 격으로, 오랫동안 비가 내리지 않았다.

➡ _____

44 농부 1: 이제 나는 남은 소가 없어!

➡ _____

45 소 1: 안녕.

➡ _____

46 이장: 공유지에 무슨 일이 일어난 거지?

➡ _____

47 과거에는 비가 오지 않는 해에도 공유지에 있는 적은 수의 소들이 먹을 것을 항상 찾을 수 있었다.

➡ _____

48 하지만, 지금은 소가 너무 많아서 풀이 남지 않았다.

➡ _____

49 상황은 마을 사람들에게 가혹했다; 많은 소들이 죽었다.

➡ _____

50 즐겨라, 그러나 규칙을 기억해라: 가구당 오직 소 한 마리.

➡ _____

51 마침내 목초지가 회복되었다.

➡ _____

52 이제는 가구당 한 마리의 소만 감당할 수 있게 되었다.

➡ _____

53 마을은 '한 가구, 한 마리 소' 규칙으로 돌아갔다.

➡ _____

54 마을 사람들 모두는 중요한 교훈을 배웠다. 즉, 자원이 공유될 때는 모두가 그 자원을 소중히 여기고 공평하게 사용하는 것이 중요하다는 것이다.

➡ _____

55 이제 마을 사람들은 이 이야기를 자신들의 후손에게 들려준다.

➡ _____

56 그들은 이 이야기를 '공유지 이야기'라고 부른다.

➡ _____

[01~03] 다음 글을 읽고 물음에 답하시오.

The Commons: Space for Everyone

Head of a village: Let's share the commons.
Villager 1: My cow can get enough grass.
Villager 2: Yeah, there's plenty for every cow.

Everyone was allowed to use the grassland.
____ⓐ____, it was called "the commons." ____ⓑ____
tradition, each family only had one cow, so
it was easy for each cow in the village (A)
to find enough grass to eat. The grass on the
commons was green all summer long.

01 위 글의 빈칸 ⓐ에 들어갈 알맞은 말을 고르시오.

① Similarly   ② However
③ Therefore   ④ In addition
⑤ That is

02 위 글의 빈칸 ⓑ에 알맞은 전치사를 쓰시오.

➡ _____

03 위 글의 밑줄 친 (A)to find와 to부정사의 용법이 같은 것을 모두 고르시오.

① I make it a rule to take a walk early in
   the morning.
② It is high time to go to bed now.
③ He cannot be a gentleman to do such a
   thing.
④ I decided to go there with Kate.
⑤ I'm looking for a bigger house to live in.

[04~06] 다음 글을 읽고 물음에 답하시오.

A few days later, the farmer visited a close
friend who had four children. He wanted to
help ①his friend, so he told ②him in secret,
"If I were ③you, I would bring in one more
cow and raise it on the commons." The friend
thanked ④him and did ⓐas ⑤he was told the
next day.

04 밑줄 친 ①~⑤ 중에서 가리키는 대상이 나머지 넷과 다른
것은?

①   ②   ③   ④   ⑤

05 위 글의 밑줄 친 ⓐas와 같은 의미로 쓰인 것을 고르시오.

① He came up as I was speaking.
② They cut down on salty food as I
   advised.
③ As it was getting dark, we soon turned
   back.
④ As one grows older, one becomes more
   silent.
⑤ Take as much as you want.

06 What did the farmer advise his close friend to do? Fill in
the blanks (A) and (B) with suitable words.

> He advised him to bring in (A)_____
> _____ _____ and raise it on
> (B)_____ _____.

[07~09] 다음 글을 읽고 물음에 답하시오.

The Commons: Space for ⓐ

Head of a village: Let's share the commons.

Villager 1: My cow can get enough grass.

Villager 2: Yeah, there's plenty for every cow.

Everyone was allowed to use the grassland. Therefore, ⓑit was called "the commons." By tradition, each family only had one cow, so it was easy for each cow in the village to find enough grass to eat. The grass on the commons was green all summer long.

07 위 글의 빈칸 ⓐ에 들어갈 알맞은 말을 고르시오.

① Common People　　② Everyone

③ Grown-ups　　④ Nobody

⑤ Some Villagers

서답형

08 위 글의 밑줄 친 ⓑit이 가리키는 것을 본문에서 찾아 쓰시오.

➡ _____

09 According to the passage, which is NOT true?

① The head of a village suggested sharing the commons.

② Villager 1 and 2 think that their cows can get enough grass.

③ By tradition, there was no limit to the number of cows each family could have.

④ Each cow in the village easily found enough grass to eat.

⑤ The grass on the commons was green throughout the summer.

[10~13] 다음 글을 읽고 물음에 답하시오.

At last, the grass came back. Now it was able to support only one cow per family. The village went back to (A)'한 가구, 한 마리 소' 규칙. The villagers all learned an important (B)lesson: when resources ⓐ _____, it is important for everyone to value the resources and use them fairly. The villagers now tell this story to their children. They call it "The Story of the Commons."

서답형

10 위 글의 빈칸 ⓐ에 share를 알맞은 형태로 쓰시오.

➡ _____

서답형

11 위 글의 밑줄 친 (A)의 우리말에 맞게 영작하시오.

➡ _____

12 위 글의 밑줄 친 (B)lesson과 같은 의미로 쓰인 것을 고르시오.

① Our first lesson on Tuesdays is French.

② We will study Lesson Three today.

③ I have no lesson today.

④ Let her fate be a lesson to you.

⑤ What did we do last lesson?

13 위 글의 주제로 알맞은 것을 고르시오.

① the importance of using the shared resources fairly

② the effective way to protect Mother Nature

③ the recovery of the commons and enough grass for the cows

④ the importance of the protection of the environment

⑤ the harsh situation of the commons

[14~17] 다음 글을 읽고 물음에 답하시오.

Soon, other villagers did the same. Some secretly brought one more cow to the commons, ⓐwhile others brought even more to the grassland without telling anyone. ⓑ그들은 추가된 소에게도 충분한 풀이 있을 것이라고 생각했다. ⓒSoon the village was full of happy-looking farmers!

14 위 글의 앞에 올 내용으로 가장 알맞은 것을 고르시오.

① People managed the commons well together.
② People became richer than before.
③ Some people secretly brought one more cow to the commons.
④ People lived poor lives in the village.
⑤ Some people helped one another.

15 위 글의 밑줄 친 ⓐwhile과 같은 의미로 쓰인 것을 고르시오.

① Make hay while the sun shines.
② Where have you been all this while?
③ It took him a while to calm down.
④ The walls are green, while the ceiling is white.
⑤ I fell asleep while I was reading.

서답형

16 위 글의 밑줄 친 ⓑ의 우리말에 맞게 주어진 어휘를 알맞게 배열하시오.

enough / cows / grass / be / they / there / additional / the / that / for / would / thought

➡ _____
_____

서답형

17 위 글의 밑줄 친 ⓒ와 같은 뜻이 되도록 빈칸에 들어갈 알맞은 말을 쓰시오.

➡ Soon the village was _____ happy-looking farmers!

[18~22] 다음 글을 읽고 물음에 답하시오.

Enjoy, but remember the rule: ONLY ONE COW PER FAMILY.

ⓐAt last, the grass came back. (①) The village went back to ⓑthe one-family-one-cow rule. (②) The villagers all learned an important lesson: when resources are shared, it is important for everyone to value the resources and use ⓒthem fairly. (③) The villagers now tell this story to their children. (④) They call it "The Story of the Commons." (⑤)

18 위 글의 밑줄 친 ⓐAt last와 바꿔 쓸 수 있는 말을 모두 고르시오.

① Actually   ② Finally   ③ In the end
④ Lastly   ⑤ Eventually

19 위 글의 흐름으로 보아, 주어진 문장이 들어가기에 가장 적절한 곳은?

Now it was able to support only one cow per family.

①   ②   ③   ④   ⑤

서답형

20 다음 빈칸에 알맞은 단어를 넣어 위 글의 밑줄 친 ⓑ에 대한 설명을 완성하시오.

It means that each family should have only _____ _____.

서답형

21 위 글의 밑줄 친 ⓒthem이 가리키는 것을 본문에서 찾아 쓰시오.

➡ _____

서답형

22 What is the lesson from the story? Fill in the blanks (A) and (B) with suitable words.

> When people share (A)_____, everyone should value the shared resources and use them (B)_____.

[23~25] 다음 글을 읽고 물음에 답하시오.

Everyone was allowed to use the grassland. Therefore, it was called "the commons." By tradition, each family only had one cow, so it was easy for each cow in the village to find enough grass to eat. The grass on the commons was green all summer long.

But one day a villager broke ⓐthe rule. He brought another cow and let it graze on the commons. He thought that nobody would notice it. A happy feeling filled his heart when he thought of the milk and cheese that the second cow would bring to his family.

서답형

23 위 글의 내용으로 미루어 보아, 밑줄 친 ⓐthe rule의 내용을 다음과 같이 정리하고자 한다. 빈칸 (A)와 (B)에 들어갈 알맞은 단어를 본문에서 찾아 쓰시오.

> Each family should let only (A)_____ _____ graze on (B)_____ _____.

중요

24 위 글의 두 번째 단락에 어울리는 속담으로 알맞지 <u>않은</u> 것을 고르시오.

① Heaven helps those who help themselves.

② Greed knows no limits.

③ Don't count your chickens before they are hatched.

④ Give him an inch, and he will take a mile.

⑤ Appetite comes with eating.

25 Which question CANNOT be answered after reading the passage?

① Why was the grassland called "the commons"?

② How many cows did each family have by tradition?

③ Did each cow in the village find enough grass to eat easily?

④ How was the grass on the commons throughout the summer?

⑤ How much milk and cheese did the second cow bring to his family?

[26~29] 다음 글을 읽고 물음에 답하시오.

A few days later, the farmer visited a close friend who had four children. He wanted to help his friend, so he told him ⓐin secret, "If I were you, I would bring in one more cow and ⓑraise ⓒit on the commons." The friend thanked him and ⓓdid as he was told the next day.

서답형

26 위 글의 밑줄 친 ⓐin secret를 한 단어로 고치시오.

➡ _____

27 위 글의 밑줄 친 ⓑraise와 같은 의미로 쓰인 것을 고르시오.

① He tried to <u>raise</u> a hand in greeting.

② How can we <u>raise</u> standards in schools?

③ She didn't <u>raise</u> cattle at that time.

④ He told me how to <u>raise</u> money for a charity.

⑤ We <u>raise</u> a national flag on a national holiday.

서답형

28 위 글의 밑줄 친 ⓒit이 가리키는 것을 본문에서 찾아 쓰시오.

➡ _____

서답형

29 다음 빈칸 (A)와 (B)에 알맞은 단어를 넣어, 위 글의 밑줄 친 ⓓ가 의미하는 것을 완성하시오.

> (A)_____ in one more cow and (B)_____ it on the commons as his friend told him to do the previous day

[30~33] 다음 글을 읽고 물음에 답하시오.

　Soon, other villagers did the same. Some secretly brought one more cow to the commons, while others brought (A)<u>even</u> more to the grassland without telling anyone. They thought that there would be enough grass for the additional cows. Soon the village was full 　ⓐ 　 happy-looking farmers!

　The number of cows rose slowly at first. Then the cow population grew more quickly. The grass on the commons began to

disappear, and it became harder 　ⓑ 　 the cows to find grass to eat. (B)<u>To make matters worse</u>, it did not rain for a long time.

중요

30 위 글의 빈칸 ⓐ와 ⓑ에 들어갈 전치사가 바르게 짝지어진 것은?

	ⓐ	ⓑ		ⓐ	ⓑ
①	with	of	②	of	by
③	in	for	④	with	of
⑤	of	for			

31 위 글의 밑줄 친 (A)even과 바꿔 쓸 수 없는 말을 고르시오.

① much　　　② very

③ still　　　④ far

⑤ a lot

서답형

32 위 글의 밑줄 친 (B)를 다음과 같이 바꿔 쓸 때 빈칸에 들어갈 알맞은 단어를 쓰시오.

➡ _____ was worse

중요

33 위 글을 읽고 알 수 없는 것을 고르시오.

① What did the villagers bring to the commons?

② What did the villagers think about the commons?

③ How many cows were there on the commons?

④ Did the number of cows rise quickly from the beginning?

⑤ Did it rain a lot on the commons?

[01~03] 다음 글을 읽고 물음에 답하시오.

"If I (A)[have / had] two cows, I would be richer."

"No one will notice it."

But one day a villager broke the rule. He brought (B)[another / the other] cow and let it (C)[graze / grazing] on the commons. He thought that nobody would notice ⓐ it. ⓑA happy feeling filled his heart when he thought of the milk and cheese that the second cow would bring to his family.

01 위 글의 괄호 (A)~(C)에서 어법상 알맞은 낱말을 골라 쓰시오.

➡ (A) _____ (B) _____ (C) _____

02 위 글의 밑줄 친 ⓐit이 가리키는 것을 우리말로 쓰시오.

➡ _____

_____

03 위 글의 밑줄 친 ⓑ를 수동태로 고치시오.

➡ _____

[04~07] 다음 글을 읽고 물음에 답하시오.

Once upon a time there was a small village in a forest. The villagers were farmers and raised cows. (A)Luckily, some good grassland lied in the middle of the village.

Everyone was allowed ___ⓐ___ the grassland. Therefore, it was called "the commons." By tradition, each family only had one cow, (B) 그래서 마을에 있는 소들이 충분히 먹을 풀을 찾는 것은 쉬운 일이었다. The grass on the commons was green all summer long.

04 위 글의 빈칸 ⓐ에 use를 알맞은 형태로 쓰시오.

➡ _____

05 위 글의 밑줄 친 (A)에서 어법상 틀린 부분을 찾아 고치시오.

_____ ➡ _____

06 위 글의 밑줄 친 (B)의 우리말에 맞게 주어진 어휘를 알맞게 배열하시오.

| each cow / to find / easy / it / so / in the village / to eat / for / was / enough grass |

➡ _____

_____

07 위 글의 내용을 다음과 같이 정리하고자 한다. 빈칸 (A)와 (B)에 들어갈 알맞은 단어를 본문에서 찾아 쓰시오.

| In the middle of a small village in a forest, there was some (A)_____ _____ which was called "(B)_____ _____" because everyone was allowed to use it. |

[08~10] 다음 글을 읽고 물음에 답하시오.

Soon, other villagers did the same. Some secretly brought one more cow to the commons, while others brought even more to the grassland (A)without telling anyone. They thought that there would be enough grass for the ____@____ cows. Soon the village was full of happy-looking farmers!

The number of cows rose slowly at first. Then the cow population grew more quickly. The grass on the commons began to disappear, and it became harder for the cows to find grass to eat. To make matters worse, it did not rain for a long time.

08 위 글의 빈칸 ⓐ에 add를 알맞은 형태로 쓰시오.

➡ _____

09 위 글의 밑줄 친 (A)without telling anyone과 바꿔 쓸 수 있는 한 단어를 본문에서 찾아 쓰시오.

➡ _____

10 본문의 내용과 일치하도록 다음 빈칸 (A)와 (B)에 들어갈 알맞은 단어를 본문에서 찾아 쓰시오.

> The (A)_____ _____ grew quickly because the villagers brought additional cows to the commons, so it became (B)_____ for the cows to find grass to eat.

[11~12] 다음 글을 읽고 물음에 답하시오.

In the past, when a dry year came, the small number of cows on the commons always found something to eat. However, no grass was left now because there were too many cows. ⓐThings were favorable for the villagers; many of the cows died.

11 위 글의 밑줄 친 ⓐ에서 흐름상 어색한 부분을 찾아 고치시오. (철자 h로 시작할 것)

_____ ➡ _____

12 다음 빈칸 (A)와 (B)에 알맞은 단어를 넣어, '비가 오지 않는 해일 때의 공유지의 상태'를 쓰시오.

> • **In the past:** The small number of cows on the commons always (A)_____
>
> _____ _____ _____.
>
> • **Now:** No grass was left because there were (B)_____ _____ _____, and many of them died.

[13~14] 다음 글을 읽고 물음에 답하시오.

At last, the grass came back. Now it was able to support only one cow per family. The village went back to the one-family-one-cow rule. The villagers all learned an important lesson: when resources are shared, it is important for everyone to value the resources and use them ____ⓐ____. The villagers now tell this story to their children. They call it "The Story of the Commons."

13 주어진 영영풀이를 참고하여 빈칸 ⓐ에 철자 f로 시작하는 단어를 쓰시오.

> with justice

➡ _____

14 How many cows was the grass able to support per family? Answer in English in a full sentence.

➡ _____

구석구석

My Speaking Portfolio - Step 2

A: How should I solve the population problem in my town?

B: If I were you, I'd give support to families with children.
If+주어+동사의 과거형 주어+would/could+동사원형

C: I think you should welcome people from other towns.

A: Okay. Thank you all for your advice.

구문해설 ・solve: 해결하다 ・population: 인구 ・advice: 조언

A: 제가 어떻게 우리 마을의 인구 문제를 해결해야 할까요?

B: 저라면 아이가 있는 가정에 지원을 해 줄 것입니다.

C: 저는 당신이 다른 마을에서 오는 사람들을 기쁘게 맞이해야 한다고 생각합니다.

A: 알겠습니다. 조언 감사합니다.

My Speaking Portfolio - Step 3

A Problem in My Town

Rareville

The population is becoming smaller and smaller in my town. To solve
비교급 and 비교급: 점점 더 ~한   부사적 용법(목적)
this serious problem, I will give support to families with children. I
                                       (소유・구비) ~을 가지고, ~이 있는
will also welcome people from other towns. In addition, I will reduce stress
(의향・속셈) ~할 작정이다, ~하겠다
for working parents. I am sure that these steps will help solve the population
명사를 앞에서 수식하는 현재분사(능동의 의미)   앞에서 취하겠다고 한 조치들
problem in my town.

구문해설 ・give support to: ~을 지지[후원]하다 ・in addition: 게다가 ・reduce: 줄이다, 축소하다

우리 마을의 문제

Rareville

우리 마을의 인구수가 점점 줄어들고 있습니다. 이 심각한 문제를 해결하기 위해 저는 아이가 있는 가정을 지원하겠습니다. 또한, 다른 마을에서 오는 사람들을 기쁘게 맞이하겠습니다. 덧붙여, 맞벌이 부모들의 스트레스를 덜어 주겠습니다. 저는 이러한 조치가 우리 마을의 인구 문제를 해결하는 데에 도움이 될 것이라고 확신합니다.

After You Read Graphic Organizer

Story Mountain

Each family raised one cow on the commons.

Villagers secretly started to bring additional cows.
                              = bringing
The grass began to disappear, and it did not rain for a long time.
                     = disappearing   비인칭 주어(날씨)
Many cows could not find enough grass to eat and died.
                                     to부정사의 형용사적 용법
The grass finally came back.
                  = returned
The villagers went back to the one-family-one-cow rule.
                                     '한 가구, 한 마리 소' 규칙

구문해설 ・raise: 기르다 ・common: 공유지 ・secretly: 몰래, 비밀리에 ・additional: 추가의
・disappear: 사라지다 ・finally: 마침내

이야기 산

각 가정은 공유지에서 소를 한 마리씩 길렀다.

마을 사람들은 몰래 소를 더 데려오기 시작했다.

풀이 사라지기 시작했고, 오랫동안 비가 오지 않았다.

많은 소들이 충분히 먹을 풀을 찾지 못해서 죽었다.

목초지가 마침내 회복되었다.

마을 사람들은 '한 가구, 한 마리 소' 규칙으로 돌아갔다.

영역별 핵심문제

01 다음 영영풀이가 가리키는 것을 고르시오.

> a source of supply, support, or aid

① grassland　　　② view
③ resource　　　④ pleasure
⑤ volunteer

02 다음 중 밑줄 친 부분의 뜻풀이가 바르지 <u>않은</u> 것은?

① I have a fever and a <u>runny nose</u>. (콧물)
② It is wrong to <u>break a rule</u> or tell a lie. (규칙을 어기다)
③ <u>The number of</u> tourists has decreased dramatically because of Covid-19. (많은)
④ May I have a <u>window seat</u>? (창가 자리)
⑤ Cindy hid under the bed <u>in secret</u>. (몰래)

03 다음 우리말에 맞게 빈칸에 알맞은 말을 쓰시오.

(1) 새해 인사인 세배는 한국의 오래된 전통이다.
　➡ *Sebae*, the New Year's bow, is a long _____ in Korea.

(2) Mike는 답을 알지 못했고, 나 역시 그랬다.
　➡ Mike didn't know the answer, and I didn't, _____.

(3) 일부 지역에서는 소들이 흔히 초지에서 풀을 뜯는다.
　➡ In some areas, cows usually _____ in green fields.

(4) 우리는 배를 빌리기 위해서 시간당 20달러를 내야 한다.
　➡ We should pay 20 dollars _____ hour to rent a boat.

04 다음 문장의 빈칸에 들어갈 말을 〈보기〉에서 골라 쓰시오.

> ┤ 보기 ├
> to make matters worse / in secret / senior citizens / once upon a time / in the middle of

(1) _____, there was a man who liked hunting.
(2) These days, he often wakes up _____ the night.
(3) _____, it started to snow heavily again.
(4) Many _____ need help when they go grocery shopping.
(5) Linda studied music _____ because her parents wanted her to be a lawyer.

[05~06] 다음 대화를 읽고 물음에 답하시오.

Gina: My stomach growls every morning. What should I do?
Tom: Ha ha. Do you usually have breakfast?
Gina: No, I have no time to eat anything at home.
Tom: If I were you, I'd bring some snacks.
Gina: That's a good idea.

05 What's the matter with Gina?

➡ _____

06 What does Tom advise Gina to do?

➡ _____

[07~08] 다음 대화를 읽고 물음에 답하시오.

Sora: Wow, it feels great to be on this ship, Dad.

Dad: I feel the same, Sora. Here (A)[is / are] our seats, 20A and 20B.

Sora: Yeah. Do you mind if I take the window seat? I like to see the view outside.

Dad: No problem.

Sora: By the way, I want to eat something like noodles or sandwiches.

Dad: If I were you, I wouldn't eat anything like that.

Sora: Why is that?

Dad: They may make you seasick.

Sora: Oh, I see. Then, I'll have some ice cream.

Dad: That's not a good idea, (B)[too / either]. Let's eat after we (C)[arrive / arrival].

07 위 대화의 괄호 (A)~(C)에서 어법상 알맞은 말이 바르게 짝지어진 것은?

	(A)	(B)	(C)
①	is	too	arrive
②	is	either	arrival
③	are	either	arrive
④	are	either	arrival
⑤	are	too	arrive

08 위 대화를 읽고 대답할 수 없는 것은?

① Where are Sora and her dad?

② Which seat does Sora want to take?

③ What does Sora want to eat?

④ What can cause seasick?

⑤ Which does Sora like better, noodles or sandwiches?

[09~10] 다음 대화를 읽고 물음에 답하시오.

Jimin: Thanks for letting me volunteer here, Ms. Yun.

Ms. Yun: It's my pleasure, Jimin. I'm glad you decided to help.

Jimin: Well, what should I do?

Ms. Yun: Today's lesson is about taking photos with smartphones. Why don't you help the slow learners?

Jimin: Okay. Is there anything I should know?

Ms. Yun: Yes. Please be patient and kind to the learners.

Jimin: I'll keep that in mind. By the way, do you mind if I use your charger? My battery is a little low.

Ms. Yun: ___(A)___ Go right ahead.

09 위 대화의 빈칸 (A)에 들어갈 말로 나머지와 의도가 다른 것은?

① Of course not.　② No, not at all.

③ Certainly not.　④ Yes, I do.

⑤ No problem.

10 위 대화의 내용과 일치하지 않는 것은?

① 지민이는 봉사활동을 할 수 있게 되어 감사해 한다.

② 오늘 수업은 스마트폰으로 사진을 찍는 것에 관한 것이다.

③ 윤 선생님은 지민이에게 학습 속도가 느린 사람들을 도와줄 것을 부탁하였다.

④ 윤 선생님은 지민이에게 인내심을 갖고 학습자들에게 친절히 대해 줄 것을 부탁하였다.

⑤ 지민이는 배터리가 별로 남지 않아 자신의 충전기를 사용하여 충전할 것이다.

11 다음 대화가 자연스럽게 이어지도록 순서대로 배열하시오.

> *(The phone rings.)*
> Hi, Kevin. What's up?
> (A) No, not at all.
> (B) What is it?
> (C) Hi, Aunt Victoria. I called to ask you a favor.
> (D) I need a sleeping bag for my science camp. Do you mind if I borrow yours?

➡ _____

Grammar

12 다음 중 밑줄 친 if의 쓰임이 나머지와 다른 하나를 고르시오.

① If I were you, I wouldn't eat anything like that.
② If I liked horror movies, I would see *Blue Friday*.
③ Please let me know if you would like to participate in the meeting.
④ I would help the poor if I was rich.
⑤ Minho would be surprised if he heard the news.

13 다음 중 어법상 어색한 문장은?

① It was natural for them to do their best.
② Was it impossible for him to finish the job on time?
③ It is difficult for her to act in a play.
④ It is important for children to exercise.
⑤ It was very foolish for you to park the car in the middle of the road.

14 다음 주어진 문장을 가정법으로 바르게 고친 것은?

> As I don't speak Spanish, I won't tell him to stop.

① If I spoke Spanish, I won't tell him to stop.
② If I spoke Spanish, I would tell him to stop.
③ If I spoke Spanish, I wouldn't tell him to stop.
④ If I speak Spanish, I will tell him to stop.
⑤ If I speak Spanish, I would tell him to stop.

[15~16] 우리말에 맞게 주어진 어휘를 이용하여 빈칸에 알맞은 말을 쓰시오.

15
> 아이들이 컴퓨터 게임을 많이 하는 것은 위험할 수 있다.
> = It can be dangerous _____ computer games too much. (kids, play)

16
> 나에게 만약 우주로 가는 표가 두 장 있다면, 나는 나의 개 Pluto와 함께 명왕성에 갈 텐데.
> = If I _____ two tickets to space, I _____ to Pluto with my dog, Pluto. (have, go)

17 다음 문장에서 어법상 어색한 것을 바르게 고치시오.

(1) If I am you, I'd send the soup back and ask for a refund.

_____ ➡ _____

(2) If Mr. Kim taught us math, we will be very pleased.

_____ ➡ _____

(3) It was heartless for him to fire an employee for such a thing.

_____ ➡ _____

(4) It was hard of him to not stare at her.

_____ ➡ _____

18 두 문장이 비슷한 뜻이 되도록 빈칸에 알맞은 것을 쓰시오.

(1) Elsa needed to find somewhere to sleep.
= It was necessary _____ somewhere to sleep.

(2) Megan was kind enough to give me some advice.
= It was kind _____ me some advice.

Reading

[19~21] 다음 글을 읽고 물음에 답하시오.

Helping the Elderly

Last Saturday, I went to the community center in my neighborhood. I volunteered with senior citizens who were taking a smartphone class there. The day's lesson was about taking photos with smartphones. I helped the slow learners in the class. It was a little difficult for me to explain the same thing ⓐagain and again. However, I felt really proud when I saw "my students" take pictures with their smartphones after the class. I think I am going to volunteer more often.

19 위 글의 밑줄 친 ⓐagain and again과 바꿔 쓸 수 없는 말을 모두 고르시오.

① immediately   ② repeatedly
③ over and over   ④ actually
⑤ time and again

20 위 글에서 알 수 있는 'I'의 심경으로 가장 알맞은 것을 고르시오.

① puzzled   ② ashamed
③ satisfied   ④ arrogant
⑤ disappointed

21 위 글을 읽고 알 수 없는 것을 고르시오.

① When did the writer volunteer?
② Where did the writer volunteer?
③ Could "the writer's students" take pictures with their smartphones after the class?
④ What did the writer do there?
⑤ How long did the writer volunteer?

[22~24] 다음 글을 읽고 물음에 답하시오.

Everyone was allowed to use the grassland. ⓐTherefore, it was called "the commons." ⓑ전통에 따라 각 가정은 소가 한 마리만 있었다, so it was easy for each cow in the village to find enough grass ⓒto eat. The grass on the commons was green all summer long.

22 위 글의 밑줄 친 ⓐ를 능동태로 고치시오.

➡ _____

23 위 글의 밑줄 친 ⓑ의 우리말에 맞게 주어진 어휘를 이용하여 8 단어로 영작하시오.

By, only, had

➡ _____

24 아래 〈보기〉에서 위 글의 밑줄 친 ⓒ와 to부정사의 용법이 다른 것의 개수를 고르시오.

┌─── 보기 ───┐
① It is dangerous for children to play with matches.
② She is too young to understand it.
③ He was the first man to land on the moon.
④ The water in this cup is not good to drink.
⑤ I found it useless to teach him English.
└──────────┘

① 1개 ② 2개 ③ 3개 ④ 4개 ⑤ 5개

[25~26] 다음 글을 읽고 물음에 답하시오.

Soon, other villagers did the same. Some secretly brought one more cow to the commons, while others brought even more to the grassland without telling anyone. They thought that there would be enough grass for the additional cows. Soon the village was full of happy-looking farmers!

The number of cows rose slowly at first. Then the cow population grew more quickly. The grass on the commons began to disappear, and it became harder for the cows to find grass to eat. To make matters worse, it did not rain for a long time.

25 위 글의 제목으로 알맞은 것을 고르시오.

① The Smart Way to Increase Wealth
② Greed Caused the Unhappy Result
③ Don't Worry. We Have Enough Grass!
④ The More Cows They Had, the Happier They Became
⑤ What Was Worse, There Was No Rain!

26 According to the passage, which is NOT true?

① Some villagers secretly brought one more cow to the grassland.
② Other villagers brought even more cows to the commons.
③ The number of cows rose slowly at first.
④ As time went by, the cow population grew more quickly.
⑤ Though there were many cows, it wasn't difficult for the cows to find grass to eat.

[27~28] 다음 글을 읽고 물음에 답하시오.

Farmer 1: I don't have any cows (A)[leaving / left]!
Cow 1: Good bye.
Head of a village: What (B)[happened / was happened] to the commons?

In the past, when a dry year came, the small number of cows on the commons always found something to eat. ___ⓐ___, no grass was left now (C)[though / because] there were too many cows. Things were harsh for the villagers; many of the cows died.

27 위 글의 빈칸 ⓐ에 들어갈 알맞은 말을 고르시오.

① As a result   ② However
③ For example   ④ Moreover
⑤ Thus

28 위 글의 괄호 (A)~(C)에서 문맥이나 어법상 알맞은 낱말을 골라 쓰시오.

➡ (A) _____ (B) _____ (C) _____

01 다음 짝지어진 단어의 관계가 같도록 빈칸에 알맞은 말을 쓰시오. *출제율 100%*

> decide : decision = pollute : _____

02 다음 문장의 빈칸에 들어갈 말을 〈보기〉에서 골라 쓰시오. *출제율 95%*

> ┌─ 보기 ├─
> laid / lay / lied / sat / seat / raised / risen

(1) I have never _____ to my parents about my grades.

(2) Clara was tired and _____ on the floor to take a nap.

(3) The vegetable prices have _____ sharply since August.

(4) Have you _____ a new carpet in the living room?

(5) The lecturer is coming, so please _____ yourselves.

(6) I have never _____ on such a comfortable chair before.

(7) When the teacher asked the students a difficult question, no hand was _____.

03 다음 우리말에 맞게 주어진 단어를 사용하여 영작하시오. *출제율 90%*

(1) 그 공원의 가운데에는 동상이 하나 있다. (there, statue, middle)

➡ _____

_____

(2) 그 박물관에서 사진을 찍는 것은 허용되지 않는다. (you, allowed, picture)

➡ _____

_____

(3) Sally는 버스에서 노인 한 분에게 자리를 양보해 드렸다. (seat, offered, senior)

➡ _____

_____

[04~06] 다음 대화를 읽고 물음에 답하시오.

Brian: Jimin, have you decided where to volunteer?

Jimin: Not yet. Do you know a good place to volunteer?

Brina: If I were you, I'd go to the community center.

Jimin: The community center? What can I do there?

Brian: There's a smartphone class for senior citizens, and they're looking for volunteers.

Jimin: That sounds interesting, but I've never taught anyone.

Brian: Don't worry. All you need to do is help the teacher there.

Jimin: Okay. Thanks for your advice.

04 What does Brian advise Jimin to do? *출제율 90%*

➡ _____

05 For whom is the smartphone class in the community center? *출제율 95%*

➡ _____

06 What does Jimin need to do in the smartphone class? *출제율 90%*

➡ _____

07 다음 중 짝지어진 대화가 <u>어색한</u> 것은?

① A: Do you mind if I eat your sausage?
  B: Not at all. Go ahead.
② A: Do you mind if I use your phone?
  B: No, I don't.
③ A: If I were you, I'd sit up straight.
  B: Thank you for your advice.
④ A: I broke my friend's umbrella.
  B: If I were you, I'd say sorry and buy an umbrella for him.
⑤ A: I've spent almost all my weekly allowance already.
  B: If I were you, I'd pick it out and eat the soup.

[08~10] 다음 대화를 읽고 물음에 답하시오.

Sora: Wow, it feels great to be on this ship, Dad.
Dad: I feel the same, Sora. Here are our seats, 20A and 20B.
Sora: Yeah. Do you mind if I take the window seat? I like to see the view outside.
Dad: (A)<u>No problem.</u>
Sora: By the way, I want to eat something like noodles or sandwiches.
Dad: If I were you, I wouldn't eat anything like that.
Sora: Why is that?
Dad: They may make you seasick.
Sora: Oh, I see. Then, I'll have some ice cream.
Dad: That's not a good idea, either. Let's eat after we arrive.

08 위 대화의 밑줄 친 (A)와 바꾸어 쓸 수 있는 것을 <u>모두</u> 고르시오.

① Yes, I do.
② Of course.
③ I'm sorry but you can't.
④ Of course not.
⑤ Certainly not.

09 위 대화에서 다음 영영풀이가 나타내는 말을 찾아 쓰시오.

> feeling sick or wanting to vomit when you are travelling on a boat or ship

➡ _____

10 위 대화의 내용과 일치하지 <u>않는</u> 것은?

① 소라와 아빠는 배를 타서 기분이 매우 좋다.
② 소라와 아빠의 자리는 20A와 20B이다.
③ 소라는 창가 자리에 앉고 싶어 한다.
④ 소라는 국수나 샌드위치 같은 걸 먹고 싶어 한다.
⑤ 소라와 아빠는 도착하기 전에 국수나 샌드위치 대신 아이스크림을 먹을 것이다.

11 다음 중 어법상 올바른 문장은?

① If I have my cell phone, I would take pictures of those cute cats.
② If there were no TVs, we will read more books.
③ Without your help, I would be in danger.
④ If were it not for laws in the world, it would be dangerous.
⑤ But for the Internet, we will go to the library and get necessary information.

12 다음 우리말을 괄호 안에 주어진 조건대로 영작하시오.

출제율 90%

(1) 만약 슈퍼 영웅이 있다면, 세상이 더 안전할 텐데. (if로 시작하고, there, superheroes, safer 이용)

➡ _____

(2) 만약 내가 고양이라면, 하루 종일 자고 놀 수 있을 텐데. (if로 시작하고, play all day long 이용)

➡ _____

(3) 그가 수학에 집중하는 것은 어렵다. (to부정사와 it, difficult, concentrate on 이용)

➡ _____

(4) 나를 차로 데려다주다니 그녀는 친절했다. (to부정사와 it, kind, give me a ride 이용)

➡ _____

13 어법상 바른 것을 모두 고르시오.

출제율 100%

① It is impossible of Mina to do it because she is not a good dancer.
② It is necessary for you to take a rest.
③ It was possible for he to answer the question.
④ That is hard for some people to make friends.
⑤ It was difficult for Jimmy to talk to strangers.

14 괄호 안에 주어진 어휘를 이용하여 어법에 맞게 문장을 완성하시오.

출제율 95%

(1) It was kind _____ the elderly man. (she, help)
(2) It is dangerous _____ in this river. (she, swim)

[15~17] 다음 글을 읽고 물음에 답하시오.

Soon, other villagers did the same. ____ⓐ____ secretly brought one more cow to the commons, while ____ⓑ____ brought even more to the grassland ⓒ아무에게도 말하지 않고. They thought that there would be enough grass for the additional cows. ⓓSoon the village was full of happy-looked farmers!

15 위 글의 빈칸 ⓐ와 ⓑ에 들어갈 알맞은 말을 고르시오.

출제율 90%

① One – the other
② Some – others
③ The others – another
④ Others – the others
⑤ Some – the other

16 위 글의 밑줄 친 ⓒ의 우리말에 맞게 3 단어로 영작하시오.

출제율 95%

➡ _____

17 위 글의 밑줄 친 ⓓ에서 어법상 틀린 부분을 찾아 고치시오.

출제율 90%

_____ ➡ _____

[18~20] 다음 글을 읽고 물음에 답하시오.

But one day a villager broke the rule. He brought another cow and let it ____ⓐ____ on the commons. He thought that nobody would notice it. A happy feeling filled his heart when he thought of the milk and cheese that the second cow would bring to his family.

A few days later, the farmer visited a close friend who had four children. He wanted to help his friend, so he told him in secret, "If I were you, I would bring in one more cow and raise it on the commons." The friend thanked him and did as he was told the next day.

✏️ 출제율 90%

18 주어진 영영풀이를 참고하여 빈칸 ⓐ에 철자 g로 시작하는 단어를 쓰시오.

> feed in a meadow or pasture

➡ _____

✏️ 출제율 95%

19 위 글의 주제로 알맞은 것을 고르시오.

① the effective way to use the commons
② how to form friendship between friends
③ two friends who satisfied their selfish interests and desires
④ the increased profit based on cooperation
⑤ the first step to rise out of poverty

✏️ 출제율 100%

20 According to the passage, which is NOT true?

① A villager brought another cow to the commons.
② The villagers got angry to find the farmer's injustice.
③ The thought of the extra milk and cheese made the farmer feel happy.
④ The farmer advised his close friend to bring in one more cow to the commons.
⑤ The farmer's close friend thanked him for the advice.

[21~23] 다음 글을 읽고 물음에 답하시오.

Volunteering in the Subway

Last Sunday, I worked as a student volunteer in Gyeongbokgung Station. My job was to help people buy tickets. (①) Mostly, I helped visitors to Korea from other countries. (②) ⓐ I explained how to use the ticket machines. (③) It was a little difficult for me to explain everything in English. (④) I'm excited about helping people again in the future. (⑤)

✏️ 출제율 90%

21 위 글의 흐름으로 보아, 주어진 문장이 들어가기에 가장 적절한 곳은?

> However, I felt really pleased when the visitors smiled and said thank you.

①　　②　　③　　④　　⑤

✏️ 출제율 95%

22 위 글의 밑줄 친 ⓐ를 다음과 같이 바꿔 쓸 때 빈칸에 들어갈 알맞은 말을 두 단어로 쓰시오.

➡ I explained how _____ _____ use the ticket machines.

✏️ 출제율 90%

23 What was difficult for the writer? Fill in the blanks with suitable words.

> It was a little difficult for the writer _____ _____ _____ _____ _____.

[01~03] 다음 대화를 읽고 물음에 답하시오.

> Jimin: Thanks for letting me volunteer here, Ms. Yun.
>
> Ms. Yun: It's my pleasure, Jimin. I'm glad you decided to help.
>
> Jimin: Well, what should I do?
>
> Ms. Yun: Today's lesson is about taking photos with smartphones. Why don't you help the slow learners?
>
> Jimin: Okay. Is there anything I should know?
>
> Ms. Yun: Yes. Please be patient and kind to the learners.
>
> Jimin: I'll keep that in mind. By the way, _____(A)_____ My battery is a little low.
>
> Ms. Yun: Of course not. Go right ahead.

01 위 대화의 빈칸 (A)에 들어갈 말을 〈보기〉에 주어진 단어들을 모두 배열하여 완성하시오.

┌─── 보기 ├───
│ you / your / use / mind / charger / if /
│ I / do / ?
└──────────

➡ _____

02 What does Ms. Yun ask Jimin to do?

➡ _____

_____

03 Why does Jimin need Ms. Yun's charger?

➡ _____

04 다음 문장을 주어진 어휘로 시작하는 문장으로 바꿔 쓰시오.

(1) If I were a good cook, I would make you delicious food. (as)

➡ _____

_____

(2) If I had enough time, I would take a walk with you. (because)

➡ _____

_____

(3) As we do not have ten more dollars, we can't buy the sweater for Mom. (if)

➡ _____

_____

(4) Since I am not an English teacher, I don't know the answers. (were)

➡ _____

_____

(5) If there were no rain, we couldn't live. (without)

➡ _____

_____

05 다음 문장을 주어진 조건대로 바꿔 쓰시오.

(1) I can solve the problem easily. (it 이용)

➡ _____

_____

(2) They should cook *ramyeon*. (necessary 이용)

➡ _____

_____

(3) Greg is silly enough to think that chocolate solves anything. (it 이용)

➡ _____

_____

06 다음 문장에서 어법상 어색한 부분을 찾아 고치시오.

(1) If they give me a chance, I would take it.

_____ ➡ _____

(2) Is it necessary of her to rewrite the report?

_____ ➡ _____

[07~09] 다음 글을 읽고 물음에 답하시오.

Cow 1: Hey, stop (A)[pushing / to push] me!

Cow 2: Move over!

Cow 3: This is my spot!

Cow 1: We need rain!

Cow 2: I'm hungry.

Cow 3: ⓐMe, too.

ⓑThe number of cows raised slowly at first. Then the cow population grew more quickly. The grass on the commons began to (B)[appear / disappear], and it became harder (C)[for / of] the cows to find grass to eat. To make matters worse, it did not rain for a long time.

07 위 글의 괄호 (A)~(C)에서 문맥이나 어법상 알맞은 낱말을 골라 쓰시오.

➡ (A) _____ (B) _____ (C) _____

08 위 글의 밑줄 친 ⓐMe, too.를 다음과 같이 바꿔 쓸 때 빈칸에 들어갈 알맞은 말을 쓰시오.

➡ _____ am I.

09 위 글의 밑줄 친 ⓑ에서 어법상 틀린 부분을 찾아 고치시오.

_____ ➡ _____

[10~12] 다음 글을 읽고 물음에 답하시오.

In the past, when a dry year came, the small number of cows on the commons always found something to eat. However, no grass was left now because there were too many cows. Things were harsh for the villagers; many of the cows died.

At last, the grass came back. Now it was able to support only one cow per family. The village went back to the one-family-one-cow rule. The villagers all learned an important lesson: when resources are shared, ⓐ모두가 그 자원을 소중히 여기고 공평하게 사용하는 것이 중요하다는 것이다. The villagers now tell this story to their children. They call ⓑit "The Story of the Commons."

10 Write the reason why there was no grass left on the commons?

It's because there were _____ _____ _____.

11 위 글의 밑줄 친 ⓐ의 우리말에 맞게 주어진 어휘를 알맞게 배열하시오.

to value / fairly / important / them / for / the resources / it is / use / everyone / and

➡ _____

_____

12 위 글의 밑줄 친 ⓑit이 가리키는 것을 본문에서 찾아 쓰시오.

➡ _____

01 다음 대화의 내용과 일치하도록 팝업창을 수정하시오.

Brian: Jimin, have you decided where to volunteer?

Jimin: Not yet. Do you know a good place to volunteer?

Brina: If I were you, I'd go to the community center.

Jimin: The community center? What can I do there?

Brian: There's a smartphone class for senior citizens, and they're looking for volunteers.

Jimin: That sounds interesting, but I've never taught anyone.

Brian: Don't worry. All you need to do is help the teacher there.

Jimin: Okay. Thanks for your advice.

Volunteers Needed ⊖ ⊡ ⊗

Helpers in a Smartphone Class for Kids

• Help the teacher with the class
• Teaching experience is necessary.

➡ _____ ,
_____

02 다음 내용을 바탕으로, 봉사 활동을 한 뒤에 쓴 글을 쓰시오.

• When did you volunteer? — last Sunday
• Where did you go? — Gyeongbokgung Station
• What did you do there? — helped visitors from other countries to use the subway ticket machines
• What was difficult for you? — explaining everything in English
• How did you feel? — felt pleased when they said thank you
• What are you going to do? — am going to help people again in the future

---

Volunteering in the Subway

(A)_____, I worked as a student volunteer in (B)_____.
My job was to help people to buy tickets. Mostly, I helped visitors to Korea from
(C)_____. I explained how to use (D)_____. It was a little
difficult for me (E)_____. However, I felt really (F)_____
when the visitors smiled and said thank you. I'm going to help people (G)_____.

단원별 모의고사

01 다음 영영풀이가 가리키는 것을 고르시오.

> the total number of persons or animals

① population   ② charger
③ pollution   ④ secret
⑤ lesson

02 다음 주어진 문장의 밑줄 친 mind와 같은 의미로 쓰인 것은?

> Do you <u>mind</u> if I borrow your new dress?

① Jimin replayed the scene in his <u>mind</u>.
② I don't <u>mind</u> what people think about me.
③ What I have in <u>mind</u> is that we should not break a rule.
④ When you change your <u>mind</u>, please let me know.
⑤ The <u>mind</u> as well as the body needs exercise.

03 다음 우리말과 일치하도록 주어진 어구를 배열하여 완성하시오.

(1) 학생들은 캠퍼스에서 애완동물을 키우는 것이 허락되지 않는다.
(on / to / not / are / have / campus / students / pets / allowed)

➡ _____

(2) 나는 작은 보트를 탈 때 약간의 뱃멀미가 났다.
(in / a little / a small / when / I / I / boat / got / seasick / rode)

➡ _____

(3) 이 음악 동아리에 가입하는 것은 내게 큰 기쁨을 주었다.
(club / it / me / to / great / this / gave / music / pleasure / join)

➡ _____

[04~05] 다음 대화를 읽고 물음에 답하시오.

Gina: My stomach growls every morning. What should I do?
Tom: Ha ha. Do you usually have breakfast?
Gina: No, I have no time to eat anything at home.
Tom: (A)<u>Why don't you bring some snacks?</u> (were, if, would)
Gina: That's a good idea.

04 위 대화의 밑줄 친 (A)와 의도가 같도록 주어진 단어들을 사용하여 다시 쓰시오.

➡ _____

05 위 대화의 내용과 일치하지 <u>않는</u> 것은?

① Gina seems to get stress because of her growling stomach every morning.
② Gina usually doesn't have breakfast.
③ Gina doesn't have time to eat anything at home in the evening.
④ Tom advises Gina to bring some snacks.
⑤ Gina likes Tom's advice.

[06~07] 다음 대화를 읽고 물음에 답하시오.

Sora: Wow, it feels great to be on this ship, Dad.
Dad: I feel the same, Sora. Here are our seats, 20A and 20B.
Sora: Yeah. Do you mind if I take the window seat? I like to see the view outside.

Dad: No problem.

Sora: By the way, I want to eat something like noodles or sandwiches.

Dad: (A)If I were you, I wouldn't eat anything like that.

Sora: Why is that?

Dad: They may make you seasick.

Sora: Oh, I see. Then, I'll have some ice cream.

Dad: That's not a good idea, either. Let's eat after we arrive.

06 위 대화의 밑줄 친 (A)와 바꾸어 쓸 수 없는 것은?

① I think you shouldn't eat anything like that.

② Why don't you eat anything like that?

③ You'd better not eat anything like that.

④ I advise you not to eat anything like that.

⑤ I recommend that you should not eat anything like that.

07 위 대화의 내용과 일치하도록 그림의 빈칸을 완성하시오.

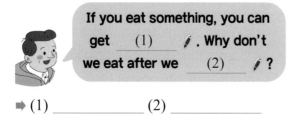

If you eat something, you can get ___(1)___ ✏. Why don't we eat after we ___(2)___ ✏?

➡ (1) _____ (2) _____

[08~09] 다음 대화를 읽고 물음에 답하시오.

Brian: Jimin, have you decided where ⓐto volunteer?

Jimin: Not yet. Do you know a good place to volunteer?

Brina: If I ⓑwere you, I'd go to the community center.

Jimin: The community center? What can I do there?

Brian: There's a smartphone class for senior citizens, and they're looking for volunteers.

Jimin: That sounds ⓒinteresting, but I've never ⓓtaught anyone.

Brian: Don't worry. All you need to do ⓔare help the teacher there.

Jimin: Okay. Thanks for your advice.

08 위 대화의 밑줄 친 ⓐ~ⓔ 중 어법상 틀린 것을 찾아 바르게 고치시오.

_____ ➡ _____

09 위 대화를 읽고 대답할 수 없는 것은?

① What is Jimin looking for?

② What does Brian advise Jimin to do?

③ What kind of class in the community center is for senior citizens?

④ What can Jimin do in the community center?

⑤ Why didn't Brian teach anyone?

10 다음 문장의 뜻이 나머지 넷과 다른 것은?

① If my grandmother were here now, I would be very happy.

② Were my grandmother here now, I would be very happy.

③ Since my grandmother is here now, I am very happy.

④ As my grandmother is not here now, I am not very happy.

⑤ My grandmother is not here now, so I am not very happy.

11 다음 중 밑줄 친 부분의 쓰임이 어색한 것은?

① It was hard for my uncle to find a good job.

② It was very thoughtful for you to send the flowers.

③ It is important for students to have breakfast every day.

④ It was easy for him to do his homework by himself.

⑤ It was polite of her to give you a chance.

12 다음 중 〈보기〉의 밑줄 친 부분과 바꿔 쓸 수 없는 것은?

┌─ 보기 ┐

What would happen if there were no cars?

└────────┘

① If it were not for cars
② without cars
③ but for cars
④ were it no cars
⑤ were it not for cars

13 괄호 안에 주어진 어휘를 활용하여 우리말과 일치하도록 영작하시오.

(1) 중력이 없다면, 무슨 일이 일어날까? (there, happen, no gravity)

➡ _____
_____

(2) Sarah가 건강하면, 파티에 올 텐데. (if, healthy, come, to)

➡ _____
_____

(3) Kevin이 지금 도착한다면, 우리는 함께 영화를 볼 수 있을 텐데. (arrive, together, watch, movie)

➡ _____
_____

(4) 그녀가 창의적인 해결책을 찾는 것은 쉬웠다. (find, easy, a creative solution)

➡ _____
_____

[14~16] 다음 글을 읽고 물음에 답하시오.

Farmer 1: ⓐIf I had two cows, I would be richer.

Farmer 1: No one will notice it.

But one day a villager broke the rule. ⓑ그는 다른 소를 데려와 공유지에서 풀을 뜯게 했다. He thought that nobody would notice it. A happy feeling filled his heart when he thought of the milk and cheese that the second cow would bring to his family.

14 위 글의 밑줄 친 ⓐ를 as로 시작하는 직설법 문장으로 고치시오.

➡ _____

15 위 글의 밑줄 친 ⓑ의 우리말에 맞게 주어진 어휘를 이용하여 11 단어로 영작하시오.

┌──────────────────────────┐
│   brought, let, commons   │
└──────────────────────────┘

➡ _____
_____

16 What made the farmer feel happy? Fill in the blanks (A) and (B) with suitable words.

┌──────────────────────────┐
│ The thought of (A)_____ _____ │
│ _____ _____ that (B)_____ │
│ _____ _____ would bring to his │
│ family made him feel happy. │
└──────────────────────────┘

[17~19] 다음 글을 읽고 물음에 답하시오.

Soon, other villagers did the same. Some secretly brought one more cow to the commons, while others brought even more to the grassland without telling anyone. They thought that there would be enough grass for the ⓐaddition cows. Soon the village was full of happy-looking farmers!

The number of cows rose slowly at first. Then the cow population grew more quickly. The grass on the commons began to disappear, and ⓑit became harder for the cows to find grass to eat. To make matters worse, it did not rain for a long time.

17 위 글의 밑줄 친 ⓐaddition을 알맞은 형태로 고치시오.

➡ _____

18 위 글의 밑줄 친 ⓑit과 문법적 쓰임이 같은 것을 고르시오. (2개)

① It is impossible to master English in a month or two.
② It is rather warm today.
③ I make it a rule to get up early.
④ It's kind of you to help me.
⑤ It is 2 miles from here to the airport.

19 Why did the grass on the commons disappear? Fill in the blanks (A) and (B) with suitable words.

Because there were too many (A)_____ on the commons, and it did not (B)_____ for a long time.

[20~22] 다음 글을 읽고 물음에 답하시오.

At last, the grass came back. Now ⓐit was able to support only one cow per family. The village went back to the one-family-one-cow rule. The villagers all learned an important lesson: when resources are shared, it is important for everyone to value the resources and use them fairly. The villagers now tell this story to their children. They call it "The Story of the Commons."

20 위 글의 밑줄 친 ⓐit이 가리키는 것을 본문에서 찾아 쓰시오.

➡ _____

21 위 글의 제목으로 알맞은 것을 고르시오.

① Too Much Greed Is Human Nature
② Enjoy the Green Grass Heartily
③ Remember the Rule: Only One Cow per Family
④ An Important Lesson: Haste Makes Waste
⑤ The Golden Rule Is Difficult to Obey

22 According to the passage, which is NOT true?

① The grass came back finally.
② The grass was able to support only one cow a family.
③ The villagers all learned an important lesson.
④ It is important to value the sources and protect them carefully.
⑤ The villagers now tell "The Story of the Commons" to their children.

Reading for Fun 3

The Last Class

교과서
Words & Expressions

Key Words

- **almost**[ɔ́ːlmoust] ⓟ 거의
- **anger**[ǽŋɡər] ⓜ 화, 분노
- **back**[bæk] ⓜ 뒤쪽, 뒷부분
- **board**[bɔːrd] ⓜ 게시판
- **carefully**[kɛ́ərfəli] ⓟ 주의 깊게
- **exam**[igzǽm] ⓜ 시험
- **ex-mayor**[eksméiər] ⓜ 전직 시장
- **ex-postman**[ekspóstmən] ⓜ 전직 우체부
- **French**[frentʃ] ⓜ 프랑스어
- **German**[dʒɔ́ːrmən] ⓜ 독일어, 독일인
- **heart**[hɑːrt] ⓜ 마음
- **however**[hauévər] ⓟ 하지만, 그러나
- **inviting**[inváitiŋ] ⓗ 유혹적인, 솔깃한
- **kindly**[káindli] ⓟ 친절하게, 다정하게
- **language**[lǽŋɡwidʒ] ⓜ 언어
- **last**[læst] ⓗ 마지막의
- **lovely**[lʌ́vli] ⓗ 사랑스러운
- **mayor**[méiər] ⓜ 시장
- **Monsieur** (프랑스어) ~씨(= Mr., Sir)
- **nervously**[nə́ːrvəsli] ⓟ 초조하게
- **noise**[nɔiz] ⓜ 시끄러움, 소란
- **notice**[nóutis] ⓜ 공고문 ⓥ 알아차리다
- **office**[ɔ́ːfis] ⓜ 사무실
- **order**[ɔ́ːrdər] ⓜ 명령, 지시
- **place**[pleis] ⓜ 자리, 좌석
- **post**[poust] ⓥ (안내문 등을) 게시[공고]하다
- **ready**[rédi] ⓗ 준비가 된
- **sentence**[séntəns] ⓜ 문장
- **shame**[ʃeim] ⓜ 부끄러움
- **silence**[sáiləns] ⓜ 고요, 적막, 침묵
- **smell**[smel] ⓥ 냄새가 나다
- **special**[spéʃəl] ⓗ 특별한
- **strange**[streindʒ] ⓗ 이상한, 낯선
- **surprisingly**[sərpráiziŋli] ⓟ 놀랍게도
- **sweet**[swiːt] ⓗ 달콤한
- **through**[θruː] 젠 ~을 통해[관통하여]
- **warm**[wɔːrm] ⓗ 따뜻한
- **wear**[wɛər] ⓥ 입다
- **whole**[houl] ⓗ 전체의, 모든
- **without**[wiðáut] 젠 ~ 없이
- **wonder**[wʌ́ndər] ⓥ 궁금하다, 궁금해하다
- **worried**[wə́ːrid] ⓗ 걱정하는, 걱정스러워 하는

Key Expressions

- **as+형용사/부사+as I can** 가능한 한 ~한[하게]
- **be late for** ~에 늦다
- **break one's heart** 매우 슬프게 하다
- **for a while[moment]** 잠시 동안
- **get angry** 화나다
- **in the middle of** ~의 도중에, ~의 중앙에
- **nothing but** 오직, 그저[단지] ~일 뿐인
- **stay away from** ~을 멀리하다
- **take an exam** 시험을 치다[보다]
- **with no sign of anger** 화난 기색 없이

118 Special Lesson. The Last Class

Word Power

※ 서로 비슷한 뜻을 가진 어휘

- □ **anger** (화, 분노) : **temper** (화, 노여움)
- □ **notice** (알아차리다) : **perceive** (알아차리다)
- □ **order** (명령) : **command** (명령)

- □ **warm** (따뜻한, 온화한) : **mild** (온화한)
- □ **worried** (걱정하는) : **anxious** (걱정하는)

※ 서로 반대의 뜻을 가진 어휘

- □ **whole** (전체의) ↔ **partial** (부분적인)
- □ **back** (뒤쪽) ↔ **front** (앞쪽)
- □ **carefully** (조심스럽게) ↔ **uncarefully** (부주의하게)

- □ **inviting** (유혹적인) ↔ **uninviting** (마음을 끌지 못하는)
- □ **noise** (시끄러움, 소란) ↔ **silence** (고요함, 침묵)

English Dictionary

- □ **anger**: 화, 분노
  - → the feeling of being angry
  - 화난 감정

- □ **exam**: 시험
  - → an important test of your knowledge, especially one that you take at school
  - 여러분의 지식의 중요한 시험, 특히 학교에서 보는 것

- □ **inviting**: 유혹적인, 솔깃한
  - → attractive in a way that makes you want to do something, go somewhere, be near someone, etc.
  - 어떤 일을 하고 싶어지게, 어떤 곳에 가고 싶어지게, 어떤 사람과 가까워지고 싶어지게 하거나 할 정도로 매력적인

- □ **lovely**: 사랑스러운
  - → attractive or beautiful especially in a graceful way
  - 특히 우아하게 매력적이거나 아름다운

- □ **mayor**: 시장
  - → an official who is elected to be the head of the government of a city or town
  - 크고 작은 도시 정부의 우두머리로 선출된 관리

- □ **noise**: 시끄러움, 소란
  - → a sound, especially when it is loud, unpleasant, or disturbing
  - 특히 시끄럽고 불쾌하거나 방해가 될 때 나는 소리

- □ **notice**: 알아차리다
  - → to become aware of something or someone by seeing, hearing, etc.
  - 보고, 듣기 등을 통해 어떤 것 또는 어떤 사람을 인식하게 되는 것

- □ **order**: 명령, 지시
  - → an instruction given by someone in a position of authority
  - 권위 있는 위치에 있는 사람이 내린 지시

- □ **post**: (안내문 등을) 게시[공고]하다
  - → to put up a sign, notice, etc. so that it can be seen by many people
  - 많은 사람이 볼 수 있도록 표지판, 게시문 등을 붙이다

- □ **shame** 부끄러움
  - → a guilty and embarrassed feeling that you have when you or someone else has behaved badly
  - 당신이나 다른 누군가가 나쁘게 행동했을 때 당신이 가지고 있는 죄스럽고 당혹스러운 감정

- □ **silence**: 고요, 적막
  - → a lack of sound or noise
  - 소리나 소음이 없음

- □ **strange**: 낯선
  - → not familiar because you have not been there before or met the person before
  - 전에 가본 적이 없거나 그 사람을 만난 적이 없기 때문에 익숙하지 않은

- □ **wear**: 입다
  - → to have something on your body as clothing, decoration, or protection
  - 어떤 것을 옷, 장식 또는 보호로서 몸에 지니다

- □ **whole**: 전체의, 모든
  - → all of something
  - 어떤 것의 전부

Reading

The Last Class

I was late for school that morning, and I was worried Monsieur
worrying(×)
Hamel would get angry. A few days before, he had told us that we
get/become/grow+형용사: ~해지다
would take an exam about French sentences that day, and I was not
ready. It was such a warm, lovely day, and the fields along the road
such+a+형용사+명사
smelled sweet and inviting. For a moment, I thought of staying away
감각동사 smell+형용사 보어   invited(×)
from school and walking around the fields. However, I ran as fast as I
as+형용사/부사+as one can: 가능한 한 ~하게 = as fast as possible
could to school.

As I passed the mayor's office, I saw people reading the notices on
지각동사 saw의 목적보어로 현재분사 reading 사용
the board. For two years all our bad news had come from that board. I
wondered, "What is it now?" I ran faster.
fast의 비교급

Usually, there was noise in the morning at school—sounds of
students talking and laughing. However, that day everything was
noise in the morning at school의 구체적인 내용
quiet. Through the windows I saw my classmates in their places and
my classmates를 지칭
Monsieur Hamel walking nervously around the classroom. I opened
V1
the door and entered in the middle of the strange silence. My face
V2
felt hot with shame!
감각동사 felt+형용사 보어

Monsieur (프랑스어) ~씨 (= Mr.,
Sir)

inviting 유혹적인, 솔깃한

stay away from ~에서 떨어져 있다.
~을 멀리하다

mayor 시장

notice 공고문; 알아차리다

nervously 초조하게

in the middle of ~의 도중에, ~의
중앙에

shame 부끄러움

확인문제

● 다음 문장이 본문의 내용과 일치하면 T, 일치하지 않으면 F를 쓰시오.

1   A few days before, Monsieur Hamel said that the students would take an exam
    about French sentences that day. ☐

2   The writer was ready for the exam about French sentences. ☐

3   For a moment, the writer thought of staying away from school and walking around
    the fields. ☐

4   As usual, there was noise at school that day. ☐

5   Through the windows the writer saw Monsieur Hamel walking nervously around
    the classroom. ☐

6   The writer entered the class in the middle of the familiar noise. ☐

Surprisingly, Monsieur Hamel looked at me with no sign of anger
화난 기색 없이
and said kindly, "Go to your seat, my little Frantz; we almost began
without you."
= Frantz

I sat down at my desk. It was then that I noticed Monsieur Hamel's
It is ~ that 강조 구문. I noticed Monsieur Hamel's blue coat then.에서 then을 강조한 형태
blue coat. He was wearing the coat he only wore on special days. Also
there was something strange about the whole class. What surprised me
무언가 이상한 것. -thing이나 -body로   선행사를 포함하는 관계대명사. What
끝나는 부정대명사는 형용사가 뒤에서 수식   이 이끄는 절이 문장의 주어 역할을 함.
most was to see people sitting at the back of the room: old Hauser was
지각동사 see의 목적보어로 현재분사 sitting 사용
there, and so were the ex-mayor, the ex-postman, and many others.
'so+be동사+주어' 형태의 도치 구문: 긍정의 동의를 나타냄.
They all seemed so sad.

While I was wondering at all this, Monsieur Hamel walked slowly to
the front. He thought for a while and kindly said:
잠시 동안
"My children, this is the last time that I'll teach you. Orders have
come from Berlin to teach nothing but German in the schools of Alsace
형용사적 용법의 to부정사   but: ~ 외에'(전치사). nothing but: 오직(only)
and Lorraine. The new teacher arrives tomorrow. This is the last class
in French, so I want you to listen carefully."
프랑스어로 하는   want+목적어+to부정사
Those few words broke my heart and made me angry. So, this
                      V1   V2
was what they had posted at the mayor's office. It was the last class
선행사를 포함하는 관계대명사
in my own language!
= in French

with no sign of anger 화난 기색 없이

ex-mayor 전직 시장

break one's heart 매우 슬프게 하다

확인문제

● 다음 문장이 본문의 내용과 일치하면 T, 일치하지 않으면 F를 쓰시오.

1 Frantz noticed Monsieur Hamel's blue coat only after he sat down at his desk. ☐

2 There was something interesting about the whole class. ☐

3 Old Hauser, the ex-mayor, the ex-postman, and many others were sitting at the back of the room. ☐

4 Orders have come from Berlin to teach only French in the schools of Alsace and Lorraine. ☐

5 The new teacher will arrive tomorrow. ☐

6 It was the last class in German. ☐

● 우리말을 참고하여 빈칸에 알맞은 말을 쓰시오.

1 The _____ Class

2 I was late for school that morning, and I was _____ Monsieur Hamel would _____ _____.

3 A few days before, he had told us that we would _____ _____ _____ about French sentences that day, and I was not _____.

4 It was _____ a warm, lovely day, and the fields along the road smelled _____ and _____.

5 For a moment, I thought of _____ _____ _____ school and _____ around the fields.

6 However, I ran _____ _____ _____ _____ _____ to school.

7 As I passed the mayor's office, I _____ _____ _____ the notices on the board.

8 For two years all our bad news _____ _____ _____ that board.

9 I _____, "What is it now?"

10 I ran _____.

11 Usually, _____ _____ _____ in the morning at school— sounds of students talking and laughing.

12 However, that day everything was _____.

13 _____ the windows I saw my classmates in their places and Monsieur Hamel _____ _____ around the classroom.

14 I opened the door and entered _____ _____ _____ the strange silence.

15 My face felt hot _____ _____!

16 Surprisingly, Monsieur Hamel looked at me _____ _____ _____ _____ _____ and said kindly, "Go to your seat, my little Frantz; we almost began _____ you."

17 I sat down _____ my desk.

18 _____ _____ then _____ I noticed Monsieur Hamel's blue coat.

19 He was wearing the coat _____ _____ _____ on special days.

20 Also there was _____ _____ about the whole class.

21 _____ surprised me most was _____ _____ people sitting at the back of the room: old Hauser was there, and _____ _____ the ex-mayor, the ex-postman, and many others.

22 They all seemed so _____.

23 While I was _____ _____ all this, Monsieur Hamel walked slowly to the front.

24 He thought _____ _____ _____ and kindly said: "My children, this is _____ _____ _____ that I'll teach you.

25 _____ have come from Berlin to teach _____ _____ _____ in the schools of Alsace and Lorraine.

26 The new teacher _____ tomorrow.

27 This is the last class _____ _____, so I want you _____ _____ carefully."

28 Those few words broke my heart and _____ _____ _____.

29 So, this was _____ they had posted at the mayor's office.

30 It was the last class _____ _____ _____ _____!

16 놀랍게도 Hamel 선생님은 화난 기색이 전혀 없이 나를 보시고 자상하게 말씀하셨다. "Frantz 야, 네 자리로 가서 앉아라. 너 없이 수업을 시작할 뻔했구나."

17 나는 내 책상으로 가서 앉았다.

18 내가 Hamel 선생님의 파란색 외투를 알아차린 것은 바로 그때였다.

19 선생님은 특별한 날에만 입는 외투를 입고 계셨다.

20 더구나 교실 전체도 무언가 이상했다.

21 나는 교실 뒤에 앉아 있는 사람들을 보고 가장 놀랐다. Hauser 할아버지가 앉아 계셨고 전직 시장님, 전직 우체부 아저씨를 비롯한 많은 사람들이 있었다.

22 그들은 모두 슬퍼 보였다.

23 내가 이 모든 것에 대해 의아해 하는 동안, Hamel 선생님이 천천히 교실 앞으로 걸어가셨다.

24 그는 잠시 생각에 잠긴 후 다정하게 말씀하셨다: "어린이 여러분, 이것이 내가 여러분을 가르치는 마지막 시간입니다.

25 Alsace와 Lorraine에 있는 학교에서는 독일어만 가르치라는 명령이 베를린에서 내려왔습니다.

26 새로운 선생님이 내일 오실 겁니다.

27 이 시간이 프랑스어로 하는 마지막 수업이니 여러분이 주의 깊게 들어 주기 바랍니다."

28 이 몇 마디는 내 마음을 아프게 하고 또 화가 나게 했다.

29 그래, 이게 바로 시장 집무실 게시판에 공고되어 있던 것이다.

30 내 모국어로 하는 마지막 수업이라니!

● 우리말을 참고하여 본문을 영작하시오.

1 마지막 수업

➡ _____

2 그날 아침 나는 수업에 늦었고, Hamel 선생님이 화를 내실까 걱정되었다.

➡ _____

3 며칠 전에 선생님은 그날 프랑스어 문장 시험을 보겠다고 말씀하셨는데, 나는 준비가 되어 있지 않았다.

➡ _____

_____

4 날씨는 무척 포근하고 사랑스러웠으며 길가의 들판에서는 달콤하고 유혹적인 향기가 났다.

➡ _____

5 잠깐 동안 나는 학교에 가지 않고 들판을 거닐까 생각했다.

➡ _____

6 하지만 나는 최대한 빨리 학교로 달려갔다.

➡ _____

7 시장의 집무실을 지나면서 나는 사람들이 게시판에 붙어 있는 공고문을 읽고 있는 것을 보았다.

➡ _____

8 지난 2년 동안 모든 나쁜 소식은 저 게시판에서 나왔다.

➡ _____

9 나는 "이번에는 뭐지?"라는 궁금증이 들었다.

➡ _____

10 나는 더욱 빨리 달렸다.

➡ _____

11 보통, 아침에는 학생들이 떠들고 웃는 소리로 학교가 소란스러웠다.

➡ _____

12 그러나 그날은 모든 것이 고요했다.

➡ _____

13 창문을 통해 나는 학급 친구들이 제자리에 앉아 있고 Hamel 선생님이 초조하게 교실을 돌아다니시는 것을 보았다.

➡ _____

_____

14 나는 문을 열고 낯선 침묵 속으로 들어갔다.

➡ _____

15 부끄러워서 얼굴이 화끈거렸다!

➡ _____

16 놀랍게도 Hamel 선생님은 화난 기색이 전혀 없이 나를 보시고 자상하게 말씀하셨다. "Frantz
야, 네 자리로 가서 앉아라. 너 없이 수업을 시작할 뻔했구나."

➡ _____

_____

17 나는 내 책상으로 가서 앉았다.

➡ _____

18 내가 Hamel 선생님의 파란색 외투를 알아차린 것은 바로 그때였다.

➡ _____

19 선생님은 특별한 날에만 입는 외투를 입고 계셨다.

➡ _____

20 더구나 교실 전체도 무언가 이상했다.

➡ _____

21 나는 교실 뒤에 앉아 있는 사람들을 보고 가장 놀랐다. Hauser 할아버지가 앉아 계셨고 전직
시장님, 전직 우체부 아저씨를 비롯한 많은 사람들이 있었다.

➡ _____

_____

22 그들은 모두 슬퍼 보였다.

➡ _____

23 내가 이 모든 것에 대해 의아해하는 동안, Hamel 선생님이 천천히 교실 앞으로 걸어가셨다.

➡ _____

24 그는 잠시 생각에 잠긴 후 다정하게 말씀하셨다: "어린이 여러분, 이것이 내가 여러분을 가르치
는 마지막 시간입니다.

➡ _____

25 Alsace와 Lorraine에 있는 학교에서는 독일어만 가르치라는 명령이 베를린에서 내려왔습니다.

➡ _____

26 새로운 선생님이 내일 오실 겁니다.

➡ _____

27 이 시간이 프랑스어로 하는 마지막 수업이니 여러분이 주의 깊게 들어 주기 바랍니다."

➡ _____

28 이 몇 마디는 내 마음을 아프게 하고 또 화가 나게 했다.

➡ _____

29 그래, 이게 바로 시장 집무실 게시판에 공고되어 있던 것이다.

➡ _____

30 내 모국어로 하는 마지막 수업이라니!

➡ _____

01 다음 짝지어진 단어의 관계가 같도록 빈칸에 알맞은 말을 쓰시오.

> arrival : _____ = departure : depart

02 다음 문장의 빈칸에 들어갈 말을 〈보기〉에서 골라 쓰시오.

> ┌── 보기 ──┐
>
> in the middle of / with no sign of anger / break my heart / stay away from

(1) The doctor advised him to _____ sweets.

(2) She made the announcement in a calm way _____.

(3) Tim stopped suddenly _____ his speech.

(4) It will _____ if you leave home.

03 다음 우리말에 맞게 빈칸에 알맞은 말을 쓰시오.

(1) 그는 세 번 시장으로 선출되었다.
   ➡ He was elected _____ three times.

(2) 중요한 회의에 대한 공지가 있었다.
   ➡ There was a _____ about an important meeting.

(3) Jack은 초조하게 그의 상사가 나타나길 기다렸다.
   ➡ Jack waited _____ for his boss to appear.

(4) 그는 그 순간에 깊은 수치심을 느꼈다.
   ➡ He felt a deep sense of _____ at that moment.

04 다음 문장에서 어법상 어색한 것을 바르게 고치시오.

(1) Don't ask so a silly question.
   _____ ➡ _____

(2) I noticed him stole into the small room.
   _____ ➡ _____

(3) When elephants fight, it is the grass where suffers.
   _____ ➡ _____

(4) You can go swimming during you stay here.
   _____ ➡ _____

[05~07] 다음 글을 읽고 물음에 답하시오.

Usually, there was noise in the morning at school — sounds of students talking and laughing. However, that day everything was quiet. Through the windows I saw my classmates in their places and Monsieur Hamel walking nervously around the classroom. ⓐI opened the door and entered in the middle of the familiar silence. My face felt hot with shame!

Surprisingly, Monsieur Hamel looked at me ⓑ화난 기색이 전혀 없이 and said kindly, "Go to your seat, my little Frantz; we almost began without you."

05 위 글의 밑줄 친 ⓐ에서 흐름상 어색한 부분을 찾아 고치시오.

_____ ➡ _____

06 위 글의 밑줄 친 ⓑ의 우리말에 맞게 주어진 어휘를 이용하여 5 단어로 영작하시오.

> with, sign

➡ _____

07 본문의 내용과 일치하도록 다음 빈칸에 알맞은 단어를 쓰시오.

> The usual sound at school in the morning was a lot of _____ of the students who talked and laughed.

[08~10] 다음 글을 읽고 물음에 답하시오.

I was late for school that morning, and I was (A)[worrying / worried] Monsieur Hamel would get angry. A few days before, he had told us that we would take an exam about French sentences that day, and I was not ready. It was (B)[so / such] a warm, lovely day, and the fields along the road smelled (C)[sweet / sweetly] and inviting. For a moment, I thought of staying away from school and walking around the fields. However, I ran as fast as ⓐI could to school.

08 위 글의 괄호 (A)~(C)에서 문맥이나 어법상 알맞은 낱말을 골라 쓰시오.

➡ (A) _____ (B) _____ (C) _____

09 위 글의 밑줄 친 ⓐI could와 바꿔 쓸 수 있는 한 단어를 쓰시오.

➡ _____

10 주어진 영영풀이에 해당하는 숙어를 본문에서 찾아 쓰시오.

> avoiding becoming involved in something

➡ _____

[11~13] 다음 글을 읽고 물음에 답하시오.

I sat down at my desk. It was then that I noticed Monsieur Hamel's blue coat. He was wearing the coat he only wore on special days. Also there was something strange about the whole class. ⓐ _____ surprised me most was to see people sitting at the back of the room: old Hauser was there, and ⓑso were the ex-mayor, the ex-postman, and many others. They all seemed so sad.

11 위 글의 빈칸 ⓐ에 들어갈 알맞은 단어를 쓰시오.

➡ _____

12 위 글의 밑줄 친 ⓑ를 다음과 같이 바꿔 쓸 때 빈칸에 들어갈 알맞은 말을 두 단어로 쓰시오.

➡ the ex-mayor, the ex-postman, and many others were _____, _____

13 위 글을 읽고 평소와 다른 교실 모습 두 가지를 우리말로 쓰시오.

➡ (1) _____

(2) _____

출제율 95%

01 다음 영영풀이가 가리키는 것을 고르시오.

> a painful feeling that one gets after doing something wrong or embarrassing

① notice
② shame
③ silence
④ sign
⑤ field

출제율 100%

02 다음 문장의 빈칸에 들어갈 말을 〈보기〉에서 골라 쓰시오.

┌─ 보기 ─┐
posted / mayor / enter / strange / shame
└────────┘

(1) She is a good _____, so she is respected by the citizens.
(2) A _____ thing happened this morning.
(3) You are not allowed to _____ this area without the permission.
(4) The interview results will be _____ on the Internet.
(5) It is a _____ that he lied to his parents.

출제율 90%

03 다음 우리말에 맞게 빈칸에 알맞은 말을 쓰시오.

(1) 사실을 말하면, 나는 그녀의 이야기 도중에 잠들었다.
  ➡ To tell the truth, I fell asleep _____ _____ _____ _____ her talk.
(2) 선생님은 화난 기색 없이 수업을 하셨다.
  ➡ My teacher gave the lesson _____ _____ _____ _____ _____.
(3) 나쁜 소식이 나를 슬프게 하여 나는 많이 울었다.
  ➡ I cried a lot because the bad news _____ _____ _____.

(4) 그녀는 자기 아이들이 불에서 떨어져 있기를 원했다.
  ➡ She wanted her children to _____ _____ _____ the fire.

출제율 95%

04 다음 중 밑줄 친 부분의 뜻풀이가 바르지 않은 것은?

① The ex-mayor was in favor of the housing plan. (전직 시장)
② When I passed the office, I heard someone calling me. (지나갔다)
③ I wonder why we need to change our original plan. (궁금해 하다)
④ He shook his legs nervously, waiting for the doctor. (초조하게)
⑤ I got a notice from a company that there was a problem in my project. (알아차리다)

출제율 95%

05 다음 주어진 문장의 밑줄 친 의미와 다른 뜻으로 쓰인 것은?

> We're going to take an exam about the French sentences.

① The criminal was given the heavy sentence.
② What does this sentence mean?
③ This complex sentence was wrongly translated.
④ Do you think it is a grammatically correct sentence?
⑤ You need to capitalize the first letter of an English sentence.

06 우리말과 일치하도록 괄호 안에 주어진 어구를 배열하여 영작하시오.

(1) 나는 손을 흔들었지만 그는 알아차리지 못했다. (he / my / I / not / but / waved / notice / did / hand)

➡ _____

_____

(2) 뉴욕시의 시장으로서 그는 그 도시 계획을 설명했다. (as / of / plan / the / city / New York City / explained / he / the mayor)

➡ _____

_____

(3) 많은 사람들 앞에서 넘어졌을 때, 나는 부끄러웠다. (down / many / felt / I / front / I / of / in / people / when / shame / fell)

➡ _____

_____

07 다음 우리말을 주어진 단어를 이용하여 영작하시오.

(1) 그들은 새 사업을 중지하라는 명령을 무시했다. (disregard, order)

➡ _____

_____

(2) 물이 정말로 유혹하는 것 같다. (inviting)

➡ _____

_____

(3) 그들은 말없이 서서 버스를 기다렸다. (silence, in)

➡ _____

_____

08 다음 중 어법상 어색한 것을 고르시오.

① What is good for the environment is also good for us.

② Fans and supporters want him to do his best.

③ My careless remarks made her angrily.

④ He was wise enough to understand it.

⑤ The next flight to Tokyo leaves tomorrow at 4:00 PM.

09 다음 밑줄 친 부정사와 쓰임이 같은 것을 고르시오.

> Orders have come from Berlin to teach nothing but German in the schools of Alsace and Lorraine.

① He is the last man to tell a lie.

② She makes it a rule to get up at six in the morning.

③ We are so happy to announce the engagement of our daughter.

④ He tasted freedom only to lose it again.

⑤ It is important for them to get the best education possible.

10 다음 중 어법상 올바른 것을 고르시오.

① It was so excited to watch the view as we went higher and higher.

② She was only a little pounds overweight.

③ Sarah heard her brother closed the door angrily.

④ It was then that a British scientist began a serious study of the subject.

⑤ As rust eats away iron, so care eats away the heart.

11 다음 문장에서 어법상 <u>어색한</u> 것을 바르게 고쳐 다시 쓰시오. *출제율 95%*

(1) I heard the girl sang a song this morning.

➡ _____

(2) I made him tell me that was on his mind.

➡ _____

(3) It was on the day which we met in the heavy rain.

➡ _____

(4) Hannah has such nice an appearance.

➡ _____

(5) My husband agrees with me, and so my friends do.

➡ _____

12 괄호 안에 주어진 어휘를 활용하여 영작하시오. *출제율 95%*

(1) 그녀는 그가 코를 푸는 것을 보았다. (see, blow his nose)

➡ _____

(2) 그는 그렇게 큰 집을 산 그 날을 후회했다. (regret, buy, such, when, large, 12 단어)

➡ _____

(3) 모든 학생들이 웃었고, 선생님도 또한 웃었다. (all the students, and, so, the teacher, 9 단어)

➡ _____

(4) Arnold가 가장 방문하고 싶은 곳은 바로 서울이었다. (most, it, visit, that, 9 단어)

➡ _____

[13~14] 다음 글을 읽고 물음에 답하시오.

Usually, there was noise in the morning at school—sounds of students talking and laughing. (①) Through the windows I saw my classmates in their places and Monsieur Hamel walking nervously around the classroom. (②) I opened the door and entered in the middle of the strange silence. (③) My face felt hot with shame! (④)

Surprisingly, Monsieur Hamel looked at me with no sign of anger and said kindly, "Go to your seat, my little Frantz; we almost began without you." (⑤)

13 위 글의 흐름으로 보아, 주어진 문장이 들어가기에 가장 적절한 곳은? *출제율 100%*

However, that day everything was quiet.

①　　②　　③　　④　　⑤

14 According to the passage, which is NOT true? *출제율 95%*

① Through the windows Frantz saw his classmates in their places.

② Monsieur Hamel was walking nervously around the classroom.

③ Frantz opened the door and entered in the middle of the strange silence.

④ Monsieur Hamel looked at Frantz in a rage.

⑤ Monsieur Hamel kindly told Frantz to go to his seat.

[15~17] 다음 글을 읽고 물음에 답하시오.

While I was wondering at all this, Monsieur Hamel walked slowly to the front. He thought for a while and kindly said:

"My children, this is the last time that I'll teach you. ⓐOrders have come from Berlin to teach ⓑnothing but German in the schools of Alsace and Lorraine. The new teacher arrives tomorrow. This is the last class in French, so I want you to listen carefully."

출제율 95%

15 위 글의 밑줄 친 ⓐOrders와 같은 의미로 쓰인 것을 고르시오.

① May I have your order, please?
② Dogs can be trained to obey orders.
③ He orders lunch for eleven o'clock.
④ Last orders at the bar now please!
⑤ The general orders a retreat.

출제율 90%

16 위 글의 밑줄 친 ⓑnothing but과 바꿔 쓸 수 있는 한 단어를 쓰시오.

➡ _____

출제율 100%

17 위 글의 제목으로 가장 알맞은 것을 고르시오.

① The Sorrow of Monsieur Hamel
② How to Teach German in the Schools
③ Orders from Berlin
④ The Last Class in French!
⑤ Expectations about the New Teacher

[18~20] 다음 글을 읽고 물음에 답하시오.

I was late ____ⓐ____ school that morning, and I was worried Monsieur Hamel would get angry. A few days before, he had told us that we would take an exam about French sentences that day, and I was not ready. It was such a warm, lovely day, and the fields along the road smelled sweet and inviting. For a moment, I thought of staying away ____ⓑ____ school and walking around the fields. ____ⓒ____, I ran as fast as I could to school.

As I passed the mayor's office, I saw people reading the notices on the board. For two years all our bad news had come from that board. I wondered, "What is it now?" I ran faster.

출제율 95%

18 위 글의 빈칸 ⓐ와 ⓑ에 들어갈 전치사가 바르게 짝지어진 것은?

　　　ⓐ　　ⓑ　　　　　　ⓐ　　ⓑ
① for – from　　　② in – by
③ on – from　　　④ for – to
⑤ on – by

출제율 90%

19 위 글의 빈칸 ⓒ에 들어갈 알맞은 말을 고르시오.

① Thus　　　　② Moreover
③ However　　　④ In other words
⑤ As a result

출제율 100%

20 위 글의 마지막 부분에서 알 수 있는 'I'의 심경으로 가장 알맞은 것을 고르시오.

① embarrassed　　② regretful
③ satisfied　　　　④ disappointed
⑤ curious

[21~23] 다음 글을 읽고 물음에 답하시오.

I sat down at my desk. It was then (A)[that / what] I noticed Monsieur Hamel's blue coat. He was wearing the coat he only wore on special days. Also there was something strange about the whole class. What surprised me most was (a)to see people (B)[sat / sitting] at the back of the room: old Hauser was there, and so (C)[was / were] the ____ⓐ____-mayor, the ____ⓑ____-postman, and many others. They all seemed so sad.

✏️ 출제율 90%

21 주어진 영영풀이를 참고하여 빈칸 ⓐ와 ⓑ에 철자 e로 시작하는 단어를 쓰시오.

> This word is used to show that someone is no longer what they were.

➡ _____

✏️ 출제율 100%

22 위 글의 괄호 (A)~(C)에서 문맥이나 어법상 알맞은 낱말을 골라 쓰시오.

➡ (A) _____ (B) _____ (C) _____

✏️ 출제율 95%

23 위 글의 밑줄 친 (a)to see와 to부정사의 용법이 같은 것을 모두 고르시오.

① She tried to see the show.
② This is a rare chance to see such good scenery.
③ It makes my heart ache to see her suffer.
④ Please tell me what to see there.
⑤ She lived to see her first grandchild.

[24~26] 다음 글을 읽고 물음에 답하시오.

While I was wondering at all this, Monsieur Hamel walked slowly to the front. He thought for a while and kindly said:

"My children, this is the last time that I'll teach you. Orders have come from Berlin to teach nothing ⓐbut German in the schools of Alsace and Lorraine. The new teacher arrives tomorrow. This is the last class in French, so I want you to listen carefully."

Those few words broke my heart and made me angry. So, this was what they had posted at the mayor's office. It was the last class in ⓑmy own language!

✏️ 출제율 95%

24 위 글의 밑줄 친 ⓐbut과 같은 의미로 쓰인 것을 모두 고르시오.

① His mother won't be there, but his father might.
② Everyone was there but him.
③ You may not believe it, but that's true.
④ He is but a child.
⑤ I came last but one in the race.

✏️ 출제율 90%

25 위 글의 밑줄 친 ⓑmy own language가 가리키는 것을 본문에서 찾아 쓰시오.

➡ _____

✏️ 출제율 100%

26 According to the passage, which is NOT true?

① This was the last time that Monsieur Hamel would teach the writer's class.
② In the schools of Alsace and Lorraine, only German will be taught.
③ The new teacher who will teach German will arrive tomorrow.
④ The writer got angry after hearing Monsieur Hamel's words.
⑤ What they had posted at the mayor's office was to introduce the new teacher.

Lesson 7

Watch Out

의사소통 기능

- 당부하기
  A: Make sure you don't play with the knives.
  B: I'll keep that in mind.

- 부탁하기
  A: Can you do me a favor?
  B: Sure. What is it?

언어 형식

- 분사구문
  I study math, **listening to** music.

- 조동사가 포함된 수동태
  The party **will be held** at 7 p.m.

Words & Expressions

Key Words

- **active** [ǽktiv] 형 활동 중인
- **area** [ɛ́əriə] 명 지역
- **ash** [æʃ] 명 재
- **chance** [tʃæns] 명 가능성, 기회
- **circle** [sə́:rkl] 동 둘러싸다
- **cold wave** 한파
- **crop** [krɑp] 명 농작물
- **destroy** [distrɔ́i] 동 파괴하다
- **discover** [diskʌ́vər] 동 발견하다
- **disturb** [distə́:rb] 동 방해하다
- **drought** [draut] 명 가뭄
- **dust** [dʌst] 명 먼지
- **earphone** [íərfòun] 명 이어폰
- **earthquake** [ə́:rθkweik] 명 지진
- **effect** [ifékt] 명 영향, 효과, 결과
- **entire** [intáiər] 형 전체의, 온
- **erupt** [irʌ́pt] 동 분출하다
- **eruption** [irʌ́pʃən] 명 분출
- **fantastic** [fæntǽstik] 형 환상적인
- **favor** [féivər] 명 친절, 부탁
- **flat** [flæt] 형 평평한
- **flood** [flʌd] 동 범람하다 명 홍수
- **heat** [hi:t] 동 데우다
- **helmet** [hélmit] 명 헬멧, 안전모
- **hit** [hit] 동 (태풍 등이) 덮치다, 엄습하다
- **hopeful** [hóupfəl] 형 희망적인
- **hot spring** 온천
- **hurricane** [hə́:rəkèin] 명 허리케인
- **issue** [íʃu:] 발표하다, 발행하다
- **Jupiter** [dʒú:pitər] 명 목성
- **landslide** [lǽndslaid] 명 산사태

- **lie** [lai] 동 위치해 있다
- **locate** [lóukeit] 동 ~의 위치를 찾아내다
- **Mars** [mɑ:rz] 명 화성
- **nearby** [nìərbái] 형 근처의 부 근처에
- **occur** [əkə́:r] 동 일어나다, 발생하다
- **overnight** [óuvərnait] 부 하룻밤 사이에, 하룻밤 동안
- **planet** [plǽnit] 명 행성
- **prevent** [privént] 동 막다, 예방하다
- **produce** [prədjú:s] 동 생산하다
- **rainfall** [réinfɔl] 명 강우, 강우량
- **relieve** [rilí:v] 동 완화하다, 줄이다
- **resource** [rí:sɔ:rs] 명 자원
- **ring** [riŋ] 명 고리, 반지
- **sandstorm** [sǽndstɔrm] 명 모래 폭풍
- **scenery** [sí:nəri] 명 경치, 풍경
- **soil** [sɔil] 명 토양
- **solar system** 태양계
- **spread** [spred] 동 퍼지다
- **sudden** [sʌ́dn] 형 갑작스러운
- **threaten** [θrétn] 동 위협하다
- **traffic** [trǽfik] 명 교통
- **tsunami** [tsuná:mi] 명 해일
- **typhoon** [taifú:n] 명 태풍
- **underwater** [ʌndərwɔ́tər] 형 수중의
- **volcano** [vɑlkéinou] 명 화산
- **volume** [válju:m] 명 부피, 용적
- **warning** [wɔ́:rniŋ] 명 주의, 경고
- **weather** [wéðər] 명 날씨
- **wildfire** [wáildfaiər] 명 산불
- **yellow dust** 명 황사

Key Expressions

- **do ~ a favor** ~의 부탁을 들어주다
- **do harm** 해를 입히다
- **get hurt** 다치다
- **get stuck in** ~에 갇히다
- **have an effect on** ~에 영향을 미치다
- **have ~ in common** ~을 공통점으로 가지다
- **in harmony with** ~와 조화를 이루어
- **keep ~ in mind** ~을 명심하다
- **millions of** 수백만의

- **make use of** ~을 이용하다
- **name after** ~을 따라 이름 짓다
- **on one's way back** 돌아오는 길에
- **prevent A from -ing** A가 ~하지 못하게 하다
- **put A in danger** A를 위험하게 하다
- **shoot ~ into ...** ~을 …으로 내뿜다
- **so far** 지금까지
- **take care of** ~을 돌보다, ~을 처리하다
- **take off** ~을 벗다

Word Power

※ 서로 비슷한 뜻을 가진 어휘

- □ **chance** 가능성 – **possibility** 가능성
- □ **effect** 영향 – **influence** 영향
- □ **erupt** 분출하다 – **burst** 터뜨리다
- □ **heat** 데우다 – **warm** 데우다
- □ **produce** 생산하다 – **yield** 생산하다
- □ **threaten** 위협하다 – **scare** 겁주다

- □ **discover** 발견하다 – **detect** 탐지하다
- □ **entire** 전체의, 온 – **whole** 전체의
- □ **fantastic** 환상적인 – **wonderful** 훌륭한
- □ **prevent** 막다 – **stop** 가로막다
- □ **sudden** 갑작스러운 – **abrupt** 갑작스러운

※ 서로 반대의 뜻을 가진 어휘

- □ **active** 활동 중인 ↔ **inactive** 활동하지 않는
- □ **destroy** 파괴하다 ↔ **construct** 건축하다
- □ **heat** 데우다 ↔ **cool** 식히다
- □ **nearby** 근처의 ↔ **faraway** 멀리 떨어진

- □ **cold wave** 한파 ↔ **heat wave** 혹서, 열기
- □ **entire** 전체의, 온 ↔ **partial** 부분적인
- □ **hopeful** 희망적인 ↔ **hopeless** 절망적인
- □ **sudden** 갑작스러운 ↔ **expected** 예상된

※ 동사 → 명사

- □ **destroy** 파괴하다 – **destruction** 파괴
- □ **disturb** 방해하다 – **disturbance** 방해
- □ **prevent** 막다 – **prevention** 예방
- □ **threaten** 위협하다 – **threat** 위협

- □ **discover** 발견하다 – **discovery** 발견
- □ **erupt** 분출하다 – **eruption** 분출
- □ **produce** 생산하다 – **production** 생산

※ 명사 → 형용사

- □ **action** 행동 – **active** 활동 중인
- □ **fantasy** 환상 – **fantastic** 환상적인
- □ **hope** 희망 – **hopeful** 희망적인

- □ **effect** 영향, 효과 – **effective** 효과적인
- □ **favor** 친절 – **favorable** 우호적인
- □ **volcano** 화산 – **volcanic** 화산의

English Dictionary

- □ **active** 활동 중인
  → involved in a particular activity 특정한 활동에 몰두한
- □ **ash** 재
  → the grey powder that remains after something has burnt 어떤 것이 불타고 난 후 남은 회색 가루
- □ **circle** 둘러싸다
  → to make a line in the shape of a ring 둥근 모양으로 선을 만들다
- □ **dust** 먼지
  → dry powder that consists of very small bits of earth or sand 흙이나 모래의 매우 작은 조각으로 구성된 마른 가루
- □ **earthquake** 지진
  → a sudden shaking of Earth's surface 지구 표면의 갑작스러운 흔들림
- □ **eruption** 분출
  → a sudden outbreak of something 무엇인가의 갑작스러운 발생

- □ **flat** 평평한
  → even and smooth without curved or high parts 곡선이나 도드라지는 부분 없이 매끈하고 평평한
- □ **planet** 행성
  → a large round object in space that moves around a star 별 주변을 도는 우주에 있는 크고 둥근 물체
- □ **prevent** 막다, 예방하다
  → to keep something from happening 어떤 것이 발생하지 못하게 하다
- □ **traffic** 교통
  → the movement of cars, ships or aircraft 차, 선박, 비행기의 움직임
- □ **volcano** 화산
  → a mountain with a big hole at the top, through which lava is pushed up 꼭대기에 용암이 솟아나오는 구멍이 있는 산

서답형

01 다음 짝지어진 단어의 관계가 같도록 빈칸에 알맞은 말을 쓰시오.

> action : active = effect : _____

02 다음 영영풀이가 가리키는 것을 고르시오.

> a mountain with a big hole at the top, through which lava is pushed up

① volcano
② earthquake
③ flood
④ drought
⑤ tornado

03 다음 중 밑줄 친 부분의 뜻풀이가 바르지 않은 것은?

① People cleaned the ashes left by the forest fire. (재)
② Rice is the main crop of the country. (농작물)
③ The war is bad because it destroys everything. (건설하다)
④ Please do not disturb me when I am sleeping. (방해하다)
⑤ The desk was covered with dust. (먼지)

서답형

04 다음 우리말에 맞게 빈칸에 알맞은 말을 쓰시오.

(1) 그 나라의 모든 도시에 홍수가 났다.
➡ All the cities of the country have been _____.

(2) 도로 한복판에서 차 사고가 발생했다.
➡ The car accident _____ in the middle of the road.

(3) 그 여행객은 하룻밤 묵을 곳을 찾고 있다.
➡ The traveler is looking for a place to stay _____.

서답형

05 다음 문장의 빈칸에 들어갈 말을 〈보기〉에서 골라 쓰시오.

> ┤ 보기 ├
> shot ~ into / solar system / on his way
> back / have ~ in common / do harm

(1) My dad bought a cake _____ _____ _____ _____ home.
(2) My brother and I _____ nothing _____ _____.
(3) Mars and Jupiter belong to the same _____ _____.
(4) Some animals _____ _____ to crops.
(5) The old truck _____ bad gas _____ the air.

중요

06 다음 빈칸 (A)~(C)에 공통으로 들어갈 말이 바르게 짝지어진 것은?

- I don't (A)_____ nothing in common with my younger brother.
- Colors (A)_____ an effect on our moods.
- There was a car accident, but anyone didn't (B)_____ hurt.
- We left earlier than usual, so we didn't (B)_____ stuck in the rush-hour traffic.
- Would you (C)_____ care of my pet for a week?
- You should (C)_____ off your hat in the classroom.

① make – take – get
② make – get – take
③ have – get – take
④ have – put – do
⑤ put – take – get

01 다음 짝지어진 단어의 관계가 같도록 빈칸에 알맞은 말을 쓰시오.

sudden : expected = _____ : partial

02 다음 우리말에 맞게 빈칸에 알맞은 말을 쓰시오.

(1) 쌍둥이 언니와 나는 많은 것들을 공통적으로 가지고 있다.

➡ My twin sister and I _____ lots of things _____ _____.

(2) 우리는 자연과 조화를 이루며 살아야 한다.

➡ We should live _____ _____ _____ nature.

(3) Paul이라는 이름은 그의 아버지에게서 따온 것이다.

➡ Paul was _____ _____ his father.

03 다음 문장의 빈칸에 들어갈 말을 〈보기〉에서 골라 쓰시오.

┌─ 보기 ─
prevent / scenery / threaten /
volume / warnings
└─

(1) She stopped her car to enjoy the beautiful _____.

(2) The bad boys often _____ children in his neighborhood.

(3) If you want to _____ car accidents, do not use your phone while driving.

(4) They gave _____ about the dangers of smoking.

(5) Which of these bottles has the greater _____?

04 우리말과 일치하도록 주어진 단어를 모두 배열하여 영작하시오.

(1) 스트레칭은 목의 통증을 완화하는 데 좋은 방법이다.

(neck / stretching / way / pain / a / to / your / good / relieve / is)

➡ _____
_____

(2) 나의 가족은 겨울에 온천에 가는 것을 좋아한다.

(likes / to / my / in / hot / winter / family / springs / visit)

➡ _____

(3) 세균이 공기 중에 퍼질 수 있다.

(the / can / through / germs / air / spread)

➡ _____
_____

05 다음 우리말에 맞게 주어진 단어를 사용하여 영작하시오.

(1) 자전거를 탈 때에는 헬멧을 착용해야 한다.
(wear, ride)

➡ _____
_____

(2) 폭염 주의보가 발효되었다. (heatwave, warnings, were)

➡ _____

(3) 이 앱은 당신의 아이의 위치를 찾아내도록 도와준다. (locate, app)

➡ _____
_____

(4) 도둑은 가게주인을 협박하고 현금을 훔쳤다.
(the shopkeeper, stole, cash)

➡ _____
_____

Conversation

① **당부하기**

> **A** Make sure you don't play with the knives. 절대로 칼을 가지고 놀지 않도록 해라.
>
> **B** I'll keep that in mind. 명심할게요.

- 당부하는 의미로 상대방에게 '꼭 ~해라.'라고 말할 때는 'Make sure ~.'라고 한다. 'make sure'는 '~을 확실하게 하다'의 뜻으로 명령문으로 나타내게 되면 '확실하게 해라.'의 의미이다. 'be sure to ~'도 마찬 가지로 '반드시 ~해라.'의 의미가 된다.

- 'Make sure'는 'Make sure (that) 주어+동사 ~.', 'Make sure to부정사 ~.'의 형태로 쓰고, 상대방에게 '~하지 마라., ~할 것을 잊지 마라., ~할 것을 기억해라.'라고 당부할 때는 부정 명령문으로 'Don't+동 사원형 ~.', 'Don't forget to+동사원형 ~.'으로 말할 수 있고 'Remember to+동사원형 ~.'으로 나타내 기도 한다.

- 상대방에게 권고하는 의미가 될 때는 '~하는 편이 더 낫다.'는 의미로 'You had better+동사원형 ~.'을 쓰게 된다. '~해야 한다'의 의미로 'be supposed to ~'도 일상적으로 많은 쓰는 표현이다.

당부하기

- Make sure to+동사원형 / (that) ~. 반드시 ~해라.
- Make certain that ~. 반드시 ~해라.
- Be sure to ~. 반드시 ~해라.
- Don't forget to ~. ~하는 것을 잊지 마라.
- Please remember to ~. ~할 것을 기억해 주세요.

핵심 Check

1. 다음 대화의 밑줄 친 우리말에 맞게 영작하시오.

(The phone rings.)

B: Hi, Mom.

W: Hi, Junho. Are you having a good time with Dad?

B: Yeah. Today we visited Dokdo.

W: That sounds cool. What are you going to do tomorrow?

B: We're going fishing on a boat.

W: Great. <u>반드시 구명조끼를 입도록 해라.</u>(a life jacket, make)

B: Okay, Mom. I'll keep that in mind.

➡ _____

② 부탁하기

A Can you do me a favor? 부탁해도 됩니까?

B Sure. What is it? 물론. 그게 무엇입니까?

A Can you feed the dog? 개에게 먹이를 줄 수 있니?

B No problem. 물론이지.

- 'Can you do me a favor?'는 상대에게 부탁을 하는 말로 '부탁 하나 해도 될까요?'의 의미이다. 조동사 can 대신 could, would 등을 사용하여 'Could you do me a favor?', 'Would you do me favor, please?'라고 할 수 있다.

- 부탁하는 말로 'Can I ask you a favor?'도 '부탁 하나 해도 될까요?'의 뜻이고, 'May I ask you a favor?' 또는 'May I ask for a favor?'라고 할 수도 있다. 'do A a favor'는 'A에게 부탁을 들어주다'의 의미이고, 'ask A a favor'는 'A에게 부탁하다'라는 뜻이다.

- '상대방에게 직설적으로 도움을 부탁을 할 때는 'Can you help me+동사원형 ~?', 'Can/Could you help me with+명사?(~ 좀 도와주시겠습니까?)'라고 할 수 있다. 이 표현은 'Do you mind helping me with ~?', 'Would you mind helping me ~?'라고 해도 같은 의도의 표현이 된다.

- 상대방에게 부탁을 하거나 허락을 요청할 때는 허락을 요청하는 조동사를 사용하여 'Can you ~?', 'May I ~?'라고 할 수 있고, 'Is it okay if I ~?' 등을 사용하여 구체적인 부탁의 내용을 말할 수 있다.

부탁하기

- Can you do me a favor? 부탁해도 될까요?
- Could/Would you do me a favor? 부탁해도 될까요?
- Can/May I ask you a favor? 부탁해도 될까요?
- Could/Would you ~ for me? ~ 좀 해 주시겠습니까?
- Could you help me with ~? ~ 좀 도와 주시겠습니까?

핵심 Check

2. 다음 대화를 가장 자연스러운 순서로 배열한 것은?

(A) Sure. What is it?

(B) No problem. Anything else?

(C) Can you do me a favor?

(D) Can you feed the dog?

① (A) – (C) – (D) – (B)　　　② (C) – (A) – (D) – (B)

③ (D) – (A) – (C) – (B)　　　④ (C) – (B) – (D) – (A)

⑤ (A) – (B) – (D) – (C)

Listen - Listen & Answer Talk 1

M: Hi, this is Cha Gisang from the Weather Station. Here is today's weather. ❶Typhoon Doni is moving north and is going to ❷hit Jejudo tonight. A typhoon warning has been ❸issued. There will be lots of rainfall with a high chance of flooding in some areas. Please ❹stay inside because Typhoon Doni will come with strong winds. Also, please ❺make sure you keep listening to our reports. Thank you.

남: 안녕하세요. 기상대에서 차 기상입니다. 오늘 날씨를 말씀드리겠습니다. 태풍 도니가 북상 중이며 오늘 밤에 제주도를 강타할 예정입니다. 태풍주의보가 발효되었습니다. 많은 양의 비가 내릴 예정이고 일부 지역에서는 홍수의 가능성이 높습니다. 태풍 도니는 강한 바람을 동반하므로 실내에 머무십시오. 또, 보도를 계속 청취해 주시기를 당부 드립니다. 감사합니다.

❶ typhoon: 태풍
❷ hit: 강타하다
❸ issue: 발표하다, 발행하다
❹ 동사원형으로 시작하는 명령문이다.
❺ 'make sure+주어+동사: 꼭 ~ 해라, 반드시 ~해라'의 뜻으로 당부의 표현이다.

Check(√) True or False

(1) The man is talking about the weather forecast.　　　　　T ☐　F ☐

(2) Typhoon Doni is coming with heavy rain and snow from the north area.　　T ☐　F ☐

 Listen - Listen & Answer Dialog 2

M: Sora, ❶can you do me a favor?

G: What is it, Dad?

M: A typhoon is coming tonight. Can you bring in the clothes from outside?

G: No problem. What about your bike?

M: I'll take care of ❷it after I finish the dishes.

G: Okay. Do you want me to call Grandma and tell ❸her about the typhoon?

M: Yes. Please tell ❸her to ❹stay home.

G: Okay, Dad.

남: 소라야, 부탁 좀 들어줄래?
여: 뭔데요, 아빠?
남: 오늘 밤 태풍이 온다는구나. 바깥에서 옷가지들을 들여와 주겠니?
여: 그럴게요. 아빠의 자전거는 어떻게 할까요?
남: 자전거는 설거지를 끝낸 후에 내가 처리하마.
여: 알겠어요. 할머니께 전화해서 태풍에 관해 말씀드릴까요?
남: 그래. 할머니께 집안에 계시라고 말씀드리렴.
여: 네, 아빠.

❶ 상대에게 부탁하는 말로 '부탁 하나 해도 될까요?'를 의미한다.
❷ it은 Dad's bike를 가리킨다.
❸ her는 모두 Grandma를 가리킨다.
❹ stay home: 집에 머물다

Check(√) True or False

(3) Dad is going to do dishes after bringing in his bike from outside.　　T ☐　F ☐

(4) The girl is going to call Grandma and ask her not to go outside.　　T ☐　F ☐

Listen - Listen More

B: Jimin, are you ❶going out?

G: Yeah. I'm going to buy some sandwiches at Choi's.

B: Are you walking there?

G: No. I'll ride my bike.

B: That's good. ❷Can you do me a favor?

G: Sure. What is it?

B: Can you buy chocolate ice cream for me ❸on your way back?

G: No problem.

B: Thanks. ❹Please make sure you wear a helmet and no ear phones!

G: Don't worry about that.

❶ go out: 외출하다

❷ 'Can you help me?' 또는 'Would you do me a favor?' 등으로 바꾸어 표현할 수 있다.

❸ on one's way back: 돌아오는 길에

❹ 당부하는 표현으로 'Be certain that ~.' 또는 'Remember that ~.' 등으로 바꾸어 표현할 수 있다.

Speak - Talk in pairs.

A: Can I start now?

B: ❶Wash your hands before you start.

A: Okay. No problem.

B: One more thing. Make sure you don't play with the ❷knives.

A: I'll keep ❸that in mind.

❶ 동사로 시작하는 명령문이다.

❷ knife의 복수형이다.

❸ that은 칼을 갖고 놀지 않겠다는 것을 뜻한다.

Wrap Up 5

(The phone rings.)

B: Hi, Mom.

W: Hi, Junho. Are you having a good time with Dad?

B: Yeah. Today we visited Dokdo.

W: That sounds cool. ❶What are you going to do tomorrow?

B: We're going fishing on a boat.

W: Great. Please make sure you wear ❷a life jacket.

B: Okay, Mom. I'll ❸keep ❹that in mind.

❶ 내일 계획을 묻는 표현으로 'What are you planning to do?' 등으로 바꾸어 표현할 수 있다.

❷ life jacket: 구명조끼

❸ keep ~ in mind: ~을 명심하다

❹ that은 구명조끼를 입어야 한다는 것을 가리킨다.

Wrap Up 6

W: ❶Can you do me a favor?

B: Sure, Grandma. What is it?

W: I want to go to the Tom Dylan concert on Christmas. Can you buy some tickets for me?

B: No problem. How many tickets do you want?

W: Two tickets, please.

❶ 상대에게 부탁을 하는 말로 'Can you give me a hand?' 등으로 바꾸어 표현할 수 있다.

● 다음 우리말과 일치하도록 빈칸에 알맞은 말을 쓰시오.

Listen - Listen & Answer Talk 1

M: Hi, this is Cha Gisang from the Weather Station. Here is today's weather. Typhoon Doni is moving north and is going to _____ Jejudo tonight. A typhoon _____ has been _____. There will be lots of _____ with a high chance of _____ in some areas. Please stay _____ because Typhoon Doni will come with strong winds. Also, please _____ _____ you keep listening to our reports. Thank you.

Listen - Listen & Answer Dialog 2

M: Sora, can you do me a _____?

G: What is it, Dad?

M: A _____ is coming tonight. Can you _____ _____ the clothes from outside?

G: _____ problem. What about your _____?

M: I'll take _____ of it after I finish the _____.

G: Okay. Do you want me to call Grandma and tell her about the _____?

M: Yes. Please tell her to _____ _____.

G: Okay, Dad.

Listen - Listen More

B: Jimin, are you going out?

G: Yeah. I'm going to buy some _____ at Choi's.

B: Are you walking there?

G: No. I'll _____ _____ _____.

B: That's _____. Can you do me _____ _____?

G: Sure. What is it?

B: Can you buy chocolate ice cream for me _____ _____?

G: No _____.

B: Thanks. Please _____ _____ you _____ a helmet and _____ ear phones!

G: Don't _____ about that.

해석

남: 안녕하세요, 기상대에서 차기상입니다. 오늘 날씨를 말씀드리겠습니다. 태풍 도니가 북상 중이며 오늘 밤에 제주도를 강타할 예정입니다. 태풍 주의보가 발효되었습니다. 많은 양의 비가 내릴 예정이고 일부 지역에서는 홍수의 가능성이 높습니다. 태풍 도니는 강한 바람을 동반하므로 실내에 머무십시오. 또, 보도를 계속 청취해 주시기를 당부 드립니다. 감사합니다.

남: 소라야, 부탁 좀 들어줄래?
여: 뭔데요, 아빠?
남: 오늘 밤 태풍이 온다는구나. 바깥에서 옷가지들을 들여와 주겠니?
여: 그럴게요. 아빠의 자전거는 어떻게 할까요?
남: 자전거는 설거지를 끝낸 후에 내가 처리하마.
여: 알겠어요. 할머니께 전화해서 태풍에 관해 말씀드릴까요?
남: 그래. 할머니께 집안에 계시라고 말씀드리렴.
여: 네, 아빠.

남: 지민아, 외출하니?
여: 응. '최가네'에서 샌드위치 좀 사려고.
남: 그곳에 걸어서 갈 거니?
여: 아니. 자전거를 타고 갈 거야.
남: 잘됐다. 부탁 좀 들어줄래?
여: 그럼. 뭔데?
남: 돌아오는 길에 초콜릿 아이스크림 좀 사다 줄 수 있어?
여: 물론이야.
남: 고마워. 헬멧 꼭 쓰고, 이어폰은 안 돼!
여: 걱정하지 마.

Speak - Talk in pairs.

A: Can I start now?

B: _____ _____ _____ before you start.

A: Okay. No problem.

B: One _____ thing. Make sure _____ _____ _____ _____

 _____ _____.

A: I'll keep that in _____.

A: 이제 시작할까요?
B: 시작하기 전에 손을 씻어라.
A: 네. 알겠어요.
B: 하나 더. 칼을 갖고 놀면 안 된다는 것을 명심해라.
A: 명심할게요.

Wrap Up 5

(The phone rings.)

B: Hi, Mom.

W: Hi, Junho. Are you _____ _____ _____ _____ with Dad?

B: Yeah. Today we visited Dokdo.

W: That sounds _____. What are you _____ to do tomorrow?

B: We're going _____ on a boat.

W: Great. Please make sure you _____ _____ _____ _____.

B: Okay, Mom. I'll _____ that _____ _____.

(전화벨이 울린다.)
남: 여보세요, 엄마.
여: 그래, 준호야. 아빠랑 좋은 시간 보내고 있니?
남: 네. 오늘 우리는 독도에 다녀왔어요.
여: 굉장하구나. 내일은 뭘 할 거니?
남: 우리는 보트를 타고 낚시하러 갈 거예요.
여: 좋겠구나. 구명조끼를 꼭 입도록 해라.
남: 네, 엄마. 명심할게요.

Wrap Up 6

W: Can you _____ _____ _____ _____?

B: Sure, Grandma. What is it?

W: I want to go to the Tom Dylan concert _____ _____. Can you

 buy some _____ for me?

B: No problem. How many _____ _____ _____ _____?

W: Two tickets, please.

여: 부탁 좀 들어줄 수 있니?
남: 물론이죠, 할머니. 뭔데요?
여: 크리스마스에 Tom Dylan 콘서트에 가고 싶구나. 나를 위해 표를 좀 구매해 주겠니?
남: 문제없어요. 표가 몇 장 필요하세요?
여: 두 장을 부탁한다.

[01~02] 다음 대화를 읽고 물음에 답하시오.

> *(The phone rings.)*
>
> **Junho:** Hi, Mom.
>
> **Mom:** Hi, Junho. Are you having a good time with Dad?
>
> **Junho:** Yeah. Today we ⓐ<u>visited</u> Dokdo.
>
> **Mom:** That ⓑ<u>sounds</u> cool. What are you going to do tomorrow?
>
> **Junho:** We're going fishing ⓒ<u>on</u> a boat.
>
> **Mom:** Great. Please make sure you ⓓ<u>wearing</u> a life jacket.
>
> **Junho:** Okay, Mom. I'll keep ⓔ<u>that</u> in mind.

01 위 대화의 밑줄 친 ⓐ~ⓔ 중 어법상 어색한 것을 찾아 바르게 고치시오.

➡ _____

02 위 대화를 읽고 대답할 수 없는 것은?

① Where did Junho visit?

② With whom did Junho visit Dokdo?

③ What is Junho planning to do tomorrow?

④ What does Mom advise to Junho?

⑤ What should Dad keep in mind?

[03~04] 다음 대화를 읽고 물음에 답하시오.

> **Grandma:** Can you do me a favor?
>
> **Jack:** Sure, Grandma. What is it?
>
> **Grandma:** I want to go to the Tom Dylan concert on Christmas. Can you buy some tickets for me?
>
> **Jack:** No problem. How many tickets do you want?
>
> **Grandma:** Two tickets, please.

03 Where does Grandma want to go on Christmas?

➡ _____

04 What does Grandma want Jack to do?

➡ _____

[01~03] 다음 대화를 읽고 물음에 답하시오.

Girl: Can I start now?

Man: Wash your hands before you start.

Girl: Okay. No problem.

Man: One more thing. Make sure you don't play with the knives.

Girl: I'll keep that in mind.

01 위 대화가 일어나는 장소로 가장 적절한 것은?

① hospital   ② post office

③ kitchen   ④ airport

⑤ grocery store

서답형

02 What does the man ask the girl to do first?

➡ _____

서답형

03 남자가 여자에게 하지 말도록 당부한 것을 10자 내외의 우리말로 쓰시오.

➡ _____

[04~05] 다음 대화를 읽고 물음에 답하시오.

Dad: Sora, (A)can you do me a favor?

Sora: What is it, Dad?

Dad: A typhoon is coming tonight. Can you bring in the clothes from outside?

Sora: No problem. What about your bike?

Dad: I'll take care of it after I finish the dishes.

Sora: Okay. Do you want me to call Grandma and tell her about the typhoon?

Dad: Yes. Please tell her to stay home.

Sora: Okay, Dad.

04 위 대화의 밑줄 친 (A)와 바꾸어 쓰기에 <u>어색한</u> 것은?

① would you do me a favor?

② can you help me?

③ can you give me a hand?

④ may I ask you a favor?

⑤ what can I do for you?

05 위 대화를 읽고 대답할 수 <u>없는</u> 것은?

① What does Dad ask Sora to do?

② Who will take care of the bike?

③ How's the weather tonight?

④ What will Sora tell her grandmother about?

⑤ What is Sora going to bring to her grandmother?

[06~08] 다음 대화를 읽고 물음에 답하시오.

M: Hi, this is Cha Gisang from the Weather Station. Here is today's weather. Typhoon Doni is moving north and is going to hit Jejudo tonight. A typhoon warning has been issued. There will be lots of rainfall with a high chance of flooding in some areas. Please stay inside because Typhoon Doni will come with strong winds. Also, (A)please make sure you keep listening to our reports. Thank you.

서답형

06 위 대화에서 다음의 영영풀이가 뜻하는 것을 찾아 쓰시오.

a violent tropical storm with very strong winds

➡ _____

07 위 대화의 밑줄 친 (A)와 바꾸어 쓰기에 어색한 것은?

① make certain that you should keep listening to our reports

② don't forget to keep listening to our reports

③ remember to keep listening to our reports

④ be sure to keep listening to our reports

⑤ I'm not certain that you should keep listening to our reports

08 위 대화의 내용과 일치하지 <u>않는</u> 것은?

① 태풍 도니가 북상 중이다.

② 태풍은 오늘 밤에 제주도를 강타할 예정이다.

③ 태풍주의보가 해제되었다.

④ 많은 양의 비가 내릴 예정이고 일부 지역에서는 홍수의 가능성이 높다.

⑤ 태풍 도니는 강한 바람을 동반하므로 실내에 머물 것을 당부한다.

[09~11] 다음 대화를 읽고 물음에 답하시오.

Brian: Jimin, are you going out?

Jimin: Yeah. I'm going to buy some sandwiches at Choi's. (A)

Brian: Are you walking there?

Jimin: No. I'll ride my bike. (B)

Brian: That's good. (C)

Jimin: Sure. What is it?

Brian: Can you buy chocolate ice cream for me on your way back?

Jimin: No problem. (D)

Brian: Thanks. Please make sure you wear a helmet and no ear phones! (E)

Jimin: Don't worry about that.

09 위 대화의 (A)~(E) 중 주어진 문장이 들어가기에 적절한 곳은?

> Can you do me a favor?

① (A) ② (B) ③ (C) ④ (D) ⑤ (E)

10 Choose all the places that Jimin is going to visit.

① ② ③ ④ ⑤ ⑥

11 위 대화를 읽고 대답할 수 <u>없는</u> 것은?

① Where is Jimin going?

② What is Jimin going to buy?

③ What does Brian ask Jimin to do?

④ What shouldn't Jimin wear when she rides her bike?

⑤ How can Brian help Jimin?

12 다음 중 짝지어진 대화가 <u>어색한</u> 것을 고르시오.

① A: Can you do me a favor?
   B: Sure. What is it?

② A: Can I ask you a favor?
   B: Sure. What can I do for you?

③ A: Could you take out the trash?
   B: No problem. I'll do that for you.

④ A: Would you do me a favor?
   B: I'm sorry to hear that. Anything else?

⑤ A: Can you help me? Please take me to the flower shop.
   B: Umm. I can take you to the bus stop.

01 다음 대화가 자연스럽게 이어지도록 순서대로 배열하시오.

(A) Two tickets, please.
(B) Can you do me a favor?
(C) Sure, Grandma. What is it?
(D) No problem. How many tickets do you want?
(E) I want to go to the Tom Dylan concert on Christmas. Can you buy some tickets for me?

➡ _____

02 다음 대화의 내용과 일치하도록 빈칸을 완성하시오.

Dad: Sora, can you do me a favor?
Sora: What is it, Dad?
Dad: A typhoon is coming tonight. Can you bring in the clothes from outside?
Sora: No problem. What about your bike?
Dad: I'll take care of it after I finish the dishes.
Sora: Okay. Do you want me to call Grandma and tell her about the typhoon?
Dad: Yes. Please tell her to stay home.
Sora: Okay, Dad.

↓

Sora: Hello, this is Sora.
Grandma: Hi, Sweety. What's up?
Sora: Grandma, you should ____(A)____ because ____(B)____.
Grandma: Oh, I see. Thank you for letting me know that.
Sora: You're welcome.

(A) _____
(B) _____

[03~05] 다음 글을 읽고 물음에 답하시오.

M: Hi, this is Cha Gisang from the Weather Station. Here is today's weather. Typhoon Doni is moving north and is going to hit Jejudo tonight. A typhoon warning has been issued. There will be lots of rainfall with a high chance of flooding in some areas. Please stay inside because Typhoon Doni will come with strong winds. Also, please make sure you keep listening to our reports. Thank you.

03 When is Typhoon Doni going to hit Jejudo?

➡ _____

04 What will Typhoon Doni cause in some areas?

➡ _____

중요
05 What does the man ask the listeners to do?

➡ _____
_____

06 다음 대화가 자연스럽게 이어지도록 순서대로 배열하시오.

(The phone rings.)
Junho: Hi, Mom.
Mom: Hi, Junho. Are you having a good time with Dad?
(A) Okay, Mom. I'll keep that in mind.
(B) We're going fishing on a boat.
(C) Yeah. Today we visited Dokdo.
(D) Great. Please make sure you wear a life jacket.
(E) That sounds cool. What are you going to do tomorrow?

➡ _____

Grammar

① 분사구문

> • I study math, **listening** to music. 나는 음악을 들으면서 수학을 공부한다.

■ 분사가 이끄는 구를 분사구문이라고 하며, 이유, 조건, 시간, 동시동작, 양보 등의 뜻을 나타낸다. 분사
구문은 '접속사+주어+동사'로 이루어진 부사절의 주어가 주절의 주어와 일치할 때 접속사와 주어를 생
략하고 동사를 분사(동사원형+-ing)로 만들어 부사구로 표현한 것이다.

   • While I was walking along the street, I met Mr. White.
   → **Walking** along the street, I met Mr. White. (시간)

■ 부사절과 주절의 주어가 다를 때는 부사절의 주어를 생략하지 않고 사용하며 이것을 독립분사구문이라
고 한다. 일반인이 주어일 경우에는 생략한다. (비인칭 독립분사구문)

   • As it was getting dark, we soon turned back.
   → It **being** getting dark, we soon turned back. 어두워지기 시작하였으므로 이내 우리는 돌아왔다.

■ 분사구문의 부정은 분사 앞에 'not'이나 'never'를 쓴다.

   • She had to leave early because she didn't have much time.
   → **Not having** much time, she had to leave early. 그녀는 시간이 촉박해서 빨리 떠나야 했다.

■ 분사구문의 의미를 분명히 하기 위해 분사 앞에 접속사를 쓰는 경우도 있다. 이 경우는 부사절에서 '주
어+be동사'를 생략한 것과 같은 형태가 된다.

   • While **taking** this medicine, avoid alcohol. 이 약을 복용하는 동안 술은 피해라.

■ 부사절의 시제가 주절보다 앞선 경우에는 완료분사구문(having+과거분사)으로 쓴다.

   • After I had been sick, I realized how precious health is.
   = **Having been** sick, I realized how precious health is. 아프고 난 후, 나는 건강의 소중함을 알았다.

■ 분사구문에서 Being이나 Having been은 대부분 생략하지만, 보어가 명사일 경우나 분사가 아닌 경우
에 보통 접속사 없이 being을 생략하지 않는다.

   • Though she was lonely, she was good-humored.
   → Though (**being**) lonely, she was good-humored. 그녀는 외로웠음에도 불구하고 유머 감각이 넘쳤다.

■ 과거분사로 시작되는 분사구문은 being이 생략된 것으로 수동의 의미를 갖는다.

   • (Being) **Seen** from above, hurricanes look peaceful. 상공에서 봤을 때 허리케인들은 평온해 보인다.

핵심 Check

1. 다음 괄호 안에서 알맞은 말을 고르시오.

(1) (Live / Living) next door, I seldom see her.

(2) (Being / To be) rich, he could buy such a big house.

② 조동사가 포함된 수동태

• The party **will be held** at 7 p.m. 파티는 오후 7시에 열릴 것이다.

■ 수동태는 행위자보다는 행위의 대상에 중점을 두고 말할 때 쓰며, 조동사가 있는 문장의 수동태는 '조동사+be+과거분사'의 형태로 나타낸다.

　• You must keep accurate records. 너는 정확한 기록을 간직해야 한다.

　 = Accurate records **must be kept** by you. 정확한 기록이 너에 의해 간직되어야 한다.

■ 부정문은 '조동사+not+be+과거분사'의 형태로, 의문문은 '조동사+주어+be+과거분사 ~?'의 형태로 쓴다.

　• The value of regular exercise **should not be underestimated**. 규칙적인 운동의 가치를 과소평가하면 안 된다.

cf. 　1. 수동태 구문에서 행위자가 일반인이거나 강조할 필요가 없을 때에는 'by+행위자'를 생략하고 쓸 수 있다.

　• The textbooks **will be used** in schools nationwide beginning next year.
그 교과서들은 내년부터 전국의 학교에서 사용될 것이다.

　2. 수동태로 쓰지 않는 동사

　　자동사는 목적어가 없으므로 수동태로 쓸 수 없으며 '상태'나 '소유'를 나타내는 타동사도 수동태로 쓰이지 않음에 주의해야 한다.

　• The accident **happened** late last year. 그 사고는 작년 말에 일어났다.
　 The accident was happened late last year. (×)

　• The scorpion **has** a sting in its tail. 전갈은 꼬리에 독침이 있다.
　 A sting is had in its tail by the scorpion. (×)

핵심 Check

2. 다음 우리말과 일치하도록 주어진 어휘를 이용하여 빈칸에 알맞게 쓰시오.

　(1) 그 법을 어떻게 개정할 것인지 숙고할 필요가 있다. (might, reform)

　　➡ We need to consider how the law ＿＿＿＿ ＿＿＿＿ ＿＿＿＿.

　(2) 그녀의 허락 없이는 아무것도 할 수 없을 것이다. (could, do)

　　➡ Nothing ＿＿＿＿ ＿＿＿＿ ＿＿＿＿ without her say-so.

01 다음 빈칸에 들어갈 말로 알맞은 것은?

_____ hungry, he ate much.

① Being   ② Been   ③ Am

④ Was   ⑤ Be

02 다음 괄호 안에서 알맞은 말을 고르시오.

(1) (Feel / Feeling) sick, I went to the doctor.

(2) She stared blankly into space, (knowing not / not knowing) what to say next.

(3) The chair (will be delivered / will deliver) on Thursday.

(4) Costs (should be kept / should be keep) to a minimum.

03 다음 우리말에 맞게 빈칸에 알맞은 것은?

텔레비전을 보다가 그는 잠이 들었다.
= _____ television, he fell asleep.

① Watch   ② Watches   ③ Watched

④ To watch   ⑤ Watching

04 다음 문장을 수동태로 고쳤을 때 알맞은 것은?

We can see germs through a microscope.

① Germs can see us through a microscope.

② Germs are seen through a microscope.

③ Germs can be seen through a microscope.

④ Germs be seen through a microscope.

⑤ Germs can seen through a microscope.

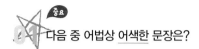

01 다음 중 어법상 어색한 문장은?

① After dinner, we sat talking on the veranda.
② The boys and girls danced, singing together.
③ Every Friday evening, we dance together, listen to music.
④ He was covered with dust while walking along the road.
⑤ Turning to the left, you will find the police station.

02 다음 대화의 빈칸에 들어갈 말로 알맞은 것은?

> M: Did you finish the work?
> B: No. Not yet.
> M: Why? Do you have any problems?
> B: Yes. They gave no indication of how the work _____.

① does
② is done
③ should do
④ should done
⑤ should be done

03 다음 빈칸에 알맞은 말이 바르게 짝지어진 것은?

> • Not _____ his phone number, I couldn't call him.
> • Creativity can _____.

① knowing – teach
② knowing – be taught
③ know – teach
④ knew – be taught
⑤ knew – be teach

04 다음 문장의 밑줄 친 부분 중 어법상 어색한 것은?

> I always give ⓐ<u>myself</u> allowances, ⓑ <u>know</u> that things ⓒ<u>may not</u> always ⓓ<u>go</u> as ⓔ<u>planned</u>.

① ⓐ
② ⓑ
③ ⓒ
④ ⓓ
⑤ ⓔ

서답형

05 다음 괄호 안에서 알맞은 말을 고르시오.

(1) As usual, up to five books (can be borrowed / can borrow) at a time for two weeks.
(2) Some vitamins (can be not / cannot be) manufactured by our bodies.
(3) Slowly, an image began to (appear / be appeared) on the screen.
(4) Many changes (took place / were taken place) between the two world wars.
(5) (Finish / Finishing) dinner, he went out to walk his dog.
(6) While (wait / waiting) for a bus, she met her best friend.
(7) He took the last Wednesday off, (feeling not / not feeling) well.
(8) (Being / It being) a sunny day, she went swimming.

06 다음 중 어법상 바르지 <u>않은</u> 것은?

① The work should finished by 7 p.m. by us.
② Safety rules must be followed by everyone.
③ Many herbs can be grown indoors.
④ This essay will have to be completely rewritten.
⑤ The highway will be closed this Wednesday.

07 주어진 두 문장을 한 문장으로 바꿀 때 옳지 <u>않은</u> 것은?

> • They saw the dog.
> • The sheep gathered together.

① The sheep gathered together as they saw the dog.
② Seeing the dog, the sheep gathered together.
③ When seeing the dog, the sheep gathered together.
④ When they saw the dog, the sheep gathered together.
⑤ When saw the dog, the sheep gathered together.

서답형

08 다음 두 문장을 한 문장으로 바꿔 쓸 때 빈칸에 들어갈 한 단어를 쓰시오.

> • He was walking around the park.
> • He met his neighbor Ms. Marple.
> ➡ _____ around the park, he met his neighbor Ms. Marple.

[09~10] 다음 우리말을 바르게 영작한 것을 고르시오.

09

> 동물들이 오락거리로 이용되어서는 안 된다.

① Animals should not use for entertainment.
② Animals should not be use for entertainment.
③ Animals should not be used for entertainment.
④ Animals should use not for entertainment.
⑤ Animals should be not used for entertainment.

10

> 매우 추웠기 때문에, 그녀는 따뜻한 차 한 잔을 마셨다.

① Because very cold, she drank a cup of hot tea.
② Because she very cold, she drank a cup of hot tea.
③ Being she felt very cold, she drank a cup of hot tea.
④ Feeling very cold, she drank a cup of hot tea.
⑤ Feeling she very cold, she drank a cup of hot tea.

서답형

11 다음 괄호 안의 어휘를 바르게 배열하시오.

(1) This book (be, read, can) by children.
➡ _____

(2) Such rude manners (be, not, should, accepted).
➡ _____

12 밑줄 친 부분의 쓰임이 주어진 문장과 같은 것은?

> Feeling tired, she went to bed early.

① She wouldn't change it, knowing it was wrong.
② Being tired, every player went home right after the game.
③ Receiving payment, I will send the book to you.
④ I study math, listening to music.
⑤ Seeing him, give him this note.

13 다음 문장을 수동태로 고쳤을 때 올바른 것은?

> We should keep the meeting room clean.

① The meeting room should keep clean by us.
② The meeting room is kept clean by us.
③ The meeting room be kept clean by us.
④ The meeting room should kept clean by us.
⑤ The meeting room should be kept clean by us.

서답형

14 다음 문장에서 생략할 수 있는 것을 찾아 쓰시오.

(1) John broke his arm while he was building his house.

➡ _____

(2) Although she was tired, she continued to work on her report.

➡ _____

(3) I'm sure you were very good-looking when you were young.

➡ _____

15 다음 우리말에 맞도록 빈칸에 들어갈 알맞은 것은?

> 내년 봄에 학교 구내 식당이 지어질 것이다.
> = A school cafeteria _____ next spring.

① builds
② will build
③ will built
④ will be built
⑤ will be build

[16~17] 다음 우리말을 참고하여 주어진 문장의 틀린 부분을 찾아 바르게 고친 것을 고르시오.

16

> 나는 돈을 잃어버렸기 때문에 그 시계를 살 수 없다.
> = Lose the money, I can't buy the watch.

① Having lost the money, I can't buy the watch.
② Losing the money, I can't buy the watch.
③ As losing the money, I can't buy the watch.
④ Lost the money, I can't buy the watch.
⑤ Though lost the money, I can't buy the watch.

17

> 날씨가 좋다면, 나는 수영하러 갈 것이다.
> = Being fine, I'll go swimming.

① Fine, I'll go swimming.
② Being fine the weather, I'll go swimming.
③ The weather being fine, I'll go swimming.
④ As the weather fine, I'll go swimming.
⑤ The weather fine, I'll go swimming.

01 다음 주어진 문장을 분사구문으로 바꿔 쓰시오.

(1) Because she got up late, she was late for school yesterday.

➡ _____

_____

(2) The girl got off the bus, and said goodbye to her friend.

➡ _____

_____

(3) If you climb to the top of the hill, you can see the garden well.

➡ _____

_____

(4) Although she studied hard, she failed the exam.

➡ _____

_____

(5) Since I didn't know the way to the theater, I asked the girl sitting next to me to tell me the way.

➡ _____

_____

(6) If it is fine tomorrow, I'll go hiking on Dobong Mountain.

➡ _____

_____

(7) As she had lost her job, she had to leave the office.

➡ _____

_____

(8) As she is interested in history, she likes her history class.

➡ _____

_____

02 주어진 문장을 수동태로 바꿔 쓰시오. 바꿔 쓸 수 <u>없는</u> 것은 '불가'라고 쓰고 그 이유를 쓰시오.

(1) You should return new books in a week.

➡ _____

_____

(2) People will love this song for a long time.

➡ _____

_____

(3) We have to slow down the population growth.

➡ _____

_____

(4) She may doubt the sincerity of his decision.

➡ _____

_____

(5) You resemble your mother very closely.

➡ _____

(6) The airline has an excellent safety record.

➡ _____

_____

03 다음 문장에서 어법상 어색한 부분을 분사구문을 이용하여 바르게 고치시오. (생략하지 말 것.)

(1) Embarrassing to wear the clothes to work, she wore them only at home.

_____ ➡ _____

(2) Meeting him several times, she can remember him.

_____ ➡ _____

04 다음 그림을 보고, 주어진 어휘를 이용하여 빈칸을 알맞게 채우시오.

The burned skin _____ with running water. (must, cool)

05 다음 그림을 보고, 주어진 어휘를 이용하여 빈칸을 알맞게 채우시오.

Mike fell down the steps, _____ his arm. (break)

06 다음 우리말에 맞게 주어진 어구를 바르게 배열하시오.

(1) 기차역에 도착한 후에 Mike는 그의 친구들을 찾기 시작했다. (Mike, his friends, the train station, arriving, look, began, to, for, at)

➡ _____

_____

(2) 어찌할 바를 몰라 그녀는 나에게 조언을 구했다. (she, my advice, knowing, asked, what, do, not, for, to)

➡ _____

(3) 이 지역에서는 더 많은 금이 발견될 수 있다. (region, gold, this, be, can, more, found, in)

➡ _____

(4) 조리실은 항상 청결하게 유지되어야 한다. (the cooking room, all times, be, clean, kept, should, at)

➡ _____

_____

07 다음 문장에서 어법상 <u>어색한</u> 것을 바르게 고쳐 다시 쓰시오.

(1) Knives must keep in a safe place.

➡ _____

_____

(2) The department denies responsibility for what was occurred.

➡ _____

_____

(3) Arrived home, he cleaned the whole house.

➡ _____

_____

(4) Being chilly outside, I wanted to stay home.

➡ _____

(5) Writing in haste, the book has many mistakes.

➡ _____

_____

교과서

Reading

The Power of Volcanoes

What do Jejudo, Sicily, and Hawaii have in common? They are islands, of course. In fact, they are all islands <u>made</u> from volcanic
made 앞에 '관계대명사+be동사(which[that] are)' 생략
eruptions. Volcanoes are very powerful, so they are named after Vulcan, the Roman god of fire. They can <u>make big islands appear</u> or
사역동사 make+목적어+목적보어(동사원형): (목적어)가 ~하게 만들다
destroy entire cities like Pompeii. Therefore, they <u>should be studied</u>
조동사가 포함된 수동태: 조동사+be+과거분사(studied와 understood는 and로 병렬 연결)
and <u>understood</u>.

Nobody knows for sure <u>how many volcanoes there are in the world.</u>
간접의문문: 의문사+주어+동사
According to scientists, there are about 1,500 active volcanoes above sea level. Many more are underwater, and they are hard to locate. Still, scientists have discovered a large number of them so far.
현재완료: 과거의 어떤 시점에 시작한 일이 지금도 계속되고 있음을 나타냄.

Many of the volcanoes on Earth are located along the Ring of Fire that circles the Pacific Ocean. The ring is about 40,000 kilometers long, and it is home to around 75% of the world's active volcanoes. Indonesia alone has over 120 active volcanoes <u>since</u> the country lies on
이유를 나타내는 부사절을 이끄는 접속사: ~ 때문에
the Ring of Fire. This ring is also the area <u>where</u> most of the world's
장소를 나타내는 관계부사
earthquakes occur.

---

volcano 화산

have ~ in common ~을 공통적으로 가지다

eruption 분출

name after ~을 따서 이름 짓다

destroy 파괴하다

entire 전체의, 온

active 활동 중인

underwater 수중의

locate ~의 위치를 찾아내다

discover 발견하다

ring 고리, 반지

circle 둘러싸다

lie 위치해 있다

earthquake 지진

 확인문제

● 다음 문장이 본문의 내용과 일치하면 T, 일치하지 <u>않으면</u> F를 쓰시오.

1   Jejudo, Sicily, and Hawaii are all islands made from volcanic eruptions. ☐

2   According to scientists, there are about 1,500 active volcanoes underwater. ☐

3   Many of the volcanoes on Earth are located along the Ring of Fire that circles the Pacific Ocean. ☐

A Sudden Volcano

Working on a cornfield one day in 1943, farmers in Mexico found
= While they were working on a cornfield one day in 1943
something surprising. A volcano appeared overnight on a flat cornfield.
-thing이나 -body로 끝나는 대명사는 형용사가 뒤에서 수식
Residents watched the volcano grow over 100 meters tall within
지각동사 watch+목적어+목적보어(동사원형 grow)
a week. The volcano, called Paricutin, kept growing, and it finally
stopped growing at 424 meters in 1952.

You may think volcanoes can be found only on Earth. However, they
조동사가 포함된 수동태: 조동사+be+과거분사
have been discovered on other planets, too, such as Mars and Jupiter.
현재완료 수동태: have been+과거분사
In fact, "Olympus Mons" on Mars is the largest known volcano in the
가장 크다고 알려진
solar system. Its volume is about 100 times greater than that of Mauna
~ times+비교급+than A: A보다 ~ 배 더 …한 = 100 times as great as   = the volume
Loa, the largest volcano on Earth.
the largest volcano on Earth는 Mauna Loa와 동격
Being very powerful and dangerous, volcanoes do harm to people in
= Because volcanoes are very powerful and dangerous
many ways. Sometimes people get hurt, or they may lose their houses.

Crops may be destroyed, and air traffic can be threatened. Volcanoes
조동사가 포함된 수동태: 조동사+be+과거분사   조동사가 포함된 수동태: 조동사+be+과거분사
can also have serious effects on world weather. A volcanic eruption
shoots lots of ash and dust into the air, preventing some of the sunlight
= and it prevents(부대상황)
from reaching Earth and thus disturbing usual weather patterns.
prevent A from -ing: A가 ~하는 것을 막다   = and thus disturbs(부대상황)

---

sudden 갑작스러운

overnight 하룻밤 사이에

flat 평평한

planet 행성

Mars 화성

Jupiter 목성

solar system 태양계

volume 부피

do harm 해를 입히다

get hurt 다치다

crop 농작물

traffic 교통

threaten 위협하다

effect 영향, 효과, 결과

shoot ~ into … ~을 …으로 내뿜다

ash 재

dust 먼지

prevent 막다, 방해하다

 확인문제

● 다음 문장이 본문의 내용과 일치하면 T, 일치하지 <u>않으면</u> F를 쓰시오.

1 Volcanoes have been discovered on other planets, too, such as Mars and Jupiter. ☐

2 The volume of Mauna Loa, the largest volcano on Earth, is about 100 times greater
   than that of "Olympus Mons" on Mars. ☐

A Deadly Volcano

Mt. Tambora, an active volcano on the island of Sumbawa, Indonesia, erupted in 1815. The eruption killed more than 10,000 residents. It also caused an unusually cold summer around the world the following year.

What volcanoes do is not always bad for humans, however. The soil near a volcano is good for farming. Volcanoes are also a great tourist attraction. Looking for fantastic scenery, millions of tourists visit Mt. Halla in Jejudo, Mt. Etna in Sicily, or Diamond Head in Hawaii every year. Volcanoes can be used to produce electricity, too. Iceland, for example, actively turns its volcanoes' heat energy into electricity. Today people around the world are studying ways to live in greater harmony with volcanoes, and they are hopeful that more ways will be found soon.

선행사를 포함하는 관계대명사 *'언제나 ~인 것은 아닌'이라는 의미로 부분 부정*

= Because millions of tourists are looking for fantastic scenery

조동사가 포함된 수동태: 조동사+be+과거분사 *to부정사의 부사적 용법(목적)*

to부정사의 형용사적 용법

human 인간
soil 토양
fantastic 환상적인
scenery 경치
millions of 수백만의
produce 생산하다
electricity 전기
in harmony with ~와 조화를 이루어
hopeful 희망적인

확인문제

● 다음 문장이 본문의 내용과 일치하면 T, 일치하지 <u>않으면</u> F를 쓰시오.

1 Because volcanoes are very powerful and dangerous, they do harm to people in many ways ☐

2 What volcanoes do is always bad for humans. ☐

우리말을 참고하여 빈칸에 알맞은 말을 쓰시오.

1 The _____ of Volcanoes

2 What do Jejudo, Sicily, and Hawaii _____ _____ _____?

3 They are islands, _____ _____.

4 In fact, they are all islands made from _____ _____.

5 Volcanoes are very powerful, so they _____ _____ _____ Vulcan, the Roman god of fire.

6 They can _____ _____ _____ _____ or destroy entire cities like Pompeii.

7 Therefore, they _____ _____ _____ _____ _____.

8 Nobody knows for sure _____ _____ _____ _____ _____ in the world.

9 _____ _____ scientists, there are about 1,500 active volcanoes _____ _____ _____.

10 Many more are underwater, and they are _____ _____ _____.

11 Still, scientists have discovered _____ _____ _____ them so far.

12 Many of the volcanoes on Earth _____ _____ along the Ring of Fire that circles the Pacific Ocean.

13 The ring is about 40,000 kilometers long, and it is _____ _____ around 75% of the world's active volcanoes.

14 Indonesia _____ has over 120 active volcanoes since the country _____ _____ the Ring of Fire.

15 This ring is also the area _____ most of the world's earthquakes _____.

16 A _____ Volcano

17 Working on a cornfield one day in 1943, farmers in Mexico found _____ _____.

18 A volcano _____ _____ on a flat cornfield.

19 Residents watched the volcano _____ over 100 meters tall within a week.

20 The volcano, called Paricutin, _____ _____, and it finally _____ _____ at 424 meters in 1952.

1 화산의 힘
2 제주도, 시칠리아, 하와이의 공통점은 무엇일까?
3 물론, 그것들은 섬이다.
4 사실, 그것들은 모두 화산 분출에 의해 형성된 섬이다.
5 화산은 매우 강력한 힘을 가지고 있어서 로마의 불의 신, 불카누스에서 이름을 따왔다.
6 화산은 큰 섬이 생겨나게 하거나 폼페이 같은 도시 전체를 파멸시킬 수도 있다.
7 그러므로 화산은 연구되고, 이해되어야 한다.
8 세계에 얼마나 많은 화산이 있는지 누구도 정확히 알지 못한다.
9 과학자들에 따르면, 해수면 위에 대략 1,500개의 활화산이 있다.
10 더 많은 화산이 해저에 존재하는데, 그것들은 정확한 위치를 파악하기가 어렵다.
11 그럼에도 불구하고, 과학자들은 지금까지 그중 많은 수를 발견했다.
12 지구상에 있는 많은 화산들은 태평양을 둘러싸는 '불의 고리(환태평양조산대)'를 따라 위치한다.
13 그 고리는 길이가 약 40,000km에 달하며, 전 세계 활화산의 약 75%가 여기에 있다.
14 인도네시아에만 120개가 넘는 활화산이 있는데, 이 나라가 '불의 고리'에 위치하고 있기 때문이다.
15 이 고리는 또한 전 세계 지진의 대부분이 발생하는 곳이다.
16 갑작스럽게 생겨난 화산
17 1943년 어느 날 옥수수 밭에서 일을 하다가 멕시코의 농부들이 놀라운 것을 발견했다.
18 밤사이에 평평한 옥수수 밭 위로 화산이 생겨난 것이다.
19 주민들은 그 화산이 일주일이 못 되는 사이 100m 넘게 자라는 것을 지켜보았다.
20 'Paricutin(파리쿠틴)'이라고 불리는 이 화산은 계속 자랐고, 1952년에 424m로 드디어 성장을 멈추었다.

21 You may think volcanoes _____ _____ _____ only on Earth.

22 However, they _____ _____ _____ on other planets, too, such as Mars and Jupiter.

23 In fact, "Olympus Mons" on Mars is _____ _____ _____ volcano in the solar system.

24 Its volume is about _____ _____ _____ _____ _____ _____ Mauna Loa, the largest volcano on Earth.

25 Being very powerful and dangerous, volcanoes _____ _____ _____ people in many ways.

26 Sometimes people _____ _____, or they may lose their houses.

27 Crops _____ _____ _____, and air traffic _____ _____ _____.

28 Volcanoes can also _____ _____ world weather.

29 A volcanic eruption _____ lots of ash and dust _____ the air, _____ some of the sunlight _____ _____ Earth and thus _____ usual weather patterns.

30 A _____ Volcano

31 Mt. Tambora, an active volcano on the island of Sumbawa, Indonesia, _____ in 1815.

32 The _____ killed more than 10,000 residents.

33 It also caused an _____ cold summer around the world the following year.

34 _____ _____ _____ is _____ bad for humans, however.

35 The soil near a volcano _____ _____ _____ farming.

36 Volcanoes are also a great _____ _____.

37 _____ _____ fantastic scenery, millions of tourists visit Mt. Halla in Jejudo, Mt. Etna in Sicily, or Diamond Head in Hawaii every year.

38 Volcanoes _____ _____ _____ to produce electricity, too.

39 Iceland, for example, actively _____ its volcanoes' heat energy _____ electricity.

40 Today people around the world are studying ways to live in _____ _____ _____ volcanoes, and they are hopeful that more ways will be found soon.

---

21 화산이 지구에만 존재한다고 생각할지 모른다.

22 그러나 화산은 화성이나 목성 같은 다른 행성에서도 발견되어 왔다.

23 사실 화성에 있는 Olympus Mons(올림푸스 몬스)가 태양계에서 가장 크다고 알려진 화산이다.

24 그것의 부피는 지구에서 가장 큰 화산 Mauna Loa(마우나로아)의 부피보다 약 100배 더 크다.

25 매우 강력하고 위험하기 때문에, 화산은 여러 면에서 사람들에게 해를 끼친다.

26 때로는 사람들이 다치기도 하고, 집을 잃기도 한다.

27 작물이 파괴되거나, 항공 교통이 위협받을 수도 있다.

28 화산은 또한 세계 날씨에 심각한 영향을 미치기도 한다.

29 화산 분출은 다량의 화산재와 먼지를 공중으로 내뿜어, 태양 광선의 일부가 지구에 도달하는 것을 방해하고 그리하여 정상적인 기상 패턴을 깨뜨린다.

30 목숨을 앗아 가는 화산

31 인도네시아 Sumbawa(숨바와) 섬에 위치한 활화산, Tambora(탐보라) 산이 1815년에 분출했다.

32 분출은 주민 1만 명 이상을 죽음에 이르게 했다.

33 또한 이듬해 전 세계에 비정상적으로 추운 여름을 초래했다.

34 그러나 화산이 인류에게 항상 나쁜 것만은 아니다.

35 화산 인근의 토양은 농사에 좋다.

36 화산은 또한 매우 훌륭한 관광 명소이다.

37 환상적인 경관을 찾아 매년 수백만 명의 여행객들이 제주도의 한라산, 시칠리아의 Etna(에트나) 산, 하와이의 Diamond Head(다이아몬드헤드)를 방문한다.

38 화산은 또한 전기를 생산하는 데에도 이용될 수 있다.

39 예를 들어, 아이슬란드는 적극적으로 화산의 열에너지를 전기로 바꾼다.

40 오늘날 전 세계에서 사람들이 화산과 더 조화롭게 살 방법을 연구하고 있으며, 더 많은 방법이 곧 발견될 것으로 기대하고 있다.

● 우리말을 참고하여 본문을 영작하시오.

1 화산의 힘
➡ _____

2 제주도, 시칠리아, 하와이의 공통점은 무엇일까?
➡ _____

3 물론, 그것들은 섬이다.
➡ _____

4 사실, 그것들은 모두 화산 분출에 의해 형성된 섬이다.
➡ _____

5 화산은 매우 강력한 힘을 가지고 있어서 로마의 불의 신, 불카누스에게서 이름을 따왔다.
➡ _____

6 화산은 큰 섬이 생겨나게 하거나 폼페이 같은 도시 전체를 파멸시킬 수도 있다.
➡ _____

7 그러므로 화산은 연구되고, 이해되어야 한다.
➡ _____

8 세계에 얼마나 많은 화산이 있는지 누구도 정확히 알지 못한다.
➡ _____

9 과학자들에 따르면, 해수면 위에 대략 1,500개의 활화산이 있다.
➡ _____

10 더 많은 화산이 해저에 존재하는데, 그것들은 정확한 위치를 파악하기가 어렵다.
➡ _____

11 그럼에도 불구하고, 과학자들은 지금까지 그중 많은 수를 발견했다.
➡ _____

12 지구상에 있는 많은 화산들은 태평양을 둘러싸는 '불의 고리(환태평양조산대)'를 따라 위치한다.
➡ _____

13 그 고리는 길이가 약 40,000km에 달하며, 전 세계 활화산의 약 75%가 여기에 있다.
➡ _____

14 인도네시아에만 120개가 넘는 활화산이 있는데, 이 나라가 '불의 고리'에 위치하고 있기 때문이다.
➡ _____

15 이 고리는 또한 전 세계 지진의 대부분이 발생하는 곳이다.
➡ _____

16 갑작스럽게 생겨난 화산
➡ _____

17 1943년 어느 날 옥수수 밭에서 일을 하다가 멕시코의 농부들이 놀라운 것을 발견했다.
➡ _____

18 밤사이에 평평한 옥수수 밭 위로 화산이 생겨난 것이다.
➡ _____

19 주민들은 그 화산이 일주일이 못 되는 사이 100m 넘게 자라는 것을 지켜보았다.
➡ _____

20 'Paricutin(파리쿠틴)'이라 불리는 이 화산은 계속 자랐고, 1952년에 424m로 드디어 성장을 멈추었다.
➡ _____

21 화산이 지구에만 존재한다고 생각할지 모른다.

➡ _____

22 그러나 화산은 화성이나 목성 같은 다른 행성에서도 발견되어 왔다.

➡ _____

23 사실 화성에 있는 Olympus Mons(올림푸스 몬스)가 태양계에서 가장 크다고 알려진 화산이다.

➡ _____

24 그것의 부피는 지구에서 가장 큰 화산 Mauna Loa(마우나 로아)의 부피보다 약 100배 더 크다.

➡ _____

25 매우 강력하고 위험하기 때문에, 화산은 여러 면에서 사람들에게 해를 끼친다.

➡ _____

26 때로는 사람들이 다치기도 하고, 집을 잃기도 한다.

➡ _____

27 작물이 파괴되거나, 항공 교통이 위협받을 수도 있다.

➡ _____

28 화산은 또한 세계 날씨에 심각한 영향을 미치기도 한다.

➡ _____

29 화산 분출은 다량의 화산재와 먼지를 공중으로 내뿜어, 태양 광선의 일부가 지구에 도달하는 것을 방해하고 그리하여 정상적인 기상 패턴을 깨트린다.

➡ _____

30 목숨을 앗아 가는 화산

➡ _____

31 인도네시아 Sumbawa(숨바와) 섬에 위치한 활화산, Tambora(탐보라) 산이 1815년에 분출했다.

➡ _____

32 분출은 주민 1만 명 이상을 죽음에 이르게 했다.

➡ _____

33 또한 이듬해 전 세계에 비정상적으로 추운 여름을 초래했다.

➡ _____

34 그러나 화산이 인류에게 항상 나쁜 것만은 아니다.

➡ _____

35 화산 인근의 토양은 농사에 좋다.

➡ _____

36 화산은 또한 매우 훌륭한 관광 명소이다.

➡ _____

37 환상적인 경관을 찾아 매년 수백만 명의 여행객들이 제주도의 한라산, 시칠리아의 Etna(에트나) 산, 하와이의 Diamond Head(다이아몬드헤드)를 방문한다.

➡ _____

38 화산은 또한 전기를 생산하는 데에도 이용될 수 있다.

➡ _____

39 예를 들어, 아이슬란드는 적극적으로 화산의 열에너지를 전기로 바꾼다.

➡ _____

40 오늘날 전 세계에서 사람들이 화산과 더 조화롭게 살 방법을 연구하고 있으며, 더 많은 방법이 곧 발견될 것으로 기대하고 있다.

➡ _____

_____

[01~03] 다음 글을 읽고 물음에 답하시오.

What do Jejudo, Sicily, and Hawaii have in common? ⓐThey are islands, of course. In fact, ⓑthey are all islands made from volcanic eruptions. Volcanoes are very powerful, so ⓒthey are named after Vulcan, the Roman god of fire. ⓓThey can make big islands appear or destroy entire cities like Pompeii. ___(A)___ , ⓔthey should be studied and understood.

01 위 글의 빈칸 (A)에 들어갈 알맞은 말을 고르시오.

① However ② In addition
③ In other words ④ For example
⑤ Therefore

02 밑줄 친 ⓐ~ⓔ 중에서 가리키는 대상이 같은 것을 고르시오.

① ⓐ와 ⓑ ② ⓐ와 ⓒ
③ ⓐ와 ⓓ ④ ⓑ와 ⓒ
⑤ ⓑ와 ⓔ

서답형

03 본문의 내용과 일치하도록 다음 빈칸에 알맞은 단어를 본문에서 찾아 쓰시오.

Jejudo, Sicily, and Hawaii are all islands which are made from _____ _____.

[04~06] 다음 글을 읽고 물음에 답하시오.

Nobody knows for sure how many volcanoes there are in the world. ⓐ According as scientists, there are about 1,500 active volcanoes above sea level. Many more are underwater, and they are hard ⓑto locate. Still, scientists have discovered a large number of them so far.

04 위 글의 제목으로 알맞은 것을 고르시오.

① What's the Origin of the Name of Volcanoes?
② How Many Volcanoes Are There in the World?
③ There Are Many Active Volcanoes above Sea Level
④ Underwater Volcanoes Are Hard to Locate
⑤ How Amazing the Achievement of Scientists Are!

서답형

05 위 글의 밑줄 친 ⓐ에서 어법상 틀린 부분을 찾아 고치시오.

_____ ➡ _____

06 아래 〈보기〉에서 위 글의 밑줄 친 ⓑto locate와 to부정사의 용법이 같은 것의 개수를 고르시오.

┤ 보기 ├
① He is too busy to go to the movies.
② It is very dangerous to play on the street.
③ I was surprised to find a bomb in the box.
④ The subway is a great way to get around Seoul.
⑤ I don't know how to drive a car.

① 1개 ② 2개 ③ 3개 ④ 4개 ⑤ 5개

[07~08] 다음 글을 읽고 물음에 답하시오.

A Sudden Volcano

ⓐWorking on a cornfield one day in 1943, farmers in Mexico found something surprising. A volcano appeared overnight on a flat cornfield. Residents watched the volcano grow over 100 meters tall within a week. ⓑThe volcano, called Paricutin, kept growing, and it finally stopped to grow at 424 meters in 1952.

서답형

07 위 글의 밑줄 친 분사구문 ⓐ를 부사절로 고치시오.

➡ _____
_____
_____

서답형

08 위 글의 밑줄 친 ⓑ에서 어법상 틀린 부분을 찾아 고치시오.

_____ ➡ _____

[09~11] 다음 글을 읽고 물음에 답하시오.

You may think volcanoes can be found only on Earth. However, they have been discovered on other planets, too, such as Mars and Jupiter. In fact, "Olympus Mons" on Mars is the largest known volcano in the solar system. ⓐIts volume is about 100 times greater than ⓑthat of Mauna Loa, the largest volcano on Earth.

서답형

09 위 글의 밑줄 친 ⓐIts가 가리키는 것을 본문에서 찾아 쓰시오.

➡ _____

10 위 글의 밑줄 친 ⓑthat과 문법적 쓰임이 같은 것을 고르시오.

① Look at that man over there.
② That's a nice dress.
③ This year's fashion is quite different from that of last year.
④ He is the greatest novelist that has ever lived.
⑤ Are you sure she's that young?

서답형

11 본문의 내용과 일치하도록 다음 빈칸 (A)와 (B)에 알맞은 단어를 쓰시오.

"Olympus Mons" is the largest known volcano (A)_____ _____ _____ _____ and "Mauna Loa" is the largest volcano (B)_____ _____ .

[12~14] 다음 글을 읽고 물음에 답하시오.

_____ ⓐ _____

Mt. Tambora, an active volcano on the island of Sumbawa, Indonesia, erupted in 1815. The eruption killed more than 10,000 residents. ⓑIt also caused an unusually cold summer around the world the following year.

12 위 글의 빈칸 ⓐ에 들어갈 제목으로 가장 알맞은 것을 고르시오.

① The Definition of an Active Volcano
② A Deadly Volcano
③ Volcanoes on Sumbawa, Indonesia
④ The Volume of the Mt. Tambora
⑤ the Largest Active Volcano on Earth

서답형

13 위 글의 밑줄 친 ⓑ이 가리키는 것을 본문에서 찾아 쓰시오.

➡ _____

14 위 글을 읽고 알 수 없는 것을 고르시오.

① Where is Mt. Tambora?
② When did Mt. Tambora erupt?
③ How many residents did the eruption of Mt. Tambora kill?
④ When Mt. Tambora erupted in 1815, how long did it erupt?
⑤ How was the weather around the world in the summer of 1816?

[15~17] 다음 글을 읽고 물음에 답하시오.

ⓐBeing very powerful and dangerous, volcanoes do harm to people in many ways. Sometimes people get hurt, or they may lose their houses. Crops may be destroyed, and air traffic can be threatened. Volcanoes can also have serious effects on world weather. A volcanic eruption shoots lots of ash and dust into the air, ⓑ태양 광선의 일부가 지구에 도달하는 것을 방해하고 그리하여 정상적인 기상 패턴을 깨뜨리며.

15 위 글의 밑줄 친 ⓐ와 분사구문의 의미가 같은 것을 모두 고르시오.

① Having no money, I had to go home on foot.
② Feeling sick, I had to take the test.
③ Drinking lots of water, you will get healthy.
④ Not feeling hungry, she didn't have lunch.
⑤ Waiting for her, I read the fashion magazine.

16 위 글의 밑줄 친 ⓑ의 우리말에 맞게 주어진 어휘를 알맞게 배열하시오.

> disturbing / from / some of the sunlight / preventing / and thus / usual weather patterns / reaching Earth

➡ _____

_____

17 위 글의 주제로 알맞은 것을 고르시오.

① the measures to reduce global warming due to greenhouse effect

② climate change caused by the eruption of volcanoes

③ the harmful effects of volcanoes on human life

④ the most powerful volcano in history

⑤ the abnormal weather patterns of the world

[18~19] 다음 글을 읽고 물음에 답하시오.

What volcanoes do is not always bad for humans, however. (①) The soil near a volcano is good for farming. (②) Looking for fantastic scenery, millions of tourists visit Mt. Halla in Jejudo, Mt. Etna in Sicily, or Diamond Head in Hawaii every year. (③) Volcanoes can be used to produce electricity, too. (④) Iceland, ___ⓐ___, actively turns its volcanoes' heat energy into electricity. (⑤) Today people around the world are studying ways to live in greater harmony with volcanoes, and they are hopeful that more ways will be found soon.

18 위 글의 빈칸 ⓐ에 들어갈 알맞은 말을 고르시오.

① in addition ② as a result

③ however ④ on the other hand

⑤ for example

19 위 글의 흐름으로 보아, 주어진 문장이 들어가기에 가장 적절한 곳은?

> Volcanoes are also a great tourist attraction.

①　　②　　③　　④　　⑤

[20~22] 다음 글을 읽고 물음에 답하시오.

What do Jejudo, Sicily, and Hawaii have in common? (①) They are islands, of course. (②) In fact, they are all islands made from volcanic eruptions. (③) Volcanoes are very powerful, so they are named after Vulcan, the Roman god of fire. (④) Therefore, they should be studied and understood. (⑤)

Nobody knows for sure how many volcanoes there are in the world. According to scientists, there are about 1,500 active volcanoes above sea level. Many more are underwater, and they are hard to locate. Still, scientists ____ⓐ____ a large number of them so far.

서답형

20 위 글의 빈칸 ⓐ에 discover를 알맞은 형태로 쓰시오.

➡ _____

21 위 글의 흐름으로 보아, 주어진 문장이 들어가기에 가장 적절한 곳은?

> They can make big islands appear or destroy entire cities like Pompeii.

①   ②   ③   ④   ⑤

중요

22 According to the passage, which is NOT true?

① Jejudo, Sicily, and Hawaii are all islands made from volcanic eruptions.
② Volcanoes are named after Vulcan, the Roman god of fire.
③ We should study and understand volcanoes.
④ Nobody surely knows the exact number of volcanoes in the world.
⑤ According to scientists, there are about 1,500 active volcanoes underwater.

[23~24] 다음 글을 읽고 물음에 답하시오.

A Sudden Volcano

Working on a cornfield one day in 1943, farmers in Mexico found something (A)[surprising / surprised]. A volcano appeared overnight on a flat cornfield. Residents watched the volcano (B)[grow / to grow] over 100 meters tall within a week. The volcano, (C)[calling / called] Paricutin, kept growing, and it finally stopped growing at 424 meters in 1952.

서답형

23 위 글의 괄호 (A)~(C)에서 어법상 알맞은 낱말을 골라 쓰시오.

(A) _____ (B) _____ (C) _____

24 According to the passage, which is NOT true?

① One day farmers in Mexico found something surprising in 1943.
② Paricutin appeared on a flat cornfield during the night.
③ The inhabitants watched Paricutin grow more than 100 meters tall within a week.
④ Paricutin kept growing for over 10 years.
⑤ Paricutin is a 424-meter-high volcano.

[01~03] 다음 글을 읽고 물음에 답하시오.

What do Jejudo, Sicily, and Hawaii have in common? They are islands, of course. (A)In fact, they are all islands made from volcanic ⓐ_____. Volcanoes are very powerful, so they are named after Vulcan, the Roman god of fire. They can make big islands appear or destroy entire cities like Pompeii. Therefore, they should be studied and understood.

01 주어진 영영풀이를 참고하여 빈칸 ⓐ에 철자 e로 시작하는 단어를 쓰시오.

> the sudden occurrences of a violent discharge of steam and volcanic material

➡ _____

02 위 글의 밑줄 친 (A)In fact와 바꿔 쓸 수 있는 말을 쓰시오.

➡ _____

03 Why should volcanoes be studied and understood? Answer in English beginning with "Because".

➡ _____
_____

[04~06] 다음 글을 읽고 물음에 답하시오.

Many of the volcanoes on Earth are located along the Ring of Fire that circles the Pacific Ocean. The ring is about 40,000 kilometers long, and ⓐit is home to around ⓑ75% of the world's active volcanoes. Indonesia alone has over 120 active volcanoes since the country lies on the Ring of Fire. This ring is also the area where most of the world's earthquakes occur.

04 위 글의 밑줄 친 ⓐit이 가리키는 것을 본문에서 찾아 쓰시오.

➡ _____

05 위 글의 밑줄 친 ⓑ75%를 분수로 읽는 법을 쓰시오.

➡ _____

06 How many active volcanoes are there in Indonesia? Answer in English in a full sentence. (8 words)

➡ _____

[07~09] 다음 글을 읽고 물음에 답하시오.

You may think volcanoes can be found only on Earth. However, they have been discovered on (A)[another / other] planets, too, such as Mars and Jupiter. In fact, "Olympus Mons" on Mars (B)[are / is] the largest (C)[knowing / known] volcano in the solar system. ⓐIts volume is about 100 times greater than Mauna Loa, the largest volcano on Earth.

07 위 글의 괄호 (A)~(C)에서 어법상 알맞은 낱말을 골라 쓰시오.

(A) _____ (B) _____ (C) _____

08 위 글의 밑줄 친 ⓐ에서 어법상 틀린 부분을 찾아 고치시오.

⟶ _____

09 Which is larger, Olympus Mons or Mauna Loa? Answer in English. (2 words)

➡ _____

[10~13] 다음 글을 읽고 물음에 답하시오.

(A)화산이 하는 것이 인류에게 항상 나쁜 것만은 아니다, however. The soil near a volcano is good for farming. Volcanoes are also a great tourist attraction. Looking for fantastic scenery, millions of tourists visit Mt. Halla in Jejudo, Mt. Etna in Sicily, or Diamond Head in Hawaii every year. Volcanoes can ____ⓐ____ to produce electricity, too. Iceland, for example, actively turns its volcanoes' heat energy into electricity. Today people around the world are studying ways to live in greater harmony with volcanoes, and they are hopeful that more ways will be found soon.

10 위 글의 밑줄 친 (A)의 우리말에 맞게 주어진 어휘를 이용하여 9 단어로 영작하시오.

what, always, for humans

➡ _____

11 위 글의 빈칸 ⓐ에 use를 알맞은 형태로 쓰시오.

➡ _____

12 위 글을 읽고 화산의 좋은 점 세 가지를 우리말로 쓰시오.

(1) _____
(2) _____
(3) _____

13 다음 문장에서 위 글의 내용과 다른 부분을 찾아서 고치시오.

Iceland actively turns its volcanoes' explosive power into electricity.

➡ _____ ➡ _____

[14~16] 다음 글을 읽고 물음에 답하시오.

You may think volcanoes can be found only on Earth. However, they have been discovered on other planets, too, ⓐsuch as Mars and Jupiter. In fact, "Olympus Mons" on Mars is the largest known volcano in the solar system. Its volume is about ⓑ100 times greater than that of Mauna Loa, the largest volcano on Earth.

14 위 글의 밑줄 친 ⓐsuch as와 바꿔 쓸 수 있는 한 단어를 쓰시오.

➡ _____

15 위 글의 밑줄 친 ⓑ를 다음과 같이 바꿔 쓸 때 빈칸에 들어갈 알맞은 말을 세 단어로 쓰시오.

100 times _____

16 본문의 내용과 일치하도록 다음 빈칸에 알맞은 단어를 쓰시오.

Volcanoes can be found not only on Earth but also on _____.

My Speaking Portfolio Step 1

a. The electricity is out.

b. The pan caught on fire.
   불이 붙었다

c. I got stuck in the elevator.
   (엘리베이터 등에) 갇혔다

d. I burned my finger in hot water.

e. I fell down the steps and broke my arm.
   넘어졌다

구문해설 • **electricity** 전기 • **burn** 데우다, 화상을 입다

해석

a. 정전됐어요.

b. 프라이팬에 불이 붙었어요.

c. 나는 엘리베이터에 갇혔어요.

d. 나는 뜨거운 물에 손을 데었어요.

e. 나는 계단에서 넘어져서 팔이 부러졌어요.

After You Read Details

The name "volcano" comes from the Roman god of fire. – Mila

75% of the world's active volcanoes are located along the Ring of Fire. – James
부분을 나타내는 말은 다음에 나오는 명사의 수에 동사를 일치시킨다. is(✗)

The volcano Paricutin in Mexico stopped growing. – Lucy
                                    stop+~ing: ~하기를 멈추다

The eruption of Mt. Tambora brought about an unusually cold summer in
                              bring about: ~을 초래하다
1816. – David

구문해설 • **active**: 활동 중인 • **locate**: ~의 위치를 찾아내다 • **ring**: 고리, 반지 • **eruption**: 분출

"화산"이라는 이름은 로마의 불의 신에게서 이름을 따왔다. – Mila

전 세계 활화산의 75%는 '불의 고리(환태평양조산대)'를 따라 위치한다. – James

멕시코의 Paricutin 화산은 성장을 멈추었다. – Lucy

Tambora산의 분출은 1816년에 비정상적으로 추운 여름을 초래했다. – David

My Writing Portfolio

The Perfect Storm

I saw the movie *The Perfect Storm* last weekend. The movie came out in 2000,
                                                                    연도 앞에 전치사 in
and it was directed by the German director Wolfgang Petersen. It is about a
         수동태   ~에 관한
big storm in the Atlantic Ocean that put a fishing boat in danger. I liked the
                                  주격 관계대명사
movie because the scenes were exciting and very realistic. Also, I liked the
                        감정동사가 감정을 유발하는 경우 현재분사
good acting of the leading actor George Clooney. From the movie, I learned
that natural disasters like storms can be very dangerous.
명사절 접속사   ~ 같은(전치사)

구문해설 • **storm**: 폭풍(우) • **direct**: (영화·연극 따위를) 감독하다 • **the Atlantic Ocean**: 대서양
       • **scene**: 장면 • **realistic**: 현실적인, 사실적인 • **leading actor**: 주연 배우
       • **natural disaster**: 자연재해

퍼펙트 스톰

나는 지난 주말에 영화 '퍼펙트 스톰'을 봤다. 그 영화는 2000년에 개봉했고, 독일 감독 Wolfgang Petersen이 연출했다. 그것은 어선을 위험에 빠뜨린 대서양의 거대한 폭풍에 관한 것이다. 나는 장면들이 흥미진진하고 매우 사실적이었기 때문에 이 영화가 좋았다. 또한, 나는 주연 배우 George Clooney의 훌륭한 연기도 마음에 들었다. 이 영화를 통해 나는 폭풍과 같은 자연재해가 매우 위험할 수 있다는 것을 배웠다.

영역별 핵심문제

01 다음 짝지어진 단어의 관계가 같도록 빈칸에 알맞은 말을 쓰시오.

> destroy : destruction = discover : _____

02 다음 중 밑줄 친 부분의 뜻풀이가 바르지 않은 것은?

① A big typhoon is coming to Korea. (태풍)
② A powerful earthquake hit Indonesia last summer. (덮쳤다, 엄습했다)
③ A yellow dust warning was issued this morning. (경고)
④ The government issued a statement on current economic problems. (경고했다)
⑤ The rainfall has been below average this year. (강우량)

03 다음 우리말을 주어진 단어를 이용하여 영작하시오.

(1) 다른 행성에 생명체가 있을 수도 있다. (there, may)
➡ _____

(2) 올 여름에는 호우가 예상된다. (heavy)
➡ _____

(3) 우리 태양계에는 8개의 행성이 있다. (are, there)
➡ _____

04 다음 주어진 문장의 밑줄 친 volume과 같은 의미로 쓰인 것은?

> I will explain how to calculate the volume of this box.

① Kathy gave me her latest volume of poetry.
② Please turn the volume down.

③ Sugar is sold by weight, not volume.
④ I used to listen to rock music at full volume.
⑤ The volume control of a CD player is broken down.

05 우리말과 일치하도록 주어진 어구를 배열하여 영작하시오.

(1) 집에 있는 모든 것들이 화재 후에 재로 변하였다.
(the fire / the house / everything / into / in / ash / after / turned)
➡ _____

(2) 방바닥이 먼지로 덮여 있었다.
(the room / with / the floor / covered / dust / was / of)
➡ _____

(3) 올해 농부들은 풍작을 기대한다.
(this / a / farmers / have / expect / crop / year / good / to)
➡ _____

06 다음 주어진 문장의 밑줄 친 issue와 같은 의미로 쓰인 것은?

> A tornado warnings have been issued.

① We issue a monthly newsletter.
② In my plan, money is not an issue.
③ This is a big issue, so we need more time to think about it.
④ She usually writes about health issues.
⑤ You're just avoiding the issue.

Conversation

[07~08] 다음 글을 읽고 물음에 답하시오.

M: Hi, this is Cha Gisang from the Weather Station. Here is today's weather. Typhoon Doni is ⓐmoving north and is going to hit Jejudo tonight. A typhoon ⓑwarning has been issued. There will be lots of rainfall with a high chance of ⓒflooding in some areas. Please stay ⓓoutside because Typhoon Doni will come with strong winds. Also, please make sure you keep ⓔlistening to our reports. Thank you.

07 위 글의 밑줄 친 ⓐ~ⓔ에서 내용의 흐름상 어색한 곳을 찾아 바르게 고치시오.

➡ _____

08 위 글의 내용과 일치하는 것은?

① Typhoon Doni is moving south.
② Typhoon Doni is coming with heavy snow.
③ Cha Gisang is talking about tomorrow's weather.
④ Typhoon Doni will bring strong winds and lots of rainfall.
⑤ People are asked to watch the news about Jejudo.

[09~11] 다음 대화를 읽고 물음에 답하시오.

(*The phone rings.*)
Junho: Hi, Mom.
Mom: Hi, Junho. Are you having a good time with Dad?
Junho: Yeah. Today we visited Dokdo.

Mom: That sounds cool. What are you going to do tomorrow?
Junho: We're going fishing on a boat.
Mom: Great. Please make sure you wear a _____(A)_____ .
Junho: Okay, Mom. _____(B)_____

09 위 대화의 빈칸 (A)에 '구명조끼'를 나타내는 표현을 쓰시오.

➡ _____

10 위 대화의 빈칸 (B)에 들어갈 말로 적절한 것은?

① I'll keep that in mind.
② Thank you for your great efforts.
③ I'm sorry, but I can't.
④ Of course not.
⑤ No, not at all.

11 위 대화에서 알 수 있는 준호의 기분으로 적절한 것은?

① worried   ② nervous
③ excited   ④ disappointed
⑤ frightened

[12~13] 다음 대화를 읽고 물음에 답하시오.

Grandma: (A)Can you do me a favor? (hand, give)
Jack: Sure, Grandma. What is it?
Grandma: I want to go to the Tom Dylan concert on Christmas. Can you buy some tickets for me?
Jack: No problem. How many tickets do you want?
Grandma: Two tickets, please.

12 위 대화의 밑줄 친 (A)와 의도가 같도록 주어진 단어를 사용하여 다시 쓰시오.

➡ _____

13 위 대화의 내용과 일치하지 <u>않는</u> 것은?

① 할머니는 Jack에게 부탁할 것이 있다.
② 할머니는 Tom Dylan의 콘서트에 가고 싶어 하신다.
③ 할머니는 Jack에게 콘서트 표를 구매해 줄 것을 부탁하였다.
④ 할머니는 두 장의 표를 구매하기를 원하신다.
⑤ 할머니는 Jack과 함께 크리스마스에 콘서트에 가고 싶어 하신다.

14 다음 중 짝지어진 대화가 <u>어색한</u> 것을 고르시오.

① A: Remember that you must not taste or smell chemicals.
 B: OK. I will.
② A: Make sure you should take off your shoes before entering the room.
 B: Never mind. Cheer up!
③ A: Be sure you wear a helmet when you ride your bike.
 B: Sure, but now I'm going out to hike.
④ A: Make sure you are patient and kind.
 B: Okay. I'll keep that in mind.
⑤ A: Make certain that you don't run.
 B: Sure. No problem.

Grammar

15 다음 중 어법상 <u>어색한</u> 문장을 고르시오.

① A flying car will be developed in the near future.
② The work should be finished by 7 p.m.
③ Lions and tigers are belonged to the cat family.
④ Today people around the world are studying ways to live in greater harmony with volcanoes, and they are hopeful that more ways will be found soon.
⑤ Phones must be turned off.

16 다음 문장을 바꾸어 쓸 때 가장 적절한 것은?

> Getting up late, I rode my bike to school.

① I got up late, for I rode my bike to school.
② I rode my bike to school, and I got up late.
③ I got up late, or I rode my bike to school.
④ If I got up late, I rode my bike to school.
⑤ Because I got up late, I rode my bike to school.

17 수동태로 바꾼 문장 중 <u>틀린</u> 것은?

① We have to take him to hospital to get treated.
 → He has to be taken to hospital to get treated.
② My uncle will pick up John.
 → John is picked up by my uncle.
③ They cannot fix my bike today.
 → My bike cannot be fixed today by them.
④ Should you clean the shoes quickly?
 → Should the shoes be cleaned quickly by you?
⑤ People may use art as a vehicle for advertisement.
 → Art may be used as a vehicle for advertisement.

18 다음 중 어법상 올바른 문장을 고르시오.

① Ridden in a flying car, you will be able to go places faster.
② Having not much work to do, I have time to see a movie.
③ The sun rose, we made wishes.
④ Singing and dance together, we had a great time.
⑤ Having appeared overnight, Paricutin is a sudden volcano.

19 다음 그림을 보고, 주어진 어휘를 이용하여 빈칸을 알맞게 채우시오.

_____ out, Emily stopped studying math. (the electricity)

20 다음 빈칸에 알맞은 말이 순서대로 짝지어진 것은?

- He made dinner, _____ a baseball game.
- The energy inside the earth _____ in different ways.

① watches – can be felt
② watches – can feel
③ watching – can be felt
④ watching – can is felt
⑤ to watch – is can felt

Reading

[21~23] 다음 글을 읽고 물음에 답하시오.

Nobody knows for sure how many volcanoes there are in the world. According to scientists, there are about 1,500 active volcanoes above sea level. Many more are underwater, and they are hard to locate. ⓐStill, scientists ⓑhave discovered a large number of them ⓒso far.

21 위 글의 밑줄 친 ⓐStill과 같은 의미로 쓰인 것을 고르시오.

① I wrote to them last month and I'm still waiting for a reply.
② The next day was still warmer.
③ The weather was cold and wet. Still, we had a great time.
④ Keep still while I brush your hair.
⑤ It was, and still is, my favourite movie.

22 위 글의 밑줄 친 ⓑhave discovered와 현재완료 용법이 같은 것을 모두 고르시오.

① She has just come.
② How long have you studied English?
③ He has lost his watch.
④ He has watched the movie twice.
⑤ She has been sick since last Friday.

23 위 글의 밑줄 친 ⓒso far와 바꿔 쓸 수 있는 말을 두 단어로 쓰시오.

➡ _____

[24~25] 다음 글을 읽고 물음에 답하시오.

ⓐ _____

Working on a cornfield one day in 1943, farmers in Mexico found something surprising. A volcano appeared overnight on a flat cornfield. Residents watched the volcano grow over 100 meters tall within a week. The volcano, called Paricutin, kept _____ⓑ_____, and it finally stopped growing at 424 meters in 1952.

24 위 글의 빈칸 ⓐ에 들어갈 제목으로 가장 알맞은 것을 고르시오.

① The Origin of a Volcano
② The Proper Condition for Volcanic Formation
③ A Sudden Volcano
④ The Reason Paricutin Kept Growing
⑤ The Highest Volcano in the World

25 위 글의 빈칸 ⓑ에 grow를 알맞은 형태로 쓰시오.

➡ _____

[26~28] 다음 글을 읽고 물음에 답하시오.

ⓐBeing very powerful and dangerous, volcanoes do harm ___①___ people ___②___ many ways. Sometimes people get hurt, or they may lose their houses. Crops may be destroyed, and air traffic can be threatened. Volcanoes can also have serious effects ___③___ world weather. A volcanic eruption shoots lots of ash and dust ___④___ the air, preventing some of the sunlight ___⑤___ reaching Earth and thus disturbing usual weather patterns.

26 위 글의 빈칸 ①~⑤에 들어갈 전치사로 옳지 않은 것은?

① to   ② in
③ on   ④ into
⑤ with

27 위 글의 밑줄 친 분사구문 ⓐ를 부사절로 고치시오.

➡ _____

28 위 글에서 설명하고 있는 화산이 끼치는 해에 속하지 <u>않는</u> 것을 고르시오.

① 사람들을 다치게 하고 집을 잃게 한다.
② 작물을 파괴하고 항공 교통을 위협한다.
③ 세계의 날씨에 심각한 영향을 미친다.
④ 다량의 용암을 분출시킨다.
⑤ 정상적인 기상 패턴을 깨뜨린다.

[29~30] 다음 글을 읽고 물음에 답하시오.

I saw the movie *The Perfect Storm* last weekend. The movie came out in 2000, and it was directed by the German director Wolfgang Petersen. It is about a big storm in the Atlantic Ocean that put a fishing boat in danger. I liked the movie because the scenes were exciting and very realistic. Also, I liked the good acting of the leading actor George Clooney. From the movie, I learned that natural disasters like storms can be very dangerous.

29 위 글의 종류로 알맞은 것을 고르시오.

① article   ② review   ③ essay
④ summary   ⑤ book report

30 위 글을 읽고 알 수 <u>없는</u> 것을 고르시오.

① What is the title of the movie?
② Who is the director?
③ When did the movie come out?
④ What is the movie about?
⑤ With whom did the writer see the movie?

출제율 95%

01 다음 영영풀이가 가리키는 것을 고르시오.

> a sudden shaking of Earth's surface

① ash ② earthquake

③ eruption ④ dust

⑤ planet

출제율 90%

02 다음 우리말에 맞게 빈칸에 알맞은 말을 쓰시오.

(1) 지진은 도시에 있는 집과 건물의 60%를 파괴했다.

➡ The _____ _____ 60% of houses and buildings in the city.

(2) 신체 활동이 뇌에 미치는 효과는 굉장하다.

➡ The _____ of _____ exercise on the brain is great.

(3) 섬에 도착했을 때, 화산이 분출하기 시작했다.

➡ When we arrived at the island, the _____ started to _____.

[03~04] 다음 글을 읽고 물음에 답하시오.

M: Hi, this is Cha Gisang from the Weather Station. Here is today's weather. Typhoon Doni is moving north and is going to hit Jejudo tonight. A typhoon warning has been (A)[issuing / issued]. There will be lots of rainfall with a high chance of flooding in some areas. Please stay inside (B)[because / because of] Typhoon Doni will come with strong winds. Also, please make sure you keep (C)[to listen / listening] to our reports. Thank you.

출제율 90%

03 위 글을 읽고 (A)~(C)에 알맞은 말이 바르게 짝지어진 것은?

	(A)	(B)	(C)
①	issuing	because	to listen
②	issuing	because of	listening
③	issued	because	listening
④	issued	because of	listening
⑤	issued	because	to listen

출제율 100%

04 위 글을 읽고 대답할 수 <u>없는</u> 것은?

① What does Cha Gisang do?

② Where is a typhoon moving toward?

③ What has been issued?

④ What does Cha Gisang ask to do?

⑤ When will it stop raining?

[05~06] 다음 대화를 읽고 물음에 답하시오.

(*The phone rings.*)

Junho: Hi, Mom.

Mom: Hi, Junho. Are you having a good time with Dad?

Junho: Yeah. Today we visited Dokdo.

Mom: That sounds cool. What are you going to do tomorrow?

Junho: We're going fishing on a boat.

Mom: Great. Please make sure you wear a life jacket.

Junho: Okay, Mom. I'll keep that in mind.

출제율 95%

05 What did Junho do with his father today?

➡ _____

출제율 90%

06 What should Junho make sure when he goes fishing?

➡ _____

[07~08] 다음 대화를 읽고 물음에 답하시오.

Brian: Jimin, are you going ⓐout?

Jimin: Yeah. I'm going to buy ⓑsome sandwiches at Choi's.

Brian: Are you walking there?

Jimin: No. I'll ride my bike.

Brian: That's good. Can you do me ⓒa favor?

Jimin: Sure. What is it?

Brian: Can you buy chocolate ice cream for me ⓓon your way back?

Jimin: No problem.

Brian: Thanks. Please make sure you ⓔto wear a helmet and no ear phones!

Jimin: Don't worry about that.

출제율 90%

07 위 대화의 밑줄 친 ⓐ~ⓔ 중 어법상 어색한 것을 찾아 바르게 고치시오.

➡ _____

출제율 95%

08 위 대화의 내용과 일치하지 <u>않는</u> 것은?

① 지민이는 샌드위치를 사러 외출한다.

② 지민이는 자전거를 타고 '최가네'에 갈 것이다.

③ Brian은 지민이에게 돌아오는 길에 초콜릿 아이스크림을 사다 줄 것을 부탁하였다.

④ Brian은 지민이에게 헬멧을 쓰고 이어폰을 낄 것을 당부하였다.

⑤ 지민이는 Brian에게 걱정하지 말라고 안심시켰다.

[09~10] 다음 대화를 읽고 물음에 답하시오.

Brian: Sora, (A)<u>부탁 좀 들어줄래?</u> (favor, can)

Sora: What is it, Dad?

Dad: A typhoon is coming tonight. Can you bring in the clothes from outside?

Sora: No problem. What about your bike?

Dad: I'll take care of it after I finish the dishes.

Sora: Okay. Do you want me to call Grandma and tell her about the typhoon?

Dad: Yes. Please tell her to stay home.

Sora: Okay, Dad.

출제율 90%

09 위 대화의 밑줄 친 (A)의 우리말을 주어진 단어들을 사용하여 영작하시오.

➡ _____

출제율 100%

10 위 대화의 내용과 일치하지 <u>않는</u> 것은?

① 오늘 밤 태풍이 온다.

② 아빠는 소라에게 옷가지들을 바깥으로 내놓을 것을 요청했다.

③ 자전거는 아빠가 설거지를 한 후 처리할 것이다.

④ 아빠는 소라가 할머니에게 전화하기를 원하신다.

⑤ 소라는 할머니에게 집안에 계시라고 말씀드릴 것이다.

출제율 95%

11 다음 그림을 보고, 주어진 어휘를 이용하여 빈칸을 알맞게 채우시오.

When the pan caught on fire, what _____? (be, should)

12 다음 중 어법상 어색한 문장을 고르시오.

① This book must be returned by Nov. 30.
② They produce heat energy that can is turned into electricity.
③ The project will be completed soon.
④ The disease may be infected.
⑤ Foods should be kept cool.

13 다음 주어진 문장을 분사구문을 써서 바꿔 쓰시오.

> While he was listening to music, he read the novel he had bought the other day.

➡ _____

_____

14 다음 ⓐ~ⓗ 중 어법상 옳은 것을 모두 고르시오.

> ⓐ Felt tired, I went to bed early.
> ⓑ Having not enough time, I was unable to finish my homework in time.
> ⓒ Being Sunday, most shops were closed.
> ⓓ The airplane was flying in the sky, making a big noise.
> ⓔ A new school uniform must design soon.
> ⓕ You may think volcanoes can be found only on Earth.
> ⓖ The matter will discuss tomorrow.
> ⓗ The news will known to the classmates soon.

➡ _____

[15~17] 다음 글을 읽고 물음에 답하시오.

Many of the volcanoes on Earth are located along the Ring of Fire that circles the Pacific Ocean. The ring is about 40,000 kilometers long, and it is home to ⓐaround 75% of the world's active volcanoes. Indonesia alone has over 120 active volcanoes since the country lies on the Ring of Fire. ⓑThis ring is also the area where most of the world's earthquakes occurs.

15 위 글의 밑줄 친 ⓐaround와 같은 의미로 쓰인 것을 고르시오.

① I could hear laughter all around.
② He arrived around five o'clock.
③ He put his arms around her.
④ We were all running around trying to get ready in time.
⑤ I can't arrange everything around your timetable!

16 위 글의 밑줄 친 ⓑ에서 어법상 틀린 부분을 찾아 고치시오.

_____ ➡ _____

17 Which question CANNOT be answered after reading the passage?

① Where are many of the volcanoes on Earth located?
② How long is the Ring of Fire that circles the Pacific Ocean?
③ How often do the active volcanoes erupt in Indonesia?
④ Why are there many active volcanoes in Indonesia?
⑤ Where do most of the world's earthquakes occur?

[18~19] 다음 글을 읽고 물음에 답하시오.

You may think volcanoes can be found only on Earth. ___ⓐ___, they have been discovered on other planets, too, such as Mars and Jupiter. ___ⓑ___, "Olympus Mons" on Mars is the largest known volcano in the solar system. Its volume is about 100 times greater than that of Mauna Loa, the largest volcano on Earth

✎ 출제율 100%

18 위 글의 빈칸 ⓐ와 ⓑ에 들어갈 말이 바르게 짝지어진 것은?

① However – Therefore
② In addition – In fact
③ In fact – However
④ For example – On the other hand
⑤ However – In fact

✎ 출제율 95%

19 According to the passage, which is NOT true?

① Volcanoes can be found only on Earth.
② "Olympus Mons" is on Mars.
③ "Olympus Mons" is the largest known volcano in the solar system.
④ "Mauna Loa" is not so large as "Olympus Mons".
⑤ "Mauna Loa" is the largest volcano on Earth.

[20~21] 다음 글을 읽고 물음에 답하시오.

___ⓐ___ volcanoes do is not always bad for humans, however. The soil near a volcano is good for farming. Volcanoes are also a great tourist attraction. Looking for fantastic scenery, millions of tourists visit Mt. Halla in Jejudo, Mt. Etna in Sicily, or Diamond Head in Hawaii every year. ⓑVolcanoes can use to

produce electricity, too. Iceland, for example, actively turns its volcanoes' heat energy into electricity.

✎ 출제율 90%

20 위 글의 빈칸 ⓐ에 들어갈 알맞은 말을 고르시오.

① How   ② Which   ③ That
④ What   ⑤ Why

✎ 출제율 90%

21 위 글의 밑줄 친 ⓑ에서 어법상 어색한 것을 고치시오.

_____ ➡ _____

[22~23] 다음 글을 읽고 물음에 답하시오.

The energy inside the earth can be felt in different ways. First, we can see this energy in volcanoes. (①) Another way to feel the earth's power is to visit a hot spring. (②) ⓐThis is a spring of water which is usually heated by volcanic activity. (③) People say that hot spring do us good. (④) They help relieve stress and can bring on a good night's sleep. (⑤) The earth's energy is both amazing and helpful.

✎ 출제율 90%

22 위 글의 흐름으로 보아, 주어진 문장이 들어가기에 가장 적절한 곳은?

As the hot rock comes out of the earth, it changes the ground and makes hills and mountains.

①   ②   ③   ④   ⑤

✎ 출제율 95%

23 위 글의 밑줄 친 ⓐThis가 가리키는 것을 본문에서 찾아 쓰시오.

➡ _____

서술형 실전문제

다음 대화를 읽고 물음에 답하시오.

> Brian: Jimin, are you going out?
>
> Jimin: Yeah. I'm going to buy some sandwiches at Choi's.
>
> Brian: Are you walking there?
>
> Jimin: No. I'll ride my bike.
>
> Brian: That's good. Can you do me a favor?
>
> Jimin: Sure. What is it?
>
> Brian: Can you buy chocolate ice cream for me on your way back?
>
> Jimin: No problem.
>
> Brian: Thanks. Please make sure you wear a helmet and no ear phones!
>
> Jimin: Don't worry about that.

01 Where is Jimin going now and why? (Answer with 9 words.)

➡ _____

02 What does Brian ask Jimin to do?

➡ _____

_____

03 What should Jimin keep in mind?

➡ _____

_____

04 분사구문은 부사절로, 부사절은 분사구문으로 바꿔 쓰시오.

(1) Walking home after school, Tom found a soccer ball on the street.

➡ _____

_____

(2) Sleeping on the bus, I missed my stop.

➡ _____

_____

(3) He started to cry as he admitted his fault.

➡ _____

_____

(4) As it was not so cold outside, she went out without a coat.

➡ _____

_____

05 다음 우리말을 괄호 안에 주어진 어휘를 활용하여 영작하시오.

(1) 그녀는 부모님께 손을 흔들며 집을 떠났다.
(leave, wave, at)

➡ _____

(2) 나는 피곤해서 평소보다 일찍 집에 왔다.
(feel, early, usual)

➡ _____

(3) 이 프로젝트는 오늘까지 마무리될 수 없다.
(this project, finish, by)

➡ _____

(4) 연주회는 다음 주에 열릴 것이다.
(the concert, hold)

➡ _____

06 다음 문장을 수동태는 능동태로, 능동태는 수동태로 바꾸어 쓰시오.

(1) School rules must be followed by all students.

➡ _____

(2) The project should be finished tonight.

➡ _____

(3) Who will solve the problem?

➡ _____

(4) You can add eggs and cheese according to your taste.

➡ _____

_____

[07~09] 다음 글을 읽고 물음에 답하시오.

ⓐ세계에 얼마나 많은 화산이 있는지 누구도 정확히 알지 못한다. According to scientists, there are about ⓑ1,500 active volcanoes above sea level. Many more are underwater, and ⓒ they are hard to locate. Still, scientists have discovered a large number of them so far.

07 위 글의 밑줄 친 ⓐ의 우리말에 맞게 주어진 어휘를 알맞게 배열하시오.

how many volcanoes / are / knows / in the world / for sure / nobody / there

➡ _____

_____

08 위 글의 밑줄 친 ⓑ1,500을 영어로 읽는 법을 쓰시오.

➡ _____

09 위 글의 밑줄 친 ⓒ를 다음과 같이 바꿔 쓸 때 빈칸에 들어갈 알맞은 말을 한 단어를 쓰시오.

it is hard to locate _____

[10~12] 다음 글을 읽고 물음에 답하시오.

Being very powerful and dangerous, volcanoes do harm to people in many ways. Sometimes people get hurt, or they may lose their houses. Crops may be destroyed, and air traffic can be threatened. ⓐVolcanoes can also have serious effects on world weather. A volcanic eruption shoots lots of ash and dust into the air, ⓑpreventing some of the sunlight from reaching Earth and thus disturbing usual weather patterns.

10 위 글의 밑줄 친 ⓐ를 다음과 같이 바꿔 쓸 때 빈칸에 공통으로 들어갈 알맞은 한 단어를 쓰시오.

• Volcanoes can also have serious _____s on world weather.
• Volcanoes can also _____ world weather seriously.

11 위 글의 밑줄 친 분사구문 ⓑ를 절로 고치시오.

and _____ _____ some of the sunlight from reaching Earth and thus _____ usual weather patterns

12 본문의 내용과 일치하도록 다음 빈칸 (A)와 (B)에 알맞은 단어를 쓰시오.

Volcanoes can hurt people and destroy (A)_____ as well as houses. They can also threaten (B)_____ _____ and change world weather.

창의사고력 서술형 문제

01 다음 대화의 내용과 일치하도록 빈칸을 완성하시오.

Brian: Jimin, are you going out?

Jimin: Yeah. I'm going to buy some sandwiches at Choi's.

Brian: Are you walking there?

Jimin: No. I'll ride my bike.

Brian: That's good. Can you do me a favor?

Jimin: Sure. What is it?

Brian: Can you buy chocolate ice cream for me on your way back?

Jimin: No problem.

Brian: Thanks. Please make sure you wear a helmet and no ear phones!

Jimin: Don't worry about that.

▼

Jimin is going to Choi's by (A)_____ to buy (B)_____. Brian asks her to (C)_____ for him on her way back. Brian reminds her that she should (D)_____.

02 다음 내용을 바탕으로 영화 'The Perfect Storm'의 감상문을 쓰시오.

- What is the title of the movie? – *The Perfect Storm*
- Who is the director? – Wolfgang Petersen
- When did the movie come out? – 2000
- What is the movie about? – a big storm in the Atlantic Ocean that put a fishing boat in danger
- What do you like about the movie? – • exciting and realistic scenes • the good acting of the leading actor
- What did you learn from the movie? – natural disasters can be very dangerous

The Perfect Storm

I saw the movie (A)_____ last weekend. The movie came out (B)_____, and it was directed by the German director (C)_____. It is about (D)_____. I liked the movie because the scenes were exciting and very realistic. Also, I liked the (E)_____ of the leading actor George Clooney. From the movie, I learned that (F)_____ like storms can be very dangerous.

단원별 모의고사

01 다음 영영풀이가 가리키는 것은?

> a large round object in space that moves around a star

① Mars   ② planet
③ Jupiter   ④ eruption
⑤ typhoon

02 다음 주어진 어휘 중 성격이 나머지와 다른 것은?

① typhoon   ② earthquake
③ snowstorm   ④ heat wave
⑤ solar system

03 다음 문장의 빈칸에 들어갈 말을 〈보기〉에서 골라 쓰시오.

> ┌─ 보기 ┤
> favor / volcano / chance / flooding / area

(1) Sodam Park is closed today because of _____.

(2) There is little _____ of rain tomorrow morning.

(3) I am familiar with this _____.

(4) I want to ask you a _____.

(5) _____ s are major tourist attractions in the region.

[04~05] 다음 대화를 읽고 물음에 답하시오.

Grandma: Can you do me a favor?
Jack: Sure, Grandma. What is it?
Grandma: I want to go to the Tom Dylan concert on Christmas. Can you buy some tickets for me?
Jack: No problem. _____(A)_____ (want, many)
Grandma: Two tickets, please.

04 위 대화의 빈칸 (A)에 들어갈 질문을 주어진 단어를 사용하여 영작하시오.

➡ _____

05 위 대화의 내용과 일치하지 않는 것은?

① Grandma needs Jack's help.
② Grandma wants to enjoy the Tom Dylan concert on Christmas.
③ Grandma wants Jack to buy tickets for her.
④ Grandma needs two tickets of the Tom Dylan concert.
⑤ Grandma is in favor of Jack's plan for Christmas.

[06~08] 다음 대화를 읽고 물음에 답하시오.

Dad: Sora, can you do me a favor?
Sora: What is it, Dad?
Dad: A typhoon is coming tonight. Can you bring in the clothes from outside?
Sora: No problem. What about your bike?
Dad: I'll take care of it after I finish the dishes.
Sora: Okay. Do you want me to call Grandma and tell her about the typhoon?
Dad: Yes. Please tell her to stay home.
Sora: Okay, Dad.

06 What does Dad want Sora to do?

➡ _____
_____

07 What is Dad going to do after washing the dishes?

➡ _____

08 What will Sora tell her grandma to do?

➡ _____

09 다음 대화가 자연스럽게 이어지도록 순서대로 배열하시오.

> Dad: Jimin, are you going out?
>
> Jimin: Yeah. I'm going to buy some sandwiches at Choi's.
>
> Brian: Are you walking there?
>
> (A) No problem.
>
> (B) No. I'll ride my bike.
>
> (C) Sure. What is it?
>
> (D) That's good. Can you do me a favor?
>
> (E) Can you buy chocolate ice cream for me on your way back?

➡ _____

[10~11] 다음 대화를 읽고 물음에 답하시오.

> (*The phone rings.*)
>
> Junho: Hi, Mom.
>
> Mom: Hi, Junho. Are you having a good time with Dad?
>
> Junho: Yeah. Today we visited Dokdo.
>
> Mom: That sounds cool. What are you going to do tomorrow?
>
> Junho: We're going fishing on a boat.
>
> Mom: Great. (A)Please make sure you wear a life jacket.
>
> Junho: Okay, Mom. I'll keep that in mind.

10 위 대화의 밑줄 친 (A)와 바꾸어 쓰기에 어색한 것은?

① Don't forget to wear a life jacket.

② Please remember that you should wear a life jacket.

③ Be sure to wear a life jacket.

④ I'm wondering if you wear a life jacket.

⑤ Please make certain that you should wear a life jacket.

11 위 대화의 내용과 일치하지 <u>않는</u> 것은?

① 준호는 아빠와 좋은 시간을 보내고 있다.

② 준호는 아빠와 독도를 방문했다.

③ 준호는 내일 낚시를 갈 것이다.

④ 엄마는 준호에게 구명조끼를 입을 것을 당부했다.

⑤ 준호는 내일 부모님과 함께 보트를 탈 것이다.

12 다음 대화가 자연스럽게 이어지도록 순서대로 배열하시오.

> Dad: Sora, can you do me a favor?
>
> Sora: What is it, Dad?
>
> (A) I'll take care of it after I finish the dishes.
>
> (B) No problem. What about your bike?
>
> (C) Yes. Please tell her to stay home.
>
> (D) Okay. Do you want me to call Grandma and tell her about the typhoon?
>
> (E) A typhoon is coming tonight. Can you bring in the clothes from outside?
>
> Sora: Okay, Dad.

➡ _____

13 다음 두 문장의 의미가 같도록 빈칸을 완성하시오.

(1) We can use volcanoes to produce electricity.

= Volcanoes _____ to produce electricity.

(2) We should not allow young children to use smartphones.

= Young children _____ to use smartphones.

(3) They will build a tourist information center next year.

= A tourist information center _____ _____ next year.

14 다음 중 어법상 옳은 문장을 고르시오. (2개)

① Walked down the street, Sora met her PE teacher.

② Working on a cornfield one day in 1943, farmers in Mexico found something surprising.

③ Very powerful and dangerous, volcanoes do harm to people in many ways.

④ Homework should be handed in by Friday.

⑤ Therefore, they should study and understood.

15 다음 우리말을 주어진 어휘를 이용하여 영작하시오.

(1) 피자가 30분 내로 배달될 것이다.
(the pizza, deliver, within, 8 단어)

➡ _____

(2) 그 문제는 즉시 해결되어야 한다.
(the problem, should, now, solve, 7 단어)

➡ _____

(3) Dana는 시장을 향해 걷다가 우연히 역사 선생님을 만났다. (to the market, her history teacher, come across, 10 단어)

➡ _____
_____

(4) 추위를 느껴서 Susan은 그녀의 코트를 입었다.
(her coat, cold, put, 7 단어)

➡ _____

16 Which is grammatically WRONG? Select ALL.

① This medicine must taken after meal.

② The library will be closed during lunch break to encourage students to go outdoors and play sports.

③ Finding his mom, the little boy quickly ran to her.

④ Tina sat back in the sofa, closed her eyes.

⑤ A volcanic eruption shoots lots of ash and dust into the air, preventing some of the sunlight from reaching Earth and thus disturbing usual weather patterns.

17 다음 문장에서 어법상 어색한 것을 바르게 고쳐 다시 쓰시오.

(1) Food and drinks must not brought into the library.

➡ _____
_____

(2) The computer should fix Mr. Hinkle.

➡ _____

(3) Tiring after the game, the players took a rest for a while.

➡ _____
_____

(4) Having not any money, I borrowed some from my older brother.

➡ _____
_____

[18~19] 다음 글을 읽고 물음에 답하시오.

Many of the volcanoes on Earth are located along the Ring of Fire that circles the Pacific Ocean. The ring is about 40,000 kilometers long, and it is home to around 75% of the world's active volcanoes. Indonesia alone has over 120 active volcanoes (A)since the country lies on the Ring of Fire. This ring is also the area ____ⓐ____ most of the world's earthquakes occur.

18 위 글의 빈칸 ⓐ에 들어갈 알맞은 말을 고르시오.

① which ② when ③ why
④ where ⑤ how

19 위 글의 밑줄 친 (A)since와 같은 의미로 쓰인 것을 고르시오.

① She hasn't phoned me since she went to Berlin.
② I did it since he told me to.
③ How long is it since we last went there?
④ I've been busy since I came here.
⑤ It's twenty years since she came up to Seoul.

[20~21] 다음 글을 읽고 물음에 답하시오.

What volcanoes do is not always bad for humans, however. The soil near a volcano is good (A)[at / for] farming. Volcanoes are also a great tourist attraction. Looking for fantastic scenery, millions of tourists visit Mt. Halla in Jejudo, Mt. Etna in Sicily, or Diamond Head in Hawaii every year. Volcanoes can be used to (B)[produce / producing] electricity, too. Iceland, for example, actively turns its volcanoes' heat energy into electricity. Today people around the world are studying ways to live in greater (C)[conflict / harmony] with volcanoes, and they are hopeful that more ways will be found soon.

20 위 글의 괄호 (A)~(C)에서 문맥이나 어법상 알맞은 낱말을 골라 쓰시오.

(A) _____ (B) _____ (C) _____

21 According to the passage, which is NOT true?

① What volcanoes do is sometimes good for humans.
② The soil near a volcano is suitable for farming.
③ It's impossible to produce electricity by using volcanoes.
④ Iceland actively turns its volcanoes' heat energy into electricity.
⑤ People are hopeful that more ways will be found soon.

[22~23] 다음 글을 읽고 물음에 답하시오.

A Sudden Volcano

Working on a cornfield one day in 1943, farmers in Mexico found something surprising. A volcano appeared overnight on a flat cornfield. ⓐ주민들은 그 화산이 일주일도 못 되는 사이에 100미터 넘게 자라는 것을 지켜보았다. The volcano, called Paricutin, kept growing, and it ⓑfinally stopped growing at 424 meters in 1952.

22 위 글의 밑줄 친 ⓐ의 우리말에 맞게 주어진 어휘를 이용하여 12 단어로 영작하시오.

residents, watched, grow, over, within

➡ _____
_____

23 위 글의 밑줄 친 ⓑfinally와 바꿔 쓸 수 없는 말을 고르시오.

① all at once ② eventually ③ at last
④ in the end ⑤ in the long run

Lesson 8

All Your Dreams Are Worth Chasing

 의사소통 기능

- 후회 표현하기
  A: I should have saved food for the winter.
  B: Don't worry. I'll share my food with you.

- 수정하기
  A: People in Brazil speak Spanish, right?
  B: I'm afraid you're mistaken. They speak
  Portuguese.

 언어 형식

- 조동사+have p.p.
  They **must have been** hungry.

- 관계대명사의 계속적 용법
  My favorite writer is Ken Kuller, **who** lives in
  New York.

교과서 Words & Expressions

Key Words

- **achieve** [ətʃíːv] 동 이루다, 달성[성취]하다
- **activity** [æktívəti] 명 활동, 행동
- **audition** [ɔːdíʃən] 명 오디션 동 오디션을 보다
- **banner** [bǽnər] 명 현수막
- **batting title** 타격왕
- **calm** [kɑːm] 형 침착한, 냉정한
- **capital** [kǽpətl] 명 수도
- **challenging** [tʃǽlindʒiŋ] 형 도전적인
- **chase** [tʃeis] 동 쫓다, 추적하다
- **cheerful** [tʃíərfəl] 형 기분 좋은, 즐거운
- **completely** [kəmplíːtli] 부 완전히, 전적으로
- **confident** [kánfədənt] 형 확신하는, 자신만만한
- **connect** [kənékt] 동 연결하다
- **create** [kriéit] 동 만들다, 창조하다
- **decision** [disíʒən] 명 결정, 판단
- **delighted** [diláitid] 형 아주 기뻐하는
- **express** [iksprés] 동 표현하다
- **found** [faund] 동 설립하다
- **imagination** [imædʒənéiʃən] 명 상상, 상상력
- **impatient** [impéiʃənt] 형 짜증 난, 참지 못하는
- **improve** [imprúːv] 동 향상시키다, 개선하다
- **include** [inklúːd] 동 포함하다
- **join** [dʒɔin] 동 결합하다, 합류하다, 가담하다
- **league** [liːg] 명 리그, 연맹
- **lifelong** [láiflɔŋ] 형 일생[평생]의

- **Mars** [mɑːrz] 명 화성
- **mistaken** [mistéikən] 형 잘못 알고 있는
- **offer** [ɔ́ːfər] 명 제의, 제안
- **opportunity** [ùpərtʃúːnəti] 명 기회
- **pick** [pik] 동 뽑다, 고르다
- **practice** [prǽktis] 동 연습하다, 훈련하다
- **protection** [prətékʃən] 명 보호
- **quite** [kwait] 부 꽤, 상당히
- **read** [riːd] 동 ~라고 적혀 있다
- **regret** [rigrét] 동 후회하다
- **repair** [ripɛ́ər] 동 수리하다
- **rest** [rest] 명 나머지, 휴식
- **right** [rait] 부 바로
- **rule** [ruːl] 명 규칙
- **save** [seiv] 동 구하다, 절약하다, 저축하다
- **scared** [skɛərd] 형 무서워하는, 겁먹은
- **serious** [síəriəs] 형 심각한, 진지한
- **share** [ʃɛər] 동 공유하다
- **skill** [skil] 명 기량, 기술
- **stuck** [stʌk] 형 갇힌, (~에 빠져) 꼼짝 못 하는
- **suit** [suːt] 명 정장
- **tryout** [tráiaut] 명 심사, 테스트
- **worried** [wɔ́ːrid] 형 난처한, 걱정[근심]스러운
- **worth** [wəːrθ] 형 ~할 가치가 있는

Key Expressions

- **animal doctor** 수의사
- **apply for** ~에 지원하다, ~을 신청하다
- **be ashamed of** ~을 부끄러워하다
- **break down** 고장나다
- **break out** 발발[발생]하다
- **deal with** ~을 다루다
- **do one's hair** 머리를 손질하다
- **even if** 비록 ~일지라도
- **get off** (자동차 등에서) 내리다
- **go after** ~을 추구하다, ~을 얻기 위해 노력하다
- **go by** 지나가다, 흐르다
- **hang out with** ~와 시간을 보내다
- **How come?** 왜 그렇지?, 어쩌다 그렇게 됐니?

- **I'd[I would] say ~.** 내 생각에 ~인 것 같다.
- **may[might] have p.p.** ~했을지도 모른다
- **must have p.p.** ~했음에 틀림없다
- **not ~ anymore** 더 이상 ~ 않다
- **over and over** 반복해서
- **prepare for** ~을 준비하다
- **set one's alarm** 알람을 맞추다
- **should have p.p.** ~했어야 한다
- **spend+시간+-ing** ~하면서 시간을 보내다
- **too ~ to부정사** ~하기에 너무 …하다
- **traffic jam** 교통 체증
- **used to** (과거에) ~이었다[했다]
- **You can make it!** 넌 해낼 수 있어!

Word Power

※ 서로 비슷한 뜻을 가진 어휘

- □ **achieve** 이루다, 달성[성취]하다 – **accomplish** 이루다, 성취하다
- □ **decision** 결정, 판단 – **determination** 결심, 결단(력)
- □ **improve** 향상시키다, 개선하다 – **enhance** 향상시키다
- □ **offer** 제의, 제안 – **proposal** 제안, 제의
- □ **practice** 연습하다, 훈련하다 – **exercise** 연습하다
- □ **regret** 후회하다 – **repent** 후회하다
- □ **save** 구하다 – **rescue** 구조하다

- □ **completely** 완전히, 전적으로 – **entirely** 완전히
- □ **found** 설립하다 – **establish** 설립하다
- □ **include** 포함하다 – **contain** 포함하다
- □ **opportunity** 기회 – **chance** 기회
- □ **join** 결합하다 – **connect** 잇다, 연결하다
- □ **repair** 수리하다 – **fix** 수리하다
- □ **worth** ~할 가치가 있는 – **worthy** 가치 있는

※ 서로 반대의 뜻을 가진 어휘

- □ **impatient** 참지 못하는 ↔ **patient** 인내심이 강한
- □ **include** 포함하다 ↔ **exclude** 제외[배제]하다
- □ **save** 구하다, 절약하다 ↔ **waste** 낭비하다

- □ **improve** 향상시키다 ↔ **worsen** 악화시키다
- □ **join** 결합하다 ↔ **divide** 나누다, 분할하다 **separate** 분리하다
- □ **worth** ~할 가치가 있는 ↔ **worthless** 가치 없는

※ 감정을 나타내는 형용사

- □ **ashamed** 부끄러이 여기는
- □ **calm** 침착한, 냉정한
- □ **cheerful** 기분 좋은, 즐거운
- □ **confident** 확신하는, 자신만만한
- □ **curious** 호기심 있는

- □ **delighted** 아주 기뻐하는
- □ **disappointed** 실망한
- □ **embarrassed** 난처한
- □ **gloomy** 우울한
- □ **jealous** 질투심이 많은

- □ **lonely** 외로운, 고독한
- □ **regretful** 후회하는
- □ **relieved** 안도하는
- □ **scared** 무서워하는, 겁먹은
- □ **worried** 난처한, 걱정[근심]스러운

English Dictionary

- □ **banner** 현수막
  → a long piece of cloth with words written on it
  위에 글씨가 쓰여진 긴 천 조각

- □ **be ashamed of** ~을 부끄러워하다
  → to feel embarrassed and guilty about something you did 당신이 한 일에 대해 난처하거나 죄스러움을 느끼다

- □ **create** 만들다, 창조하다
  → to make something new 무언가 새로운 것을 만들다

- □ **challenging** 도전적인
  → difficult in a way that is usually enjoyable
  보통 즐길 수 없는 방식으로 어려운

- □ **connect** 연결하다
  → to join together 함께 연결하다

- □ **decision** 결정, 판단
  → the act of making up one's mind 결정하는 행위

- □ **found** 설립하다
  → to establish 설립하다

- □ **go after** ~을 추구하다, ~을 얻기 위해 노력하다
  → to pursue or run after 추구하거나 뒤쫓다

- □ **include** 포함하다
  → to have something as part of a group or total
  단체나 전체의 일부로 어떤 것을 갖다

- □ **league** 리그, 연맹
  → a group of sports teams that play against each other
  서로 상대하여 경기하는 스포츠 팀의 단체

- □ **opportunity** 기회
  → chance for doing something
  어떤 것을 할 기회

- □ **over and over** 반복해서
  → repeatedly 반복해서

- □ **read** ~라고 적혀 있다
  → to have or give information 정보를 갖거나 주다

- □ **regret** 후회하다
  → to feel sorry about something that you did in the past
  과거에 한 것에 대해 미안함을 느끼다

- □ **rest** 나머지
  → the part that is left 남아 있는 부분

- □ **serious** 심각한, 진지한
  → acting or speaking sincerely and without joking
  농담하지 않고 진심으로 행하거나 말하는

- □ **suit** 정장
  → a set of clothes usually consisting of a jacket and pants or skirt
  보통 재킷과 바지나 치마로 이루어진 한 벌의 옷

- □ **tryout** 심사, 테스트
  → a test of the potential of someone
  누군가의 가능성을 점검하는 것

- □ **worth** ~할 가치가 있는
  → good or important enough for something
  어떤 것에 대해 좋거나 충분히 중요한

01 다음 짝지어진 단어의 관계가 같도록 빈칸에 알맞은 말을 쓰시오.

> achieve : accomplish = entirely : _____

02 다음 영영풀이가 가리키는 것을 고르시오.

> to pursue or run after

① go after   ② break down

③ break out   ④ get off

⑤ be ashamed of

03 다음 중 밑줄 친 부분의 뜻풀이가 바르지 <u>않은</u> 것은?

① If I'm not <u>mistaken</u>, this book belongs to Henry. (잘못 알고 있는)

② You should <u>prepare for</u> the trip well in advance. (~을 준비하다)

③ She made up her mind to <u>apply for</u> the job. (~에 적응하다)

④ Wait until the paint has <u>completely</u> dried. (완전히)

⑤ There are many ways to <u>express</u> sad feelings. (표현하다)

04 다음 우리말을 주어진 어휘를 이용하여 영작하시오.

(1) 하버드 대학교는 1636년에 설립되었다. (Harvard University, found)

➡ _____

(2) 그 작가의 소설은 여러 번 읽을 가치가 있다. (over, read, worth)

➡ _____

05 다음 문장의 빈칸에 들어갈 말을 〈보기〉에서 골라 쓰시오. (필요하면 어형을 변화할 것)

> 보기
>
> be ashamed of / deal with / do her hair /
> hang out with / go by

(1) As time _____, things got more dangerous.

(2) He has some unfinished business to _____.

(3) You should _____ yourself for telling such lies.

(4) Tell her to go and _____ and nails.

(5) He's very friendly and really fun to _____.

06 다음 빈칸 (A)~(B)에 각각 공통으로 들어갈 말이 바르게 짝지어진 것은?

> • We had gone about fifty miles when the car (A)_____ down.
> • They had escaped to America shortly before the war (A)_____ out in 1939.
> • I think we should (B)_____ after an increase in production this year.
> • Days (B)_____ by, and his father does not come, but Alex decides to wait.

① made – go   ② made – get

③ broke – go   ④ broke – get

⑤ put – do

01 다음 짝지어진 단어의 관계가 같도록 빈칸에 알맞은 말을 쓰시오.

> lend : borrow = _____ : exclude

02 다음 우리말에 맞게 빈칸에 알맞은 말을 쓰시오.

(1) 네가 정말 원하는 직업을 추구해라.

➡ _____ _____ the job you really want.

(2) 그녀는 시험에서 부정행위를 한 것을 부끄럽게 생각했다.

➡ She _____ _____ _____ herself for cheating on the test.

(3) 그는 그녀가 그 상황을 처리할 것으로 믿어도 된다는 것을 알고 있었다.

➡ He knew he could depend upon her to _____ _____ the situation.

03 다음 문장의 빈칸에 들어갈 말을 〈보기〉에서 골라 쓰시오.

> ┤ 보기 ├
> impatient / opportunity / offer / read / include

(1) The price of pizza does not _____ the delivery fee.

(2) Don't be _____ with the children.

(3) The sign on the bench _____s "Wet Paint."

(4) Traveling abroad can give you a good _____ to learn about other cultures.

(5) Rex is considering job _____s from several companies.

04 우리말과 일치하도록 주어진 어구를 배열하여 영작하시오.

(1) 그 책은 당신의 상상력을 넓히는 데에 도움이 될 것이다. (you / your / the book / imagination / will / expand / help)

➡ _____

(2) 그녀는 자신의 관심사를 추구해서 동물원 사육사가 되었다. (she / she / a zookeeper / became / was / going / interested / what / in / by / after)

➡ _____
_____

(3) 그는 도전 의식을 북돋우고 보람이 있는 일을 찾고 있다. (he / job / rewarding / challenging / looking / is / and / a / for)

➡ _____
_____

05 다음 우리말에 맞게 주어진 어구를 사용하여 영작하시오.

(1) 원숭이들은 놀거나 서로를 뒤쫓을 때 웃는다. (chase, play, each other)

➡ _____
_____

(2) 우리 가게의 모든 샌드위치 가격은 음료를 포함한다. (the price, drinks, store, include)

➡ _____
_____

(3) 그 병원은 가난한 사람들을 치료하기 위해 설립되었다. (treat, poor, found)

➡ _____
_____

Conversation

1 후회 표현하기

> **A** I should have saved food for the winter. 나는 겨울용 식량을 저장해 놓았어야 해.
> **B** Don't worry. I'll share my food with you. 걱정하지 마. 내가 내 식량을 나눠 줄게.

■ 과거의 일에 대한 안타까움이나 후회를 나타낼 때 should have+p.p.로 표현한다. should have p.p.는 '~했어야 했는데 (하지 못했다)'는 의미이고, should not have p.p.는 '~하지 말았어야 했는데 (했다)' 는 뜻이다. 'I ought to have+p.p.', 'I had to ~, but I didn't.', 'I regret ~.', 'It would have been better if ~', 'I'm very sorry for ~', 'It's a pity that ~.' 등으로 유감이나 후회를 나타낼 수도 있다.

  • I should have gone to bed early. 나는 일찍 잤어야 했어.

  • I shouldn't have spent so much money on buying pens. 나는 펜을 사는 데 그렇게 많은 돈을 쓰지 말았어야 했어.

■ 'I should have+p.p. ~.'는 'I ought to have+p.p.', 'I'm sorry I didn't[wasn't] ~.' 또는 'I regret I didn't[wasn't] ~.' 등으로 바꿔 쓸 수 있다.

  • I should have studied math harder.

  = I ought to have studied math harder. 나는 수학을 더 열심히 공부했어야 했는데.

  = I'm sorry I didn't study math harder. 나는 수학을 더 열심히 공부하지 않은 것이 유감이다.

  = I regret I didn't study math harder. 나는 수학을 더 열심히 공부하지 않은 것을 후회한다.

유사 표현

  • You could have told me before. 당신이 전에 내게 말을 해 줄 수도 있었잖아요.

  • I wish I could give up smoking. 난 담배를 끊을 수 있으면 좋겠어.

  • I really regret not listening to her. 그녀의 말을 듣지 않은 걸 정말 후회해.

핵심 Check

1. 다음 대화의 밑줄 친 우리말을 주어진 단어를 포함하여 영작하시오.

  A: I got up late this morning. <u>알람을 맞췄어야 했어.</u> (set, alarm)

  B: I'm sorry to hear that.

  ➡ _____

2 상대방의 말 수정하기

A People in Brazil speak Spanish, right? 브라질 사람들은 스페인어를 사용해, 그렇지?

B I'm afraid you're mistaken. They speak Portuguese.
미안하지만 네가 잘못 아는 거야. 그들은 포르투칼어를 사용해.

- 상대방의 말을 수정하기 위해서 'That's not right[true].', 'I don't think that's right.', 'That's wrong.', 'You're mistaken.' 등의 표현을 사용한다.
  - **A:** Shanghai is the biggest city in China. 상해가 중국에서 가장 큰 도시야.
  - **B:** That's not true. Beijing is the biggest one in China. 사실이 아니야. 중국에서 가장 큰 도시는 북경이야.

- 상대방의 말이 잘못되어서 수정하고 싶을 때, 앞에 'I'm sorry, but ~.', 'I'm afraid ~.' 등을 붙여 좀 더 부드럽게 말할 수 있다.
  - **A:** Vincent van Gogh was French, wasn't he? Vincent van Gogh는 프랑스 사람이었지, 그렇지 않니?
  - **B:** I'm afraid you're mistaken. He was Dutch. 네가 잘못 생각하는 거야. 그는 네덜란드 사람이야.

상대방의 말 수정하기

- I'm sorry, but ~ 미안하지만, ~
- I'm afraid ~ 미안하지만, ~

핵심 Check

2. 다음 대화의 빈칸에 적절하지 <u>않은</u> 것은?

G: What made you late?

B: Well, I got up early. But it took me some time to do my hair.

G: Oh, I see. We're stuck in a heavy traffic jam. We should get off and run.

B: No, _____. The traffic is starting to move again. Let's stay on.

G: Okay. I just hope we're not terribly late.

① you're mistaken
② we shouldn't have got off
③ that's not right
④ I don't think that's right
⑤ that's wrong

Listen - Listen & Answer Dialog 1

B: Hi, Sora. What are you doing?

G: I'm drawing cartoons. I'm preparing for the exam for Mana Animation High School.

B: Oh, ❶are you? When is the exam?

G: On Friday, so I only have two days ❷left.

B: How's ❸it going?

G: ❹It's not easy to draw what I want to express. ❺I should have practiced more.

B: Don't worry! ❻You can make it!

G: Thanks.

남: 안녕, 소라야. 뭘 하고 있니?
여: 만화를 그리고 있어. 마나 애니메이션 고등학교 입학시험을 준비하고 있어.
남: 아, 그래? 시험이 언제야?
여: 금요일. 그래서 이틀밖에 안 남았어.
남: 어떻게 되고 있어?
여: 내가 표현하고 싶은 것을 그리기가 쉽지 않아. 나는 더 연습했어야 해.
남: 걱정하지 마! 넌 해낼 수 있어!
여: 고마워.

❶ preparing for the exam ~ 이하가 생략되어 있다. ❷ 과거분사로 two days를 수식하고 있다. ❸ 비인칭 주어이다.
❹ 가주어 It, 진주어로 to부정사가 쓰이고 있다. 의문사 what에 이끌리는 절이 draw의 목적어로 쓰이고 있다.
❺ should have p.p.'는 '~했어야 한다'는 의미로 과거의 행동이나 사실에 관한 추측이나 후회를 나타낸다.
❻ You can make it!: 넌 해낼 수 있어!

Check(√) True or False

(1) Sora has two days left for the exam. T ☐ F ☐

(2) Sora doesn't think it difficult to draw what she wants to express. T ☐ F ☐

Listen - Listen & Answer Dialog 2

M: Nice to meet you, Sora. Did you do well on the drawing exam?

G: I'm not sure, but I did my best.

M: Okay. Let's start the interview. ❶What made you apply for Mana Animation High School?

G: Well, ❷I've really loved drawing cartoons since I was a little child.

M: So, ❸you want to be a cartoon artist?

G: ❹That's not quite right. I want to be a game designer.

M: I see. ❺What do you think is the most important skill a game designer needs?

G: ❻I'd say imagination. A good designer should create a completely new world in a game.

M: Sounds good.

남: 소라 학생, 만나서 반가워요. 소묘 시험은 잘 봤나요?
여: 잘 모르겠지만 최선을 다했습니다.
남: 알겠어요. 면접을 시작합시다. 왜 마나 애니메이션 고등학교에 지원했나요?
여: 음, 저는 어렸을 때부터 만화 그리는 것을 정말 좋아했습니다.
남: 그렇다면, 만화가가 되고 싶나요?
여: 꼭 그렇지는 않습니다. 저는 게임 디자이너가 되고 싶습니다.
남: 그렇군요. 게임 디자이너에게 필요한 가장 중요한 기량이 무엇이라고 생각하나요?
여: 상상력이라고 말씀드리겠습니다. 훌륭한 게임 디자이너는 게임 속에서 완전히 새로운 세계를 창조해야 하거든요.
남: 좋습니다.

❶ 'Why did you apply for ~?'로 바꿔 쓸 수 있다. ❷ 현재완료의 계속 용법이다.
❸ 구어체에서 평서문의 어순으로 의문문을 대신하고 있다. ❹ 상대방의 말을 수정해 주고 있다.
❺ think 동사로 인해 간접의문문의 의문사가 문두에 쓰이고 있는 문장이다.
❻ I'd[I would] say ~.: 내 생각에 ~인 것 같다.

Check(√) True or False

(3) Sora is not sure if she did well on the drawing exam. T ☐ F ☐

(4) Sora thinks the most important skill in a game is imagination. T ☐ F ☐

Get Ready

A: We need 100 candles.

B: ❶That's not quite right. We need 101 candles.

A: ❷We should have prepared 110 candles.

❶ 상대방의 말을 수정하려고 쓴 문장이다.
❷ 'We ought to have prepared 110 candles.'와 같은 말이다.

Listen - Listen More

G: Hi, Jiho.

B: Hi, Amber. It's nice to see you on the bus.

G: Yeah, but I'm afraid we're going to be late.

B: Yeah. I hate to be late for the school festival.

G: Me, too. ❶I should have set my alarm. I forgot.

B: I understand. ❷That happens a lot to me when I'm tired, too.

G: How about you? ❸What made you late?

B: Well, I got up early. But it took me some time to do my hair.

G: Oh, I see. We're stuck in a heavy traffic jam. We should get off and run.

B: ❹No, you're mistaken. The traffic is starting to move again. Let's stay on.

G: Okay. I just hope we're not terribly late.

❶ 'should have p.p.'는 '~했어야 한다'는 의미로 과거의 행동이나 사실에 관한 추측이나 후회를 나타낸다.
❷ happens는 자동사이므로 수동태로 쓰이지 않고 a lot은 부사구로 쓰였다.
❸ 'Why were you late?'와 같은 말이다.
❹ 상대방의 말을 수정할 때 쓰는 표현이다.

Speak - Talk in pairs.

A: ❶What's the matter?

B: I feel hungry. ❷I should have saved food for the winter.

A: Don't worry. ❸I'll share my food with you.

B: Thanks.

❶ What's up?, What's the problem? 등으로 바꿔 쓸 수 있다.
❷ 과거에 대한 후회를 나타낸다.
❸ share A with B: A를 B와 공유하다

My Speaking Portfolio

G1: I didn't study English hard. I should have practiced more ❶to improve my speaking skills.

B1: I hung out with only a few close friends. ❷I regret that I didn't make more friends.

G1: ❸I should have read more books. ❹I'm afraid that I won't have time for reading when I go to high school.

B1: I ❺spent too much time on my cell phone. I should have played basketball more often.

❶ 부사적 용법으로 '목적'을 나타낸다.
❷ 'I regret that ~'으로 과거에 대한 후회를 나타낸다.
❸ 'should have p.p.'로 과거에 대한 후회를 나타낸다.
❹ 미래의 일에 대한 걱정을 표현하고 있다.
❺ spend+시간/돈+on ~ing: ~에 시간이나 돈을 쓰다

Wrap Up 6

B: What do you want to do when you grow up?

G: I want to work with robots.

B: Are you interested in making robots?

G: ❶No, that's not quite right. I want to repair robots.

B: I see. But why?

G: Because I think it'll be a good job in the future.

❶ 상대방의 말을 수정할 때 쓰는 표현이다.

Wrap Up 7

G: My computer has viruses.

B: ❶How come?

G: I opened an e-mail from a stranger. ❷I shouldn't have done that.

B: ❸If I were you, I'd get help from a computer service center right now.

❶ 'How come?'은 이어지는 어순이 평서문의 어순임에 주의해야 한다. 즉, 뒤에 'your computer has viruses'가 생략되어 있다.
❷ 'I shouldn't have p.p.'로 하지 말았어야 하는 일을 한 것에 대한 후회를 나타내고 있다.
❸ 가정법 과거로 현재 사실에 대해 반대되는 일에 대해 가정하고 있다.

• 다음 우리말과 일치하도록 빈칸에 알맞은 말을 쓰시오.

Listen - Listen & Answer Dialog 1

B: Hi, Sora. _____ are you doing?

G: I'm drawing cartoons. I'm preparing _____ the exam for Mana Animation High School.

B: Oh, _____ you? _____ is the exam?

G: _____ Friday, so I only have two days _____.

B: _____ it _____?

G: _____'s not easy _____ _____ _____ I want to express. I _____ _____ _____ more.

B: Don't worry! You can _____ _____!

G: Thanks.

남: 안녕, 소라야. 뭘 하고 있니?
여: 만화를 그리고 있어. 마나 애니메이션 고등학교 입학시험을 준비하고 있어.
남: 아, 그래? 시험이 언제야?
여: 금요일, 그래서 이틀밖에 안 남았어.
남: 어떻게 되고 있니?
여: 내가 표현하고 싶은 것을 그리기가 쉽지 않아. 나는 더 연습했어야 해.
남: 걱정하지 마! 넌 해낼 수 있어!
여: 고마워.

Listen - Listen & Answer Dialog 2

M: Nice _____ _____ you, Sora. Did you _____ _____ _____ the drawing exam?

G: I'm not _____, but I _____ _____ _____.

M: Okay. Let's start the interview. _____ _____ you apply _____ Mana Animation High School?

G: Well, I'_____ really _____ drawing cartoons _____ I was a little child.

M: So, you want to be a cartoon artist?

G: That's not _____ _____. I want to be a game designer.

M: I see. _____ do you _____ is the most important skill a game designer needs?

G: _____ _____ imagination. A good designer should create a _____ new world in a game.

M: Sounds good.

남: 소라 학생, 만나서 반가워요. 소묘 시험은 잘 봤나요?
여: 잘 모르겠지만 최선을 다했습니다.
남: 알겠어요. 면접을 시작합시다. 왜 마나 애니메이션 고등학교에 지원했나요?
여: 음, 저는 어렸을 때부터 만화 그리는 것을 정말 좋아했습니다.
남: 그렇다면, 만화가가 되고 싶나요?
여: 꼭 그렇지는 않습니다. 저는 게임 디자이너가 되고 싶습니다.
남: 그렇군요. 게임 디자이너에게 필요한 가장 중요한 기량이 무엇이라고 생각하나요?
여: 상상력이라고 말씀드리겠습니다. 훌륭한 게임 디자이너는 게임 속에서 완전히 새로운 세계를 창조해야 하거든요.
남: 좋습니다.

Speak - Talk in pairs.

A: What's the matter?

B: I feel hungry. I should have _____ food for the winter.

A: Don't worry. I'll _____ my food _____ you.

B: Thanks.

A: 무슨 일이야?
B: 배가 고파. 나는 겨울용 식량을 저장해 놨어야 해.
A: 걱정하지 마. 내가 내 식량을 나눠 줄게.
B: 고마워.

Listen - Listen More

G: Hi, Jiho.

B: Hi, Amber. It's nice _____ _____ you on the bus.

G: Yeah, but _____ _____ we're going to be late.

B: Yeah. I _____ _____ _____ late for the school festival.

G: Me, too. I _____ _____ _____ my alarm. I forgot.

B: I understand. That _____ _____ _____ to me when I'm _____, too.

G: How about you? _____ _____ you late?

B: Well, I got up early. But it took me some time to _____ _____ _____.

G: Oh, I see. _____ _____ _____ a heavy traffic jam. We should _____ _____ and run.

B: No, _____ _____. The traffic is starting to move again. Let's _____ _____.

G: Okay. I just hope we're not _____ late.

Wrap Up 6

B: What do you want to do _____ you grow up?

G: I want to work _____ robots.

B: Are you interested in _____ robots?

G: No, _____ not _____ _____. I want to repair robots.

B: I see. But _____?

G: Because I _____ it'll be a good job in the future.

Wrap Up 7

G: My computer has viruses.

B: _____ come?

G: I opened an e-mail from a stranger. I _____ _____ _____ that.

B: If I _____ _____, _____ _____ help from a computer service center right now.

해석

여: 지호야, 안녕.
남: Amber, 안녕. 버스에서 너를 보다니 반갑다.
여: 맞아, 그런데 걱정스럽게도 우리가 늦을 것 같아.
남: 그러게. 학교 축제에 늦고 싶지 않은데.
여: 나도 그래. 알람을 맞출걸. 내가 깜빡했어.
남: 이해해. 나도 피곤할 때 그런 일이 많이 일어나.
여: 너는? 무슨 일로 늦었어?
남: 음, 난 일찍 일어났어. 그런데 머리를 손질하느라 시간이 좀 걸렸어.
여: 아, 그렇구나. 우리 교통 체증에 갇혔어. 버스에서 내려서 뛰어가자.
남: 아니, 네가 잘못 생각하는 거야. 차들이 다시 움직이기 시작해. 내리지 말자.
여: 알았어. 너무 늦지 않기를 바랄 뿐이야.

남: 너는 커서 무엇을 하고 싶니?
여: 나는 로봇과 관련된 일을 하고 싶어.
남: 로봇 제작하는 것에 관심 있니?
여: 아니, 꼭 그렇지는 않아. 나는 로봇을 수리하고 싶어.
남: 그렇구나. 그런데 왜?
여: 그것이 미래에 좋은 직업이 될 거라고 생각하기 때문이야.

여: 내 컴퓨터가 바이러스에 걸렸어.
남: 어쩌다가 그랬니?
여: 모르는 사람에게서 온 이메일을 열었지. 그러지 말았어야 해.
남: 내가 너라면, 지금 바로 컴퓨터 서비스 센터에서 도움을 받겠어.

[01~02] 다음 대화를 읽고 물음에 답하시오.

B: Hi, Sora. What are you doing?

G: I'm drawing cartoons. I'm ⓐpreparing for the exam for Mana Animation High School.

B: Oh, ⓑare you? When is the exam?

G: On Friday, so I only have two days ⓒleft.

B: How's it going?

G: It's not easy to draw what I want to express. ⓓI must have practiced more.

B: Don't worry! ⓔYou can make it!

G: Thanks.

01 위 대화의 밑줄 친 ⓐ~ⓔ 중 흐름상 어색한 것을 찾아 바르게 고치시오.

➡ _____

02 위 대화를 읽고 대답할 수 없는 것은?

① What is Sora doing?

② When is the exam for Mana Animation High School?

③ How many days does Sora have for the exam?

④ Is it easy for Sora to draw what she wants to express?

⑤ Why does Sora want to attend Mana Animation High School?

[03~04] 다음 대화를 읽고 물음에 답하시오.

B: What do you want to do when you grow up?

G: I want to work with robots.

B: Are you interested in making robots?

G: No, that's not quite right. I want to repair robots.

B: I see. But why?

G: Because I think it'll be a good job in the future.

03 What does the girl want to do when she grows up?

➡ _____

04 Why does the girl want to repair robots?

➡ _____

[01~03] 다음 대화를 읽고 물음에 답하시오.

M: Nice to meet you, Sora. Did you do well on the drawing exam?

G: I'm not sure, but I did my best.

M: Okay. Let's start the interview. What made you apply for Mana Animation High School?

G: Well, I've really loved drawing cartoons since I was a little child.

M: So, you want to be a cartoon artist?

G: _____(A)_____ I want to be a game designer.

M: I see. What do you think is the most important skill a game designer needs?

G: (B)상상력이라고 말씀드리겠습니다. A good designer should create a completely new world in a game.

M: Sounds good.

01 위 대화의 빈칸 (A)에 알맞은 것은?

① It's true.
② Of course.
③ You can say that again.
④ How did you know?
⑤ That's not quite right.

02 위 대화에 나오는 M과 G의 관계로 적절한 것은?

① teacher – student
② doctor – patient
③ interviewer – interviewee
④ customer – clerk
⑤ star – fan

서답형

03 위 대화의 밑줄 친 (B)의 우리말을 3 단어로 영작하시오.

➡ _____

[04~06] 다음 대화를 읽고 물음에 답하시오.

G: Hi, Jiho.

B: Hi, Amber. It's nice to see you on the bus.

G: Yeah, but I'm afraid we're going to be late.

B: Yeah. I hate to be late for the school festival.

G: Me, too. (A)I should have set my alarm. I forgot.

B: I understand. That happens a lot to me when I'm tired, too.

G: How about you? What made you late?

B: Well, I got up early. But it took me some time to do my hair.

G: Oh, I see. We're stuck in a heavy traffic jam. We should get off and run.

B: No, you're mistaken. The traffic is starting to move again. Let's stay on.

G: Okay. I just hope we're not terribly late.

04 위 대화의 밑줄 친 (A)와 바꾸어 쓰기에 어색한 것은?

① I ought to have set my alarm.
② I may have set my alarm.
③ I'm sorry I didn't set my alarm.
④ I wish I could have set my alarm.
⑤ I regret I didn't set my alarm.

05 위 대화를 읽고 대답할 수 없는 것은?

① Why is Amber late?
② Where do Jiho and Amber meet?
③ What did Amber forget to do last night?
④ How late are Jiho and Amber?
⑤ Why is Jiho late?

서답형

06 위 대화에서 다음의 영영풀이가 뜻하는 것을 찾아 쓰시오.

> difficult to move from one position to another

➡ _____

[07~08] 다음 글을 읽고 물음에 답하시오.

G1: I didn't study English hard. I should have practiced more to improve my speaking skills.

B1: I hung out with only a few close friends. I (A)[regret / wonder] that I didn't make more friends.

B2: I should have read more books. I'm (B)[afraid / sure] that I won't have time for reading when I go to high school.

G2: I spent too much time (C)[at / on] my cell phone. I should have played basketball more often.

07 위 글의 괄호 (A)~(C)에서 알맞은 것을 바르게 짝지은 것을 고르시오.

	(A)	(B)	(C)
①	regret	afraid	at
②	regret	sure	on
③	regret	afraid	on
④	wonder	sure	at
⑤	wonder	afraid	at

중요

08 위 글의 내용과 일치하지 <u>않는</u> 것은?

① G1은 말하기 실력을 키우기 위해 열심히 영어 공부를 하지 않은 것을 후회하고 있다.

② B1은 친구 몇 명하고만 어울렸다.

③ B1은 많은 친구를 사귀지 않은 것을 후회한다.

④ B2는 고등학교에 가면 책을 읽을 시간이 없을까 봐 걱정한다.

⑤ G2는 휴대 전화에 많은 시간을 쓰고 싶어 한다.

09 다음 중 짝지어진 대화가 <u>어색한</u> 것을 고르시오.

① A: That's not quite right. I want to be a game designer.
   B: I'm sorry to hear that.

② A: I fell down on the stairs. I shouldn't have run down the stairs.
   B: I'm sorry to hear that.

③ A: I should have saved food for the winter.
   B: Don't worry. I'll share my food with you.

④ A: We're stuck in a heavy traffic jam. We should get off and run.
   B: No, you're mistaken. The traffic is starting to move again.

⑤ A: Mauna Loa is the largest known volcano in the solar system.
   B: I'm afraid you're mistaken. "Olympus Mons" on Mars is the largest known volcano in the solar system.

[10~11] 다음 대화를 읽고 물음에 답하시오.

G: My computer has viruses.
B: (A)How come?
G: I opened an e-mail from a stranger. I shouldn't have done (B)that.
B: If I were you, I'd get help from a computer service center right now.

서답형

10 위 대화의 밑줄 친 (A)를 완전한 문장으로 쓰시오.

➡ _____

서답형

11 위 대화를 읽고 밑줄 친 (B)that이 가리키는 것을 우리말로 쓰시오.

➡ _____

[01~04] 다음 대화를 읽고 물음에 답하시오.

B: What do you want to do when you grow up?

(A) No, (a)that's not quite right. I want to repair robots.

(B) I want to work with robots.

(C) Are you interested in making robots?

(D) Because I think it'll be a good job in the future.

(E) I see. But (b)why?

01 주어진 글에 대화가 자연스럽게 이어지도록 순서대로 배열하시오.

➡ _____

02 위 대화의 내용과 일치하도록 빈칸 (A)와 (B)에 알맞은 말을 쓰시오.

> G wants to (A)_____ robots because she thinks it'll be (B)_____ _____ _____ in the future.

03 위 대화의 밑줄 친 (a)와 같은 뜻의 말을 주어진 어휘를 이용하여 쓰시오.

> mistaken, afraid

➡ _____

04 위 대화의 밑줄 친 (b)why 다음에 생략되어 있는 말을 쓰시오.

➡ _____

[05~07] 다음 대화를 읽고 물음에 답하시오.

B: Hi, Sora. What are you doing?

G: I'm drawing cartoons. I'm preparing for the exam for Mana Animation High School.

B: Oh, are you? When is the exam?

G: On Friday, so I only have two days left.

B: How's it going?

G: It's not easy to draw what I want to express. I should have practiced more.

B: Don't worry! You can make it!

G: Thanks.

05 What does Sora regret?

➡ _____

06 When does Sora have the exam for Mana Animation High School? Answer in English with 6 words.

➡ _____

07 What is difficult for Sora?

➡ _____
_____

08 다음 대화가 자연스럽게 이어지도록 순서대로 배열하시오.

(A) Thanks.

(B) I feel hungry. I should have saved food for the winter.

(C) What's the matter?

(D) Don't worry. I'll share my food with you.

➡ _____

Grammar

교과서

1 조동사+have p.p.

> • They **must have been** hungry. 그들은 배고팠던 것이 틀림없다.

■ 형태: 조동사+have p.p.
의미: 과거의 행동이나 사실에 관한 추측이나 후회 등을 나타낸다.

(1) must have p.p.: ~했음이 틀림없다 (강한 추측)

• That dress **must have cost** a bomb! 저 드레스는 돈이 엄청 들었을 거야!

(2) may[might] have p.p.: ~했을지도 모른다 (약한 추측)

• He **may have missed** his train. 그가 기차를 놓쳤는지도 모른다.

• She was worried that he **might have met** with an accident.
그녀는 그가 사고를 당했을지도 모른다고 걱정했다.

(3) should[ought to] have p.p.: ~했어야 한다(그런데 하지 못했다) (후회)

• I **should have told** you the truth. 내가 너에게 진실을 말했어야 한다.

• You **ought to have come** to the meeting. 네가 그 모임에 왔더라면 좋았을 걸 그랬어.

(4) should not[ought not to] have p.p.: ~하지 않았어야 했는데(그런데 했다) (후회)

• This error **should not have happened**. 이 실수는 일어나서는 안 될 일이었습니다.

• You **ought not to have done** that. 너는 그렇게 해서는 안 되었었다.

(5) cannot have p.p.: ~했을 리가 없다(강한 부정의 추측) (↔ must have p.p.)

• He **cannot have said** so. 그가 그렇게 말했을 리가 없다.

(6) could have p.p.: ~했을 수도 있었는데[있었다] (과거와 관련된 가능성)

• The accident **could have been avoided**. 그 사고는 방지할 수도 있었을 것이다.

(7) would have p.p.: ~했을 텐데[했을 것이다] (과거와 관련된 가정이나 상상, 과거의 의지)

• He was so desperate for a job that he **would have done** anything.
그는 일자리가 너무도 절실히 필요해서 무슨 일이라도 했을 것이다.

핵심 Check

1. 다음 괄호 안에서 알맞은 단어를 고르시오.

(1) I gained some weight. I _____ _____ _____ so much fast food. (should, eat)

(2) He looks fatter than before. He _____ _____ _____ on several kilos. (put)

2 관계대명사의 계속적 용법

> • My favorite writer is Ken Kuller, **who** lives in New York.
> 내가 가장 좋아하는 작가는 Ken Kuller인데, 그는 뉴욕에 산다.

- 형태: 콤마(,) + who/which
  쓰임: 관계대명사절이 선행사를 보충해서 설명하는 역할을 한다.

- 관계대명사의 계속적 용법은 관계대명사 앞에 콤마(,)를 붙인 형태로 선행사를 보충해서 설명한다. 제한적 용법과 마찬가지로 선행사가 사람이면 who, 사물이면 which를 쓴다. 제한적 용법은 관계사가 이끄는 절부터 해석하고, 계속적 용법은 앞에서부터 해석한다.

  • Ben has two sons **who** are doctors. Ben은 의사인 아들이 둘 있다. (제한적 용법 → 아들이 둘인지 더 있는지 모름.)

  • Ben has two sons, **who** are doctors. Ben은 아들이 둘인데, 그들은 의사이다. (계속적 용법 → 아들이 둘만 있음.)

- 계속적 용법의 관계대명사는 '접속사(and, but, for, though 등)+대명사'로 고쳐 쓸 수 있다.

  • I began to read the book, **which** was very exciting.

    = I began to read the book, **and it** was very exciting.
    나는 그 책을 읽기 시작했는데 그것은 손에 땀을 쥐게 했다.

- 관계대명사 that과 what은 계속적 용법으로 사용할 수 없으며, 관계대명사가 계속적 용법으로 쓰였을 때는 생략하지 않는다.

  • Thank you for your invitation, **which** I am very pleased to accept. (○)

  • Thank you for your invitation, that I am very pleased to accept. (×)
    초대해 주셔서 고맙습니다. 기쁜 마음으로 응하겠습니다.

- which는 선행사로 구나 절을 가질 수도 있다.

  • The movie slowly brings them together, **which** I love.
    그 영화는 그들을 천천히 함께 하게 만들죠. 저는 그것을 좋아해요.

핵심 Check

2. 다음 빈칸에 알맞은 관계대명사를 쓰시오.

(1) The policeman arrested a criminal, _____ had been hiding in the forest.

(2) The letter contains a number of typing errors, _____ I must correct.

(3) I had very strong ambitions about acting, _____ I still have.

01 다음 빈칸에 알맞은 것은?

> Mr. Decker, _____ is a teacher, works at an elementary school.

① who   ② which   ③ how
④ that   ⑤ what

02 다음 괄호 안에서 알맞은 말을 고르시오.

(1) He (must / should) have spread the news. Everyone knows it.
(2) Jinsu got up late this morning. He (must / might) have been late for school.
(3) I didn't pass the audition. I (should / may) have practiced more for the audition.

03 다음 두 문장을 한 문장으로 바꾸어 쓸 때 알맞게 표현한 것을 고르시오.

> • My favorite writer is Ken Kuller.
> • The writer lives in New York.

① My favorite writer, which lives in New York, is Ken Kuller.
② My favorite writer, what lives in New York is Ken Kuller.
③ My favorite writer, who lives in New York, is Ken Kuller.
④ My favorite writer, whom lives in New York, is Ken Kuller.
⑤ My favorite writer, that lives in New York, is Ken Kuller.

04 다음 우리말에 맞게 주어진 어휘를 바르게 배열하시오.

(1) 너는 너무 많이 먹지 말았어야 한다.

(you, so, eaten, shouldn't, much, have)

➡ _____

(2) 나는 방학 중에 너의 집을 방문할 예정인데, 방학은 내일 시작한다.

(I'll, you, the vacation, tomorrow, visit, begins, which, during)

➡ _____

01 다음 중 어법상 <u>어색한</u> 것은?

① I ran into an old gentleman, who looked just like my grandfather.

② My dad painted the door pink, that is my favorite color.

③ Josh likes to eat tacos, which are a traditional Mexican dish.

④ Rose Austin, whom I saw on the subway, is a famous singer.

⑤ The Sydney Opera House, which is designed by Jørn Utzon, is in Australia.

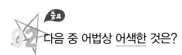

02 다음 중 어법상 <u>어색한</u> 것은?

① He should have brushed his teeth.

② They may have liked to draw something on the wall.

③ I should have build it with stronger material.

④ I shouldn't have played online games so much.

⑤ She must have loved the sport very much.

03 다음 빈칸에 알맞은 말이 바르게 짝지어진 것은?

• I should _____ nicer to my teachers and classmates.

• My grandmother, _____ lives in Busan, has 13 grandchildren.

---

① have been – who

② have been – that

③ have be – which

④ have be – that

⑤ be – what

서답형

04 다음 괄호 안에서 알맞은 말을 고르시오.

(1) My hero is King Sejong, (who / that) invented Hangeul.

(2) He painted his room blue, (who / which) is his favorite color.

(3) Tom visited her, (that / which) made him feel good.

(4) There were fish bones. They (must / should) have eaten fish in the cave.

(5) I got a bad grade in math. I (must / should) have studied harder.

(6) We went back home thinking that our pet dog (might / should) have already returned home.

05 다음 주어진 문장과 의미가 같은 것은?

I'm sure that they had a good time at the party.

---

① They should have had a good time at the party.

② They can have had a good time at the party.

③ They cannot have had a good time at the party.

④ They must have a good time at the party.

⑤ They must have had a good time at the party.

06 다음 밑줄 친 부분을 바꿔 쓸 때, 의미상 가장 적절한 것은?

This is *The Potato Eaters*, <u>which</u> was painted by Vincent van Gogh in 1885.

---

① for it ② but it ③ or it

④ and it ⑤ because it

07 Which is suitable for the blank?

> Linda was late for school again. She
> _____ have been late so often.

① can't   ② may   ③ must
④ shouldn't   ⑤ ought to

서답형

08 다음 빈칸에 알맞은 관계대명사를 쓰시오.

(1) He said nothing, _____ made her angry.
(2) He likes painting pictures very much, _____ is his number-one free time activity.
(3) I'd like to introduce my friend Mike, _____ wants to be an artist in the future.
(4) Did they climb up the Eiffel Tower, _____ is in Paris?

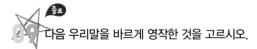

다음 우리말을 바르게 영작한 것을 고르시오.

> 나는 시카고에 갔어야 했다.

① I must have gone to Chicago.
② I should have gone to Chicago.
③ I may have gone to Chicago.
④ I can have gone to Chicago.
⑤ I would have gone to Chicago.

10 다음 문장의 밑줄 친 부분 중 어법상 어색한 것은?

> The robber ⓐstole a car, ⓑthat a woman
> ⓒparked ⓓoutside ⓔher house.

① ⓐ   ② ⓑ   ③ ⓒ   ④ ⓓ   ⑤ ⓔ

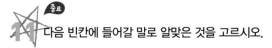

다음 빈칸에 들어갈 말로 알맞은 것을 고르시오.

> I felt sleepy all day. I _____
> up late last night.

① must have stayed
② can't have stayed
③ shouldn't have stayed
④ should have stayed
⑤ ought to have stayed

서답형

12 계속적 용법의 관계대명사를 사용하여 주어진 두 문장을 한 문장으로 바꾸시오.

> • My dad gave me a birthday present.
> • I got much happiness from it.

➡ _____
_____

13 다음 대화의 빈칸에 들어갈 말을 고르시오.

> A: Mike lost his smartphone again.
> B: Oh, that's too bad.
> A: _____

① He must be more careful.
② He should have been more careful.
③ He ought not to have been more careful.
④ You can't have been more careful.
⑤ You may have been more careful.

서답형

14 다음 밑줄 친 부분을 바꿔 쓸 때, 빈칸에 적절한 말을 쓰시오.

> He'd dyed his hair, <u>but it</u> was almost unheard-of in the 1960s.
> = He'd dyed his hair, _____ was almost unheard-of in the 1960s.

중요

15 다음 빈칸에 알맞은 말이 순서대로 바르게 짝지어진 것을 고르시오.

> • Look at the letters. They _____ have had their own alphabet.
> • He _____ have smoked so much. He has lung cancer now.

① must – must
② must – should not
③ should – must
④ should – should not
⑤ cannot – might

서답형

16 다음 각 문장에서 어법상 어색한 부분을 하나씩 찾아서 알맞게 고치시오.

(1) Yesterday I called my aunt, which lives in Mexico.

➡ _____

(2) Tom also showed me a book, that had Ken Kuller's autograph on it.

➡ _____
_____

(3) You should have not broken the rule.

➡ _____

(4) They must have leave some messages with their own letters.

➡ _____
_____

중요

17 다음 중 어법상 옳은 문장을 고르시오.

① He went to the Lost and Found, that was open until 6:00 p.m.
② John is a movie star, who often come to Korea.
③ Mozart was a composer, whom wrote a large amount of good music.
④ My sister likes this book, which has many colorful pictures.
⑤ He said nothing, who made her get angry.

18 다음 우리말과 의미가 같도록 빈칸에 들어갈 말로 알맞은 것을 고르시오.

> Smith 씨는 전에 그 영화를 봤음에 틀림없다.
> = Mr. Smith _____ the movie before.

① should have seen
② must have seen
③ cannot have seen
④ might have seen
⑤ may have seen

서답형

19 우리말 의미에 맞도록, 괄호 안의 어구를 알맞게 배열하시오.

(1) Molly 씨는 손녀 이름을 'Daisy'라고 지었는데, 그것은 꽃 이름이다. (Ms. Molly, Daisy, flower, the name, named, is, her granddaughter, which, a, of)

➡ _____
_____

(2) 그 작가는 소설 집필을 마쳤을지도 모른다. (the writer, his novel, might, finished, have)

➡ _____
_____

Grammar 서술형 시험대비

⭐중요

01 다음 빈칸에 알맞은 관계대명사를 쓰시오.

(1) Jake has two cousins, _____ live in Canada.

(2) My family had dinner at a Mexican restaurant, _____ is near the community center.

(3) My aunt, _____ lives next door, takes care of nine dogs.

(4) Mary accepted his idea of going out, _____ made him happy.

02 다음 우리말에 맞게 주어진 어구를 바르게 배열하시오. (2), (3)은 계속적 용법의 관계대명사를 쓰시오.

(1) 너는 비를 맞으면서 축구를 하지 말았어야 한다. (soccer, you, have, the rain, played, shouldn't, in)

➡ _____

(2) 그가 주연한 영화가 흥행에 성공했다. (the film, big hit, the leading role, he, which, is, plays, a, in)

➡ _____

_____

(3) 그 노부인을 내가 지하철에서 봤는데, 그녀는 유명한 배우였다. (the subway, I, the old lady, famous actress, was, saw, whom, a, on)

➡ _____

_____

고난이도

03 다음 괄호 안의 단어를 활용하여 주어진 조건대로 빈칸을 알맞게 채우시오.

(1) There are no seats left at the restaurant. We _____ a reservation. (make, 후회하는 문장을 쓸 것.)

(2) Kimberly was absent from school yesterday. She _____ yesterday. (sick, 추측하는 문장을 쓸 것.)

(3) There were loud noises all night long. He _____ through all that noise. (sleep, 부정의 추측하는 문장을 쓸 것.)

04 다음 두 문장을 해석하고 그 차이를 설명하시오.

(1) Anne has two sons who are teachers.

(2) Anne has two sons, who are teachers.

➡ 해석 _____

➡ 차이 _____

_____

_____

_____

_____

05 다음 상황에 맞게 후회하는 문장을 10 단어로 쓰시오.

> I spent all my money buying clothes. I need to buy some pens today.

➡ _____

_____

06 다음 그림을 보고, 주어진 어휘를 이용하여 빈칸을 알맞게 채우시오.

Brian is my best friend, _____
_____ pass the exam. (encourage)

07 다음 우리말을 영작하시오.

(1) 그녀는 그 영화를 보지 말았어야 했다.
➡ _____
(2) 그녀는 그 영화를 봤을 리가 없다.
➡ _____
(3) 그녀는 그 영화를 봤을지도 모른다.
➡ _____
(4) 그녀는 그 영화를 봤음에 틀림없다.
➡ _____

08 다음 문장에서 틀린 것을 고쳐 다시 쓰시오.

I'm fond of the actor, who name is not known well.

➡ _____
_____

09 다음 관계대명사의 계속적 용법을 이용하여 주어진 두 문장을 하나의 문장으로 쓰시오.

(1) • Harry invited Lindsey to the party.
 • And it made her feel happy.
➡ _____
_____

(2) • Do you know Thomas Edison?
 • He invented the light bulb.
➡ _____
_____

(3) • The book contains very good contents.
 • The book is cheap.
➡ _____
_____

10 다음 문장에서 어법상 어색한 것을 바르게 고치시오.

(1) My mom is wearing a necklace, who my dad gave her for her birthday.
_____ ➡ _____
(2) Let me introduce Jane Goodall, which studied chimpanzees all her life.
_____ ➡ _____
(3) Spanish people are proud of Antoni Gaudi, that was a great architect.
_____ ➡ _____
(4) Emma got a terrible score on the test. She must have studied harder.
_____ ➡ _____
(5) Several people are coming out. The train cannot have already arrived.
_____ ➡ _____
(6) Lisa is very wise. She must have done such a foolish thing.
_____ ➡ _____

MY GRANDMOTHER'S BASEBALL DREAMS

My grandmother Helen used to be a cook in a restaurant in a small
town near South Bend, Indiana. She does not work anymore, but she
still enjoys making delicious food, which I love so much. Food is one
of the many things that connect us. What connects us most strongly,
however, is baseball.

When I visit her on weekends, my grandmother often tells me
exciting stories about playing baseball back in the 1940s. She must
have loved the sport very much. I listen to these stories over and over.
She always says, "Go after what you want, Sarah. Don't be afraid of
trying something new or challenging. Don't be ashamed of failing."
In 1943, the All-American Girls Professional Baseball League was
founded. This league was created for baseball fans because many of
America's young men were fighting in World War II.

Helen was told that there would be local tryouts right in South Bend.
She wondered, "What would it be like to be on a baseball team and to
make it to the finals for my hometown?" She imagined a large banner
hanging at the baseball field which included the name Helen Baker.

used to (과거에) ～이었다[했다]

not ～ anymore 더 이상 ～ 않다

connect 연결하다

over and over 반복해서

go after ～을 추구하다. ～을 얻기 위해 노력하다

challenging 도전적인

be ashamed of ～을 부끄러워하다

league 리그, 연맹

found 설립하다

create 만들다, 창조하다

tryout 심사, 테스트

banner 현수막

include 포함하다

● 다음 문장이 본문의 내용과 일치하면 T, 일치하지 않으면 F를 쓰시오.

1   Sarah's grandmother Helen was a cook in a restaurant in a small town near South
    Bend, Indiana, but she isn't a cook now. ☐

2   What connects Sarah and her grandmother most strongly is food. ☐

3   When Sarah visits her grandmother on weekends, her grandmother often tells her
    exciting stories about playing baseball back in the 1940s. ☐

4   A large banner hung at the baseball field which included the name Helen Baker. ☐

On the day of the tryouts, all the rules were explained by an old man in a suit, who sounded very serious and unkind. She thought that
_{앞의 an old man을 추가 설명하기 위해 쓰인 계속적 용법의 관계대명사}
wearing a suit in the hot sun might have made him impatient. On that
_{동명사 주어}　　　　　　　　_{과거에 대한 추측(~했을지도 모른다)}
day, Helen played baseball for hours with many other young women. She was excited to go after her baseball dreams!
_{to부정사 부사적 용법(감정의 원인)}

About a week later, Helen found a letter in the mailbox. It was from people who worked for the girls' baseball league in Chicago. It read that she had been invited to the league's main tryouts in Chicago!
_{본심사에 초청된 것은 편지를 읽은 것보다 앞선 시제이므로 과거완료(had p.p.)로 표현}

As the days went by, however, Helen became worried that she might fail. She also became worried about traveling alone to Chicago, which
_{앞의 Chicago를 추가 설명하기 위해 쓰인 계속적 용법의 관계대명사}
was far away from home. When the day of the main tryouts came, she was too afraid to go.
_{너무 ~해서 …하지 않다}

My grandmother has spent the rest of her life regretting her decision.
_{spend+시간+-ing: ~하면서 시간을 보내다}
When she watches a baseball game on TV, she often says, "I should
_{갔어야 한다}
have gone to Chicago. You know, all your dreams are worth chasing,
_{be worth -ing: ~할 가치가 있다}
even if you catch only a few of them. Never miss an opportunity."
_{= your dreams}

suit 정장

serious 심각한, 진지한

impatient 짜증 난, 참지 못하는

read ~라고 적혀 있다

go by 지나가다, 흐르다

rest 나머지

regret 후회하다

decision 결정, 판단

worth ~할 가치가 있는

even if 비록 ~하더라도

opportunity 기회

 **확인문제**

● 다음 문장이 본문의 내용과 일치하면 T, 일치하지 <u>않으면</u> F를 쓰시오.

1　On the day of the tryouts, an old man in a suit explained all the rules. ☐

2　On the day of the tryouts, Helen played baseball alone for hours. ☐

3　Helen received an invitation letter from people who worked for the girls' baseball league in Chicago. ☐

4　When the day of the main tryouts came, Helen started for Chicago with many other young women. ☐

5　The writer's grandmother has spent the rest of her life regretting her decision. ☐

6　The writer's grandmother must have gone to Chicago. ☐

● 우리말을 참고하여 빈칸에 알맞은 말을 쓰시오.

1 MY GRANDMOTHER'S BASEBALL _____

2 My grandmother Helen _____ _____ _____ a cook in a restaurant in a small town near South Bend, Indiana.

3 She does not work _____, but she still enjoys making delicious food, _____ I love so much.

4 Food is one of the many things _____ _____ _____.

5 _____ connects us most strongly, however, _____ baseball.

6 When I visit her _____ _____, my grandmother often tells me exciting stories about playing baseball _____ in the 1940s.

7 She _____ _____ _____ the sport very much.

8 I listen to these stories _____ _____ _____.

9 She always says, "_____ _____ what you want, Sarah.

10 Don't be afraid of trying _____ _____ _____ _____.

11 _____ _____ _____ _____ failing."

12 In 1943, the All-American Girls Professional Baseball League _____ _____.

13 This league _____ _____ for baseball fans because many of America's young men _____ _____ in World War II.

14 Helen was told that _____ _____ _____ local tryouts right in South Bend.

15 She wondered, "_____ _____ _____ _____ _____ _____ to be on a baseball team and to make it to the finals for my hometown?"

16 She imagined a large banner _____ at the baseball field _____ _____ the name Helen Baker.

1 할머니의 야구 꿈

2 우리 할머니 Helen은 Indiana주 South Bend 근처 작은 마을에 있는 식당의 요리사였다.

3 할머니는 더 이상 일을 하지 않지만 여전히 맛있는 음식을 즐겨 만드시고, 나는 그 음식들을 무척 좋아한다.

4 음식은 우리를 연결하는 많은 것 가운데 하나이다.

5 하지만 우리를 가장 강하게 연결하는 것은 바로 야구이다.

6 주말마다 할머니 댁에 가면, 할머니는 종종 과거 1940년대의 야구 경기에 관해 흥미로운 이야기를 내게 들려주신다.

7 그녀는 야구를 무척 좋아했던 게 분명하다.

8 나는 이 이야기들을 몇 번이고 듣는다.

9 그녀는 항상 "네가 원하는 것을 이루려고 노력하렴, Sarah.

10 새로운 것이나 도전적인 것을 시도해 보기를 두려워하지 말거라.

11 실패하는 것을 부끄러워하지 마라."라고 말씀하신다.

12 1943년, 전미 여자 프로야구 리그가 창립되었다.

13 미국의 청년 중 많은 사람들이 제2차 세계대전에 참전해 있었기 때문에 이 리그가 야구 팬들을 위해 만들어졌다.

14 Helen 할머니는 지역 심사가 바로 South Bend에서 있을 거라고 들었다.

15 그녀는 "야구 팀에 들어가서 고향을 위해 결승전까지 진출한다는 건 어떤 기분일까?"라며 궁금해했다.

16 그녀는 Helen Baker라는 이름이 포함된 큰 현수막이 야구장에 걸려 있는 것을 상상했다.

17 On the day of the tryouts, all the rules _____ _____ by an old man _____ _____ _____, who sounded very serious and unkind.

18 She thought that _____ _____ _____ in the hot sun might have made him _____.

19 On that day, Helen played baseball _____ _____ with many other young women.

20 She was excited _____ _____ _____ her baseball dreams!

21 About a week later, Helen _____ _____ _____ in the mailbox.

22 _____ _____ _____ people who worked for the girls' baseball league in Chicago.

23 _____ _____ that she _____ _____ _____ to the league's main tryouts in Chicago!

24 _____ the days went by, however, Helen became _____ that she might fail.

25 She also became worried about traveling alone to Chicago, _____ was _____ _____ _____ home.

26 When the day of the main tryouts came, she was _____ afraid _____ go.

27 My grandmother has spent the rest of her life _____ her decision.

28 When she watches a baseball game on TV, she often says, "I _____ _____ _____ to Chicago.

29 You know, all your dreams _____ _____ _____, even if you catch only a few of them.

30 _____ _____ an opportunity."

---

17 심사 당일 모든 규칙이 정장을 입은 나이 든 남자에 의해 설명되었는데, 그는 무척 진지하고 불친절하게 들렸다.

18 뜨거운 태양 아래 정장을 입고 있는 것이 그를 짜증나게 만들었을지도 모른다고 그녀는 생각했다.

19 그날, Helen 할머니는 다른 젊은 여성들과 함께 몇 시간 동안 야구를 했다.

20 그녀는 자신의 야구 꿈을 쫓아가게 되어 신이 났다!

21 일주일쯤 지나, Helen 할머니는 우편함에서 편지 한 통을 발견했다.

22 그것은 시카고에 있는 여자 야구리그에서 일하는 사람들이 보낸 것이었다.

23 그 편지에는 그녀가 시카고에서 열리는 리그의 본심사에 초청되었다고 적혀 있었다!

24 하지만 하루하루 갈수록, Helen 할머니는 심사에 떨어질까봐 걱정되었다.

25 그녀는 또한 시카고까지 혼자 여행하는 것이 걱정되었는데, 시카고는 집에서 멀리 떨어진 곳이었다.

26 본심사가 있는 날이 되었을 때, 그녀는 너무 두려워서 갈 수 없었다.

27 할머니는 남은 인생을 자신의 결정을 후회하며 보내셨다.

28 텔레비전에서 야구 경기를 볼 때, 그녀는 종종 "난 시카고에 갔어야 해.

29 너도 알겠지만, 모든 꿈은 추구할 가치가 있단다. 비록 일부만 이루게 되더라도 말이야.

30 절대 기회를 놓치지 마라."라고 말씀하신다.

● 우리말을 참고하여 본문을 영작하시오.

1 할머니의 야구 꿈

➡ _____

2 우리 할머니 Helen은 Indiana주 South Bend 근처 작은 마을에 있는 식당의 요리사였다.

➡ _____

_____

3 할머니는 더 이상 일을 하지 않지만 여전히 맛있는 음식을 즐겨 만드시고, 나는 그 음식들을 무척 좋아한다.

➡ _____

4 음식은 우리를 연결하는 많은 것 가운데 하나이다.

➡ _____

5 하지만 우리를 가장 강하게 연결하는 것은 바로 야구이다.

➡ _____

6 주말마다 할머니 댁에 가면, 할머니는 종종 과거 1940년대의 야구 경기에 관해 흥미로운 이야기를 내게 들려주신다

➡ _____

_____

7 그녀는 야구를 무척 좋아했던 게 분명하다.

➡ _____

8 나는 이 이야기들을 몇 번이고 듣는다.

➡ _____

9 그녀는 항상 "네가 원하는 것을 이루려고 노력하렴, Sarah.

➡ _____

10 새로운 것이나 도전적인 것을 시도해 보기를 두려워하지 말거라.

➡ _____

11 실패하는 것을 부끄러워하지 마라."라고 말씀하신다.

➡ _____

12 1943년, 전미 여자 프로야구 리그가 창립되었다.

➡ _____

13 미국의 청년 중 많은 사람들이 제2차 세계대전에 참전해 있었기 때문에 이 리그가 야구 팬들을 위해 만들어졌다.

➡ _____

_____

14 Helen 할머니는 지역 심사가 바로 South Bend에서 있을 거라고 들었다.

➡ _____

15 그녀는 "야구 팀에 들어가서 고향을 위해 결승전까지 진출한다는 건 어떤 기분일까?"라며 궁금해했다.

➡ _____

_____

16 그녀는 Helen Baker라는 이름이 포함된 큰 현수막이 야구장에 걸려 있는 것을 상상했다.

➡ _____

_____

17 심사 당일 모든 규칙이 정장을 입은 나이 든 남자에 의해 설명되었는데, 그는 무척 진지하고 불친절하게 들렸다.

➡ _____

_____

18 뜨거운 태양 아래 정장을 입고 있는 것이 그를 짜증나게 만들었을지도 모른다고 그녀는 생각했다.

➡ _____

19 그날, Helen 할머니는 다른 젊은 여성들과 함께 몇 시간 동안 야구를 했다.

➡ _____

20 그녀는 자신의 야구 꿈을 좇아가게 되어 신이 났다!

➡ _____

21 일주일쯤 지나, Helen 할머니는 우편함에서 편지 한 통을 발견했다.

➡ _____

22 그것은 시카고에 있는 여자 야구 리그에서 일하는 사람들이 보낸 것이었다.

➡ _____

23 그 편지에는 그녀가 시카고에서 열리는 리그의 본심사에 초청되었다고 적혀 있었다!

➡ _____

24 하지만 하루하루 갈수록, Helen 할머니는 심사에 떨어질까봐 걱정되었다.

➡ _____

25 그녀는 또한 시카고까지 혼자 여행하는 것이 걱정되었는데, 시카고는 집에서 멀리 떨어진 곳이었다.

➡ _____

26 본심사가 있는 날이 되었을 때, 그녀는 너무 두려워서 갈 수 없었다.

➡ _____

27 할머니는 남은 인생을 자신의 결정을 후회하며 보내셨다.

➡ _____

28 텔레비전에서 야구 경기를 볼 때, 그녀는 종종 "난 시카고에 갔어야 해.

➡ _____

29 너도 알겠지만, 모든 꿈은 추구할 가치가 있단다, 비록 일부만 이루게 되더라도 말이야.

➡ _____

30 절대 기회를 놓치지 마라."라고 말씀하신다.

➡ _____

[01~03] 다음 글을 읽고 물음에 답하시오.

My grandmother Helen (A)[used to / would] be a cook in a restaurant in a small town near South Bend, Indiana. She does not work anymore, but she still enjoys making delicious food, which I love so much. Food is one of the many things that connect us. (B)[That / What] connects us most strongly, however, is baseball.

When I visit her on weekends, my grandmother often tells me exciting stories about playing baseball back in the 1940s. She (C)[must / should] have loved the sport very much. I listen to these stories over and over. She always says, "Go after what you want, Sarah. ⓐDon't be afraid of trying something new or challenging. Don't be ashamed of failing."

서답형

01 위 글의 괄호 (A)~(C)에서 어법상 알맞은 낱말을 골라 쓰시오.

(A) _____ (B) _____ (C) _____

02 위 글의 밑줄 친 ⓐ에서 알 수 있는 Sarah의 할머니의 성격으로 가장 알맞은 것을 고르시오.

① stubborn　　② indecisive
③ adventurous　　④ conservative
⑤ timid

03 According to the passage, which is NOT true?

① Though Sarah's grandmother isn't a cook now, she was a cook in a restaurant.
② Sarah's grandmother still enjoys making delicious food.
③ Sarah and her grandmother have a common interest in baseball.
④ Sarah often tells her grandmother exciting stories about baseball.
⑤ It is certain that Sarah's grandmother loved baseball very much.

[04~06] 다음 글을 읽고 물음에 답하시오.

ⓐAs the days went by, however, Helen became worried that she might fail. She also became worried about traveling alone to Chicago, which was far away from home. When the day of the main tryouts came, she was too afraid to go.

My grandmother has spent the rest of her life regretting her decision. When she watches a baseball game on TV, she often says, "I should have gone to Chicago. You know, ⓑall your dreams are worth chasing, even if you catch only a few of them. Never miss an opportunity."

04 위 글의 밑줄 친 ⓐAs와 같은 의미로 쓰인 것을 고르시오.

① Leave the papers as they are.
② He is famous as a statesman.
③ As we go up, the air grows colder.
④ This is twice as large as that.
⑤ As I was tired, I soon fell asleep.

서답형

05 밑줄 친 ⓑ를 다음과 같이 바꿔 쓸 때 빈칸에 들어갈 알맞은 말을 쓰시오.

> it is worth while to chase _____
>
> _____ _____

중요

06 위 글에 어울리는 속담으로 알맞은 것을 두 개 고르시오.

① Haste makes waste.
② Make hay while the sun shines.
③ It never rains but it pours.
④ Look before you leap.
⑤ Strike the iron while it is hot.

[07~09] 다음 글을 읽고 물음에 답하시오.

In 1943, the All-American Girls Professional Baseball League was founded. This league was created for baseball fans because many of America's young men were fighting in ⓐWorld War Ⅱ.

Helen was told that there would be local tryouts right in South Bend. She wondered, "What would it be like to be on a baseball team and ⓑto make it to the finals for my hometown?" She imagined a large banner hanging at the baseball field which included the name Helen Baker.

서답형

07 위 글의 밑줄 친 ⓐWorld War Ⅱ를 영어로 읽는 법을 쓰시오.

➡ _____

08 아래 〈보기〉에서 위 글의 밑줄 친 ⓑto make와 to부정사의 용법이 다른 것의 개수를 고르시오.

> ┤ 보기 ├
> ① She went to the library to borrow books.
> ② It's important for me to practice English.
> ③ She has a special way to cook rice.
> ④ I am so happy to hear that.
> ⑤ It is about time to play basketball.

① 1개　② 2개　③ 3개　④ 4개　⑤ 5개

서답형

09 Why was the All-American Girls Professional Baseball League founded? Fill in the blanks (A) and (B) with suitable words.

> Many of America's (A)_____ _____ were fighting in World War Ⅱ, so the All-American Girls Professional Baseball League was founded in 1943 for (B)_____ _____.

[10~12] 다음 글을 읽고 물음에 답하시오.

About a week later, Helen found a letter in the mailbox. It was from people who worked for the girls' baseball league in Chicago. It read that she had been invited to the league's main tryouts in Chicago!

As the days went by, ____ⓐ____, Helen became worried that she might fail. She also became worried about traveling alone to Chicago, which was far away from home. When the day of the main tryouts came, she was too afraid to go.

중요

10 위 글의 빈칸 ⓐ에 들어갈 알맞은 말을 고르시오.

① for example　　② that is
③ in addition　　④ however
⑤ thus

중요

11 위 글의 제목으로 가장 알맞은 것은?

① The Girls' Baseball League Held in Chicago
② Wow! I Was Invited to the League's Main Tryouts!
③ An Unfulfilled Dream out of Fear
④ What If I Fail?
⑤ Travel Alone to Chicago? No Way!

12 According to the passage, which is NOT true?

① Helen found a letter in the mailbox about a week later.
② People who worked for the girls' baseball league in Chicago sent an invitation letter to Helen.
③ Helen became worried that she might fail as the days went by.
④ Though Chicago wasn't far away from home, Helen became worried about traveling alone there.
⑤ When the day of the main tryouts came, Helen was so afraid that she couldn't go.

[13~14] 다음 글을 읽고 물음에 답하시오.

On the day of the tryouts, all the rules were explained by an old man ___ⓐ___ a suit, who sounded very serious and unkind. She thought that (A)뜨거운 태양 아래 정장을 입고 있는 것이 그를 짜증나게 만들었을지도 모른다. On that day, Helen played baseball for hours

with many other young women. She was excited to go ___ⓑ___ her baseball dreams!

13 위 글의 빈칸 ⓐ와 ⓑ에 들어갈 전치사가 바르게 짝지어진 것은?

　　ⓐ　　ⓑ　　　　ⓐ　　ⓑ　　　　ⓐ　　ⓑ
① for – on　　② in – after　　③ in – on
④ for – to　　⑤ on – after

서답형

14 밑줄 친 (A)의 우리말에 맞게 주어진 어휘를 이용하여 12 단어로 영작하시오.

wearing, in, might, made, impatient

➡ _____

_____

15 주어진 글 다음에 이어질 글의 순서로 가장 적절한 것은?

My grandmother Helen used to be a cook in a restaurant in a small town near South Bend, Indiana. She does not work anymore, but she still enjoys making delicious food, which I love so much.

(A) I listen to these stories over and over. She always says, "Go after what you want, Sarah. Don't be afraid of trying something new or challenging. Don't be ashamed of failing."

(B) Food is one of the many things that connect us. What connects us most strongly, however, is baseball.

(C) When I visit her on weekends, my grandmother often tells me exciting stories about playing baseball back in the 1940s. She must have loved the sport very much.

① (A) – (C) – (B)   ② (B) – (A) – (C)
③ (B) – (C) – (A)   ④ (C) – (A) – (B)
⑤ (C) – (B) – (A)

[16~18] 다음 글을 읽고 물음에 답하시오.

My grandmother Helen ⓐused to be a cook in a restaurant in a small town near South Bend, Indiana. She does not work anymore, but she still enjoys making delicious food, which I love so much. Food is one of the many things that connect us. ⓑWhat connect us most strongly, however, is baseball.

When I visit her on weekends, my grandmother often tells me exciting stories about playing baseball back in the 1940s. She must have loved the sport very much. I listen to these stories over and over. She always says, "Go after what you want, Sarah. Don't be afraid of trying something new or challenging. Don't be ashamed of failing."

16 위 글의 밑줄 친 ⓐused to와 문법적 쓰임이 다른 것을 고르시오.

① Love <u>used to</u> be something more romantic than it is now.
② He isn't what he <u>used to</u> be three years ago.
③ There <u>used to</u> be many tall trees in front of the school buildings.
④ She <u>used to</u> live in Korea.
⑤ He <u>used to</u> call on me every Sunday.

서답형

17 위 글의 밑줄 친 ⓑ에서 어법상 틀린 부분을 찾아 고치시오.

_____ ➡ _____

18 위 글의 주제로 알맞은 것을 고르시오.

① Sarah's grandmother's love for cooking
② Sarah's grandmother's special dish
③ Sarah's grandmother's love for baseball
④ the exciting stories about playing baseball back in the 1940s
⑤ Sarah's grandmother's nursery story

[19~20] 다음 글을 읽고 물음에 답하시오.

On the day of the tryouts, all the rules were explained by an old man in a suit, who sounded very (A)[serious and unkind / seriously and unkindly]. She thought that wearing a suit in the hot sun might have made him (B)[impatient / impatiently]. On that day, Helen played baseball for hours with many other young women. She was excited to go after her baseball dreams!

About a week later, Helen found a letter in the mailbox. It was from people who worked for the girls' baseball league in Chicago. It (C)[read / was read] that she had been invited to the league's main tryouts in Chicago!

서답형

19 위 글의 괄호 (A)~(C)에서 문맥이나 어법상 알맞은 낱말을 골라 쓰시오.

(A) _____
(B) _____ (C) _____

20 위 글을 읽고 알 수 <u>없는</u> 것은?

① Who explained all the rules?
② With whom did Helen play baseball on the day of the tryouts?
③ Who sent the invitation letter to Helen?
④ Where would the league's main tryouts be held?
⑤ Did Helen participate in the league's main tryouts?

[01~03] 다음 글을 읽고 물음에 답하시오.

My grandmother Helen used to be a cook in a restaurant in a small town near South Bend, Indiana. ⓐShe does not work anymore, but she still enjoys making delicious food, that I love so much. Food is one of the many things that connect us. What connects us most strongly, however, is baseball.

When I visit her on weekends, my grandmother often tells me exciting stories about playing baseball back in the 1940s. ⓑ She must have loved the sport very much. I listen to these stories over and over. She always says, "Go after what you want, Sarah. Don't be afraid of trying something new or challenging. Don't be ashamed of failing."

01 위 글의 밑줄 친 ⓐ에서 어법상 틀린 부분을 찾아 고치시오.

_____ ➡ _____

02 위 글의 밑줄 친 ⓑ를 다음과 같이 바꿔 쓸 때 빈칸에 들어갈 알맞은 한 단어를 쓰시오.

> It is certain that she _____ the sport very much.

03 다음 빈칸 (A)와 (B)에 알맞은 단어를 넣어 Sarah의 할머니에 대한 소개를 완성하시오.

> Sarah's grandmother (A)_____ a cook in a restaurant, but now she isn't a cook anymore. Nevertheless, she still enjoys making delicious food, and (B)_____ loves it so much.
>
> *nevertheless: 그렇기는 하지만, 그럼에도 불구하고

[04~07] 다음 글을 읽고 물음에 답하시오.

As the days went by, however, Helen became worried that she might fail. She also became worried about traveling alone to Chicago, which was far away from home. When the day of the main tryouts came, (A)she was too afraid to go.

My grandmother has spent the rest of her life ___ⓐ___ her decision. When she watches a baseball game on TV, she often says, "(B)I must have gone to Chicago. You know, all your dreams are worth chasing, even if you catch only a few of them. Never miss an opportunity."

04 위 글의 빈칸 ⓐ에 regret를 알맞은 형태로 쓰시오.

➡ _____

05 위 글의 밑줄 친 (A)를 다음과 같이 바꿔 쓸 때 빈칸에 들어갈 알맞은 말을 쓰시오.

> she was _____ afraid _____ she _____ go

06 위 글의 밑줄 친 (B)에서 흐름상 어색한 부분을 찾아 고치시오.

_____ ➡ _____

07 Helen이 시카고에 가지 못한 이유 두 가지를 우리말로 쓰시오.

(1) _____
(2) _____

[08~10] 다음 글을 읽고 물음에 답하시오.

My grandmother Helen used to be a cook in a restaurant in a small town near South Bend, Indiana. She does not work anymore, but she still enjoys making delicious food, which I love so much. Food is one of the many things that connect us. ⓐ우리를 가장 강하게 연결하는 것은, however, is baseball.

When I visit her ⓑon weekends, my grandmother often tells me exciting stories about playing baseball back in the 1940s. She must have loved the sport very much. I listen to ⓒthese stories over and over. She always says, "Go after what you want, Sarah. Don't be afraid of trying something new or challenging. Don't be ashamed of failing."

08 위 글의 밑줄 친 ⓐ의 우리말에 맞게 관계대명사를 사용하여 5 단어로 영작하시오.

➡ _____

09 위 글의 밑줄 친 ⓑon weekends와 바꿔 쓸 수 있는 말을 쓰시오.

➡ _____

10 위 글의 밑줄 친 ⓒthese stories가 가리키는 것을 본문에서 찾아 쓰시오.

➡ _____

[11~13] 다음 글을 읽고 물음에 답하시오.

On the day of the tryouts, all the rules were explained by an old man in a suit, ⓐ who sounded very serious and unkind. She thought that wearing a suit in the hot sun might have made him impatient. On that day, Helen played baseball for hours with many other young women. She was excited to go after her baseball dreams!

About a week later, Helen found a letter in the mailbox. It was from people who worked for the girls' baseball league in Chicago. It read that she had been invited to the league's main tryouts in Chicago!

11 위 글의 밑줄 친 ⓐwho를 접속사를 포함한 두 단어로 바꿔 쓰시오.

➡ _____

12 What was written on the invitation letter? Fill in the blanks (A) and (B) with suitable words.

> The fact that she _____ _____ _____ to the league's main tryouts in Chicago was written on the invitation letter.

13 본문의 내용과 일치하도록 다음 빈칸 (A)와 (B)에 알맞은 단어를 쓰시오.

> Helen thought that (A)_____ _____ _____ in the hot sun might have caused an old man who explained all the rules to be impatient, and as a result, he sounded very (B)_____ _____ _____.

해석

After You Read Graphic Organizer

Cause

The Second World War broke out.
발발했다

She loved baseball so much.

She was not sure of her success. Also, she was afraid of traveling alone.
~에 확신을 가졌다   동명사   = by herself

Effect

In 1943, the All-American Girls Professional Baseball League was founded.
                                                        found–founded–founded

She joined the local tryouts in South Bend.
= participated in

She didn't go to the main tryouts.

구문해설
- break out: 발발하다 · be sure of: ~에 확신을 가지다, ~을 믿다
- be afraid of: ~을 무서워하다 · league: 리그, 연맹 · found: 설립하다
- tryout: 심사, 테스트

원인

제2차 세계대전이 발발했다. 그녀는 야구를 무척 좋아했다. 그녀는 자신의 성공을 확신하지 못했다. 또한 그녀는 혼자 여행하는 것을 두려워했다.

결과

1943년, 전미 여자 프로야구 리그가 창립되었다. 그녀는 **South Bend**의 지역 심사에 참가했다. 그녀는 본심사에 가지 않았다.

My Writing Portfolio

JANE GOODALL, MOTHER OF CHIMPANZEES

Jane Goodall was born in London, England, in 1934. Her interest in
borne(✗)
chimpanzees began when she first read about Tarzan. She has been studying
                                                        현재완료진행형
wild chimpanzees in Africa since her twenties. She has also been working for
                            since+시간 명사. for+기간 명사   현재완료진행형
the protection of chimpanzees. In 1995, she received the Hubbard Medal for
protecting wild animals. Thanks to her lifelong study, we have come to know a
                                                                ~하게 되다
lot about chimpanzees. Jane Goodall is one of the greatest scientists in history.
                                        one of+복수 명사: ~ 중의 하나

구문해설 · protection: 보호 · wild animal: 야생 동물 · thanks to: ~ 덕분에 · lifelong: 일생[평생]의

Jane Goodall, 침팬지의 어머니

Jane Goodall은 1934년 영국 런던에서 태어났다. 침팬지에 대한 관심은 그녀가 타잔에 관해 읽었을 때 시작되었다. 그녀는 20대 때부터 아프리카에서 야생 침팬지를 연구해 오고 있다. 그녀는 침팬지 보호를 위해서도 노력해 오고 있다. 1995년에 그녀는 야생 동물 보호에 대한 공로를 인정받아 허버드상을 받았다. 일생을 바친 그녀의 연구 덕분에, 우리는 침팬지에 관해 많이 알게 되었다. Jane Goodall은 역사상 가장 위대한 과학자 중 한 명이다.

Words in Action

The Cheetahs are winning the game, and their fans are singing a cheerful
song. If Jason stays calm and catches the ball, the game ends. Oh my! He
조건의 부사절을 이끄는 접속사
misses the ball! The Ducks make two runs, and the game continues. Jason
looks ashamed and nervous. The Ducks fans are going wild, while the
감정동사의 과거분사형(감정을 느낄 때 사용)   반면에(대조를 나타내는 접속사)
Cheetahs fans look scared and worried.
감정동사의 과거분사형(감정을 느낄 때 사용)

구문해설
- cheerful: 발랄한, 쾌활한, 즐거운 · stay calm: 침착함을 유지하다
- make two runs: 2루로 진루하다 · continue: 계속하다 · ashamed: 부끄러운, 창피한
- nervous: 불안해[초조해] 하는 · go wild: 미친 듯 열중하다
- scared: 무서워하는, 겁먹은 · worried: 걱정[우려]하는, 걱정스러워 하는

Cheetahs가 경기를 이기고 있고, 팬들이 신나는 노래를 부르고 있습니다. **Jason**이 침착함을 유지해서 공을 잡으면 경기가 끝납니다. 오, 이럴수가! 그가 공을 놓칩니다! **Ducks**는 2루로 진루하고, 경기는 계속됩니다. **Jason**은 창피하고 긴장한 것처럼 보입니다. **Ducks** 팬들은 열광하고 있는 반면, **Cheetahs** 팬들은 두렵고 걱정스러운 것처럼 보입니다.

영역별 핵심문제

01 다음 짝지어진 단어의 관계가 같도록 빈칸에 알맞은 말을 쓰시오.

> offer : proposal = determination : _____

02 다음 중 밑줄 친 부분의 뜻풀이가 바르지 않은 것은?

① As time <u>went by</u>, he got more and more wrinkles on his face. (지나갔다, 흘렀다)
② He spent the <u>rest</u> of his money on dinner. (나머지)
③ His speech is <u>worth</u> listening to over and over again. (~할 가치가 있는)
④ My sister was very nervous all night before the <u>tryouts</u>. (노력)
⑤ <u>Even if</u> you don't like it, you must do it. (비록 ~하더라도)

03 다음 주어진 문장의 밑줄 친 apply와 같은 의미로 쓰인 것은?

> You can <u>apply</u> for citizenship after five years' residency.

① <u>Apply</u> the paint with a fine brush.
② The rules don't <u>apply</u> here.
③ I should like to <u>apply</u> for the position of Sales Director.
④ He had to <u>apply</u> some force to open the door.
⑤ This rule doesn't <u>apply</u> to your case.

04 다음 우리말을 주어진 어구를 이용하여 영작하시오.

(1) 왜 이 선생님은 항상 야근을 하세요?
(come, Mr. Lee, work overtime)
➡ _____

(2) 네 꿈을 이루고 싶다면, 너는 그것을 추구해야만 한다. (accomplish, should, go, it)
➡ _____
_____

(3) 그 조리법은 달걀과 우유를 포함하나요?
(recipe, eggs, include)
➡ _____

05 다음 주어진 문장의 밑줄 친 rest와 같은 의미로 쓰인 것은?

> He spent the <u>rest</u> of his life in France.

① Jack divided up the <u>rest</u> of the cash.
② The doctor told me to <u>rest</u>.
③ I had a good night's <u>rest</u>.
④ <u>Rest</u> your head on my shoulder.
⑤ I don't want to <u>rest</u> on my past glory.

06 다음 영영풀이에 해당하는 단어로 알맞은 것은?

> to feel sorry about something that you did in the past

① practice　　② achieve
③ improve　　④ connect
⑤ regret

Conversation

[07~10] 다음 대화를 읽고 물음에 답하시오.

M: Nice to meet you, Sora. Did you do well on the drawing exam?

G: I'm not sure, but I did my best.

M: Okay. (①) What made you apply for Mana Animation High School?

G: Well, I've really loved drawing cartoons since I was a little child. (②)

M: (③) So, you want to be a cartoon artist?

G: (A)That's not quite right. I want to be a game designer. (④)

M: I see. (⑤) What do you think is the most important skill a game designer needs?

G: I'd say imagination. A good designer should create a completely new world in a game.

M: Sounds good.

07 위 대화의 (①)~(⑤) 중에서 주어진 문장이 들어가기에 가장 적절한 곳은?

> Let's start the interview.

①   ②   ③   ④   ⑤

08 위 대화의 밑줄 친 (A)와 의도가 같도록 2 단어로 쓰시오. (단어 wrong은 사용하지 말 것.)

➡ _____

09 위 대화의 내용과 일치하지 <u>않는</u> 것은?

① 남자는 소라에게 소묘 시험을 잘 봤는지 묻는다.
② 소라는 최선을 다했다고 답한다.

③ 소라는 어렸을 때부터 만화 그리는 것을 정말 좋아해서 마나 애니메이션 고등학교에 지원했다.
④ 소라는 만화가가 되고 싶다.
⑤ 소라는 게임 디자이너에게 필요한 가장 중요한 기량은 상상력이라고 생각한다.

10 Why does Sora think imagination is the most important skill a game designer needs? Answer in English beginning with "Because".

➡ _____
_____

[11~13] 다음 대화를 읽고 물음에 답하시오.

G: My computer has viruses.

B: (A)어쩌다가 그랬니?

G: I opened an e-mail from a stranger.
_____(a)_____ (should, that)

B: (B)내가 너라면, 지금 바로 컴퓨터 서비스 센터에서 도움을 받겠어. (a computer service center, help, get, right, from)

11 빈칸 (a)에 알맞은 말을 주어진 단어를 이용해서 5 단어로 쓰시오.

➡ _____

12 위 대화의 밑줄 친 (A)의 우리말을 두 단어로 영작하시오.

➡ _____

13 위 대화의 밑줄 친 (B)의 우리말을 주어진 어휘를 이용하여 14 단어로 영작하시오.

➡ _____
_____

14 다음 중 짝지어진 대화가 <u>어색한</u> 것을 고르시오.

① A: The capital of Australia is Sydney, right?

B: I'm afraid you're wrong. The capital of Australia is Canberra.

② A: What's the matter?

B: My nose is getting longer. I should have told lies.

③ A: I should have sent her a thank-you letter.

B: I think texting might have been better.

④ A: Tom, I hear you're from Pittsburg.

B: That's not quite right. I'm from Gettysburg.

⑤ A: Tomatoes were first grown in Europe, weren't they?

B: I'm afraid you're mistaken. They were first grown in South America.

Grammar

15 다음 빈칸에 들어갈 말로 알맞은 것은?

Tom showed me a picture, _____ he took yesterday.

① where ② who ③ what
④ that ⑤ which

16 다음 중 어법상 <u>어색한</u> 문장을 <u>모두</u> 고르시오.

① You should have came to the meeting on time.

② She must have loved flowers.

③ He may be in Paris when Irene went to Finland.

④ I should have read more books because I want to be a writer.

⑤ She thought that wearing a suit in the hot sun might have made him impatient.

17 다음 그림을 참고하여 빈칸에 알맞게 쓰시오.

This morning, I met Audrey, _____
_____ I ran to school not to be late.

18 다음 두 문장의 의미가 비슷하도록 할 때, 빈칸에 알맞은 말을 쓰시오.

(1) I'm sorry you didn't go to the movies with her yesterday.

➡ You _____ to the movies with her yesterday.

(2) I'm sure you didn't go to the movies with her yesterday.

➡ You _____ to the movies with her yesterday.

(3) I'm sure you went to the movies with her yesterday.

➡ You _____ to the movies with her yesterday.

(4) It's a pity that you went to the movies with her yesterday.

➡ You _____ to the movies with her yesterday.

(5) It is probable that you went to the movies with her yesterday.

➡ You _____ to the movies with her yesterday.

19 다음 문장을 의미에 맞게 바르게 바꿔 쓴 문장을 고르시오.

> Maryanne, who was young, had to work every day.

① Maryanne, for she was young, had to work every day.
② Maryanne, though she was young, had to work every day.
③ Maryanne, and she was young, had to work every day.
④ Maryanne, so she was young, had to work every day.
⑤ Maryanne, unless she was young, had to work every day.

20 다음 빈칸에 알맞은 것은?

> He had a beautiful wife, _____ he loved greatly.

① that   ② what   ③ which
④ whom   ⑤ whose

21 다음 ⓐ~ⓕ 중 어법상 옳은 것을 모두 고르시오.

> ⓐ You may have left it in the classroom.
> ⓑ Minsu must have eat it. He was near the table a few minutes ago.
> ⓒ Thank you for helping me. I might have gotten lost without you.
> ⓓ My fish in the fish tank were dead. I should have forgotten to feed them.
> ⓔ Nick lost an umbrella, which he bought yesterday.
> ⓕ Dorothy Kamenshek, that was called "Dottie," was only 17 when she first played in the All-American Girls Professional Baseball League.

➡ _____

Reading

[22~24] 다음 글을 읽고 물음에 답하시오.

My grandmother Helen used to be a cook in a restaurant in a small town near South Bend, Indiana. (①) She does not work anymore, but she still enjoys making delicious food, which I love so much. (②) Food is one of the many things that connect us. (③)

When I visit her on weekends, my grandmother often tells me exciting stories about playing baseball back in the 1940s. (④) She must have loved the sport very much. (⑤) I listen to these stories over and over. She always says, "Go after what you want, Sarah. ⓐ새로운 것이나 도전적인 것을 시도해 보기를 두려워하지 말거라. Don't be ashamed of failing."

22 위 글의 흐름으로 보아, 주어진 문장이 들어가기에 가장 적절한 곳은?

> What connects us most strongly, however, is baseball.

①   ②   ③   ④   ⑤

23 위 글의 제목으로 알맞은 것을 고르시오.

① My Grandma, the Greatest Cook Ever
② Grandma Still Enjoys Making Delicious Food!
③ Baseball, What Connects Us Most Strongly
④ Playing Baseball Back in the 1940s
⑤ How to Go after What You Want

24 위 글의 밑줄 친 ⓐ의 우리말에 맞게 주어진 어휘를 알맞게 배열하시오.

> trying / don't / be / new / afraid / challenging / of / or / something

➡ _____

_____

[25~26] 다음 글을 읽고 물음에 답하시오.

In 1943, the All-American Girls Professional Baseball League was (A)[found / founded]. This league was created for baseball fans because many of America's young men were fighting in World War Ⅱ.

Helen was told that there would be local tryouts right in South Bend. She (B)[wandered / wondered], "(C)[How / What] would it be like to be on a baseball team and to make it to the finals for my hometown?" She imagined a large banner hanging at the baseball field which included the name Helen Baker.

25 위 글의 괄호 (A)~(C)에서 문맥이나 어법상 알맞은 낱말을 골라 쓰시오.

(A) _____ (B) _____ (C) _____

26 According to the passage, which is NOT true?

① The All-American Girls Professional Baseball League was created for baseball fans.

② In 1943, many of America's young men were fighting in World War Ⅱ.

③ Someone told Helen that there would be local tryouts right in South Bend.

④ Helen was on a baseball team and made it to the finals for her hometown.

⑤ Helen imagined a large banner hanging at the baseball field which included her name.

[27~28] 다음 글을 읽고 물음에 답하시오.

On the day of the tryouts, all the rules were explained by an old man in a suit, who sounded very serious and unkind. She thought that ⓐwearing a suit in the hot sun might have made him impatient. On that day, Helen played baseball for hours with many other young women. She was excited to go after her baseball dreams!

About a week later, Helen found a letter in the mailbox. ⓑIt was from people who worked for the girls' baseball league in Chicago. It read that she had been invited to the league's main tryouts in Chicago!

27 위 글의 밑줄 친 ⓐwearing과 문법적 쓰임이 같은 것을 모두 고르시오.

① He was thinking about wearing a suit.

② Do you know the man wearing a suit?

③ He is wearing a suit.

④ I saw him wearing a suit.

⑤ He didn't mind wearing a suit in the hot sun.

28 위 글의 밑줄 친 ⓑIt이 가리키는 것을 본문에서 찾아 쓰시오.

➡ _____

01 출제율 90%

다음 영영풀이가 가리키는 것을 고르시오.

> to have something as part of a group or total

① improve ② include ③ create
④ chase ⑤ found

02 출제율 95%

다음 〈보기〉에서 알맞은 단어를 골라 문장을 완성하시오.

┌─ 보기 ─┐
gloomy regretful curious jealous
relieved
└─────┘

(1) I am _____ about your opinion on the new employee.

(2) If you don't study hard now, you will be _____ later.

(3) They are very _____ of my good reputation.

(4) You'll be _____ to know your jobs are safe.

(5) Cloudy days like this make me feel _____.

[03~05] 다음 대화를 읽고 물음에 답하시오.

W: Nice to meet you, Seongho.
B: Nice to meet you, (A)[either / too].
W: Are you nervous?
B: A bit, but I'm fine.
W: Okay, let's start the interview. (a)왜 우리 학교에 지원했나요?
B: I like the curriculum of this school (B)[because / because of] it has various subjects. I'm certain (C)[that / if] (b)they'll help me in many ways.
W: I see. Good luck to you.
B: Thank you.

03 출제율 100%

위 대화의 (A)~(C)에 들어갈 말로 바르게 짝지어진 것은?

	(A)	(B)	(C)
①	either	because	if
②	either	because of	if
③	too	because	that
④	too	because of	that
⑤	too	because	if

04 출제율 90%

위 대화의 밑줄 친 (a)의 우리말을 make를 이용하여 영작하시오.

➡ _____

05 출제율 95%

위 대화의 밑줄 친 (b)they가 가리키는 것을 찾아 쓰시오.

➡ _____

[06~07] 다음 대화를 읽고 물음에 답하시오.

B: Hi, Sora. What are you doing?
G: I'm drawing cartoons. I'm preparing for the exam for Mana Animation High School.
B: Oh, do you? When is the exam?
G: On Friday, so I only have two days left.
B: How's it going?
G: It's not easy to draw what I want to express. I should have practiced more.
B: Don't worry! You can make it!
G: Thanks.

06 출제율 95%

위 대화에서 어법상 어색한 것을 하나 찾아 바르게 고치시오.

_____ ➡ _____

07 위 대화에 나타난 소라의 심경으로 적절한 것을 고르시오.

① delighted　② nervous　③ peaceful
④ regretful　⑤ relieved

[08~09] 다음 대화를 읽고 물음에 답하시오.

M: Nice to meet you, Sora. Did you do well on the drawing exam?

G: I'm not sure, but I did my best.

M: Okay. Let's start the interview. What made you apply for Mana Animation High School?

G: Well, I've really loved drawing cartoons since I was a little child.

M: So, you want to be a cartoon artist?

G: (A)꼭 그렇지는 않습니다. I want to be a game designer.

M: I see. What do you think is the most important skill a game designer needs?

G: I'd say imagination. A good designer should create a completely new world in a game.

M: Sounds good.

08 위 대화를 읽고 답할 수 <u>없는</u> 질문을 고르시오.

① Did Sora do her best on the drawing exam?
② Why did Sora apply for Mana Animation High School?
③ Does Sora want to be a cartoon artist?
④ Since when has Sora wanted to be a game designer?
⑤ Why does Sora think imagination is the most important skill a game designer needs?

09 위 대화의 밑줄 친 (A)의 우리말을 right를 이용하여 4 단어로 영작하시오.

➡ _____

10 다음 중 짝지어진 대화가 <u>어색한</u> 것을 고르시오.

① A: Pad thai is a famous Vietnamese dish.
　B: I'm afraid you're mistaken. Pad thai is a famous Thai dish.
② A: A volcano called Paricutin appeared in three days.
　B: I'm afraid you're wrong. A volcano called Paricutin appeared overnight.
③ A: Are you nervous?
　B: A bit, but I'm fine.
④ A: You're late again. You're always late.
　B: I'm so sorry. I should have made you wait.
⑤ A: My house has blown away. I should have built it with stronger material.
　B: Don't worry. I'll help you to build your house again.

11 다음 빈칸에 들어갈 수 있는 말이 <u>다른</u> 하나는?

① Einstein, _____ was born in Germany, is famous for the theory of relativity.
② I visited my friend in Mokpo, _____ welcomed me.
③ Our homeroom teacher is Mr. Hong, _____ teaches us history.
④ Uncle Ben went on a trip to Africa, _____ was his lifelong dream.
⑤ The writer, _____ was taking a walk in the park, sat down on the bench.

12 출제율 100%

다음 중 어법상 적절한 문장을 <u>모두</u> 고르시오.

① I should have practice more to improve my speaking skills.

② I think sending text messages might have be better.

③ You shouldn't have made the same mistake again.

④ It must rain last night.

⑤ Mike may have been sick last weekend.

13 출제율 90%

다음 두 문장이 같은 뜻이 되도록 빈칸에 알맞은 말을 두 단어로 쓰시오.

This painting is *Sunflowers*, which was painted by Vincent van Gogh.

= This painting is *Sunflowers*, _____ _____ was painted by Vincent van Gogh.

14 출제율 95%

'should'와 괄호 안의 단어를 이용하여 다음 상황에 알맞은 충고의 말을 완성하시오.

(1) I spent all the money on snacks. I need some money to buy the book.

➡ You _____ money more carefully. (spend)

(2) I wasted my time playing computer games. I need more time to finish the project.

➡ You _____ your time. (waste)

(3) It's very dark. I need a light to find the way.

➡ You _____ a lantern. (bring)

15 출제율 95%

다음 빈칸에 들어갈 알맞은 말을 순서대로 묶은 것은?

• It's very hot here. You _____ have worn a T-shirt and shorts.

• My favorite city is Sydney, _____ is located on the east coast of Australia.

① should – who   ② should – which

③ must – who   ④ must – which

⑤ may – that

[16~18] 다음 글을 읽고 물음에 답하시오.

My grandmother Helen used to be a cook in a restaurant in a small town near South Bend, Indiana. She does not work anymore, but she still enjoys ⓐ_____ delicious food, which I love so much. Food is one of the many things that connect us. ⓑWhat connects us most strongly, however, is baseball.

When I visit her on weekends, my grandmother often tells me exciting stories about playing baseball back in the 1940s. She must have loved the sport very much. I listen to these stories ⓒover and over. She always says, "Go after what you want, Sarah. Don't be afraid of trying something new or challenging. Don't be ashamed of failing."

16 출제율 90%

위 글의 빈칸 ⓐ에 make를 알맞은 형태로 쓰시오.

➡ _____

17 출제율 95%

위 글의 밑줄 친 ⓑWhat과 문법적 쓰임이 같은 것을 고르시오.

① What is your name?

② He always does what he believes is right.

③ What kind of music do you like?

④ What do you think this is?

⑤ What day of the week is it today?

④ Helen's excitement from going after her baseball dreams

⑤ the girls' baseball league in Chicago

출제율 90%

18 위 글의 밑줄 친 ⓒover and over와 바꿔 쓸 수 없는 말을 고르시오.

① time and again ② repeatedly

③ step by step ④ many times

⑤ time after time

출제율 95%

21 위 글에서 알 수 있는 Helen의 심경으로 가장 알맞은 것을 고르시오.

① regretful ② afraid

③ puzzled ④ disappointed

⑤ excited

[19~21] 다음 글을 읽고 물음에 답하시오.

On the day of the tryouts, all the rules were explained by an old man in a suit, who sounded very serious and unkind. (①) She thought that wearing a suit in the hot sun might have made him impatient. (②) On that day, Helen played baseball for hours with many other young women. (③) She was excited to go after her baseball dreams!

(④) It was from people who worked for the girls' baseball league in Chicago. (⑤) It read that she had been invited to the league's main tryouts in Chicago!

[22~23] 다음 글을 읽고 물음에 답하시오.

My grandmother has spent the rest of her life regretting her decision. When she watches a baseball game on TV, she often says, "ⓐI should have gone to Chicago. You know, all your dreams are worth chasing, even if you catch only a few of ⓑthem. Never miss an opportunity."

출제율 95%

19 위 글의 흐름으로 보아, 주어진 문장이 들어가기에 가장 적절한 곳은?

About a week later, Helen found a letter in the mailbox.

① ② ③ ④ ⑤

출제율 95%

22 위 글의 밑줄 친 ⓐ를 다음과 같이 바꿔 쓸 때 빈칸에 들어갈 알맞은 말을 두 단어로 쓰시오.

I am sorry that I ＿＿＿＿ ＿＿＿＿ to Chicago.

출제율 100%

20 위 글의 주제로 알맞은 것을 고르시오.

① the hot weather on the day of the tryouts

② the importance of wearing a suit

③ to play baseball with other women

출제율 90%

23 위 글의 밑줄 친 ⓑ가 가리키는 것을 본문에서 찾아 쓰시오.

➡ ＿＿＿＿＿＿＿＿＿＿＿＿＿

[01~03] 다음 대화를 읽고 물음에 답하시오.

G: Hi, Jiho.

B: Hi, Amber. It's nice to see you on the bus.

G: Yeah, but I'm afraid we're going to be late.

B: Yeah. I hate to be late for the school festival.

G: Me, too. I should have set my alarm. I forgot.

B: I understand. That happens a lot to me when I'm tired, too.

G: How about you? What made you late?

B: Well, I got up early. But it took me some time to do my hair.

G: Oh, I see. We're stuck in a heavy traffic jam. We should get off and run.

B: No, you're mistaken. The traffic is starting to move again. Let's stay on.

G: Okay. I just hope we're not terribly late.

01 Where are Jiho and Amber going now? Answer with 7 words.

➡ _____

02 Why is Jiho late? Answer in English beginning with "Because".

➡ _____
_____

03 Why did Amber suggest that they get off the bus and run? Answer in English beginning with "Because".

➡ _____
_____

04 계속적 용법의 관계대명사를 사용하여 주어진 두 문장을 한 문장으로 바꾸시오.

(1) • This book is about Abraham Lincoln.
 • Abraham Lincoln was the 16th President of the U.S.

➡ _____
_____

(2) • My grandmother's house is still nice to live in.
 • My grandmother's house was built 100 years ago.

➡ _____
_____

(3) • She enjoys making delicious food.
 • She finds satisfaction from making delicious food.

➡ _____
_____

05 다음 문장에서 틀린 것을 고쳐 다시 쓰시오.

(1) Fallen leaves are on the ground. It should have been windy.

➡ _____
_____

(2) Sam looks very tired this morning. He should have stayed up late last night.

➡ _____
_____

(3) His favorite place is his house, that is next to mine.

➡ _____
_____

(4) My brother, who major was history, is a professor of the university.

➡ _____
_____

06 다음 우리말을 주어진 어휘를 이용하여 영작하시오.

(1) 기차가 역에 도착했을지도 모른다.
(arrive, the station)

➡ _____

_____

(2) 그가 이것을 혼자 했을 리가 없다.
(do, this, by himself)

➡ _____

_____

(3) 이 스마트폰은 내가 지난달에 샀는데, 디자인이 매우 좋다. (have a great design)

➡ _____

_____

[07~09] 다음 글을 읽고 물음에 답하시오.

My grandmother Helen used to be a cook in a restaurant in a small town near South Bend, Indiana. She does not work anymore, but she still enjoys making delicious food, ⓐwhich I love so much. Food is one of the many things that connect us. What connects us most strongly, however, is baseball.

When I visit her on weekends, my grandmother often tells me exciting stories about playing baseball back in the ⓑ1940s. She must have loved the sport very much. I listen to these stories over and over. She always says, "Go after what you want, Sarah. Don't be afraid of trying something new or challenging. Don't be ashamed of failing."

07 위 글의 밑줄 친 ⓐ를 접속사를 사용하여 바꿔 쓰시오.

➡ _____

08 위 글의 밑줄 친 ⓑ1940s를 영어로 읽는 법을 쓰시오.

➡ _____

09 본문의 내용과 일치하도록 다음 빈칸에 알맞은 단어를 쓰시오.

Sarah's grandmother always tells Sarah to go after _____ _____ _____.

[10~12] 다음 글을 읽고 물음에 답하시오.

On the day of the tryouts, (A)all the rules were explained by an old man in a suit, who sounded very serious and unkind. She thought that wearing a suit in the hot sun might have made him impatient. On that day, Helen played baseball for hours with many other young women. She was excited to go after her baseball dreams!

About a week later, Helen found a letter in the mailbox. It was from people who worked for the girls' baseball league in Chicago. It read that she ___ⓐ___ to the league's main tryouts in Chicago!

10 위 글의 빈칸 ⓐ에 invite를 알맞은 형태로 쓰시오.

➡ _____

11 위 글의 밑줄 친 (A)를 능동태로 고치시오.

➡ _____

12 본문의 내용과 일치하도록 다음 빈칸 (A)와 (B)에 알맞은 단어를 쓰시오.

Helen received an invitation (A)_____ from people who worked for the girls' baseball league in Chicago where the league's (B)_____ _____ would be held.

01 다음 내용에서 필자가 후회하고 있는 것을 찾아 우리말로 쓰시오.

> My school life was mostly fun, but there are some things that I regret. First of all, I should have read more books because I want to be a writer. Second, I shouldn't have played online games so much. Thirdly, I should have been nicer to my teachers and classmates. Lastly, I shouldn't have eaten so much fast food. In high school, I'll try my best so that there won't be anything that I'll regret.

(1) _____

(2) _____

(3) _____

(4) _____

02 '조동사+have p.p.'를 사용하여 빈칸에 본인만의 문장을 쓰시오.

(1) In the morning the road is muddy. _____

(2) Emma doesn't answer my call. _____

(3) I didn't get a good grade in the math test. _____

03 다음 내용을 바탕으로 전기문을 쓰시오.

> • What is the person's name?
>   - Jane Goodall
> • Where and when was the person born?
>   - London, England / 1934
> • What did the person do?
>   - studied wild chimpanzees in Africa, worked for the protection of chimpanzees
> • What are other facts about the person?
>   - received the Hubbard Medal

> ### JANE GOODALL, MOTHER OF CHIMPANZEES
> Jane Goodall was born (A)_____, in 1934. Her interest in chimpanzees began when she first read about Tarzan. She has been studying (B)_____ in Africa since her twenties. She has also been working for (C)_____. In 1995, she received (D)_____ for protecting wild animals. Thanks to her lifelong study, we have come to know a lot about chimpanzees. Jane Goodall is one of the greatest scientists in history.

단원별 모의고사

01 다음의 영영풀이가 가리키는 것은?

> good or important enough for something

① calm ② worth ③ lifelong
④ serious ⑤ challenging

02 다음 빈칸에 알맞은 것을 고르시오.

> _____ you do not like it, you must do it.

① As ② Despite ③ Even if
④ If ⑤ When

03 다음 우리말에 맞게 빈칸에 알맞은 말을 쓰시오.

(1) 약간의 상상력을 이용하면 너는 정답을 알 수 있다.
→ You can get the answer if you use a little _____.

(2) 나는 내 대답이 맞다고 자신한다.
→ I'm _____ that my answer is correct.

(3) 팬들은 그들의 팀이 또 다른 경기에서 지자 실망했다.
→ The fans were _____ that their team lost another game.

[04~05] 다음 대화를 읽고 물음에 답하시오.

B: Hi, Sora. What are you doing?
G: I'm drawing cartoons. I'm preparing for the exam for Mana Animation High School.
B: Oh, are you? When is the exam?
G: On Friday, so I only have two days left.
B: How's it going?
G: It's not easy to draw what I want to express. I should have practiced more.
B: Don't worry! (A)넌 해낼 수 있어! (make)
G: Thanks.

04 위 대화의 밑줄 친 (A)의 우리말을 주어진 단어를 사용하여 영작하시오.

→ _____

05 When will Sora have the exam for Mana Animation High School?

→ _____
_____

[06~08] 다음 대화를 읽고 물음에 답하시오.

G: Hi, Jiho.
B: Hi, Amber. It's nice to see you on the bus.
G: Yeah, but I'm afraid we're going to be late.
B: Yeah. I hate to be late for the school festival.
G: Me, too. I should have set my alarm. I forgot.
B: (①) I understand. That happens a lot to me when I'm tired, too.
G: How about you? What made you late?
B: (②) Well, I got up early. But it took me some time to do my hair.
G: (③) Oh, I see. We're stuck in a heavy traffic jam. We should get off and run.
B: (④) The traffic is starting to move again. Let's stay on.
G: (⑤) Okay. I just hope we're not terribly late.

06 위 대화의 (①)~(⑤) 중에서 주어진 문장이 들어가기에 가장 적절한 곳은?

> No, you're mistaken.

① ② ③ ④ ⑤

07 What did Amber forget to do last night?

➡ _____

08 Why did Amber suggest they get off the bus and run?

➡ _____

_____

09 주어진 두 문장 사이에 대화가 자연스럽게 이어지도록 순서 대로 배열하시오.

W: Are you nervous?

(A) Okay, let's start the interview. What made you apply for our school?
(B) A bit, but I'm fine.
(C) I see. Good luck to you.
(D) I like the curriculum of this school because it has various subjects. I'm certain that they'll help me in many ways.

B: Thank you.

➡ _____

[10~11] 다음 대화를 읽고 물음에 답하시오.

B: What do you want to do when you grow up?
G: I want to work with robots.
B: Are you interested in making robots?
G: No, (A)that's not quite right. I want to repair robots.
B: I see. But why?
G: Because I think it'll be a good job in the future.

10 위 대화의 밑줄 친 (A)와 바꾸어 쓰기 어색한 것은?

① That's not true.
② I don't think that's right.
③ That's wrong.
④ You're quite correct.
⑤ You're mistaken.

11 Write the reason why G wants to repair robots. Answer in English beginning with "It's because".

➡ _____

_____

12 다음 그림을 보고 우리말에 맞게 괄호 안에 주어진 단어를 활용하여 주어진 조건대로 영작하시오. (두 문장으로 쓰고 필요시 1 단어를 추가할 것.)

Mina는 커피를 타다가 손가락을 데었는데 커피는 그녀가 가장 좋아하는 음료이다. 그녀는 더 조심했어야 했다.
(coffee, got her finger, her favorite drink, making, ought, while, burned)

(1) 조건: 콤마와 관계대명사를 이용할 것.
➡ _____

_____

(2) 조건: 접속사 and와 조동사 should를 이용할 것.
➡ _____

_____

13 다음 중 어법상 옳은 문장을 <u>모두</u> 고르시오.

① He is my son, which works at the amusement park.

② I got up late. I may have set my alarm.

③ I must have left my wallet in the movie theater.

④ One of my friends, that wants to be a teacher, is Abigail.

⑤ On the day of the tryouts, all the rules were explained by an old man in a suit, who sounded very serious and unkind.

⑥ You should not have wasted your pocket money on useless things.

⑦ She also became worried about traveling alone to Chicago, who was far away from home.

14 다음 그림을 보고 우리말에 맞게 괄호 안에 주어진 단어를 활용하여 주어진 조건대로 영작하시오. (두 문장으로 쓰고 필요시 1 단어를 추가할 것.)

Uncle Ben went on a trip to Turkey. He _____ _____ _____ very happy to make his lifelong dream come true. (be)

15 다음 빈칸에 알맞은 말로 짝지어진 것을 고르시오.

- You _____ up earlier.
- You _____ too much fast food.

① should have get – should have not eaten
② should have get – should not have eaten
③ should have got – should not have ate
④ should have got – should not have eaten
⑤ should got – should have not eaten

16 다음 밑줄 친 부분과 바꿔 쓸 수 있는 것은?

Mike didn't keep his promise, <u>and it</u> made Kay really upset.

① which ② that ③ what
④ who ⑤ where

17 다음 문장에서 어법상 어색한 것을 바르게 고쳐 다시 쓰시오.

(1) She does not work anymore, but she still enjoys making delicious food, that I love it so much.

➡ _____

_____

(2) She is my friend, Nida, which I met in Germany.

➡ _____

_____

(3) Gogh met Gauguin in Arles, that changed his life.

➡ _____

_____

(4) The rabbit should have slept during the race to beat the turtle.

➡ _____

_____

(5) Hanju ought to have lost his umbrella in the subway. He doesn't have it now.

➡ _____

_____

19 위 글의 밑줄 친 ⓑthese stories가 가리키는 것을 본문에서 찾아 쓰시오.

➡ _____

_____

[20~21] 다음 글을 읽고 물음에 답하시오.

In 1943, the All-American Girls Professional Baseball League was founded. This league was created ___ⓐ___ baseball fans because many of America's young men were fighting in World War Ⅱ.

Helen was told that there would be local tryouts (A)right in South Bend. She wondered, "What would it be like to be ___ⓑ___ a baseball team and to make it to the finals for my hometown?" She imagined a large banner hanging at the baseball field which included the name Helen Baker.

[18~19] 다음 글을 읽고 물음에 답하시오.

My grandmother Helen used to be a cook in a restaurant in a small town near South Bend, Indiana. She does not work anymore, but she still enjoys making delicious food, which I love so much. Food is one of the many things that connect us. What connects us most strongly, ___ⓐ___, is baseball.

When I visit her on weekends, my grandmother often tells me exciting stories about playing baseball back in the 1940s. She must have loved the sport very much. I listen to ⓑthese stories over and over. She always says, "Go after what you want, Sarah. Don't be afraid of trying something new or challenging. Don't be ashamed of failing."

20 위 글의 빈칸 ⓐ와 ⓑ에 들어갈 전치사가 바르게 짝지어진 것은?

	ⓐ	ⓑ		ⓐ	ⓑ		ⓐ	ⓑ
①	by	at	②	for	to	③	for	on
④	to	at	⑤	by	on			

18 위 글의 빈칸 ⓐ에 들어갈 알맞은 말을 고르시오.

① therefore　　② moreover

③ in other words　　④ as a result

⑤ however

21 위 글의 밑줄 친 (A)right와 같은 의미로 쓰인 것을 고르시오.

① She gave the right answer.

② Lee was standing right behind her.

③ What gives you the right to do that?

④ Keep on the right side of the road.

⑤ I hope we're doing the right thing.

[22~23] 다음 글을 읽고 물음에 답하시오.

On the day of the tryouts, all the rules were explained by an old man in a suit, who sounded very serious and unkind. She thought that wearing a suit in the hot sun might have made him impatient. On that day, Helen played baseball for hours with many other young women. She was excited to go after her baseball dreams!

About a week later, Helen found a letter in the mailbox. It was from people who worked for the girls' baseball league in Chicago. It ⓐ read that she had been invited to the league's main tryouts in Chicago!

22 위 글의 밑줄 친 ⓐread와 같은 의미로 쓰인 것을 고르시오.

① The sign read 'No admittance'.
② He liked to read to his grandchildren.
③ She's still learning to read.
④ She read us a story.
⑤ I can't read your writing.

23 According to the passage, which is NOT true?

① An old man in a suit explained all the rules on the day of the tryouts.
② The old man sounded very serious and unkind.
③ Helen played baseball for hours with many other young women on the day of the tryouts.
④ The old man who explained all the rules on the day of the tryouts sent an invitation letter to Helen.
⑤ Helen had been invited to the league's main tryouts in Chicago.

[24~25] 다음 글을 읽고 물음에 답하시오.

As the days went by, however, Helen became worried that she might fail. (①) When the day of the main tryouts came, she was too afraid to go. (②)

My grandmother has spent the rest of her life regretting her decision. (③) When she watches a baseball game on TV, she often says, "ⓐI should have gone to Chicago. (④) You know, all your dreams are worth chasing, even if you catch only a few of them. (⑤) Never miss an opportunity."

24 위 글의 흐름으로 보아, 주어진 문장이 들어가기에 가장 적절한 곳은?

> She also became worried about traveling alone to Chicago, which was far away from home.

①   ②   ③   ④   ⑤

25 위 글의 밑줄 친 ⓐ에서 알 수 있는 필자의 할머니 심경으로 가장 알맞은 것을 고르시오.

① confused   ② regretful
③ ashamed   ④ nervous
⑤ depressed

MEMO

Reading for Fun 4

Keep Out

Words & Expressions

교과서

Key Words

- **actually** [ǽktʃuəli] 부 실제(로)는, 사실은
- **breathe** [briːð] 동 숨 쉬다
- **cast** [kæst] 명 석고붕대, 깁스
- **cycle** [sáikl] 동 자전거를 타다
- **dirt** [dəːrt] 명 흙, 먼지
- **entrance** [éntrəns] 명 입구, 입장
- **gateway** [géitwei] 명 입구, 관문
- **hurt** [həːrt] 동 고통을 주다, 아프다
- **lesson** [lésn] 명 교훈
- **manager** [mǽnidʒər] 명 경영자, 관리자
- **opening** [óupəniŋ] 명 열린 구멍, 창(窓), 구멍, 틈, 입구
- **particular** [pərtíkjulər] 형 특별한

- **record** [rékərd] 명 기록
- **relief** [rilíːf] 명 안도, 안심
- **safety product** 안전 제품
- **scream** [skriːm] 명 비명
- **shout** [ʃaut] 동 외치다, 소리[고함]치다
- **thick** [θik] 형 두터운, 빽빽한
- **though** [ðou] 부 그러나, 그래도
- **throughout** [θruːáut] 전 ~ 내내, ~ 동안 쭉
- **thumping** [θʌ́mpiŋ] 형 쿵쾅거리는
- **whisper** [hwíspər] 동 속삭이다
- **wooden** [wúdn] 형 나무로 된, 목재의
- **would** [wəd] 조 ~하곤 했다(과거의 불규칙적 습관)

Key Expressions

- **after a while** 얼마 후에
- **all of a sudden** 갑자기
- **as ~ as one can** 최대한[가능한 한] ~한[하게]
- **as soon as** ~하자마자
- **as usual** 여느 때처럼
- **at first** 처음에는
- **day in and day out** 매일
- **in other words** 다시 말해서, 즉
- **in reply** 대답으로
- **inch by inch** 조금씩

- **keep out** 들어가지 않다
- **manage to** 간신히 ~하다
- **one behind the other** 한 사람 뒤에 다른 한 사람
- **reach out** (손·팔·다리 등을) 뻗다
- **set off** 출발하다
- **side by side** 나란히
- **stop ~ from -ing** ~가 …하는 것을 막다
- **thanks to** ~ 덕분에
- **used to** ~하곤 했다(과거의 규칙적이고 반복적인 동작이나 상태)

Word Power

※ 서로 비슷한 뜻을 가진 어휘

☐ **acatually** 실제(로)는, 사실은 – **really** 사실, 참으로

☐ **all of a sudden** 갑자기 – **suddenly** 갑자기

☐ **at first** 처음에는 – **in the beginning** 처음에는

☐ **day in and day out** 매일 – **day after day** 매일

☐ **entrance** 입구 – **gateway** 입구

☐ **hurt** 고통을 주다, 아프다 – **ache** 아프다, 쑤시다

☐ **lesson** 교훈 – **instruction** 교훈, 가르침

☐ **particular** 특별한 – **special** 특별한

☐ **shout** 외치다, 소리[고함]치다 – **cry** 소리치다, 외치다

☐ **stop ~ from -ing** ~가 …하는 것을 막다
   keep ~ from -ing ~가 …하는 것을 막다

※ 서로 반대의 뜻을 가진 어휘

☐ **at first** 처음에는 ↔ **at last** 마침내, 드디어

☐ **hurt** 고통을 주다, 아프다 ↔ **heal** 고치다, 낫게 하다

☐ **entrance** 입구 ↔ **exit** 출구

☐ **thick** 두터운, 빽빽한 ↔ **thin** 얇은, 드문드문한

English Dictionary

☐ **breathe** 숨 쉬다
   → to take a breath
      숨을 쉬다

☐ **cycle** 자전거를 타다
   → to ride a bicycle
      자전거를 타다

☐ **dirt** 흙, 먼지
   → loose or packed soil or sand
      흐트러지거나 뭉친 흙이나 모래

☐ **entrance** 입구
   → the way you go in
      안으로 들어가는 길

☐ **gateway** 입구
   → an opening for a gate
      문으로 향하는 열린 구멍

☐ **manager** 경영자, 관리자
   → a person who is responsible for running part of a business organization
      사업 조직의 일부를 운영하는 책임을 지는 사람

☐ **particular** 특별한
   → worthy of notice; special; unusual
      주목할 가치가 있는; 특별한; 평범하지 않은

☐ **relief** 안도, 안심
   → removal of something painful
      고통스러운 어떤 것의 제거

☐ **scream** 비명
   → a loud sharp cry or noise
      크고 날카로운 울음이나 소음

☐ **thick** 두터운, 빽빽한
   → close-packed with units or individuals
      단일체나 개체로 밀집한

☐ **throughout** ~ 내내, ~ 동안 쭉
   → during the whole period of
      전체 기간 동안

☐ **thumping** 쿵쾅거리는
   → hitting something in a heavy, continuous way
      심하게, 그리고 계속해서 무엇인가를 때리는

☐ **wooden** 나무로 된, 목재의
   → made of wood
      나무로 만들어진

Reading

Keep Out

Every summer, my family used to go on holiday to the coast.
'~하곤 했다'라는 뜻으로 과거의 규칙적이고 반복적인 동작이나 상태를 나타냄.
We always went to the same place and stayed at the same small
guesthouse. We would stay for two weeks, swimming in the sea and
과거의 불규칙적인 습관을 나타내는 조동사(~하곤 했다)   분사구문(~하면서)
walking around the little town. In other words, we never did anything
분사 구문(~하면서)
special, and nothing ever really happened on these vacations.

At the time of this story I was twelve years old. Most people can
remember this particular summer, as it was the hottest summer England
이유를 나타내는 접속사(~ 때문에)
had had since records began. It did not rain throughout June and July,
관계대명사 that이 생략된 형용사절. 주절보다 먼저 있었던 일을 언급하므로 과거완료 (had had)
and the sun shone day in and day out.

But Ron and I loved the heat and the sun. Every day, we would ride
our bicycles further and further away from the guesthouse.
far의 비교급
One day Ron decided that we should ride our bikes along the old
~을 따라
train tracks to see where they would take us. I was happy to follow
to부정사의 부사적 용법(목적)   동사 see의 목적어 역할을 하는 간접의문문
Ron, as usual, and we set off after breakfast.

in other words 다시 말해서, 즉 (= namely)
particular 특별한
throughout ~ 내내, ~ 동안 쭉
day in and day out 매일 (= day after day)
as usual 여느 때처럼
set off 출발하다

확인문제

● 다음 문장이 본문의 내용과 일치하면 T, 일치하지 <u>않으면</u> F를 쓰시오.

1 Every summer, the writer's family used to go on holiday to the coast. ☐

2 Every summer, the writer's family did something special. ☐

3 Ron and the writer loved the heat and the sun. ☐

4 Ron and the writer would ride their bicycles near the guesthouse every day. ☐

5 One day Ron decided that they should ride their bikes along the old train tracks to
see where they would take them. ☐

6 Ron and the writer set off before breakfast. ☐

At first, the tracks were easy to follow, and we cycled along side
by side. After a while, the grass grew thicker, and we had to ride one
behind the other. Ron was ahead. The tracks went toward the woods
and it grew darker as the trees stood tall and formed a roof over the
tracks.

Ron stopped suddenly. "Look ahead!" he shouted. I stopped next to
him and saw a white, wooden gateway across a black opening.

"It's a tunnel," I said.

"Yes, and it says, 'Keep Out' on the gate," replied Ron. "Do you want
to have a look inside?"

Actually, I did not want to go inside. I felt a little cold all of a sudden,
and I wanted to go back into the sunlight. But I answered, "Sure," and
moved ahead.

We left our bikes at the gate and climbed over. We entered the cool
tunnel. The air inside was heavy. Above our heads there was a sound
that grew louder and louder.

"What's that?" I called out.

"Bats," said Ron, "Keep your head down." Then he moved on.

"Don't go so fast." I called after him. I meant, "Don't leave me
behind" but I didn't say so.

cycle 자전거를 타다
side by side 나란히
after a while 얼마 후에
thick 두터운, 빽빽한
wooden 나무로 된, 목재의
gateway 입구
all of a sudden 갑자기

📎 **확인문제**

● 다음 문장이 본문의 내용과 일치하면 T, 일치하지 않으면 F를 쓰시오.

1 At first, the tracks were easy to follow, and Ron and the writer cycled along side by side. ☐

2 Ron and the writer saw a white, wooden gateway next to a black opening. ☐

3 Ron asked, "Do you want to have a look inside?" ☐

4 The writer wanted to go inside. ☐

5 Ron and the writer left their bikes at the gate and climbed over. ☐

6 Above their heads there was a sound that faded away. ☐

The next thing I heard was a loud noise right above us, a thumping
_{The next thing과 I heard 사이에는 관계대명사 that이 생략되었다.}　　　　_{a loud noise와 a thumping sound는 동격}
sound like an express train and then a scream.

"Ron!" I shouted. "Ron, what's up? Can you hear me?" No reply.

"Speak to me, Ron. Tell me what's happened."
_{= what has}

I slowly walked toward where Ron had been and found only dirt and
_{관계부사 where 앞에 선행사 the place가 생략되어 있음.}
small rocks. As I reached out my hands, I felt something wet—Ron's

face! His eyes were closed, and he was breathing weakly. "It's okay,

Ron," I whispered. "I'll get you out."

"I think I've broken my leg. It really hurts. Just go and get help, Ben."

"No," I replied. "I'll get you out of here to safety first." I started
_{= a safe place}
moving away the dirt and rocks with my hands.

I felt calm, and I felt in control. It took a long time to clear away the
_{It takes+시간+to부정사: ~하는 데 …의 시간이 걸리다}
earth covering Ron. Finally, I managed to free his body. Holding him
_{현재분사 covering은 앞의 명사 the earth를 수식}　　　　　_{부대상황을 나타내는 분사 구문. = As I held}
under the arms, I pulled him backward, inch by inch, toward the tunnel

entrance.

thumping 쿵쾅거리는
scream 비명
dirt 흙, 먼지
breathe 숨 쉬다
safety 안전, 안전한 곳
manage to 간신히 ~하다
entrance 입구

📎 **확인문제**

● 다음 문장이 본문의 내용과 일치하면 T, 일치하지 <u>않으면</u> F를 쓰시오.

1　There was a thumping sound like an express train. ☐

2　Ron said to me, "Speak to me. Tell me what's happened." ☐

3　Ron's eyes were closed, and he was breathing weakly. ☐

4　Ben started moving away the dirt and rocks with his hands. ☐

5　Ron and the writer walked toward the tunnel entrance. ☐

It seemed to take ages, but finally I was able to get Ron out of the
tunnel. He didn't look too well, though. His face was white, and he
was trying hard to stop himself from crying out. I found our bikes and
brought the two water bottles to Ron.

"Here, drink these," I said. "I'll go and get help. I'll be as quick as I
can." In reply, Ron simply pressed my hands.

I got on my bicycle and raced back along the tracks until I got to the
nearest farmhouse. I ran past the gate and found a woman washing
some dishes in the kitchen.

Thanks to her, Ron was taken to the hospital, where his leg was put
in a cast. As soon as our parents arrived at the hospital and saw us,
my mother cried with relief. But all my father said was, "Let that be a
lesson to you."

And what was the lesson? It was "*Keep out* means *Stay out of
trouble*." Ron is now the manager of a big company which produces
helmets and other safety products. And me? I am a fire fighter.

thanks to ~ 덕분에

relief 안도, 안심

manager 경영자, 관리자

확인문제

● 다음 문장이 본문의 내용과 일치하면 T, 일치하지 <u>않으면</u> F를 쓰시오.

1 Finally the writer was able to get Ron out of the tunnel. ☐

2 Ron couldn't stop himself from crying out. ☐

3 The writer found their bikes and brought the two water bottles to Ron. ☐

4 Ron said, "Come back as soon as you can." ☐

5 The writer got on his bicycle and raced back along the tracks until he got to the
    nearest farmhouse. ☐

6 As soon as their parents arrived at the hospital and saw them, their father cried with
    relief. ☐

• 우리말을 참고하여 빈칸에 알맞은 말을 쓰시오.

1 _____ _____

2 Every summer, my family _____ _____ _____ on holiday to the coast.

3 We always went to the same place and _____ _____ the same small guesthouse.

4 We would stay for two weeks, _____ in the sea and _____ around the little town.

5 _____ _____ _____, we never did _____ _____, and nothing ever really happened on these vacations.

6 _____ _____ _____ _____ this story I was twelve years old.

7 Most people can remember this particular summer, as it was the hottest summer England _____ _____ since records began.

8 It did not rain throughout June and July, and the sun shone _____ _____ _____ _____ _____.

9 But Ron and I loved _____ _____ and the sun.

10 Every day, we would ride our bicycles _____ _____ _____ away from the guesthouse.

11 One day Ron decided that we should ride our bikes along the old train tracks to see where they would _____ _____.

12 I was happy to follow Ron, _____ _____, and we _____ _____ after breakfast.

13 At first, the tracks were easy to follow, and we cycled along _____ _____ _____.

---

1 들어가지 마시오

2 여름마다 나의 가족은 해안으로 휴가를 가곤 했다.

3 우리는 항상 같은 곳에 가서 똑같은 작은 게스트하우스에 묵었다.

4 우리는 2주 가량 머물며 바다에서 수영하고 작은 마을 주위를 돌아다니곤 했다.

5 다시 말해서, 그런 휴가에서 우리는 특별한 일을 하지 않았고 정말 아무 일도 일어나지 않았다.

6 이 이야기는 내가 12살 때 일이다.

7 관측 이래 영국이 겪은 가장 더운 여름이었기 때문에, 대부분의 사람들은 이 특별한 여름을 기억할 수 있다.

8 6월과 7월 내내 비가 오지 않았고 태양은 연일 쨍쨍했다.

9 하지만 Ron과 나는 그 더위와 태양을 사랑했다.

10 매일 우리는 게스트하우스에서 조금씩 먼 곳으로 자전거를 타고 가곤 했다.

11 어느 날, Ron은 낡은 철로가 우리를 어디로 데려다줄지 알아보려고 그 철로를 따라 자전거를 타기로 결정했다.

12 난 늘 그랬듯 Ron을 따르는 게 즐거웠고, 아침 식사 후에 우리는 출발했다.

13 처음에는 철길을 따라가는 게 어렵지 않아 우리는 나란히 자전거를 타고 갔다.

14 After a while, the grass grew thicker, and we had to ride _____ _____ _____ _____.

15 Ron was _____.

16 The tracks went toward the woods and it _____ _____ as the trees stood tall and _____ _____ _____ over the tracks.

17 Ron stopped suddenly. "_____ _____!" he shouted.

18 I stopped _____ _____ _____ and saw a white, wooden gateway across a black opening.

19 "It's _____ _____," I said.

20 "Yes, and it says, '_____ _____' on the gate," replied Ron.

21 "Do you want to _____ _____ _____ inside?"

22 _____, I did not want to go inside.

23 I felt a little cold _____ _____ _____ _____, and I wanted to go back into the sunlight.

24 But I answered, "Sure," and _____ _____.

25 We _____ our bikes at the gate and climbed over.

26 We _____ the cool tunnel.

27 The air inside was _____.

28 Above our heads there was a sound that _____ _____ _____ _____.

29 "What's that?" I _____ _____.

30 "Bats," said Ron, "_____ your head _____." Then he moved on.

31 "Don't go so fast." I _____ _____ him.

14 한참 후, 풀이 점점 우거져서 우리는 한 사람이 앞서가고 다른 사람이 뒤에서 가야 했다.

15 Ron이 앞서가고 있었다.

16 철길은 숲으로 이어졌고 나무가 높이 자라 철길 위로 지붕을 형성하며 점점 더 어두워졌다.

17 Ron이 갑자기 멈췄다. "앞을 봐!"라고 그가 외쳤다.

18 나는 그의 옆에 멈춰서 캄캄한 입구를 가로지르는 흰색 나무문을 보았다.

19 "터널이네." 내가 말했다.

20 "맞아. 그리고 문에 '들어가지 마시오'라고 적혀 있어." Ron이 대답했다.

21 "안을 보고 싶니?"

22 사실, 난 안으로 들어가고 싶지 않았다.

23 갑자기 나는 한기를 살짝 느꼈고 햇빛 속으로 되돌아가고 싶었다.

24 그렇지만 나는 "물론이지."라고 답하며 앞으로 움직였다.

25 우리는 문 앞에 자전거를 남겨두고 넘어갔다.

26 우리는 서늘한 터널로 들어갔다.

27 안의 공기는 묵직했다.

28 우리 머리 위로 점점 더 커지는 소리가 났다.

29 "저게 뭐야?"라고 내가 소리쳤다.

30 "박쥐야." Ron이 말했다. "머리를 숙여." 그러고 나서 그는 계속 움직였다.

31 "너무 빨리 가지 마." 나는 그를 부르며 뒤쫓았다.

32 I meant, "Don't _____ me _____" but I didn't say so.

33 The next thing I heard was a loud noise right above us, a _____ sound _____ _____ _____ _____ and then a scream.

34 "Ron!" I shouted. "Ron, _____ _____? Can you hear me?" No reply.

35 "Speak to me, Ron. Tell me _____ _____."

36 I slowly walked toward _____ _____ _____ _____ and found only dirt and small rocks.

37 As I reached out my hands, I felt _____ _____ — Ron's face!

38 His eyes _____ _____, and he was breathing weakly.

39 "It's okay, Ron," I whispered. "I'll _____ _____ _____."

40 "I think I'_____ _____ my leg. It really hurts. Just _____ _____ _____ _____, Ben."

41 "No," I replied. "I'll _____ _____ _____ _____ to safety first."

42 I started _____ _____ the dirt and rocks with my hands.

43 I felt calm, and I felt _____ _____.

44 It took a long time to clear away the earth _____ Ron.

45 Finally, I _____ _____ _____ his body.

46 _____ him under the arms, I pulled him backward, _____ _____ _____, toward the tunnel entrance.

47 It seemed _____ _____ _____, but finally I was able to get Ron out of the tunnel.

48 He didn't _____ _____ _____, though.

---

32 '나를 두고 가지 마'라고 말하고 싶었지만, 나는 그렇게 말하지 않았다.

33 그다음 내가 들은 것은 바로 앞에서 나는 큰 소음이었는데, 그 것은 마치 고속열차 같은 쿵쾅거리는 소리였다. 이어서 비명이 들렸다.

34 "Ron!" 나는 외쳤다. "Ron, 무슨 일이야? 내 말 들려?" 아무 응답이 없었다.

35 "Ron, 나에게 말해 봐. 무슨 일이 생겼는지 말해 줘."

36 나는 천천히 Ron이 있던 곳으로 걸어갔고 흙과 작은 자갈만을 발견했다.

37 손을 뻗었을 때 나는 축축한 무언가를 느꼈다. Ron의 얼굴이었다!

38 그의 눈은 감겨 있었고 약하게 숨을 쉬고 있었다.

39 "괜찮아, Ron." 나는 속삭였다. "내가 꺼내 줄게."

40 "다리가 부러진 것 같아. 정말 아파. 그냥 가서 도움을 요청해, Ben."

41 "안 돼." 나는 대답했다. "우선 안전한 곳까지 여기에서 형을 꺼낼 거야."

42 나는 손으로 흙과 자갈을 치우기 시작했다.

43 나는 침착했고 내가 잘할 수 있다고 느꼈다.

44 Ron을 뒤덮은 흙을 치우는 데에 오랜 시간이 걸렸다.

45 드디어 나는 그의 몸을 자유롭게 할 수 있었다.

46 팔 밑으로 그를 안고서 그를 터널 입구 쪽으로 조금씩 뒤로 끌어당겼다.

47 오랜 시간이 걸린 듯했지만 결국 나는 Ron을 터널 밖으로 데리고 나올 수 있었다.

48 그는 별로 좋아 보이지 않았다.

49 His face was white, and he was trying hard to _____ himself _____ _____ _____ from crying out.

50 I found our bikes and brought the _____ _____ _____ to Ron.

51 "Here, drink these," I said. "I'll _____ _____ _____ _____. I'll be as quick as I can."

52 _____ _____, Ron simply _____ _____ _____.

53 I got on my bicycle and _____ _____ along the tracks until I got to the nearest farmhouse.

54 I ran past the gate and found a woman _____ _____ _____ in the kitchen.

55 _____ _____ _____, Ron was taken to the hospital, _____ his leg was put in a cast.

56 As soon as our parents arrived at the hospital and saw us, my mother cried _____ _____.

57 But all my father said was, "_____ _____ _____ _____ to you."

58 And what was the lesson? It was "*Keep out* means _____ _____ _____ _____."

59 Ron is now the manager of a big company which produces helmets and other _____ _____.

60 And me? I am a _____ _____.

● 우리말을 참고하여 본문을 영작하시오.

1 들어가지 마시오

➡ _____

2 여름마다 나의 가족은 해안으로 휴가를 가곤 했다.

➡ _____

3 우리는 항상 같은 곳에 가서 똑같은 작은 게스트하우스에 묵었다.

➡ _____

4 우리는 2주 가량 머물며 바다에서 수영하고 작은 마을 주위를 돌아다니곤 했다.

➡ _____

5 다시 말해서, 그런 휴가에서 우리는 특별한 일을 하지 않았고 정말 아무 일도 일어나지 않았다.

➡ _____

_____

6 이 이야기는 내가 12살 때 일이다.

➡ _____

7 관측 이래 영국이 겪은 가장 더운 여름이었기 때문에, 대부분의 사람들은 이 특별한 여름을 기억할 수 있다.

➡ _____

_____

8 6월과 7월 내내 비가 오지 않았고 태양은 연일 쨍쨍했다.

➡ _____

9 하지만 Ron과 나는 그 더위와 태양을 사랑했다.

➡ _____

10 매일 우리는 게스트하우스에서 조금씩 먼 곳으로 자전거를 타고 가곤 했다.

➡ _____

11 어느 날, Ron은 낡은 철로가 우리를 어디로 데려다줄지 알아보려고 그 철로를 따라 자전거를 타기로 결정했다.

➡ _____

_____

12 난 늘 그랬듯 Ron을 따르는 게 즐거웠고, 아침 식사 후에 우리는 출발했다.

➡ _____

13 처음에는 철길을 따라가는 게 어렵지 않아 우리는 나란히 자전거를 타고 갔다.

➡ _____

14 한참 후, 풀이 점점 우거져서 우리는 한 사람이 앞서가고 다른 사람이 뒤에서 가야 했다.

➡ _____

15 Ron이 앞서가고 있었다.

➡ _____

16 철길은 숲으로 이어졌고 나무가 높이 자라 철길 위로 지붕을 형성하며 점점 더 어두워졌다.

➡ _____

_____

17 Ron이 갑자기 멈췄다. "앞을 봐!"라고 그가 외쳤다.

➡ _____

18 나는 그의 옆에 멈춰서 캄캄한 입구를 가로지르는 흰색 나무문을 보았다.

➡ _____

19 "터널이네." 내가 말했다.

➡ _____

20 "맞아. 그리고 문에 '들어가지 마시오'라고 적혀 있어." Ron이 대답했다.

➡ _____

21 "안을 보고 싶니?"

➡ _____

22 사실, 난 안으로 들어가고 싶지 않았다.

➡ _____

23 갑자기 나는 한기를 살짝 느꼈고 햇빛 속으로 되돌아가고 싶었다.

➡ _____

24 그렇지만 나는 "물론이지."라고 답하며 앞으로 움직였다.

➡ _____

25 우리는 문 앞에 자전거를 남겨 두고 넘어갔다.

➡ _____

26 우리는 서늘한 터널로 들어갔다.

➡ _____

27 안의 공기는 묵직했다.

➡ _____

28 우리 머리 위로 점점 더 커지는 소리가 났다.

➡ _____

29 "저게 뭐야?"라고 내가 소리쳤다.

➡ _____

30 "박쥐야." Ron이 말했다. "머리를 숙여." 그러고 나서 그는 계속 움직였다.

➡ _____

31 "너무 빨리 가지 마." 나는 그를 부르며 뒤쫓았다.

➡ _____

32 '나를 두고 가지 마.'라고 말하고 싶었지만, 나는 그렇게 말하지 않았다.

➡ _____

33 그다음 내가 들은 것은 바로 앞에서 나는 큰 소음이었는데, 그것은 마치 고속열차 같은 쿵쾅거리는 소리였다. 이어서 비명이 들렸다.

➡ _____

34 "Ron!" 나는 외쳤다. "Ron, 무슨 일이야? 내 말 들려?" 아무 응답이 없었다.

➡ _____

35 "Ron, 나에게 말해 봐. 무슨 일이 생겼는지 말해 줘."

➡ _____

36 나는 천천히 Ron이 있던 곳으로 걸어갔고 흙과 작은 자갈만을 발견했다.

➡ _____

37 손을 뻗었을 때 나는 축축한 무언가를 느꼈다. Ron의 얼굴이었다!

➡ _____

38 그의 눈은 감겨 있었고 약하게 숨을 쉬고 있었다.

➡ _____

39 "괜찮아, Ron." 나는 속삭였다. "내가 꺼내 줄게."

➡ _____

40 "다리가 부러진 것 같아. 정말 아파. 그냥 가서 도움을 요청해, Ben."

➡ _____

41 "안 돼." 나는 대답했다. "우선 안전한 곳까지 여기에서 형을 꺼낼 거야."

➡ _____

42 나는 손으로 흙과 자갈을 치우기 시작했다.

➡ _____

43 나는 침착했고 내가 잘할 수 있다고 느꼈다.

➡ _____

44 Ron을 뒤덮은 흙을 치우는 데에 오랜 시간이 걸렸다.

➡ _____

45 드디어 나는 그의 몸을 자유롭게 할 수 있었다.

➡ _____

46 팔 밑으로 그를 안고서 그를 터널 입구 쪽으로 조금씩 뒤로 끌어당겼다.

➡ _____

47 오랜 시간이 걸린 듯했지만 결국 나는 Ron을 터널 밖으로 데리고 나올 수 있었다.

➡ _____

48 그는 별로 좋아 보이지 않았다.

➡ _____

49 그의 얼굴은 창백했고 울음을 터뜨리지 않으려고 몹시 애쓰고 있었다.

➡ _____

50 나는 우리 자전거를 찾아서 Ron에게 물병 두 개를 가져다주었다.

➡ _____

51 "여기, 이거 마셔." 나는 말했다. "내가 가서 도움을 구할게. 최대한 빨리 올게."

➡ _____

52 대답으로 Ron은 그저 내 손을 꽉 잡았다.

➡ _____

53 나는 자전거를 타고 왔던 철길을 따라 달려, 마침내 가장 가까운 농가에 도착했다.

➡ _____

54 대문을 지나 달려가 나는 부엌에서 설거지를 하고 있는 부인을 발견했다.

➡ _____

55 그 부인 덕분에 Ron은 병원으로 이송되었고, 병원에서 다리에 석고붕대를 했다.

➡ _____

56 부모님이 병원에 도착해서 우리를 보자마자, 어머니는 안도감에 울음을 터뜨리셨다.

➡ _____

57 하지만 아버지가 하신 말씀은 "이 일이 너희에게 교훈이 되기를 바란다."가 전부였다.

➡ _____

58 그래서 교훈이 무엇이었을까? 그것은 '들어가지 마시오'라는 말은 '곤경을 멀리하라'는 뜻이라는 것이다.

➡ _____

59 Ron은 지금 안전모와 여러 안전 제품을 생산하는 큰 회사의 관리자이다.

➡ _____

60 그럼 나는? 나는 소방관이다.

➡ _____

서술형 실전문제

01 다음 짝지어진 단어의 관계가 같도록 빈칸에 알맞은 단어를 주어진 철자로 시작하여 쓰시오.

> entrance : exit = thick : t_____

02 다음 문장의 빈칸에 들어갈 말을 〈보기〉에서 골라 쓰시오.

> ┤ 보기 ├─
> all of a sudden / thumping / managed to
> / in other words

(1) The washing machine made a _____ sound.

(2) He was broke. _____ _____ _____, he had no money.

(3) He _____ _____ fix the computer by himself.

(4) _____ _____ _____ _____, there was a scream behind us.

03 다음 우리말에 맞게 빈칸에 알맞은 말을 쓰시오.

(1) 그녀는 자신의 문제들에도 불구하고 평상시처럼 일을 계속했다.
➡ Despite her problems, she carried on working _____ _____.

(2) 내가 처음에는 그 일이 힘들었지만 곧 익숙해졌다.
➡ I found the job tiring _____ _____ but I soon got used to it.

(3) 나는 그 방에 들어서는 순간 뭔가가 잘못되었다는 것을 알았다.
➡ _____ _____ _____ I walked in the room, I knew that something was wrong.

04 다음 중 어법상 어색한 것을 골라 바르게 고쳐 쓰시오.

① The next thing I heard was a loud noise right above us, a thumping sound like an express train and then a scream.
② I slowly walked toward where Ron had been and found only dirt and small rocks.
③ Ron decided that we ride our bikes along the old train tracks.
④ We must stop him from seeing her somehow.
⑤ Being no objection, the meeting was put off.

➡ _____
_____

05 다음 문장에서 어법상 틀린 곳을 찾아 바르게 고쳐 쓰시오.

(1) He would be a pilot, but now he has a desk job.
_____ ➡ _____

(2) We had many difficulties, while covered this case.
_____ ➡ _____

(3) Is this the building which the accident happened?
_____ ➡ _____

(4) Tell me that has happened.
_____ ➡ _____

(A)Every summer, my family used to go on holiday to the coast. We always went to the same place and stayed at the same small guesthouse. We would stay for two weeks, swimming in the sea and walking around the little town. In other words, we never did anything special, and nothing ever really happened on these vacations.

At the time of this story I was twelve years old. Most people can remember this particular summer, as it was the hottest summer England ⓐ since records began. It did not rain throughout June and July, and the sun shone day in and day out.

But Ron and I loved the heat and the sun. Every day, we would ride our bicycles further and further away from the guesthouse.

06 위 글의 빈칸 ⓐ에 have를 알맞은 형태로 쓰시오.

➡ _____

07 위 글의 밑줄 친 (A)를 다음과 같이 바꿔 쓸 때 빈칸에 들어갈 알맞은 단어를 쓰시오.

(1) Every summer, my family was in the habit of _____ on holiday to the coast.

(2) Every summer, my family made it a rule _____ _____ on holiday to the coast.

08 Why does the writer say that most people can remember this particular summer? Answer in English beginning with "Because".

➡ _____

_____

I slowly walked toward (A)[which / where] Ron had been and found only dirt and small rocks. As I reached out my hands, I felt something wet—Ron's face! His eyes were closed, and he was breathing weakly. "It's okay, Ron," I whispered. "I'll get you out."

"I think I've broken my leg. It really hurts. Just go and get help, Ben."

"No," I replied. "I'll get you out of here to safety first." I started moving away the dirt and rocks with my hands.

I felt (B)[calm / calmly], and I felt in control. ⓐRon을 뒤덮은 흙을 치우는 데에 오랜 시간이 걸렸다. Finally, I managed (C)[to free / freeing] his body. Holding him under the arms, I pulled him backward, inch by inch, toward the tunnel entrance.

09 위 글의 괄호 (A)~(C)에서 문맥이나 어법상 알맞은 낱말을 골라 쓰시오.

(A) _____ (B) _____ (C) _____

10 위 글의 밑줄 친 ⓐ의 우리말에 맞게 주어진 어휘를 이용하여 12 단어로 영작하시오.

| took, time, clear away, earth, covering |

➡ _____

_____

11 다음 문장에서 위 글의 내용과 다른 부분을 찾아서 고치시오.

| Ben started moving away the dirt and rocks with a shovel. |

_____ ➡ _____

01 다음 문장의 빈칸에 들어갈 말을 〈보기〉에서 골라 쓰시오.

| 보기 |

thanks to / wooden / relief /
after a while / cast

(1) There is a _____ table in the living room.
(2) My _____ is finally off and there's serious muscle loss.
(3) I met a lot of nice people, _____ _____ you.
(4) _____ _____ _____ , we naturally started talking about the children.
(5) My mother breathed a sigh of _____.

[02~03] 다음 영영풀이가 가리키는 것을 고르시오.

02

a loud sharp cry or noise

① scream   ② treat   ③ dirt
④ lesson   ⑤ breath

03

removal of something painful

① thick   ② entrance   ③ hurt
④ relief   ⑤ whisper

04 다음 중 밑줄 친 부분의 뜻풀이가 바르지 <u>않은</u> 것은?

① Where is the <u>entrance</u> of the museum? (입구)
② You should keep a <u>record</u> of your expenses. (기록)
③ We <u>set off</u> for the station after lunch. (출발하다)
④ She must try to <u>stop</u> him <u>from</u> going fishing. (~가 …하는 것을 막다)
⑤ Three girls were walking along the bank <u>side by side</u>. (한 줄로)

05 다음 문장에 공통으로 들어갈 말을 쓰시오.

- I was thankful that he hadn't been _____.
- None of the passengers were badly _____.
- There was _____ and real anger in her voice.

06 다음 우리말과 일치하도록 주어진 어구를 배열하여 영작하시오.

(1) 그녀가 몸을 기울여 그의 귀에 대고 뭔가를 속삭였다. (she / his / something / ear / whispered / leaned / and / over / in)

➡ _____

_____

(2) 나는 빈 녹음실에서 종종 각본을 읽는 연습을 하곤 했다. (I / the scripts / the / recording room / reading / practice / would / empty / often / in)

➡ _____

_____

(3) 제 연기가 조금씩 향상되고 있다는 걸 보여주고 싶었어요. (I / I / inch / inch / show / wanted / improve / could / acting / that / my / by / to)

➡ _____

_____

07 다음 우리말을 주어진 어구를 이용하여 영작하시오.

(1) 매일 같은 식당에서 밥 먹는 것도 이젠 신물이 나. (day, so tired, eating, in, out)

➡ _____

_____

(2) 저 방에는 들어가지 마세요. (that, please, keep, of)

➡ _____

(3) 손을 뻗었을 때 나는 축축한 무언가를 느꼈다. (my hand, reach, wet, as)

➡ _____

08 다음 중 어법상 올바른 것을 고르시오.

① It took a long time to clear away the earth covering Ron.

② Most people can remember this particular summer, as it was the hottest summer England has had since records began.

③ It makes my heart to ache seeing her suffer.

④ He was trying hard to stop himself to cry out.

⑤ After a while, the grass grew thicker, and the two boys had to ride one behind other.

09 다음 괄호 안에 주어진 조건대로 바꿔 쓰시오.

(1) It did not rain throughout June and July, and the sun shone day in and day out. (분사구문으로)

➡ _____

_____

(2) As it was the hottest summer England had had since records began, most people can remember this particular summer. (분사구문으로)

➡ _____

_____

(3) Ron decided that we should ride our bikes along the old train tracks so that we could see where they would take us. (to부정사를 이용하여)

➡ _____

_____

(4) I'd like to see. Can she give me a hand? (if를 이용하여 한 문장으로)

➡ _____

_____

10 다음 문장에서 어법상 어색한 것을 바르게 고쳐 다시 쓰시오.

(1) The book is a detailed piece of work covered all aspects of the subject.

➡ _____

(2) The two men were walking quickly, one behind other.

➡ _____

(3) Ron was taken to the hospital, in where his leg was put in a cast.

➡ _____

(4) It took her some time realizing the dangers of her situation.

➡ _____

11 다음 중 어법상 어색한 것을 고르시오.

① Holding him under the arms, I pulled him backward, inch by inch, toward the tunnel entrance.

② It seemed that it took ages, but finally I was able to get Ron out of the tunnel.

③ Mike was trying hard to stop himself from crying out.

④ I'll be as quickly as I can.

⑤ It was easy to follow the tracks.

[12~13] 다음 글을 읽고 물음에 답하시오.

At the time of this story I was twelve years old. Most people can remember this particular summer, ⓐas it was the hottest summer England had had since records began. It did not rain throughout June and July, and the sun shone day in and day out.

But Ron and I loved the heat and the sun. Every day, we would ride our bicycles further and further away from the guesthouse.

12 위 글의 밑줄 친 문장 ⓐ의 had had와 과거완료 용법이 같은 것을 모두 고르시오.

① I had never seen such a strange animal before.

② He had lived there for ten years when his father died.

③ When I reached the station, the train had already started.

④ I bought an umbrella yesterday, for I had lost my old one.

⑤ When we called on her, she had been ill in bed for a week.

13 According to the passage, which is NOT true?

① At the time of this story the writer was twelve years old.

② It was the hottest summer England had had since records began.

③ It did not rain throughout June and July.

④ Ron and the writer loved the heat and the sun.

⑤ Every day, Ron and the writer would ride their bicycles near the guesthouse.

[14~16] 다음 글을 읽고 물음에 답하시오.

One day Ron decided that we should ride our bikes along the old train tracks to see where ⓐthey would take us. (①) I was happy to follow Ron, as usual, and we set off after breakfast. (②)

At first, the tracks were easy ⓑto follow, and we cycled along side by side. (③) Ron was ahead. (④) The tracks went toward the woods and it grew darker as the trees stood tall and formed a roof over the tracks. (⑤)

14 위 글의 밑줄 친 ⓐthey가 가리키는 것을 본문에서 찾아 쓰시오.

➡ _____

15 위 글의 흐름으로 보아, 주어진 문장이 들어가기에 가장 적절한 곳은?

After a while, the grass grew thicker, and we had to ride one behind the other.

①   ②   ③   ④   ⑤

16 아래 <보기>에서 위 글의 밑줄 친 ⓑto follow와 to부정사의 용법이 같은 것의 개수를 고르시오.

> ┌─ 보기 ─
> ① There is no one to do it.
> ② He can't be rich to ask me for some money.
> ③ My hobby is to collect stamps.
> ④ They came here to ask me a question.
> ⑤ It is important to use your time well.

① 1개　② 2개　③ 3개　④ 4개　⑤ 5개

[17~19] 다음 글을 읽고 물음에 답하시오.

> Ron stopped ⓐsuddenly. "Look ahead!" he shouted. I stopped next to him and ⓑ캄캄한 입구를 가로지르는 흰색 나무 문을 보았다.
>
> "It's a tunnel," I said.
>
> "Yes, and it says, 'Keep Out' on the gate," replied Ron. "Do you want to have a look inside?"
>
> Actually, I did not want to go inside. I felt a little cold all of a sudden, and I wanted to go back into the sunlight. But I answered, "Sure," and moved ahead.

17 위 글의 밑줄 친 ⓐsuddenly와 바꿔 쓸 수 있는 말을 본문에서 찾아 쓰시오.

➡ _____

18 위 글의 밑줄 친 ⓑ의 우리말에 맞게 주어진 어휘를 알맞게 배열하시오.

> across / opening / saw / gateway / a / wooden / black / a / white / , /

➡ _____
_____

19 What words were written on the gate? Fill in the blanks with suitable words.

> The warning words, _____ _____,
> were written on the gate.

[20~22] 다음 글을 읽고 물음에 답하시오.

> We left our bikes at the gate and climbed over. We entered the cool tunnel. The air inside was heavy. Above our heads there was a sound that grew louder and louder.
>
> "What's that?" I called out.
>
> "Bats," said Ron, "Keep ⓐyour head down." Then he moved on.
>
> "Don't go so fast." I called after ⓑhim. I meant, "Don't leave ⓒme behind" but I didn't say so.
>
> The next thing ⓓI heard was a loud noise right above us, a thumping sound like an express train and then a scream.
>
> "Ron!" I shouted. "Ron, what's up? Can ⓔyou hear me?" No reply. "Speak to me, Ron. Tell me what's happened."

20 밑줄 친 ⓐ~ⓔ 중에서 가리키는 대상이 서로 같은 것은?

① ⓐ - ⓑ　　② ⓑ - ⓒ
③ ⓑ - ⓓ　　④ ⓑ - ⓔ
⑤ ⓓ - ⓔ

출제율 100%

21 위 글의 분위기로 가장 알맞은 것을 고르시오.

① exciting   ② urgent

③ festive   ④ gloomy

⑤ monotonous

출제율 95%

22 Which question CANNOT be answered after reading the passage?

① Where did they leave their bikes?

② Where did they enter?

③ What were there above their heads?

④ Who said "Keep your head down"?

⑤ What's happened to Ron?

[23~25] 다음 글을 읽고 물음에 답하시오.

Thanks to her, Ron was taken to the hospital, ⓐwhere his leg was put in a cast. As soon as our parents arrived at the hospital and saw us, my mother cried with relief. But all my father said was, "ⓑLet that being a lesson to you."

And what was the lesson? It was "Keep out means Stay out of trouble." Ron is now the manager of a big company which produces helmets and other safety products. And me? I am a fire fighter.

출제율 95%

23 위 글의 밑줄 친 ⓐ를 다음과 같이 바꿔 쓸 때 빈칸에 들어갈 알맞은 말을 한 칸에 한 단어씩 쓰시오.

and _____ his leg was put in a cast

= and _____ _____ _____ his leg was put in a cast

출제율 90%

24 위 글의 밑줄 친 ⓑ에서 어법상 틀린 부분을 찾아 고치시오.

_____ ➡ _____

출제율 85%

25 What did they learn from the accident? Fill in the blanks with suitable words.

They learned "*Keep out* means _____ _____ _____ _____."

MEMO

MEMO

INSIGHT
on the textbook
교과서 파헤치기

※ 다음 영어를 우리말로 쓰시오.

01 arrival _____

02 poet _____

03 literature _____

04 copy _____

05 particular _____

06 charge _____

07 literary _____

08 express _____

09 loneliness _____

10 childhood _____

11 freedom _____

12 publish _____

13 rare _____

14 further _____

15 library _____

16 government _____

17 achieve _____

18 graduation _____

19 movement _____

20 poetry _____

21 celebrate _____

22 whole _____

23 harsh _____

24 remain _____

25 sew _____

26 poem _____

27 treatment _____

28 wallet _____

29 present _____

30 publication _____

31 independence _____

32 longing _____

33 author _____

34 editor _____

35 give up _____

36 in a hurry _____

37 check out _____

38 be well known for _____

39 hang out with _____

40 take part in _____

41 have ~ in mind _____

42 look good on _____

43 give it a try _____

※ 다음 우리말을 영어로 쓰시오.

01 가혹한, 혹독한 _____

02 전체의, 모든 _____

03 체포하다 _____

04 외로움 _____

05 도착 _____

06 독립 _____

07 기소, 혐의 _____

08 (한 편의) 시 _____

09 문학의, 문학적인 _____

10 졸업 _____

11 편집자 _____

12 졸업 앨범 _____

13 선사하다, 주다 _____

14 이루다, 얻다 _____

15 빌리다 _____

16 기념하다, 축하하다 _____

17 동경, 갈망 _____

18 운동 _____

19 자유 _____

20 희귀한 _____

21 남아 있다, 계속 ∼하다 _____

22 더, 더 멀리 _____

23 정부, 정권 _____

24 저자 _____

25 (문학 장르) 시 _____

26 출판하다 _____

27 바느질하다 _____

28 문학 _____

29 출판, 발행 _____

30 대우, 처리 _____

31 어린 시절 _____

32 표현하다 _____

33 시인 _____

34 추천하다 _____

35 포기하다 _____

36 세우다, 내걸다 _____

37 ∼에 참가하다 _____

38 서둘러 _____

39 ∼에 잘 어울리다 _____

40 ∼을 염두에 두다 _____

41 시도하다 _____

42 ∼을 기대하다 _____

43 ∼와 시간을 보내다 _____

※ 다음 영영풀이에 알맞은 단어를 <보기>에서 골라 쓴 후, 우리말 뜻을 쓰시오.

1 _____ : not divided; all: _____

2 _____ : not common; unusual: _____

3 _____ : a person who writes poems: _____

4 _____ : the receiving of an academic degree: _____

5 _____ : written works which are of artistic value: _____

6 _____ : a strong feeling of wanting something: _____

7 _____ : to suggest as being good or worthy: _____

8 _____ : the town where someone was born and grew up: _____

9 _____ : the state of not being governed by another country: _____

10 _____ : to make or mend with needle and thread: _____

11 _____ : unpleasant and causing pain to the body or senses: _____

12 _____ : a feeling of being unhappy because you are away from other people:

_____

13 _____ : a piece of writing, arranged in patterns of lines and of sounds:

_____

14 _____ : the action of making something known to the public: _____

15 _____ : a person who prepares a book to be published, for example by checking

and correcting the text, making improvements, etc.: _____

16 _____ : to do something special or enjoyable for an important event, occasion,

holiday, etc.: _____

보기

sew	independence	literature	poet
editor	celebrate	rare	longing
loneliness	recommend	harsh	hometown
poem	publication	whole	graduation

Step1

※ 다음 우리말과 일치하도록 빈칸에 알맞은 말을 쓰시오.

Listen - Listen & Answer Dialog 1

Minjun: Hello, Ms. Seo.

Ms. Seo: Hi, Minjun. _____ time _____ see. What _____ you here?

Minjun: I _____ _____ write _____ _____ _____. Can you _____ a good novel _____ _____?

Ms. Seo: How _____ a mystery? There's a new Ken Kuller book, *22nd Street*.

Minjun: Oh, I've _____ _____ him. Can you _____ _____ the book?

Ms. Seo: It's in the "_____ _____" area. It's really _____ _____ teens in Great Britain.

Minjun: Thank you for your help. Can I _____ it _____?

Ms. Seo: Sure. You can _____ new books _____ _____ _____.

Minjun: Okay.

민준: 안녕하세요, 서 선생님.
서 선생님: 안녕, 민준아. 오랜만이구나. 무슨 일로 여기에 온 거니?
민준: 독후감을 써야 해서요. 읽기에 좋은 소설을 추천해 주시겠어요?
서 선생님: 추리 소설은 어떠니? Ken Kuller의 신간, '22번가'가 있단다.
민준: 아, 그에 관해 들어 본 적이 있어요. 책을 보여 주실 수 있나요?
서 선생님: '신착 도서' 서가에 있단다. 그 책은 영국의 십 대들 사이에서 많은 인기를 끌고 있어.
민준: 도와주셔서 감사합니다. 그 책을 대출할 수 있을까요?
서 선생님: 물론이지. 신간은 7일간 빌릴 수 있어.
민준: 알겠습니다.

Listen - Listen & Answer Dialog 2

Sora: Hey, Minjun. What _____ you _____?

Minjun: I'm reading a _____ for a _____ _____.

Sora: Let _____ _____. Oh, is this a new book by Ken Kuller?

Minjun: Yeah, I _____ it this morning. Do you know Ken Kuller?

Sora: Of _____. I'm a _____ of his. I've read _____ of his _____ _____.

Minjun: I think he's a great _____. I can't _____ _____ this book.

Sora: You know _____? His novel *Four Eyes* _____ _____ _____ _____ a movie.

Minjun: Yeah. I saw the movie poster. It _____ _____.

Sora: It'll _____ _____ next Thursday. I'm _____ _____ _____ it!

Minjun: Maybe we can see the movie _____.

소라: 안녕, 민준아. 뭐 하고 있니?
민준: 나는 독후감을 쓰려고 소설을 읽고 있어.
소라: 어디 봐. 아, 이거 Ken Kuller의 신간이지?
민준: 맞아, 오늘 아침에 이걸 대출했어. 너는 Ken Kuller를 알고 있니?
소라: 물론이지. 난 그의 열렬한 팬이야. 그의 추리 소설은 모두 읽었어.
민준: 내 생각에 그는 위대한 작가야. 이 책을 손에서 놓을 수가 없어.
소라: 그거 알아? 그의 소설 '네 개의 눈'이 영화로 만들어졌어.
민준: 맞아. 나도 영화 포스터를 봤어. 재미있어 보이더라.
소라: 영화는 다음 주 목요일에 개봉한대. 그걸 보는 게 기대돼!
민준: 아마 우리 영화를 같이 볼 수 있겠다.

Listen More - Listen and complete

Mike: Good morning, Jiho.

Jiho: Good morning.

Mike: _____ _____ _____, please. _____ _____ _____ _____ your hair done?

Jiho: Well, I'm _____ my pictures for the _____. So I want to look _____.

Mike: When do you _____ the pictures?

Jiho: This Friday at Dream & Joy Park.

Mike: Sounds good. Do you have a _____ style in _____?

Jiho: No. Can you _____ one for me?

Mike: _____ _____ this. How about this style? It'll _____ _____ _____ you.

Jiho: Wow, I like it. I _____ _____ _____ _____ how I'll look in the pictures.

Mike: I'm _____ you'll _____ _____.

My Speaking Portfolio

Jane: Nice _____ _____ you, Mr. Henry. Is O. Henry your _____ _____?

Mr. Henry: No. My real name is William Sydney Porter.

Jane: Can you tell me _____ _____ _____?

Mr. Henry: I'm _____ the U.S.

Jane: What do you _____ _____?

Mr. Henry: I'm a _____ _____ _____. I _____ _____ about 300 short stories.

Jane: Wow! You're great! What is _____ about your short stories?

Mr. Henry: They're _____ _____ _____ their _____ _____.

Jane: Can you _____ a popular story _____ a _____ _____?

Mr. Henry: Sure. I _____ *The Last Leaf*.

Jane: What is it _____?

Mr. Henry: It's about a sick girl and an old artist _____ _____ _____ _____.

Jane: Oh, I want to read it. I _____ _____.

Mike: 안녕, 지호야.

지호: 안녕하세요.

Mike: 자리에 앉으렴. 머리를 어떻게 해 줄까?

지호: 음, 저는 졸업 앨범에 들어갈 사진을 찍을 거예요. 그래서 멋져 보이고 싶어요.

Mike: 언제 사진을 찍니?

지호: 이번 금요일에 Dream & Joy Park에서요.

Mike: 멋지구나. 마음에 둔 특별한 스타일이 있니?

지호: 아니요. 저를 위해 하나 추천해 주시겠어요?

Mike: 이걸 보렴. 이 스타일은 어떠니? 너에게 잘 어울릴 거야.

지호: 와, 마음에 들어요. 제가 사진에서 어떻게 보일지 빨리 보고 싶네요.

Mike: 틀림없이 멋져 보일 거야.

Jane: 만나서 반갑습니다, Henry 씨. O. Henry가 당신의 본명인가요?

Mr. Henry: 아니요. 제 본명은 William Sydney Porter입니다.

Jane: 어디 출신이신지 말씀해 주시겠어요?

Mr. Henry: 저는 미국 출신입니다.

Jane: 주로 무엇을 쓰시나요?

Mr. Henry: 저는 단편 소설 작가입니다. 300여 편의 단편 소설을 썼죠.

Jane: 와! 대단하시네요! 당신의 단편 소설은 무엇이 특별한가요?

Mr. Henry: 그것들은 뜻밖의 결말로 유명합니다.

Jane: 뜻밖의 결말이 있는 유명한 이야기를 하나 추천해 주실 수 있나요?

Mr. Henry: 물론이죠. 저는 '마지막 잎새'를 추천합니다.

Jane: 그것은 무엇에 관한 이야기인가요?

Mr. Henry: 아픈 소녀와 그녀의 목숨을 구하는 늙은 화가의 이야기예요.

Jane: 아, 그것을 읽고 싶네요. 무척 기대됩니다.

※ 다음 우리말에 맞도록 대화를 영어로 쓰시오.

Listen - Listen & Answer Dialog 1

Minjun: _____

Ms. Seo: _____

Minjun: _____

Ms. Seo: _____

Minjun: _____

Ms. Seo: _____

_____

Minjun: _____

Ms. Seo: _____

Minjun: _____

해석

민준: 안녕하세요, 서 선생님.
서 선생님: 안녕, 민준아. 오랜만이구나. 무슨 일로 여기에 온 거니?
민준: 독후감을 써야 해서요. 읽기에 좋은 소설을 추천해 주시겠어요?
서 선생님: 추리 소설은 어떠니? Ken Kuller의 신간, '22번가'가 있단다.
민준: 아, 그에 관해 들어 본 적이 있어요. 책을 보여 주실 수 있나요?
서 선생님: '신착 도서' 서가에 있단다. 그 책은 영국의 십 대들 사이에서 많은 인기를 끌고 있어.
민준: 도와주셔서 감사합니다. 그 책을 대출할 수 있을까요?
서 선생님: 물론이지. 신간은 7일간 빌릴 수 있어.
민준: 알겠습니다.

Listen - Listen & Answer Dialog 2

Sora: _____

Minjun: _____

Sora: _____

Minjun: _____

Sora: _____

Minjun: _____

Sora: _____

Minjun: _____

Sora: _____

Minjun: _____

소라: 안녕, 민준아. 뭐 하고 있니?
민준: 나는 독후감을 쓰려고 소설을 읽고 있어.
소라: 어디 봐. 아, 이거 Ken Kuller의 신간이지?
민준: 맞아, 오늘 아침에 이걸 대출했어. 너는 Ken Kuller를 알고 있니?
소라: 물론이지. 난 그의 열렬한 팬이야. 그의 추리 소설은 모두 읽었어.
민준: 내 생각에 그는 위대한 작가야. 이 책을 손에서 놓을 수가 없어.
소라: 그거 알아? 그의 소설 '네 개의 눈'이 영화로 만들어졌어.
민준: 맞아. 나도 영화 포스터를 봤어. 재미있어 보이더라.
소라: 영화는 다음 주 목요일에 개봉한대. 그걸 보는 게 기대돼!
민준: 아마 우리 영화를 같이 볼 수 있겠다.

Listen More - Listen and complete

Mike: _____

Jiho: _____

Mike: _____

Jiho: _____

Mike: _____

Jiho: _____

Mike: _____

Jiho: _____

Mike: _____

Jiho: _____

Mike: _____

Mike: 안녕, 지호야.

지호: 안녕하세요.

Mike: 자리에 앉으렴. 머리를 어떻게 해 줄까?

지호: 음, 저는 졸업 앨범에 들어갈 사진 을 찍을 거예요. 그래서 멋져 보이 고 싶어요.

Mike: 언제 사진을 찍니?

지호: 이번 금요일에 Dream & Joy Park에서요.

Mike: 멋지구나. 마음에 둔 특별한 스타 일이 있니?

지호: 아니요. 저를 위해 하나 추천해 주 시겠어요?

Mike: 이걸 보렴. 이 스타일은 어떠니? 너에게 잘 어울릴 거야.

지호: 와, 마음에 들어요. 제가 사진에서 어떻게 보일지 빨리 보고 싶네요.

Mike: 틀림없이 멋져 보일 거야.

My Speaking Portfolio

Jane: _____

Mr. Henry: _____

Jane: _____

Mr. Henry: _____

Jane: _____

Mr. Henry: _____

Jane: _____

Mr. Henry: _____

Jane: _____

Mr. Henry: _____

Jane: _____

Mr. Henry: _____

Jane: _____

Jane: 만나서 반갑습니다, Henry 씨. O. Henry가 당신의 본명인가요?

Mr. Henry: 아니요. 제 본명은 William Sydney Porter입니다.

Jane: 어디 출신이신지 말씀해 주시겠 어요?

Mr. Henry: 저는 미국 출신입니다.

Jane: 주로 무엇을 쓰시나요?

Mr. Henry: 저는 단편 소설 작가입니 다. 300여 편의 단편 소설을 썼 죠.

Jane: 와! 대단하시네요! 당신의 단편 소설은 무엇이 특별한가요?

Mr. Henry: 그것들은 뜻밖의 결말로 유 명합니다.

Jane: 뜻밖의 결말이 있는 유명한 이야 기를 하나 추천해 주실 수 있나 요?

Mr. Henry: 물론이죠. 저는 '마지막 잎 새'를 추천합니다.

Jane: 그것은 무엇에 관한 이야기인가 요?

Mr. Henry: 아픈 소녀와 그녀의 목숨을 구하는 늙은 화가의 이야기예요.

Jane: 아, 그것을 읽고 싶네요. 무척 기 대됩니다.

※ 다음 우리말과 일치하도록 빈칸에 알맞은 것을 골라 쓰시오.

1 A _____ _____ _____ Stars
A. Loved   B. Poet   C. Who

2 In the sky _____ seasons pass _____ _____ _____
A. hurry   B. where   C. a   D. in

3 _____ _____ the _____ .
A. fills   B. autumn   C. air

4 And _____ I _____ , _____ a _____ ,
A. without   B. ready   C. worry   D. stand

5 _____ _____ all the _____ there.
A. stars   B. count   C. to

6 _____ for _____ star,
A. one   B. memory

7 _____ for _____ star,
A. another   B. love

8 _____ for _____ star,
A. another   B. loneliness

9 _____ for _____ star,
A.another   B. longing

10 _____ _____ another _____ ,
A. poetry   B. star   C. for

11 And, oh, mother, mother _____ _____ _____ .
A. another   B. for   C. star

12 _____ you _____ these _____ before?
A. lines   B. read   C. have

13 They are _____ _____ the _____ "Counting Stars at Night" _____ Yoon Dong-ju.
A. by   B. of   C. poem   D. part

14 The poem was _____ a long time ago but _____ _____ one of Korea's favorite _____ .
A. remains   B. poems   C. written   D. still

15 Dong-ju _____ _____ _____ 1917 _____ Yanbin, China.
A. near   B. born   C. in   D. was

16 _____ a young boy, he loved sports, and he was a soccer player _____ his _____ .
A. for   B. as   C. school

17 He also loved _____ _____ much _____ he _____ the numbers on all his friends' soccer uniforms.
A. that   B. sewed   C. so   D. sewing

1 별을 사랑한 시인

2 계절이 지나가는 하늘에는

3 가을로 가득 차 있습니다.

4 나는 아무 걱정도 없이

5 가을 속의 별들을 다 헤일 듯합니다.

6 별 하나에 추억과

7 별 하나에 사랑과

8 별 하나에 쓸쓸함과

9 별 하나에 동경과

10 별 하나에 시와

11 별 하나에 어머니, 어머니,

12 당신은 이 시 구절을 읽어 본 적이 있는가?

13 이것은 윤동주의 시 '별 헤는 밤'의 일부이다.

14 시는 오래 전에 쓰였지만 여전히 한국이 가장 좋아하는 시 중의 하나로 남아 있다.

15 동주는 중국 연변 근처에서 1917년에 태어났다.

16 어린 소년이었을 때 그는 운동을 좋아했고, 학교의 축구 선수였다.

17 그는 또한 바느질하는 것을 무척 좋아해서 친구들의 축구 유니폼에 번호를 바느질해 주기도 했다.

18 However, _____ literature _____ he loved _____ .

A. most   B. that   C. was   D. it

19 In elementary school he _____ a _____ of _____ .

A. poems   B. lot   C. wrote

20 He even made a _____ _____ _____ his _____ , Song Mong-gyu.

A. cousin   B. literary   C. with   D. magazine

21 In middle school he once _____ a _____ book by a famous poet of the time, Baek Seok, and _____ the _____ book by hand.

A. copied   B. borrowed   C. whole   D. poetry

22 He really wanted to _____ his _____ _____ of the _____ book.

A. rare   B. own   C. have   D. copy

23 His parents wanted him to be a _____ , but Dong-ju _____ to study _____ at a _____ in Seoul.

A. literature   B. college   C. chose   D. doctor

24 During his college years, he often _____ _____ with other young poets and wrote poetry where he _____ feelings about his hometown and _____ country.

A. expressed   B. hung   C. lost   D. out

25 To _____ his _____ , he wished to _____ 19 of his poems _____ the title, *Heaven, Wind, Stars, and Poetry*.

A. publish   B. celebrate   C. under   D. graduation

26 He made _____ _____ of the book _____ _____ .

A. by   B. copies   C. three   D. hand

27 One was _____ to his close friend, Jeong Byeong-uk, _____ was _____ to his favorite professor, and the last one was _____ for himself.

A. another   B. kept   C. given   D. presented

28 However, his professor _____ _____ his plan _____ he thought the Japanese government would not allow the _____ .

A. against   B. publication   C. advised   D. because

18 그러나 그가 가장 사랑한 것은 문학이었다.

19 초등학교에 다닐 때 그는 많은 시를 썼다.

20 심지어 사촌 송몽규와 문학잡지를 만들기도 했다.

21 그가 중학교에 다니던 때 한번은 당대의 유명한 시인 백석의 시집을 빌려 와서 책 전체를 필사하기도 했다.

22 그는 정말로 그 희귀한 책을 한 부 갖고 싶었던 것이다.

23 그의 부모는 그가 의사가 되기를 바랐지만 동주는 서울에 있는 대학에서 문학 공부를 하기로 했다.

24 대학 시절에 그는 종종 다른 젊은 시인들과 어울려 다녔고, 고향과 잃어버린 조국에 대한 심정을 표현하는 시를 썼다.

25 졸업을 기념하여 그는 '하늘과 바람과 별과 시'라는 제목으로 자신의 시 19편을 출판하고 싶어 했다.

26 그는 책 세 부를 손으로 만들었다.

27 한 부는 가까운 친구인 정병욱에게 주었고, 또 하나는 그가 가장 좋아하는 교수에게 선물했으며, 마지막 하나는 자신이 보관했다.

28 그러나 그의 교수는 일본 정부가 출판을 허가하지 않으리라 여겨, 그의 계획에 반대하는 충고를 했다.

29 Dong-ju _____ his _____ and _____ _____ the idea.

    A. up   B. followed   C. gave   D. advice

30 Dong-ju decided to _____ _____ in the country where his father _____ _____ before.

    A. further   B. studied   C. study   D. had

31 So, _____ 1942, Dong-ju and his cousin _____ _____ _____ in Japan.

    A. study   B. in   C. to   D. began

32 On July 10 the _____ year, his cousin was _____ by the Japanese police for talking _____ in an _____ movement.

    A. part   B. arrested   C. following   D. independence

33 Four days _____, Dong-ju was also _____ on the _____.

    A. same   B. later   C. charges   D. arrested

34 In 1945, Dong-ju and his cousin died in _____ _____ _____ _____ by the police.

    A. prison   B. treatment   C. harsh   D. after

35 _____ was just a _____ months later _____ Korea _____ independence from Japan.

    A. achieved   B. it   C. that   D. few

36 In 1948, Jeong Byeong-uk _____ Dong-ju's poems to the _____ brother, and they were _____ _____.

    A. finally   B. brought   C. poet's   D. published

37 The book _____ _____ the title the poet _____ _____ of many years before.

    A. thought   B. given   C. had   D. was

38 His poems are loved by people of all _____, and thus they still shine _____ in our _____ _____ the stars in the autumn night sky.

    A. hearts   B. ages   C. brightly   D. like

---

29 동주는 그의 충고를 따랐고 그 생각을 포기했다.

30 동주는 그의 아버지가 예전에 공부했던 나라에서 학업을 이어 가기로 했다.

31 그리하여 1942년에 동주와 그의 사촌은 일본에서 공부를 시작했다.

32 다음 해 7월 10일에 그의 사촌은 독립운동에 가담했다는 이유로 일본 경찰에게 체포되었다.

33 나흘 뒤 동주 역시 같은 혐의로 체포되었다.

34 1945년에 동주와 그의 사촌은 경찰의 가혹 행위를 당한 후 감옥에서 사망했다.

35 한국이 일본으로부터 독립을 이룬 것은 그로부터 불과 몇 달 후의 일이었다.

36 1948년에 정병욱이 동주의 시를 시인의 동생에게 가져다주었고, 마침내 그것들은 출판되었다.

37 그 책에는 시인이 수년 전에 생각해 두었던 제목이 붙었다.

38 그의 시는 모든 세대의 사랑을 받고 있고, 따라서 그것들은 가을밤 하늘의 별처럼 우리 가슴 속에 여전히 밝게 빛나고 있다.

※ 다음 우리말과 일치하도록 빈칸에 알맞은 것을 골라 쓰시오.

1 A _____ _____ Loved Stars

2 In the sky _____ seasons pass _____ _____ _____

3 Autumn _____ the air.

4 And ready I stand, _____ _____ _____,

5 To _____ all the stars there.

6 _____ for one star,

7 Love for _____ star,

8 _____ for another star,

9 _____ for another star,

10 _____ _____ another star,

11 And, oh, mother, mother _____ _____ _____.

12 _____ you _____ _____ _____ before?

13 They are _____ _____ the poem "Counting Stars at Night" _____ Yoon Dong-ju.

14 The poem _____ _____ a long time ago but _____ _____ one of Korea's favorite _____.

15 Dong-ju _____ _____ _____ 1917 near Yanbin, China.

16 _____ a young boy, he loved sports, and he was a soccer player _____ _____ _____.

17 He also loved _____ _____ much _____ he _____ the numbers on all his friends' soccer uniforms.

1 별을 사랑한 시인

2 계절이 지나가는 하늘에는

3 가을로 가득 차 있습니다.

4 나는 아무 걱정도 없이

5 가을 속의 별들을 다 헤일 듯합니다.

6 별 하나에 추억과

7 별 하나에 사랑과

8 별 하나에 쓸쓸함과

9 별 하나에 동경과

10 별 하나에 시와

11 별 하나에 어머니, 어머니.

12 당신은 이 시 구절을 읽어 본 적이 있는가?

13 이것은 윤동주의 시 '별 헤는 밤'의 일부이다.

14 시는 오래 전에 쓰였지만 여전히 한국이 가장 좋아하는 시 중의 하나로 남아 있다.

15 동주는 중국 연변 근처에서 1917년에 태어났다.

16 어린 소년이었을 때 그는 운동을 좋아했고, 학교의 축구 선수였다.

17 그는 또한 바느질하는 것을 무척 좋아해서 친구들의 축구 유니폼에 번호를 바느질해 주기도 했다.

18 However, _____ _____ literature _____ he loved _____ .

19 In elementary school he _____ _____ _____ _____
_____ .

20 He even made _____ _____ _____ _____ his cousin,
Song Mong-gyu.

21 In middle school he once _____ a poetry book by a famous poet
of the time, Baek Seok, and _____ the whole book _____
_____ .

22 He really wanted _____ _____ _____ _____ _____
of the _____ _____ .

23 His parents wanted him _____ _____ _____ _____ _____ ,
but Dong-ju _____ _____ _____ _____ at a college in
Seoul.

24 _____ his college years, he often _____ _____ _____
_____ _____ _____ and wrote poetry _____ he _____
_____ about his hometown and _____ _____ .

25 _____ _____ _____ _____ _____ _____ , he wished to _____ 19
of his poems _____ _____ _____ , *Heaven, Wind, Stars,
and Poetry*.

26 He made _____ _____ of the book _____ _____ .

27 One _____ _____ _____ his close friend, Jeong
Byeong-uk, _____ was presented to his favorite professor, and
_____ _____ _____ _____ was kept _____ _____ .

28 However, his professor _____ _____ his plan _____
he thought the Japanese government would not _____ the
_____ .

18 그러나 그가 가장 사랑한 것은 문학이었다.

19 초등학교에 다닐 때 그는 많은 시를 썼다.

20 심지어 사촌 송몽규와 문학잡지를 만들기도 했다.

21 그가 중학교에 다니던 때 한번은 당대의 유명한 시인 백석의 시집을 빌려 와서 책 전체를 필사하기도 했다.

22 그는 정말로 그 희귀한 책을 한 부 갖고 싶었던 것이다.

23 그의 부모는 그가 의사가 되기를 바랐지만 동주는 서울에 있는 대학에서 문학 공부를 하기로 했다.

24 대학 시절에 그는 종종 다른 젊은 시인들과 어울려 다녔고, 고향과 잃어버린 조국에 대한 심정을 표현하는 시를 썼다.

25 졸업을 기념하여 그는 '하늘과 바람과 별과 시'라는 제목으로 자신의 시 19편을 출판하고 싶어 했다.

26 그는 책 세 부를 손으로 만들었다.

27 한 부는 가까운 친구인 정병욱에게 주었고, 또 하나는 그가 가장 좋아하는 교수에게 선물했으며, 마지막 하나는 자신이 보관했다.

28 그러나 그의 교수는 일본 정부가 출판을 허가하지 않으리라 여겨, 그의 계획에 반대하는 충고를 했다.

29 Dong-ju _____ his advice and _____ _____ the idea.

30 Dong-ju _____ _____ _____ _____ in the country where his father _____ _____ _____.

31 So, in 1942, Dong-ju and his cousin _____ _____ _____ in Japan.

32 On July 10 the _____ _____, his cousin was arrested by the Japanese police _____ _____ _____ _____ an _____ _____.

33 Four days _____, Dong-ju was also _____ _____ _____ _____ _____.

34 In 1945, Dong-ju and his cousin died in prison _____ _____ _____ _____ _____ _____.

35 _____ _____ just a few months later _____ Korea _____ _____ from Japan.

36 In 1948, Jeong Byeong-uk _____ Dong-ju's poems _____ the poet's brother, and _____ _____ _____ _____.

37 The book _____ _____ the title the poet _____ _____ _____ many years _____.

38 His poems _____ _____ _____ people of all ages, and thus they still _____ _____ in our hearts _____ the stars in the autumn night sky.

29 동주는 그의 충고를 따랐고 그 생각을 포기했다.

30 동주는 그의 아버지가 예전에 공부했던 나라에서 학업을 이어 가기로 했다.

31 그리하여 1942년에 동주와 그의 사촌은 일본에서 공부를 시작했다.

32 다음 해 7월 10일에 그의 사촌은 독립운동에 가담했다는 이유로 일본 경찰에게 체포되었다.

33 나흘 뒤 동주 역시 같은 혐의로 체포되었다.

34 1945년에 동주와 그의 사촌은 경찰의 가혹 행위를 당한 후 감옥에서 사망했다.

35 한국이 일본으로부터 독립을 이룬 것은 그로부터 불과 몇 달 후의 일이었다.

36 1948년에 정병욱이 동주의 시를 시인의 동생에게 가져다주었고, 마침내 그것들은 출판되었다.

37 그 책에는 시인이 수년 전에 생각해 두었던 제목이 붙었다.

38 그의 시는 모든 세대의 사랑을 받고 있고, 따라서 그것들은 가을밤 하늘의 별처럼 우리 가슴 속에 여전히 밝게 빛나고 있다.

※ 다음 문장을 우리말로 쓰시오.

1 A Poet Who Loved Stars

➡ _____

2 In the sky where seasons pass in a hurry

➡ _____

3 Autumn fills the air.

➡ _____

4 And ready I stand, without a worry,

➡ _____

5 To count all the stars there.

➡ _____

6 Memory for one star,

➡ _____

7 Love for another star,

➡ _____

8 Loneliness for another star,

➡ _____

9 Longing for another star,

➡ _____

10 Poetry for another star,

➡ _____

11 And, oh, mother, mother for another star.

➡ _____

12 Have you read these lines before?

➡ _____

13 They are part of the poem "Counting Stars at Night" by Yoon Dong-ju.

➡ _____

14 The poem was written a long time ago but still remains one of Korea's favorite poems.

➡ _____

15 Dong-ju was born in 1917 near Yanbin, China.

➡ _____

16 As a young boy, he loved sports, and he was a soccer player for his school.

➡ _____

17 He also loved sewing so much that he sewed the numbers on all his friends' soccer uniforms.

➡ _____

18 However, it was literature that he loved most.

➡ _____

19 In elementary school he wrote a lot of poems.

➡ _____

20 He even made a literary magazine with his cousin, Song Mong-gyu.

➡ _____

21 In middle school he once borrowed a poetry book by a famous poet of the time, Baek Seok, and copied the whole book by hand.

➡ _____

22 He really wanted to have his own copy of the rare book.

➡ _____

23 His parents wanted him to be a doctor, but Dong-ju chose to study literature at a college in Seoul.

➡ _____

24 During his college years, he often hung out with other young poets and wrote poetry where he expressed feelings about his hometown and lost country.

➡ _____

25 To celebrate his graduation, he wished to publish 19 of his poems under the title, *Heaven, Wind, Stars, and Poetry*.

➡ _____

26 He made three copies of the book by hand.

➡ _____

27 One was given to his close friend, Jeong Byeong-uk, another was presented to his favorite professor, and the last one was kept for himself.

➡ _____

_____

28 However, his professor advised against his plan because he thought the Japanese government would not allow the publication.

➡ _____

29 Dong-ju followed his advice and gave up the idea.

➡ _____

30 Dong-ju decided to study further in the country where his father had studied before.

➡ _____

31 So, in 1942, Dong-ju and his cousin began to study in Japan.

➡ _____

32 On July 10 the following year, his cousin was arrested by the Japanese police for taking part in an independence movement.

➡ _____

33 Four days later, Dong-ju was also arrested on the same charges.

➡ _____

34 In 1945, Dong-ju and his cousin died in prison after harsh treatment by the police.

➡ _____

35 It was just a few months later that Korea achieved independence from Japan.

➡ _____

36 In 1948, Jeong Byeong-uk brought Dong-ju's poems to the poet's brother, and they were finally published.

➡ _____

37 The book was given the title the poet had thought of many years before.

➡ _____

38 His poems are loved by people of all ages, and thus they still shine brightly in our hearts like the stars in the autumn night sky.

➡ _____

_____

※ 다음 괄호 안의 단어들을 우리말에 맞도록 바르게 배열하시오.

1 (Poet / A / Loved / Who / Stars)
➡ _____

2 (the / in / where / sky / pass / seasons / a / in / hurry)
➡ _____

3 (fills / autumn / air. / the)
➡ _____

4 (ready / and / stand, / I / a / without / worry,)
➡ _____

5 (count / to / the / all / there. / stars)
➡ _____

6 (for / memory / star, / one)
➡ _____

7 (for / love / star, / another)
➡ _____

8 (for / loneliness / star, / another)
➡ _____

9 (for / longing / star, / another)
➡ _____

10 (for / poetry / star, / another)
➡ _____

11 (oh, / and, / mother / mother, / another / for / star.)
➡ _____

12 (you / have / these / read / before? / lines)
➡ _____

13 (are / they / of / part / poem / the / Stars / "Counting / Night" / at / Yoon / by / Dong-ju.)
➡ _____

14 (poem / the / written / was / long / a / time / but / ago / remains / still / of / one / favorite / Korea's / poems.)
➡ _____

_____

15 (was / Dong-ju / in / born / near / 1917 / China. / Yanbin,)
➡ _____

16 (a / as / boy, / young / loved / he / sports, / he / and / a / was / player / soccer / his / school. / for)
➡ _____

_____

17 (also / he / sewing / loved / much / so / he / that / the / sewed / numbers / all / on / friends' / his / uniforms. / soccer)
➡ _____

_____

---

1 별을 사랑한 시인

2 계절이 지나가는 하늘에는

3 가을로 가득 차 있습니다.

4 나는 아무 걱정도 없이

5 가을 속의 별들을 다 헤일 듯합니다.

6 별 하나에 추억과

7 별 하나에 사랑과

8 별 하나에 쓸쓸함과

9 별 하나에 동경과

10 별 하나에 시와

11 별 하나에 어머니, 어머니,

12 당신은 이 시 구절을 읽어 본 적이 있는가?

13 이것은 윤동주의 시 '별 헤는 밤'의 일부이다.

14 시는 오래 전에 쓰였지만 여전히 한국이 가장 좋아하는 시 중의 하나로 남아 있다.

15 동주는 중국 연변 근처에서 1917년에 태어났다.

16 어린 소년이었을 때 그는 운동을 좋아했고, 학교의 축구 선수였다.

17 그는 또한 바느질하는 것을 무척 좋아해서 친구들의 축구 유니폼에 번호를 바느질해 주기도 했다.

18 (it / however, / was / that / literature / loved / he / most.)

➡ _____

19 (elementary / in / school / wrote / he / lot / a / poems. / of)

➡ _____

20 (even / he / a / made / magazine / literary / his / with / cousin, / Mong-gyu. / Song)

➡ _____

21 (middle / in / he / school / borrowed / once / poetry / a / by / book / famous / a / of / poet / time, / the / Seok, / Baek / and / the / copied / book / whole / hand. / by)

➡ _____

22 (really / he / to / wanted / have / own / his / of / copy / the / book. / rare)

➡ _____

23 (parents / his / him / wanted / be / to / doctor, / a / but / chose / Dong-ju / study / to / at / literature / college / a / Seoul. / in)

➡ _____

➡ _____

24 (his / during / years, / college / often / he / out / hung / other / with / poets / young / and / poetry / wrote / he / where / feelings / expressed / his / about / hometown / and / country. / lost)

➡ _____

➡ _____

25 (celebrate / to / graduation, / his / wished / he / publish / to / of / 19 / poems / his / the / under / title, / *Wind,* / *Heaven,* / *and* / *Stars,* / *Poetry*.)

➡ _____

➡ _____

26 (made / he / copies / three / the / of / book / hand. / by)

➡ _____

27 (was / one / given / his / to / friend, / close / Byeong-uk, / Jeong / was / another / to / presented / his / professor, / favorite / and / last / the / was / one / for / kept / himself.)

➡ _____

➡ _____

28 (his / however, / professor / against / advised / plan / his / he / because / the / thought / Japanese / would / government / allow / not / publication. / the)

➡ _____

➡ _____

18 그러나 그가 가장 사랑한 것은 문학이었다.

19 초등학교에 다닐 때 그는 많은 시를 썼다.

20 심지어 사촌 송몽규와 문학잡지를 만들기도 했다.

21 그가 중학교에 다니던 때 한번은 당대의 유명한 시인 백석의 시집을 빌려 와서 책 전체를 필사하기도 했다.

22 그는 정말로 그 희귀한 책을 한 부 갖고 싶었던 것이다.

23 그의 부모는 그가 의사가 되기를 바랐지만 동주는 서울에 있는 대학에서 문학 공부를 하기로 했다.

24 대학 시절에 그는 종종 다른 젊은 시인들과 어울려 다녔고, 고향과 잃어버린 조국에 대한 심정을 표현하는 시를 썼다.

25 졸업을 기념하여 그는 '하늘과 바람과 별과 시'라는 제목으로 자신의 시 19편을 출판하고 싶어 했다.

26 그는 책 세 부를 손으로 만들었다.

27 한 부는 가까운 친구인 정병욱에게 주었고, 또 하나는 그가 가장 좋아하는 교수에게 선물했으며, 마지막 하나는 자신이 보관했다.

28 그러나 그의 교수는 일본 정부가 출판을 허가하지 않으리라 여겨, 그의 계획에 반대하는 충고를 했다.

29 (followed / Dong-ju / advice / his / and / up / gave / idea. / the)

➡ _____

30 (decided / Dong-ju / study / to / in / further / the / country / his / where / father / studied / before. / had)

➡ _____

_____

31 (in / so, / 1942, / Dong-ju / his / and / cousin / to / began / in / study / Japan.)

➡ _____

32 (July / on / the / 10 / year, / following / cousin / his / arrested / was / the / by / police / Japanese / for / part / taking / an / in / movement. / independence)

➡ _____

_____

33 (days / four / later, / was / Dong-ju / arrested / also / the / on / charges. / same)

➡ _____

34 (1945, / in / and / Dong-ju / cousin / his / in / died / prison / harsh / after / by / treatment / police. / the)

➡ _____

_____

35 (was / it / a / just / months / few / that / later / achieved / Korea / from / independence / Japan.)

➡ _____

_____

36 (1948, / in / Byeong-uk / Jeong / brought / poems / Dong-ju's / to / poet's / the / and / brother, / were / they / published. / finally)

➡ _____

_____

37 (book / the / given / was / title / the / poet / the / thought / had / many / of / before. / years)

➡ _____

_____

38 (poems / his / loved / are / people / by / ages, / all / of / and / thus / still / they / brightly / shine / our / in / like / hearts / the / in / stars / the / night / autumn / sky.)

➡ _____

_____

29 동주는 그의 충고를 따랐고 그 생각을 포기했다.

30 동주는 그의 아버지가 예전에 공부했던 나라에서 학업을 이어 가기로 했다.

31 그리하여 1942년에 동주와 그의 사촌은 일본에서 공부를 시작했다.

32 다음 해 7월 10일에 그의 사촌은 독립운동에 가담했다는 이유로 일본 경찰에게 체포되었다.

33 나흘 뒤 동주 역시 같은 혐의로 체포되었다.

34 1945년에 동주와 그의 사촌은 경찰의 가혹 행위를 당한 후 감옥에서 사망했다.

35 한국이 일본으로부터 독립을 이룬 것은 그로부터 불과 몇 달 후의 일이었다.

36 1948년에 정병욱이 동주의 시를 시인의 동생에게 가져다주었고, 마침내 그것들은 출판되었다.

37 그 책에는 시인이 수년 전에 생각해 두었던 제목이 붙었다.

38 그의 시는 모든 세대의 사랑을 받고 있고, 따라서 그것들은 가을밤 하늘의 별처럼 우리 가슴 속에 여전히 밝게 빛나고 있다.

※ 다음 우리말을 영어로 쓰시오.

1 별을 사랑한 시인

➡ _____

2 계절이 지나가는 하늘에는

➡ _____

3 가을로 가득 차 있습니다.

➡ _____

4 나는 아무 걱정도 없이

➡ _____

5 가을 속의 별들을 다 헤일 듯합니다.

➡ _____

6 별 하나에 추억과

➡ _____

7 별 하나에 사랑과

➡ _____

8 별 하나에 쓸쓸함과

➡ _____

9 별 하나에 동경과

➡ _____

10 별 하나에 시와

➡ _____

11 별 하나에 어머니, 어머니,

➡ _____

12 당신은 이 시 구절을 읽어 본 적이 있는가?

➡ _____

13 이것은 윤동주의 시 '별 헤는 밤'의 일부이다.

➡ _____

14 시는 오래 전에 쓰였지만 여전히 한국이 가장 좋아하는 시 중의 하나로 남아 있다.

➡ _____

15 동주는 중국 연변 근처에서 1917년에 태어났다.

➡ _____

16 어린 소년이었을 때 그는 운동을 좋아했고, 학교의 축구 선수였다.

➡ _____

17 그는 또한 바느질하는 것을 무척 좋아해서 친구들의 축구 유니폼에 번호를 바느질해 주기도 했다.

➡ _____

18 그러나 그가 가장 사랑한 것은 문학이었다.

➡ _____

19 초등학교에 다닐 때 그는 많은 시를 썼다.

➡ _____

20 심지어 사촌 송몽규와 문학잡지를 만들기도 했다.

➡ _____

21 그가 중학교에 다니던 때 한번은 당대의 유명한 시인 백석의 시집을 빌려 와서 책 전체를 필사
하기도 했다.

➡ _____

_____

22 그는 정말로 그 희귀한 책을 한 부 갖고 싶었던 것이다.

➡ _____

23 그의 부모는 그가 의사가 되기를 바랐지만 동주는 서울에 있는 대학에서 문학 공부를 하기로 했다.

➡ _____

_____

24 대학 시절에 그는 종종 다른 젊은 시인들과 어울려 다녔고, 고향과 잃어버린 조국에 대한 심정을
표현하는 시를 썼다.

➡ _____

_____

25 졸업을 기념하여 그는 '하늘과 바람과 별과 시'라는 제목으로 자신의 시 19편을 출판하고 싶어
했다.

➡ _____

_____

26 그는 책 세 부를 손으로 만들었다.

➡ _____

27 한 부는 가까운 친구인 정병욱에게 주었고, 또 하나는 그가 가장 좋아하는 교수에게 선물했으며,
마지막 하나는 자신이 보관했다.

➡ _____

_____

28 그러나 그의 교수는 일본 정부가 출판을 허가하지 않으리라 여겨, 그의 계획에 반대하는 충고를 했다.

➡ _____

_____

29 동주는 그의 충고를 따랐고 그 생각을 포기했다.

➡ _____

30 동주는 그의 아버지가 예전에 공부했던 나라에서 학업을 이어 가기로 했다.

➡ _____

31 그리하여 1942년에 동주와 그의 사촌은 일본에서 공부를 시작했다.

➡ _____

32 다음 해 7월 10일에 그의 사촌은 독립운동에 가담했다는 이유로 일본 경찰에게 체포되었다.

➡ _____

_____

33 나흘 뒤 동주 역시 같은 혐의로 체포되었다.

➡ _____

34 1945년에 동주와 그의 사촌은 경찰의 가혹 행위를 당한 후 감옥에서 사망했다.

➡ _____

35 한국이 일본으로부터 독립을 이룬 것은 그로부터 불과 몇 달 후의 일이었다.

➡ _____

36 1948년에 정병욱이 동주의 시를 시인의 동생에게 가져다주었고, 마침내 그것들은 출판되었다.

➡ _____

_____

37 그 책에는 시인이 수년 전에 생각해 두었던 제목이 붙었다.

➡ _____

38 그의 시는 모든 세대의 사랑을 받고 있고, 따라서 그것들은 가을밤 하늘의 별처럼 우리 가슴 속에 여전히 밝게 빛나고 있다.

➡ _____

_____

※ 다음 우리말과 일치하도록 빈칸에 알맞은 말을 쓰시오.

Communicate: Speak

1. Tom: Hi, Sora. You _____ _____.
2. Sora: Yeah. I'm really _____ _____ _____ this Tuesday.
3. Tom: This Tuesday? What's _____ Tuesday?
4. Sora: There's a big _____ _____ . I _____ _____!

1. Tom: 안녕, 소라. 너 신나 보여.
2. Sora: 응. 나는 정말로 이번 주 화요일이 기대돼.
3. Tom: 이번 주 화요일? 화요일에 무슨 일이 있니?
4. Sora: 큰 컬링 게임이 있어. 나는 너무 기대돼!

Before You Read

1. _____ _____ we _____ August 15 in our class.
2. We _____ _____ pictures of people who _____ _____ through _____ _____ and _____ _____ _____ independence.
3. Also, there was a talk on _____ who _____ _____ their _____ _____ _____ in _____ _____.

1. 지난주에 우리는 반에서 8월 15일을 기념했습니다.
2. 우리는 가혹한 시대를 살면서 독립을 쟁취하려고 노력한 사람들의 사진을 전시했습니다.
3. 또한, 자유를 향한 동경을 문학 작품에 표현한 작가들에 관한 강연도 있었습니다.

Wrap Up READING

1. Do you enjoy plays, _____, novels, or _____?
2. They are _____ _____ _____ literature, and people _____ _____ _____ _____ _____ _____.
3. However, all of them _____ _____ _____ _____ our own small world _____ _____ _____ _____.
4. When we read literature, we _____ _____ the ideas of great _____ _____ _____ long ago.
5. We can even imagine _____ someone else or _____ in a _____ _____ _____.
6. _____ _____, literature opens up for us new worlds that we _____ _____ _____ before.

1. 당신은 희곡, 시, 소설 또는 만화를 즐기는가?
2. 그것들은 다양한 종류의 문학으로, 어떤 종류를 선호하는지는 사람에 따라 다르다.
3. 그러나 그것들은 모두 우리를 우리가 사는 작은 세계 너머로 가게 해 준다.
4. 문학을 읽을 때, 우리는 오래 전에 살았던 위대한 작가들의 생각과 마주치게 된다.
5. 심지어 우리는 다른 누군가가 되거나 완전히 다른 장소에서 사는 상상을 할 수도 있다.
6. 요컨대, 문학은 이전에 가 본 적이 없는 새로운 세계를 우리 앞에 펼쳐 준다.

※ 다음 우리말을 영어로 쓰시오.

Communicate: Speak

1. Tom: 안녕, 소라. 너 신나 보여.

   ➡ _____

2. Sora: 응. 나는 정말로 이번 주 화요일이 기대돼.

   ➡ _____

3. Tom: 이번 주 화요일? 화요일에 무슨 일이 있니?

   ➡ _____

4. Sora: 큰 컬링 게임이 있어. 나는 너무 기대돼!

   ➡ _____

Before You Read

1. 지난주에 우리는 반에서 8월 15일을 기념했습니다.

   ➡ _____

2. 우리는 가혹한 시대를 살면서 독립을 쟁취하려고 노력한 사람들의 사진을 전시했습니다.

   ➡ _____

3. 또한, 자유를 향한 동경을 문학 작품에 표현한 작가들에 관한 강연도 있었습니다.

   ➡ _____

Wrap Up READING

1. 당신은 희곡, 시, 소설 또는 만화를 즐기는가?

   ➡ _____

2. 그것들은 다양한 종류의 문학으로, 어떤 종류를 선호하는지는 사람에 따라 다르다.

   ➡ _____

3. 그러나 그것들은 모두 우리를 우리가 사는 작은 세계 너머로 가게 해 준다.

   ➡ _____

4. 문학을 읽을 때, 우리는 오래 전에 살았던 위대한 작가들의 생각과 마주치게 된다.

   ➡ _____

5. 심지어 우리는 다른 누군가가 되거나 완전히 다른 장소에서 사는 상상을 할 수도 있다.

   ➡ _____

6. 요컨대, 문학은 이전에 가 본 적이 없는 새로운 세계를 우리 앞에 펼쳐 준다.

   ➡ _____

※ 다음 영어를 우리말로 쓰시오.

01 additional _____

02 local _____

03 proud _____

04 raise _____

05 company _____

06 senior _____

07 volunteer _____

08 serious _____

09 view _____

10 population _____

11 harsh _____

12 messy _____

13 common _____

14 support _____

15 growl _____

16 disappoint _____

17 pollute _____

18 lesson _____

19 fairly _____

20 notice _____

21 carry _____

22 pollution _____

23 value _____

24 resource _____

25 seasick _____

26 patient _____

27 disappear _____

28 grassland _____

29 graze _____

30 charger _____

31 secret _____

32 per _____

33 sleepy _____

34 pleasure _____

35 in secret _____

36 by the way _____

37 once upon a time _____

38 take care of _____

39 be full of _____

40 ask a favor _____

41 the number of _____

42 to make matters worse _____

43 break a rule _____

※ 다음 우리말을 영어로 쓰시오.

01	오염	
02	빌리다	
03	진지한	
04	충전기	
05	교훈	
06	꽤	
07	개체 수, 인구	
08	지역의	
09	직접적으로	
10	~당, ~마다	
11	초래하다	
12	오염시키다	
13	비밀	
14	인내심이 있는; 환자	
15	추가적인	
16	졸리는	
17	초지, 풀밭	
18	공유지, 공원	
19	지지하다, 부양하다	
20	풀을 뜯다	
21	두다, 놓다	

22	뱃멀미가 나는	
23	지저분한	
24	실망하게 하다	
25	전망, 경관	
26	소중히 여기다	
27	알아채다	
28	꼬르륵 소리가 나다	
29	가혹한, 냉혹한	
30	신경을 쓰다, 싫어하다	
31	자랑스러운	
32	함께함, 동행	
33	자원	
34	사라지다	
35	조화롭게	
36	규칙을 어기다	
37	~을 돌보다	
38	몰래, 비밀리에	
39	~의 수	
40	~으로 가득 차다	
41	옛날에	
42	부탁하다	
43	~을 명심하다	

※ 다음 영영풀이에 알맞은 단어를 <보기>에서 골라 쓴 후, 우리말 뜻을 쓰시오.

1 _____ : added; more: _____

2 _____ : for each: _____

3 _____ : to become aware of: _____

4 _____ : to feed on grass: _____

5 _____ : land with grass: _____

6 _____ : unpleasantly severe: _____

7 _____ : a natural ability to do something well: _____

8 _____ : something to be learned: _____

9 _____ : to become impossible to see: _____

10 _____ : a piece of land used jointly: _____

11 _____ : the total number of persons or animals: _____

12 _____ : a source of supply, support, or aid: _____

13 _____ : to supply things that are needed: _____

14 _____ : to think that someone or something is important: _____

15 _____ : a piece of equipment for loading a battery with electricity: _____

16 _____ : to take and use something that belongs to someone else, and return it to them at a later time: _____

보기			
borrow	talent	charger	lesson
common	per	disappear	additional
support	grassland	value	harsh
population	graze	resource	notice

※ 다음 우리말과 일치하도록 빈칸에 알맞은 말을 쓰시오.

Listen - Listen & Answer Dialog 1

B: Jimin, have you decided _____ _____ _____?

G: Not yet. Do you know a _____ _____ _____ _____?

B: If I _____ you, I'd go to the _____ _____.

G: The _____ _____? What can I do there?

B: There's a smartphone class for _____ _____, and they're _____ _____ volunteers.

G: That _____ interesting, but I've _____ _____ anyone.

B: Don't worry. All you need _____ _____ _____ _____ the teacher there.

G: Okay. Thanks for your _____.

소년: 지민아, 어디에서 봉사 활동 할지 결정했니?
소녀: 아직. 봉사 활동을 하기에 좋은 장소를 알고 있어?
소년: 내가 너라면, 지역 주민 센터에서 봉사 활동을 할 거야.
소녀: 지역 주민 센터? 거기에서 무엇을 할 수 있는데?
소년: 어르신들을 위한 스마트폰 수업이 있는데 거기에서 자원봉사자를 찾고 있어.
소녀: 그거 좋겠다, 하지만 난 누군가를 가르쳐 본 적이 없어.
소년: 걱정하지 마. 너는 그곳에서 선생님을 돕기만 하면 돼.
소녀: 알겠어. 조언해 줘서 고마워.

Listen - Listen & Answer Dialog 2

G: Thanks for _____ _____ _____ here, Ms. Yun.

W: It's my _____, Jimin. I'm glad you _____ _____ help.

G: Well, what _____ I do?

W: Today's _____ is about _____ _____ with smartphones. _____ _____ _____ help the _____ _____?

G: Okay. Is _____ _____ I should know?

W: Yes. Please be _____ and _____ to the _____.

G: I'll _____ _____ _____ _____. _____ _____ _____, _____ _____ _____ _____ _____ I use your _____? My battery is _____ _____ _____.

W: Of course _____. Go right ahead.

소녀: 윤 선생님, 이곳에서 봉사 활동을 하게 해 주셔서 감사해요.
선생님: 천만에, 지민아. 네가 돕겠다고 해 줘서 나는 기쁘단다.
소녀: 음, 제가 무엇을 해야 하나요?
선생님: 오늘 수업은 스마트폰으로 사진을 찍는 것에 관한 거란다. 학습 속도가 느린 사람들을 도와주는 게 어떨까?
소녀: 네. 제가 알아 두어야 할 것이 있나요?
선생님: 그래. 인내심을 갖고 학습자들에게 친절히 대해 주렴.
소녀: 명심할게요. 그런데, 제가 선생님의 충전기를 사용해도 될까요? 제 배터리가 별로 남지 않아서요.
선생님: 물론이지. 사용하렴.

Listen - Listen More

G: Wow, it feels great to be _____ _____ _____, Dad.

M: I feel _____ _____, Sora. Here are our _____, 20A and 20B.

G: Yeah. _____ _____ _____ I take the _____ _____? I like to see the _____ _____.

M: No _____.

G: By the way, I want to eat something _____ _____ or _____.

소녀: 와! 배에 타니 정말 좋아요, 아빠.
남: 나도 그렇단다, 소라야. 20A와 20B, 여기가 우리 자리야.
소녀: 네. 제가 창가 자리에 앉아도 괜찮을까요? 바깥 풍경을 보고 싶어요.
남: 그렇게 하렴.
소녀: 그런데, 국수나 샌드위치 같은 걸 먹고 싶어요.

M: _____ _____ _____ _____, I _____ _____ anything _____ that.

G: Why is that?

M: They may _____ you _____.

G: Oh, I see. Then, I'll have _____ ice cream.

M: That's not a good idea, _____. _____ eat _____ _____ _____.

남: 나라면, 그런 것들을 먹지 않을 거야.
소녀: 왜 그렇죠?
남: 그런 음식들이 뱃멀미하게 할 수 있단다.
소녀: 오, 알겠어요. 그렇다면, 아이스크림을 먹을래요.
남: 그것도 좋은 생각이 아니야. 우리 도착한 뒤에 먹자.

Speak - Talk in groups

A: I didn't _____ my science homework.

B: _____ I _____ you, I'd do it _____ _____.

A: Thanks _____ your _____.

A: 과학 숙제를 가져오지 않았어.
B: 내가 너라면, 쉬는 시간에 할 거야.
A: 조언 고마워.

Speak - Talk in pairs.

A: Do you _____ _____ I eat your sausage?

B: Not _____ _____. Go _____.

A: Thank you.

A: 내가 네 소시지를 먹어도 될까?
B: 물론이지, 그럼.
A: 고마워.

Wrap Up 5

(The phone rings.)

W: Hi, Kevin. _____ _____?

B: Hi, Aunt Victoria. I _____ to _____ _____.

W: What is it?

B: I need a _____ _____ for my science camp. _____ _____ _____ _____ I _____ yours?

W: _____, not at all.

(전화벨이 울린다.)
여: Kevin, 안녕. 무슨 일이니?
소년: Victoria 이모, 안녕하세요. 부탁 좀 드리려고 전화했어요.
여: 그게 뭔데?
소년: 과학 캠프에 침낭이 필요해요. 제가 이모 것을 빌려도 될까요?
여: 물론이지.

Wrap Up 6

G: My _____ _____ every morning. What should I do?

B: Ha ha. Do you usually _____ _____?

G: No, I have _____ _____ _____ _____ anything at home.

B: _____ _____ _____ _____, I'd _____ some snacks.

G: That's a good idea.

소녀: 아침마다 나는 배가 꼬르륵거려. 어떻게 해야 할까?
소년: 하하. 너는 보통 아침을 먹니?
소녀: 아니, 집에서 뭘 먹을 시간이 없어.
소년: 내가 너라면, 간식을 좀 가져오겠다.
소녀: 그거 좋은 생각이야.

Step2

※ 다음 우리말에 맞도록 대화를 영어로 쓰시오.

Listen - Listen & Answer Dialog 1

B: _____

G: _____

B: _____

G: _____

B: _____

G: _____

B: _____

G: _____

해석

소년: 지민아, 어디에서 봉사 활동 할지 결정했니?

소녀: 아직. 봉사 활동을 하기에 좋은 장소를 알고 있어?

소년: 내가 너라면, 지역 주민 센터에서 봉사 활동을 할 거야.

소녀: 지역 주민 센터? 거기에서 무엇을 할 수 있는데?

소년: 어르신들을 위한 스마트폰 수업이 있는데 거기에서 자원봉사자를 찾고 있어.

소녀: 그거 좋겠다. 하지만 난 누군가를 가르쳐 본 적이 없어.

소년: 걱정하지 마. 너는 그곳에서 선생님을 돕기만 하면 돼.

소녀: 알겠어. 조언해 줘서 고마워.

Listen - Listen & Answer Dialog 2

G: _____

W: _____

G: _____

W: _____

_____

G: _____

W: _____

G: _____

_____

W: _____

소녀: 윤 선생님, 이곳에서 봉사 활동을 하게 해 주셔서 감사해요.

선생님: 천만에, 지민아. 네가 돕겠다고 해 줘서 나는 기쁘단다.

소녀: 음, 제가 무엇을 해야 하나요?

선생님: 오늘 수업은 스마트폰으로 사진을 찍는 것에 관한 거란다. 학습 속도가 느린 사람들을 도와주는 게 어떨까?

소녀: 네. 제가 알아 두어야 할 것이 있나요?

선생님: 그래. 인내심을 갖고 학습자들에게 친절히 대해 주렴.

소녀: 명심할게요. 그런데, 제가 선생님의 충전기를 사용해도 될까요? 제 배터리가 별로 남지 않아서요.

선생님: 물론이지. 사용하렴.

Listen - Listen More

G: _____

M: _____

G: _____

M: _____

G: _____

소녀: 와! 배에 타니 정말 좋아요, 아빠.

남: 나도 그렇단다, 소라야. 20A와 20B, 여기가 우리 자리야.

소녀: 네. 제가 창가 자리에 앉아도 괜찮을까요? 바깥 풍경을 보고 싶어요.

남: 그렇게 하렴.

소녀: 그런데, 국수나 샌드위치 같은 걸 먹고 싶어요.

M: _____

G: _____

M: _____

G: _____

M: _____

남: 나라면, 그런 것들을 먹지 않을 거야.

소녀: 왜 그렇죠?

남: 그런 음식들이 뱃멀미하게 할 수 있단다.

소녀: 오, 알겠어요. 그렇다면, 아이스크림을 먹을래요.

남: 그것도 좋은 생각이 아니야. 우리 도착한 뒤에 먹자.

Speak - Talk in groups

A: _____

B: _____

A: _____

A: 과학 숙제를 가져오지 않았어.

B: 내가 너라면, 쉬는 시간에 할 거야.

A: 조언 고마워.

Speak - Talk in pairs.

A: _____

B: _____

A: _____

A: 내가 네 소시지를 먹어도 될까?

B: 물론이지, 그러렴.

A: 고마워.

Wrap Up 5

(The phone rings.)

W: _____

B: _____

W: _____

B: _____

W: _____

(전화벨이 울린다.)

여: Kevin, 안녕. 무슨 일이니?

소년: Victoria 이모, 안녕하세요. 부탁 좀 드리려고 전화했어요.

여: 그게 뭔데?

소년: 과학 캠프에 침낭이 필요해요. 제가 이모 것을 빌려도 될까요?

여: 물론이지.

Wrap Up 6

G: _____

B: _____

G: _____

B: _____

G: _____

소녀: 아침마다 나는 배가 꼬르륵거려. 어떻게 해야 할까?

소년: 하하. 너는 보통 아침을 먹니?

소녀: 아니, 집에서 뭘 먹을 시간이 없어.

소년: 내가 너라면, 간식을 좀 가져오겠다.

소녀: 그거 좋은 생각이야.

※ 다음 우리말과 일치하도록 빈칸에 알맞은 것을 골라 쓰시오.

1 The _____ of the _____
A. Commons　　B. Story

2 _____ _____ a time there was a small _____ in a _____.
A. upon　　B. forest　　C. once　　D. village

3 The _____ were _____ and _____ _____.
A. farmers　　B. cows　　C. villagers　　D. raised

4 _____, some good grassland _____ in the _____ of the _____.
A. lay　　B. luckily　　C. village　　D. middle

5 The Commons: _____ _____ _____
A. for　　B. Space　　C. Everyone

6 **Head of a village:** _____ _____ the _____.
A. commons　　B. share　　C. let's

7 **Villager 1:** My _____ can get _____ _____.
A. grass　　B. cow　　C. enough

8 **Villager 2:** Yeah, there's _____ for _____ _____.
A. every　　B. plenty　　C. cow

9 Everyone was _____ _____ _____ the grassland.
A. allowed　　B. use　　C. to

10 _____, it was _____ "the _____."
A. called　　B. commons　　C. therefore

11 By _____, each family only had one cow, so it was _____ for each cow in the village to find _____ _____ to eat.
A. enough　　B. easy　　C. tradition　　D. grass

12 The _____ on the commons was green _____ _____.
A. long　　B. grass　　C. summer　　D. all

13 **Farmer 1:** If I _____ two cows, I _____ _____.
A. be　　B. had　　C. would　　D. richer

14 **Farmer 1:** _____ _____ will _____ it.
A. one　　B. no　　C. notice

15 But _____ day a villager _____ the _____.
A. broke　　B. one　　C. rule

16 He brought _____ cow and _____ it _____ on the _____.
A. graze　　B. another　　C. let　　D. commons

17 He _____ that _____ _____ it.
A. would　　B. nobody　　C. thought　　D. notice

18 A happy feeling _____ his _____ when he _____ of the milk and cheese that the second cow would _____ to his family.
A. filled　　B. bring　　C. thought　　D. heart

1 공유지 이야기

2 옛날, 숲속에 작은 마을이 있었다.

3 마을 주민들은 농부였고 소를 길렀다.

4 다행히도, 마을 한 가운데에 좋은 목초지가 있었다.

5 공유지: 모두를 위한 장소

6 이장: 공유지를 함께 나누어 씁시다.

7 마을 사람 1: 내 소가 풀을 충분히 뜯을 수 있겠어.

8 마을 사람 2: 맞아. 모든 소에게 충분한 양이야.

9 모든 사람들이 목초지를 사용하도록 허락되었다.

10 그러므로 목초지는 '공유지'라고 불렸다.

11 전통에 따라 각 가정은 소가 한 마리만 있었고, 그래서 마을에 있는 소들이 충분히 먹을 풀을 찾는 것은 쉬운 일이었다.

12 공유지의 풀은 여름 내내 푸르렀다.

13 농부 1: 만약 소가 두 마리 있다면, 내가 더 부유할 텐데.

14 농부 1: 아무도 눈치 채지 못할 거야.

15 그러나 어느 날 마을 사람 하나가 규칙을 깨뜨렸다.

16 그는 또 다른 소를 가져와 공유지에서 풀을 뜯게 했다.

17 그는 아무도 그것을 눈치 채지 못할 거라고 생각했다.

18 두 번째 소가 가족에게 가져다 줄 우유와 치즈를 생각하자 그의 마음은 행복감으로 충만했다.

19 Farmer 1: He _____ _____ _____.
A. four   B. has   C. children

20 Farmer 1: If I _____ you, I _____ _____ _____ cow.
A. would   B. were   C. another   D. raise

21 Farmer 2: _____ _____ the _____!
A. for   B. thanks   C. tip

22 A _____ days _____, the farmer visited a _____ friend _____ had four children.
A. who   B. few   C. close   D. later

23 He wanted to help his friend, so he told him _____ _____, "If I were you, I would _____ in one more cow and _____ it on the commons."
A. raise   B. secret   C. bring   D. in

24 The friend _____ him and did _____ he was _____ the _____ day.
A. told   B. thanked   C. as   D. next

25 Cow 1: _____ are _____?
A. you   B. who

26 Cow 2: _____ _____.
A. new   B. I'm

27 Cow 3: Who _____ _____ _____?
A. lying   B. is   C. there

28 Cow 4: I _____ _____.
A. know   B. don't

29 Farmer 3: I can be _____ _____ _____ in this _____.
A. village   B. farmer   C. richest   D. the

30 Soon, _____ villagers _____ _____ _____.
A. did   B. other   C. same   D. the

31 Some _____ brought one more cow to the commons, _____ others brought _____ more to the grassland _____ telling anyone.
A. while   B. without   C. secretly   D. even

32 They _____ that there _____ be _____ grass for the _____ cows.
A. additional   B. enough   C. thought   D. would

33 Soon the _____ was _____ of _____ _____!
A. full   B. village   C. farmers   D. happy-looking

34 Cow 1: Hey, _____ _____ _____!
A. me   B. stop   C. pushing

35 Cow 2: _____ _____!
A. over   B. move

36 Cow 3: _____ is _____ _____!
A. my   B. this   C. spot

37 Cow 1: We _____ _____!
A. rain   B. need

38 Cow 2: _____ _____.
A. hungry   B. I'm

19 농부 1: 그는 아이가 네 명이나 있어.

20 농부 1: 내가 당신이라면, 소를 한 마리 더 기르겠어요.

21 농부 2: 조언 고마워요!

22 며칠 후, 그 농부는 아이가 네 명 있는 친한 친구 집을 방문했다.

23 그는 친구를 도와주고 싶어서 몰래 그에게 말했다. "내가 당신이라면, 소를 한 마리 더 데려와 공유지에서 키우겠어요."

24 친구는 그에게 고마워했고 그다음 날 자신이 들은 대로 했다.

25 소 1: 넌 누구니?

26 소 2: 난 새로 왔어.

27 소 3: 누가 저기 누워 있는 거야?

28 소 4: 몰라.

29 농부 3: 내가 마을에서 가장 부유한 농부가 될 수 있어.

30 곧, 다른 사람들도 그렇게 했다.

31 어떤 사람들은 은밀하게 소를 한 마리 더 공유지에 데려왔고, 또 어떤 사람들은 아무에게도 말하지 않고 훨씬 많은 소를 목초지에 데려왔다.

32 그들은 추가된 소에게도 충분한 풀이 있을 것이라고 생각했다.

33 곧 마을은 행복해 보이는 농부들로 가득 찼다!

34 소 1: 이봐, 밀지 마!

35 소 2: 저기로 가!

36 소 3: 여긴 내 자리야!

37 소 1: 비가 필요해!

38 소 2: 배고파.

39 Cow 3: _____, _____.

    A. too   B. me

40 The _____ _____ cows _____ _____ at first.

    A. of   B. slowly   C. number   D. rose

41 Then the _____ _____ _____ _____ quickly.

    A. grew   B. cow   C. more   D. population

42 The grass on the commons began to _____, and it became _____ for the cows to _____ grass to _____.

    A. harder   B. disappear   C. eat   D. find

43 _____ _____ _____ _____, it did not rain for a long time.

    A. worse   B. make   C. matters   D. to

44 Farmer 1: I don't _____ any _____ _____!

    A. have   B. left   C. cows

45 Cow 1: _____ _____.

    A. bye   B. good

46 Head of a village: What _____ _____ the _____?

    A. to   B. happened   C. commons

47 In the _____, when a dry year came, the small _____ of cows on the commons always found _____ to _____.

    A. something   B. past   C. number   D. eat

48 _____, no grass was _____ now _____ _____ were too many cows.

    A. because   B. however   C. left   D. there

49 _____ were _____ for the _____; many of the cows _____.

    A. villagers   B. harsh   C. died   D. things

50 **Enjoy, but _____ the _____: _____ ONE COW _____ FAMILY.**

    A. rule   B. PER   C. remember   D. ONLY

51 _____ _____, the grass _____ _____.

    A. came   B. at   C. back   D. last

52 Now it was _____ to _____ only one cow _____ family.

    A. support   B. per   C. able

53 The _____ _____ _____ to the one-family-one-cow _____.

    A. rule   B. back   C. village   D. went

54 The villagers all learned an important _____: when resources are _____, it is important for everyone to _____ the resources and use them _____.

    A. shared   B. fairly   C. value   D. lesson

55 The _____ now _____ this story _____ their _____.

    A. tell   B. children   C. to   D. villagers

56 They _____ _____ "The _____ of the _____."

    A. it   B. call   C. Commons   D. Story

---

39 소 3: 나도.

40 처음에는 소의 수가 천천히 늘어났다.

41 그러더니 소의 개체 수는 더 빨리 증가했다.

42 공유지의 풀은 사라지기 시작했고, 소들이 먹을 풀을 찾기가 더 힘들어졌다.

43 엎친 데 덮친 격으로, 오랫동안 비가 내리지 않았다.

44 농부 1: 이제 나는 남은 소가 없어!

45 소 1: 안녕.

46 이장: 공유지에 무슨 일이 일어난 거지?

47 과거에는 비가 오지 않는 해에도 공유지에 있는 적은 수의 소들이 먹을 것을 항상 찾을 수 있었다.

48 하지만, 지금은 소가 너무 많아서 풀이 남지 않았다.

49 상황은 마을 사람들에게 가혹했다; 많은 소들이 죽었다.

50 즐겨라, 그러나 규칙을 기억해라: 가구당 오직 소 한 마리.

51 마침내 목초지가 회복되었다.

52 이제는 가구당 한 마리의 소만 감당할 수 있게 되었다.

53 마을은 '한 가구, 한 마리 소' 규칙으로 돌아갔다.

54 마을 사람들 모두는 중요한 교훈을 배웠다. 즉, 자원이 공유될 때는 모두가 그 자원을 소중히 여기고 공평하게 사용하는 것이 중요하다는 것이다.

55 이제 마을 사람들은 이 이야기를 자신들의 후손에게 들려준다.

56 그들은 이 이야기를 '공유지 이야기'라고 부른다.

※ 다음 우리말과 일치하도록 빈칸에 알맞은 것을 골라 쓰시오.

1 The Story of the _____

2 _____ _____ _____ _____ there _____ a small village in a _____.

3 The villagers were _____ and _____ _____.

4 _____, some good grassland _____ in the middle of the village.

5 The Commons: _____ _____

6 Head of a village: _____ _____ the _____.

7 Villager 1: My cow can get _____ _____.

8 Villager 2: Yeah, _____ _____ for every cow.

9 Everyone _____ _____ _____ _____ the grassland.

10 Therefore, it _____ _____ "the commons."

11 _____ _____, each family only had one cow, so it was easy _____ each cow in the village _____ find _____ _____ _____ _____.

12 The grass on the commons was green _____ _____ _____.

13 Farmer 1: If I _____ two cows, I _____ _____ _____ _____.

14 Farmer 1: No one will _____ it.

15 But _____ _____ a villager _____ _____ _____ _____.

16 He _____ another cow and _____ _____ _____ on the commons.

17 He _____ that _____ _____ _____ it.

18 A happy feeling _____ his heart when he _____ _____ the milk and cheese that the second cow _____ _____ to his family.

1 공유지 이야기

2 옛날, 숲속에 작은 마을이 있었다.

3 마을 주민들은 농부였고 소를 길렀다.

4 다행히도, 마을 한 가운데에 좋은 목초지가 있었다.

5 공유지: 모두를 위한 장소

6 이장: 공유지를 함께 나누어 씁시다.

7 마을 사람 1: 내 소가 풀을 충분히 뜯을 수 있겠어.

8 마을 사람 2: 맞아, 모든 소에게 충분한 양이야.

9 모든 사람들이 목초지를 사용하도록 허락되었다.

10 그러므로 목초지는 '공유지'라고 불렸다.

11 전통에 따라 각 가정은 소가 한 마리만 있었고, 그래서 마을에 있는 소들이 충분히 먹을 풀을 찾는 것은 쉬운 일이었다.

12 공유지의 풀은 여름 내내 푸르렀다.

13 농부 1: 만약 소가 두 마리 있다면, 내가 더 부유할 텐데.

14 농부 1: 아무도 눈치 채지 못할 거야.

15 그러나 어느 날 마을 사람 하나가 규칙을 깨뜨렸다.

16 그는 또 다른 소를 가져와 공유지에서 풀을 뜯게 했다.

17 그는 아무도 그것을 눈치 채지 못할 거라고 생각했다.

18 두 번째 소가 가족에게 가져다 줄 우유와 치즈를 생각하자 그의 마음은 행복감으로 충만했다.

19 Farmer 1: He _____ four _____.

20 Farmer 1: If I _____ you, I _____ _____ another cow.

21 Farmer 2: _____ _____ the tip!

22 A few days _____, the farmer visited a close friend _____ had four children.

23 He wanted to help his friend, so he told him _____ _____, "If I _____ you, I _____ _____ _____ one more cow and _____ _____ on the commons."

24 The friend thanked him and did _____ _____ _____ _____ the next day.

25 Cow 1: _____ are you?

26 Cow 2: I'm _____.

27 Cow 3: Who is _____ there?

28 Cow 4: I _____ _____.

29 Farmer 3: I can be _____ _____ _____ in this village.

30 Soon, _____ villagers _____ _____ _____ _____.

31 Some _____ brought one more cow to the commons, while others brought _____ _____ to the grassland _____ _____ _____.

32 They thought that there would be _____ _____ for the _____ cows.

33 Soon the village was _____ _____ _____ farmers!

34 Cow 1: Hey, _____ _____ me!

35 Cow 2: Move _____!

36 Cow 3: This is my _____!

37 Cow 1: We need _____!

38 Cow 2: I'm _____.

---

19 농부 1: 그는 아이가 네 명이나 있어.

20 농부 1: 내가 당신이라면, 소를 한 마리 더 기르겠어요.

21 농부 2: 조언 고마워요!

22 며칠 후, 그 농부는 아이가 네 명 있는 친한 친구 집을 방문했다.

23 그는 친구를 도와주고 싶어서 몰래 그에게 말했다. "내가 당신이라면, 소를 한 마리 더 데려와 공유지에서 키우겠어요."

24 친구는 그에게 고마워했고 그다음 날 자신이 들은 대로 했다.

25 소 1: 넌 누구니?

26 소 2: 난 새로 왔어.

27 소 3: 누가 저기 누워 있는 거야?

28 소 4: 몰라.

29 농부 3: 내가 마을에서 가장 부유한 농부가 될 수 있어.

30 곧, 다른 사람들도 그렇게 했다.

31 어떤 사람들은 은밀하게 소를 한 마리 더 공유지에 데려왔고, 또 어떤 사람들은 아무에게도 말하지 않고 훨씬 많은 소를 목초지에 데려왔다.

32 그들은 추가된 소에게도 충분한 풀이 있을 것이라고 생각했다.

33 곧 마을은 행복해 보이는 농부들로 가득 찼다!

34 소 1: 이봐, 밀지 마!

35 소 2: 저기로 가!

36 소 3: 여긴 내 자리야!

37 소 1: 비가 필요해!

38 소 2: 배고파.

39 Cow 3: _____ , _____ .

40 _____ of cows _____ slowly at first.

41 Then the _____ _____ _____ more quickly.

42 The grass on the commons began _____ _____ , and it became _____ for the cows to find _____ _____ _____ .

43 _____ _____ _____ _____ , it did not rain _____ _____ _____ _____ .

44 Farmer 1: I don't have _____ _____ _____ !

45 Cow 1: Good bye.

46 Head of a village: What _____ _____ the commons?

47 In the past, when a dry year came, the small number of cows on the commons always found _____ _____ _____ .

48 However, no grass was left now _____ _____ _____ _____ _____ cows.

49 Things were _____ for the villagers; many of the cows died.

50 **Enjoy, but remember the _____ : ONLY ONE COW _____ _____ .**

51 _____ _____ , the grass _____ _____ .

52 Now it _____ _____ _____ _____ _____ _____ _____ per family.

53 The village went back to the _____ _____ .

54 The villagers all learned an important _____ : when resources _____ _____ , it is important _____ _____ _____ the resources and use them _____ .

55 The _____ now tell this story _____ their children.

56 They _____ _____ "The Story of the _____ ."

---

39 소 3: 나도.

40 처음에는 소의 수가 천천히 늘어났다.

41 그러더니 소의 개체 수는 더 빨리 증가했다.

42 공유지의 풀은 사라지기 시작했고, 소들이 먹을 풀을 찾기가 더 힘들어졌다.

43 엎친 데 덮친 격으로, 오랫동안 비가 내리지 않았다.

44 농부 1: 이제 나는 남은 소가 없어!

45 소 1: 안녕.

46 이장: 공유지에 무슨 일이 일어난 거지?

47 과거에는 비가 오지 않는 해에도 공유지에 있는 적은 수의 소들이 먹을 것을 항상 찾을 수 있었다.

48 하지만, 지금은 소가 너무 많아서 풀이 남지 않았다.

49 상황은 마을 사람들에게 가혹했다; 많은 소들이 죽었다.

50 즐겨라, 그러나 규칙을 기억해라: 가구당 오직 소 한 마리.

51 마침내 목초지가 회복되었다.

52 이제는 가구당 한 마리의 소만 감당할 수 있게 되었다.

53 마을은 '한 가구, 한 마리 소' 규칙으로 돌아갔다.

54 마을 사람들 모두는 중요한 교훈을 배웠다. 즉, 자원이 공유될 때는 모두가 그 자원을 소중히 여기고 공평하게 사용하는 것이 중요하다는 것이다.

55 이제 마을 사람들은 이 이야기를 자신들의 후손에게 들려준다.

56 그들은 이 이야기를 '공유지 이야기'라고 부른다.

※ 다음 문장을 우리말로 쓰시오.

1 The Story of the Commons
➡ _____

2 Once upon a time there was a small village in a forest.
➡ _____

3 The villagers were farmers and raised cows.
➡ _____

4 Luckily, some good grassland lay in the middle of the village.
➡ _____

5 The Commons: Space for Everyone
➡ _____

6 Head of a village: Let's share the commons.
➡ _____

7 Villager 1: My cow can get enough grass.
➡ _____

8 Villager 2: Yeah, there's plenty for every cow.
➡ _____

9 Everyone was allowed to use the grassland.
➡ _____

10 Therefore, it was called "the commons."
➡ _____

11 By tradition, each family only had one cow, so it was easy for each cow in the village to find enough grass to eat.
➡ _____

12 The grass on the commons was green all summer long.
➡ _____

13 Farmer 1: If I had two cows, I would be richer.
➡ _____

14 Farmer 1: No one will notice it.
➡ _____

15 But one day a villager broke the rule.
➡ _____

16 He brought another cow and let it graze on the commons.
➡ _____

17 He thought that nobody would notice it.
➡ _____

18 A happy feeling filled his heart when he thought of the milk and cheese that the second cow would bring to his family.
➡ _____

19 Farmer 1: He has four children.
➡ _____

20 Farmer 1: If I were you, I would raise another cow.
➡ _____

21 Farmer 2: Thanks for the tip!
➡ _____

22 A few days later, the farmer visited a close friend who had four children.
➡ _____

23 He wanted to help his friend, so he told him in secret, "If I were you, I would bring in one more cow and raise it on the commons."
➡ _____

24 The friend thanked him and did as he was told the next day.
➡ _____

25 Cow 1: Who are you?
➡ _____

26 Cow 2: I'm new.
➡ _____

27 Cow 3: Who is lying there?
➡ _____

28 Cow 4: I don't know.
➡ _____

29 Farmer 3: I can be the richest farmer in this village.
➡ _____

30 Soon, other villagers did the same.
➡ _____

31 Some secretly brought one more cow to the commons, while others brought even more to the grassland without telling anyone.
➡ _____

_____

32 They thought that there would be enough grass for the additional cows.
➡ _____

33 Soon the village was full of happy-looking farmers!
➡ _____

34 Cow 1: Hey, stop pushing me!
➡ _____

35 Cow 2: Move over!
➡ _____

36 Cow 3: This is my spot!
➡ _____

37 Cow 1: We need rain!
➡ _____

38 Cow 2: I'm hungry.
➡ _____

39 Cow 3: Me, too.
➡ _____

40 The number of cows rose slowly at first.
➡ _____

41 Then the cow population grew more quickly.
➡ _____

42 The grass on the commons began to disappear, and it became harder for the cows to find grass to eat.
➡ _____

43 To make matters worse, it did not rain for a long time.
➡ _____

44 Farmer 1: I don't have any cows left!
➡ _____

45 Cow 1: Good bye.
➡ _____

46 Head of a village: What happened to the commons?
➡ _____

47 In the past, when a dry year came, the small number of cows on the commons always found something to eat.
➡ _____

48 However, no grass was left now because there were too many cows.
➡ _____

49 Things were harsh for the villagers; many of the cows died.
➡ _____

50 Enjoy, but remember the rule: ONLY ONE COW PER FAMILY.
➡ _____

51 At last, the grass came back.
➡ _____

52 Now it was able to support only one cow per family.
➡ _____

53 The village went back to the one-family-one-cow rule.
➡ _____

54 The villagers all learned an important lesson: when resources are shared, it is important for everyone to value the resources and use them fairly.
➡ _____

55 The villagers now tell this story to their children.
➡ _____

56 They call it "The Story of the Commons."
➡ _____

※ 다음 괄호 안의 단어들을 우리말에 맞도록 바르게 배열하시오.

1 (Story / the / The / of / Commons)
➡ _____

2 (upon / once / time / a / there / a / was / village / small / a / in / forest.)
➡ _____

3 (villagers / the / farmers / were / and / cows. / raised)
➡ _____

4 (some / luckily, / good / lay / grassland / in / middle / the / of / village. / the)
➡ _____

5 (Commons: / The / for / Everyone / Space)
➡ _____

6 (Head of a village: / share / let's / commons. / the)
➡ _____

7 (Villager 1: / cow / my / get / can / grass. / enough)
➡ _____

8 (Villager 2: / there's / yeah, / for / plenty / cow. / every)
➡ _____

9 (was / everyone / to / allowed / the / use / grassland.)
➡ _____

10 (it / therefore, / called / was / commons." / "the)
➡ _____

11 (tradition, / by / family / each / had / only / cow, / one / it / so / easy / was / each / for / in / cow / the / village / enough / find / to / eat. / to / grass)
➡ _____

12 (grass / the / the / on / commons / green / was / summer / all / long.)
➡ _____

13 (Farmer 1: / I / if / two / had / cows, / would / I / richer. / be)
➡ _____

14 (Farmer 1: / one / no / notice / will / it.)
➡ _____

15 (one / but / a / day / broke / villager / rule. / the)
➡ _____

16 (brouhght / he / cow / another / and / it / let / on / graze / commons. / the)
➡ _____

17 (thought / he / nobody / that / notice / would / it.)
➡ _____

18 (happy / a / filled / feeling / heart / his / he / when / of / thought / the / and / milk / cheese / the / that / cow / second / bring / would / his / to / family.)
➡ _____
_____

1 공유지 이야기

2 옛날, 숲속에 작은 마을이 있었다.

3 마을 주민들은 농부였고 소를 길렀다.

4 다행히도, 마을 한 가운데에 좋은 목초지가 있었다.

5 공유지: 모두를 위한 장소

6 이장: 공유지를 함께 나누어 씁시다.

7 마을 사람 1: 내 소가 풀을 충분히 뜯을 수 있겠어.

8 마을 사람 2: 맞아, 모든 소에게 충분한 양이야.

9 모든 사람들이 목초지를 사용하도록 허락되었다.

10 그러므로 목초지는 '공유지'라고 불렸다.

11 전통에 따라 각 가정은 소가 한 마리만 있었고, 그래서 마을에 있는 소들이 충분히 먹을 풀을 찾는 것은 쉬운 일이었다.

12 공유지의 풀은 여름 내내 푸르렀다.

13 농부 1: 만약 소가 두 마리 있다면, 내가 더 부유할 텐데.

14 농부 1: 아무도 눈치 채지 못할 거야.

15 그러나 어느 날 마을 사람 하나가 규칙을 깨뜨렸다.

16 그는 또 다른 소를 가져와 공유지에서 풀을 뜯게 했다.

17 그는 아무도 그것을 눈치 채지 못할 거라고 생각했다.

18 두 번째 소가 가족에게 가져다 줄 우유와 치즈를 생각하자 그의 마음은 행복감으로 충만했다.

19 (Farmer 1: / has / he / children. / four)
➡ _____

20 (Farmer 1: / I / if / you, / were / would / I / another / raise / cow.)
➡ _____

21 (Farmer 2: / for / thanks / tip! / the)
➡ _____

22 (few / a / later, / days / farmer /the / a / visited / friend / close / had / who / children. / four)
➡ _____

23 (wanted / he / help / to / friend, / his / he / so / him / told / secret, / in / I / "if / were / you, / would / I / in / bring / more / one / cow / and / it / raise / the / on / commons.")
➡ _____
_____

24 (friend / the / him / thanked / and / as / did / was / he / the / told / day. / next)
➡ _____

25 (Cow 1: / are / you? / who)
➡ _____

26 (Cow 2: / new. / I'm)
➡ _____

27 (Cow 3: / is / who / there? / lying)
➡ _____

28 (Cow 4: / don't / I / know.)
➡ _____

29 (Farmer 3: / can / I / the / be / farmer / richest / this / in / village.)
➡ _____

30 (other / soon, / did / villagers / same. / the)
➡ _____

31 (secretly / some / one / brought / cow / more / the / to / commons, / others / while / even / brought / more / the / to / without / grassland / anyone. / telling)
➡ _____
_____

32 (thought / they / there / that / be / would / enough / for / grass / the / cows. / additional)
➡ _____

33 (the / soon / was / village / of / full / farmers! / happy-looking)
➡ _____

34 (Cow 1: / stop / hey, / me! / pushing)
➡ _____

35 (Cow 2: / over! / move)
➡ _____

36 (Cow 3: / is / this / spot! / my)
➡ _____

37 (Cow 1: / need / we / rain!)
➡ _____

38 (Cow 2: / hungry. / I'm)
➡ _____

---

19 농부 1: 그는 아이가 네 명이나 있어.

20 농부 1: 내가 당신이라면, 소를 한 마리 더 기르겠어요.

21 농부 2: 조언 고마워요!

22 며칠 후, 그 농부는 아이가 네 명 있는 친한 친구 집을 방문했다.

23 그는 친구를 도와주고 싶어서 몰래 그에게 말했다. "내가 당신이라면, 소를 한 마리 더 데려와 공유지에서 키우겠어요."

24 친구는 그에게 고마워했고 그다음 날 자신이 들은 대로 했다.

25 소 1: 넌 누구니?

26 소 2: 난 새로 왔어.

27 소 3: 누가 저기 누워 있는 거야?

28 소 4: 몰라.

29 농부 3: 내가 마을에서 가장 부유한 농부가 될 수 있어.

30 곧, 다른 사람들도 그렇게 했다.

31 어떤 사람들은 은밀하게 소를 한 마리 더 공유지에 데려왔고, 또 어떤 사람들은 아무에게도 말하지 않고 훨씬 많은 소를 목초지에 데려왔다.

32 그들은 추가된 소에게도 충분한 풀이 있을 것이라고 생각했다.

33 곧 마을은 행복해 보이는 농부들로 가득 찼다!

34 소 1: 이봐, 밀지 마!

35 소 2: 저기로 가!

36 소 3: 여긴 내 자리야!

37 소 1: 비가 필요해!

38 소 2: 배고파.

39 (Cow 3: / too. / me,)
➡ _____

40 (number / the / cows / of / slowly / rose / first. / at)
➡ _____

41 (the / then / population / cow / more / grew / quickly.)
➡ _____

42 (grass / the / the / on / commons / to / began / disappear, / it / and / harder / became / the / for / cows / to / grass / find / eat. / to)
➡ _____

43 (make / to / worse, / matters / did / it / rain / not / for / long / a / time.)
➡ _____

44 (Farmer 1: / don't / I / any / have / left! / cows)
➡ _____

45 (Cow 1: / bye. / good)
➡ _____

46 (Head of a village: / happened / what / the / to / commons?)
➡ _____

47 (the / in / past, / a / when / year / dry / came, / small / the / number / cows / of / on / commons / the / found / always / to / something / eat.)
➡ _____

48 (no / however, / was / grass / now / let / because / were / there / many / too / cows.)
➡ _____

49 (were / things / for / harsh / villagers; / the / of / many / cows / the / died.)
➡ _____

50 (but / enjoy, / the / remember / rule: / ONE / ONLY / PER / COW / FAMILY.)
➡ _____

51 (last, / at / grass / the / back. / came)
➡ _____

52 (it / now / able / was / to / only / support / one / cow / family. / per)
➡ _____

53 (village / the / back / went / the / to / rule. / one-family-one-cow)
➡ _____

54 (villagers / the / learned / all / important / an / lesson: / resources / when / shared, / are / is / it / for / important / to / everyone / value / resources / the / use / and / fairly. / them)
➡ _____

55 (villagers / the / tell / now / story / this / their / to / children.)
➡ _____

56 (call / they / it / Story / "The / of / Commons." / the)
➡ _____

39 소 3: 나도.

40 처음에는 소의 수가 천천히 늘어났다.

41 그러더니 소의 개체 수는 더 빨리 증가했다.

42 공유지의 풀은 사라지기 시작했고, 소들이 먹을 풀을 찾기가 더 힘들어졌다.

43 엎친 데 덮친 격으로, 오랫동안 비가 내리지 않았다.

44 농부 1: 이제 나는 남은 소가 없어!

45 소 1: 안녕.

46 이장: 공유지에 무슨 일이 일어난 거지?

47 과거에는 비가 오지 않는 해에도 공유지에 있는 적은 수의 소들이 먹을 것을 항상 찾을 수 있었다.

48 하지만, 지금은 소가 너무 많아서 풀이 남지 않았다.

49 상황은 마을 사람들에게 가혹했다; 많은 소들이 죽었다.

50 즐겨라, 그러나 규칙을 기억해라: 가구당 오직 소 한 마리.

51 마침내 목초지가 회복되었다.

52 이제는 가구당 한 마리의 소만 감당할 수 있게 되었다.

53 마을은 '한 가구, 한 마리 소' 규칙으로 돌아갔다.

54 마을 사람들 모두는 중요한 교훈을 배웠다. 즉, 자원이 공유될 때는 모두가 그 자원을 소중히 여기고 공평하게 사용하는 것이 중요하다는 것이다.

55 이제 마을 사람들은 이 이야기를 자신들의 후손에게 들려준다.

56 그들은 이 이야기를 '공유지 이야기'라고 부른다.

※ **다음 우리말을 영어로 쓰시오.**

1 공유지 이야기
➡ _____

2 옛날, 숲속에 작은 마을이 있었다.
➡ _____

3 마을 주민들은 농부였고 소를 길렀다.
➡ _____

4 다행히도, 마을 한 가운데에 좋은 목초지가 있었다.
➡ _____

5 공유지: 모두를 위한 장소
➡ _____

6 이장: 공유지를 함께 나누어 씁시다.
➡ _____

7 마을 사람 1: 내 소가 풀을 충분히 뜯을 수 있겠어.
➡ _____

8 마을 사람 2: 맞아, 모든 소에게 충분한 양이야.
➡ _____

9 모든 사람들이 목초지를 사용하도록 허락되었다.
➡ _____

10 그러므로 목초지는 '공유지'라고 불렸다.
➡ _____

11 전통에 따라 각 가정은 소가 한 마리만 있었고, 그래서 마을에 있는 소들이 충분히 먹을 풀을 찾는 것은 쉬운 일이었다.
➡ _____
_____

12 공유지의 풀은 여름 내내 푸르렀다.
➡ _____

13 농부 1: 만약 소가 두 마리 있다면, 내가 더 부유할 텐데.
➡ _____

14 농부 1: 아무도 눈치 채지 못할 거야.
➡ _____

15 그러나 어느 날 마을 사람 하나가 규칙을 깨뜨렸다.
➡ _____

16 그는 또 다른 소를 가져와 공유지에서 풀을 뜯게 했다.
➡ _____

17 그는 아무도 그것을 눈치 채지 못할 거라고 생각했다.
➡ _____

18 두 번째 소가 가족에게 가져다줄 우유와 치즈를 생각하자 그의 마음은 행복감으로 충만했다.
➡ _____
_____

19 농부 1: 그는 아이가 네 명이나 있어.

➡️ _____

20 농부 1: 내가 당신이라면, 소를 한 마리 더 기르겠어요.

➡️ _____

21 농부 2: 조언 고마워요!

➡️ _____

22 며칠 후, 그 농부는 아이가 네 명 있는 친한 친구 집을 방문했다.

➡️ _____

23 그는 친구를 도와주고 싶어서 몰래 그에게 말했다. "내가 당신이라면, 소를 한 마리 더 데려와 공유지에서 키우겠어요."

➡️ _____

➡️ _____

24 친구는 그에게 고마워했고 그다음 날 자신이 들은 대로 했다.

➡️ _____

25 소 1: 넌 누구니?

➡️ _____

26 소 2: 난 새로 왔어.

➡️ _____

27 소 3: 누가 저기 누워 있는 거야?

➡️ _____

28 소 4: 몰라.

➡️ _____

29 농부 3: 내가 마을에서 가장 부유한 농부가 될 수 있어.

➡️ _____

30 곧, 다른 사람들도 그렇게 했다.

➡️ _____

31 어떤 사람들은 은밀하게 소를 한 마리 더 공유지에 데려왔고, 또 어떤 사람들은 아무에게도 말하지 않고 훨씬 많은 소를 목초지에 데려왔다.

➡️ _____

➡️ _____

32 그들은 추가된 소에게도 충분한 풀이 있을 것이라고 생각했다.

➡️ _____

33 곧 마을은 행복해 보이는 농부들로 가득 찼다!

➡️ _____

34 소 1: 이봐, 밀지 마!

➡️ _____

35 소 2: 저기로 가!

➡️ _____

36 소 3: 여긴 내 자리야!

➡️ _____

37 소 1: 비가 필요해!

➡️ _____

38 소 2: 배고파.
➡

39 소 3: 나도.
➡

40 처음에는 소의 수가 천천히 늘어났다.
➡

41 그러더니 소의 개체 수는 더 빨리 증가했다.
➡

42 공유지의 풀은 사라지기 시작했고, 소들이 먹을 풀을 찾기가 더 힘들어졌다.
➡

43 엎친 데 덮친 격으로, 오랫동안 비가 내리지 않았다.
➡

44 농부 1: 이제 나는 남은 소가 없어!
➡

45 소 1: 안녕.
➡

46 이장: 공유지에 무슨 일이 일어난 거지?
➡

47 과거에는 비가 오지 않는 해에도 공유지에 있는 적은 수의 소들이 먹을 것을 항상 찾을 수 있었다.
➡

48 하지만, 지금은 소가 너무 많아서 풀이 남지 않았다.
➡

49 상황은 마을 사람들에게 가혹했다; 많은 소들이 죽었다.
➡

50 즐겨라, 그러나 규칙을 기억해라: 가구당 오직 소 한 마리.
➡

51 마침내 목초지가 회복되었다.
➡

52 이제는 가구당 한 마리의 소만 감당할 수 있게 되었다.
➡

53 마을은 '한 가구, 한 마리 소' 규칙으로 돌아갔다.
➡

54 마을 사람들 모두는 중요한 교훈을 배웠다. 즉, 자원이 공유될 때는 모두가 그 자원을 소중히 여기고 공평하게 사용하는 것이 중요하다는 것이다.
➡

55 이제 마을 사람들은 이 이야기를 자신들의 후손에게 들려준다.
➡

56 그들은 이 이야기를 '공유지 이야기'라고 부른다.
➡

※ 다음 우리말과 일치하도록 빈칸에 알맞은 말을 쓰시오.

My Speaking Portfolio - Step 2

1. A: How _____ I _____ the _____ _____ in my town?
2. B: _____ I _____ you, I'd _____ _____ _____ _____
   with children.
3. C: I think you _____ _____ people from _____ _____ .
4. A: Okay. Thank you all _____ _____ _____ .

1. A: 제가 어떻게 우리 마을의 인구 문제를 해결해야 할까요?
2. B: 저라면 아이가 있는 가정에 지원을 해 줄 것입니다.
3. C: 저는 당신이 다른 마을에서 오는 사람들을 기쁘게 맞이해야 한다고 생각합니다.
4. A: 알겠습니다. 조언 감사합니다.

My Speaking Portfolio - Step 3

1. A _____ in _____ _____
2. Rareville
3. The population is _____ _____ _____ _____ _____ in my town.
4. _____ _____ this serious problem, I will _____ _____ to families _____ children.
5. I _____ also _____ people _____ _____ _____ .
6. _____ _____ , I will _____ _____ for _____ _____ .
7. I am sure that _____ _____ will _____ _____ the _____ in my town.

1. 우리 마을의 문제
2. Rareville
3. 우리 마을의 인구수가 점점 줄어들고 있습니다.
4. 이 심각한 문제를 해결하기 위해 저는 아이가 있는 가정을 지원하겠습니다.
5. 또한, 다른 마을에서 오는 사람들을 기쁘게 맞이하겠습니다.
6. 덧붙여, 맞벌이 부모들의 스트레스를 덜어 주겠습니다.
7. 저는 이러한 조치가 우리 마을의 인구 문제를 해결하는 데에 도움이 될 것이라고 확신합니다.

After You Read Graphic Organizer

1. **Story** _____
2. _____ family _____ one cow _____ _____ _____ .
3. _____ _____ started _____ _____ _____ _____ .
4. The grass began _____ _____ , and _____ did not rain _____ _____ _____ _____ .
5. Many cows could not _____ _____ _____ _____ _____ and died.
6. The grass _____ _____ _____ .
7. The villagers _____ _____ _____ the one-family-one-cow _____ .

1. 이야기 산
2. 각 가정은 공유지에서 소를 한 마리씩 길렀다.
3. 마을 사람들은 몰래 소를 더 데려오기 시작했다.
4. 풀이 사라지기 시작했고, 오랫동안 비가 오지 않았다.
5. 많은 소들이 충분히 먹을 풀을 찾지 못해서 죽었다.
6. 목초지가 마침내 회복되었다.
7. 마을 사람들은 '한 가구, 한 마리 소' 규칙으로 돌아갔다.

※ 다음 우리말을 영어로 쓰시오.

My Speaking Portfolio - Step 2

1. A: 제가 어떻게 우리 마을의 인구 문제를 해결해야 할까요?
➡ _____

2. B: 저라면 아이가 있는 가정에 지원을 해 줄 것입니다.
➡ _____

3. C: 저는 당신이 다른 마을에서 오는 사람들을 기쁘게 맞이해야 한다고 생각합니다.
➡ _____

4. A: 알겠습니다. 조언 감사합니다.
➡ _____

My Speaking Portfolio - Step 3

1. 우리 마을의 문제
➡ _____

2. Rareville
➡ _____

3. 우리 마을의 인구수가 점점 줄어들고 있습니다.
➡ _____

4. 이 심각한 문제를 해결하기 위해 저는 아이가 있는 가정을 지원하겠습니다.
➡ _____

5. 또한, 다른 마을에서 오는 사람들을 기쁘게 맞이하겠습니다.
➡ _____

6. 덧붙여, 맞벌이 부모들의 스트레스를 덜어 주겠습니다.
➡ _____

7. 저는 이러한 조치가 우리 마을의 인구 문제를 해결하는 데에 도움이 될 것이라고 확신합니다.
➡ _____

After You Read Graphic Organizer

1. 이야기 산
➡ _____

2. 각 가정은 공유지에서 소를 한 마리씩 길렀다.
➡ _____

3. 마을 사람들은 몰래 소를 더 데려오기 시작했다.
➡ _____

4. 풀이 사라지기 시작했고, 오랫동안 비가 오지 않았다.
➡ _____

5. 많은 소들이 충분히 먹을 풀을 찾지 못해서 죽었다.
➡ _____

6. 목초지가 마침내 회복되었다.
➡ _____

7. 마을 사람들은 '한 가구, 한 마리 소' 규칙으로 돌아갔다.
➡ _____

※ 다음 영어를 우리말로 쓰시오.

01 carefully _____

02 exam _____

03 wear _____

04 without _____

05 inviting _____

06 silence _____

07 worried _____

08 post _____

09 ready _____

10 surprisingly _____

11 almost _____

12 ex-postman _____

13 whole _____

14 however _____

15 strange _____

16 through _____

17 ex-mayor _____

18 last _____

19 mayor _____

20 anger _____

21 nervously _____

22 shame _____

23 order _____

24 sentence _____

25 noise _____

26 notice _____

27 heart _____

28 warm _____

29 special _____

30 wonder _____

31 place _____

32 sweet _____

33 lovely _____

34 office _____

35 get angry _____

36 nothing but _____

37 stay away from _____

38 take an exam _____

39 for a while[moment] _____

40 in the middle of _____

41 break one's heart _____

42 with no sign of anger _____

43 as+형용사/부사+as I can _____

※ 다음 우리말을 영어로 쓰시오.

01 시장

02 (안내문 등을) 게시[공고]하다

03 자리, 좌석

04 문장

05 고요, 적막, 침묵

06 공고문; 알아차리다

07 사랑스러운

08 언어

09 전직 시장

10 입다

11 시끄러움, 소란

12 화, 분노

13 뒤쪽, 뒷부분

14 특별한

15 초조하게

16 사무실

17 마음

18 따뜻한

19 하지만, 그러나

20 이상한, 낯선

21 ~을 통해[관통하여]

22 준비가 된

23 놀랍게도

24 주의 깊게

25 시험

26 전체의, 모든

27 거의

28 전직 우체부

29 ~ 없이

30 유혹적인, 솔깃한

31 부끄러움

32 명령, 지시

33 걱정하는, 걱정스러워 하는

34 친절하게, 다정하게

35 오직, 그저[단지] ~일 뿐인

36 ~에 늦다

37 잠시 동안

38 화나다

39 시험을 치다[보다]

40 ~을 멀리하다

41 매우 슬프게 하다

42 화난 기색 없이

43 ~의 도중에, ~의 중앙에

※ 다음 영영풀이에 알맞은 단어를 <보기>에서 골라 쓴 후, 우리말 뜻을 쓰시오.

1 _____ : all of something: _____

2 _____ : the feeling of being angry: _____

3 _____ : a lack of sound or noise: _____

4 _____ : to think about something with curiosity: _____

5 _____ : a sound, especially when it is loud, unpleasant, or disturbing: _____

6 _____ : attractive or beautiful especially in a graceful way: _____

7 _____ : an instruction given by someone in a position of authority: _____

8 _____ : an important test of your knowledge, especially one that you take at school: _____

9 _____ : to become aware of something or someone by seeing, hearing, etc.: _____

10 _____ : to have something on your body as clothing, decoration, or protection: _____

11 _____ : an official who is elected to be the head of the government of a city or town: _____

12 _____ : a room, set of rooms, or building where people work, usually sitting at desks: _____

13 _____ : to put up a sign, notice, etc. so that it can be seen by many people: _____

14 _____ : not familiar because you have not been there before or met the person before: _____

15 _____ : attractive in a way that makes you want to do something, go somewhere, be near someone, etc.: _____

16 _____ : a guilty and embarrassed feeling that you have when you or someone else has behaved badly: _____

wear	noise	post	exam
inviting	anger	mayor	whole
notice	order	shame	lovely
strange	wonder	office	silence

※ 다음 우리말과 일치하도록 빈칸에 알맞은 것을 골라 쓰시오.

1 The _____ _____
A. Class   B. Last

2 I was _____ for school that morning, and I was _____ Monsieur Hamel would _____ _____.
A. worried   B. get   C. late   D. angry

3 A few days before, he had told us that we would _____ an _____ about French _____ that day, and I was not _____.
A. exam   B. ready   C. take   D. sentences

4 It was _____ a warm, lovely day, and the fields _____ the road smelled _____ and _____.
A. inviting   B. along   C. such   D. sweet

5 For a moment, I thought of _____ _____ _____ school and _____ around the fields.
A. away   B. from   C. staying   D. walking

6 However, I ran as _____ _____ _____ _____ to school.
A. I   B. fast   C. as   D. could

7 As I _____ the _____ office, I saw people _____ the _____ on the board.
A. notices   B. passed   C. reading   D. mayor's

8 _____ two years all our bad news _____ _____ _____ that board.
A. come   B. for   C. had   D. from

9 I _____, " _____ is it _____?"
A. now   B. wondered   C. what

10 I _____ _____.
A. faster   B. ran

11 Usually, _____ _____ _____ in the morning at school— sounds of students talking and _____.
A. was   B. laughing   C. there   D. noise

12 _____, that day _____ was _____.
A. quiet   B. however   C. everything

13 _____ the windows I saw my classmates in their places and Monsieur Hamel _____ _____ _____ the classroom.
A. around   B. through   C. nervously   D. walking

14 I opened the door and _____ in the _____ of the _____.
A. silence   B. entered   C. strange   D. middle

15 My face felt _____ _____ _____!
A. shame   B. with   C. hot

---

1 마지막 수업

2 그날 아침 나는 수업에 늦었고, Hamel 선생님이 화를 내실까 걱정되었다.

3 며칠 전에 선생님은 그날 프랑스어 문장 시험을 보겠다고 말씀하셨는데, 나는 준비가 되어 있지 않았다.

4 날씨는 무척 포근하고 사랑스러웠으며 길가의 들판에서는 달콤하고 유혹적인 향기가 났다.

5 잠깐 동안 나는 학교에 가지 않고 들판을 거닐까 생각했다.

6 하지만 나는 최대한 빨리 학교로 달려갔다.

7 시장의 집무실을 지나면서 나는 사람들이 게시판에 붙어 있는 공고문을 읽고 있는 것을 보았다.

8 지난 2년 동안 모든 나쁜 소식은 저 게시판에서 나왔다.

9 나는 "이번에는 뭐지?"라는 궁금증이 들었다.

10 나는 더욱 빨리 달렸다.

11 보통, 아침에는 학생들이 떠들고 웃는 소리로 학교가 소란스러웠다.

12 그러나 그날은 모든 것이 고요했다.

13 창문을 통해 나는 학급 친구들이 제자리에 앉아 있고 Hamel 선생님이 초조하게 교실을 돌아다니시는 것을 보았다.

14 나는 문을 열고 낯선 침묵 속으로 들어갔다.

15 부끄러워서 얼굴이 화끈거렸다!

16 Surprisingly, Monsieur Hamel looked at me _____ no sign of
_____ and said kindly, "Go to your _____, my little Frantz;
we almost began _____ you."

   A. without   B. anger   C. with   D. seat

17 I _____ _____ _____ my desk.

   A. at   B. sat   C. down

18 _____ _____ then _____ I _____ Monsieur Hamel's
blue coat.

   A. noticed   B. was   C. that   D. it

19 He was _____ the coat he _____ _____ on _____
days.

   A. wore   B. wearing   C. only   D. special

20 Also there was _____ _____ about the _____ _____.

   A. class   B. something   C. whole   D. strange

21 _____ surprised me most was to see people _____ at the
back of the room: old Hauser was there, and _____ _____
the ex-mayor, the ex-postman, and many others.

   A. were   B. what   C. so   D. sitting

22 They all _____ _____ _____.

   A. so   B. seemed   C. sad

23 _____ I was _____ _____ all this, Monsieur Hamel
walked slowly to the _____.

   A. front   B. wondering   C. while   D. at

24 He thought _____ a _____ and _____ said: "My children,
this is the _____ time that I'll teach you.

   A. while   B. last   C. for   D. kindly

25 _____ have come _____ Berlin to teach _____ _____
German in the schools of Alsace and Lorraine.

   A. but   B. orders   C. nothing   D. from

26 The _____ _____ _____ tomorrow.

   A. arrives   B. new   C. teacher

27 This is the _____ class _____ French, so I want you _____
_____ carefully."

   A. last   B. in   C. listen   D. to

28 Those _____ words _____ my heart and _____ me
_____.

   A. broke   B. angry   C. made   D. few

29 So, this was _____ they had _____ at the _____ _____.

   A. posted   B. what   C. office   D. mayor's

30 It was the _____ class _____ my _____ _____!

   A. own   B. last   C. in   D. language

16 놀랍게도 Hamel 선생님은 화난 기색이 전혀 없이 나를 보시고 자상하게 말씀하셨다. "Frantz야, 네 자리로 가서 앉아라. 너 없이 수업을 시작할 뻔했구나."

17 나는 내 책상으로 가서 앉았다.

18 내가 Hamel 선생님의 파란색 외투를 알아차린 것은 바로 그 때였다.

19 선생님은 특별한 날에만 입는 외투를 입고 계셨다.

20 더구나 교실 전체도 무언가 이상했다.

21 나는 교실 뒤에 앉아 있는 사람들을 보고 가장 놀랐다. Hauser 할아버지가 앉아 계셨고 전직 시장님, 전직 우체부 아저씨를 비롯한 많은 사람들이 있었다.

22 그들은 모두 슬퍼 보였다.

23 내가 이 모든 것에 대해 의아해 하는 동안, Hamel 선생님이 천천히 교실 앞으로 걸어가셨다.

24 그는 잠시 생각에 잠긴 후 다정하게 말씀하셨다: "어린이 여러분, 이것이 내가 여러분을 가르치는 마지막 시간입니다.

25 Alsace와 Lorraine에 있는 학교에서는 독일어만 가르치라는 명령이 베를린에서 내려왔습니다.

26 새로운 선생님이 내일 오실 겁니다.

27 이 시간이 프랑스어로 하는 마지막 수업이니 여러분이 주의 깊게 들어 주기 바랍니다."

28 이 몇 마디는 내 마음을 아프게 하고 또 화가 나게 했다.

29 그래, 이게 바로 시장 집무실 게시판에 공고되어 있던 것이다.

30 내 모국어로 하는 마지막 수업이라니!

※ 다음 우리말과 일치하도록 빈칸에 알맞은 것을 골라 쓰시오.

1 The _____ _____

2 I was _____ _____ school that morning, and I was _____ Monsieur Hamel would _____ _____ .

3 A few days before, he had told us that we would _____ _____ _____ about French _____ that day, and I was not _____ .

4 It was _____ a warm, lovely day, and the fields along the road _____ _____ and _____ .

5 For a moment, I thought of _____ _____ _____ school and _____ _____ the fields.

6 However, I ran _____ _____ _____ _____ _____ to school.

7 _____ I _____ the mayor's office, I _____ _____ _____ the _____ on the board.

8 For two years all our bad news _____ _____ _____ that board.

9 I _____ , "What is it now?"

10 I ran _____ .

11 Usually, _____ _____ _____ in the morning at school— sounds of students _____ and _____ .

12 However, that day everything _____ _____ .

13 _____ the windows I saw my classmates in their places and Monsieur Hamel _____ _____ _____ the classroom.

14 I opened the door and entered _____ _____ _____ the _____ _____ .

15 My face felt hot _____ _____ !

1 마지막 수업

2 그날 아침 나는 수업에 늦었고, Hamel 선생님이 화를 내실까 걱정되었다.

3 며칠 전에 선생님은 그날 프랑스어 문장 시험을 보겠다고 말씀하셨는데, 나는 준비가 되어 있지 않았다.

4 날씨는 무척 포근하고 사랑스러웠으며 길가의 들판에서는 달콤하고 유혹적인 향기가 났다.

5 잠깐 동안 나는 학교에 가지 않고 들판을 거닐까 생각했다.

6 하지만 나는 최대한 빨리 학교로 달려갔다.

7 시장의 집무실을 지나면서 나는 사람들이 게시판에 붙어 있는 공고문을 읽고 있는 것을 보았다.

8 지난 2년 동안 모든 나쁜 소식은 저 게시판에서 나왔다.

9 나는 "이번에는 뭐지?"라는 궁금증이 들었다.

10 나는 더욱 빨리 달렸다.

11 보통, 아침에는 학생들이 떠들고 웃는 소리로 학교가 소란스러웠다.

12 그러나 그날은 모든 것이 고요했다.

13 창문을 통해 나는 학급 친구들이 제자리에 앉아 있고 Hamel 선생님이 초조하게 교실을 돌아다니시는 것을 보았다.

14 나는 문을 열고 낯선 침묵 속으로 들어갔다.

15 부끄러워서 얼굴이 화끈거렸다!

16 Surprisingly, Monsieur Hamel looked at me _____ _____ _____ _____ _____ and said kindly, "Go to your seat, my little Frantz; we almost began _____ you."

17 I _____ _____ _____ my desk.

18 _____ _____ then _____ I _____ Monsieur Hamel's blue coat.

19 He _____ _____ the coat _____ _____ _____ _____ special days.

20 Also there was _____ _____ about the _____ _____.

21 _____ surprised me most was _____ _____ people sitting at the back of the room: old Hauser was there, and _____ _____ the _____, the _____, and many others.

22 They all _____ so _____.

23 _____ I was _____ _____ all this, Monsieur Hamel walked slowly to the front.

24 He thought _____ _____ _____ and kindly said: "My children, this is _____ _____ _____ that I'll teach you.

25 _____ have _____ _____ Berlin to teach _____ _____ _____ in the schools of Alsace and Lorraine.

26 The new teacher _____ tomorrow.

27 This is the last class _____ _____, so I want you _____ _____ _____."

28 Those few words _____ my heart and _____ _____ _____.

29 So, this was _____ they had posted at the _____ _____.

30 It was the last class _____ _____ _____ _____ _____!

16 놀랍게도 Hamel 선생님은 화난 기색이 전혀 없이 나를 보시고 자상하게 말씀하셨다. "Frantz야, 네 자리로 가서 앉아라. 너 없이 수업을 시작할 뻔했구나."

17 나는 내 책상으로 가서 앉았다.

18 내가 Hamel 선생님의 파란색 외투를 알아차린 것은 바로 그 때였다.

19 선생님은 특별한 날에만 입는 외투를 입고 계셨다.

20 더구나 교실 전체도 무언가 이상했다.

21 나는 교실 뒤에 앉아 있는 사람들을 보고 가장 놀랐다. Hauser 할아버지가 앉아 계셨고 전직 시장님, 전직 우체부 아저씨를 비롯한 많은 사람들이 있었다.

22 그들은 모두 슬퍼 보였다.

23 내가 이 모든 것에 대해 의아해하는 동안, Hamel 선생님이 천천히 교실 앞으로 걸어가셨다.

24 그는 잠시 생각에 잠긴 후 다정하게 말씀하셨다: "어린이 여러분, 이것이 내가 여러분을 가르치는 마지막 시간입니다.

25 Alsace와 Lorraine에 있는 학교에서는 독일어만 가르치라는 명령이 베를린에서 내려왔습니다.

26 새로운 선생님이 내일 오실 겁니다.

27 이 시간이 프랑스어로 하는 마지막 수업이니 여러분이 주의 깊게 들어 주기 바랍니다."

28 이 몇 마디는 내 마음을 아프게 하고 또 화가 나게 했다.

29 그래, 이게 바로 시장 집무실 게시판에 공고되어 있던 것이다.

30 내 모국어로 하는 마지막 수업이라니!

※ 다음 문장을 우리말로 쓰시오.

1 The Last Class

➡ _____

2 I was late for school that morning, and I was worried Monsieur Hamel would get angry.

➡ _____

3 A few days before, he had told us that we would take an exam about French sentences that day, and I was not ready.

➡ _____

4 It was such a warm, lovely day, and the fields along the road smelled sweet and inviting.

➡ _____

5 For a moment, I thought of staying away from school and walking around the fields.

➡ _____

6 However, I ran as fast as I could to school.

➡ _____

7 As I passed the mayor's office, I saw people reading the notices on the board.

➡ _____

8 For two years all our bad news had come from that board.

➡ _____

9 I wondered, "What is it now?"

➡ _____

10 I ran faster.

➡ _____

11 Usually, there was noise in the morning at school—sounds of students talking and laughing.

➡ _____

12 However, that day everything was quiet.

➡ _____

13 Through the windows I saw my classmates in their places and Monsieur Hamel walking nervously around the classroom.

➡ _____

14 I opened the door and entered in the middle of the strange silence.

➡ _____

15 My face felt hot with shame!

➡ _____

16 ▸ Surprisingly, Monsieur Hamel looked at me with no sign of anger and said kindly, "Go to your seat, my little Frantz; we almost began without you."

➡ _____

17 ▸ I sat down at my desk.

➡ _____

18 ▸ It was then that I noticed Monsieur Hamel's blue coat.

➡ _____

19 ▸ He was wearing the coat he only wore on special days.

➡ _____

20 ▸ Also there was something strange about the whole class.

➡ _____

21 ▸ What surprised me most was to see people sitting at the back of the room: old Hauser was there, and so were the ex-mayor, the ex-postman, and many others.

➡ _____

_____

22 ▸ They all seemed so sad.

➡ _____

23 ▸ While I was wondering at all this, Monsieur Hamel walked slowly to the front.

➡ _____

24 ▸ He thought for a while and kindly said: "My children, this is the last time that I'll teach you.

➡ _____

25 ▸ Orders have come from Berlin to teach nothing but German in the schools of Alsace and Lorraine.

➡ _____

26 ▸ The new teacher arrives tomorrow.

➡ _____

27 ▸ This is the last class in French, so I want you to listen carefully."

➡ _____

28 ▸ Those few words broke my heart and made me angry.

➡ _____

29 ▸ So, this was what they had posted at the mayor's office.

➡ _____

30 ▸ It was the last class in my own language!

➡ _____

※ 다음 괄호 안의 단어들을 우리말에 맞도록 바르게 배열하시오.

1 (Last / The / Class)
➡ _____

2 (was / I / for / late / that / school / morning, / I / and / worried / was / Hamel / Monsieur / get / would / angry.)
➡ _____

3 (few / a / before, / days / had / he / us / told / we / that / would / an / take / about / exam / sentences / French / day, / that / I / and / not / was / ready.)
➡ _____

4 (was / it / a / such / warm, / day, / lovely / and / fields / the / the / along / smelled / road / sweet / inviting. / and)
➡ _____

5 (a / for / moment, / thought / I / staying / of / from / away / school / and / around / walking / fields. / the)
➡ _____

6 (I / however, / ran / fast / as / I / as / could / school. / to)
➡ _____

7 (I / as / the / passed / office, / mayor's / saw / I / reading / people / notices / the / the / on / board.)
➡ _____

8 (two / for / all / years / bad / our / had / news / from / come / board. / that)
➡ _____

9 (wondered, / I / "what / it / is / now?")
➡ _____

10 (ran / I / faster.)
➡ _____

11 (there / usually, / noise / was / the / in / morning / school / at / – / of / sounds / talking / students / laughing. / and)
➡ _____

12 (that / however, / everything / day / quiet. / was)
➡ _____

13 (the / through / windows / saw / I / classmates / my / their / in / places / and / Hamel / Monsieur / nervously / walking / the / around / classroom.)
➡ _____

14 (opened / I / door / the / and / in / entered / middle / the / strange / of / the / silence.)
➡ _____

15 (face / my / hot / felt / shame! / with)
➡ _____

1 마지막 수업

2 그날 아침 나는 수업에 늦었고, Hamel 선생님이 화를 내실까 걱정되었다.

3 며칠 전에 선생님은 그날 프랑스어 문장 시험을 보겠다고 말씀하셨는데, 나는 준비가 되어 있지 않았다.

4 날씨는 무척 포근하고 사랑스러웠으며 길가의 들판에서는 달콤하고 유혹적인 향기가 났다.

5 잠깐 동안 나는 학교에 가지 않고 들판을 거닐까 생각했다.

6 하지만 나는 최대한 빨리 학교로 달려갔다.

7 시장의 집무실을 지나면서 나는 사람들이 게시판에 붙어 있는 공고문을 읽고 있는 것을 보았다.

8 지난 2년 동안 모든 나쁜 소식은 저 게시판에서 나왔다.

9 나는 "이번에는 뭐지?"라는 궁금증이 들었다.

10 나는 더욱 빨리 달렸다.

11 보통, 아침에는 학생들이 떠들고 웃는 소리로 학교가 소란스러웠다.

12 그러나 그날은 모든 것이 고요했다.

13 창문을 통해 나는 학급 친구들이 제자리에 앉아 있고 Hamel 선생님이 초조하게 교실을 돌아다니시는 것을 보았다.

14 나는 문을 열고 낯선 침묵 속으로 들어갔다.

15 부끄러워서 얼굴이 화끈거렸다!

16 (Monsieur / surprisingly, / Hamel / at / looked / with / me / sign / no / anger / of / and / kindly, / said / "go / your / to / seat, / little / my / Frantz; / almost / we / without / began / you.")

➡ _____

17 (sat / I / down / my / at / desk.)

➡ _____

18 (was / it / that / then / noticed / I / Hamel's / Monsieur / coat. / blue)

➡ _____

19 (was / he / the / wearing / coat / only / he / on / wore / days. / special)

➡ _____

20 (there / also / something / was / about / strange / whole / the / class.)

➡ _____

21 (surprised / what / most / me / to / was / see / sitting / people / the / at / of / back / room: / the / Hauser / old / there, / was / so / and / the / were / ex-mayor, / ex-postman, / the / many / and / others.)

➡ _____

22 (all / they / so / seemed / sad.)

➡ _____

23 (I / while / wondering / was / all / at / this, / Hamel / Monsieur / slowly / walked / the / to / front.)

➡ _____

24 (thought / he / a / for / while / and / said: / kindly / children, / "my / is / this / last / the / time / I'll / that / you. / teach)

➡ _____

25 (have / orders / from / come / Berlin / teach / to / but / nothing / in / German / the / of / schools / Alsace / Lorraine. / and)

➡ _____

26 (new / the / arrives / teacher / tomorrow.)

➡ _____

27 (is / this / last / the / in / class / French, / I / so / you / want / listen / to / carefully.")

➡ _____

28 (few / those / broke / words / heart / my / and / me / made / angry.)

➡ _____

29 (this / so, / what / was / had / they / at / posted / mayor's / the / office.)

➡ _____

30 (was / it / last / the / in / class / own / my / language!)

➡ _____

16 놀랍게도 Hamel 선생님은 화난 기색이 전혀 없이 나를 보시고 자상하게 말씀하셨다. "Frantz야, 네 자리로 가서 앉아라. 너 없이 수업을 시작할 뻔했구나."

17 나는 내 책상으로 가서 앉았다.

18 내가 Hamel 선생님의 파란색 외투를 알아차린 것은 바로 그 때였다.

19 선생님은 특별한 날에만 입는 외투를 입고 계셨다.

20 더구나 교실 전체도 무언가 이상했다.

21 나는 교실 뒤에 앉아 있는 사람들을 보고 가장 놀랐다. Hauser 할아버지가 앉아 계셨고 전직 시장님, 전직 우체부 아저씨를 비롯한 많은 사람들이 있었다.

22 그들은 모두 슬퍼 보였다.

23 내가 이 모든 것에 대해 의아해 하는 동안, Hamel 선생님이 천천히 교실 앞으로 걸어가셨다.

24 그는 잠시 생각에 잠긴 후 다정하게 말씀하셨다: "어린이 여러분, 이것이 내가 여러분을 가르치는 마지막 시간입니다.

25 Alsace와 Lorraine에 있는 학교에서는 독일어만 가르치라는 명령이 베를린에서 내려왔습니다.

26 새로운 선생님이 내일 오실 겁니다.

27 이 시간이 프랑스어로 하는 마지막 수업이니 여러분이 주의 깊게 들어 주기 바랍니다."

28 이 몇 마디는 내 마음을 아프게 하고 또 화가 나게 했다.

29 그래, 이게 바로 시장 집무실 게시판에 공고되어 있던 것이다.

30 내 모국어로 하는 마지막 수업이라니!

※ **다음 우리말을 영어로 쓰시오.**

1 마지막 수업

➡ _____

2 그날 아침 나는 수업에 늦었고, Hamel 선생님이 화를 내실까 걱정되었다.

➡ _____

3 며칠 전에 선생님은 그날 프랑스어 문장 시험을 보겠다고 말씀하셨는데, 나는 준비가 되어 있지 않았다.

➡ _____

_____

4 날씨는 무척 포근하고 사랑스러웠으며 길가의 들판에서는 달콤하고 유혹적인 향기가 났다.

➡ _____

5 잠깐 동안 나는 학교에 가지 않고 들판을 거닐까 생각했다.

➡ _____

6 하지만 나는 최대한 빨리 학교로 달려갔다.

➡ _____

7 시장의 집무실을 지나면서 나는 사람들이 게시판에 붙어 있는 공고문을 읽고 있는 것을 보았다.

➡ _____

8 지난 2년 동안 모든 나쁜 소식은 저 게시판에서 나왔다.

➡ _____

9 나는 "이번에는 뭐지?"라는 궁금증이 들었다.

➡ _____

10 나는 더욱 빨리 달렸다.

➡ _____

11 보통, 아침에는 학생들이 떠들고 웃는 소리로 학교가 소란스러웠다.

➡ _____

12 그러나 그날은 모든 것이 고요했다.

➡ _____

13 창문을 통해 나는 학급 친구들이 제자리에 앉아 있고 Hamel 선생님이 초조하게 교실을 돌아다니시는 것을 보았다.

➡ _____

_____

14 나는 문을 열고 낯선 침묵 속으로 들어갔다.

➡ _____

15 부끄러워서 얼굴이 화끈거렸다!

➡ _____

16 놀랍게도 Hamel 선생님은 화난 기색이 전혀 없이 나를 보시고 자상하게 말씀하셨다. "Frantz야, 네 자리로 가서 앉아라. 너 없이 수업을 시작할 뻔했구나."

➡ _____

_____

17 나는 내 책상으로 가서 앉았다.

➡ _____

18 내가 Hamel 선생님의 파란색 외투를 알아차린 것은 바로 그때였다.

➡ _____

19 선생님은 특별한 날에만 입는 외투를 입고 계셨다.

➡ _____

20 더구나 교실 전체도 무언가 이상했다.

➡ _____

21 나는 교실 뒤에 앉아 있는 사람들을 보고 가장 놀랐다. Hauser 할아버지가 앉아 계셨고 전직 시장님, 전직 우체부 아저씨를 비롯한 많은 사람들이 있었다.

➡ _____

_____

22 그들은 모두 슬퍼 보였다.

➡ _____

23 내가 이 모든 것에 대해 의아해하는 동안, Hamel 선생님이 천천히 교실 앞으로 걸어가셨다.

➡ _____

24 그는 잠시 생각에 잠긴 후 다정하게 말씀하셨다: "어린이 여러분, 이것이 내가 여러분을 가르치는 마지막 시간입니다.

➡ _____

25 Alsace와 Lorraine에 있는 학교에서는 독일어만 가르치라는 명령이 베를린에서 내려왔습니다.

➡ _____

26 새로운 선생님이 내일 오실 겁니다.

➡ _____

27 이 시간이 프랑스어로 하는 마지막 수업이니 여러분이 주의 깊게 들어 주기 바랍니다."

➡ _____

28 이 몇 마디는 내 마음을 아프게 하고 또 화가 나게 했다.

➡ _____

29 그래, 이게 바로 시장 집무실 게시판에 공고되어 있던 것이다.

➡ _____

30 내 모국어로 하는 마지막 수업이라니!

➡ _____

※ 다음 영어를 우리말로 쓰시오.

01	dust		22	volcano
02	disturb		23	tsunami
03	earthquake		24	entire
04	relieve		25	sudden
05	sandstorm		26	threaten
06	drought		27	landslide
07	effect		28	rainfall
08	erupt		29	locate
09	crop		30	nearby
10	resource		31	occur
11	eruption		32	ash
12	destroy		33	chance
13	issue		34	circle
14	flood		35	put A in danger
15	typhoon		36	make use of
16	volume		37	get hurt
17	scenery		38	name after
18	wildfire		39	keep ~ in mind
19	prevent		40	have an effect on
20	yellow dust		41	prevent A from -ing
21	warning		42	shoot ~ into …
			43	in harmony with

※ 다음 우리말을 영어로 쓰시오.

01	강우, 강우량	
02	가뭄	
03	활동 중인	
04	농작물	
05	파괴하다	
06	지진	
07	방해하다	
08	분출	
09	완화하다, 줄이다	
10	위협하다	
11	해일	
12	범람하다; 홍수	
13	일어나다, 발생하다	
14	먼지	
15	부피, 용적	
16	경치, 풍경	
17	주의, 경고	
18	산사태	
19	영향, 효과, 결과	
20	재	
21	산불	

22	황사	
23	전체의, 온	
24	자원	
25	모래 폭풍	
26	태풍	
27	화산	
28	갑작스러운	
29	분출하다	
30	막다, 예방하다	
31	발표하다, 발행하다	
32	토양	
33	둘러싸다	
34	하룻밤 사이에	
35	수백만의	
36	~을 …으로 내뿜다	
37	갇히다	
38	~을 따라 이름 짓다	
39	~에 영향을 미치다	
40	~을 이용하다	
41	A를 위험하게 하다	
42	~와 조화를 이루어	
43	돌아오는 길에	

※ 다음 영영풀이에 알맞은 단어를 <보기>에서 골라 쓴 후, 우리말 뜻을 쓰시오.

1 _____ : a sudden outbreak of something: _____

2 _____ : involved in a particular activity: _____

3 _____ : to make a line in the shape of a ring: _____

4 _____ : the movement of cars, ships or aircraft: _____

5 _____ : a sudden shaking of Earth's surface: _____

6 _____ : even and smooth without curved or high parts: _____

7 _____ : to keep something from happening: _____

8 _____ : the grey powder that remains after something has burnt: _____

9 _____ : a large amount of water covering an area that is usually dry: _____

10 _____ : the amount of rain that falls on a particular area: _____

11 _____ : a plant such as a grain or fruit grown in large amounts: _____

12 _____ : dry powder that consists of very small bits of earth or sand: _____

13 _____ : a large round object in space that moves around a star: _____

14 _____ : to interrupt someone when they are trying to work, sleep, etc.: _____

15 _____ : a mountain with a big hole at the top, through which lava is pushed up: _____

16 _____ : a mass of earth, rock, etc. that falls down the slope of a mountain or a cliff: _____

disturb	earthquake	landslide	flat
crop	active	dust	eruption
volcano	ash	planet	prevent
rainfall	traffic	flood	circle

※ 다음 우리말과 일치하도록 빈칸에 알맞은 말을 쓰시오.

Listen - Listen & Answer Talk 1

M: Hi, this is Cha Gisang from the Weather Station. Here is today's weather. Typhoon Doni is moving north and is going to _____ Jejudo tonight. A typhoon _____ has been _____. There will be lots of _____ with a high chance of _____ in some areas. Please stay _____ because Typhoon Doni will come with strong winds. Also, please _____ _____ you _____ _____ _____ our reports. Thank you.

남: 안녕하세요, 기상대에서 차기상입니다. 오늘 날씨를 말씀드리겠습니다. 태풍 도니가 북상 중이며 오늘 밤에 제주도를 강타할 예정입니다. 태풍 주의보가 발효되었습니다. 많은 양의 비가 내릴 예정이고 일부 지역에서는 홍수의 가능성이 높습니다. 태풍 도니는 강한 바람을 동반하므로 실내에 머무십시오. 또, 보도를 계속 청취해 주시기를 당부 드립니다. 감사합니다.

Listen - Listen & Answer Dialog 2

M: Sora, can you _____ me _____ _____?

G: What is it, Dad?

M: A _____ is coming tonight. Can you _____ _____ the clothes from _____?

G: _____ problem. What about your _____?

M: I'll _____ _____ _____ it after I finish the _____.

G: Okay. Do you want me to call Grandma and tell her about the _____?

M: Yes. Please _____ her _____ _____ _____.

G: Okay, Dad.

남: 소라야, 부탁 좀 들어줄래?
여: 뭔데요, 아빠?
남: 오늘 밤 태풍이 온다는구나. 바깥에서 옷가지들을 들여와 주겠니?
여: 그럴게요. 아빠의 자전거는 어떻게 할까요?
남: 자전거는 설거지를 끝낸 후에 내가 처리하마.
여: 알겠어요. 할머니께 전화해서 태풍에 관해 말씀드릴까요?
남: 그래. 할머니께 집안에 계시라고 말씀드리렴.
여: 네, 아빠.

Listen - Listen More

B: Jimin, are you _____ _____?

G: Yeah. I'm going to buy some _____ at Choi's.

B: Are you walking there?

G: No. I'll _____ _____ _____.

B: That's _____. Can you do me _____ _____?

G: Sure. What is it?

B: Can you buy chocolate ice cream for me _____ _____ _____ _____?

G: No _____.

B: Thanks. Please _____ _____ you _____ a helmet and _____ ear phones!

G: _____ _____ about that.

남: 지민아, 외출하니?
여: 응. '최가네'에서 샌드위치 좀 사려고.
남: 그곳에 걸어서 갈 거니?
여: 아니. 자전거를 타고 갈 거야.
남: 잘됐다. 부탁 좀 들어줄래?
여: 그럼. 뭔데?
남: 돌아오는 길에 초콜릿 아이스크림 좀 사다 줄 수 있어?
여: 물론이야.
남: 고마워. 헬멧 꼭 쓰고, 이어폰은 안 돼!
여: 걱정하지 마.

Speak - Talk in pairs.

A: Can I start now?

B: _____ _____ _____ before you start.

A: Okay. No _____.

B: One _____ thing. Make sure _____ _____ _____ _____

_____ _____.

A: I'll _____ that in _____.

Wrap Up 5

(The phone rings.)

B: Hi, Mom.

W: Hi, Junho. Are you _____ _____ _____ _____ with Dad?

B: Yeah. Today we visited Dokdo.

W: That sounds _____. What are you _____ to do tomorrow?

B: We're _____ _____ on a boat.

W: Great. Please _____ _____ you _____ _____ _____

_____.

B: Okay, Mom. I'll _____ that _____ _____.

Wrap Up 6

W: Can you _____ _____ _____ _____ _____?

B: _____, Grandma. What is it?

W: I want to go to the Tom Dylan concert _____ _____. Can you

_____ some _____ for me?

B: No _____. How many _____ _____ _____ _____?

W: Two tickets, please.

※ 다음 우리말에 맞도록 대화를 영어로 쓰시오.

Listen - Listen & Answer Talk 1

M: _____

_____

_____

_____

_____

남: 안녕하세요, 기상대에서 차기상입니다. 오늘 날씨를 말씀드리겠습니다. 태풍 도니가 북상 중이며 오늘 밤에 제주도를 강타할 예정입니다. 태풍 주의보가 발효되었습니다. 많은 양의 비가 내릴 예정이고 일부 지역에서는 홍수의 가능성이 높습니다. 태풍 도니는 강한 바람을 동반하므로 실내에 머무십시오. 또, 보도를 계속 청취해 주시기를 당부 드립니다. 감사합니다.

Listen - Listen & Answer Dialog 2

M: _____

G: _____

M: _____

G: _____

M: _____

G: _____

M: _____

G: _____

남: 소라야, 부탁 좀 들어줄래?
여: 뭔데요, 아빠?
남: 오늘 밤 태풍이 온다는구나. 바깥에서 옷가지들을 들여와 주겠니?
여: 그럴게요. 아빠의 자전거는 어떻게 할까요?
남: 자전거는 설거지를 끝낸 후에 내가 처리하마.
여: 알겠어요. 할머니께 전화해서 태풍에 관해 말씀드릴까요?
남: 그래. 할머니께 집안에 계시라고 말씀드리렴.
여: 네, 아빠.

Listen - Listen More

B: _____

G: _____

B: _____

G: _____

B: _____

G: _____

B: _____

G: _____

B: _____

G: _____

남: 지민아, 외출하니?
여: 응. '최가네'에서 샌드위치 좀 사려고.
남: 그곳에 걸어서 갈 거니?
여: 아니. 자전거를 타고 갈 거야.
남: 잘됐다. 부탁 좀 들어줄래?
여: 그럼. 뭔데?
남: 돌아오는 길에 초콜릿 아이스크림 좀 사다 줄 수 있어?
여: 물론이야.
남: 고마워. 헬멧 꼭 쓰고, 이어폰은 안 돼!
여: 걱정하지 마.

Speak - Talk in pairs.

A: _____

B: _____

A: _____

B: _____

A: _____

A: 이제 시작할까요?
B: 시작하기 전에 손을 씻어라.
A: 네. 알겠어요.
B: 하나 더. 칼을 갖고 놀면 안 된다는 것을 명심해라.
A: 명심할게요.

Wrap Up 5

(The phone rings.)

B: _____

W: _____

B: _____

W: _____

B: _____

W: _____

B: _____

(전화벨이 울린다.)
남: 여보세요, 엄마.
여: 그래, 준호야. 아빠랑 좋은 시간 보내고 있니?
남: 네. 오늘 우리는 독도에 다녀왔어요.
여: 굉장하구나. 내일은 뭘 할 거니?
남: 우리는 보트를 타고 낚시하러 갈 거예요.
여: 좋겠구나. 구명조끼를 꼭 입도록 해라.
남: 네, 엄마. 명심할게요.

Wrap Up 6

W: _____

B: _____

W: _____

_____

B: _____

W: _____

여: 부탁 좀 들어줄 수 있니?
남: 물론이죠, 할머니. 뭔데요?
여: 크리스마스에 Tom Dylan 콘서트에 가고 싶구나. 나를 위해 표를 좀 구매해 주겠니?
남: 문제없어요. 표가 몇 장 필요하세요?
여: 두 장을 부탁한다.

※ 다음 우리말과 일치하도록 빈칸에 알맞은 것을 골라 쓰시오.

1 The _____ of _____
A. Volcanoes   B. Power

2 What do Jejudo, Sicily, and Hawaii _____ _____ _____?
A. common   B. have   C. in

3 They are _____, _____ _____.
A. of   B. islands   C. course

4 In _____, they are all _____ made from _____ _____.
A. volcanic   B. fact   C. eruptions   D. islands

5 Volcanoes are very _____, _____ they are _____ Vulcan, the Roman god of fire.
A. named   B. so   C. after   D. powerful

6 They can _____ big islands _____ or _____ _____ cities like Pompeii.
A. appear   B. entire   C. make   D. destroy

7 _____, they _____ be _____ and _____.
A. studied   B. therefore   C. understood   D. should

8 Nobody knows _____ _____ how many _____ _____ are in the world.
A. volcanoes   B. sure   C. there   D. for

9 _____ to scientists, there are about 1,500 _____ volcanoes _____ sea _____.
A. above   B. according   C. active   D. level

10 Many more are _____, and they are _____ _____ _____.
A. underwater   B. hard   C. locate   D. to

11 _____, scientists have _____ a large _____ of them so _____.
A. far   B. discovered   C. number   D. still

12 Many of the _____ on Earth are _____ _____ the Ring of Fire that _____ the Pacific Ocean.
A. located   B. volcanoes   C. along   D. circles

13 The ring is _____ 40,000 kilometers _____, and it is _____ to _____ 75% of the world's active volcanoes.
A. home   B. long   C. about   D. around

---

1 화산의 힘

2 제주도, 시칠리아, 하와이의 공통점은 무엇일까?

3 물론, 그것들은 섬이다.

4 사실, 그것들은 모두 화산 분출에 의해 형성된 섬이다.

5 화산은 매우 강력한 힘을 가지고 있어서 로마의 불의 신, 불카누스에게서 이름을 따왔다.

6 화산은 큰 섬이 생겨나게 하거나 폼페이 같은 도시 전체를 파멸시킬 수도 있다.

7 그러므로 화산은 연구되고, 이해되어야 한다.

8 세계에 얼마나 많은 화산이 있는지 누구도 정확히 알지 못한다.

9 과학자들에 따르면, 해수면 위에 대략 1,500개의 활화산이 있다.

10 더 많은 화산이 해저에 존재하는데, 그것들은 정확한 위치를 파악하기가 어렵다.

11 그럼에도 불구하고, 과학자들은 지금까지 그중 많은 수를 발견했다.

12 지구상에 있는 많은 화산들은 태평양을 둘러싸는 '불의 고리(환태평양조산대)'를 따라 위치한다.

13 그 고리는 길이가 약 40,000km에 달하며, 전 세계 활화산의 약 75%가 여기에 있다.

14 Indonesia _____ has over 120 active volcanoes _____ the country _____ _____ the Ring of Fire.

   A. since   B. lies   C. alone   D. on

15 This ring is also the _____ where _____ of the world's _____ _____.

   A. occur   B. most   C. area   D. earthquakes

16 A _____ _____

   A. Volcano   B. Sudden

17 _____ on a _____ one day in 1943, farmers in Mexico found _____ _____.

   A. something   B. cornfield   C. working   D. surprising

18 A volcano _____ _____ on a _____ _____.

   A. flat   B. appeared   C. cornfield   D. overnight

19 _____ watched the volcano _____ _____ 100 meters tall _____ a week.

   A. grow   B. within   C. residents   D. over

20 The volcano, _____ Paricutin, _____ growing, and it finally _____ _____ at 424 meters in 1952.

   A. stopped   B. kept   C. called   D. growing

21 You _____ think volcanoes _____ _____ _____ only on Earth.

   A. be   B. may   C. found   D. can

22 However, they have _____ _____ on other planets, too, _____ _____ Mars and Jupiter.

   A. such   B. been   C. discovered   D. as

23 In _____, "Olympus Mons" on Mars is the _____ _____ volcano in the _____ system.

   A. solar   B. fact   C. known   D. largest

24 Its volume is about 100 _____ _____ than that of Mauna Loa, the _____ _____ on Earth.

   A. greater   B. volcano   C. times   D. largest

---

14 인도네시아에만 120개가 넘는 활화산이 있는데, 이 나라가 '불의 고리'에 위치하고 있기 때문이다.

15 이 고리는 또한 전 세계 지진의 대부분이 발생하는 곳이다.

16 갑작스럽게 생겨난 화산

17 1943년 어느 날 옥수수 밭에서 일을 하다가 멕시코의 농부들이 놀라운 것을 발견했다.

18 밤사이에 평평한 옥수수 밭 위로 화산이 생겨난 것이다.

19 주민들은 그 화산이 일주일이 못 되는 사이 100m 넘게 자라는 것을 지켜보았다.

20 'Paricutin(파리쿠틴)'이라고 불리는 이 화산은 계속 자라났고, 1952년에 424m로 드디어 성장을 멈추었다.

21 화산이 지구에만 존재한다고 생각할지 모른다.

22 그러나 화산은 화성이나 목성 같은 다른 행성에서도 발견되어 왔다.

23 사실 화성에 있는 Olympus Mons(올림푸스 몬스)가 태양계에서 가장 크다고 알려진 화산이다.

24 그것의 부피는 지구에서 가장 큰 화산 Mauna Loa(마우나로아)의 부피보다 약 100배 더 크다.

25 _____ very powerful and _____, volcanoes do _____ to people in many _____.

    A. harm   B. dangerous   C. ways   D. being

26 Sometimes people _____ _____, or they _____ _____ their houses.

    A. hurt   B. lose   C. get   D. may

27 Crops _____ be _____, and air traffic can _____ _____.

    A. destroyed   B. may   C. threatened   D. be

28 Volcanoes can also _____ _____ _____ _____ world weather.

    A. effects   B. have   C. serious   D. on

29 A volcanic eruption _____ lots of ash and dust into the air, _____ some of the sunlight from _____ Earth and thus _____ usual weather patterns.

    A. preventing   B. disturbing   C. shoots   D. reaching

30 A _____ _____

    A. Volcano   B. Deadly

31 Mt. Tambora, an _____ _____ on the _____ of Sumbawa, Indonesia, _____ in 1815.

    A. erupted   B. island   C. volcano   D. active

32 The _____ killed _____ _____ 10,000 _____.

    A. residents   B. eruption   C. than   D. more

33 It also _____ an _____ cold summer _____ the world the _____ year.

    A. around   B. unusually   C. caused   D. following

34 _____ _____ do is not always bad for _____, _____.

    A. humans   B. volcanoes   C. what   D. however

35 The _____ near a _____ is _____ for _____.

    A. farming   B. soil   C. good   D. volcano

36 _____ are also a _____ _____ _____.

    A. tourist   B. volcanoes   C. attraction   D. great

37 _____ for fantastic _____, _____ of _____ visit Mt. Halla in Jejudo, Mt. Etna in Sicily, or Diamond Head in Hawaii every year.

    A. millions   B. scenery   C. tourists   D. looking

38 Volcanoes can _____ _____ to _____ _____, too.

    A. produce   B. be   C. electricity   D. used

39 Iceland, _____ example, actively _____ its _____ heat energy _____ electricity.

    A. turns   B. for   C. volcanoes'   D. into

40 Today people around the world are studying _____ to live in greater _____ with volcanoes, and they are _____ that more ways will be _____ soon.

    A. ways   B. harmony   C. hopeful   D. found

---

25 매우 강력하고 위험하기 때문에, 화산은 여러 면에서 사람들에게 해를 끼친다.

26 때로는 사람들이 다치기도 하고, 집을 잃기도 한다.

27 작물이 파괴되거나, 항공 교통이 위협받을 수도 있다.

28 화산은 또한 세계 날씨에 심각한 영향을 미치기도 한다.

29 화산 분출은 다량의 화산재와 먼지를 공중으로 내뿜어, 태양 광선의 일부가 지구에 도달하는 것을 방해하고 그리하여 정상적인 기상 패턴을 깨뜨린다.

30 목숨을 앗아 가는 화산

31 인도네시아 Sumbawa(숨바와) 섬에 위치한 활화산, Tambora(탐보라) 산이 1815년에 분출했다.

32 분출은 주민 1만 명 이상을 죽음에 이르게 했다.

33 또한 이듬해 전 세계에 비정상적으로 추운 여름을 초래했다.

34 그러나 화산이 인류에게 항상 나쁜 것만은 아니다.

35 화산 인근의 토양은 농사에 좋다.

36 화산은 또한 매우 훌륭한 관광 명소이다.

37 환상적인 경관을 찾아 매년 수백만 명의 여행객들이 제주도의 한라산, 시칠리아의 Etna(에트나) 산, 하와이의 Diamond Head(다이아몬드헤드)를 방문한다.

38 화산은 또한 전기를 생산하는 데에도 이용될 수 있다.

39 예를 들어, 아이슬란드는 적극적으로 화산의 열에너지를 전기로 바꾼다.

40 오늘날 전 세계에서 사람들이 화산과 더 조화롭게 살 방법을 연구하고 있으며, 더 많은 방법이 곧 발견될 것으로 기대하고 있다.

※ 다음 우리말과 일치하도록 빈칸에 알맞은 말을 쓰시오.

1 The _____ of _____

2 What do Jejudo, Sicily, and Hawaii _____ _____ _____ ?

3 They are _____, _____ _____.

4 In _____, they are all islands made from _____ _____.

5 Volcanoes are very powerful, so they _____ _____ _____ Vulcan, the Roman god of fire.

6 They can _____ _____ _____ _____ or _____ entire cities like Pompeii.

7 Therefore, they _____ _____ _____ _____ _____.

8 Nobody knows for sure _____ _____ _____ _____ _____ in the world.

9 _____ _____ scientists, there are _____ 1,500 active volcanoes _____ _____ _____.

10 Many more are _____, and they are _____ _____ _____.

11 Still, scientists have discovered _____ _____ _____ them _____ _____.

12 Many of the volcanoes on Earth _____ _____ _____ _____ the Ring of Fire that circles the Pacific Ocean.

13 The ring is about 40,000 kilometers long, and it is _____ _____ around 75% of the world's _____.

14 Indonesia _____ has over 120 active volcanoes _____ the country _____ _____ the Ring of Fire.

15 This ring is also the area _____ most of the world's earthquakes _____.

16 A _____ Volcano

17 _____ on a cornfield one day in 1943, farmers in Mexico found _____ _____.

18 A volcano _____ _____ on a _____ _____.

19 Residents watched the volcano _____ over 100 meters tall _____ a week.

20 The volcano, called Paricutin, _____ _____, and it finally _____ _____ at 424 meters in 1952.

1 화산의 힘
2 제주도, 시칠리아, 하와이의 공통점은 무엇일까?
3 물론, 그것들은 섬이다.
4 사실, 그것들은 모두 화산 분출에 의해 형성된 섬이다.
5 화산은 매우 강력한 힘을 가지고 있어서 로마의 불의 신, 불카누스에게서 이름을 따왔다.
6 화산은 큰 섬이 생겨나게 하거나 폼페이 같은 도시 전체를 파멸시킬 수도 있다.
7 그러므로 화산은 연구되고, 이해되어야 한다.
8 세계에 얼마나 많은 화산이 있는지 누구도 정확히 알지 못한다.
9 과학자들에 따르면, 해수면 위에 대략 1,500개의 활화산이 있다.
10 더 많은 화산이 해저에 존재하는데, 그것들은 정확한 위치를 파악하기가 어렵다.
11 그럼에도 불구하고, 과학자들은 지금까지 그중 많은 수를 발견했다.
12 지구상에 있는 많은 화산들은 태평양을 둘러싸는 '불의 고리(환태평양조산대)'를 따라 위치한다.
13 그 고리는 길이가 약 40,000km에 달하며, 전 세계 활화산의 약 75%가 여기에 있다.
14 인도네시아에만 120개가 넘는 활화산이 있는데, 이 나라가 '불의 고리'에 위치하고 있기 때문이다.
15 이 고리는 또한 전 세계 지진의 대부분이 발생하는 곳이다.
16 갑작스럽게 생겨난 화산
17 1943년 어느 날 옥수수 밭에서 일을 하다가 멕시코의 농부들이 놀라운 것을 발견했다.
18 밤사이에 평평한 옥수수 밭 위로 화산이 생겨난 것이다.
19 주민들은 그 화산이 일주일이 못 되는 사이 100m 넘게 자라는 것을 지켜보았다.
20 'Paricutin(파리쿠틴)'이라고 불리는 이 화산은 계속 자랐고, 1952년에 424m로 드디어 성장을 멈추었다.

21 You may think volcanoes _____ _____ _____ only on Earth.

22 However, they _____ _____ _____ on other planets, too, _____ _____ Mars and Jupiter.

23 In fact, "Olympus Mons" on Mars is _____ _____ _____ volcano in the _____ _____.

24 Its volume is about _____ _____ _____ _____ _____ _____ Mauna Loa, the largest volcano on Earth.

25 Being very powerful and dangerous, volcanoes _____ _____ _____ people _____ _____ _____ _____.

26 Sometimes people _____ _____, or they may lose their houses.

27 Crops _____ _____ _____, and air traffic _____ _____ _____.

28 Volcanoes can also _____ _____ _____ _____ _____ world weather.

29 A volcanic eruption _____ lots of ash and dust _____ the air, _____ some of the sunlight _____ _____ Earth and thus _____ usual weather patterns.

30 A _____ _____

31 Mt. Tambora, an _____ _____ on the island of Sumbawa, Indonesia, _____ in 1815.

32 The _____ killed _____ _____ 10,000 residents.

33 It also caused an _____ cold summer around the world the _____ _____.

34 _____ _____ _____ is _____ _____ bad for humans, however.

35 The soil near a volcano _____ _____ _____ _____ farming.

36 Volcanoes are also a great _____ _____.

37 _____ _____ fantastic scenery, _____ _____ tourists visit Mt. Halla in Jejudo, Mt. Etna in Sicily, or Diamond Head in Hawaii every year.

38 Volcanoes _____ _____ _____ to produce electricity, too.

39 Iceland, for example, actively _____ its volcanoes' heat energy _____ _____.

40 Today people around the world are studying ways to live in _____ _____ _____ volcanoes, and they are hopeful that more ways _____ _____ _____ soon.

21 화산이 지구에만 존재한다고 생각할지 모른다.

22 그러나 화산은 화성이나 목성 같은 다른 행성에서도 발견되어 왔다.

23 사실 화성에 있는 Olympus Mons(올림푸스 몬스)가 태양계에서 가장 크다고 알려진 화산이다.

24 그것의 부피는 지구에서 가장 큰 화산 Mauna Loa(마우나로아)의 부피보다 약 100배 더 크다.

25 매우 강력하고 위험하기 때문에, 화산은 여러 면에서 사람들에게 해를 끼친다.

26 때로는 사람들이 다치기도 하고, 집을 잃기도 한다.

27 작물이 파괴되거나, 항공 교통이 위협받을 수도 있다.

28 화산은 또한 세계 날씨에 심각한 영향을 미치기도 한다.

29 화산 분출은 다량의 화산재와 먼지를 공중으로 내뿜어, 태양 광선의 일부가 지구에 도달하는 것을 방해하고 그리하여 정상적인 기상 패턴을 깨뜨린다.

30 목숨을 앗아 가는 화산

31 인도네시아 Sumbawa(숨바와) 섬에 위치한 활화산, Tambora(탐보라) 산이 1815년에 분출했다.

32 분출은 주민 1만 명 이상을 죽음에 이르게 했다.

33 또한 이듬해 전 세계에 비정상적으로 추운 여름을 초래했다.

34 그러나 화산이 인류에게 항상 나쁜 것만은 아니다.

35 화산 인근의 토양은 농사에 좋다.

36 화산은 또한 매우 훌륭한 관광 명소이다.

37 환상적인 경관을 찾아 매년 수백만 명의 여행객들이 제주도의 한라산, 시칠리아의 Etna(에트나) 산, 하와이의 Diamond Head(다이아몬드헤드)를 방문한다.

38 화산은 또한 전기를 생산하는 데에도 이용될 수 있다.

39 예를 들어, 아이슬란드는 적극적으로 화산의 열에너지를 전기로 바꾼다.

40 오늘날 전 세계에서 사람들이 화산과 더 조화롭게 살 방법을 연구하고 있으며, 더 많은 방법이 곧 발견될 것으로 기대하고 있다.

※ 다음 문장을 우리말로 쓰시오.

1 The Power of Volcanoes
➡ _____

2 What do Jejudo, Sicily, and Hawaii have in common?
➡ _____

3 They are islands, of course.
➡ _____

4 In fact, they are all islands made from volcanic eruptions.
➡ _____

5 Volcanoes are very powerful, so they are named after Vulcan, the Roman god of fire.
➡ _____

6 They can make big islands appear or destroy entire cities like Pompeii.
➡ _____

7 Therefore, they should be studied and understood.
➡ _____

8 Nobody knows for sure how many volcanoes there are in the world.
➡ _____

9 According to scientists, there are about 1,500 active volcanoes above sea level.
➡ _____

10 Many more are underwater, and they are hard to locate.
➡ _____

11 Still, scientists have discovered a large number of them so far.
➡ _____

12 Many of the volcanoes on Earth are located along the Ring of Fire that circles the Pacific Ocean.
➡ _____

13 The ring is about 40,000 kilometers long, and it is home to around 75% of the world's active volcanoes.
➡ _____

14 Indonesia alone has over 120 active volcanoes since the country lies on the Ring of Fire.
➡ _____

15 This ring is also the area where most of the world's earthquakes occur.
➡ _____

16 A Sudden Volcano
➡ _____

17 Working on a cornfield one day in 1943, farmers in Mexico found something surprising.
➡ _____

18 A volcano appeared overnight on a flat cornfield.
➡ _____

19 Residents watched the volcano grow over 100 meters tall within a week.
➡ _____

20 The volcano, called Paricutin, kept growing, and it finally stopped growing at 424 meters in 1952.
➡ _____

21 You may think volcanoes can be found only on Earth.
➡ _____

22 However, they have been discovered on other planets, too, such as Mars and Jupiter.
➡ _____

23 In fact, "Olympus Mons" on Mars is the largest known volcano in the solar system.
➡ _____

24 Its volume is about 100 times greater than that of Mauna Loa, the largest volcano on Earth.
➡ _____

25 Being very powerful and dangerous, volcanoes do harm to people in many ways.
➡ _____

26 Sometimes people get hurt, or they may lose their houses.
➡ _____

27 Crops may be destroyed, and air traffic can be threatened.
➡ _____

28 Volcanoes can also have serious effects on world weather.
➡ _____

29 A volcanic eruption shoots lots of ash and dust into the air, preventing some of the sunlight from reaching Earth and thus disturbing usual weather patterns.
➡ _____

30 A Deadly Volcano
➡ _____

31 Mt. Tambora, an active volcano on the island of Sumbawa, Indonesia, erupted in 1815.
➡ _____

32 The eruption killed more than 10,000 residents.
➡ _____

33 It also caused an unusually cold summer around the world the following year.
➡ _____

34 What volcanoes do is not always bad for humans, however.
➡ _____

35 The soil near a volcano is good for farming.
➡ _____

36 Volcanoes are also a great tourist attraction.
➡ _____

37 Looking for fantastic scenery, millions of tourists visit Mt. Halla in Jejudo, Mt. Etna in Sicily, or Diamond Head in Hawaii every year.
➡ _____

38 Volcanoes can be used to produce electricity, too.
➡ _____

39 Iceland, for example, actively turns its volcanoes' heat energy into electricity.
➡ _____

40 Today people around the world are studying ways to live in greater harmony with volcanoes, and they are hopeful that more ways will be found soon.
➡ _____
_____

※ 다음 괄호 안의 단어들을 우리말에 맞도록 바르게 배열하시오.

1 (Power / The / Volcanoes / of)
➡ _____

2 (do / what / Sicily, / Jejudo, / and / have / Hawaii / common? / in)
➡ _____

3 (are / they / of / islands, / course.)
➡ _____

4 (fact, / in / are / they / islands / all / from / made / eruptions. / volcanic)
➡ _____

5 (are / volcanoes / powerful, / very / they / so / named / are / Vulcan, / after / Roman / the / of / god / fire.)
➡ _____
_____

6 (can / they / big / make / appear / islands / or / entire / destroy / like / cities / Pompeii.)
➡ _____

7 (they / therefore, / be / should / studied / understood. / and)
➡ _____

8 (knows / nobody / sure / for / many / how / volacnoes / are / there / the / in / world.)
➡ _____

9 (to / according / scientists, / are / there / 1,500 / about / volcanoes / active / sea / above / level.)
➡ _____
_____

10 (more / many / underwater, / are / they / and / hard / are / locate. / to)
➡ _____

11 (scientists / still, / discovered / have / large / a / number / them / of / far. / so)
➡ _____

12 (of / many / volcanoes / the / Earth / on / located / are / the / along / of / Ring / Fire / circles / that / the / Ocean. / Pacific)
➡ _____
_____

13 (ring / the / about / is / kilometers / 40,000 / long, / it / and / is / to / home / around / of / 75% / active / world's / the / volcanoes.)
➡ _____
_____

1 화산의 힘

2 제주도, 시칠리아, 하와이의 공통점은 무엇일까?

3 물론, 그것들은 섬이다.

4 사실, 그것들은 모두 화산 분출에 의해 형성된 섬이다.

5 화산은 매우 강력한 힘을 가지고 있어서 로마의 불의 신, 불카누스에서 이름을 따왔다.

6 화산은 큰 섬이 생겨나게 하거나 폼페이 같은 도시 전체를 파멸시킬 수도 있다.

7 그러므로 화산은 연구되고, 이해되어야 한다.

8 세계에 얼마나 많은 화산이 있는지 누구도 정확히 알지 못한다.

9 과학자들에 따르면, 해수면 위에 대략 1,500개의 활화산이 있다.

10 더 많은 화산이 해저에 존재하는데, 그것들은 정확한 위치를 파악하기가 어렵다.

11 그럼에도 불구하고, 과학자들은 지금까지 그중 많은 수를 발견했다.

12 지구상에 있는 많은 화산들은 태평양을 둘러싸는 '불의 고리(환태평양조산대)'를 따라 위치한다.

13 그 고리는 길이가 약 40,000km에 달하며, 전 세계 활화산의 약 75%가 여기에 있다.

14 (alone / Indonesia / over / has / active / 120 / volcanoes / the / since / country / on / lies / Ring / the / Fire. / of)

➡ _____

_____

15 (ring / this / also / is / area / the / most / where / the / of / earthquakes / world's / occur.)

➡ _____

16 (Sudden / A / Volcano)

➡ _____

17 (on / working / cornfield / a / day / one / 1943, / in / in / farmers / found / Mexico / surprising. / something)

➡ _____

_____

18 (volcano / a / overnight / appeared / a / on / cornfield. / flat)

➡ _____

19 (watched / residents / volcano / the / over / grow / meters / 100 / tall / a / within / week.)

➡ _____

20 (volcano, / the / Paricutin, / called / growing, / kept / it / and / stopped / finally / at / growing / 424 / in / meters / 1952.)

➡ _____

_____

21 (may / you / volcanoes / think / be / can / only / found / Earth. / on)

➡ _____

22 (they / however, / been / have / on / discovered / planets, / other / too, / as / such / Jupiter. / and / Mars)

➡ _____

_____

23 (fact, / in / Mons" / "Olympus / on / is / Mars / largest / the / volcano / known / the / in / system. / solar)

➡ _____

_____

24 (volume / its / about / is / times / 100 / greater / that / than / Mauna / of / Loa, / largest / the / on / volcano / Earth.)

➡ _____

_____

14 인도네시아에만 120개가 넘는 활화산이 있는데, 이 나라가 '불의 고리'에 위치하고 있기 때문이다.

15 이 고리는 또한 전 세계 지진의 대부분이 발생하는 곳이다.

16 갑작스럽게 생겨난 화산

17 1943년 어느 날 옥수수 밭에서 일을 하다가 멕시코의 농부들이 놀라운 것을 발견했다.

18 밤사이에 평평한 옥수수 밭 위로 화산이 생겨난 것이다.

19 주민들은 그 화산이 일주일이 못 되는 사이 100m 넘게 자라는 것을 지켜보았다.

20 'Paricutin(파리쿠틴)'이라고 불리는 이 화산은 계속 자라났고, 1952년에 424m로 드디어 성장을 멈추었다.

21 화산이 지구에만 존재한다고 생각할지 모른다.

22 그러나 화산은 화성이나 목성 같은 다른 행성에서도 발견되어 왔다.

23 사실 화성에 있는 Olympus Mons(올림푸스 몬스)가 태양계에서 가장 크다고 알려진 화산이다.

24 그것의 부피는 지구에서 가장 큰 화산 Mauna Loa(마우나로아)의 부피보다 약 100배 더 크다.

25 (very / being / and / powerful / dangerous, / do / volcanoes / harm / people / to / many / in / ways.)
➡ _____

26 (people / sometimes / hurt, / get / they / or / lose / may / houses. / their)
➡ _____

27 (may / crops / destroyed, / be / air / and / can / traffic / threatened. / be)
➡ _____

28 (can / volanoes / have / also / effects / serious / world / on / weather.)
➡ _____

29 (volcanic / a / shoots / eruption / of / lots / ash / dust / and / into / air, / the / some / preventing / the / of / from / sunlight / reaching / and / Earth / disturbing / thus / weather / usual / patterns.)
➡ _____
_____

30 (Deadly / A / Volcano)
➡ _____

31 (Tambora, / Mt. / active / an / on / volcano / the / of / island / Sumbawa / erupted / Indonesia, / 1815. / in)
➡ _____

32 (eruption / the / more / killed / 10,000 / than / residents.)
➡ _____

33 (also / it / an / caused / cold / unusually / around / summer / the / world / following / the / year.)
➡ _____

34 (volcanoes / what / is / do / always / not / for / bad / however. / humans,)
➡ _____

35 (soil / the / a / near / is / volcano / for / good / farming.)
➡ _____

36 (are / volcanoes / a / also / tourist / great / attraction.)
➡ _____

37 (for / lookiing / scenery, / fantastic / of / millions / visit / tourists / Halla / Mt. / Jejudo, / in / Etna / Mt. / Sicily, / in / Diamond / or / in / Head / every / Hawaii / year.)
➡ _____

38 (can / volcanoes / be / used / produce / to / too. / electricity,)
➡ _____

39 (for / Iceland, / example, / turns / actively / volcanoes' / its / energy / heat / electricity. / into)
➡ _____

40 (people / today / the / around / world / studying / are / to / ways / in / live / harmony / greater / volcanoes, / with / they / and / hopeful / are / more / that / will / ways / found / be / soon.)
➡ _____
_____

25 매우 강력하고 위험하기 때문에, 화산은 여러 면에서 사람들에게 해를 끼친다.

26 때로는 사람들이 다치기도 하고, 집을 잃기도 한다.

27 작물이 파괴되거나, 항공 교통이 위협받을 수도 있다.

28 화산은 또한 세계 날씨에 심각한 영향을 미치기도 한다.

29 화산 분출은 다량의 화산재와 먼지를 공중으로 내뿜어, 태양 광선의 일부가 지구에 도달하는 것을 방해하고 그리하여 정상적인 기상 패턴을 깨뜨린다.

30 목숨을 앗아 가는 화산

31 인도네시아 Sumbawa(숨바와) 섬에 위치한 활화산, Tambora(탐보라) 산이 1815년에 분출했다.

32 분출은 주민 1만 명 이상을 죽음에 이르게 했다.

33 또한 이듬해 전 세계에 비정상적으로 추운 여름을 초래했다.

34 그러나 화산이 인류에게 항상 나쁜 것만은 아니다.

35 화산 인근의 토양은 농사에 좋다.

36 화산은 또한 매우 훌륭한 관광 명소이다.

37 환상적인 경관을 찾아 매년 수백만 명의 여행객들이 제주도의 한라산, 시칠리아의 Etna(에트나) 산, 하와이의 Diamond Head(다이아몬드헤드)를 방문한다.

38 화산은 또한 전기를 생산하는 데에도 이용될 수 있다.

39 예를 들어, 아이슬란드는 적극적으로 화산의 열에너지를 전기로 바꾼다.

40 오늘날 전 세계에서 사람들이 화산과 더 조화롭게 살 방법을 연구하고 있으며, 더 많은 방법이 곧 발견될 것으로 기대하고 있다.

※ **다음 우리말을 영어로 쓰시오.**

1 화산의 힘
➡ _____

2 제주도, 시칠리아, 하와이의 공통점은 무엇일까?
➡ _____

3 물론, 그것들은 섬이다.
➡ _____

4 사실, 그것들은 모두 화산 분출에 의해 형성된 섬이다.
➡ _____

5 화산은 매우 강력한 힘을 가지고 있어서 로마의 불의 신, 불카누스에게서 이름을 따왔다.

6 화산은 큰 섬이 생겨나게 하거나 폼페이 같은 도시 전체를 파멸시킬 수도 있다.
➡ _____

7 그러므로 화산은 연구되고, 이해되어야 한다.
➡ _____

8 세계에 얼마나 많은 화산이 있는지 누구도 정확히 알지 못한다.
➡ _____

9 과학자들에 따르면, 해수면 위에 대략 1,500개의 활화산이 있다.
➡ _____

10 더 많은 화산이 해저에 존재하는데, 그것들은 정확한 위치를 파악하기가 어렵다.
➡ _____

11 그럼에도 불구하고, 과학자들은 지금까지 그중 많은 수를 발견했다.
➡ _____

12 지구상에 있는 많은 화산들은 태평양을 둘러싸는 '불의 고리(환태평양조산대)'를 따라 위치한다.
➡ _____

13 그 고리는 길이가 약 40,000km에 달하며, 전 세계 활화산의 약 75%가 여기에 있다.
➡ _____

14 인도네시아에만 120개가 넘는 활화산이 있는데, 이 나라가 '불의 고리'에 위치하고 있기 때문이다.
➡ _____

15 이 고리는 또한 전 세계 지진의 대부분이 발생하는 곳이다.
➡ _____

16 갑작스럽게 생겨난 화산
➡ _____

17 1943년 어느 날 옥수수 밭에서 일을 하다가 멕시코의 농부들이 놀라운 것을 발견했다.
➡ _____

18 밤사이에 평평한 옥수수 밭 위로 화산이 생겨난 것이다.
➡ _____

19 주민들은 그 화산이 일주일이 못 되는 사이 100m 넘게 자라는 것을 지켜보았다.
➡ _____

20 'Paricutin(파리쿠틴)'이라 불리는 이 화산은 계속 자라났고, 1952년에 424m로 드디어 성장을 멈추었다.
➡ _____

21 화산이 지구에만 존재한다고 생각할지 모른다.
➡ _____

22 그러나 화산은 화성이나 목성 같은 다른 행성에서도 발견되어 왔다.
➡ _____

23 사실 화성에 있는 Olympus Mons(올림푸스 몬스)가 태양계에서 가장 크다고 알려진 화산이다.
➡ _____

24 그것의 부피는 지구에서 가장 큰 화산 Mauna Loa(마우나 로아)의 부피보다 약 100배 더 크다.
➡ _____

25 매우 강력하고 위험하기 때문에, 화산은 여러 면에서 사람들에게 해를 끼친다.
➡ _____

26 때로는 사람들이 다치기도 하고, 집을 잃기도 한다.
➡ _____

27 작물이 파괴되거나, 항공 교통이 위협받을 수도 있다.
➡ _____

28 화산은 또한 세계 날씨에 심각한 영향을 미치기도 한다.
➡ _____

29 화산 분출은 다량의 화산재와 먼지를 공중으로 내뿜어, 태양 광선의 일부가 지구에 도달하는 것을 방해하고 그리하여 정상적인 기상 패턴을 깨트린다.
➡ _____

30 목숨을 앗아 가는 화산
➡ _____

31 인도네시아 Sumbawa(숨바와) 섬에 위치한 활화산, Tambora(탐보라) 산이 1815년에 분출했다.
➡ _____

32 분출은 주민 1만 명 이상을 죽음에 이르게 했다.
➡ _____

33 또한 이듬해 전 세계에 비정상적으로 추운 여름을 초래했다.
➡ _____

34 그러나 화산이 인류에게 항상 나쁜 것만은 아니다.
➡ _____

35 화산 인근의 토양은 농사에 좋다.
➡ _____

36 화산은 또한 매우 훌륭한 관광 명소이다.
➡ _____

37 환상적인 경관을 찾아 매년 수백만 명의 여행객들이 제주도의 한라산, 시칠리아의 Etna(에트나) 산, 하와이의 Diamond Head(다이아몬드헤드)를 방문한다.
➡ _____

38 화산은 또한 전기를 생산하는 데에도 이용될 수 있다.
➡ _____

39 예를 들어, 아이슬란드는 적극적으로 화산의 열에너지를 전기로 바꾼다.
➡ _____

40 오늘날 전 세계에서 사람들이 화산과 더 조화롭게 살 방법을 연구하고 있으며, 더 많은 방법이 곧 발견될 것으로 기대하고 있다.
➡ _____
_____

※ 다음 우리말과 일치하도록 빈칸에 알맞은 말을 쓰시오.

My Speaking Portfolio Step 1

1. The _____ is _____ .
2. The pan _____ _____ _____ .
3. I _____ _____ in the elevator.
4. I _____ _____ _____ in hot water.
5. I _____ _____ the steps and _____ my arm.

1. 정전됐어요.
2. 프라이팬에 불이 붙었어요.
3. 나는 엘리베이터에 갇혔어요.
4. 나는 뜨거운 물에 손을 데었어요.
5. 나는 계단에서 넘어져서 팔이 부러졌어요.

After You Read Details

1. The name "_____" _____ _____ the Roman god of fire. - Mila
2. 75% of _____ _____ _____ _____ _____ _____ _____ the Ring of Fire. - James
3. The volcano Paricutin in Mexico _____ _____ . - Lucy
4. _____ _____ of Mt. Tambora _____ _____ _____ _____ _____ _____ in 1816. - David

1. "화산"이라는 이름은 로마의 불의 신에게서 이름을 따왔다. – Mila
2. 전 세계 활화산의 75%는 '불의 고리(환태평양조산대)'를 따라 위치한다. – James
3. 멕시코의 Paricutin 화산은 성장을 멈추었다. – Lucy
4. Tambora산의 분출은 1816년에 비정상적으로 추운 여름을 초래했다. – David

My Writing Portfolio

1. The _____ _____
2. I _____ the movie *The Perfect Storm* _____ _____ .
3. The movie _____ _____ in 2000, and it _____ _____ _____ the German director Wolfgang Petersen.
4. It is _____ a big storm _____ _____ _____ _____ that put a fishing boat _____ _____ .
5. I liked the movie _____ _____ and very _____ .
6. Also, I liked the _____ _____ _____ _____ _____ George Clooney.
7. From the movie, I _____ that _____ _____ _____ can be very _____ .

1. 퍼펙트 스톰
2. 나는 지난 주말에 영화 '퍼펙트 스톰'을 봤다.
3. 그 영화는 2000년에 개봉했고, 독일 감독 Wolfgang Petersen이 연출했다.
4. 그것은 어선을 위험에 빠뜨린 대서양의 거대한 폭풍에 관한 것이다.
5. 나는 장면들이 흥미진진하고 매우 사실적이었기 때문에 이 영화가 좋았다.
6. 또한, 나는 주연 배우 George Clooney의 훌륭한 연기도 마음에 들었다.
7. 이 영화를 통해 나는 폭풍과 같은 자연재해가 매우 위험할 수 있다는 것을 배웠다.

※ 다음 우리말을 영어로 쓰시오.

My Speaking Portfolio Step 1

1. A: 정전됐어요.
   ➡ _____

2. 프라이팬에 불이 붙었어요.
   ➡ _____

3. 나는 엘리베이터에 갇혔어요.
   ➡ _____

4. 나는 뜨거운 물에 손을 데었어요.
   ➡ _____

5. 나는 계단에서 넘어져서 팔이 부러졌어요.
   ➡ _____

After You Read Details

1. "화산"이라는 이름은 로마의 불의 신에게서 이름을 따왔다. – Mila
   ➡ _____

2. 전 세계 활화산의 75%는 '불의 고리(환태평양조산대)'를 따라 위치한다. – James
   ➡ _____

3. 멕시코의 Paricutin 화산은 성장을 멈추었다. – Lucy
   ➡ _____

4. Tambora산의 분출은 1816년에 비정상적으로 추운 여름을 초래했다. – David
   ➡ _____

My Writing Portfolio

1. 퍼펙트 스톰
   ➡ _____

2. 나는 지난 주말에 영화 '퍼펙트 스톰'을 봤다.
   ➡ _____

3. 그 영화는 2000년에 개봉했고, 독일 감독 Wolfgang Petersen이 연출했다.
   ➡ _____

4. 그것은 어선을 위험에 빠뜨린 대서양의 거대한 폭풍에 관한 것이다.
   ➡ _____

5. 나는 장면들이 흥미진진하고 매우 사실적이었기 때문에 이 영화가 좋았다.
   ➡ _____

6. 또한, 나는 주연 배우 George Clooney의 훌륭한 연기도 마음에 들었다.
   ➡ _____

7. 이 영화를 통해 나는 폭풍과 같은 자연재해가 매우 위험할 수 있다는 것을 배웠다.
   ➡ _____

※ 다음 영어를 우리말로 쓰시오.

01	achieve	22	scared
02	confident	23	cheerful
03	banner	24	regret
04	tryout	25	challenging
05	worried	26	found
06	calm	27	imagination
07	capital	28	improve
08	offer	29	repair
09	opportunity	30	include
10	lifelong	31	mistaken
11	chase	32	decision
12	protection	33	rest
13	worth	34	skill
14	completely	35	break down
15	impatient	36	may[might] have p.p.
16	connect	37	deal with
17	delighted	38	break out
18	rule	39	used to
19	save	40	be ashamed of
20	serious	41	apply for
21	express	42	hang out with
		43	over and over

※ 다음 우리말을 영어로 쓰시오.

01 확신하는, 자신만만한

02 향상시키다, 개선하다

03 현수막

04 완전히, 전적으로

05 포함하다

06 일생[평생]의

07 이루다, 달성[성취]하다

08 침착한, 냉정한

09 표현하다

10 연결하다

11 설립하다

12 기분 좋은, 즐거운

13 아주 기뻐하는

14 쫓다, 추적하다

15 연습하다, 훈련하다

16 후회하다

17 수도

18 심사, 테스트

19 보호

20 도전적인

21 짜증 난, 참지 못하는

22 기회

23 ~할 가치가 있는

24 상상, 상상력

25 수리하다

26 기량, 기술

27 결정, 판단

28 구하다, 절약하다

29 무서워하는, 겁먹은

30 심각한, 진지한

31 잘못 알고 있는

32 나머지, 휴식

33 뽑다, 고르다

34 꽤, 상당히

35 지나가다, 흐르다

36 반복해서

37 고장 나다

38 ~했음에 틀림없다

39 ~을 부끄러워하다

40 발발[발생]하다

41 ~와 시간을 보내다

42 ~을 다루다

43 ~에 지원하다, ~을 신청하다

※ 다음 영영풀이에 알맞은 단어를 <보기>에서 골라 쓴 후, 우리말 뜻을 쓰시오.

1 _____ : to establish: _____

2 _____ : to join together: _____

3 _____ : the part that is left: _____

4 _____ : to make something new: _____

5 _____ : to have or give information: _____

6 _____ : chance for doing something: _____

7 _____ : showing a lack of patience: _____

8 _____ : the act of making up one's mind: _____

9 _____ : difficult in a way that is usually enjoyable: _____

10 _____ : a test of the potential of someone: _____

11 _____ : a long piece of cloth with words written on it: _____

12 _____ : to have something as part of a group or total: _____

13 _____ : acting or speaking sincerely and without joking: _____

14 _____ : a group of sports teams that play against each other: _____

15 _____ : to feel sorry about something that you did in the past: _____

16 _____ : good or important enough for something: _____

보기			
regret	decision	league	opportunity
banner	found	challenging	rest
worth	read	serious	impatient
tryout	connect	include	create

※ 다음 우리말과 일치하도록 빈칸에 알맞은 말을 쓰시오.

Listen - Listen & Answer Dialog 1

B: Hi, Sora. _____ are you doing?

G: I'm _____ _____. I'm _____ _____ the exam for Mana Animation High School.

B: Oh, _____ you? _____ is the exam?

G: _____ Friday, so I only have two days _____.

B: _____ it _____?

G: _____'s not easy _____ _____ _____ I want _____ _____. I _____ _____ _____ more.

B: Don't _____! You can _____ _____!

G: Thanks.

Listen - Listen & Answer Dialog 2

M: Nice _____ _____ you, Sora. Did you _____ _____ _____ the _____ _____?

G: I'm not _____, but I _____ _____ _____.

M: Okay. Let's start the interview. _____ _____ you _____ _____ Mana Animation High School?

G: Well, I'_____ really _____ drawing cartoons _____ I was a _____ _____.

M: So, you want to be a _____ _____?

G: That's not _____ _____. I want to be a game designer.

M: I see. _____ do you _____ is the _____ _____ a game designer needs?

G: _____ _____ imagination. A good designer should create a _____ new world in a game.

M: Sounds good.

Speak - Talk in pairs.

A: What's the _____?

B: I feel _____. I should have _____ food for the winter.

A: _____ worry. I'll _____ my food _____ you.

B: Thanks.

Listen - Listen More

G: Hi, Jiho.

B: Hi, Amber. It's nice _____ _____ you on the bus.

G: Yeah, but _____ _____ we're going to _____ _____.

B: Yeah. I _____ _____ _____ _____ _____ the school festival.

G: Me, too. I _____ _____ _____ my alarm. I forgot.

B: I understand. That _____ _____ _____ to me when I'm _____, too.

G: How about you? _____ _____ you _____?

B: Well, I _____ _____ early. But _____ _____ me some time to _____ _____ _____.

G: Oh, I see. _____ _____ _____ a heavy _____ _____. We should _____ _____ and run.

B: No, _____ _____. The traffic is starting to move again. Let's _____ _____.

G: Okay. I just hope we're not _____ late.

여: 지호야, 안녕.
남: Amber, 안녕. 버스에서 너를 보다니 반갑다.
여: 맞아, 그런데 걱정스럽게도 우리가 늦을 것 같아.
남: 그러게. 학교 축제에 늦고 싶지 않은데.
여: 나도 그래. 알람을 맞출걸. 내가 깜빡했어.
남: 이해해. 나도 피곤할 때 그런 일이 많이 일어나.
여: 너는? 무슨 일로 늦었어?
남: 음, 난 일찍 일어났어. 그런데 머리를 손질하느라 시간이 좀 걸렸어.
여: 아, 그렇구나. 우리 교통 체증에 갇혔어. 버스에서 내려서 뛰어가자.
남: 아니, 네가 잘못 생각하는 거야. 차들이 다시 움직이기 시작해. 내리지 말자.
여: 알았어. 너무 늦지 않기를 바랄 뿐이야.

Wrap Up 6

B: What do you want to do _____ you _____ _____?

G: I want to work _____ robots.

B: Are you _____ _____ _____ robots?

G: No, _____ not _____ _____. I want to _____ robots.

B: I see. But _____?

G: _____ I _____ it'll be a good job in the future.

남: 너는 커서 무엇을 하고 싶니?
여: 나는 로봇과 관련된 일을 하고 싶어.
남: 로봇 제작하는 것에 관심 있니?
여: 아니, 꼭 그렇지는 않아. 나는 로봇을 수리하고 싶어.
남: 그렇구나. 그런데 왜?
여: 그것이 미래에 좋은 직업이 될 거라고 생각하기 때문이야.

Wrap Up 7

G: My computer _____ _____.

B: _____ come?

G: I opened an e-mail from a stranger. I _____ _____ _____ that.

B: If I _____ _____, _____ _____ help from a computer service center _____ _____.

여: 내 컴퓨터가 바이러스에 걸렸어.
남: 어쩌다가 그랬니?
여: 모르는 사람에게서 온 이메일을 열었지. 그러지 말았어야 해.
남: 내가 너라면, 지금 바로 컴퓨터 서비스 센터에서 도움을 받겠어.

※ 다음 우리말에 맞도록 대화를 영어로 쓰시오.

Listen - Listen & Answer Dialog 1

B: _____

G: _____

_____

B: _____

G: _____

B: _____

G: _____

B: _____

G: _____

남: 안녕, 소라야. 뭘 하고 있니?

여: 만화를 그리고 있어. 마나 애니메이션 고등학교 입학시험을 준비하고 있어.

남: 아, 그래? 시험이 언제야?

여: 금요일. 그래서 이틀밖에 안 남았어.

남: 어떻게 되고 있니?

여: 내가 표현하고 싶은 것을 그리기가 쉽지 않아. 나는 더 연습했어야 해.

남: 걱정하지 마! 넌 해낼 수 있어!

여: 고마워.

Listen - Listen & Answer Dialog 2

M: _____

G: _____

M: _____

_____

G: _____

M: _____

G: _____

M: _____

G: _____

M: _____

남: 소라 학생, 만나서 반가워요. 소묘 시험은 잘 봤나요?

여: 잘 모르겠지만 최선을 다했습니다.

남: 알겠어요. 면접을 시작합시다. 왜 마나 애니메이션 고등학교에 지원했나요?

여: 음, 저는 어렸을 때부터 만화 그리는 것을 정말 좋아했습니다.

남: 그렇다면, 만화가가 되고 싶나요?

여: 꼭 그렇지는 않습니다. 저는 게임 디자이너가 되고 싶습니다.

남: 그렇군요. 게임 디자이너에게 필요한 가장 중요한 기량이 무엇이라고 생각하나요?

여: 상상력이라고 말씀드리겠습니다. 훌륭한 게임 디자이너는 게임 속에서 완전히 새로운 세계를 창조해야 하거든요.

남: 좋습니다.

Speak - Talk in pairs.

A: _____

B: _____

A: _____

B: _____

A: 무슨 일이야?

B: 배가 고파. 나는 겨울용 식량을 저장해 놨어야 해.

A: 걱정하지 마. 내가 내 식량을 나눠 줄게.

B: 고마워.

Listen - Listen More

G: _____

B: _____

G: _____

B: _____

G: _____

B: _____

G: _____

B: _____

G: _____

B: _____

G: _____

Wrap Up 6

B: _____

G: _____

B: _____

G: _____

B: _____

G: _____

Wrap Up 7

G: _____

B: _____

G: _____

B: _____

여: 지호야, 안녕.

남: Amber, 안녕. 버스에서 너를 보다니 반갑다.

여: 맞아, 그런데 걱정스럽게도 우리가 늦을 것 같아.

남: 그러게. 학교 축제에 늦고 싶지 않은데.

여: 나도 그래. 알람을 맞출걸. 내가 깜빡했어.

남: 이해해. 나도 피곤할 때 그런 일이 많이 일어나.

여: 너는? 무슨 일로 늦었어?

남: 음, 난 일찍 일어났어. 그런데 머리를 손질하느라 시간이 좀 걸렸어.

여: 아, 그렇구나. 우리 교통 체증에 갇혔어. 버스에서 내려서 뛰어가자.

남: 아니, 네가 잘못 생각하는 거야. 차들이 다시 움직이기 시작해. 내리지 말자.

여: 알았어. 너무 늦지 않기를 바랄 뿐이야.

남: 너는 커서 무엇을 하고 싶니?

여: 나는 로봇과 관련된 일을 하고 싶어.

남: 로봇 제작하는 것에 관심 있니?

여: 아니, 꼭 그렇지는 않아. 나는 로봇을 수리하고 싶어.

남: 그렇구나. 그런데 왜?

여: 그것이 미래에 좋은 직업이 될 거라고 생각하기 때문이야.

여: 내 컴퓨터가 바이러스에 걸렸어.

남: 어쩌다가 그랬니?

여: 모르는 사람에게서 온 이메일을 열었지. 그러지 말았어야 해.

남: 내가 너라면, 지금 바로 컴퓨터 서비스 센터에서 도움을 받겠어.

※ 다음 우리말과 일치하도록 빈칸에 알맞은 것을 골라 쓰시오.

1 MY _____ _____ _____
A. DREAMS   B. BASEBALL   C. GRANDMOTHER'S

2 My grandmother Helen _____ be a _____ in a restaurant in a small town _____ South Bend, Indiana.
A. near   B. to   C. cook   D. used

3 She does not _____ _____, but she still enjoys making _____ food, _____ I love so much.
A. which   B. anymore   C. delicious   D. work

4 Food is _____ of the many things _____ _____ _____.
A. connect   B. one   C. us   D. that

5 _____ _____ us most _____, _____, is baseball.
A. however   B. what   C. strongly   D. connects

6 _____ I visit her on _____, my grandmother often tells me _____ stories about playing baseball _____ in the 1940s.
A. back   B. weekends   C. exciting   D. when

7 She _____ _____ _____ the sport very much.
A. have   B. must   C. loved

8 I _____ these stories _____ _____ over.
A. over   B. to   C. and   D. listen

9 She always _____, " _____ _____ _____ you want, Sarah.
A. after   B. go   C. says   D. what

10 Don't be _____ of trying _____ _____ or _____.
A. challenging   B. afraid   C. something   D. new

11 _____ be _____ _____ _____ ."
A. ashamed   B. don't   C. of   D. failing

12 _____ 1943, the All-American Girls _____ Baseball League _____ _____.
A. founded   B. in   C. was   D. Professional

13 This league was _____ for baseball fans _____ many of America's young men _____ _____ in World War II.
A. fighting   B. created   C. because   D. were

14 Helen was told that _____ _____ be _____ _____ right in South Bend.
A. would   B. tryouts   C. there   D. local

15 She wondered, " _____ _____ it be _____ to be on a baseball team and to make it to the _____ for my hometown?"
A. like   B. what   C. finals   D. would

16 She _____ a large banner _____ at the baseball field _____ the name Helen Baker.
A. included   B. imagined   C. which   D. hanging

1 할머니의 야구 꿈

2 우리 할머니 Helen은 Indiana주 South Bend 근처 작은 마을에 있는 식당의 요리사였다.

3 할머니는 더 이상 일을 하지 않지만 여전히 맛있는 음식을 즐겨 만드시고, 나는 그 음식들을 무척 좋아한다.

4 음식은 우리를 연결하는 많은 것 가운데 하나이다.

5 하지만 우리를 가장 강하게 연결하는 것은 바로 야구이다.

6 주말마다 할머니 댁에 가면, 할머니는 종종 과거 1940년대의 야구 경기에 관해 흥미로운 이야기를 내게 들려주신다.

7 그녀는 야구를 무척 좋아했던 게 분명하다.

8 나는 이 이야기들을 몇 번이고 듣는다.

9 그녀는 항상 "네가 원하는 것을 이루려고 노력하렴, Sarah.

10 새로운 것이나 도전적인 것을 시도해 보기를 두려워하지 말거라.

11 실패하는 것을 부끄러워하지 마라."라고 말씀하신다.

12 1943년, 전미 여자 프로야구 리그가 창립되었다.

13 미국의 청년 중 많은 사람들이 제2차 세계대전에 참전해 있었기 때문에 이 리그가 야구 팬들을 위해 만들어졌다.

14 Helen 할머니는 지역 심사가 바로 South Bend에서 있을 거라고 들었다.

15 그녀는 "야구 팀에 들어가서 고향을 위해 결승전까지 진출한다는 건 어떤 기분일까?"라며 궁금해했다.

16 그녀는 Helen Baker라는 이름이 포함된 큰 현수막이 야구장에 걸려 있는 것을 상상했다.

17 On the day of the tryouts, all the rules were _____ by an old man in a _____, who sounded very _____ and _____.

    A. suit   B. unkind   C. explained   D. serious

18 She _____ that _____ a suit in the hot sun might have _____ him _____.

    A. impatient   B. wearing   C. made   D. thought

19 _____ that day, Helen played baseball _____ _____ with many _____ young women.

    A. hours   B. on   C. other   D. for

20 She was _____ _____ _____ _____ her baseball dreams!

    A. after   B. excited   C. go   D. to

21 _____ a week _____, Helen _____ a letter in the _____.

    A. mailbox   B. about   C. found   D. later

22 _____ was _____ people who _____ _____ the girls' baseball league in Chicago.

    A. worked   B. from   C. for   D. it

23 It _____ that she _____ been invited to the league's _____ in Chicago!

    A. main   B. had   C. tryouts   D. read

24 _____ the days _____ _____, however, Helen became _____ that she might fail.

    A. worried   B. as   C. went   D. by

25 She also became worried about _____ alone to Chicago, _____ was _____ _____ from home.

    A. which   B. away   C. traveling   D. far

26 When the day of the main _____ came, she was _____ _____ _____ go.

    A. too   B. tryouts   C. to   D. afraid

27 My grandmother has _____ the _____ of her life _____ her _____.

    A. regretting   B. spent   C. decision   D. rest

28 When she _____ a baseball game on TV, she often says, "I _____ _____ _____ to Chicago.

    A. have   B. watches   C. should   D. gone

29 You know, all your dreams are _____ _____, _____ if you catch only a _____ of them.

    A. chasing   B. few   C. worth   D. even

30 _____ _____ an _____."

    A. miss   B. never   C. opportunity

---

17 심사 당일 모든 규칙이 정장을 입은 나이 든 남자에 의해 설명되었는데, 그는 무척 진지하고 불친절하게 들렸다.

18 뜨거운 태양 아래 정장을 입고 있는 것이 그를 짜증나게 만들었을지도 모른다고 그녀는 생각했다.

19 그날, Helen 할머니는 다른 젊은 여성들과 함께 몇 시간 동안 야구를 했다.

20 그녀는 자신의 야구 꿈을 좇아가게 되어 신이 났다!

21 일주일쯤 지나, Helen 할머니는 우편함에서 편지 한 통을 발견했다.

22 그것은 시카고에 있는 여자 야구리그에서 일하는 사람들이 보낸 것이었다.

23 그 편지에는 그녀가 시카고에서 열리는 리그의 본심사에 초청되었다고 적혀 있었다!

24 하지만 하루하루 갈수록, Helen 할머니는 심사에 떨어질까봐 걱정되었다.

25 그녀는 또한 시카고까지 혼자 여행하는 것이 걱정되었는데, 시카고는 집에서 멀리 떨어진 곳이었다.

26 본심사가 있는 날이 되었을 때, 그녀는 너무 두려워서 갈 수 없었다.

27 할머니는 남은 인생을 자신의 결정을 후회하며 보내셨다.

28 텔레비전에서 야구 경기를 볼 때, 그녀는 종종 "난 시카고에 갔어야 해.

29 너도 알겠지만, 모든 꿈은 추구할 가치가 있단다, 비록 일부만 이루게 되더라도 말이야.

30 절대 기회를 놓치지 마라."라고 말씀하신다.

※ 다음 우리말과 일치하도록 빈칸에 알맞은 것을 골라 쓰시오.

1 MY _____ BASEBALL _____

2 My grandmother Helen _____ _____ _____
_____ in a restaurant in a small town _____ South Bend,
Indiana.

3 She does not work _____, but she still _____ _____
delicious food, _____ I love so much.

4 Food is _____ of the many things _____ _____ _____.

5 _____ _____ us most _____, however, _____ baseball.

6 When I visit her _____ _____, my grandmother often tells
me _____ _____ about playing baseball _____ in the
1940s.

7 She _____ _____ _____ the sport very much.

8 I _____ _____ _____ these stories _____ _____ _____.

9 She always says, "_____ _____ _____ you want, Sarah.

10 Don't be _____ _____ trying _____ _____ _____
_____.

11 _____ _____ _____ _____ failing."

12 In 1943, the All-American Girls Professional Baseball League
_____ _____.

13 This league _____ _____ for baseball fans because many of
America's young men _____ _____ in World War II.

14 Helen was told that _____ _____ _____ _____
_____ right in South Bend.

15 She wondered, "_____ _____ _____ _____ _____
to be on a baseball team and to make it to _____ _____ for
my hometown?"

16 She _____ a large banner _____ at the baseball field
_____ _____ the name Helen Baker.

1 할머니의 야구 꿈

2 우리 할머니 Helen은 Indiana주 South Bend 근처 작은 마을에 있는 식당의 요리사였다.

3 할머니는 더 이상 일을 하지 않지만 여전히 맛있는 음식을 즐겨 만드시고, 나는 그 음식들을 무척 좋아한다.

4 음식은 우리를 연결하는 많은 것 가운데 하나이다.

5 하지만 우리를 가장 강하게 연결하는 것은 바로 야구이다.

6 주말마다 할머니 댁에 가면, 할머니는 종종 과거 1940년대의 야구 경기에 관해 흥미로운 이야기를 내게 들려주신다.

7 그녀는 야구를 무척 좋아했던 게 분명하다.

8 나는 이 이야기들을 몇 번이고 듣는다.

9 그녀는 항상 "네가 원하는 것을 이루려고 노력하렴, Sarah.

10 새로운 것이나 도전적인 것을 시도해 보기를 두려워하지 말거라.

11 실패하는 것을 부끄러워하지 마라."라고 말씀하신다.

12 1943년, 전미 여자 프로야구 리그가 창립되었다.

13 미국의 청년 중 많은 사람들이 제2차 세계대전에 참전해 있었기 때문에 이 리그가 야구 팬들을 위해 만들어졌다.

14 Helen 할머니는 지역 심사가 바로 South Bend에서 있을 거라고 들었다.

15 그녀는 "야구 팀에 들어가서 고향을 위해 결승전까지 진출한다는 건 어떤 기분일까?"라며 궁금해했다.

16 그녀는 Helen Baker라는 이름이 포함된 큰 현수막이 야구장에 걸려 있는 것을 상상했다.

17 On the day of the tryouts, all the rules _____ _____ by an old man _____ _____ _____, who sounded very _____ and unkind.

18 She thought that _____ _____ _____ in the hot sun _____ _____ _____ him _____.

19 On that day, Helen played baseball _____ _____ with many _____ young _____.

20 She was excited _____ _____ _____ her baseball dreams!

21 About a week _____, Helen _____ _____ _____ in the mailbox.

22 _____ _____ _____ people who worked for the girls' baseball league in Chicago.

23 _____ _____ that she _____ _____ _____ to the _____ _____ _____ in Chicago!

24 _____ the days _____ _____, however, Helen became _____ that she might fail.

25 She also became _____ _____ traveling alone to Chicago, _____ was _____ _____ _____ home.

26 When the day of the _____ _____ came, she was _____ afraid _____ go.

27 My grandmother _____ _____ the rest of her life _____ her decision.

28 When she watches a baseball game on TV, she often says, "I _____ _____ _____ to Chicago.

29 You know, all your dreams _____ _____ _____, _____ _____ you catch only a few of them.

30 _____ _____ an _____."

---

17 심사 당일 모든 규칙이 정장을 입은 나이 든 남자에 의해 설명되었는데, 그는 무척 진지하고 불친절하게 들렸다.

18 뜨거운 태양 아래 정장을 입고 있는 것이 그를 짜증나게 만들었을지도 모른다고 그녀는 생각했다.

19 그날, Helen 할머니는 다른 젊은 여성들과 함께 몇 시간 동안 야구를 했다.

20 그녀는 자신의 야구 꿈을 좇아가게 되어 신이 났다!

21 일주일쯤 지나, Helen 할머니는 우편함에서 편지 한 통을 발견했다.

22 그것은 시카고에 있는 여자 야구리그에서 일하는 사람들이 보낸 것이었다.

23 그 편지에는 그녀가 시카고에서 열리는 리그의 본심사에 초청되었다고 적혀 있었다!

24 하지만 하루하루 갈수록, Helen 할머니는 심사에 떨어질까봐 걱정되었다.

25 그녀는 또한 시카고까지 혼자 여행하는 것이 걱정되었는데, 시카고는 집에서 멀리 떨어진 곳이었다.

26 본심사가 있는 날이 되었을 때, 그녀는 너무 두려워서 갈 수 없었다.

27 할머니는 남은 인생을 자신의 결정을 후회하며 보내셨다.

28 텔레비전에서 야구 경기를 볼 때, 그녀는 종종 "난 시카고에 갔어야 해.

29 너도 알겠지만, 모든 꿈은 추구할 가치가 있단다, 비록 일부만 이루게 되더라도 말이야.

30 절대 기회를 놓치지 마라."라고 말씀하신다.

※ 다음 문장을 우리말로 쓰시오.

1 MY GRANDMOTHER'S BASEBALL DREAMS
➡ _____

2 My grandmother Helen used to be a cook in a restaurant in a small town near South Bend, Indiana.
➡ _____

3 She does not work anymore, but she still enjoys making delicious food, which I love so much.
➡ _____

4 Food is one of the many things that connect us.
➡ _____

5 What connects us most strongly, however, is baseball.
➡ _____

6 When I visit her on weekends, my grandmother often tells me exciting stories about playing baseball back in the 1940s.
➡ _____

7 She must have loved the sport very much.
➡ _____

8 I listen to these stories over and over.
➡ _____

9 She always says, "Go after what you want, Sarah.
➡ _____

10 Don't be afraid of trying something new or challenging.
➡ _____

11 Don't be ashamed of failing."
➡ _____

12 In 1943, the All-American Girls Professional Baseball League was founded.
➡ _____

13 This league was created for baseball fans because many of America's young men were fighting in World War II.
➡ _____

14 Helen was told that there would be local tryouts right in South Bend.
➡ _____

15 She wondered, "What would it be like to be on a baseball team and to make it to the finals for my hometown?"
➡ _____

16 She imagined a large banner hanging at the baseball field which included the name Helen Baker.

➡ _____

17 On the day of the tryouts, all the rules were explained by an old man in a suit, who sounded very serious and unkind.

➡ _____

18 She thought that wearing a suit in the hot sun might have made him impatient.

➡ _____

19 On that day, Helen played baseball for hours with many other young women.

➡ _____

20 She was excited to go after her baseball dreams!

➡ _____

21 About a week later, Helen found a letter in the mailbox.

➡ _____

22 It was from people who worked for the girls' baseball league in Chicago.

➡ _____

23 It read that she had been invited to the league's main tryouts in Chicago!

➡ _____

24 As the days went by, however, Helen became worried that she might fail.

➡ _____

25 She also became worried about traveling alone to Chicago, which was far away from home.

➡ _____

26 When the day of the main tryouts came, she was too afraid to go.

➡ _____

27 My grandmother has spent the rest of her life regretting her decision.

➡ _____

28 When she watches a baseball game on TV, she often says, "I should have gone to Chicago.

➡ _____

29 You know, all your dreams are worth chasing, even if you catch only a few of them.

➡ _____

30 Never miss an opportunity."

➡ _____

※ 다음 괄호 안의 단어들을 우리말에 맞도록 바르게 배열하시오.

1   (GRANDMOTHER'S / MY / DREAMS / BASEBALL)
➡ _____

2   (grandmother / my / used / Helen / be / to / cook / a / a / in / in / restarant / a / small / near / town / Bend, / South / Indiana.)
➡ _____

3   (does / she / work / not / anymore, / she / but / enjoys / still / delicious / making / food, / I / which / so / love / much.)
➡ _____

4   (is / food / of / one / many / the / things / connect / that / us.)
➡ _____

5   (connects / what / most / us / however, / strongly, / baseball. / is)
➡ _____

6   (I / when / visit / on / her / weekends, / grandmother / my / often / me / tells / stories / exciting / playing / about / back / baseball / the / in / 1940s.)
➡ _____

7   (must / she / loved / have / sport / the / much. / very)
➡ _____

8   (listen / I / these / to / over / stories / over. / and)
➡ _____

9   (always / she / says, / after / "go / you / what / Sarah. / want,)
➡ _____

10   (be / don't / of / afraid / something / trying / or / new / challenging.)
➡ _____

11   (be / don't / of / ashamed / failing.")
➡ _____

12   (1943, / in / All-American / the / Professional / Girls / League / Baseball / founded. / was)
➡ _____

13   (league / this / created / was / baseball / for / because / fans / of / many / young / America's / were / men / in / fighting / War / World / II.)
➡ _____

14   (was / Helen / that / told / would / there / local / be / right / tryouts / in / Bend. / South)
➡ _____

15   (wondered, / she / would / "what / be / it / to / like / on / be / a / team / baseball / and / make / to / it / the / to / for / finals / hometown?" / my)
➡ _____

---

1   할머니의 야구 꿈

2   우리 할머니 Helen은 Indiana주 South Bend 근처 작은 마을에 있는 식당의 요리사였다.

3   할머니는 더 이상 일을 하지 않지만 여전히 맛있는 음식을 즐겨 만드시고, 나는 그 음식들을 무척 좋아한다.

4   음식은 우리를 연결하는 많은 것 가운데 하나이다.

5   하지만 우리를 가장 강하게 연결하는 것은 바로 야구이다.

6   주말마다 할머니 댁에 가면, 할머니는 종종 과거 1940년대의 야구 경기에 관해 흥미로운 이야기를 내게 들려주신다.

7   그녀는 야구를 무척 좋아했던 게 분명하다.

8   나는 이 이야기들을 몇 번이고 듣는다.

9   그녀는 항상 "네가 원하는 것을 이루려고 노력하렴, Sarah.

10   새로운 것이나 도전적인 것을 시도해 보기를 두려워하지 말거라.

11   실패하는 것을 부끄러워하지 마라."라고 말씀하신다.

12   1943년, 전미 여자 프로야구 리그가 창립되었다.

13   미국의 청년 중 많은 사람들이 제2차 세계대전에 참전해 있었기 때문에 이 리그가 야구 팬들을 위해 만들어졌다.

14   Helen 할머니는 지역 심사가 바로 South Bend에서 있을 거라고 들었다.

15   그녀는 "야구 팀에 들어가서 고향을 위해 결승전까지 진출한다는 건 어떤 기분일까?"라며 궁금해했다.

16 (imagined / she / large / a / hanging / banner / the / at / field / baseball / included / which / name / the / Baker. / Helen)

➡ _____

17 (the / on / of / day / tryouts, / the / all / were / rules / by / explained / an / man / old / a / in / suit, / sounded / who / serious / very / unkind. / and)

➡ _____

18 (thought / she / wearing / that / suit / a / the / in / sun / hot / have / might / him / made / impatient.)

➡ _____

19 (that / on / day, / played / Helen / for / baseball / hours / many / with / young / ohter / women.)

➡ _____

20 (was / she / to / excited / go / her / after / dreams! / baseball)

➡ _____

21 (a / about / later, / week / found / Helen / letter / a / the / in / mailbox.)

➡ _____

22 (was / it / people / from / worked / who / the / for / baseball / girls' / in / league / Chicago.)

➡ _____

23 (read / it / she / that / been / had / invited / the / to / main / league's / tryouts / Chicago! / in)

➡ _____

24 (the / as / went / days / by, / Helen / however, / worried / became / she / that / fail. / might)

➡ _____

25 (also / she / worried / became / traveling / about / to / alone / which / Chicago, / far / was / from / away / home.)

➡ _____

26 (the / when / day / the / of / tryouts / main / came, / was / she / afraid / too / go. / to)

➡ _____

27 (grandmother / my / spent / has / rest / the / her / of / regretting / life / decision. / her)

➡ _____

28 (she / when / a / watches / game / baseball / TV, / on / often / she / says, / should / "I / gone / have / Chicago. / to)

➡ _____

29 (know, / you / your / all / are / dreams / chasing, / worth / if / even / catch / you / a / only / of / few / them.)

➡ _____

30 (miss / never / opportunity." / an)

➡ _____

16 그녀는 Helen Baker라는 이름이 포함된 큰 현수막이 야구장에 걸려 있는 것을 상상했다.

17 심사 당일 모든 규칙이 정장을 입은 나이 든 남자에 의해 설명되었는데, 그는 무척 진지하고 불친절하게 들렸다.

18 뜨거운 태양 아래 정장을 입고 있는 것이 그를 짜증나게 만들었을지도 모른다고 그녀는 생각했다.

19 그날, Helen 할머니는 다른 젊은 여성들과 함께 몇 시간 동안 야구를 했다.

20 그녀는 자신의 야구 꿈을 좇아가게 되어 신이 났다!

21 일주일쯤 지나, Helen 할머니는 우편함에서 편지 한 통을 발견했다.

22 그것은 시카고에 있는 여자 야구리그에서 일하는 사람들이 보낸 것이었다.

23 그 편지에는 그녀가 시카고에서 열리는 리그의 본심사에 초청되었다고 적혀 있었다!

24 하지만 하루하루 갈수록, Helen 할머니는 심사에 떨어질까봐 걱정되었다.

25 그녀는 또한 시카고까지 혼자 여행하는 것이 걱정되었는데, 시카고는 집에서 멀리 떨어진 곳이었다.

26 본심사가 있는 날이 되었을 때, 그녀는 너무 두려워서 갈 수 없었다.

27 할머니는 남은 인생을 자신의 결정을 후회하며 보내셨다.

28 텔레비전에서 야구 경기를 볼 때, 그녀는 종종 "난 시카고에 갔어야 해.

29 너도 알겠지만, 모든 꿈은 추구할 가치가 있단다. 비록 일부만 이루게 되더라도 말이야.

30 절대 기회를 놓치지 마라."라고 말씀하신다.

※ 다음 우리말을 영어로 쓰시오.

1 할머니의 야구 꿈

➡ _____

2 우리 할머니 Helen은 Indiana주 South Bend 근처 작은 마을에 있는 식당의 요리사였다.

➡ _____

_____

3 할머니는 더 이상 일을 하지 않지만 여전히 맛있는 음식을 즐겨 만드시고, 나는 그 음식들을 무척 좋아한다.

➡ _____

4 음식은 우리를 연결하는 많은 것 가운데 하나이다.

➡ _____

5 하지만 우리를 가장 강하게 연결하는 것은 바로 야구이다.

➡ _____

6 주말마다 할머니 댁에 가면, 할머니는 종종 과거 1940년대의 야구 경기에 관해 흥미로운 이야기를 내게 들려주신다.

➡ _____

_____

7 그녀는 야구를 무척 좋아했던 게 분명하다.

➡ _____

8 나는 이 이야기들을 몇 번이고 듣는다.

➡ _____

9 그녀는 항상 "네가 원하는 것을 이루려고 노력하렴, Sarah.

➡ _____

10 새로운 것이나 도전적인 것을 시도해 보기를 두려워하지 말거라.

➡ _____

11 실패하는 것을 부끄러워하지 마라."라고 말씀하신다.

➡ _____

12 1943년, 전미 여자 프로야구 리그가 창립되었다.

➡ _____

13 미국의 청년 중 많은 사람들이 제2차 세계대전에 참전해 있었기 때문에 이 리그가 야구 팬들을 위해 만들어졌다.

➡ _____

_____

14 Helen 할머니는 지역 심사가 바로 South Bend에서 있을 거라고 들었다.

➡ _____

15 그녀는 "야구 팀에 들어가서 고향을 위해 결승전까지 진출한다는 건 어떤 기분일까?"라며 궁금해했다.

➡ _____

_____

16 그녀는 Helen Baker라는 이름이 포함된 큰 현수막이 야구장에 걸려 있는 것을 상상했다.

➡ _____

_____

17 심사 당일 모든 규칙이 정장을 입은 나이 든 남자에 의해 설명되었는데, 그는 무척 진지하고 불친절하게 들렸다.

➡ _____

_____

18 뜨거운 태양 아래 정장을 입고 있는 것이 그를 짜증나게 만들었을지도 모른다고 그녀는 생각했다.

➡ _____

19 그날, Helen 할머니는 다른 젊은 여성들과 함께 몇 시간 동안 야구를 했다.

➡ _____

20 그녀는 자신의 야구 꿈을 좇아가게 되어 신이 났다!

➡ _____

21 일주일쯤 지나, Helen 할머니는 우편함에서 편지 한 통을 발견했다.

➡ _____

22 그것은 시카고에 있는 여자 야구 리그에서 일하는 사람들이 보낸 것이었다.

➡ _____

23 그 편지에는 그녀가 시카고에서 열리는 리그의 본심사에 초청되었다고 적혀 있었다!

➡ _____

24 하지만 하루하루 갈수록, Helen 할머니는 심사에 떨어질까봐 걱정되었다.

➡ _____

25 그녀는 또한 시카고까지 혼자 여행하는 것이 걱정되었는데, 시카고는 집에서 멀리 떨어진 곳이었다.

➡ _____

26 본심사가 있는 날이 되었을 때, 그녀는 너무 두려워서 갈 수 없었다.

➡ _____

27 할머니는 남은 인생을 자신의 결정을 후회하며 보내셨다.

➡ _____

28 텔레비전에서 야구 경기를 볼 때, 그녀는 종종 "난 시카고에 갔어야 해.

➡ _____

29 너도 알겠지만, 모든 꿈은 추구할 가치가 있단다, 비록 일부만 이루게 되더라도 말이야.

➡ _____

30 절대 기회를 놓치지 마라."라고 말씀하신다.

➡ _____

※ 다음 우리말과 일치하도록 빈칸에 알맞은 말을 쓰시오.

After You Read Graphic Organizer

Cause

1. The Second World War _____ _____.

2. She loved baseball _____ _____.

3. She _____ not _____ her success. Also, she _____ _____ _____ _____.

Effect

4. In 1943, the All-American Girls Professional Baseball League was _____.

5. She _____ _____ _____ _____ in South Bend.

6. She didn't go to the _____ _____.

My Writing Portfolio

1. JANE GOODALL, _____ _____ _____

2. Jane Goodall _____ _____ _____ _____, _____, in 1934.

3. _____ _____ chimpanzees began _____ _____ _____ _____ about Tarzan.

4. She _____ _____ _____ wild chimpanzees in Africa _____ _____ _____.

5. She _____ also _____ _____ for the _____ _____.

6. In 1995, she _____ the Hubbard Medal _____ _____ _____ _____.

7. _____ _____ _____ _____ _____, we have _____ _____ _____ a lot about chimpanzees.

8. Jane Goodall is _____ _____ _____ _____ _____ in history.

Words in Action

1. The Cheetahs _____ _____ the game, and their fans _____ _____ _____ _____ _____.

2. _____ Jason _____ _____ and _____ the ball, the game ends.

3. Oh my! He _____ the ball!

4. The Ducks _____ _____ _____, and the _____ _____.

5. Jason _____ _____ and _____.

6. The Ducks fans are _____ _____, _____ the Cheetahs fans _____ _____ and _____.

원인
1. 제2차 세계대전이 발발했다.
2 그녀는 야구를 무척 좋아했다.
3. 그녀는 자신의 성공을 확신하지 못했다. 또한 그녀는 혼자 여행하는 것을 두려워했다.

결과
4. 1943년, 전미 여자 프로야구 리그가 창립되었다.
5. 그녀는 South Bend의 지역 심사에 참가했다.
6. 그녀는 본심사에 가지 않았다.

1. Jane Goodall, 침팬지의 어머니
2. Jane Goodall은 1934년 영국 런던에서 태어났다.
3. 침팬지에 대한 관심은 그녀가 타잔에 관해 읽었을 때 시작되었다.
4. 그녀는 20대 때부터 아프리카에서 야생 침팬지를 연구해 오고 있다.
5. 그녀는 침팬지 보호를 위해서도 노력해 오고 있다.
6. 1995년에 그녀는 야생 동물 보호에 대한 공로를 인정받아 허버드상을 받았다.
7. 일생을 바친 그녀의 연구 덕분에, 우리는 침팬지에 관해 많이 알게 되었다.
8. Jane Goodall은 역사상 가장 위대한 과학자 중 한 명이다.

1. Cheetahs가 경기를 이기고 있고, 팬들이 신나는 노래를 부르고 있습니다.
2. Jason이 침착함을 유지해서 공을 잡으면 경기가 끝납니다.
3. 오, 이럴수가! 그가 공을 놓칩니다!
4. Ducks는 2루로 진루하고, 경기는 계속됩니다.
5. Jason은 창피하고 긴장한 것처럼 보입니다.
6. Ducks 팬들은 열광하고 있는 반면, Cheetahs 팬들은 두렵고 걱정스러운 것처럼 보입니다.

※ 다음 우리말을 영어로 쓰시오.

After You Read Graphic Organizer

원인

1. 제2차 세계대전이 발발했다.
➡ _____

2. 그녀는 야구를 무척 좋아했다.
➡ _____

3. 그녀는 자신의 성공을 확신하지 못했다. 또한 그녀는 혼자 여행하는 것을 두려워했다.
➡ _____

결과

4. 1943년, 전미 여자 프로야구 리그가 창립되었다.
➡ _____

5. 그녀는 South Bend의 지역 심사에 참가했다.
➡ _____

6. 그녀는 본심사에 가지 않았다.
➡ _____

My Writing Portfolio

1. Jane Goodall, 침팬지의 어머니
➡ _____

2. Jane Goodall은 1934년 영국 런던에서 태어났다.
➡ _____

3. 침팬지에 대한 관심은 그녀가 타잔에 관해 읽었을 때 시작되었다.
➡ _____

4. 그녀는 20대 때부터 아프리카에서 야생 침팬지를 연구해 오고 있다.
➡ _____

5. 그녀는 침팬지 보호를 위해서도 노력해 오고 있다.
➡ _____

6. 1995년에 그녀는 야생 동물 보호에 대한 공로를 인정받아 허버드상을 받았다.
➡ _____

7. 일생을 바친 그녀의 연구 덕분에, 우리는 침팬지에 관해 많이 알게 되었다.
➡ _____

8. Jane Goodall은 역사상 가장 위대한 과학자 중 한 명이다.
➡ _____

Words in Action

1. Cheetahs가 경기를 이기고 있고, 팬들이 신나는 노래를 부르고 있습니다.
➡ _____

2. Jason이 침착함을 유지해서 공을 잡으면 경기가 끝납니다.
➡ _____

3. 오, 이럴수가! 그가 공을 놓칩니다!
➡ _____

4. Ducks는 2루로 진루하고, 경기는 계속됩니다.
➡ _____

5. Jason은 창피하고 긴장한 것처럼 보입니다.
➡ _____

6. Ducks 팬들은 열광하고 있는 반면, Cheetahs 팬들은 무섭고 걱정스러운 것처럼 보입니다.
➡ _____

※ 다음 영어를 우리말로 쓰시오.

01	shout		21	record
02	relief		22	scream
03	safety product		23	thick
04	actually		24	whisper
05	hurt		25	as usual
06	lesson		26	set off
07	cycle		27	in reply
08	throughout		28	reach out
09	dirt		29	day in and day out
10	entrance		30	inch by inch
11	though		31	after a while
12	wooden		32	side by side
13	breathe		33	as soon as
14	gateway		34	at first
15	cast		35	in other words
16	manager		36	all of a sudden
17	thumping		37	manage to
18	opening		38	thanks to
19	particular		39	used to
20	would		40	stop ~ from -ing

※ 다음 우리말을 영어로 쓰시오.

01 나무로 된, 목재의 _____

02 안전 제품 _____

03 ~하곤 했다
(과거의 불규칙적 습관) _____

04 석고붕대, 깁스 _____

05 그러나, 그래도 _____

06 비명 _____

07 자전거를 타다 _____

08 흙, 먼지 _____

09 입구, 입장 _____

10 ~ 내내, ~ 동안 쭉 _____

11 교훈 _____

12 경영자, 관리자 _____

13 열린 구멍, 틈 _____

14 입구, 관문 _____

15 특별한 _____

16 기록 _____

17 쿵쾅거리는 _____

18 고통을 주다, 아프다 _____

19 속삭이다 _____

20 안도, 안심 _____

21 외치다, 소리[고함]치다 _____

22 실제(로)는, 사실은 _____

23 숨 쉬다 _____

24 두터운, 빽빽한 _____

25 처음에는 _____

26 (손 · 팔 · 다리 등을) 뻗다 _____

27 조금씩 _____

28 ~가 …하는 것을 막다 _____

29 ~ 덕분에 _____

30 출발하다 _____

31 얼마 후에 _____

32 나란히 _____

33 매일 _____

34 다시 말해서, 즉 _____

35 ~하자마자 _____

36 대답으로 _____

37 여느 때처럼 _____

38 간신히 ~하다 _____

39 갑자기 _____

40 ~하곤 했다(과거의 규칙적
이고 반복적인 동작이나 상태) _____

※ 다음 영영풀이에 알맞은 단어를 <보기>에서 골라 쓴 후, 우리말 뜻을 쓰시오.

1 _____ : to take a breath: _____

2 _____ : to ride a bicycle: _____

3 _____ : loose or packed soil or sand: _____

4 _____ : the way you go in: _____

5 _____ : close-packed with units or individuals: _____

6 _____ : a loud sharp cry or noise: _____

7 _____ : removal of something painful: _____

8 _____ : an opening for a gate: _____

9 _____ : a large amount of water covering an area that is usually dry: _____

10 _____ : during the whole period of: _____

11 _____ : something learned through experience: _____

12 _____ : worthy of notice; special; unusual: _____

13 _____ : hitting something in a heavy, continuous way: _____

14 _____ : a person who is responsible for running part of a business organization:

_____

15 _____ : a written account of something that is kept so that it can be looked at and

used in the future: _____

16 _____ : to speak very quietly to somebody so that other people cannot hear what

you are saying: _____

보기			
particular	breathe	whisper	dirt
lesson	scream	record	gateway
manager	thick	relief	cycle
flood	entrance	throughout	thumping

※ 다음 우리말과 일치하도록 빈칸에 알맞은 것을 골라 쓰시오.

1 _____ _____
   A. Keep   B. Out

2 Every summer, my family _____ _____ _____ on holiday to the _____.
   A. go   B. used   C. coast   D. to

3 We always went to the same _____ and _____ _____ the _____ small guesthouse.
   A. place   B. at   C. same   D. stayed

4 We would _____ for two weeks, _____ in the sea and _____ around the _____ town.
   A. walking   B. swimming   C. little   D. stay

5 In _____ _____, we never did _____ special, and nothing ever really _____ on these vacations.
   A. words   B. happened   C. other   D. anything

6 _____ _____ _____ _____ this story I was twelve years old.
   A. time   B. at   C. of   D. the

7 Most people can remember this _____ summer, _____ it was the hottest summer England _____ had _____ records began.
   A. since   B. had   C. particular D. as

8 It did not rain _____ June and July, and the sun _____ day _____ and day _____.
   A. shone   B. throughout C. out   D. in

9 _____ Ron and I _____ the _____ and the _____.
   A. heat   B. sun   C. but   D. loved

10 Every day, we would _____ our bicycles _____ and further _____ _____ the guesthouse.
   A. ride   B. further   C. from   D. away

11 One day Ron _____ that we should _____ our bikes _____ the old train tracks to see where they would _____ us.
   A. take   B. along   C. decided   D. ride

12 I was happy to follow Ron, _____ _____, and we _____ _____ after breakfast.
   A. usual   B. off   C. as   D. set

13 At first, the tracks were _____ to _____, and we _____ along side _____ side.
   A. follow   B. easy   C. by   D. cycled

---

1 들어가지 마시오

2 여름마다 나의 가족은 해안으로 휴가를 가곤 했다.

3 우리는 항상 같은 곳에 가서 똑같은 작은 게스트하우스에 묵었다.

4 우리는 2주 가량 머물며 바다에서 수영하고 작은 마을 주위를 돌아다니곤 했다.

5 다시 말해서, 그런 휴가에서 우리는 특별한 일을 하지 않았고 정말 아무 일도 일어나지 않았다.

6 이 이야기는 내가 12살 때 일이다.

7 관측 이래 영국이 겪은 가장 더운 여름이었기 때문에, 대부분의 사람들은 이 특별한 여름을 기억할 수 있다.

8 6월과 7월 내내 비가 오지 않았고 태양은 연일 쨍쨍했다.

9 하지만 Ron과 나는 그 더위와 태양을 사랑했다.

10 매일 우리는 게스트하우스에서 조금씩 먼 곳으로 자전거를 타고 가곤 했다.

11 어느 날, Ron은 낡은 철로가 우리를 어디로 데려다줄지 알아보려고 그 철로를 따라 자전거를 타기로 결정했다.

12 난 늘 그랬듯 Ron을 따르는 게 즐거웠고, 아침 식사 후에 우리는 출발했다.

13 처음에는 철길을 따라가는 게 어렵지 않아 우리는 나란히 자전거를 타고 갔다.

14 After a _____, the grass grew _____, and we had to ride one _____ the _____.
    A. behind   B. while   C. other   D. thicker

15 Ron _____ _____.
    A. ahead   B. was

16 The tracks went _____ the woods and it grew _____ as the trees stood tall and _____ a _____ over the tracks.
    A. formed   B. toward   C. darker   D. roof

17 Ron _____ _____. "Look _____!" he _____.
    A. shouted   B. suddenly   C. ahead   D. stopped

18 I stopped next _____ him and saw a white, _____ gateway _____ a black _____.
    A. across   B. to   C. opening   D. wooden

19 "It's _____ _____," I _____.
    A. tunnel   B. said   C. a

20 "Yes, and it says, '_____ _____' on the _____," _____ Ron.
    A. Out   B. gate   C. Keep   D. replied

21 "Do you want to _____ _____ _____ _____?"
    A. inside   B. a   C. have   D. look

22 _____, I did _____ to go _____.
    A. actually   B. inside   C. want   D. not

23 I felt a _____ cold all of a _____, and I wanted to go _____ _____ the sunlight.
    A. sudden   B. into   C. little   D. back

24 But I _____, "Sure," and _____ _____.
    A. moved   B. answered   C. ahead

25 We _____ our bikes at the _____ and _____ _____.
    A. left   B. over   C. gate   D. climbed

26 We _____ the _____.
    A. tunnel   B. entered   C. cool

27 The _____ was _____.
    A. heavy   B. inside   C. air

28 _____ our heads there was a _____ that _____ _____ and louder.
    A. sound   B. above   C. louder   D. grew

29 "What's that?" I _____ _____.
    A. out   B. called

30 "Bats," said Ron, "_____ your head _____." Then he _____ _____.
    A. on   B. keep   C. moved   D. down

31 "_____ go so _____." I _____ _____ him.
    A. after   B. fast   C. called   D. don't

---

14 한참 후, 풀이 점점 우거져서 우리는 한 사람이 앞서가고 다른 사람이 뒤에서 가야 했다.

15 Ron이 앞서가고 있었다.

16 철길은 숲으로 이어졌고 나무가 높이 자라 철길 위로 지붕을 형성하며 점점 더 어두워졌다.

17 Ron이 갑자기 멈췄다. "앞을 봐!"라고 그가 외쳤다.

18 나는 그의 옆에 멈춰서 캄캄한 입구를 가로지르는 흰색 나무문을 보았다.

19 "터널이네." 내가 말했다.

20 "맞아. 그리고 문에 '들어가지 마시오'라고 적혀 있어." Ron이 대답했다.

21 "안을 보고 싶니?"

22 사실, 난 안으로 들어가고 싶지 않았다.

23 갑자기 나는 한기를 살짝 느꼈고 햇빛 속으로 되돌아가고 싶었다.

24 그렇지만 나는 "물론이지."라고 답하며 앞으로 움직였다.

25 우리는 문 앞에 자전거를 남겨두고 넘어갔다.

26 우리는 서늘한 터널로 들어갔다.

27 안의 공기는 묵직했다.

28 우리 머리 위로 점점 더 커지는 소리가 났다.

29 "저게 뭐야?"라고 내가 소리쳤다.

30 "박쥐야." Ron이 말했다. "머리를 숙여." 그러고 나서 그는 계속 움직였다.

31 "너무 빨리 가지 마." 나는 그를 부르며 뒤쫓았다.

32 I _____, "Don't _____ me _____" but I didn't say _____.

    A. behind   B. meant   C. leave   D. so

33 The next thing I heard was a _____ noise right above us, a _____ sound like an _____ train and then a _____.

    A. thumping   B. scream   C. loud   D. express

34 "Ron!" I _____. "Ron, what's _____? Can you _____ me?" No _____.

    A. up   B. reply   C. shouted   D. hear

35 "_____ to me, Ron. _____ me _____ _____."

    A. happened   B. speak   C. what's   D. tell

36 I slowly walked _____ _____ Ron had _____ and found only _____ and small rocks.

    A. dirt   B. toward   C. been   D. where

37 As I _____ _____ my hands, I felt _____ _____ — Ron's face!

    A. out   B. wet   C. reached   D. something

38 His eyes _____ _____, and he was _____ _____.

    A. weakly   B. were   C. breathing   D. closed

39 "It's okay, Ron," I _____. "I'll _____ you _____."

    A. whispered   B. out   C. get

40 "I think I've _____ my leg. It really _____. Just go and _____ _____, Ben."

    A. hurts   B. broken   C. help   D. get

41 "No," I _____. "I'll _____ you _____ of here to _____ first."

    A. out   B. replied   C. safety   D. get

42 I started _____ _____ the _____ and rocks _____ my hands.

    A. with   B. moving   C. dirt   D. away

43 I _____ _____, and I felt _____ _____.

    A. control   B. calm   C. in   D. felt

44 It _____ a long time to _____ _____ the earth _____ Ron.

    A. covering   B. took   C. away   D. clear

45 _____, I _____ _____ _____ his body.

    A. free   B. managed   C. finally   D. to

46 _____ him under the arms, I pulled him _____, inch by inch, _____ the tunnel _____.

    A. toward   B. backward   C. holding   D. entrance

47 It _____ to take _____, but finally I was _____ to get Ron _____ of the tunnel.

    A. ages   B. able   C. seemed   D. out

48 He didn't _____ _____ _____ _____, _____.

    A. though   B. well   C. too   D. look

32 '나를 두고 가지 마'라고 말하고 싶었지만, 나는 그렇게 말하지 않았다.

33 그다음 내가 들은 것은 바로 앞에서 나는 큰 소음이었는데, 그것은 마치 고속열차 같은 쿵쾅거리는 소리였다. 이어서 비명이 들렸다.

34 "Ron!" 나는 외쳤다. "Ron, 무슨 일이야? 내 말 들려?" 아무 응답이 없었다.

35 "Ron, 나에게 말해 봐. 무슨 일이 생겼는지 말해 줘."

36 나는 천천히 Ron이 있던 곳으로 걸어갔고 흙과 작은 자갈만을 발견했다.

37 손을 뻗었을 때 나는 축축한 무언가를 느꼈다. Ron의 얼굴이었다!

38 그의 눈은 감겨 있었고 약하게 숨을 쉬고 있었다.

39 "괜찮아, Ron." 나는 속삭였다. "내가 꺼내 줄게."

40 "다리가 부러진 것 같아. 정말 아파. 그냥 가서 도움을 요청해, Ben."

41 "안 돼." 나는 대답했다. "우선 안전한 곳까지 여기에서 형을 꺼낼 거야."

42 나는 손으로 흙과 자갈을 치우기 시작했다.

43 나는 침착했고 내가 잘할 수 있다고 느꼈다.

44 Ron을 뒤덮은 흙을 치우는 데에 오랜 시간이 걸렸다.

45 드디어 나는 그의 몸을 자유롭게 할 수 있었다.

46 팔 밑으로 그를 안고서 그를 터널 입구 쪽으로 조금씩 뒤로 끌어당겼다.

47 오랜 시간이 걸린 듯했지만 결국 나는 Ron을 터널 밖으로 데리고 나올 수 있었다.

48 그는 별로 좋아 보이지 않았다.

49 His face was white, and he was trying hard to _____ himself _____ _____ _____ from crying out.

A. crying　　　　B. out　　　　C. stop　　　　D. from

50 I _____ our bikes and _____ the two _____ _____ to Ron.

A. brought　　　B. found　　　C. bottles　　　D. water

51 "Here, drink these," I said. "I'll go and _____ _____. I'll be as _____ _____ I can."

A. quick　　　　B. help　　　　C. as　　　　D. get

52 _____ _____, Ron _____ _____ my hands.

A. pressed　　　B. reply　　　C. simply　　　D. in

53 I got on my bicycle and _____ _____ along the tracks _____ I got to the _____ farmhouse.

A. nearest　　　B. back　　　C. until　　　D. raced

54 I ran _____ the _____ and found a woman _____ some _____ in the kitchen.

A. washing　　　B. past　　　C. dishes　　　D. gate

55 _____ to her, Ron was _____ to the hospital, where his leg was _____ in a _____.

A. put　　　　　B. cast　　　　C. thanks　　　D. taken

56 As _____ as our parents _____ at the hospital and saw us, my mother cried _____ _____.

A. relief　　　　B. soon　　　C. with　　　D. arrived

57 But all my father said was, "_____ that _____ a _____ to you."

A. lesson　　　　B. let　　　　C. be

58 And what was the _____? It was "*Keep* _____ means _____ *out of* _____."

A. lesson　　　　B. trouble　　　C. out　　　D. stay

59 Ron is now the _____ of a big company which _____ helmets and other _____ _____.

A. safety　　　　B. manager　　C. produces　　D. products

60 And me? I _____ a _____ _____.

A. fighter　　　　B. fire　　　C. am

49 그의 얼굴은 창백했고 울음을 터뜨리지 않으려고 몹시 애쓰고 있었다.

50 나는 우리 자전거를 찾아서 Ron 에게 물병 두 개를 가져다주었다.

51 "여기, 이거 마셔." 나는 말했다. "내가 가서 도움을 구할게. 최대한 빨리 올게."

52 대답으로 Ron은 그저 내 손을 꽉 잡았다.

53 나는 자전거를 타고 왔던 철길을 따라 달려, 마침내 가장 가까운 농가에 도착했다.

54 대문을 지나 달려가 나는 부엌에서 설거지를 하고 있는 부인을 발견했다.

55 그 부인 덕분에 Ron은 병원으로 이송되었고, 병원에서 다리에 석고붕대를 했다.

56 부모님이 병원에 도착해서 우리를 보자마자, 어머니는 안도감에 울음을 터뜨리셨다.

57 하지만 아버지가 하신 말씀은 "이 일이 너희에게 교훈이 되기를 바란다."가 전부였다.

58 그래서 교훈이 무엇이었을까? 그것은 '들어가지 마시오'라는 말은 '곤경을 멀리하라'는 뜻이라는 것이다.

59 Ron은 지금 안전모와 여러 안전 제품을 생산하는 큰 회사의 관리자이다.

60 그럼 나는? 나는 소방관이다.

※ 다음 우리말과 일치하도록 빈칸에 알맞은 말을 쓰시오.

1 _____ _____

2 _____ summer, my family _____ _____ _____ on holiday to the coast.

3 We always went to the same place and _____ _____ the same small _____.

4 We would _____ _____ two weeks, _____ in the sea and _____ around the little town.

5 _____ _____ _____, we never did _____ _____, and nothing ever really happened on these vacations.

6 _____ _____ _____ _____ this story I was twelve years old.

7 Most people can remember this particular summer, as it was the hottest summer England _____ _____ since records began.

8 It did not rain _____ June and July, and the sun _____ _____ _____ _____ _____ _____.

9 But Ron and I loved _____ _____ and the sun.

10 Every day, we would ride our bicycles _____ _____ _____ _____ _____ the guesthouse.

11 One day Ron decided that we should ride our bikes along the old train tracks to see where they would _____ _____.

12 I was happy _____ _____ Ron, _____ _____, and we _____ _____ after breakfast.

13 At first, the tracks were easy to follow, and we _____ _____ _____ _____ _____.

1 들어가지 마시오

2 여름마다 나의 가족은 해안으로 휴가를 가곤 했다.

3 우리는 항상 같은 곳에 가서 똑같은 작은 게스트하우스에 묵었다.

4 우리는 2주 가량 머물며 바다에서 수영하고 작은 마을 주위를 돌아다니곤 했다.

5 다시 말해서, 그런 휴가에서 우리는 특별한 일을 하지 않았고 정말 아무 일도 일어나지 않았다.

6 이 이야기는 내가 12살 때 일이다.

7 관측 이래 영국이 겪은 가장 더운 여름이었기 때문에, 대부분의 사람들은 이 특별한 여름을 기억할 수 있다.

8 6월과 7월 내내 비가 오지 않았고 태양은 연일 쨍쨍했다.

9 하지만 Ron과 나는 그 더위와 태양을 사랑했다.

10 매일 우리는 게스트하우스에서 조금씩 먼 곳으로 자전거를 타고 가곤 했다.

11 어느 날, Ron은 낡은 철로가 우리를 어디로 데려다줄지 알아보려고 그 철로를 따라 자전거를 타기로 결정했다.

12 난 늘 그랬듯 Ron을 따르는 게 즐거웠고, 아침 식사 후에 우리는 출발했다.

13 처음에는 철길을 따라가는 게 어렵지 않아 우리는 나란히 자전거를 타고 갔다.

14 After a while, the grass _____ _____, and we had to ride _____ _____ _____ _____.

15 Ron was _____.

16 The tracks went toward the woods and it _____ _____ as the trees stood tall and _____ _____ _____ over the tracks.

17 Ron stopped suddenly. "_____ _____!" he _____.

18 I stopped _____ _____ _____ and saw a white, wooden gateway across a _____ _____.

19 "It's _____ _____," I said.

20 "Yes, and it says, '_____ _____' on the gate," replied Ron.

21 "Do you want to _____ _____ _____ inside?"

22 _____, I did not want to _____ _____.

23 I felt a little cold _____ _____ _____ _____, and I wanted to _____ _____ _____ the sunlight.

24 But I answered, "Sure," and _____ _____.

25 We _____ our bikes at the gate and _____ _____.

26 We _____ the cool tunnel.

27 The air _____ was _____.

28 Above our heads there was a sound that _____ _____ _____ _____.

29 "What's that?" I _____ _____.

30 "Bats," said Ron, "_____ your head _____." Then he _____ _____.

31 "_____ _____ so fast." I _____ _____ him.

14 한참 후, 풀이 점점 우거져서 우리는 한 사람이 앞서가고 다른 사람이 뒤에서 가야 했다.

15 Ron이 앞서가고 있었다.

16 철길은 숲으로 이어졌고 나무가 높이 자라 철길 위로 지붕을 형성하며 점점 더 어두워졌다.

17 Ron이 갑자기 멈췄다. "앞을 봐!"라고 그가 외쳤다.

18 나는 그의 옆에 멈춰서 캄캄한 입구를 가로지르는 흰색 나무문을 보았다.

19 "터널이네." 내가 말했다.

20 "맞아. 그리고 문에 '들어가지 마시오'라고 적혀 있어." Ron이 대답했다.

21 "안을 보고 싶니?"

22 사실, 난 안으로 들어가고 싶지 않았다.

23 갑자기 나는 한기를 살짝 느꼈고 햇빛 속으로 되돌아가고 싶었다.

24 그렇지만 나는 "물론이지."라고 답하며 앞으로 움직였다.

25 우리는 문 앞에 자전거를 남겨두고 넘어갔다.

26 우리는 서늘한 터널로 들어갔다.

27 안의 공기는 묵직했다.

28 우리 머리 위로 점점 더 커지는 소리가 났다.

29 "저게 뭐야?"라고 내가 소리쳤다.

30 "박쥐야." Ron이 말했다. "머리를 숙여." 그러고 나서 그는 계속 움직였다.

31 "너무 빨리 가지 마." 나는 그를 부르며 뒤쫓았다.

32 I meant, "Don't _____ me _____" but I didn't say so.

33 The next thing I heard was a _____ _____ right above us, a _____ sound _____ _____ _____ _____ and then a _____.

34 "Ron!" I shouted. "Ron, _____ _____? Can you hear me?" No _____.

35 "Speak to me, Ron. Tell me _____ _____."

36 I slowly walked toward _____ _____ _____ _____ and found only dirt and small rocks.

37 As I _____ _____ my hands, I felt _____ _____ — Ron's face!

38 His eyes _____ _____, and he was _____ _____.

39 "It's okay, Ron," I whispered. "I'll _____ _____ _____."

40 "I think I'_____ _____ my leg. It really hurts. Just _____ _____ _____ _____, Ben."

41 "No," I replied. "I'll _____ _____ _____ _____ _____ _____ to safety first."

42 I started _____ _____ the dirt and rocks with my hands.

43 I _____ _____, and I felt _____ _____.

44 It took a long time to _____ _____ the earth _____ Ron.

45 Finally, I _____ _____ _____ his body.

46 _____ him under the arms, I pulled him backward, _____ _____ _____, toward the _____ _____.

47 It seemed _____ _____ _____, but finally I was able to get Ron _____ _____ the tunnel.

48 He didn't _____ _____ _____, _____.

32 '나를 두고 가지 마'라고 말하고 싶었지만, 나는 그렇게 말하지 않았다.

33 그다음 내가 들은 것은 바로 앞에서 나는 큰 소음이었는데, 그것은 마치 고속열차 같은 쿵쾅거리는 소리였다. 이어서 비명이 들렸다.

34 "Ron!" 나는 외쳤다. "Ron, 무슨 일이야? 내 말 들려?" 아무 응답이 없었다.

35 "Ron, 나에게 말해 봐. 무슨 일이 생겼는지 말해 줘."

36 나는 천천히 Ron이 있던 곳으로 걸어갔고 흙과 작은 자갈만을 발견했다.

37 손을 뻗었을 때 나는 축축한 무언가를 느꼈다. Ron의 얼굴이었다!

38 그의 눈은 감겨 있었고 약하게 숨을 쉬고 있었다.

39 "괜찮아, Ron." 나는 속삭였다. "내가 꺼내 줄게."

40 "다리가 부러진 것 같아. 정말 아파. 그냥 가서 도움을 요청해, Ben."

41 "안 돼." 나는 대답했다. "우선 안전한 곳까지 여기에서 형을 꺼낼 거야."

42 나는 손으로 흙과 자갈을 치우기 시작했다.

43 나는 침착했고 내가 잘할 수 있다고 느꼈다.

44 Ron을 뒤덮은 흙을 치우는 데에 오랜 시간이 걸렸다.

45 드디어 나는 그의 몸을 자유롭게 할 수 있었다.

46 팔 밑으로 그를 안고서 그를 터널 입구 쪽으로 조금씩 뒤로 끌어당겼다.

47 오랜 시간이 걸린 듯했지만 결국 나는 Ron을 터널 밖으로 데리고 나올 수 있었다.

48 그는 별로 좋아 보이지 않았다.

49 His face was white, and he was trying hard to _____ himself _____ _____ _____ from _____ _____ .

50 I found our bikes and brought the _____ _____ _____ to Ron.

51 "Here, drink these," I said. "I'll _____ _____ _____ _____ . I'll be _____ _____ _____ I _____ ."

52 _____ _____ , Ron simply _____ _____ _____ .

53 I got on my bicycle and _____ _____ along the tracks until I got to _____ _____ _____ .

54 I _____ _____ the gate and found a woman _____ _____ _____ in the kitchen.

55 _____ _____ _____ , Ron was taken to the hospital, _____ his leg was _____ in a _____ .

56 _____ _____ _____ our parents arrived at the hospital and saw us, my mother cried _____ _____ .

57 But all my father said was, " _____ _____ _____ _____ _____ to you."

58 And what was the _____ ? It was "*Keep out* means _____ _____ _____ _____ ."

59 Ron is now the manager of a big company which produces helmets and _____ _____ _____ .

60 And me? I am a _____ _____ .

49 그의 얼굴은 창백했고 울음을 터뜨리지 않으려고 몹시 애쓰고 있었다.

50 나는 우리 자전거를 찾아서 Ron에게 물병 두 개를 가져다주었다.

51 "여기, 이거 마셔." 나는 말했다. "내가 가서 도움을 구할게. 최대한 빨리 올게."

52 대답으로 Ron은 그저 내 손을 꽉 잡았다.

53 나는 자전거를 타고 왔던 철길을 따라 달려, 마침내 가장 가까운 농가에 도착했다.

54 대문을 지나 달려가 나는 부엌에서 설거지를 하고 있는 부인을 발견했다.

55 그 부인 덕분에 Ron은 병원으로 이송되었고, 병원에서 다리에 석고붕대를 했다.

56 부모님이 병원에 도착해서 우리를 보자마자, 어머니는 안도감에 울음을 터뜨리셨다.

57 하지만 아버지가 하신 말씀은 "이 일이 너희에게 교훈이 되기를 바란다."가 전부였다.

58 그래서 교훈이 무엇이었을까? 그것은 '들어가지 마시오'라는 말은 '곤경을 멀리하라'는 뜻이라는 것이다.

59 Ron은 지금 안전모와 여러 안전 제품을 생산하는 큰 회사의 관리자이다.

60 그럼 나는? 나는 소방관이다.

※ 다음 문장을 우리말로 쓰시오.

1 Keep Out

➡ _____

2 Every summer, my family used to go on holiday to the coast.

➡ _____

3 We always went to the same place and stayed at the same small guesthouse.

➡ _____

4 We would stay for two weeks, swimming in the sea and walking around the little town.

➡ _____

5 In other words, we never did anything special, and nothing ever really happened on these vacations.

➡ _____

6 At the time of this story I was twelve years old.

➡ _____

7 Most people can remember this particular summer, as it was the hottest summer England had had since records began.

➡ _____

8 It did not rain throughout June and July, and the sun shone day in and day out.

➡ _____

9 But Ron and I loved the heat and the sun.

➡ _____

10 Every day, we would ride our bicycles further and further away from the guesthouse.

➡ _____

11 One day Ron decided that we should ride our bikes along the old train tracks to see where they would take us.

➡ _____

12 I was happy to follow Ron, as usual, and we set off after breakfast.

➡ _____

13 At first, the tracks were easy to follow, and we cycled along side by side.

➡ _____

14 After a while, the grass grew thicker, and we had to ride one behind the other.

➡ _____

15 Ron was ahead.

➡ _____

16 The tracks went toward the woods and it grew darker as the trees stood tall and formed a roof over the tracks.

➡ _____

17 Ron stopped suddenly. "Look ahead!" he shouted.

➡ _____

18 I stopped next to him and saw a white, wooden gateway across a black opening.

➡ _____

19 "It's a tunnel," I said.

➡ _____

20 "Yes, and it says, 'Keep Out' on the gate," replied Ron.

➡ _____

21 "Do you want to have a look inside?"

➡ _____

22 Actually, I did not want to go inside.

➡ _____

23 I felt a little cold all of a sudden, and I wanted to go back into the sunlight.

➡ _____

24 But I answered, "Sure," and moved ahead.

➡ _____

25 We left our bikes at the gate and climbed over.

➡ _____

26 We entered the cool tunnel.

➡ _____

27 The air inside was heavy.

➡ _____

28 Above our heads there was a sound that grew louder and louder.

➡ _____

29 "What's that?" I called out.

➡ _____

30 "Bats," said Ron, "Keep your head down." Then he moved on.

➡ _____

31 "Don't go so fast." I called after him.

➡ _____

32 I meant, "Don't leave me behind" but I didn't say so.

➡ _____

33 The next thing I heard was a loud noise right above us, a thumping sound like an express
train and then a scream.

➡ _____

_____

34 "Ron!" I shouted. "Ron, what's up? Can you hear me?" No reply.

➡ _____

35 "Speak to me, Ron. Tell me what's happened."

➡ _____

36 I slowly walked toward where Ron had been and found only dirt and small rocks.

➡ _____

37 As I reached out my hands, I felt something wet — Ron's face!

➡ _____

38 His eyes were closed, and he was breathing weakly.

➡ _____

39 "It's okay, Ron," I whispered. "I'll get you out."

➡ _____

40 "I think I've broken my leg. It really hurts. Just go and get help, Ben."

➡ _____

41 "No," I replied. "I'll get you out of here to safety first."

➡ _____

42 I started moving away the dirt and rocks with my hands.

➡ _____

43 I felt calm, and I felt in control.

➡ _____

44 It took a long time to clear away the earth covering Ron.

➡ _____

45 Finally, I managed to free his body.

➡ _____

46 Holding him under the arms, I pulled him backward, inch by inch, toward the tunnel entrance.

➡ _____

47 It seemed to take ages, but finally I was able to get Ron out of the tunnel.

➡ _____

48 He didn't look too well, though.

➡ _____

49 His face was white, and he was trying hard to stop himself from crying out.

➡ _____

50 I found our bikes and brought the two water bottles to Ron.

➡ _____

51 Here, drink these," I said. "I'll go and get help. I'll be as quick as I can."

➡ _____

52 In reply, Ron simply pressed my hands.

➡ _____

53 I got on my bicycle and raced back along the tracks until I got to the nearest farmhouse.

➡ _____

54 I ran past the gate and found a woman washing some dishes in the kitchen.

➡ _____

55 Thanks to her, Ron was taken to the hospital, where his leg was put in a cast.

➡ _____

56 As soon as our parents arrived at the hospital and saw us, my mother cried with relief.

➡ _____

57 But all my father said was, "Let that be a lesson to you."

➡ _____

58 And what was the lesson? It was "*Keep out* means *Stay out of trouble*."

➡ _____

59 Ron is now the manager of a big company which produces helmets and other safety products.

➡ _____

60 And me? I am a fire fighter.

➡ _____

※ 다음 괄호 안의 단어들을 우리말에 맞도록 바르게 배열하시오.

1 (Out / Keep)
➡ _____

2 (summer, / every / family / my / to / used / on / go / holiday / to / coast. / the)
➡ _____

3 (always / we / to / went / same / the / place / and / at / stayed / the / small / same / guesthouse.)
➡ _____

4 (would / we / for / stay / weeks, / two / in / swimming / the / and / sea / around / walking / little / the / town.)
➡ _____

5 (other / in / words, / never / we / anything / did / special, / and / ever / nothing / really / happened / these / on / vacations.)
➡ _____

6 (the / at / of / time / story / this / was / I / twelve / old. / years)
➡ _____

7 (people / most / can / this / remember / summer, / particular / it / as / the / was / summer / hottest / had / England / since / had / began. / records)
➡ _____

8 (did / it / rain / not / June / throughout / July, / and / the / and / sun / shone / in / day / and / out. / day)
➡ _____

9 (Ron / but / and / loved / I / heat / the / and / sun. / the)
➡ _____

10 (day, / every / would / we / our / ride / further / bicycles / and / from / away / further / guesthoue. / the)
➡ _____

11 (day / one / decided / Ron / that / should / we / our / ride / along / bikes / old / the / tracks / train / see / to / they / where / take / would / us.)
➡ _____

12 (was / I / to / happy / Ron, / follow / usual, / as / and / set / we / off / breakfast. / after)
➡ _____

13 (first, / at / tracks / the / easy / were / follow, / to / we / and / along / cycled / by / side / side.)
➡ _____

1 들어가지 마시오

2 여름마다 나의 가족은 해안으로 휴가를 가곤 했다.

3 우리는 항상 같은 곳에 가서 똑같은 작은 게스트하우스에 묵었다.

4 우리는 2주 가량 머물며 바다에서 수영하고 작은 마을 주위를 돌아다니곤 했다.

5 다시 말해서, 그런 휴가에서 우리는 특별한 일을 하지 않았고 정말 아무 일도 일어나지 않았다.

6 이 이야기는 내가 12살 때 일이다.

7 관측 이래 영국이 겪은 가장 더운 여름이었기 때문에, 대부분의 사람들은 이 특별한 여름을 기억할 수 있다.

8 6월과 7월 내내 비가 오지 않았고 태양은 연일 쨍쨍했다.

9 하지만 Ron과 나는 그 더위와 태양을 사랑했다.

10 매일 우리는 게스트하우스에서 조금씩 먼 곳으로 자전거를 타고 가곤 했다.

11 어느 날, Ron은 낡은 철로가 우리를 어디로 데려다줄지 알아보려고 그 철로를 따라 자전거를 타기로 결정했다.

12 난 늘 그랬듯 Ron을 따르는 게 즐거웠고, 아침 식사 후에 우리는 출발했다.

13 처음에는 철길을 따라가는 게 어렵지 않아 우리는 나란히 자전거를 타고 갔다.

14 (a / after / while, / grass / the / thicker, / grew / we / and / to / had / one / ride / behind / other. / the)
➡ _____

15 (was / Ron / ahead.)
➡ _____

16 (tracks / the / toward / went / woods / the / and / grew / it / as / darker / the / stood / trees / and / tall / a / formed / roof / the / over / tracks.)
➡ _____

17 (stopped / Ron / suddenly. // ahead!" / "look / shouted. / he)
➡ _____

18 (stopped / I / to / next / and / him / a / saw / white, / gateway / wooden / a / across / opening. / black)
➡ _____

19 (a / "it's / I / tunnel," / said.)
➡ _____

20 (and / "yes, / says, / it / Out' / 'Keep / the / on / gate," / Ron. / replied)
➡ _____

21 (you / "do / to / want / a / have / inside?" / look)
➡ _____

22 (I / actually, / not / did / to / want / inside. / go)
➡ _____

23 (felt / I / little / a / cold / a / of / all / sudden, / and / wanted / I / go / to / into / back / sunlight. / the)
➡ _____

24 (I / but / anwered, / "sure," / moved / and / ahead.)
➡ _____

25 (left / we / bikes / our / the / at / and / gate / over. / climbed)
➡ _____

26 (entered / we / the / tunnel. / cool)
➡ _____

27 (air / the / inside / heavy. / was)
➡ _____

28 (our / above / there / heads / was / sound / a / grew / that / and / louder / louder.)
➡ _____

29 (that?" / "what's / called / I / out.)
➡ _____

30 (Ron, / said / "bats, / "keep / head / your / down." // he / then / on. / moved)
➡ _____

31 (go / "don't / fast." / so // called / I / him. / after)
➡ _____

14 한참 후, 풀이 점점 우거져서 우리는 한 사람이 앞서가고 다른 사람이 뒤에서 가야 했다.
15 Ron이 앞서가고 있었다.
16 철길은 숲으로 이어졌고 나무가 높이 자라 철길 위로 지붕을 형성하며 점점 더 어두워졌다.
17 Ron이 갑자기 멈췄다. "앞을 봐!"라고 그가 외쳤다.
18 나는 그의 옆에 멈춰서 캄캄한 입구를 가로지르는 흰색 나무문을 보았다.
19 "터널이네." 내가 말했다.
20 "맞아. 그리고 문에 '들어가지 마시오'라고 적혀 있어." Ron이 대답했다.
21 "안을 보고 싶니?"
22 사실, 난 안으로 들어가고 싶지 않았다.
23 갑자기 나는 한기를 살짝 느꼈고 햇빛 속으로 되돌아가고 싶었다.
24 그렇지만 나는 "물론이지."라고 답하며 앞으로 움직였다.
25 우리는 문 앞에 자전거를 남겨두고 넘어갔다.
26 우리는 서늘한 터널로 들어갔다.
27 안의 공기는 묵직했다.
28 우리 머리 위로 점점 더 커지는 소리가 났다.
29 "저게 뭐야?"라고 내가 소리쳤다.
30 "박쥐야." Ron이 말했다. "머리를 숙여." 그러고 나서 그는 계속 움직였다.
31 "너무 빨리 가지 마." 나는 그를 부르며 뒤쫓았다.

32 (meant, / I / leave / "don't / behind" / me / I / but / didn't / so. / say)

➡ _____

33 (next / the / I / thing / was / heard / a / noise / loud / above / right / us, / a / sound / thumping / like / express / an / and / train / then / scream. / a)

➡ _____

34 ("Ron!" / shouted. / I // what's / Ron, / up? // you / can / me? / hear // reply. / no)

➡ _____

35 (to / "speak / Ron. / me, // me / tell / happened." / what's)

➡ _____

36 (slowly / I / toward / walked / Ron / where / been / had / and / only / found / dirt / small / and / rocks.)

➡ _____

37 (I / as / out / reached / hands, / my / felt / I / wet / something / — / face! / Ron's)

➡ _____

38 (eyes / his / closed, / were / he / and / breathing / was / weakly.)

➡ _____

39 (okay, / "it's / Ron," / whispered. / I // get / "I'll / out." / you)

➡ _____

40 (think / "I / broken / I've / leg. / my // really / it / hurts. // go / just / and / help, / get / Ben.")

➡ _____

41 ("no," / repiled. / I / get / "I'll / out / you / here / of / safety / to / first.")

➡ _____

42 (started / I / away / moving / dirt / the / and / with / rocks / hands. / my)

➡ _____

43 (felt / I / calm, / I / and / in / felt / control.)

➡ _____

44 (took / it / long / a / to / time / away / clear / earth / the / Ron. / covering)

➡ _____

45 (I / finally, / to / managed / his / body. / free)

➡ _____

46 (him / holding / the / under / arms, / pulled / I / backward, / him / by / inch / inch, / toward / tunnel / the / entrance.)

➡ _____

47 (seemed / it / take / to / ages, / finally / but / was / I / to / able / Ron / get / of / out / tunnel. / the)

➡ _____

48 (didn't / he / too / look / though. / well,)

➡ _____

32 '나를 두고 가지 마'라고 말하고 싶었지만, 나는 그렇게 말하지 않았다.

33 그다음 내가 들은 것은 바로 앞에서 나는 큰 소음이었는데, 그것은 마치 고속열차 같은 쿵쾅거리는 소리였다. 이어서 비명이 들렸다.

34 "Ron!" 나는 외쳤다. "Ron, 무슨 일이야? 내 말 들려?" 아무 응답이 없었다.

35 "Ron, 나에게 말해 봐. 무슨 일이 생겼는지 말해 줘."

36 나는 천천히 Ron이 있던 곳으로 걸어갔고 흙과 작은 자갈만을 발견했다.

37 손을 뻗었을 때 나는 축축한 무언가를 느꼈다. Ron의 얼굴이었다!

38 그의 눈은 감겨 있었고 약하게 숨을 쉬고 있었다.

39 "괜찮아, Ron." 나는 속삭였다. "내가 꺼내 줄게."

40 "다리가 부러진 것 같아. 정말 아파. 그냥 가서 도움을 요청해, Ben."

41 "안 돼." 나는 대답했다. "우선 안전한 곳까지 여기에서 형을 꺼낼 거야."

42 나는 손으로 흙과 자갈을 치우기 시작했다.

43 나는 침착했고 내가 잘할 수 있다고 느꼈다.

44 Ron을 뒤덮은 흙을 치우는 데에 오랜 시간이 걸렸다.

45 드디어 나는 그의 몸을 자유롭게 할 수 있었다.

46 팔 밑으로 그를 안고서 그를 터널 입구 쪽으로 조금씩 뒤로 끌어당겼다.

47 오랜 시간이 걸린 듯했지만 결국 나는 Ron을 터널 밖으로 데리고 나올 수 있었다.

48 그는 별로 좋아 보이지 않았다.

49 (face / his / white, / was / he / and / trying / was / to / hard / stop / from / himself / out. / crying)

➡ _____

_____

50 (found / I / bikes / our / and / the / brought / water / two / to / bottles / Ron.)

➡ _____

51 (drink / "here, / these," said. / I // go / "I'll / get / and / help. // be / I'll / quick / as / I / as / can.")

➡ _____

_____

52 (reply, / in / simply / Ron / my / pressed / hands.)

➡ _____

53 (got / I / my / on / bicycle / and / back / raced / the / along / tracks / I / until / to / got / nearest / the / farmhouse.)

➡ _____

_____

54 (ran / I / the / past / gate / and / a / found / woman / some / washing / dishes / the / in / kitchen.)

➡ _____

_____

55 (to / thanks / her, / was / Ron / to / taken / the / where / hospital, / his / was / leg / put / cast. / a / in)

➡ _____

_____

56 (soon / as / our / as / parents / at / arrived / the / and / hospital / saw / my / us, / mother / with / cried / relief.)

➡ _____

_____

57 (all / but / father / my / was, / said, / that / "let / a / be / to / lesson / you.")

➡ _____

58 (what / and / the / was / lesson? // was / it / *out* / "*Keep* / *Stay* / means / *of* / *out* / *trouble*.")

➡ _____

59 (is / Ron / the / now / of / manager / big / a / company / produces / which / helmets / other / and / products. / safety)

➡ _____

_____

60 (me? / and / am / I / fire / fighter. / a)

➡ _____

49 그의 얼굴은 창백했고 울음을 터뜨리지 않으려고 몹시 애쓰고 있었다.

50 나는 우리 자전거를 찾아서 Ron 에게 물병 두 개를 가져다주었다.

51 "여기, 이거 마셔." 나는 말했다. "내가 가서 도움을 구할게. 최대한 빨리 올게."

52 대답으로 Ron은 그저 내 손을 꽉 잡았다.

53 나는 자전거를 타고 왔던 철길을 따라 달려, 마침내 가장 가까운 농가에 도착했다.

54 대문을 지나 달려가 나는 부엌에서 설거지를 하고 있는 부인을 발견했다.

55 그 부인 덕분에 Ron은 병원으로 이송되었고, 병원에서 다리에 석고붕대를 했다.

56 부모님이 병원에 도착해서 우리를 보자마자, 어머니는 안도감에 울음을 터뜨리셨다.

57 하지만 아버지가 하신 말씀은 "이 일이 너희에게 교훈이 되기를 바란다."가 전부였다.

58 그래서 교훈이 무엇이었을까? 그것은 '들어가지 마시오'라는 말은 '곤경을 멀리하라'는 뜻이라는 것이다.

59 Ron은 지금 안전모와 여러 안전 제품을 생산하는 큰 회사의 관리자이다.

60 그럼 나는? 나는 소방관이다.

※ 다음 우리말을 영어로 쓰시오.

1 들어가지 마시오

➡ _____

2 여름마다 나의 가족은 해안으로 휴가를 가곤 했다.

➡ _____

3 우리는 항상 같은 곳에 가서 똑같은 작은 게스트하우스에 묵었다.

➡ _____

4 우리는 2주 가량 머물며 바다에서 수영하고 작은 마을 주위를 돌아다니곤 했다.

➡ _____

5 다시 말해서, 그런 휴가에서 우리는 특별한 일을 하지 않았고 정말 아무 일도 일어나지 않았다.

➡ _____

_____

6 이 이야기는 내가 12살 때 일이다.

➡ _____

7 관측 이래 영국이 겪은 가장 더운 여름이었기 때문에, 대부분의 사람들은 이 특별한 여름을 기억할 수 있다.

➡ _____

_____

8 6월과 7월 내내 비가 오지 않았고 태양은 연일 쨍쨍했다.

➡ _____

9 하지만 Ron과 나는 그 더위와 태양을 사랑했다.

➡ _____

10 매일 우리는 게스트하우스에서 조금씩 먼 곳으로 자전거를 타고 가곤 했다.

➡ _____

11 어느 날, Ron은 낡은 철로가 우리를 어디로 데려다줄지 알아보려고 그 철로를 따라 자전거를 타기로 결정했다.

➡ _____

_____

12 난 늘 그랬듯 Ron을 따르는 게 즐거웠고, 아침 식사 후에 우리는 출발했다.

➡ _____

13 처음에는 철길을 따라가는 게 어렵지 않아 우리는 나란히 자전거를 타고 갔다.

➡ _____

14 한참 후, 풀이 점점 우거져서 우리는 한 사람이 앞서가고 다른 사람이 뒤에서 가야 했다.

➡ _____

15 Ron이 앞서가고 있었다.

➡ _____

16 철길은 숲으로 이어졌고 나무가 높이 자라 철길 위로 지붕을 형성하며 점점 더 어두워졌다.

➡ _____

_____

17 Ron이 갑자기 멈췄다. "앞을 봐!"라고 그가 외쳤다.

➡ _____

18 나는 그의 옆에 멈춰서 캄캄한 입구를 가로지르는 흰색 나무문을 보았다.

➡ _____

19 "터널이네." 내가 말했다.

➡ _____

20 "맞아. 그리고 문에 '들어가지 마시오'라고 적혀 있어." Ron이 대답했다.

➡ _____

21 "안을 보고 싶니?"

➡ _____

22 사실, 난 안으로 들어가고 싶지 않았다.

➡ _____

23 갑자기 나는 한기를 살짝 느꼈고 햇빛 속으로 되돌아가고 싶었다.

➡ _____

24 그렇지만 나는 "물론이지."라고 답하며 앞으로 움직였다.

➡ _____

25 우리는 문 앞에 자전거를 남겨 두고 넘어갔다.

➡ _____

26 우리는 서늘한 터널로 들어갔다.

➡ _____

27 안의 공기는 묵직했다.

➡ _____

28 우리 머리 위로 점점 더 커지는 소리가 났다.

➡ _____

29 "저게 뭐야?"라고 내가 소리쳤다.

➡ _____

30 "박쥐야." Ron이 말했다. "머리를 숙여." 그러고 나서 그는 계속 움직였다.

➡ _____

31 "너무 빨리 가지 마." 나는 그를 부르며 뒤쫓았다.

➡ _____

32 '나를 두고 가지 마.'라고 말하고 싶었지만, 나는 그렇게 말하지 않았다.
➡ _____

33 그다음 내가 들은 것은 바로 앞에서 나는 큰 소음이었는데, 그것은 마치 고속열차 같은 쿵쾅거리는 소리였다. 이어서 비명이 들렸다.
➡ _____

_____

34 "Ron!" 나는 외쳤다. "Ron, 무슨 일이야? 내 말 들려?" 아무 응답이 없었다.
➡ _____

35 "Ron, 나에게 말해 봐. 무슨 일이 생겼는지 말해 줘."
➡ _____

36 나는 천천히 Ron이 있던 곳으로 걸어갔고 흙과 작은 자갈만을 발견했다.
➡ _____

37 손을 뻗었을 때 나는 축축한 무언가를 느꼈다. Ron의 얼굴이었다!
➡ _____

38 그의 눈은 감겨 있었고 약하게 숨을 쉬고 있었다.
➡ _____

39 "괜찮아, Ron." 나는 속삭였다. "내가 꺼내 줄게."
➡ _____

40 "다리가 부러진 것 같아. 정말 아파. 그냥 가서 도움을 요청해, Ben."
➡ _____

41 "안 돼." 나는 대답했다. "우선 안전한 곳까지 여기에서 형을 꺼낼 거야."
➡ _____

42 나는 손으로 흙과 자갈을 치우기 시작했다.
➡ _____

43 나는 침착했고 내가 잘할 수 있다고 느꼈다.
➡ _____

44 Ron을 뒤덮은 흙을 치우는 데에 오랜 시간이 걸렸다.
➡ _____

45 드디어 나는 그의 몸을 자유롭게 할 수 있었다.
➡ _____

46 팔 밑으로 그를 안고서 그를 터널 입구 쪽으로 조금씩 뒤로 끌어당겼다.
➡ _____

47 오랜 시간이 걸린 듯했지만 결국 나는 Ron을 터널 밖으로 데리고 나올 수 있었다.
➡ _____

48 그는 별로 좋아 보이지 않았다.
➡ _____

49 그의 얼굴은 창백했고 울음을 터뜨리지 않으려고 몹시 애쓰고 있었다.

➡ _____

50 나는 우리 자전거를 찾아서 Ron에게 물병 두 개를 가져다주었다.

➡ _____

51 "여기, 이거 마셔." 나는 말했다. "내가 가서 도움을 구할게. 최대한 빨리 올게."

➡ _____

52 대답으로 Ron은 그저 내 손을 꽉 잡았다.

➡ _____

53 나는 자전거를 타고 왔던 철길을 따라 달려, 마침내 가장 가까운 농가에 도착했다.

➡ _____

54 대문을 지나 달려가 나는 부엌에서 설거지를 하고 있는 부인을 발견했다.

➡ _____

55 그 부인 덕분에 Ron은 병원으로 이송되었고, 병원에서 다리에 석고붕대를 했다.

➡ _____

56 부모님이 병원에 도착해서 우리를 보자마자, 어머니는 안도감에 울음을 터뜨리셨다.

➡ _____

57 하지만 아버지가 하신 말씀은 "이 일이 너희에게 교훈이 되기를 바란다."가 전부였다.

➡ _____

58 그래서 교훈이 무엇이었을까? 그것은 '들어가지 마시오'라는 말은 '곤경을 멀리하라'는 뜻이라는 것이다.

➡ _____

59 Ron은 지금 안전모와 여러 안전 제품을 생산하는 큰 회사의 관리자이다.

➡ _____

60 그럼 나는? 나는 소방관이다.

➡ _____

MEMO

MEMO

적중100

2학기

정답 및 해설

천재 | 이재영

중 **3**

Lesson 5

Are You into Books?

시험대비 실력평가 p.08

01 independence   02 ④   03 ②

04 ②

05 (1) poet (2) author[writer] (3) publication
   (4) hometown (5) turn   06 ④

01 주어진 관계는 반의어 관계이다. dependence: 의존, independence: 독립

02 나머지는 모두 동사와 명사로 짝지어져 있지만 ④번은 동사-형용사로 짝지어져 있다.

03 '무언가를 원하는 강한 감정'을 가리키는 말은 longing(동경, 갈망)이다.

04 look forward to~: ~을 기대하다

05 poet: 시인, poetry: 시, publication:출판, hometown: 고향, turn on: 켜다

06 주어진 문장과 나머지는 '표현하다'를 나타내지만 ④번은 '급행'을 나타낸다.

서술형 시험대비 p.09

01 borrow   02 hometown

03 (1) in a hurry (2) by hand (3) hang out with

04 (1) independence (2) charge (3) further
   (4) shine (5) graduation

05 (1) Hong Kong gained independence from the UK in 1997.
   (2) I need to check my pictures before I publish my novel.
   (3) The forest is home to some rare insects and plants.

06 (1) The graduation ceremony is being held in the gym now.
   (2) The punishment was harsh and unfair.
   (3) I arrest you in the name of the law.

01 주어진 관계는 반의어 관계이다. borrow: 빌리다, lend: 빌려주다

02 '누군가가 태어나 자란 마을'을 가리키는 말은 hometown(고향)이다.

03 in a hurry: 서둘러, by hand 손으로, hang out with ~와 시간을 보내다

04 further: 더, 더 멀리; 더 이상의, independence: 독립, charge: 기소, 혐의, graduation: 졸업, shine: 빛나다

05 independence: 독립, publish: 출판하다, rare: 희귀한

06 graduation ceremony: 졸업식, punishment: 처벌, harsh: 가혹한, arrest: 체포하다

교과서 Conversation

핵심 Check p.10~11

1 ②   2 ②

교과서 대화문 익히기

Check(√) True or False p.12

1 T 2 T 3 T 4 F

교과서 확인학습 p.14~15

Listen – Listen & Answer Dialog 1

Long, no, brings / a book report, recommend / about / show me / New Arrivals, popular / check, out / borrow

Listen – Listen & Answer Dialog 2

novel, book report / me see / borrowed / big fan, all / stop reading / what, has been made / interesting / come out, looking forward to seeing / together

Listen More – Listen and complete

Take a seat, How would you like / yearbook, cool / take / particular, mind / recommend / look good on / can't wait to see / sure

My Speaking Portfolio

real name / where you're from / usually / short story writer / special / well known for / recommend, surprise ending / recommend / who saves her life / can't wait

01 ⑤ 02 ①

03 She can't wait for the concert.

04 They will go to the Thunder concert this Friday.

01 ⑤번은 주문을 확인하겠다는 표현이며, 나머지는 모두 주문할 것인지 묻는 표현이다.

02 ①번을 제외한 나머지는 모두 추천해 주는 표현이다.

03 can't wait for 명사: ~이 너무 기대되다

04 James와 엄마는 이번 주 금요일에 Thunder 콘서트에 갈 것이다.

01 Can you recommend a good novel to read?

02 ⓐ Ken Kuller ⓑ 22nd Street

03 ⑤ 04 ②

05 It'll come out next Thursday. 06 ⑤

07 ⓔ seeing → to see 08 ⑤

09 (A) you are (B) known (C) saves 10 ⑤

03 대화의 내용으로 보아 학생과 사서 선생님과의 대화라는 것을 알 수 있다.

04 주어진 문장은 Ken Kuller를 아는지에 대한 대답으로 적절하므로 (B)에 들어간다.

06 ⑤번을 제외하고 모두 기대감을 표현한다.

07 can't wait to+동사원형

08 지호가 새로운 스타일을 보기 위해 얼마나 기다려야 할지는 알 수 없다.

09 (A)는 간접 의문문으로 '의문사+주어+동사' 어순으로 이어져야 한다. (B) be well known for: ~로 유명하다, (C) who가 가리키는 선행사가 an old artist이므로 saves가 적절하다.

10 O. Henry의 '마지막 잎새'를 추천한 이유는 뜻밖의 결말 때문이다.

01 She recommends a new Ken Kuller book, *22nd Street*.

02 He can find it out in the "New Arrivals" area.

03 (A) the yearbook (B) Dream & Joy Park
   (C) to recommend a hairstyle for him
   (D) seeing how he'll look in the pictures
   (E) Jiho will look cool

04 (D) → (A) → (C) → (E) → (B)

01 서 선생님은 민준에게 Ken Kuller의 새 책, 22nd street을 추천한다.

02 민준은 '신착 도서' 서가에서 찾을 수 있다.

03 지호는 미용사, Mike에게 갔다. 지호는 금요일에 Dream & Joy Park에서 졸업 앨범을 위해 사진을 찍을 것이다. 지호는 마음에 둔 스타일이 없어서 마이크에게 헤어스타일을 추천해 줄 것을 요청했다. Mike는 하나를 제안했다. 지호는 그가 어떻게 사진에서 보일지 기대하고 있다. Mike는 지호가 멋있어 보일 것이라 확신했다.

04 (D) Ken Kuller에 대한 의견 표현 → (A) Ken Kuller의 소설이 영화로 만들어졌다고 소개 → (C) 영화에 대한 생각 표현 → (E) 영화 개봉일 설명 및 기대감 표현 → (B) 기대 표현에 대한 반응

1 (1) had just occurred (2) had got (3) met

2 (1) It (2) that (3) whom

01 ⑤

02 (1) had already left (2) had been called
   (3) It (4) who 03 ④

04 (1) I lost the backpack that I had bought two weeks before.
   (2) He realized that he had lost the keys.
   (3) It is the movie that everybody is talking about.

01 주절의 동사가 said로 과거이고 친구를 만난 것은 그 이전의 사실이므로 과거완료(대과거)를 써야 한다.

02 (1) 귀가한 것보다 그가 떠난 것이 앞서는 것이므로 과거완료가 적절하다. (2) 징집되었음(앞선 사실)을 말하는 것이므로 과거완료가 적절하다. (3) 'It+is/was+강조어(구)+that ...'의 형태로 특정 부분을 강조하여 나타낼 때 사용한다. That이 아닌 It이 적절하다. (4) 강조되는 어구가 사람으로 주격일 때는 that 대신에 who를 쓸 수 있다.

03 'It ~ that 강조 구문'은 'It is/was ~ that ...'의 형태로, 강조하고자 하는 부분을 'It is/was'와 that 사이에 넣고, 나머지 부분을 that 뒤에 써서 주어, 목적어인 명사, 부사(구/절) 등을 강조한다. that이 들어가는 것이 적절하다.

04 (1) 잃어버린 것보다 배낭을 산 것이 앞서므로 과거완료를 이용

한다. (2) 안 것보다 잃어버린 것이 앞서므로 과거완료로 나타낸다. (3) 'It ~ that 강조 구문'은 'It is/was ~ that ...'의 형태로, 강조하고자 하는 부분을 'It is/was'와 that 사이에 넣고, 나머지 부분을 that 뒤에 쓴다.

시험대비 실력평가   p.23~25

01 ②　　　02 ③　　　03 ①

04 (1) had ever made　(2) had presented
　　(3) had lived　(4) who　(5) when　(6) where

05 ④　　　06 ③　　　07 ⑤　　　08 ③

09 ④　　　10 ①　　　11 ②

12 Sherill found the box that Adam had hidden a week before.

13 had played　　　14 ②　　　15 ③

16 (1) I looked at something I had never seen before.
　　(2) He remembered what he had read.
　　(3) It was the lamp that[which] someone broke in the room.
　　(4) It was when Mike told his wife something that she realized her mistake.
　　(5) It is in the school gym that we play basketball every Saturday.

17 ④

01 ② She strongly insisted that she had not been there.

02 ③ 'It ~ that 강조 구문'은 동사를 강조하는데는 쓰이지 않는다.

03 첫 번째 빈칸에는 'It ~ that 강조 구문'으로 that 또는 which가 적절하다. 두 번째 빈칸에는 말한 시점인 과거보다 그전날 밤에 끝낸 것이 앞서므로 과거완료가 적절하다.

04 (1) 그때까지 계속해서 한 연설이므로 과거완료가 적절하다. (2) 목걸이를 찬 시점보다 사 준 시점이 앞서므로 'had presented'가 적절하다. (3) since(~이래로)가 있으므로 '1957년 이래로 살아왔다'는 'had lived'가 적절하다. (4) 강조하는 것이 Kate로 사람이므로 who가 적절하다. (5) 강조하는 것이 시간을 나타내는 부사 yesterday이므로 when이 적절하다. (6) 강조하는 것이 장소를 나타내는 부사구 'in the library'이므로 where가 적절하다.

05 말한 시점(과거)보다 살았던 것이 앞설 때 과거완료로 나타낸다.

06 ③ have met → had met

07 (A)에는 'It ~ that 강조 구문'으로 that이 적절하고, (B)에는 그가 지금까지 많은 책을 써 온 것이므로 현재완료가 적절하다.

08 <보기>와 ③번은 강조 용법의 that이다. ① 부사. (강조를 나타내어) 그렇게, 그 정도. 나는 그렇게 멀리 걸을 수가 없다. ② 대명사 [앞서 말한 명사의 반복을 피하기 위해] (~의) 그것. 중국에 있는 한 도시의 전체 인구는 한국의 세 개 도시의 전체 인구보다 더 많다. ③ 영어를 진정 문학적인 언어로 바꿔 놓은 이는

바로 Chaucer였다. ④ 접속사. [목적어를 이끌어] ~하다는[이라는] 것을. 네가 외국에 갔다온 것을 들었다. ⑤ 지시형용사. 저기 있는 저 남자 한번 봐.

09 집에 온 것보다 방을 청소한 것이 앞서므로 과거완료가 적절하다.

10 'It ~ that 강조 구문'은 강조하고자 하는 부분을 'It is/was'와 that 사이에 넣고, 나머지 부분을 that 뒤에 쓴다.

11 'It ~ that 강조 구문'은 강조하고자 하는 부분을 'It is/was'와 that 사이에 넣고, 나머지 부분을 that 뒤에 쓴다.

12 '찾은 것(과거)'보다 '숨긴 것'이 앞서는 시제이므로 과거완료로 나타낸다.

13 8살에 축구하기 시작했으므로 8살 이래로 축구해 왔다고 과거완료로 나타낼 수 있다.

14 ②번은 'It: 가주어, that절: 진주어'이고, 나머지는 모두 'It ~ that 강조 용법'으로 쓰였다.

15 <보기>는 계속적 용법이다. ① 완료, ② 경험, ③ 계속, ④ 결과, ⑤ 대과거

16 (1) 완료시제와 어울리는 것은 ago가 아니라 before이다. (2) 읽은 것을 기억했던 것이므로 'had remembered'를 remembered로, read를 'had read'로 고치는 것이 적절하다. (3) 강조하는 것이 'the lamp'이므로 who를 that이나 which로 고치는 것이 적절하다. (4) 강조하는 것이 'when Mike told his wife something'이므로 which를 that으로 고치는 것이 적절하다. (5) that 다음에 완전한 절이 나오므로 'the school gym'을 강조하는 것이 아니라 'in the school gym'으로 장소의 부사구를 강조하는 것으로 고치는 것이 적절하다.

17 '세상 사람 누구도 본 적이 없는'이라는 의미로 그때까지의 경험을 나타내는 과거완료를 이용한다.

서술형 시험대비   p.26~27

01 had bought for me

02 (1) It was *gimbap* that Joanne ate for lunch.
　　(2) It is on Saturdays that I take a swimming lesson.
　　(3) The police officer said Mr. Green had driven through a red light.
　　(4) We had had that car for 15 years before it broke down.

03 (1) He had never studied English before he went to London.
　　(2) Daniel had never been to London until he met Jane.
　　(3) He took items that he had given to Carolyn and gave them to Dora.
　　(4) It was her wallet that[which] Judy lost on the bus.

(5) It was on a small island that I was born.

(6) He drove his car carefully.

04 (1) had already broken　(2) It was a ladybug

05 (1) had opened　(2) had already left

06 (1) It was my brother who bought the cake at the store last night.

(2) My brother did buy the cake at the store last night.

(3) It was the cake which my brother bought at the store last night.

(4) It was at the store where my brother bought the cake last night.

(5) It was last night when my brother bought the cake at the store.

07 (1) It was at the age of six that[when] I learned how to read and write.

(2) It is my dad that[who] gets up earliest in my family.

(3) It is an egg sandwich that[which] I eat when I feel blue.

(4) Was it Nick that I saw at the bookstore?

01 과거보다 앞선 시제에 일어난 것을 나타내는 과거완료를 이용한다.

02 (1) 목적어 '김밥'을 강조하는 'It ~ that 강조 용법'을 이용한다. (2) 시간을 나타내는 부사구 'on Saturdays'를 강조하는 'It ~ that 강조 용법'을 이용한다. (3) 경찰관이 말한 것을 과거시제로 하고 Green 씨가 빨간 신호등을 무시하고 운전한 것을 과거완료로 나타낸다. (4) 그 차가 고장 난 것을 과거시제로 하고 우리가 15년 동안 소유한 것을 과거완료로 나타낸다.

03 (1) 그가 런던에 가기 전에 일어난 일이므로 과거완료시제가 적절하다. (2) 그가 Jane을 만나기 전의 일이므로 과거완료로 고치는 것이 적절하다. (3) Carolyn에게 주었던 것을 Dora에게 준 것이므로 'had given'으로 고치는 것이 적절하다. (4) 강조하는 것이 'her wallet'이므로 who를 that이나 which로 고치는 것이 적절하다. (5) 'where I was born'이 완전한 절이므로 'a small island'를 강조하는 것이 아니라 'on a small island'로 장소의 부사구를 강조하는 것으로 고치는 것이 적절하다. (6) 'It ~ that ...' 강조 구문은 동사나 양태부사를 강조하는 데 쓰이지 않는다.

04 (1) 과거보다 앞서는 일이나 상태를 나타내는 과거완료(대과거)를 이용한다. (2) 목적어 'a ladybug'를 강조하는 'It ~ that 강조 용법'을 이용한다.

05 (1) 과거완료의 대과거 용법을 이용한다. (2) 과거완료의 결과 용법을 이용한다.

06 과거시제이므로 강조하고자 하는 부분을 It was와 that 사이에 넣고, 나머지 부분을 that 뒤에 쓴다. 이때 that을 사용하지 말라고

하였으므로, that 대신에 강조하고자 하는 것이 사람이면 who, 사물이면 which, 장소일 경우 where, 시간일 경우 when을 사용한다. 또한 'It is[was] ~ that ...' 구문은 동사를 강조할 수 없으므로 동사는 동사 앞에 do/does/did를 사용하여 강조한다.

07 'It ~ that 강조 구문'은 강조하고자 하는 부분을 'It is/was'와 that 사이에 넣고, 나머지 부분을 that 뒤에 쓴다. (4)번은 평서문으로 고친 후 강조 용법으로 쓰고 그것을 다시 의문문으로 바꾸면 쉽다.

교과서 Reading

확인문제　p.28

1 T　2 F　3 T　4 F

확인문제　p.29

1 T　2 F　3 T　4 F

교과서 확인학습 A　p.30~32

01 Who

02 where, in a hurry

03 fills

04 without a worry

05 count

06 Memory

07 another

08 Loneliness

09 Longing

10 for

11 for another star

12 these lines

13 part of, by

14 still remains, poems

15 was born

16 for his school

17 so, that

18 it was, that

19 a lot of poems

20 a literary magazine

21 copied, by hand

22 to have his own copy

23 to be a doctor

24 hung out with, where, lost country

25 To celebrate his graduation, under the title

26 three copies, by hand

27 was given to, another, the last one

28 advised against　29 followed, gave up

30 to study further, had studied

31 began to study　32 for taking part in

33 on the same charges　34 after harsh treatment

35 It was, that

36 they were finally published

37 was given, had thought of

38 are loved by, like

1 A Poet Who Loved Stars

2 In the sky where seasons pass in a hurry

3 Autumn fills the air.

4 And ready I stand, without a worry,

5 To count all the stars there.

6 Memory for one star,

7 Love for another star,

8 Loneliness for another star,

9 Longing for another star,

10 Poetry for another star,

11 And, oh, mother, mother for another star.

12 Have you read these lines before?

13 They are part of the poem "Counting Stars at Night" by Yoon Dong-ju.

14 The poem was written a long time ago but still remains one of Korea's favorite poems.

15 Dong-ju was born in 1917 near Yanbin, China.

16 As a young boy, he loved sports, and he was a soccer player for his school.

17 He also loved sewing so much that he sewed the numbers on all his friends' soccer uniforms.

18 However, it was literature that he loved most.

19 In elementary school he wrote a lot of poems.

20 He even made a literary magazine with his cousin, Song Mong-gyu.

21 In middle school he once borrowed a poetry book by a famous poet of the time, Baek Seok, and copied the whole book by hand.

22 He really wanted to have his own copy of the rare book.

23 His parents wanted him to be a doctor, but Dong-ju chose to study literature at a college in Seoul.

24 During his college years, he often hung out with other young poets and wrote poetry where he expressed feelings about his hometown and lost country.

25 To celebrate his graduation, he wished to publish 19 of his poems under the title, *Heaven, Wind, Stars, and Poetry*.

26 He made three copies of the book by hand.

27 One was given to his close friend, Jeong Byeong-uk, another was presented to his favorite professor, and the last one was kept for himself.

28 However, his professor advised against his plan because he thought the Japanese government would not allow the publication.

29 Dong-ju followed his advice and gave up the idea.

30 Dong-ju decided to study further in the country where his father had studied before.

31 So, in 1942, Dong-ju and his cousin began to study in Japan.

32 On July 10 the following year, his cousin was arrested by the Japanese police for taking part in an independence movement.

33 Four days later, Dong-ju was also arrested on the same charges.

34 In 1945, Dong-ju and his cousin died in prison after harsh treatment by the police.

35 It was just a few months later that Korea achieved independence from Japan.

36 In 1948, Jeong Byeong-uk brought Dong-ju's poems to the poet's brother, and they were finally published.

37 The book was given the title the poet had thought of many years before.

38 His poems are loved by people of all ages, and thus they still shine brightly in our hearts like the stars in the autumn night sky.

01 ②   02 ①, ④

03 favorite poem → favorite poems

04 ①, ③   05 (A) During (B) other (C) another

06 under the title, *Heaven, Wind, Stars, and Poetry*

07 ④   08 (A) poems (B) a literary magazine

09 ⑤   10 in which   11 ③

12 participating in   13 sewing 또는 to sew

14 ③   15 ④   16 ②

17 ⑤   18 studying → to study

19 ③   20 ⓑ In 번 → On   21 ⑤

22 ③

01 ⓐ in a hurry: 서둘러, ⓑ by: ~에 의한(저자를 나타낼 때 사용)

02 (A)와 ①, ④: 경험 용법, ②, ⑤: 계속 용법, ③: 완료 용법

03 one+of+복수명사: ~ 중의 하나

04 동주가 그의 계획에 반대하는 교수의 충고를 따랐다고 했으므로, 그 생각을 '포기했다'고 하는 것이 적절하다. abandon = give up: 포기하다, ②, ⑤: 제의[제안]했다, ④: 설명했다

05 (A) during+기간을 나타내는 명사, while+주어+동사, (B) 뒤에 복수명사인 young poets가 나오므로 other가 적절하다. another+단수명사, (C) 책 세 부 중에 두 번째에 해당하므로 another가 적절하다. (세 개의 대상을 가리킬 때 하나는 one,

또 하나는 another, 나머지 하나는 the other나 the last one, the rest 등으로 쓴다.), the other: 둘 중에서 나머지 하나를 가리킴.

06 under the title: ~의 제목으로

07 ⓐ와 ④: ~일 때, ① ~한 대로, ② ~이기 때문에, ③ ~하다시피[~하듯이], ⑤ [보통 as ~ as ...로 형용사·부사 앞에서] …와 같은 정도로, 마찬가지로, (as ~ as …에서, 앞의 as가 지시부사, 뒤의 as는 접속사)

08 동주는 초등학교에 다닐 때 많은 '시'를 썼고, 심지어 사촌 송몽규와 '문학잡지'를 만들기도 했다.

09 동주가 필사한 시집의 제목이 무엇이었는지는 대답할 수 없다. ① He was born in 1917. ② He loved soccer. ③ Because he loved sewing so much. ④ In elementary school.

10 관계부사 where는 '전치사+관계대명사(in which)'로 바꿔 쓸 수 있다.

11 ⓑ와 ③: 혐의(명사), in court: 법정에서, ① (상품·서비스에 대한) 요금(명사), ② 충전하다(동사), ④ 비난하다, 고소[고발]하다(동사), prosecutor: 검사, ⑤ (요금, 값을) 청구하다(동사)

12 글그들은 독립운동에 '가담했다'는 이유로 일본 경찰에게 체포되었다. take part in = participate in: ~에 참가하다

13 love는 목적어로 to부정사와 동명사를 둘 다 쓸 수 있다.

14 주어진 문장의 However에 주목한다. ③번 앞 문장에서 바느질하는 것을 무척 좋아한다고 한 다음에, '그러나' 그가 가장 사랑한 것은 문학이었다고 해야 하므로 ③번이 적절하다.

15 동주는 '초등학교'에 다닐 때 사촌 송몽규와 문학잡지를 만들었다.

16 그의 교수는 일본 정부가 출판을 허가하지 않으리라 여겨, 그의 계획에 '반대하는' 충고를 했다고 하는 것이 적절하다. against: ~에 반대하여

17 ⑤의 his는 동주가 가장 좋아하는 교수를 가리키고, 나머지는 다 동주를 가리킨다.

18 choose는 to부정사를 목적어로 취하기 때문에, studying을 to study로 고치는 것이 적절하다.

19 주어진 문장의 Four days later에 주목한다. ③번 앞 문장에서 말한 그의 사촌이 독립운동에 가담했다는 이유로 일본 경찰에게 체포된 날로부터 나흘 뒤를 말하는 것이므로 ③번이 적절하다.

20 날짜가 있을 때는 전치사 on을 사용하는 것이 적절하다.

21 이 글은 '동주와 그의 사촌이 독립운동에 가담했다는 이유로 일본 경찰에게 체포되어 가혹 행위를 당한 후, 한국이 일본으로부터 독립하기 불과 몇 달 전에 감옥에서 사망했다'는 내용의 글이므로, 주제로는 ⑤번 '동주와 그의 사촌의 독립 운동과 불행한 사망'이 적절하다.

22 동사는 'It is ~ that ...' 강조 구문으로 강조할 수 없고, Jeong

Byeong-uk did bring Dong-ju's poems to the poet's brother in 1948.처럼 강조의 조동사 do(es)나 did를 사용하여 강조하는 것이 적절하다.

01 where   02 in haste   03 These lines
04 (A) poems   (B) literary   (C) rare
05 it was literature that he loved most
06 bought → borrowed   07 was given
08 nineteen forty-eight   09 his poems
10 further   11 harsh treatment
12 He gave one to his close friend, Jeong Byeong-uk, presented another to his favorite professor, and kept the last one for himself.
13 졸업을 기념하여 그가 '하늘과 바람과 별과 시'라는 제목으로 자신의 시 19편을 출판하는 것
14 (A) literature   (B) a doctor

01 뒤에 완전한 문장이 이어지고 선행사가 장소이므로, 관계부사 where가 적절하다.

02 in a hurry = in haste: 서둘러

03 '이 시 구절들'을 가리킨다.

04 (A) 많은 '시'를 썼다고 해야 하므로 poems가 적절하다. poet: 시인, (B) '문학잡지'를 만들기도 했다고 해야 하므로 형용사 literary가 적절하다. literally: 문자[말] 그대로(부사), (C) 그 '희귀한' 책을 한 부 갖고 싶었던 것이라고 해야 하므로 rare가 적절하다. rare: 희귀한, common: 흔한

05 'it is ~ that ...' 강조 구문을 사용하여 it was와 that 사이에 강조하려는 말 literature를 쓰는 것이 적절하다.

06 동주가 중학교에 다니던 때 책 전체를 필사했던 백석의 시집은 그가 '산' 것이 아니라 '빌린' 것이다.

07 '책에는 시인이 수년 전에 생각해 두었던 제목이 붙었다'고 해야 하므로 수동태로 쓰는 것이 적절하다.

08 두 자리씩 끊어서 읽는 것이 적절하다.

09 '그의 시'를 가리킨다.

10 학업을 '이어가기로' 했다고 해야 하므로 further로 쓰는 것이 적절하다. far–farther–farthest: 멀리(거리), far–further–furthest: 더 이상의, 추가의(정도)

11 일본 경찰의 '가혹 행위'가 있었기 때문에 동주와 그의 사촌은 감옥에서 사망했다.

12 He를 주어로 하여 능동태로 고치는 것이 적절하다.

13 His plan was to publish 19 of his poems under the title, *Heaven, Wind, Stars, and Poetry* to celebrate his graduation.

14 그의 부모는 그가 '의사'가 되기를 바랐지만 동주는 서울에 있는 대학에서 '문학'을 전공하기로 했다. major in: ~을 전공하다

01 independence   02 ③

03 (1) poem   (2) whole   (3) rare   (4) loneliness
     (5) literature

04 ①   05 ⑤

06 (1) The robber was arrested near the bank.
     (2) Our team went through harsh training.
     (3) He tried his best to achieve his goal.
     (4) I want fair treatment.

07 (1) The professor advised against the use of
     sugar.
     (2) Let's celebrate our graduation and have a
     party.
     (3) Designers and editors try their best to make a
     gook book.

08 ⓔ to see → to seeing   09 ④   10 ②

11 What brings you here?   12 ⑤

13 (B) → (E) → (C) → (A) → (D)

14 ⑤   15 ⑤   16 ④

17 ⓐ, ⓓ, ⓔ   18 ①, ②   19 ⑤   20 ③

21 ②   22 ②   23 ①, ③, ④   24 ⑤

25 had thought   26 ①

---

01 '다른 나라의 지배를 받지 않는 상태'를 가리키는 말은 independence(독립)이다.

02 poet: 시인

03 rare: 드문, 희귀한, loneliness: 외로움, poem: 시, whole: 전체의, literature: 문학

04 check out: (도서관에서) 대출하다, come out: 나오다, hang out with: ~와 시간을 보내다

05 주어진 문장은 '주다, 제출하다'를 의미하며 이와 같은 의미를 나타내는 것은 ⑤번이다. ①, ②번은 '선물', ③, ④번은 '현재의'를 나타낸다.

06 robber: 도둑, try one's best: 최선을 다하다, achieve: (일·목적)을 이루다, fair: 공정한, treatment: 대우

07 advise against: ~에 반대하는 충고를 하다, graduation: 졸업, editor: 편집자

08 look forward to+~ing: ~하기를 기대하다

09 ④ Ken Kuller의 Four Eyes가 영화로 만들어졌다.

10 주어진 문장은 책을 추천해 달라는 요청에 대한 답변으로 적절하므로 ②번이 알맞다.

12 ⑤ '22nd Street'은 대출 가능하다.

13 (B) 언제 사진을 찍는지 대답 → (E) 마음에 둔 스타일이 있는지 질문 → (C) 대답 및 추천 요청 → (A) 제안 → (D) 반응 및 기대 표현

14 추천을 요청하는 표현에 '네 말에 전적으로 동의해.'라는 대답은 어색하다.

15 'It ~ that ...' 강조 구문에서 강조하는 대상이 장소의 부사(구/절)일 경우, that 대신에 where로 바꿔 쓸 수 있다.

16 He had already left when I returned home. 돌아오기 전에 이미 떠난 것이므로 돌아온 것은 과거로, 떠난 것은 과거완료로 써야 한다.

17 ⓑ had got → got, already began → had already begun ⓒ has → had ⓕ which → that[who] ⓖ That → It

18 ① Because she had not studied hard, she failed the test. ② It was in 2014 that my family moved to this city.

19 ⓐ 축구 유니폼 '위'에 번호를 바느질한 것이므로, 표면에 붙어서 '위'를 나타내는 on이 적절하다. ⓑ by hand: 손으로, 직접

20 이 글은 동주가 어린 소년이었을 때 운동을 좋아했고 바느질하는 것을 무척 좋아했지만, 그가 가장 사랑한 것은 문학이었다는 내용의 글이므로, 주제로는 ③번 '동주가 무엇보다도 가장 사랑한 것은 문학이었다.'가 적절하다.

21 동주가 어린 소년이었을 때 운동을 좋아한 이유는 알 수 없다. ① He was born near Yanbin, China. ③ He sewed the numbers on their soccer uniforms. ④ With his cousin, Song Mong-gyu. ⑤ Baek Seok's poetry book.

22 'he expressed feelings about his hometown and lost country in poetry'에서, 'in poetry'를 관계부사 where로 바꾸는 것이 적절하다.

23 ⓑ와 ②, ⑤: 부사적 용법, ①, ④: 형용사적 용법, ③: 명사적 용법

24 졸업을 기념하여 그는 '하늘과 바람과 별과 시'라는 제목으로 자신의 시 19편을 출판하고 싶어 했지만, 그 생각을 '포기했다.' ③ hang around with = hang out with: ~와 시간을 보내다

25 시인이 책의 제목을 생각한 것은 책에 제목을 붙인 것보다 먼저 일어난 일이므로 과거완료 had thought를 쓰는 것이 적절하다.

26 finally = at last = in the end = eventually = in the long run: 마침내, ① (여러 개를 언급할 때) 마지막으로

01 (1) take part in   (2) looking forward to
     (3) is well known for   (4) Give it a try

02 ④   03 ⓐ → a new book by Ken Kuller

04 ⑤   05 Can you recommend one for me?

06 ②   07 ③

08 Can you recommend a popular story with a
surprise ending?

09 His short stories[They] are famous because of
surprise endings.

10 It's about a sick girl and an old artist who saves
her life.

11 (1) the U.S.   (2) short stories
   (3) surprising endings   (4) *The Last Leaf*

12 She was not upset because she had bought
   some extra balloons.

13 ④

14 (1) He showed me some poems he had written
   himself.
   (2) When I came back home, I found somebody
   had turned on the TV.
   (3) It was on the bus that[where] Judy lost her
   wallet.
   (4) It was in 1776 that[when] the U.S. gained
   independence from Great Britain.

15 ②   16 ①   17 ④   18 ①
19 ②   20 ⑤
21 has studied → had studied   22 ②, ④

01 take part in: ~에 참가하다, look forward to: ~을 기대하다,
   be well known for: ~로 유명하다, give it a try: 시도하다

02 (A) stop+~ing: ~하던 것을 멈추다, stop+to부정사: ~하
   기 위해 멈추다 (B) 영화로 만들어졌으므로 made, (C) look
   forward to ~ing: ~하기를 기대하다

03 ⓐ를 제외한 나머지는 모두 영화를 가리킨다.

04 민준과 소라가 언제 그 영화를 보러 갈지는 알 수 없다.

06 위 대화는 미용사와 손님의 관계임을 알 수 있다.

07 지호가 마음에 둔 특별한 헤어 스타일은 없었다.

09 Mr. Henry의 단편 소설들은 뜻밖의 결말로 유명하다.

10 '마지막 잎새'는 아픈 소녀와 그녀의 목숨을 구하는 늙은 화가의
   이야기이다.

12 시간차가 드러나도록 하라고 했으므로 앞서는 사건을 과거완료
   시제로 나타낸다.

13 It is in the park that Patricia plays badminton every
   weekend.

14 (1) 그가 쓴 것이 보여 준 시점보다 앞서므로 과거완료로 나타
   낸다. (2) TV를 켠 것이 발견한 시점보다 앞서므로 과거완료
   로 나타낸다. (3) 'It ~ that …' 강조 구문에서 강조하는 대상이
   'on the bus'로 장소를 나타내므로, which가 아니라 that이나
   where로 써야 한다. (4) 'It ~ that …' 강조 구문이며 what이
   아닌 that이 되어야 하고 that 이하가 완전한 절이므로 강조하는
   대상이 1776이 아니라 시간의 부사구 in 1776이 되어야 한다.
   that 대신 when으로 써도 좋다.

15 첫 번째 문장에서는 빌려준 것이 잃어버린 것보다 앞선 시제이
   므로 과거완료 had lent가 적절하다. 두 번째 문장에서는 'It ~
   that …' 강조 구문에서 강조하는 대상이 시간의 부사(구/절)일
   경우, when으로 바꿔 쓸 수 있다.

16 앞에 나오는 내용과 상반되는 내용이 뒤에 이어지므로
   However가 가장 적절하다. ② 그러므로, ③ 즉[말하자면], ⑤

그 결과

17 ⓑ와 ④: '(It is[was] … that ~'의 형태로 명사[대명사]를 강
   조하여) ~하는 것은, ① 보어절을 이끄는 접속사, ② 지시형용
   사, ③ [원인·이유] ~이므로, ~ 때문에, ⑤ 동격절을 이끄는 접
   속사

18 ⓐ for oneself: 혼자 힘으로, 자기를 위하여, ⓑ 그의 교수는
   그의 계획에 '반대하는' 충고를 했다. against: ~에 반대하여[맞
   서], for: ~에 찬성[지지]하는

19 ②번 다음 문장의 the book에 주목한다. 주어진 문장에서 동주
   가 출판하고 싶어 했던 책을 받고 있으므로 ②번이 적절하다.

20 이 글은 '동주가 졸업을 기념하여 '하늘과 바람과 별과 시'라는
   제목으로 자신의 시 19편을 출판하고 싶어했지만, 그의 교수가
   일본 정부가 출판을 허가하지 않으리라 여겨 그의 계획에 반대
   하는 충고를 했고, 결국 동주는 그의 충고를 따라 자신의 생각을
   포기했다'는 내용의 글이므로, 제목으로는 ⑤번 '시집 출판이라
   는 이루지 못한 소원'이 적절하다.

21 동주의 아버지가 공부한 것은 동주가 일본에 공부하러 가기로
   결심한 것보다 앞서 일어난 일이므로, 과거완료인 had studied
   로 고치는 것이 적절하다.

22 take part in = participate in = join: ~에 참가하다, ①
   attend to: ~을 돌보다, 시중들다, ③ deal in: ~을 매매하다,
   ⑤ take into account: ~을 고려하다

서술형 실전문제
p.52~53

01 He is going to Dream & Joy Park.

02 He asks Mike to recommend a hairstyle for him.

03 He is going to take pictures for the yearbook.

04 (1) The witness admitted that he had not told the
   complete truth.
   (2) I learned that he had been sick since last
   week.
   (3) It was my parents that[who] got married in a
   small restaurant.
   (4) It was his endless efforts that[which] moved all
   the animals' hearts.

05 (1) My aunt knew London so well because she
   had visited the city many times.
   (2) It was *The Potato Eaters* that Vincent van
   Gogh painted in 1885.

06 (A) sewed   (B) that   (C) borrowed

07 a poetry book by a famous poet of the time,
   Baek Seok

08 Because he really wanted to have his own copy
   of the rare book.

09 (A) hung   (B) last   (C) followed

9

10 his professor advised against his plan because he thought the Japanese government would not allow the publication

11 He expressed feelings about his hometown and lost country.

01 지호는 이번 주 금요일에 Dream & Joy Park에 갈 것이다.

02 지호는 Mike에게 헤어스타일을 추천해 줄 것을 요청한다.

03 지호는 졸업 앨범을 위해 사진을 찍을 것이다.

04 (1) 목격자가 '진실을 말한 것이 아님을 인정했다.'라는 의미로 인정한 시점보다 진실을 말하지 않은 것이 앞선 시점이므로 과거완료로 나타내는 것이 적절하다. (2) since가 있으므로 '지난주부터 계속 아팠다'는 의미로 과거완료로 나타내는 것이 적절하다. (3) 접속사 없이 동사가 2개가 나온 형태이므로 'It ~ that ...' 강조 구문의 that이나 who를 넣어 주는 것이 적절하다. (4) 'It ~ that ...' 강조 구문에서 강조하고자 하는 것이 'his endless efforts'로 사물이므로 who를 that이나 which로 고치는 것이 적절하다.

05 (1) 잘 아는 것이 그 전에 여러 번 방문했기 때문이므로 방문했던 것을 과거완료로 나타낸다. (2) 'It ~ that 강조 구문'은 강조하고자 하는 부분을 'It is/was'와 that 사이에 넣고, 나머지 부분을 that 뒤에 쓴다.

06 (A) 친구들의 축구 유니폼에 번호를 '바느질해' 주기도 했다고 해야 하므로 sewed가 적절하다. sew-sewed-sewn: 바느질하다, 깁다, saw-sawed-sawn: 톱으로 켜다, (B) 'it is ~ that ...' 강조 구문으로 literature를 강조하는 구문이므로 that이 적절하다. (C) 백석의 시집을 '빌려 와서' 책 전체를 필사하기도 했다고 해야 하므로 borrowed가 적절하다. borrow: 빌리다, lend-lent-lent: 빌려주다

07 '당대의 유명한 시인, 백석의 시집'을 가리킨다.

08 그는 정말로 그 희귀한 책을 한 부 갖고 싶었기 때문이었다.

09 (A) '다른 젊은 시인들과 어울려 다녔다'고 해야 하므로 hung이 적절하다. hang out with: ~와 시간을 보내다, hang이 '교수형에 처하다'의 뜻일 때는 hang-hanged-hanged로 변화하지만, 그 외에는 hang-hung-hung으로 변화한다. (B) '마지막 하나'라고 해야 하므로 last가 적절하다. last: 마지막의, latest: 최근의, (C) 그의 충고를 '따라' 그 생각을 포기했다고 해야 하므로 followed가 적절하다. refuse: 거절하다

10 'against'를 보충하면 된다.

11 그는 그의 시에서 '고향과 잃어버린 조국에 대한 심정'을 표현했다.

|모범답안|

01 (A) a book report (B) all of his mystery books
(C) has been made into a movie (D) interesting

02 (A) Tommy (B) washes his face
(C) black eyes (D) jumps high (E) in my bed

01 독후감을 위해 Ken Kuller의 새 책을 읽고 있는 중에, 소라가 내게 와서 Ken Kuller에 대해 이야기했다. 나는 소라가 이미 Ken Kuller를 알고 있으며 그의 모든 미스터리 책들을 읽었다는 것을 알게 되었다. 그녀는 내게 그의 소설 Four Eyes가 영화로 만들어졌다고 이야기했다. 내가 영화 포스터를 보았을 때, 그것은 재미있어 보였다. 소라는 그걸 보는 것을 기대하고 있다.

01 (1) government (2) publication (3) literature
(4) literary

02 ⓔ → Can I check it out?   03 ⑤

04 (A) a good novel
(B) a new Ken Kuller book, *22nd Street*
(C) among teens (D) "New Arrivals" area

05 He borrowed it this morning.

06 *Four Eyes* has been made into a movie.

07 He thinks Ken Kuller is a great writer.

08 ③

09 I'm looking forward to seeing how I'll look in the pictures.

10 ⑤   11 ②   12 ⑤

13 (1) had gone (2) had fixed

14 ③   15 ④

16 (1) It is fried chicken that I eat when I feel good.
(2) It was Mr. Brown that[who] saved the child in the river.
(3) She insisted that she had not been there the previous night.
(4) When the children arrived at the camp, their parents had already started cooking.

17 ①, ③, ④, ⑥   18 literary

19 He also loved sewing so much that he sewed the numbers on all his friends' soccer uniforms.

20 literature   21 ⑤   22 copy

23 Because he thought the Japanese government would not allow the publication.

24 ②   25 ③   26 living

27 plays, poems, novels, or cartoons

01 government: 정부, publication: 출판, literature: 문학, literary: 문학의

02 '타동사+부사'로 이루어진 경우 목적어가 인칭대명사일 때 '동사+대명사 목적어+부사'의 순서에 유의한다.

03 *22nd street*이 왜 영국의 십대들에게 인기가 있는지는 알 수 없다.

04 오늘 나는 책을 빌리러 도서관에 갔다. 나는 독후감을 써야 하는데 무엇을 읽어야 할지 몰랐다. 나는 서 선생님께 좋은 소설을 추천해 주실 것을 요청했다. 선생님은 *Ken Kuller*의 신간, '22번가'를 소개해 주셨다. 나는 이 책이 영국의 십 대들 사이에서 많은 인기가 있다고 들었다. 나는 '신착 도서' 서가에서 그것을 찾았다. 나는 이 책을 읽는 것을 매우 기대하고 있다.

05 민준이는 Ken Kuller의 새 책을 오늘 아침에 빌렸다.

06 Ken Kuller의 소설 중, *Four Eyes*가 영화로 만들어졌다.

07 민준이는 Ken Kuller가 위대한 작가라고 생각한다.

08 이어지는 대답에서 마음에 두고 있는 특정한 스타일이 없다는 대답이 이어지므로 ⓒ에 들어가는 것이 알맞다.

09 look forward to+~ing: ~하기를 기대하다

10 위 대화는 미용실에서 이루어지는 대화임을 알 수 있다.

11 주어진 문장은 주로 무엇을 쓰는지에 대한 대답으로서 적절하므로 (B)가 적절하다.

12 대화를 통해 '마지막 잎새'에서 늙은 화가가 어떻게 아픈 소녀를 구했는지 알 수 없다.

13 (1) 이미 가고 없다는 과거완료의 '결과' 용법을 이용한다. (2) 과거의 어느 시점보다 먼저 일어난 일이나 상태를 나타낼 때 과거완료를 사용한다.

14 It is the car that[which] James Bond drove in the famous films called 007.

15 주어진 문장과 ④번은 과거완료의 대과거 용법이다. ① 결과 ② 계속 ③ 경험 ⑤ 완료

16 (1) eat에 맞추어 'It is'로 쓰는 것이 적절하다. 또는 'It was'에 맞추어 ate로 쓰는 것이 적절하다. (2) 접속사 없이 동사가 2개가 나온 형태이므로 'It ~ that ...' 강조 구문의 that이나 who를 넣어 주는 것이 적절하다. (3) 그 전날, 거기에 없었다고 주장하는 것이므로 과거완료로 나타내는 것이 적절하다. (4) 도착한 시점보다 시작한 시점이 앞서므로 과거완료로 쓰는 것이 적절하다.

17 ② The train had left when I arrived at the station. ⑤ It was Uncle Ben that[who] broke Plum's toy. ⑦ It was the drums that[which] he played this year.

18 literary: 문학의, 문학을 쓰거나 연구하거나 혹은 이해하는 것과 관련된

19 so를 보충하면 된다. so+형용사/부사+that ~: 너무 …해서 ~하다

20 무엇보다도 동주가 가정 사랑한 것은 '문학'이었다.

21 앞에 나오는 내용과 상반되는 내용이 뒤에 이어지므로 However가 가장 적절하다. ① 게다가, 더욱이, ② 다시 말해서, ③ 비슷하게, ④ 따라서, 그러므로

22 one은 copy를 가리킨다.

23 '일본 정부가 출판을 허가하지 않으리라고 여겨', 그의 계획에 반대하는 충고를 했다.

24 ⓐ, ②, ⑤: 동명사, ①, ③, ④: 현재분사

25 동주와 그의 사촌은 1942년에 일본에서 공부를 시작했고 '다음해(1943년)' 7월 10일에 그의 사촌은 독립운동에 가담했다는 이유로 일본 경찰에게 체포되었다.

26 동사 imagine의 목적어로 동명사 being과 병렬구조를 이루도록 쓰는 것이 적절하다.

25 '희곡, 시, 소설 또는 만화'를 가리킨다.

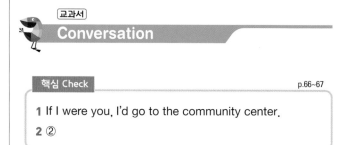

Lesson 6

Together in Our Community

시험대비 실력평가
p.64

01 (m)essy 02 ① 03 ⑤
04 (1) (n)otice (2) (v)iew (3) population 05 ④
06 (1) Jane volunteered at a children's hospital last year.
　(2) I usually go for a walk on the common.
　(3) There are many horses on the grassland.

01 주어진 단어는 반의어 관계를 나타낸다. messy: 지저분한, tidy: 깨끗한
02 '들판에서 풀을 뜯다'라는 뜻을 가리키는 말은 graze(풀을 뜯다)이다. 다.
03 주어진 문장에서 mind는 '신경을 쓰다, 싫어하다'를 나타낸다.
04 notice: 알아차리다, view: 전망, population: 인구
05 주어진 문장은 공유지를 나타내며 이와 같은 의미로 쓰인 것은 ④번이다. 나머지는 '흔한, 공동의'를 뜻한다.
06 volunteer: 자원봉사하다, common: 공유지, grassland: 풀밭

서술형 시험대비
p.65

01 impatient
02 sat – sat, seated – seated /
　lay – lain, lied – lied, laid – laid
03 (1) harsh (2) support (3) lesson (4) resources
　(5) values
04 (1) in (s)ecret (2) break a rule (3) at last
　(4) To (m)ake (m)atters worse
05 (1) Keep my advice in mind during the trip.
　(2) Students are not allowed to speak loudly in the library.
　(3) Koreans visit their relatives on New Year's Day by tradition.

01 주어진 단어는 반의어 관계를 나타낸다. patient: 인내심이 있는, impatient: 인내심이 없는
03 value: 가치; 소중하게 생각하다, harsh: 가혹한, lesson: 교훈, support: 지지하다, resource: 자원

04 in secret: 몰래, 비밀리에, break a rule: 규칙을 어기다, at last: 마침내, to make matters worse: 엎친 데 덮친 격으로
05 keep ~ in mind: ~을 명심하다, be allowed to: ~하는 것이 허용되다, by tradition: 전통에 따라

교과서
Conversation

핵심 Check
p.66~67

1 If I were you, I'd go to the community center.
2 ②

교과서 대화문 익히기

Check(√) True or False
p.68

1 F 2 F 3 F 4 T

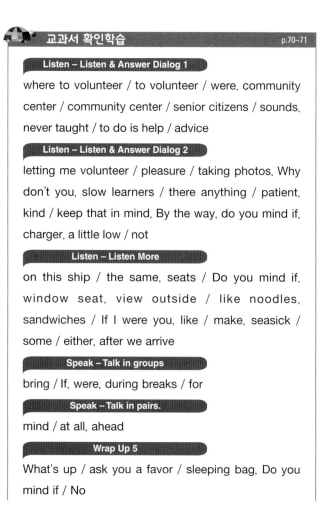

교과서 확인학습
p.70~71

Listen – Listen & Answer Dialog 1
where to volunteer / to volunteer / were, community center / community center / senior citizens / sounds, never taught / to do is help / advice

Listen – Listen & Answer Dialog 2
letting me volunteer / pleasure / taking photos, Why don't you, slow learners / there anything / patient, kind / keep that in mind, By the way, do you mind if, charger, a little low / not

Listen – Listen More
on this ship / the same, seats / Do you mind if, window seat, view outside / like noodles, sandwiches / If I were you, like / make, seasick / some / either, after we arrive

Speak – Talk in groups
bring / If, were, during breaks / for

Speak – Talk in pairs.
mind / at all, ahead

Wrap Up 5
What's up / ask you a favor / sleeping bag, Do you mind if / No

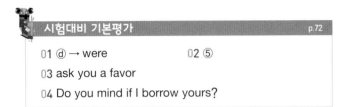

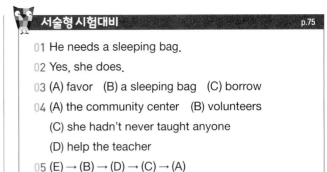

Wrap Up 6

stomach growls / have breakfast / no time / If I were you

시험대비 기본평가 p.72

01 ⓓ → were　　　　02 ⑤

03 ask you a favor

04 Do you mind if I borrow yours?

01 가정법 과거 구문으로 'If+주어+과거동사/were' 형태로 이어져야 하므로 were가 적절하다.

02 Gina는 Tom의 조언에 따라 간식을 가져올 것이다.

03 ask A a favor: A에게 부탁하다

04 'Do you mind ~?'는 상대방에게 허락을 요청하는 표현이다.

시험대비 실력평가 p.73~74

01 volunteer　　　02 ①　　　03 ⑤

04 ①　　　　　　05 ⑤

06 Do you mind if I take the window seat?

07 It's because she wants to see the view outside.

08 He doesn't want her to eat them because they may make her seasick.

09 (D) → (B) → (E) → (A) → (C)　　10 ⑤

01 '강요받지 않고 또는 돈을 지불 받지 않고 무언가를 하겠다고 하다'를 가리키는 말은 volunteer(자원봉사하다)이다.

02 ①번을 제외한 나머지는 모두 충고를 하는 표현이다. ①번은 허락을 구할 때 쓸 수 있다.

03 어르신들을 돕는 것은 지민이다.

04 ①번은 학습 속도가 느린 학습자들을 도울 수 있을지 의구심을 나타낸다.

05 위 대화에서 어떤 종류의 충전기를 지민이 필요로 하는지 알 수 없다.

07 소라는 바깥 풍경을 보고 싶기 때문에 창가 자리에 앉기를 원한다.

08 소라의 아빠는 국수나 샌드위치 같은 음식이 뱃멀미를 일으킬 수 있기 때문에 소라가 그것들을 먹기를 원하지 않는다.

09 (D) 감사 표현에 대한 반응 → (B) 무엇을 해야 하는지 질문 → (E) 수업 계획 설명 → (A) 알아두어야 할 것 질문 → (C) 알아두어야 할 사항 설명

10 대답이 허락을 의미하므로 'Of course not.'이 적절하다.

서술형 시험대비 p.75

01 He needs a sleeping bag.

02 Yes, she does.

03 (A) favor　(B) a sleeping bag　(C) borrow

04 (A) the community center　(B) volunteers

　　(C) she hadn't never taught anyone

　　(D) help the teacher

05 (E) → (B) → (D) → (C) → (A)

01 Kevin은 과학 캠프에 침낭이 필요하다.

02 Victoria는 Kevin이 그녀의 것을 빌리도록 허락해 주었다.

03 Kevin은 Victoria에게 부탁하기 위해 전화했다. 그는 과학 캠프에 침낭이 필요했다. 그가 그녀의 것을 빌릴 수 있을지 물었을 때, 그녀는 그것을 사용하는 것을 허락했다.

04 지민은 봉사활동하기에 좋은 장소를 찾고 있었다. 그녀는 Brian에게 좋은 장소를 추천해 줄 것을 요청했다. 그는 그녀에게 지역 주민 센터를 방문할 것을 조언했다, 왜냐하면 그들은 어르신들을 위한 스마트폰 수업에 자원봉사자를 찾고 있었기 때문이다. 하지만 지민은 누군가를 전혀 가르쳐 본 적이 없기 때문에 걱정했다. 다행히 그녀가 해야 할 일은 어르신들을 가르치는 것이 아니라 교사를 도와주는 것이었다.

05 (E) 문제점 설명 → (B) 아침을 먹는지 질문 → (D) 대답 → (C) 충고하기 → (A) 반응

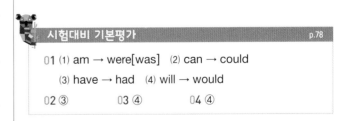

교과서

Grammar

핵심 Check p.76~77

1 (1) for　(2) for　(3) of

2 If he were on vacation, he would be in Busan now.

시험대비 기본평가 p.78

01 (1) am → were[was]　(2) can → could

　　(3) have → had　(4) will → would

02 ③　　　　03 ④　　　　04 ④

01 문제에서 모든 문장이 가정법 문장이라고 했고, 모든 문장의 구조는 '가정법 과거' 형태이므로, if절의 동사는 과거로, 주절의 조동사는 과거형으로 고치는 것이 적절하다.

02 to부정사의 의미상의 주어는 to부정사 바로 앞에 'for+목적격'으로 나타내지만 문장에서 보어로 쓰인 형용사가 nice, kind, smart, wise 등과 같이 사람의 성향, 성격을 나타내는 말일 때는 'of+목적격'으로 쓴다. to부정사의 의미상의 주어가 일반적

13

인 사람일 경우는 보통 생략한다.

03 주절에 조동사의 과거형이 나온 가정법 문장으로, 내용상 be동사의 과거형이 필요한데, 일반적으로 가정법 과거에서 be동사의 과거형은 were를 쓴다.

04 it을 가주어로 하고 to부정사를 진주어로 하며 의미상의 주어로 'for them'을 쓰는 것이 적절하다.

시험대비 실력평가   p.79~81

01 ④   02 ①   03 ②   04 ⑤
05 ③   06 (1) were (2) had (3) for (4) of
07 ③   08 ②   09 ①   10 ④
11 (1) for my dad to cook (2) for him to solve
   (3) of her to help
12 ⑤   13 ③   14 ②   15 ③
16 (1) If you were me, would you talk to the teacher?
   (2) It was wise of them to call the police directly.
17 (1) I'll → I'd (2) of → for

01 가정법 문장이라면 will을 would로, 직설법 문장이라면 knew를 know로 쓰는 것이 적절하다.

02 to부정사의 의미상의 주어는 to부정사 바로 앞에 'for+목적격'으로 나타낸다.

03 주절에 could가 나와 있고 내용상 가정법으로 보아야 하므로 have를 had로 고치는 것이 적절하다.

04 to부정사의 의미상의 주어는 to부정사 바로 앞에 'for+목적격'으로 나타내지만 문장에서 보어로 쓰인 형용사가 사람의 성향, 성격을 나타내는 말 때는 'of+목적격'으로 쓴다.

05 ①, ②, ⑤번은 직설법 전환이 잘못된 문장이며, ④번은 직설법의 인과 관계가 바뀌었다.

06 (1), (2) 주절에 조동사의 과거형이 나왔으므로, 가정법 문장이다. (3), (4) to부정사의 의미상의 주어는 'for+목적격'으로 나타내지만 문장에서 보어로 쓰인 형용사가 사람의 성향, 성격을 나타내는 말 때는 'of+목적격'으로 쓴다.

07 가정법 과거 시제의 문장으로 쓴다. 'If she had a car'로 종속절을 쓰고 주절에 조동사의 과거형 would를 쓰는 것에 유의한다.

08 it을 가주어로 하고 to부정사를 진주어로 하며 의미상의 주어로 to부정사 바로 앞에 'for+목적격'으로 쓰는 것이 적절하다.

09 ①번의 if는 간접의문문으로 명사절을 이끄는 접속사이며, 나머지는 모두 가정법의 조건절을 이끄는 종속접속사이다.

10 가정법 과거의 문장들이다. If절에는 동사의 과거형을, 주절에는 조동사의 과거형을 쓰는 것이 적절하다. Were it not for your help = If it were not for your help = Without your help = But for your help

11 to부정사의 의미상의 주어는 to부정사 바로 앞에 'for+목적격'

으로 나타내지만 문장에서 보어로 쓰인 형용사가 사람의 성향, 성격을 나타내는 말 때는 'of+목적격'으로 쓴다.

12 가정법 과거 문장은 현재시제의 직설법으로 바꿔 쓸 수 있다. 가정법은 현재 사실과 반대로 가정하는 것이므로 부정하는 것이 서로 바뀌는 것에 주의한다.

13 to부정사의 의미상의 주어가 일반적인 사람일 경우는 보통 생략한다.

14 옳은 문장은 ⓒ, ⓕ 2개이다. ⓐ am → were, ⓑ can → could, ⓓ I → me ⓔ knowing → to know ⓖ sings → to sing

15 '~가 없다면'이라는 가정법 표현은 'If there were no ~'로 나타낸다. If there were no weapons = If it were not for weapons = Were it not for weapons = Without weapons = But for weapons

16 (1) 주절에 would가 있는 가정법 과거 문장이다. are를 were로 고치는 것이 적절하다. (2) 문장에서 보어로 쓰인 형용사가 사람의 성향, 성격을 나타내는 말일 때는 to부정사의 의미상의 주어로 'of+목적격'을 쓴다.

17 (1) 가정법 과거는 'If+주어+were/동사의 과거형 ~, 주어+조동사의 과거형(would/should/could/might)+동사원형 …'의 형태이다. I'll을 I'd로 고치는 것이 적절하다. (2) 문장에서 보어로 쓰인 형용사가 사람의 성향, 성격을 나타내는 말이 아니므로 to부정사의 의미상의 주어로 'for+목적격'을 쓴다.

서술형 시험대비   p.82~83

01 If she lived in Germany, she could speak German.
02 It is wise of you to admit your mistake.
03 (1) If it were not for (2) Were it not for
   (3) If there were no (4) But for (5) As there are
04 kind of you to help   05 were
06 (1) If my mother were not busy now, we could go to the movies.
   (2) If I were[was] a teacher, I would be the students' best friend.
   (3) If there were[was] no tests, I would be happy.
   (4) If Chris finished his homework every day, he could play baseball with us.
07 (1) of him to give (2) of him to keep
   (3) for her to walk
08 knew, would
09 (1) If Ryan were[was] not busy, we would visit his house.
   (2) If you wore this dress, you would look prettier.
   (3) It is not easy for me to speak in English.
   (4) It is possible for them to repair the door.
10 (1) of → for (2) because of → because

01 가정법 과거 시제의 문장으로 쓴다. 'If she lived in Germany'로 종속절을 쓰고 주절에 조동사의 과거형 could를 쓰는 것에 유의한다.

02 문장에서 보어로 쓰인 형용사가 사람의 성향, 성격을 나타내는 말일 때는 to부정사의 의미상의 주어로 'of+목적격'을 쓴다.

03 '시험이 없다면 나는 행복할 텐데.'라는 뜻이다. 가정법 과거의 경우, Without = If it were not for = Were it not for = If there were no = But for이다. 'If it were not for' 등은 'If it was not for'보다는 'If it were not for'로 쓰는 것이 흔하다.

04 문장에서 보어로 쓰인 형용사가 kind이므로 to부정사의 의미상의 주어로 'of+목적격'을 쓴다.

05 가정법 과거는 'If+주어+were/동사의 과거형 ~, 주어+조동사의 과거형(would/should/could/might)+동사원형 …'의 형태이다. if절의 동사가 be동사인 경우 주어의 인칭과 수에 상관없이 were를 쓰는 것이 원칙이지만 주어가 1, 3인칭 단수일 때는 was를 쓰기도 한다. 단, If I were you는 관용적으로 were만 쓴다.

06 직설법 현재 문장을 가정법 과거 문장으로 바꿀 때, 종속절에는 동사의 과거형을, 주절에는 '조동사의 과거형+동사원형'을 쓰는 것에 유의한다.

07 to부정사의 의미상의 주어는 to부정사 바로 앞에 'for+목적격'으로 나타내지만 문장에서 보어로 쓰인 형용사가 사람의 성향, 성격을 나타내는 말일 때는 'of+목적격'으로 쓴다.

08 가정법 과거는 현재 사실과 반대되는 가정을 나타낼 때 사용하므로 직설법 문장을 가정법으로 나타낼 수 있다.

09 (1), (2) '가정법 과거를 이용한다. (3), (4) it을 가주어로 하고 to부정사를 진주어로 하며 문장에서 보어로 쓰인 형용사가 사람의 성향, 성격을 나타내는 말이 아니므로 의미상의 주어로 'for+목적격'을 쓴다.

10 (1) to부정사의 의미상의 주어는 'for+목적격'으로 쓴다. (2) 뒤에 절이 이어지므로 because로 써야 한다.

교과서 Reading

확인문제 p.84

1 T 2 F 3 T 4 F 5 T 6 F

확인문제 p.85

1 T 2 F 3 T 4 F 5 T 6 F

확인문제 p.86

1 T 2 F 3 T 4 F 5 T 6 T

교과서 확인학습 A p.87~89

01 Commons
02 Once upon a time
03 raised
04 lay
05 Space for Everyone
06 Let's share
07 enough grass
08 there's plenty
09 was allowed to use
10 was called
11 By tradition / enough grass to eat
12 all summer long
13 had, would be
14 notice
15 broke the rule
16 let it graze
17 nobody would notice
18 thought of, would bring
19 has
20 were, would raise
21 for
22 who
23 in secret, bring in, raise it
24 as he was told
25 Who
26 new
27 lying
28 don't know
29 the richest
30 did the same
31 secretly, even more, without telling anyone
32 additional
33 looking
34 pushing
35 over
36 spot
37 rain
38 hungry
39 Me, too
40 rose
41 cow population
42 to disappear, harder
43 To make matters worse
44 left
46 happened to
47 something to eat
48 there were too many
49 harsh
50 PER FAMILY
51 At last
52 support only one cow
53 one-family-one-cow
54 lesson, are shared, to value, fairly
55 to
56 call it

교과서 확인학습 B p.90~92

1 The Story of the Commons
2 Once upon a time there was a small village in a forest.
3 The villagers were farmers and raised cows.
4 Luckily, some good grassland lay in the middle of the village.
5 The Commons: Space for Everyone
6 Head of a village: Let's share the commons.
7 Villager 1: My cow can get enough grass.
8 Villager 2: Yeah, there's plenty for every cow.
9 Everyone was allowed to use the grassland.
10 Therefore, it was called "the commons."

11 By tradition, each family only had one cow, so it was easy for each cow in the village to find enough grass to eat.

12 The grass on the commons was green all summer long.

13 Farmer 1: If I had two cows, I would be richer.

14 Farmer 1: No one will notice it.

15 But one day a villager broke the rule.

16 He brought another cow and let it graze on the commons.

17 He thought that nobody would notice it.

18 A happy feeling filled his heart when he thought of the milk and cheese that the second cow would bring to his family.

19 Farmer 1: He has four children.

20 Farmer 1: If I were you, I would raise another cow.

21 Farmer 2: Thanks for the tip!

22 A few days later, the farmer visited a close friend who had four children.

23 He wanted to help his friend, so he told him in secret, "If I were you, I would bring in one more cow and raise it on the commons."

24 The friend thanked him and did as he was told the next day.

25 Cow 1: Who are you?

26 Cow 2: I'm new.

27 Cow 3: Who is lying there?

28 Cow 4: I don't know.

29 Farmer 3: I can be the richest farmer in this village.

30 Soon, other villagers did the same.

31 Some secretly brought one more cow to the commons, while others brought even more to the grassland without telling anyone.

32 They thought that there would be enough grass for the additional cows.

33 Soon the village was full of happy-looking farmers!

34 Cow 1: Hey, stop pushing me!

35 Cow 2: Move over!

36 Cow 3: This is my spot!

37 Cow 1: We need rain!

38 Cow 2: I'm hungry.

39 Cow 3: Me, too.

40 The number of cows rose slowly at first.

41 Then the cow population grew more quickly.

42 The grass on the commons began to disappear, and it became harder for the cows to find grass to eat.

43 To make matters worse, it did not rain for a long time.

44 Farmer 1: I don't have any cows left!

45 Cow 1: Good bye.

46 Head of a village: What happened to the commons?

47 In the past, when a dry year came, the small number of cows on the commons always found something to eat.

48 However, no grass was left now because there were too many cows.

49 Things were harsh for the villagers; many of the cows died.

50 Enjoy, but remember the rule: ONLY ONE COW PER FAMILY.

51 At last, the grass came back.

52 Now it was able to support only one cow per family.

53 The village went back to the one-family-one-cow rule.

54 The villagers all learned an important lesson: when resources are shared, it is important for everyone to value the resources and use them fairly.

55 The villagers now tell this story to their children.

56 They call it "The Story of the Commons."

시험대비 실력평가   p.93~97

01 ③   02 By   03 ①, ④
04 ④   05 ②
06 (A) one more cow   (B) the commons
07 ②   08 the grassland   09 ③
10 are shared
11 the one-family-one-cow rule   12 ④
13 ①   14 ③   15 ④
16 They thought that there would be enough grass for the additional cows.
17 filled with   18 ②, ③, ⑤   19 ①
20 one cow   21 the resources
22 (A) resources   (B) fairly
23 (A) one[a] cow   (B) the commons   24 ①
25 ⑤   26 secretly   27 ③
28 one more cow
29 (A) brought   (B) raised   30 ⑤
31 ②   32 What   33 ③

01 앞의 내용의 결과가 나오고 있으므로 Therefore가 가장 적절하다. ① 비슷하게, ④ 게다가, 더욱이, ⑤ 즉, 말하자면

02 by tradition: 전통에 따라

03 (A)와 ①, ④: 명사적 용법, ②, ⑤: 형용사적 용법, ③: 부사적 용법

04 ④는 친구 집을 방문한 농부를 가리키고, 나머지는 다 농부의 친구를 가리킨다.

05 ⓐ와 ②: ~하는 대로, ① ~하고 있을 때, ③ ~이므로, ④ ~함에 따라, ⑤ as ~ as ...로 동등 비교를 나타내어 …와 같이, …만큼 (as ~ as ...에서, 앞의 as는 지시부사, 뒤의 as는 접속사)

06 '소를 한 마리 더' 데려와 '공유지'에서 키우라고 충고했다.

07 두 번째 단락에서 '모든 사람들'이 목초지를 사용하도록 허락되었기 때문에 목초지가 '공유지'라고 불렸다고 했으므로, "공유지: '모두'를 위한 장소"라고 하는 것이 적절하다. ① 일반인, 민중, ③ 성인들, 어른들

08 '목초지'를 가리킨다.

09 전통에 따라 각 가정은 소가 한 마리만 있었다. ⑤ throughout the summer: 여름 내내

10 '자원이 공유될 때'라고 해야 하므로 수동태로 쓰는 것이 적절하다.

11 one-family-one-cow: 한 가구, 한 마리 소

12 (B)와 ④: 교훈, 그 여자의 운명을 교훈으로 삼아라. ①, ③, ⑤: 수업[교습/교육], ② (교과서 안의) 과

13 이 글은 '자원이 공유될 때는 모두가 그 자원을 소중히 여기고 공평하게 사용하는 것이 중요하다'는 내용의 글이므로, 주제로는 ①번 '공유 자원을 공평하게 사용하는 것의 중요성'이 적절하다. ② protect: 보호하다, ③ recovery: 회복

14 '곧, 다른 사람들도 그렇게 했다.'라고 하면서 어떤 사람들은 은밀하게 소를 한 마리 더 공유지에 데려왔고, 또 어떤 사람들은 아무에게도 말하지 않고 훨씬 많은 소를 목초지에 데려왔다는 내용이 이어지고 있으므로, 위 글의 앞에 올 내용으로 가장 알맞은 것은 '몇몇 사람들이 공유지에 은밀하게 소를 한 마리 더 데려오는' 내용이라고 하는 것이 적절하다.

15 ⓐ와 ④: 그런데, 한편(으로는)(접속사), ①과 ⑤: ~하고 있는 동안에(접속사), ②와 ③ 잠깐, 잠시(명사)

16 there would be enough grass: 충분한 풀이 있을 것이다

17 be full of = be filled with: ~으로 가득 차다

18 at last = finally = in the end = eventually: 마침내, 결국, ① 실제로, 정말로, ④ 마지막으로, 끝으로(무엇을 열거하면서 마지막 요소 앞에 붙이는 말)

19 주어진 문장의 it에 주목한다. ①번 앞 문장의 the grass를 받고 있으므로 ①번이 적절하다.

20 각 가정은 '소가 한 마리만' 있어야 한다는 것을 의미한다.

21 '자원'을 가리킨다.

22 사람들이 '자원'을 공유할 때는 모두가 그 공유된 자원을 소중히 여기고 '공평하게' 사용해야 한다.

23 각 가정은 '소 한 마리'만 '공유지'에서 풀을 뜯게 해야 한다.

24 이 글의 두 번째 단락은 '마을 사람 하나가 규칙을 깨뜨리고 다른 소를 데려와 공유지에서 풀을 뜯게 하면서, 두 번째 소가 가져다줄 이익 생각에 마음이 행복감으로 충만해졌다'는 내용의 글이므로, 어울리는 속담으로는 '사람의 욕심은 한이 없다' 혹은 '떡 줄 사람은 생각지도 않는데 김칫국부터 마신다.'는 속담이 적절하다. ① 하늘은 스스로 돕는 자를 돕는다. ② 탐욕은 끝이 없다. → 말 타면 종 부리고 싶다. ③ 떡 줄 사람은 생각지도 않는데 김칫국부터 마신다. ④ 1인치를 주니까 1마일을 가져가려고 한다. → 물에 빠진 것 구해주니 봇짐 내 놓으라고 한다(욕심이 끝이 없다). ⑤ 먹으면서 식욕이 생긴다. 이미 먹고 있는데 또 식욕이 생긴다, 욕심이 생긴다.

25 '두 번째 소가 가족에게 얼마나 많은 우유와 치즈를 가져다주었는지'는 대답할 수 없다. '두 번째 소가 가족에게 가져다줄 우유와 치즈를 생각하자 그의 마음은 행복감으로 충만했다'고 했을 뿐이다. ① Because everyone was allowed to use it. ② Each family only had one cow by tradition. ③ Yes. ④ It was green throughout the summer.

26 전치사+추상명사 = 부사, in secret: 몰래, 비밀리에

27 ⓐ와 ③: (동물)을 사육하다, 기르다, ① (무엇을 위로) 들어 올리다, ② (양·수준 등을) 올리다, ④ (~을 위해) [돈]을 모으다, 모금하다, ⑤ 게양하다

28 공유지에 더 데려온 '소 한 마리'를 가리킨다.

29 그 전날 친구가 그에게 하라고 말한 대로 소를 한 마리 더 '데려와' 공유지에서 '키웠다.' the previous day: 그 전날

30 ⓐ be full of: ~으로 가득 차다, ⓑ for the cows: to부정사의 의미상 주어

31 ②: 원급 강조, (A)와 나머지: 비교급 강조(훨씬)

32 to make matters worse = what was worse: 엎친 데 덮친 격으로

33 공유지에 몇 마리의 소들이 있었는지는 알 수 없다. ① They brought cows. ② They thought there would be enough grass for additional cows. ④ No. ⑤ No.

01 (A) had   (B) another   (C) graze

02 그가 규칙을 깨뜨리고 소를 한 마리 더 데려와 공유지에서 풀을 뜯게 한 것.

03 His heart was filled with a happy feeling

04 to use   05 lied → lay

06 so it was easy for each cow in the village to find enough grass to eat

07 (A) good grassland   (B) the commons

08 additional   09 secretly

10 (A) cow population   (B) harder

17

11 favorable → harsh

12 (A) found something to eat (B) too many cows

13 fairly

14 It was able to support only one[a] cow per family.

01 (A) 가정법 과거는 'If+주어+동사의 과거형 ~, 주어+조동사의 과거형+동사원형 ….'의 형태로 써야 하므로 had가 적절하다. (B) '또 다른 하나'라고 해야 하므로 another가 적절하다. another: 또 하나(의), the other: (둘 중의) 다른 하나, (C) 'let+목적어+동사원형'으로 써야 하므로 graze가 적절하다.

02 앞에 나온 내용을 가리킨다.

03 fill은 수동태로 고칠 때 be filled with로 고치는 것이 적절하다.

04 'allow+목적어+to부정사'를 수동태로 바꾼 것이므로, 'to부정사'로 쓰는 것이 적절하다.

05 다행히도, 마을 한 가운데에 좋은 목초지가 '있었다'고 해야 하므로 lied를 lay로 고치는 것이 적절하다. lie-lied-lied: 거짓말하다, lie-lay-lain: 눕다, 놓여 있다

06 it: 가주어, for each cow in the village: 의미상의 주어, to find 이하: 진주어, to eat: 형용사적 용법의 to부정사

07 숲속에 있는 작은 마을 한 가운데에, 모든 사람들이 사용하도록 허락되어 '공유지'라고 불리는 '좋은 목초지'가 있었다.

08 '추가된' 소라고 해야 하므로 additional이 적절하다.

09 without telling anyone(아무에게도 말하지 않고) = secretly(은밀하게)

10 마을 사람들이 추가로 소들을 공유지에 데려왔기 때문에 '소의 개체 수'가 빨리 증가했고 소들이 먹을 풀을 찾기가 '더 힘들어졌다.'

11 소가 너무 많아서 풀이 남지 않았다고 했기 때문에 상황은 마을 사람들에게 '가혹했다(harsh)'로 고치는 것이 적절하다. favorable: 호의적인

12 • 과거: 공유지에 있는 적은 수의 소들이 '먹을 것을 항상 찾을 수 있었다.' • 현재: '소가 너무 많아서' 풀이 남지 않아, 많은 소들이 죽었다.

13 with justice: 공정하게, 정당하게, use them fairly: 그것들을 공평하게 사용하다

14 가구당 한 마리의 소만 감당할 수 있게 되었다.

영역별 핵심문제
p.101~105

01 ③   02 ③

03 (1) tradition (2) either (3) graze (4) per[an]

04 (1) Once upon a time (2) in the middle of
   (3) To make matters worse (4) senior citizens
   (5) in secret

05 Her stomach growls every morning.

06 He advises her to bring some snacks.

07 ③   08 ⑤   09 ④   10 ⑤

11 (C) → (B) → (D) → (A)   12 ③   13 ⑤

14 ②   15 for kids to play

16 had, would go

17 (1) am → were (2) will → would
   (3) for him → of him
   (4) of him to not → for him not to

18 (1) for Elsa to find (2) of Megan to give

19 ①, ④   20 ③   21 ⑤

22 Therefore, people[they] called it "the commons."

23 By tradition, each family only had one[a] cow.

24 ④   25 ②   26 ⑤   27 ②

28 (A) left (B) happened (C) because

01 '공급, 지원 또는 후원의 근원'을 가리키는 말은 resource(자원)이다..

02 the number of: ~의 수

03 tradition: 전통, graze: 풀을 뜯다, per: ~당, ~마다(= a, an)

04 to make matters worse: 설상가상으로, in secret: 몰래, 비밀리에, senior citizens: 어르신, 노인, once upon a time: 옛날에, in the middle of: ~ 가운데

05 Gina의 배가 아침마다 꼬르륵거린다.

06 Tom은 Gina에게 약간의 간식을 가져올 것을 조언한다.

07 (A) Here is+단수 명사, Here are+복수 명사, (B) 부정문이므로 either, (C) 주어 다음에 동사가 이어져야 하므로 arrive가 적절하다.

08 위 대화에서 소라가 국수와 샌드위치 중 어느 것을 더 좋아하는지는 알 수 없다.

09 나머지는 모두 허락을 나타내지만 ④번은 허락하지 않는 표현이다.

10 지민이는 배터리가 별로 남지 않아 윤 선생님의 충전기를 사용하여 충전할 것이다.

11 (C) 전화한 이유 설명 → (B) 부탁이 무엇인지 질문 → (D) 부탁 내용 설명 → (A) 대답

12 ③번의 if는 간접의문문에 쓰였지만 나머지는 모두 가정법의 조건절을 이끌고 있다.

13 to부정사의 의미상의 주어는 to부정사 앞에 'for+목적격'으로 나타내지만 문장에서 보어로 쓰인 형용사가 사람의 성향, 성격을 나타내는 말일 때는 'of+목적격'으로 쓴다.

14 가정법 과거는 'If+주어+were/동사의 과거형 ~, 주어+조동사의 과거형+동사원형 ….'의 형태로 나타낸다.

15 to부정사의 의미상의 주어는 to부정사 앞에 'for+목적격'으로 나타낸다.

16 가정법 과거는 조건절에는 동사의 과거형이 나오고 주절에는 '조동사의 과거형(would/should/could/might)+동사원형'이 나온다.

17 (1), (2) 가정법 과거는 조건절에는 동사의 과거형이 나오고 주

절에는 '조동사의 과거형(would/should/could/might)+동사원형'이 나온다. (3) 문장에 쓰인 형용사가 사람의 성향, 성격을 나타내는 말일 때는 의미상의 주어로 'of+목적격'으로 쓴다. (4) to부정사의 의미상의 주어는 to부정사 바로 앞에 'for+목적격'으로 나타내며, to부정사의 부정은 to부정사 앞에 not이나 never를 써서 'not(never)+to부정사'로 나타낸다.

18 It을 가주어로 하고 to부정사를 진주어로 하며 의미상의 주어로 'for+목적격'을 쓴다. 단, 문장에서 보어로 쓰인 형용사가 사람의 성향, 성격을 나타내는 말이면 'of+목적격'을 쓴다.

19 again and again = repeatedly = over and over = time and again: 되풀이하여, 누차 ① 즉시, ④ 실제로

20 ③ 만족한, ① 어리둥절해하는, ② 부끄러운, ④ 거만한, 오만한, ⑤ 실망한

21 얼마나 오래 봉사 활동을 했는지는 알 수 없다. ① Last Saturday. ② At the community center in the neighborhood. ③ Yes. ④ The writer helped the slow learners in the class.

22 people[they]을 주어로 하여 능동태로 고치는 것이 적절하다.

23 By tradition: 전통에 따라

24 ⓒ와 ③: 형용사적 용법, ①, ⑤: 명사적 용법, ②, ④: 부사적 용법

25 이 글은 '마을 사람들의 탐욕으로 인해 공유지의 풀이 사라지기 시작했고, 소들이 먹을 풀을 찾기가 더 힘들어졌다'는 내용의 글이므로, 제목으로는 ②번 '탐욕이 불행한 결과를 초래했다'가 적절하다.

26 소의 개체 수가 더 빨리 증가함에 따라 공유지의 풀은 사라지기 시작했고, 소들이 먹을 풀을 찾기가 '더 힘들어졌다.'

27 앞에 나오는 내용과 상반되는 내용이 뒤에 이어지므로 However가 가장 적절하다. ① 그 결과, ④ 게다가, 더욱이, ⑤ 따라서, 그러므로

28 (A) '남은' 소리라고 해야 하므로 left가 적절하다. (B) happen은 수동태로 만들 수 없으므로 happened가 적절하다. (C) 문맥상 이유를 나타내는 접속사가 적절하다.

단원별 예상문제 p.106~109

01 pollution
02 (1) lied (2) lay (3) risen (4) laid (5) seat (6) sat
   (7) raised
03 (1) There is a statue in the middle of the park.
   (2) You are not allowed to take a picture in the museum.
   (3) Sally offered her seat to a senior citizen on the bus.
04 He advises her to go to the community center.
05 It is for senior citizens.
06 She needs to help the teacher.   07 ⑤

08 ④, ⑤   09 seasick   10 ⑤   11 ③
12 (1) If there were superheroes, the world would be safer.
   (2) If I were[was] a cat, I could sleep and play all day long.
   (3) It is difficult for him to concentrate on math.
   (4) It was kind of her to give me a ride
13 ②, ⑤
14 (1) of her to help   (2) for her to swim
15 ②   16 without telling anyone
17 happy-looked → happy-looking   18 graze
19 ③   20 ②   21 ④
22 they should
23 to explain everything in English

01 주어진 단어는 동사와 명사의 관계를 나타낸다. pollute: 오염시키다, pollution: 오염

02 lie: 거짓말하다(lie − lied − lied), 눕다(lie − lay − lain) lay: 놓다, 두다(lay − laid − laid) rise: 오르다(rise − rose − risen) raise(raise − raised − raised): 들어올리다 seat(seat − seated − seated): 앉히다 sit(sit − sat − sat): 앉다

03 in the middle of: ~의 가운데에, be allowed to: ~하는 것이 허락되다, senior citizen: 노인, 어르신

04 Brian은 지민이에게 지역 주민 센터에 가 볼 것을 조언한다.

05 지역 주민 센터의 스마트폰 수업은 어르신들을 위한 것이다.

06 지민이가 스마트폰 수업에서 해야 할 일은 교사를 도와주는 것이다.

07 allowance: 용돈, 용돈을 거의 다 썼다는 말에 대한 조언으로 적절하지 않다.

08 ①, ②, ③은 Do you mind if ~?로 물을 때 거절의 대답이다.

09 '보트나 배를 타고 여행할 때 토하고 싶거나 아픔을 느끼는' 것을 나타내 말은 seasick(뱃멀미가 나는)이다.

10 아빠는 도착한 후에 아이스크림을 먹을 것을 제안했다.

11 ① If I had my cell phone, I would take pictures of those cute cats. ② If there were no TVs, we would read more books. ④ Were it not for laws in the world, it would be dangerous. ⑤ But for the Internet, we would go to the library and get necessary information.

12 (1), (2) 가정법 과거는 'If+주어+were/동사의 과거형 ~, 주어+조동사의 과거형(would/should/could/might)+동사원형 …'의 형태이다. (3) it을 가주어로 하고 to부정사를 진주어로 하며 의미상의 주어로 'for+목적격'을 쓰며, 문장에서 보어로 쓰인 형용사가 사람의 성향, 성격을 나타내는 말이면 'of+목적격'을 쓴다.

13 ① It is impossible for Mina to do it because she is not a good dancer. ③ It was possible for him to answer

the question. ④ It is hard for some people to make friends.

14 'It(가주어) ~ for[of] ...(의미상의 주어) 진주어(to부정사)' 구문을 이용한다.

15 ② Some - others: 어떤 사람들은 - 또 어떤 사람들은, ① One - the other: (둘 중에서) 하나는 - 나머지 하나는, ③ The others - another: 나머지 전체는 - (셋 이상 중에서) 또 하나는

16 without ~ing: ~하지 않고

17 happy-looking: 행복해 보이는

18 graze 풀을 뜯다, 목장이나 목초지에서 먹을 것을 먹다

19 이 글은 '마을의 규칙을 어기고 사리사욕을 채운 두 친구'에 대한 글이므로, 주제로는 ③번 '사리사욕을 채운 두 친구'가 적절하다. satisfy one's selfish interests and desires: 사리사욕을 채우다, ④ cooperation: 협력, ⑤ rise out of poverty: 가난에서 벗어나다

20 '다른 소를 데려와 공유지에서 풀을 뜯게 한 것을 아무도 눈치 채지 못할 거라고 생각했다'고 했으므로, '마을 사람들이 농부의 부당함을 발견하고 화를 냈다'는 것은 사실이 아니다. injustice: 부당함, 부당성, ③ extra: 추가의

21 주어진 문장의 However에 주목한다. ④번 앞 문장의 내용과 상반되는 내용이 뒤에 이어지므로 ④번이 적절하다.

22 의문사+to부정사 = 의문사+주어+should+동사원형, visitors to Korea from other countries를 they로 바꿔서 쓰는 것이 적절하다.

23 '모든 것을 영어로 설명하는 것'이 약간 어려웠다.

서술형 실전문제
p.110~111

01 do you mind if I use your charger?

02 She asks her to be patient and kind to the learners.

03 It's because her battery is a little low.

04 (1) As I am[I'm] not a good cook, I won't make you delicious food.

(2) Because I don't have enough time, I won't take a walk with you.

(3) If we had ten more dollars, we could buy the sweater for Mom.

(4) Were I an English teacher, I would know the answers.

(5) Without rain, we couldn't live.

05 (1) It is easy for me to solve the problem.

(2) It is necessary for them to cook *ramyeon*

(3) It is silly of Greg to think that chocolate solves anything.

06 (1) give → gave (2) of → for

07 (A) pushing (B) disappear (C) for

08 So   09 raised → rose

10 too many cows

11 it is important for everyone to value the resources and use them fairly

12 this story

02 윤 선생님은 지민이에게 인내심을 갖고 학습자들에게 친절하게 대할 것을 요청했다.

03 지민의 배터리가 별로 남지 않아서 충전기가 필요하다.

04 (1)~(3) 가정법 과거 문장은 현재시제의 직설법으로 바꿔 쓸 수 있다. (4) 가정법으로 고친 후, if를 생략하고 were를 문두에 쓰고 도치시킨다. (5) if there were[was] no = if it were not for = were it not for = without = but for

05 it을 가주어로 하고 to부정사를 진주어로 하며 의미상의 주어로 'for+목적격'을 쓰며, 문장에서 보어로 쓰인 형용사가 사람의 성향, 성격을 나타내는 말이면 'of+목적격'을 쓴다.

06 (1) 가정법 과거에서 종속절에는 동사의 과거형을 쓴다. (2) to부정사의 의미상의 주어는 to부정사 바로 앞에 'for+목적격'으로 나타내지만 문장에서 보어로 쓰인 형용사가 사람의 성향, 성격을 나타내는 말일 때는 'of+목적격'으로 쓴다.

07 (A) '밀지 마!'라고 해야 하므로 pushing이 적절하다. stop+~ing: ~을 그만두다, stop+to부정사: ~하기 위해 멈추다, (B) '풀이 사라지기 시작했다'고 해야 하므로 disappear가 적절하다. (C) harder가 사람의 성질을 나타내는 형용사가 아니므로, to부정사의 의미상의 주어 자리에 'for+목적격'을 쓰는 것이 적절하다. 'of+목적격': 사람의 성질을 나타내는 형용사가 있을 때 사용.

08 Me, too. = So am I.: 나도 그래.

09 소의 수가 천천히 늘어났다고 해야 하므로, raised를 rose로 고치는 것이 적절하다. raise: (무엇을 위로) 들어 올리다, 기르다

10 '소가 너무 많았기' 때문이다.

11 it은 가주어이고, to value 이하가 진주어 역할을 한다. for everyone은 to부정사의 의미상의 주어이다.

12 it은 앞 문장의 this story를 가리킨다.

창의사고력 서술형 문제
p.112

|모범답안|

01 Kids → Senior Citizens , necessary → not necessary(= unnecessary)

02 (A) Last Sunday (B) Gyeongbokgung Station
(C) other countries
(D) the subway ticket machines
(E) to explain everything in English
(F) pleased (G) again in the future

p.113~116

01 ①   02 ②

03 (1) Students are not allowed to have pets on campus.
　(2) I got a little seasick when I rode in a small boat.
　(3) It gave me great pleasure to join this music club.

04 If I were you, I would bring some snacks.

05 ③   06 ②   07 (1) seasick   (2) arrive

08 ⓔ → is   09 ⑤   10 ③   11 ②

12 ④

13 (1) What would happen if there were[was] no gravity?
　(2) If Sarah were[was] healthy, she would come to the party.
　(3) If Kevin arrived now, we could watch the movie together.
　(4) It was easy for her to find a creative solution.

14 As I don't have two cows, I am not richer.

15 He brought another cow and let it graze on the commons.

16 (A) the milk and cheese   (B) the second cow

17 additional   18 ①, ④

19 (A) cows   (B) rain   20 the grass

21 ③   22 ④

사의 과거형(would/should/could/might)+동사원형 …'의 형태로 쓴다. (4) 'It(가주어) ~ for(of) …(의미상의 주어) 진주어(to부정사)' 구문을 이용한다.

14 가정법 과거는 직설법으로 고칠 때 현재 시제로 고치는 것이 적절하다.

15 사역동사인 let의 목적보어로 원형부정사인 graze를 쓰는 것이 적절하다.

16 '두 번째 소'가 가족에게 가져다줄 '우유와 치즈'에 대한 생각이 그를 행복하게 느끼도록 만들었다.

17 addition의 형용사형으로 고친다.

18 (B)와 ①, ④: 가주어, ②, ⑤: 비인칭주어, ③ 가목적어

19 공유지에 너무 많은 '소'가 있었고, 오랫동안 '비'가 내리지 않았기 때문이다.

20 '목초지'를 가리킨다.

21 이 글은 '자원이 공유될 때는 모두가 그 자원을 소중히 여기고 공평하게 사용하는 것이 중요하다는 교훈을 마을 사람들이 배웠다'는 내용의 글이므로, 제목으로는 ③번 '규칙을 기억해라: 가구 당 오직 소 한 마리'가 적절하다. ① human nature: 인간 본성, ② heartily: 실컷, 열심히, ④ Haste makes waste: 급할수록 돌아가라, 급히 서두르면 일을 망친다. ⑤ obey: (명령·법 등을) 따르다[지키다]

22 '자원'을 소중히 여기고 공평하게 사용하는 것이 중요하다. resource: 자원, source: (사물의) 원천, 근원, (자료의) 출처, ② a family = per family

---

01 '사람이나 동물의 전체 수'를 가리키는 말은 population(인구)이다.

02 주어진 문장에서 mind는 '신경 쓰다, 싫어하다'를 뜻하며 이와 같은 의미로 쓰인 것은 ②번이다. 나머지는 모두 '마음, 생각'을 나타낸다.

06 ②는 먹으라고 제안하는 것이므로 의미가 다르다.

08 주어가 'All you need to do'로 단수이므로 is가 적절하다.

09 Brian이 왜 아무도 가르치지 않았는지는 대화를 통해 알 수 없다.

10 ③ 할머니가 지금 여기 계시기 때문에, 나는 매우 기쁘다. ①, ②, ④, ⑤ 할머니가 지금 여기 계시다면, 나는 매우 기쁠 텐데. (할머니가 지금 여기 안 계시기 때문에, 나는 별로 기쁘지 않다.)

11 It was very thoughtful of you to send the flowers. to부정사의 의미상의 주어로 'for+목적격'을 쓰지만, 문장에서 보어로 쓰인 형용사가 사람의 성향, 성격을 나타내는 말이면 'of+목적격'을 쓴다.

12 If there were no ~ = If it were not for ~ = Were it not for ~ = Without ~ = But for ~

13 (1)~(3) '만약 ~라면 …할 텐데'라는 뜻으로, 현재 사실을 반대로 가정하거나 실현 가능성이 없는 일에 대해서 가정할 때 사용하는 가정법과거로 'If+주어+were/동사의 과거형 ~, 주어+조동

21

The Last Class

Reading

확인문제   p.120

1 T   2 F   3 T   4 F   5 T   6 F

확인문제   p.121

1 T   2 F   3 T   4 F   5 T   6 F

교과서 확인학습 A   p.122~123

01 Last	02 worried, get angry
03 take an exam, ready	04 such, sweet, inviting
05 staying away from, walking	
06 as fast as I could	07 saw people reading
08 had come from	09 wondered
10 faster	11 there was noise
12 quiet	
13 Through, walking nervously	
14 in the middle of	15 with shame
16 with no sign of anger, without	
17 at	18 It was, that
19 he only wore	20 something strange
21 What, to see, so were	22 sad
23 wondering at	
24 for a while, the last time	
25 Orders, nothing but German	
26 arrives	27 in French, to listen
28 made me angry	29 what
30 in my own language	

교과서 확인학습 B   p.124~125

1 The Last Class

2 I was late for school that morning, and I was worried Monsieur Hamel would get angry.

---

3 A few days before, he had told us that we would take an exam about French sentences that day, and I was not ready.

4 It was such a warm, lovely day, and the fields along the road smelled sweet and inviting.

5 For a moment, I thought of staying away from school and walking around the fields.

6 However, I ran as fast as I could to school.

7 As I passed the mayor's office, I saw people reading the notices on the board.

8 For two years all our bad news had come from that board.

9 I wondered, "What is it now?"

10 I ran faster.

11 Usually, there was noise in the morning at school—sounds of students talking and laughing.

12 However, that day everything was quiet.

13 Through the windows I saw my classmates in their places and Monsieur Hamel walking nervously around the classroom.

14 I opened the door and entered in the middle of the strange silence.

15 My face felt hot with shame!

16 Surprisingly, Monsieur Hamel looked at me with no sign of anger and said kindly, "Go to your seat, my little Frantz; we almost began without you."

17 I sat down at my desk.

18 It was then that I noticed Monsieur Hamel's blue coat.

19 He was wearing the coat he only wore on special days.

20 Also there was something strange about the whole class.

21 What surprised me most was to see people sitting at the back of the room: old Hauser was there, and so were the ex-mayor, the ex-postman, and many others.

22 They all seemed so sad.

23 While I was wondering at all this, Monsieur Hamel walked slowly to the front.

24 He thought for a while and kindly said: "My children, this is the last time that I'll teach you.

25 Orders have come from Berlin to teach nothing but German in the schools of Alsace and Lorraine.

26 The new teacher arrives tomorrow.

27 This is the last class in French, so I want you to listen carefully."

28 Those few words broke my heart and made me angry.

서술형 실전문제　　　　　　　　　p.126~127

01 arrive

02 (1) stay away from　(2) with no sign of anger
　　(3) in the middle of　(4) break my heart

03 (1) mayor　(2) notice　(3) nervously　(4) shame

04 (1) so → such　(2) stole → steal 또는 stealing
　　(3) where → that[which]　(4) during → while

05 familiar → strange

06 with no sign of anger　　　　07 noise

08 (A) worried　(B) such　(C) sweet

09 possible　　　　　　　　10 staying away from

11 What　　　　　　　　　12 there, too

13 (1) Hamel 선생님이 특별한 날에만 입는 파란색 외투를
　　입고 계셨다.
　　(2) Hauser 할아버지, 전직 시장님, 전직 우체부
　　아저씨를 비롯한 많은 사람들이 모두 슬퍼 보이는
　　모습으로 교실 뒤에 앉아 있었다.

01 주어진 관계는 명사와 동사의 관계를 나타낸다. arrive: 도착하다, depart: 출발하다

02 in the middle of: ~의 도중에, ~의 중앙에, with no sign of anger: 화난 기색 없이, break my heart: 매우 슬프게 하다, stay away from: ~에서 떨어져 있다, ~을 멀리하다

03 mayor: 시장, notice: 공지, nervously: 초조하게, shame: 수치심

04 (1) 어순에 주의한다. so+형용사+a+명사, such+a+형용사+명사 (2) notice는 지각동사로 목적격보어로 동사원형이나 현재분사가 나온다. (3) 'It is ~ that ...' 강조 구문으로 where를 that이나 which로 고쳐야 한다. (4) during+명사(구), while+절(주어+동사)

05 보통, 아침에는 학생들이 떠들고 웃는 소리로 학교가 소란스러웠지만 그날은 모든 것이 고요했다고 했기 때문에, 'familiar'를 'strange'로 고치는 것이 적절하다. familiar: 익숙한, 친숙한

06 with no sign of anger: 화난 기색 없이

07 보통, 아침에 학교에서 들리는 소리는 떠들고 웃는 학생들의 많은 '시끄러운 소리'였다.

08 (A) 감정을 나타내는 동사는 수식받는 명사가 감정을 느끼게 되는 경우에 과거분사를 써야 하므로 worried가 적절하다. (B) 뒤에 'a+형용사+명사'가 이어지므로 such가 적절하다. such+a+형용사+명사, so+형용사+a+명사, (C) 감각동사

smell 뒤에 형용사 보어를 써야 하므로 sweet가 적절하다.

09 as+형용사/부사+as+one+can = as+형용사/부사+as+possible: 가능한 한 ~하게

10 stay away from: ~에서 떨어져 있다, ~을 멀리하다, ~에 개입되는 것을 피하다, become involved in: ~에 개입되다, 관계되다

11 선행사를 포함하는 관계대명사 What이 적절하다. What이 이끄는 절이 문장의 주어 역할을 하고 있다.

12 '전직 시장님, 전직 우체부 아저씨를 비롯한 많은 사람들도 있었다.'는 뜻이다.

13 글쓴이가 책상으로 가서 앉은 뒤에 알아차린 Hamel 선생님의 파란색 외투와 교실 전체에서 무언가 이상하다고 느낀 내용을 쓰는 것이 적절하다.

단원별 예상문제　　　　　　　　　p.128~132

01 ②

02 (1) mayor　(2) strange　(3) enter　(4) posted
　　(5) shame

03 (1) in the middle of　(2) with no sign of anger
　　(3) broke my heart　(4) stay away from

04 ⑤　　　　　　05 ①

06 (1) I waved my hand, but he did not notice.
　　(2) As the mayor of New York City, he explained the city plan.
　　(3) When I fell down in front of many people, I felt shame.

07 (1) They disregarded the order to stop the new project.
　　(2) The water looks really inviting.
　　(3) They stood in silence and waited for the bus.

08 ③　　　　09 ①　　　　10 ④

11 (1) I heard the girl sing[singing] a song this morning.
　　(2) I made him tell me what was on his mind.
　　(3) It was on the day that[when] we met in the heavy rain.
　　(4) Hannah has such a nice appearance. 또는 Hannah has so nice an appearance.
　　(5) My husband agrees with me, and so do my friends.

12 (1) She saw him blow[blowing] his nose.
　　(2) He regretted the day when he had bought such a large house.
　　(3) All the students laughed and so did the teacher.
　　(4) It was Seoul that Arnold wanted to visit most.

01 '잘못되거나 당혹스러운 일을 한 후 가지게 되는 고통스러운 감정'을 나타내는 말은 'shame(부끄러움)'이다.

02 post: 게시하다, mayor: 시장, enter: ~에 들어가다 / strange: 이상한, 낯선 shame: 수치(심), 창피

03 in the middle of: ~의 도중에, ~의 중앙에, with no sign of anger: 화난 기색 없이, break my heart: 매우 슬프게 하다, stay away from: ~에서 떨어져 있다

04 notice는 '공지'를 뜻한다.

05 주어진 문장에서 sentence는 '문장'을 뜻하지만 ①번은 '선고'를 뜻한다. translate: 번역하다, capitalize: 대문자로 쓰다

06 notice: 알아차리다, mayor: 시장, fall down: 넘어지다, shame: 부끄러움, 수치

07 disregard: 무시하다, order: 명령, inviting: 유혹적인, silence: 침묵

08 ③ made의 목적격보어로 형용사 angry가 나와야 한다.

09 주어진 문장의 to teach는 Orders를 수식하는 형용사적 용법이다. ① 형용사적 용법 ②, ⑤ 명사적 용법 ③, ④ 부사적 용법

10 ① It was so exciting to watch the view as we went higher and higher. ② She was only a few pounds overweight. ③ Sarah heard her brother close[closing] the door angrily. ⑤ As rust eats away iron, so does care eat away the heart.

11 (1) hear는 지각동사이므로 목적격보어로 동사원형이나 현재분사가 나와야 한다. (2) tell의 직접목적어와 was의 주어 역할을 하도록 that을 what으로 고쳐야 한다. (3) 'It is ~ that ...' 강조 구문으로 on the day를 강조하고 있으므로 which를 that이나 when으로 고쳐야 한다. (4) 어순에 주의한다. such+a+형용사+명사, so+형용사+a+명사 (5) so가 '~도 (또한) 그렇다'라는 의미로 쓰일 때 'so+(조)동사+주어'의 형태로 도치가 이루어진다.

12 (1) 지각동사의 목적격보어로 동사원형이나 현재분사가 나온다. (2) 집을 산 것이 후회한 것보다 앞서는 시제이므로 과거완료로 나타낸다. such+a+형용사+명사 (3) so가 '~도 (또한) 그렇다'라는 의미로 쓰일 때 'so+(조)동사+주어'의 형태로 도치가 이루어진다. (4) 'It is[was] ~ that ...' 강조 구문으로 쓴다.

13 주어진 문장의 However에 주목한다. ①번 앞 문장의 내용과 상반되는 내용이 뒤에 이어지므로 ①번이 적절하다.

14 놀랍게도 Hamel 선생님은 '화난 기색이 전혀 없이' Frantz를 보시고 자상하게 말씀하셨다고 했다. in a rage: 분개하여

15 ⓐ와 ②: 명령, 지시, ① 주문, ③ 주문하다(동사), ④ 주문[주문한 음식/음료], 바에 마지막 주문을 지금 해 주세요[곧 주문 마

감입니다]! ⑤ 명령하다, 지시하다(동사)

16 nothing but = only: 오직

17 이 글은 'Alsace와 Lorraine에 있는 학교에서는 독일어만 가르치라는 명령이 베를린에서 내려와서, 이번 시간이 프랑스어로 하는 마지막 수업'이라는 내용의 글이므로, 제목으로는 ④번 '프랑스어로 하는 마지막 수업'이 적절하다.

18 ⓐ be late for: ~에 늦다, ⓑ stay away from: ~에서 떨어져 있다, ~을 멀리하다

19 앞에 나오는 내용과 상반되는 내용이 뒤에 이어지므로 However가 가장 적절하다. ① 따라서, 그러므로, ② 게다가, 더욱이, ④ 다시 말해서, ⑤ 그 결과

20 나는 "이번에는 뭐지?"라는 궁금증이 들었다고 했으므로 curious(궁금한)가 적절하다. ① 쑥스러운, 어색한, 당황스러운, ② 유감스러워 하는, 후회하는, ④ 실망한

21 ex: 전직, 어떤 사람이 더 이상 예전의 지위에 있지 않다는 것을 보여주기 위해 사용되는 단어이다.

22 (A) 'It is ~ that' 강조 구문으로, I noticed Monsieur Hamel's blue coat then.에서 then을 강조한 형태이므로 that이 적절하다. (B) 지각동사 see의 목적보어로 현재분사 sitting을 쓰는 것이 적절하다. (C) 주어가 'the ex-mayor, the ex-postman, and many others'이므로 were가 적절하다.

23 (ⓐ)와 ①, ③, ④: 명사적 용법, ②: 형용사적 용법, ⑤: 부사적 용법

24 ⓐ와 ②, ⑤: but은 '~ 외에'라는 의미의 전치사로, nothing but은 '오직(only)'이라고 해석한다. ①, ③ 그러나(접속사), ④ 단지, 그저 ~뿐(부사)

25 글쓴이의 모국어는 '프랑스어'이다.

26 시장 집무실 게시판에 공고되어 있던 것은 'Alsace와 Lorraine에 있는 학교에서는 독일어만 가르치라는 명령이 베를린에서 내려왔다'는 것이었다.

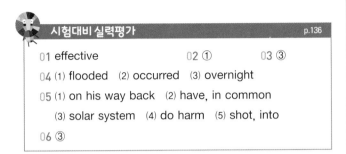

Watch Out

시험대비 실력평가
p.136

01 effective   02 ①   03 ③

04 (1) flooded (2) occurred (3) overnight

05 (1) on his way back (2) have, in common

(3) solar system (4) do harm (5) shot, into

06 ③

01 주어진 관계는 명사와 형용사의 관계를 나타낸다. active: 활동 중인, effective: 효과적인

02 '꼭대기에 용암이 솟아나오는 구멍이 있는 산'을 가리키는 말은 volcano(화산)이다.

03 destroy: 파괴하다

04 flood: 홍수가 나다, occur: 발생하다, overnight: 하룻밤 동안

05 shoot ~ into: ~을 …으로 내뿜다, solar system: 태양계, on one's way back home: 집으로 돌아오는 길에, have ~ in common: ~을 공통점으로 가지다, do harm: 해를 끼치다

06 have in common: ~을 공통점으로 갖다, have an effect on: ~에 영향을 미치다, get hurt: 다치다, get stuck in: 갇히다, take care of: ~을 돌보다, take off: ~을 벗다

서술형 시험대비
p.137

01 entire

02 (1) have, in common (2) in harmony with

(3) named after

03 (1) scenery (2) threaten (3) prevent (4) warnings

(5) volume

04 (1) Stretching is a good way to relieve your neck pain.

(2) My family likes to visit hot springs in winter.

(3) Germs can spread through the air.

05 (1) You should wear a helmet when you ride a bike.

(2) Heatwave warnings were issued.

(3) The app helps you locate your child.

(4) The thief threatened the shopkeeper and stole cash.

01 주어진 관계는 반의어 관계를 나타낸다. sudden: 갑작스러운, entire: 전체의

02 have ~ in common: ~을 공통으로 가지다, in harmony with: ~와 조화를 이루어, name after: ~을 따서 이름 짓다

03 prevent: 막다, 예방하다 scenery: 경치, 풍경 threaten: 위협하다 volume: 부피 warning: 주의, 경고

04 relieve: 완화하다, hot spring: 온천, spread: 퍼지다, germ: 세균

05 helmet: 헬멧, 안전모, issue: 발효하다, locate: ~의 위치를 찾아내다, threaten: 위협하다, thief: 도둑

교과서
Conversation

핵심 Check
p.138~139

1 Please make sure you wear a life jacket.

2 ②

교과서 대화문 익히기

Check(√) True or False
p.140

1 T 2 F 3 F 4 T

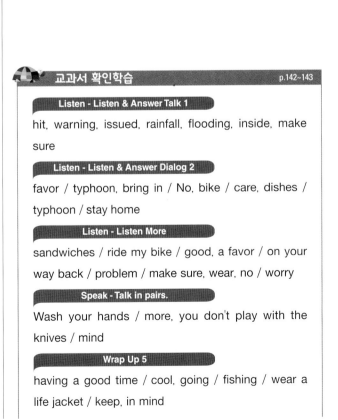

교과서 확인학습
p.142~143

Listen - Listen & Answer Talk 1

hit, warning, issued, rainfall, flooding, inside, make sure

Listen - Listen & Answer Dialog 2

favor / typhoon, bring in / No, bike / care, dishes / typhoon / stay home

Listen - Listen More

sandwiches / ride my bike / good, a favor / on your way back / problem / make sure, wear, no / worry

Speak - Talk in pairs.

Wash your hands / more, you don't play with the knives / mind

Wrap Up 5

having a good time / cool, going / fishing / wear a life jacket / keep, in mind

Wrap Up 6

do me a favor / on Christmas, tickets / tickets do you want

시험대비 기본평가　　　　　　　　　　p.144

01 ⓓ → wear　　　　　　　02 ⑤

03 She wants to go to the Tom Dylan concert.

04 She wants him to buy some concert tickets for her.

01 make sure 뒤에 접속사 that이 생략된 절이므로 동사 wear가 적절하다.

02 위 대화를 통해 아빠가 무엇을 명심해야 하는지 알 수 없다.

03 할머니는 크리스마스에 Tom Dylan 콘서트에 가고 싶어 하신다.

04 할머니는 Jack이 콘서트 표를 사주기를 원한다.

시험대비 실력평가　　　　　　　　p.145~146

01 ③　　　　　　　02 He asks her to wash her hands

first.　　03 칼을 가지고 놀지 말 것.　　04 ⑤

05 ⑤　　06 typhoon　07 ⑤　　08 ③

09 ③　　10 ①, ④　　11 ⑤　　12 ④

01 위 대화는 부엌에서 주의해야 할 사항에 대해 이야기하고 있다.

02 남자는 여자에게 먼저 손을 씻을 것을 요청한다.

03 남자는 여자에게 'Make sure you don't play with the knives.'라고 하고 있다.

04 (A)는 부탁하기를 나타내는 표현이지만, ⑤번은 도움을 주려는 의미를 나타낸다.

05 위 대화를 통해 소라가 할머니에게 무엇을 가져갈지는 알 수 없다.

06 '강한 바람을 동반한 강한 열대성 폭풍'을 가리키는 말은 typhoon(태풍)이다.

07 (A)는 당부하는 표현으로 ⑤번과 바꾸어 쓰기에 어색하다.

08 태풍주의보가 발효되었다.

09 주어진 문장은 부탁하는 표현으로 다음에 이어지는 응답으로 부탁 내용이 무엇인지 묻고 있는 (C)가 적절하다.

10 지민은 '최가네 샌드위치' 가게와 '아이스크림' 가게를 방문할 것이다.

11 어떻게 Brian이 지민을 도울 수 있을지는 알 수 없다.

12 부탁하는 표현에 '그 말을 들으니 유감이다'라는 말은 어색하다.

서술형 시험대비　　　　　　　　　　p.147

01 (B) → (C) → (E) → (D) → (A)

02 (A) stay home　(B) a typhoon is coming tonight

03 It is going to hit Jejudo tonight.

04 It will cause lots of rainfall with a high chance of flooding in some areas.

05 He asks the listeners to stay inside and keep listening to the reports.

06 (C) → (E) → (B) → (D) → (A)

01 (B) 부탁하기 → (C) 부탁 내용 질문 → (E) 부탁 내용 설명 → (D) 반응 및 구체적인 질문 → (A) 구체적인 질문에 대한 대답

03 태풍 도니는 오늘밤 제주도를 강타할 것이다.

04 태풍 도니는 일부 지역에 많은 비를 동반한 홍수를 야기할 것이다.

05 남자는 청취자들에게 실내에 머무르고 계속 보도를 청취해 주기를 부탁한다.

06 (C) 아빠와 좋은 시간을 보냈음을 설명 → (E) 반응 및 내일 계획 질문 → (B) 내일 계획 설명 → (D) 당부하기 → (A) 대답하기

교과서

Grammar

핵심 Check　　　　　　　　　　p.148~149

1 (1) Living　(2) Being

2 (1) might be reformed　(2) could be done

시험대비 기본평가　　　　　　　　　p.150

01 ①

02 (1) Feeling　(2) not knowing
　(3) will be delivered　(4) should be kept

03 ⑤　　　　　　　04 ③

01 접속사 없이 '주어+동사'가 이어지고 있으므로 빈칸에는 '접속사+주어+동사'의 역할을 할 수 있는 현재분사로(그가 배고픈 것은 능동이므로) 분사구문이 되어야 한다.

02 (1) 접속사가 없으므로 '접속사+주어+동사'의 역할을 할 수 있는 Feeling이 적절하다. (2) 분사구문의 부정은 분사 앞에 'not'이나 'never'를 쓴다. (3) 의자가 배달되는 것이므로 수동태로 나타내는 것이 적절하다. (4) 조동사가 있는 문장의 수동태는 '조동사+be+과거분사'의 형태로 나타낸다.

03 접속사 없이 '주어+동사'가 이어지고 있으므로 '접속사+주어+동사'의 역할을 할 수 있는 분사구문으로 나타내는 것이 적절하다.

04 조동사가 있는 문장의 수동태는 '조동사+be+과거분사'의 형태로 나타낸다.

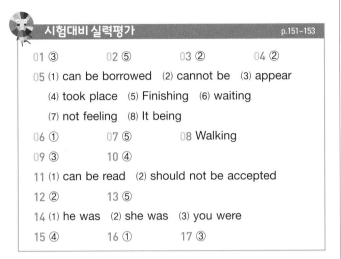

01 ③   02 ⑤   03 ②   04 ②

05 (1) can be borrowed   (2) cannot be   (3) appear

     (4) took place   (5) Finishing   (6) waiting

     (7) not feeling   (8) It being

06 ①   07 ⑤   08 Walking

09 ③   10 ④

11 (1) can be read   (2) should not be accepted

12 ②   13 ⑤

14 (1) he was   (2) she was   (3) you were

15 ④   16 ①   17 ③

01 dance라는 동사가 있고 접속사가 없으므로 listen을 listening으로 분사구문으로 만들어야 한다. Every Friday evening, we dance together, listening to music.

02 조동사가 있는 문장의 수동태는 '조동사+be+과거분사'의 형태로 나타낸다.

03 첫 번째 빈칸에는 접속사가 없으므로 '접속사+주어+동사'의 역할을 할 수 있는 knowing이 적절하다. 두 번째 빈칸에는 수동태가 나와야 하므로 'be taught'가 적절하다.

04 앞에 give라는 동사가 있고 접속사가 없으므로 know를 knowing으로 분사구문으로 만들어야 한다.

05 (1) 조동사가 있는 문장의 수동태는 '조동사+be+과거분사'의 형태로 나타내며, 책은 '빌려지는 것'이므로 수동태가 적절하다. (2) 조동사가 있는 문장의 수동태의 부정문은 '조동사+not+be+과거분사'의 형태로 쓴다. (3) appear는 자동사이므로 수동태로 쓰이지 않는다. (4) took place는 자동사로 쓰이므로 수동태로 쓰이지 않는다. (5) 접속사가 없으므로 '접속사+주어+동사'의 역할을 할 수 있는 분사구문으로 쓰는 것이 적절하다. (6) 분사구문의 뜻을 명확히 하기 위해 접속사 While을 생략하지 않고 남겨둔 경우이다. (7) 분사구문의 부정은 분사 앞에 'not'이나 'never'를 쓴다. (8) 부사절과 주절의 주어가 다르므로 부사절의 주어를 생략하지 않고 써야 한다.

06 The work should be finished by 7 p.m. 조동사가 있는 문장의 수동태는 '조동사+be+과거분사'의 형태로 나타낸다.

07 '접속사+주어+동사'의 부사절을 분사구문으로 바꾸어 쓸 수 있다. 분사구문의 뜻을 명확히 하기 위해 접속사를 생략하지 않기도 하지만 필요한 주어를 생략하지는 않는다.

08 한 문장으로 쓰면 'While he was walking around the park, he met his neighbor Ms. Marple.'이고, 분사구문으로 바꾸면 'While he was walking'을 현재분사 Walking으로 써야 한다.

09 동물들이 이용되는 것이므로 수동태로 쓰고, 부정문을 만들기 위해서는 조동사 뒤에 not을 쓴다.

10 'Because she felt very cold, she drank a cup of hot tea.'를 분사구문으로 바르게 바꾼 것은 ④번이다.

11 (1) 조동사가 있는 문장의 수동태는 '조동사+be+과거분사'의 형태로 나타낸다. (2) 조동사가 있는 문장의 수동태의 부정문은 '조동사+not+be+과거분사'의 형태로 나타낸다.

12 주어진 문장과 ②번은 '이유'를 나타낸다. ① 양보, ③ 시간, ④ 동시동작, ⑤ 조건

13 조동사가 있는 문장의 수동태는 '조동사+be+과거분사'의 형태로 나타낸다.

14 부사절에서 주어가 주절의 주어와 같을 때 '주어+be동사'를 생략할 수 있으며 이것은 분사구문으로 고쳤을 때 being을 생략하고 접속사를 남겨둔 것과 같다.

15 조동사가 있는 문장의 수동태는 '조동사+be+과거분사'의 형태로 나타낸다.

16 부사절의 시제가 주절보다 앞선 경우에는 완료분사구문 (having+과거분사)으로 쓴다.

17 부사절과 주절의 주어가 다를 때는 부사절의 주어를 생략하지 않고 사용하며 이것을 독립분사구문이라고 한다.

01 (1) Getting up late, she was late for school yesterday.

     (2) The girl got off the bus, saying goodbye to her friend.

     (3) Climbing to the top of the hill, you can see the garden well.

     (4) Studying hard, she failed the exam.

     (5) Not knowing the way to the theater, I asked the girl sitting next to me to tell me the way.

     (6) It being fine tomorrow, I'll go hiking on Dobong Mountain.

     (7) Having lost her job, she had to leave the office.

     (8) (Being) Interested in history, she likes her history class.

02 (1) New books should be returned in a week by you.

     (2) This song will be loved for a long time (by people).

     (3) The population growth has to be slowed down (by us).

     (4) The sincerity of his decision may be doubted by her.

     (5) 불가. 이유: resemble은 상태를 나타내는 동사로 수동태로 쓰이지 않는다.

27

(6) 불가. 이유: '소유'를 나타내는 타동사는 수동태로
쓰이지 않는다.

03 (1) Embarrassing → Embarrassed

(2) Meeting → Having met

04 must be cooled   05 breaking

06 (1) Arriving at the train station, Mike began to
look for his friends.

(2) Not knowing what to do, she asked for my
advice.

(3) More gold can be found in this region.

(4) The cooking room should be kept clean at all
times.

07 (1) Knives must be kept in a safe place.

(2) The department denies responsibility for what
occurred.

(3) Arriving home, he cleaned the whole house.

(4) It being chilly outside, I wanted to stay home.

(5) (Having been) Written in haste, the book has
many mistakes.

01 '접속사+주어+동사'로 이루어진 부사절의 주어가 주절의 주어
와 일치할 때 접속사와 주어를 생략하고 동사를 분사(동사원형
+-ing)로 만든다. (1) '이유', (2) '연속동작' (3) '조건' (4) '양
보' (5) 분사구문의 부정은 'not+현재분사'이다. (6) 주절의 주
어와 부사절의 주어가 다르므로 주어를 생략하면 안 된다.(독립
분사구문) (7) 부사절의 시제가 주절보다 앞선 경우에는 완료분
사구문(having+과거분사)으로 쓴다. (8) 과거분사로 시작되는
분사구문은 being이 생략된 것으로 수동의 의미를 갖는다.

02 조동사가 있는 문장의 수동태는 '조동사+be+과거분사'의 형태
로 나타낸다. 행위자가 일반인이거나 강조할 필요가 없을 때에
는 'by+행위자'를 생략하고 쓸 수 있다. (3)번의 경우 주어의 수
사 복수에서 단수로 바뀌므로 'have to'가 'has to'로 되어야 함
에 주의한다.

03 (1) 당황하게 한 것이 아니라 '당황하게 된'이라는 '수동'의 의미
가 되어야 하므로 Embarrassed로 고쳐야 한다. (2) 몇 번 만
난 것은 기억하는 것보다 먼저 일어난 일이므로 완료분사구문으
로 쓴다.

04 조동사가 있는 문장의 수동태는 '조동사+be+과거분사'의 형태
로 나타낸다. 행위자가 일반인이거나 강조할 필요가 없을 때에
는 'by+행위자'를 생략하고 쓸 수 있다.

05 'and broke'를 분사구문 breaking으로 쓴다. = Mike fell
down the steps and broke his arm.(연속 동작)

06 (1) 현재분사가 분사구문을 이끌도록 한다. (2) 분사구문의 부정
은 분사 앞에 'not'이나 'never'를 쓴다. (3), (4) 조동사가 있는
문장의 수동태는 '조동사+be+과거분사'의 형태로 나타내며 행위
자가 일반인이거나 강조할 필요가 없을 때에는 'by+행위자'를 생
략하고 쓸 수 있다.

07 (1) Knives가 주어이므로 수동태로 써야 하고, 조동사가 있
는 문장의 수동태는 '조동사+be+과거분사'의 형태로 쓴다. (2)
occur는 자동사이므로 수동태로 쓰이지 않는다. (3) 도착하는
것은 능동이므로 현재분사를 쓰쓰는 것이 적절하다. (4) 주절의
주어와 부사절의 주어가 다르므로 독립분사구문으로 써야 한다.
(5) 책이 쓰여지는 것이므로 수동의 의미인 과거분사가 나와야
하며, 책이 쓰여진 시제가 앞서므로 완료분사구문으로 써야 한
다. Having been written에서 Having been을 생략하여 써
도 좋다.

Reading

확인문제   p.156

1 T   2 F   3 T

확인문제   p.157

1 T   2 F

확인문제   p.158

1 T   2 F

교과서 확인학습 A   p.159~160

01 Power   02 have in common
03 of course   04 volcanic eruptions
05 are named after
06 make big islands appear
07 should be studied and understood
08 how many volcanoes there are
09 According to, above sea level
10 hard to locate
11 a large number of   12 are located
13 home to   14 alone, lies on
15 where, occur   16 Sudden
17 something surprising   18 appeared overnight
19 grow
20 kept growing, stopped growing
21 can be found   22 have been discovered
23 the largest known
24 100 times greater than that of
25 do harm to   26 get hurt
27 may be destoryed, can be threatened

28 have serious effects on

29 shoots, into, preventing, from reaching, disturbing

30 Deadly 31 erupted

32 eruption 33 unusually

34 What volcanoes do, not always

35 is good for 36 tourist attraction

37 Looking for 38 can be used

39 turns, into 40 greater harmony with

교과서 확인학습 B

p.161~162

1 The Power of Volcanoes

2 What do Jejudo, Sicily, and Hawaii have in common?

3 They are islands, of course.

4 In fact, they are all islands made from volcanic eruptions.

5 Volcanoes are very powerful, so they are named after Vulcan, the Roman god of fire.

6 They can make big islands appear or destroy entire cities like Pompeii.

7 Therefore, they should be studied and understood.

8 Nobody knows for sure how many volcanoes there are in the world.

9 According to scientists, there are about 1,500 active volcanoes above sea level.

10 Many more are underwater, and they are hard to locate.

11 Still, scientists have discovered a large number of them so far.

12 Many of the volcanoes on Earth are located along the Ring of Fire that circles the Pacific Ocean.

13 The ring is about 40,000 kilometers long, and it is home to around 75% of the world's active volcanoes.

14 Indonesia alone has over 120 active volcanoes since the country lies on the Ring of Fire.

15 This ring is also the area where most of the world's earthquakes occur.

16 A Sudden Volcano

17 Working on a cornfield one day in 1943, farmers in Mexico found something surprising.

18 A volcano appeared overnight on a flat cornfield.

19 Residents watched the volcano grow over 100 meters tall within a week.

20 The volcano, called Paricutin, kept growing, and it finally stopped growing at 424 meters in 1952.

21 You may think volcanoes can be found only on Earth.

22 However, they have been discovered on other planets, too, such as Mars and Jupiter.

23 In fact, "Olympus Mons" on Mars is the largest known volcano in the solar system.

24 Its volume is about 100 times greater than that of Mauna Loa, the largest volcano on Earth.

25 Being very powerful and dangerous, volcanoes do harm to people in many ways.

26 Sometimes people get hurt, or they may lose their houses.

27 Crops may be destoryed, and air traffic can be threatened.

28 Volcanoes can also have serious effects on world weather.

29 A volcanic eruption shoots lots of ash and dust into the air, preventing some of the sunlight from reaching Earth and thus disturbing usual weather patterns.

30 A Deadly Volcano

31 Mt. Tambora, an active volcano on the island of Sumbawa, Indonesia, erupted in 1815.

32 The eruption killed more than 10,000 residents.

33 It also caused an unusually cold summer around the world the following year.

34 What volcanoes do is not always bad for humans, however.

35 The soil near a volcano is good for farming.

36 Volcanoes are also a great tourist attraction.

37 Looking for fantastic scenery, millions of tourists visit Mt. Halla in Jejudo, Mt. Etna in Sicily, or Diamond Head in Hawaii every year.

38 Volcanoes can be used to produce electricity, too.

39 Iceland, for example, actively turns its volcanoes' heat energy into electricity.

40 Today people around the world are studying ways to live in greater harmony with volcanoes, and they are hopeful that more ways will be found soon.

시험대비 실력평가

p.163~167

01 ⑤ 02 ① 03 volcanic eruptions

04 ② 05 According as → According to

06 ②

07 While they were working on a cornfield one day in

29

　　　1943 또는 When[As] they worked on a cornfield one day in 1943

08 to grow → growing　　　09 Olympus Mons

10 ③　　　　　　11 (A) in the solar system　(B) on Earth

12 ②　　　　13 The eruption　　　　14 ④

15 ①, ④

16 preventing some of the sunlight from reaching Earth and thus disturbing usual weather patterns

17 ③　　　　18 ⑤　　　　19 ②

20 have discovered　　　21 ④　　　22 ⑤

23 (A) surprising　(B) grow　(C) called　　24 ④

01 앞의 내용의 결과가 나오고 있으므로 Therefore가 가장 적절하다. therefore: 그러므로, ② 게다가, 더욱이, ③ 다시 말해서

02 ⓐ과 ⓑ: 'Jejudo, Sicily, and Hawaii', ⓒ~ⓔ: '화산'

03 제주도, 시실리아, 하와이는 모두 '화산 분출'에 의해 형성된 섬이다.

04 이 글은 '세계에 얼마나 많은 화산이 있는지 누구도 정확히 알지 못하고 해수면 위에 대략 1,500개의 활화산이 있는데, 그것보다 더 많이 존재하는 해저 화산들은 정확한 위치를 파악하기가 어렵다'는 내용의 글이므로, 제목으로는 ②번 '세계에 얼마나 많은 화산이 있는가?'가 적절하다.

05 'according as+주어+동사'이므로 'According to'로 고치는 것이 적절하다.

06 ⓑ와 ①, ③: 부사적 용법, ②, ⑤: 명사적 용법, ④: 형용사적 용법

07 '때'를 나타내는 부사절로 바꿔 쓸 수 있다.

08 '1952년에 424m로 '드디어 성장을 멈추었다'고 해야 하므로 to grow를 growing으로 고치는 것이 적절하다. stop+~ing: ~하는 것을 멈추다, stop+to부정사: ~하기 위해 멈추다

09 '올림푸스 몬스'를 가리킨다.

10 ⓑ와 ③: [앞에서 말한 명사의 반복을 피하기 위해] (~의) 그것(지시대명사), ① 지시형용사, ② 저것(말하는 사람과 가까이에 있지 않은 사람이나 사물을 가리킴), ④ 관계대명사, ⑤ [수량·정도를 나타내는 말을 한정하여] 그만큼(지시부사)

11 Olympus Mons는 '태양계에서' 가장 크다고 알려진 화산이고, Mauna Loa는 '지구에서' 가장 큰 화산이다.

12 이 글은 'Tambora 산의 분출이 주민 1만 명 이상을 죽음에 이르게 했다'는 내용의 글이므로, 제목으로는 ②번 '목숨을 앗아가는 화산'이 적절하다. ① definition: 정의

13 (Tambora 산의) '분출'을 가리킨다.

14 Tambora 산이 1815년에 분출했을 때 '얼마나 오래' 분출했는지는 알 수 없다. ① It's on the island of Sumbawa, Indonesia. ② It erupted in 1815. ③ It killed more than 10,000 residents. ⑤ It was unusually cold.

15 ⓐ와 ①, ④: 이유, ② 양보, ③ 조건, ⑤ 때

16 preventing과 disturbing은 부대상황을 나타내는 분사 구문이다. prevent A from -ing: A가 ~하는 것을 막다

17 이 글은 '화산이 매우 강력하고 위험하기 때문에, 여러 면에서 사람들에게 해를 끼친다'는 내용의 글이므로, 주제로는 ③번 '인간 생활에 끼치는 화산의 해로운 영향'이 적절하다.

18 앞의 내용의 예가 나오고 있으므로 for example이 가장 적절하다. ① 게다가, 더욱이, ② 그 결과, ④ 다른 한편으로는, 반면에

19 주어진 문장의 also에 주목한다. ②번 앞 문장에서 화산이 인류에게 항상 나쁜 것만은 아닌 첫 번째 예로 화산 인근의 토양이 농사에 좋다고 말한 다음에, '또한' 화산은 매우 훌륭한 관광 명소라는 설명을 하는 것이므로 ②번이 적절하다.

20 과학자들이 (과거부터) 지금까지 해저에 존재하는 많은 수의 화산을 '발견해 왔다'라고 해야 하므로 '현재완료시제'로 쓰는 것이 적절하다.

21 주어진 문장의 They에 주목한다. ④번 앞 문장의 Volcanoes를 받고 있으므로 ④번이 적절하다.

22 과학자들에 따르면, '해수면 위에' 대략 1,500개의 활화산이 있다.

23 (A) 감정을 나타내는 동사는 감정을 유발할 때 현재분사를 쓰는 것이 적절하므로 surprising이 적절하다. (B) watch는 지각동사이므로 목적격보어 자리에 동사원형인 grow가 적절하다. (C) Paricutin(파리쿠틴)'이라 '불리는' 화산이라고 해야 하므로 called가 적절하다.

24 1943년에 생기기 시작해서 1952년에 드디어 성장을 멈추었다고 했으므로 '10년 이상 동안' 계속 자랐다는 것은 옳지 않다.

서술형 시험대비　　　　　　　p.168~169

01 eruptions

02 As a matter of fact / Actually / To tell the truth

03 Because they can make big islands appear or destroy entire cities like Pompeii.

04 the Ring of Fire　　　05 three-fourths

06 There are over 120 active volcanoes in Indonesia.

07 (A) other　(B) is　(C) known

08 Mauna Loa → that of Mauna Loa

09 Olympus Mons.

10 What volcanoes do is not always bad for humans

11 be used

12 (1) 화산 인근의 토양은 농사에 좋다.

　　(2) 화산은 또한 매우 훌륭한 관광 명소이다.

　　(3) 화산은 또한 전기를 생산하는 데에도 이용될 수 있다.

13 explosive power → heat energy

14 like　　　　15 as great as

16 other planets

01 eruption: 분출, 증기와 화산 물질의 강력한 방출이 갑작스럽게 발생하는 것

02 In fact / As a matter of fact / Actually / To tell the truth: 사실

03 화산은 큰 섬이 생겨나게 하거나 폼페이 같은 도시 전체를 파멸시킬 수도 있기 때문이다.

04 '불의 고리(환태평양조산대)'를 가리킨다.

05 75%는 4분의 3이다. 분수를 읽을 때 분자는 '기수', 분모는 '서수'로 읽는 것이 적절하다. 분자와 분모는 하이픈으로 연결하여 쓰고, 분자가 2 이상인 경우 분모 끝에 s를 붙인다.

06 인도네시아에는 120개가 넘는 활화산이 있다.

07 (A) another 뒤에는 단수 명사가 와야 하므로 other가 적절하다. (B) "Olympus Mons"가 주어이므로 is가 적절하다. (C) 태양계에서 가장 크다고 '알려진' 화산이라고 해야 하므로 known이 적절하다.

08 그것의 부피는 지구에서 가장 큰 화산 Mauna Loa의 '부피'보다 약 100배 더 크다고 해야 하므로, that of Mauna Loa로 고치는 것이 적절하다. 대명사 that은 the volume을 대신한다.

09 'Olympus Mons'는 'Mauna Loa'의 부피보다 약 100배 더 크다.

10 선행사를 포함하는 관계대명사 what을 주어로 하여 쓰는 것이 적절하다. not always는 '언제나 ~인 것은 아닌'이라는 의미로 부분 부정을 나타낸다.

11 화산은 또한 전기를 생산하는 데에도 '이용될 수' 있다고 해야 하므로 수동태로 쓰는 것이 적절하다.

12 화산이 인류에게 항상 나쁜 것만이 아니라고 말하면서 예로 든 세 가지를 쓰는 것이 적절하다.

13 아이슬란드는 적극적으로 화산의 '열에너지'를 전기로 바꾼다. explosive power: 폭발력

14 such as = like: ~와 같은

15 ~ times+비교급+than A = ~ times+as+원급+as A: A보다 ~ 배 더 …한

16 화산은 지구뿐만 아니라 '다른 행성'에서도 발견되어 왔다.

영역별 핵심문제
p.171~175

01 discovery **02** ④

03 (1) There may be life on other planets.
(2) Heavy rainfall is expected this summer.
(3) There are eight planets in our solar system.

04 ③

05 (1) Everything in the house turned into ash after the fire.
(2) The floor of the room was covered with dust.
(3) This year farmers expect to have a good crop.

06 ① **07** ⓓ → inside **08** ④

09 life jacket **10** ① **11** ③

12 Can you give me a hand? **13** ⑤

14 ② **15** ③ **16** ⑤ **17** ②

18 ⑤ **19** The electricity being **20** ③

21 ③ **22** ②, ⑤ **23** until now **24** ③

25 growing **26** ⑤

27 Because[As] they are very powerful and dangerous

28 ④ **29** ② **30** ⑤

01 주어진 단어의 관계는 동사와 명사의 관계를 나타낸다. destroy: 파괴하다, discover: 발견하다

02 주어진 문장에서 issue는 '발표하다'를 의미한다.

03 (1) planet: 행성 (2) rainfall: 강우(량) (3) solar system: 태양계

04 주어진 문장에서 volume은 '부피'를 의미하며 이와 같은 의미로 쓰인 것은 ③번이다. ① '책, (책의) 권 ②,④,⑤ 음량, 볼륨

05 (1) turn into: ~로 변하다 (2) be covered with: ~로 덮이다 (3) expect: 기대하다

06 주어진 문장에서 issue는 '발표하다'를 의미하며 이와 같은 의미로 쓰인 것은 ①번이다. 나머지는 모두 '주제, 쟁점, 문제'를 의미한다.

07 태풍이 오니 실내에 머물러 있을 것을 조언하는 것이 자연스러우므로 inside가 적절하다.

08 태풍 도니는 강한 바람과 많은 비를 동반할 것이다.

10 당부하는 말에 '명심할게요.'라는 대답이 적절하다.

11 위 대화에서 준호가 신난 것을 알 수 있다. frightened: 겁먹은

12 'Can you give me a hand?'는 '저를 도와주시겠어요?'라고 도움을 요청하는 표현이다.

13 위 대화에서 할머니가 누구와 콘서트에 갈지는 알 수 없다.

14 상대방의 당부하는 말에 '신경 쓰지 마. 기운 내!'라는 대답은 어색하다.

15 Lions and tigers belong to the cat family. 'belong to'는 '~에 속하다'라는 뜻으로 수동태로 쓰이지 않는다.

16 주어진 문장은 '이유'를 나타내는 분사구문으로 볼 수 있다.

17 조동사 will이 있으므로 'will+be+과거분사'의 형태로 쓴다.

18 ① Riding in a flying car, you will be able to go places faster. ② Not having much work to do, I have time to see a movie. ③ The sun rising, we made wishes. ④ Singing and dancing together, we had a great time. ⑤ 'Because it appeared overnight, Paricutin is a sudden volcano.'를 분사구문으로 쓴 것이다.

19 'When the electricity was out, ~'을 부사구문으로 고쳐 쓴 것이다. 주절의 주어와 부사절의 주어가 다르므로 주어를 생략하면 안 된다.(독립분사구문)

20 첫 번째 문장에서는 접속사가 없으므로 '접속사+주어+동사'의 역할을 할 수 있는 분사구문 watching이 적절하다. 두 번째 문장에서는 수동태가 나와야 하고 조동사가 있으므로 '조동사+be+과거분사'의 형태로 쓴다.

21 ⓐ와 ③: 그럼에도 불구하고(부사), ①과 ⑤: 아직(도)(부사), ② (비교급을 강조하여) 훨씬(부사), ④ 가만히 있는, 고요한(형용사)

22 ⓑ와 ②, ⑤: 계속 용법, ① 완료 용법, ③ 결과 용법, ④ 경험 용법

23 so far = until now: 지금까지

24 이 글은 '밤사이에 평평한 옥수수 밭 위로 화산이 생겨난 것'에 관한 글이므로, 제목으로는 ③번 '갑작스럽게 생겨난 화산'이 적절하다.

25 keep ~ing: 계속해서 ~하다

26 ⑤ prevent A from -ing: A가 ~하는 것을 막다, ① do harm to: ~에 해를 끼치다, ② in many ways: 여러 면에서, ③ have effects on: ~에 영향을 끼치다, ④ shoot ~ into ...: ~을 …으로 내뿜다

27 '이유'를 나타내는 부사절로 바꿔 쓸 수 있다.

28 '다량의 용암을 분출시킨다.'는 말은 위 글에 없다.

29 위 글은 '감상문'이다. review (책, 연극, 영화 등에 대한) 논평[비평], 감상문, ① (신문, 잡지의) 글, 기사, ③ 수필, ④ 요약, 개요, ⑤ 독후감

30 '글쓴이가 누구와 함께 영화를 보았는지'를 알 수 없다. ① It is *The Perfect Storm*. ② Wolfgang Petersen. ③ It came out in 2000. ④ It is about a big storm in the Atlantic Ocean that put a fishing boat in danger.

단원별 예상문제   p.176~179

01 ②

02 (1) earthquake destroyed   (2) effect, physical
   (3) volcano, erupt

03 ③   04 ⑤

05 He visited Dokdo with his father.

06 He should make sure to wear a life jacket.

07 ⓔ → wear

08 ④   09 can you do me a favor? 10 ②

11 should be done   12 ②

13 Listening to music, he read the novel he had
   bought the other day.

14 ⓓ, ⓕ   15 ②   16 occurs → occur

17 ③   18 ⑤   19 ①   20 ④

21 use → be used   22 ①

23 a hot spring

---

01 '지구 표면의 갑작스러운 흔들림'을 나타내는 말은 earthquake(지진)이다.

02 earthquake: 지진, destroy: 파괴하다, effect: 영향, 효과, physical: 신체의, volcano: 화산, erupt: 분출하다

03 (A) '발표하다'를 뜻하며 수동태로 issued, (B) because of+

명사(구), because+주어+동사, (C) keep ~ing: 계속 ~하다

04 위 대화를 통해 언제 비가 그칠지는 알 수 없다.

05 준호는 아빠와 독도를 방문했다.

06 준호는 낚시 갈 때 구명조끼를 꼭 입을 것을 명심해야 한다.

07 make sure (that) 주어+동사 ~: 꼭 ~해라, 반드시 ~해라

10 아빠는 바깥에 있는 옷가지들을 안으로 가져올 것을 부탁하였다.

11 be동사가 주어졌으므로 조동사가 있는 수동태인 '조동사+be+과거분사'의 형태로 쓴다.

12 조동사가 있는 문장의 수동태는 '조동사+be+과거분사'의 형태로 나타낸다.

13 접속사와 부사절의 주어를 생략하고 현재분사를 그대로 쓴다.

14 ⓐ Felt → Feeling. ⓑ Having not → Not having ⓒ Being → It being ⓔ design → be designed ⓖ discuss → be discussed ⓗ known → be known

15 ⓐ와 ②: 약, ~쯤, ① 사방에(서), 빙 둘러, ③ 둘레에, 주위에, ④ 이리저리, 여기저기, ⑤ (특정한 사람이나 사상 등에) 맞춰, (내가 모든 걸 당신 일정에 맞출 수는 없잖아요!)

16 'most+복수명사'는 복수로 취급해야 하므로 'occur'로 고치는 것이 적절하다.

17 '인도네시아에서 활화산이 얼마나 자주 분출하는지'는 대답할 수 없다. ① They are located along the Ring of Fire that circles the Pacific Ocean. ② It is about 40,000 kilometers long. ④ Because the country lies on the Ring of Fire. ⑤ They occur in the Ring of Fire that circles the Pacific Ocean.

18 ⓐ 앞에 나오는 내용과 상반되는 내용이 뒤에 이어지므로 However가 가장 적절하다. ⓑ 방금 한 말에 대해 자세한 내용을 덧붙이고 있으므로 In fact가 가장 적절하다. ① Therefore 그러므로, ② In addition 게다가, 더욱이, ④ on the other hand 다른 한편으로는, 반면에

19 화산은 화성이나 목성 같은 '다른 행성에서도' 발견되어 왔다.

20 선행사를 포함하는 관계대명사 what을 쓰는 것이 적절하다.

21 '조동사 can+be+p.p.'의 수동태가 되어야 한다.

22 주어진 문장은 ①번 앞 문장에서 말한 '화산에서 이 에너지를 볼 수 있다'는 것을 설명하는 문장이므로 ①번이 적절하다.

23 '온천'을 가리킨다.

서술형 실전문제   p.180~181

01 She is going to Choi's to buy some sandwiches.

02 He asks her to buy chocolate ice cream for him on her way back.

03 She should keep in mind that she wears a helmet and no ear phones.

04 (1) While he was walking home after school, Tom found a soccer ball on the street.

(2) Because[As/ Since] I slept on the bus, I missed my stop.

(3) He started to cry, admitting his fault.

(4) It not being so cold outside, she went out without a coat.

05 (1) She left home, waving at her parents.

(2) Feeling tired, I came home earlier than usual.

(3) This project cannot be finished by today.

(4) The concert will be held next week.

06 (1) All students must follow school rules.

(2) We should finish the project tonight.

(3) By whom will the problem be solved?

(4) Eggs and cheese can be added according to your taste.

07 Nobody knows for sure how many volcanoes there are in the world.

08 one thousand five hundred

09 them

10 influence

11 it prevents, disturbs

12 (A) crops   (B) air traffic

01 지민이는 지금 샌드위치를 사러 '최가네'에 간다.

02 Brian은 지민이에게 돌아오는 길에 초콜릿 아이스크림을 사다 줄 것을 요청한다.

03 지민이는 헬멧을 쓰고 이어폰을 끼지 말 것을 명심해야 한다.

04 (1) 의미상 '시간'을 나타내는 분사구문이다. (2) 의미상 '이유'를 나타내는 분사구문이다. (3) 의미상 '부대상황'을 나타내는 분사구문으로 바꾼다. (4) 주절의 주어와 다르므로 독립분사구문으로 바꾼다.

05 (1) 의미상 '동시동작'을 나타내는 분사구문이다. (2) 의미상 '이유'를 나타내는 분사구문이다. (3), (4) 조동사가 있는 문장의 수동태는 '조동사+be+과거분사'의 형태로 나타낸다.

06 조동사가 있는 수동태는 '조동사+be+과거분사'의 형태로 쓴다. (3)은 Who will the problem be solved by?로 바꿀 수도 있다.

07 동사 knows의 목적어로 '간접의문문의 순서(의문사+주어+동사)'로 쓰는 것이 적절하다.

08 'one thousand five hundreds'로 쓰지 않도록 조심해야 한다.

09 주어 they를 locate의 '목적어'로 바꾸는 것이 적절하다.

10 have an effect[influence/impact] on = influence = affect: ~에 영향을 미치다

11 ⓑ는 부대상황을 나타내는 분사구문으로, and it prevents ~ and thus disturbs ~로 바꾸어 쓸 수 있다.

12 화산은 사람들에게 해를 끼치고 집뿐만 아니라 '농작물'을 파괴할 수 있다. 또한 화산은 '항공 교통'을 위협하고 세계 날씨를 바꾼다.

|모범답안|

01 (A) bike   (B) some sandwiches

(C) buy chocolate ice cream

(D) wear a helmet and no ear phones

02 (A) *The Perfect Storm*   (B) in 2000

(C) Wolfgang Petersen

(D) a big storm in the Atlantic Ocean that put a fishing boat in danger

(E) good acting   (F) natural disasters

01 지민이는 샌드위치를 사러 자전거로 '최가네'에 갈 것이다. Brian은 그녀에게 그를 위해 돌아오는 길에 초콜릿 아이스크림을 사다 달라고 요청한다. Brian은 그녀에게 헬멧을 쓰고 이어폰을 사용하지 말 것을 상기시킨다.

01 ②   02 ⑤

03 (1) flooding   (2) chance   (3) area

(4) favor   (5) Volcanoe(s)

04 How many tickets do you want?   05 ⑤

06 He wants her to bring in the clothes from outside and call Grandma.

07 He is going to take care of the bike.

08 She will tell her to stay home.

09 (B) → (D) → (C) → (E) → (A)   10 ④

11 ⑤   12 (E) → (B) → (A) → (D) → (C)

13 (1) can be used   (2) should not be allowed

(3) will be built

14 ②, ④

15 (1) The pizza will be delivered within 30 minutes.

(2) The problem should be solved right now.

(3) Dana came across her history teacher, walking to the market.

(4) Feeling cold, Susan put on her coat.

16 ①, ④

17 (1) Food and drinks must not be brought into the library.

(2) The computer should be fixed by Mr. Hinkle.

(3) (Being) Tired after the game, the players took a rest for a while.

(4) Not having any money, I borrowed some from my older brother.

18 ④   19 ②

20 (A) for   (B) produce   (C) harmony   21 ③

33

22 Residents watched the volcano grow over 100 meters tall within a week.

23 ①

숙하다, (C) 화산과 더 '조화롭게' 살 방법이라고 해야 하므로 harmony가 적절하다. conflict: 투쟁, 전투, 분쟁

21 화산은 또한 전기를 생산하는 데에도 이용될 수 있다.

22 watch는 지각동사로 목적격보어 자리에 동사원형인 grow를 쓰는 것이 적절하다.

23 ① all at once: 갑자기, finally / at last / eventually / in the end / in the long run: 마침내

01 '별 주변을 도는 우주에 있는 크고 둥근 물체'를 가리키는 것은 planet(행성)이다.

02 주어진 단어들 중 나머지는 모두 자연 재해를 나타내지만 ⑤번은 '태양계'를 나타낸다.

03 favor: 친절, 부탁, volcano: 화산, chance: 가능성, flooding: 홍수, area: 지역

05 할머니가 Jack의 크리스마스 계획을 찬성한다는 내용은 대화를 통해 알 수 없다.

06 아빠는 소라가 바깥에서 옷가지들을 들여오고 할머니께 전화를 하길 원하신다.

07 아빠는 설거지를 끝낸 후에 자전거를 처리하실 것이다.

08 소라는 할머니께 집안에 계시라고 말할 것이다.

09 (B) 걸어가지 않고 자전거를 탈 것이라고 설명 → (D) 부탁하기 → (C) 부탁 내용 질문 → (E) 부탁 내용 설명 → (A) 허락

10 (A)는 당부하는 표현이지만 ④번은 궁금증을 나타낸다.

11 준호는 내일 '아빠'와 보트를 탈 것이다.

12 (E) 부탁 내용 설명 → (B) 대답 및 자전거 관리 질문 → (A) 자전거 관리에 대한 대답 → (D) 요구 사항 확인 → (C) 대답

13 조동사가 있는 수동태는 '조동사+be+과거분사'의 형태로 쓴다.

14 ① Walked → Walking ③ Very → Being very ⑤ study → be studied

15 (1), (2) 조동사가 있는 수동태는 '조동사+be+과거분사'의 형태로 쓴다. (3) '시간'의 분사구문을 이용한다. (4) '이유'의 분사구문을 이용한다.

16 ① This medicine must be taken after meal. ④ Tina sat back in the sofa, closing her eyes.

17 (1) 조동사가 있는 수동태는 '조동사+be+과거분사'의 형태로 쓴다. (2) 컴퓨터가 주어이므로 수동태가 되어야 한다. 조동사가 있는 수동태는 '조동사+be+과거분사'의 형태로 쓴다. (3) 주어가 피곤하게 되는 수동의 관계이므로 being이 생략된 과거분사 Tired나 Being tired로 시작하는 문장으로 바꾼다. (4) 분사구문의 부정은 분사 앞에 'not'이나 'never'를 쓴다.

18 ④ This ring is also the area. + Most of the world's earthquakes occur in the area.를 합친 문장이므로, This ring is also the area 'where[in which]' most of the world's earthquakes occur.라고 하는 것이 적절하다.

19 (A)와 ②: ~때문에, ①, ③, ④, ⑤: ~한 이후로

20 (A) 화산 인근의 토양은 농사에 '좋다'고 해야 하므로 for가 적절하다. be good at: ~을 잘하다, be good for: ~에 좋다, (B) 화산은 또한 전기를 '생산하는 데에도' 이용될 수 있다고 해야 하므로 produce가 적절하다. be used to ~ing: ~하 데 익

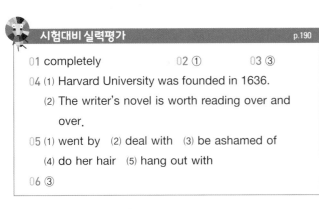

All Your Dreams Are Worth Chasing

01 completely   02 ①   03 ③

04 (1) Harvard University was founded in 1636.

  (2) The writer's novel is worth reading over and over.

05 (1) went by (2) deal with (3) be ashamed of

  (4) do her hair (5) hang out with

06 ③

01 주어진 관계는 동의어의 관계를 나타낸다. achieve: 이루다, 달성[성취]하다 accomplish: 이루다, 성취하다 entirely: 완전히 completely: 완전히, 전적으로

02 '추구하거나 뒤쫓다'를 가리키는 말은 'go after(~을 추구하다' 이다.

03 apply for: ~에 지원하다, ~을 신청하다

05 be ashamed of: ~을 부끄러워하다, deal with: ~을 다루다, do one's hair: 머리를 손질하다, hang out with: ~와 시간을 보내다, go by: 지나가다, 흐르다

06 break down: 고장나다, break out: 발발[발생]하다, go after: ~을 추구하다, go by: 지나가다, 흐르다

01 include

02 (1) Go after (2) was ashamed of (3) deal with

03 (1) include (2) impatient (3) read (4) opportunity

  (5) offer

04 (1) The book will help you expand your imagination.

  (2) She became a zookeeper by going after what she was interested in.

  (3) He is looking for a challenging and rewarding job.

05 (1) When monkeys play and chase each other, they laugh.

  (2) The price of all sandwiches in our store includes drinks.

  (3) The hospital was founded to treat poor people.

01 주어진 관계는 반의어 관계를 나타낸다. lend: 빌리다, borrow: 빌려주다, include: 포함하다, exclude: 제외[배제]하다

02 go after: ~을 추구하다, be ashamed of: ~을 부끄러워하다, deal with: ~을 다루다

03 impatient: 짜증 난, 참지 못하는 opportunity: 기회 offer: 제의, 제안 read: ~라고 적혀 있다 include: 포함하다

04 imagination: 상상, 상상력, go after: ~을 추구하다, challenging: 도전적인

05 chase: 쫓다, 추적하다, include: 포함하다, found: 설립하다

1 I should have set the alarm.

2 ②

1 T   2 F   3 T   4 F

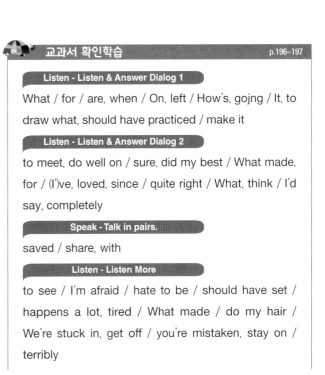

Listen - Listen & Answer Dialog 1

What / for / are, when / On, left / How's, gojng / It, to draw what, should have practiced / make it

Listen - Listen & Answer Dialog 2

to meet, do well on / sure, did my best / What made, for / (I')ve, loved, since / quite right / What, think / I'd say, completely

Speak - Talk in pairs.

saved / share, with

Listen - Listen More

to see / I'm afraid / hate to be / should have set / happens a lot, tired / What made / do my hair / We're stuck in, get off / you're mistaken, stay on / terribly

Wrap Up 6

when / with / making / that's, quite right / why / think

Wrap Up 7

How / shouldn't have done / were you, I'd get

시험대비 기본평가 p.198

01 ⓓ must → should 02 ⑤
03 She wants to work with robots.
04 Because she thinks it'll be a good job in the future.

01 'must have p.p.'는 '~했음에 틀림없다'라는 의미이고, 'should have p.p.'는 '~했어야 한다'라는 의미이므로 must를 should로 고치는 것이 적절하다.

02 위 대화를 통해 소라가 왜 마나 애니메이션 고등학교에 입학하고 싶은지 알 수 없다.

03 소녀는 로봇과 관련된 일을 하고 싶어 한다.

04 소녀는 '그것이 미래에 좋은 직업이 될 거라고 생각하기 때문이야.'라고 말하고 있다.

시험대비 실력평가 p.199~200

01 ⑤ 02 ③ 03 I'd say imagination.
04 ② 05 ④ 06 stuck 07 ③
08 ⑤ 09 ①
10 How come your computer has viruses?
11 모르는 사람에게서 온 이메일을 연 것.

01 (A)에 이어서 '저는 게임 디자이너가 되고 싶습니다.'라고 하는 것으로 보아 상대방의 말을 수정할 때 쓰는 표현이 나오는 것이 적절하다.

02 위 대화의 M과 G는 면접[인터뷰] 하는 사람과 면접[인터뷰] 받는 사람의 관계이다.

03 I'd[I would] say ~: 내 생각에 ~인 것 같다

04 'I should have+p.p. ~.'는 'I ought to have+p.p.', 'I'm sorry I didn't[wasn't] ~.' 또는 'I regret I didn't[wasn't] ~.' 등으로 바꿔 쓸 수 있다.

05 위 대화를 통해 지호와 Amber가 얼마나 늦었는지 알 수 없다.

06 '한 위치에서 다른 위치로 움직이기 힘든'을 가리키는 말은 stuck(갇힌, 꼼짝 못 하는)이다.

07 (A)는 후회하는 표현이 적절하다. (B)는 많은 책을 읽지 못한 것을 걱정하고 있으므로 afraid가 적절하다. (C) spend+시간/돈+on (동)명사: ~에 시간이나 돈을 쓰다

08 'G2는 휴대 전화에 너무 많은 시간을 썼다고 후회하고 있다.

09 상대방의 말을 수정해 주는 말에 '유감이다'라고 말하는 것은 어색하다.

10 'How come?'은 평서문의 어순이 이어지는 것에 주의해야 한다. 완전한 문장으로 쓸 때 뒤에 'your computer has viruses'라고 써야 한다.

11 '그러지 말았어야 해.'라고 말하고 있다. 즉, 모르는 사람에게서 온 이메일을 열지 말았어야 한다는 말이다.

서술형 시험대비 p.201

01 (B) → (C) → (A) → (E) → (D)
02 (A) repair (B) a good job
03 I'm afraid you're mistaken
04 do you want to repair robots
05 She regrets that she didn't practice more.
06 She has the exam this Friday.
07 To draw[Drawing] what she wants to express is difficult.
08 (C) → (B) → (D) → (A)

01 '커서 무엇을 하고 싶은지' 묻는 주어진 글에 이어 (B)에서 답하고, (C)에서 추가적인 질문을 하고, (A)에서 추가적인 질문에 답하고, (E)에서 이유를 묻고, (D)에서 답하는 순서가 자연스럽다.

02 G는 그것이 미래에 좋은 직업이 될 거라 생각하기 때문에 로봇을 수리하는 일을 하고 싶어 한다.

03 That's not quite right.는 상대방의 말을 수정하기 위해 쓰는 표현으로 'I'm afraid you're mistaken.'으로 바꿔 쓸 수 있다.

04 왜 로봇을 수리하고 싶은지 묻는 말이다.

05 '더 연습했어야 해.'라고 하는 것으로 보아 더 연습하지 않았던 것을 후회하고 있음을 알 수 있다.

06 '금요일'이라고 하면서 '이틀밖에 안 남았다'고 했으므로 이번 금요일임을 알 수 있다.

07 '내가 표현하고 싶은 것을 그리기가 쉽지 않아.'라고 하고 있다.

08 (C)에서 무슨 일인지 묻고, (B)에서 배고프다며 식량을 저장해 놓지 않았음을 후회하고, (D)에서 걱정하지 말라며 식량을 나눠 주겠다고 하자 (A)에서 고맙다고 답하는 순서가 적절하다.

[교과서]

Grammar

핵심 Check p.202~203

1 (1) shouldn't have eaten (2) must have put
2 (1) who (2) which (3) which

01 ①　　　　02 (1) must　(2) might　(3) should

03 ③

04 (1) You shouldn't have eaten so much.

  (2) I'll visit you during the vacation, which begins tomorrow.

01 Mr. Decker를 선행사로 하는 계속적 용법의 주격 관계대명사 who가 와야 한다. that이나 what은 계속적 용법의 관계대명사로 쓸 수 없다.

02 (1) 문맥상 '~했음이 틀림없다'는 강한 추측의 표현이 적절하다. (2) 문맥상 '~했을지도 모른다'는 약한 추측의 표현이 적절하다. (3) 문맥상 '~했어야 한다'는 후회의 표현이 적절하다.

03 계속적 용법의 관계대명사에서 선행사가 My favorite writer로 사람이고 is의 주어가 필요한 주격이므로 who를 쓰는 것이 적절하다.

04 (1) should not[ought not to] have p.p.: ~하지 않았어야 했는데 (그런데 했다) (후회) (2) 우리말 해석이 순차적으로 되어 있으므로 관계대명사의 계속적 용법을 이용한다.

01 ②　　　　02 ③　　　　03 ①

04 (1) who　(2) which　(3) which　(4) must　(5) should

  (6) might

05 ⑤　　　　06 ④　　　　07 ④

08 (1) which　(2) which　(3) who　(4) which

09 ②　　　　10 ②　　　　11 ③

12 My dad gave me a birthday present, from which I got much happiness.

13 ②　　　　14 which　　15 ②

16 (1) Yesterday I called my aunt, who lives in Mexico.

  (2) Tom also showed me a book, which had KenKuller's autograph on it.

  (3) You should not have broken the rule.

  (4) They must have left some messages with their own letters.

17 ④　　　　18 ②

19 (1) Ms. Molly named her granddaughter Daisy, which is the name of a flower.

  (2) The writer might have finished his novel.

01 관계대명사 that은 계속적 용법으로 사용할 수 없다.

02 'should+have+p.p.' 형태가 되어야 한다. I should have built it with stronger material.

03 첫 번째 빈칸에는 'should+have+p.p.' 형태가 적절하다. 두 번째 빈칸에는 선행사가 사람이고 주어 역할을 하는 계속적 용

법이므로 who가 적절하다.

04 (1) 선행사가 King Sejong으로 사람이고 주어 역할을 하는 계속적 용법이므로 who가 적절하다. (2) 선행사가 사물이고 주어 역할을 하는 계속적 용법이므로 which가 적절하다. (3) 선행사가 앞의 절 전체(Tom visited her)이므로 which가 적절하다. (4) must have p.p.: ~했음이 틀림없다 (강한 추측) (5) should have p.p.: ~했어야 한다 (그런데 하지 못했다) (후회) (6) might have p.p.: ~했을지도 모른다 (약한 추측)

05 'I'm sure+that 주어+과거동사(~을 확신한다, 분명히 ~하다)'은 강한 추측의 must have p.p.(~했음이 틀림없다)로 쓸 수 있다.

06 계속적 용법의 관계대명사는 '접속사+대명사'로 바꾸어 쓸 수 있다. 이것은 '감자 먹는 사람들'인데 Vincent van Gogh가 1885년에 그렸다'라는 것으로, 적절한 접속사는 and이다.

07 should not[ought not to] have p.p.: ~하지 않았어야 했는데 (그런데 했다) (후회)

08 계속적 용법에는 선행사가 사람이면 who, 동물이나 사물이면 which를 쓴다.

09 should have p.p.: ~했어야 한다(후회)

10 앞에 콤마가 있는 관계대명사의 계속적 용법에는 that을 쓰지 않는다.

11 '하루 종일 졸렸다'는 말로 보아 늦게까지 깨어 있으면 안 되었다는 후회의 말이 적절하다. should not[ought not to] have p.p.: ~하지 않았어야 했는데 (그런데 했다) (후회)

12 선행사가 앞 절 전체이므로 which를 이용한다. 전치사 from의 목적어로 쓰이는 것에 주의한다.

13 휴대폰을 잃어버린 것이므로 후회(~했어야 한다)의 의미를 가지는 should have p.p.가 적절하다.

14 계속적 용법의 관계대명사는 '접속사+대명사'로 바꾸어 쓸 수 있다.

15 첫 번째 빈칸에는 must have p.p.(~했음이 틀림없다)가 적절하다. 두 번째 빈칸에는 should not have p.p.(~하지 않았어야 했는데)가 적절하다.

16 (1) 선행사가 사람이므로 which가 아니라 who를 써야 한다. (2) 계속적 용법에는 that을 쓰지 않는다. (3) should는 조동사로 not이 바로 다음에 나와야 한다. (4) 'must have p.p.' 형태가 되어야 한다.

17 ① 계속적 용법에는 that을 쓰지 않는다. (that → which) ② 동사의 수의 일치가 부적절하다. (come → comes) ③ 주격 관계대명사가 나와야 하므로 whom을 who로 고쳐야 한다. ⑤ 선행사가 앞 절의 내용이므로 that을 which로 고쳐야 한다.

18 must have p.p.: ~했음이 틀림없다 (강한 추측)

19 (1) 관계대명사의 계속적 용법을 이용한다. 선행사를 Daisy로 하고 관계대명사 which가 수식하도록 쓴다. (2) might have p.p.: ~했을지도 모른다 (약한 추측)

01 (1) who (2) which (3) who (4) which

02 (1) You shouldn't have played soccer in the rain.

    (2) The film, in which he plays the leading role, is a big hit.

    (3) The old lady, whom I saw on the subway, was a famous actress.

03 (1) should[ought to] have made

    (2) must have been sick (3) can't have slept

04 해석: (1) Anne은 교사인 아들 두 명이 있다.

    (2) Anne은 아들 두 명이 있는데, 그들 모두 교사이다.

    차이: (1)은 관계대명사의 한정적 용법으로 선행사를 수식하는 형용사 역할을 하며 '교사인 아들 두 명'으로 해석한다. 아들이 몇 명인지 모르는데 그 중에 교사인 아들이 두 명이라는 의미이며, (2)는 관계대명사의 계속적 용법으로 선행사를 부연 설명하며 아들이 두 명으로 둘 다 교사이다.

05 I shouldn't have spent all my money on buying clothes.

06 who encouraged me to

07 (1) She should not[ought not to] have watched the movie.

    (2) She cannot have watched the movie.

    (3) She may[might] have watched the movie.

    (4) She must have watched the movie.

08 I'm fond of the actor, whose name is not known well.

09 (1) Harry invited Lindsey to the party, which made her feel happy.

    (2) Do you know Thomas Edison, who invented the light bulb?

    (3) The book, which is cheap, contains very good contents.

10 (1) who → which

    (2) which → who

    (3) that → who

    (4) must → should

    (5) cannot → may[might]

    (6) must → cannot

01 who와 which는 모두 계속적 용법에 쓰일 수 있고 선행사가 사람이면 who, 동물이나 사물이면 which를 쓴다. (1), (3) 앞의 선행사가 사람이므로 who를 쓴다. (2) 앞의 선행사가 사물이므로 which를 쓴다. (4) which는 앞의 절 전체를 선행사로 받을 수 있다.

02 (1) shouldn't have p.p.: ~하지 않았어야 했는데 (그런데 했다) (후회) (2) The film is a big hit. + He plays the leading role in the film.을 계속적 용법의 관계대명사 which로 연결한다. (3) The old lady was a famous actress. + I saw her on the subway.를 계속적 용법의 관계대명사 whom으로 연결한다. saw의 목적어 The old lady를 선행사로 하는 목적격 관계대명사 whom을 이용하여 'The old lady, whom I saw ~'로 쓴다.

03 (1) 'should[ought to] have p.p.'를 이용하여 '후회'를 나타낸다. (2) 'must have p.p.'를 이용하여 '추측'을 나타낸다. (3) 'can't have p.p.'를 이용하여 '부정의 추측'을 나타낸다.

05 '다 써버리지 말았어야 했는데'라고 후회하는 표현을 써야 하므로 'should have+과거분사'를 이용한다.

06 friend를 선행사로 하는 관계대명사 who를 이용하고, encourage는 목적격보어로 to부정사를 쓰는 것에 주의한다.

07 (1) should not[ought not to] have p.p.: ~하지 않았어야 했는데 (그런데 했다) (과거 사실에 대한 유감이나 후회) (2) cannot have p.p.: ~했을 리가 없다 (과거 사실에 대한 강한 부정의 추측) (3) may[might] have p.p.: ~했을지도 모른다 (과거 사실에 대한 약한 긍정의 추측) (4) must have p.p.: ~했음이 틀림없다 (과거 사실에 대한 강한 추측)

08 뒤에 나오는 name을 수식해 주는 소유격 whose가 적절하다.

09 (1) 앞에 나온 절 전체를 선행사로 받는 which를 이용한다. (2) 사람을 선행사로 받는 who를 이용한다. (3) 계속적 용법의 관계대명사는 '접속사(and, but, for, though 등)+대명사'로 고쳐 쓸 수 있다. 여기서는 'though+it'으로 생각할 수 있다.

10 (1) 선행사가 사물이므로 which로 나타낸다. (2) 선행사가 사람이므로 who로 나타낸다. (3) 계속적 용법의 관계대명사로는 that을 쓰지 않는다. (4) '후회'를 나타내는 'should have p.p.'가 적절하다. (5) 몇 명의 사람들이 나오고 있으므로 '약한 추측'을 나타내는 'may[might] have p.p.'가 적절하다. (6) '강한 부정의 추측'을 나타내는 'cannot have p.p.'가 적절하다.

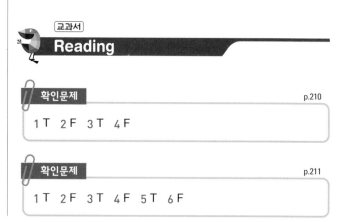

교과서

Reading

확인문제   p.210

1 T   2 F   3 T   4 F

확인문제   p.211

1 T   2 F   3 T   4 F   5 T   6 F

01 DREAMS
02 used to be
03 anymore, which
04 that connect us
05 What, is
06 on weekends, back
07 must have loved
08 over and over
09 Go after
10 something new or challenging
11 Don't be ashamed of
12 was founded
13 was created, were fighting
14 there would be
15 What would it be like
16 hanging, which included
17 were explained, in a suit
18 wearing a suit, impatient
19 for hours
20 to go after
21 found a letter
22 It was from
23 It read, had been invited
24 As, worried
25 which, far away from
26 too, to
27 regretting
28 should have gone
29 are worth chasing
30 Never miss

1 MY GRANDMOTHER'S BASEBALL DREAMS

2 My grandmother Helen used to be a cook in a restaurant in a small town near South Bend, Indiana.

3 She does not work anymore, but she still enjoys making delicious food, which I love so much.

4 Food is one of the many things that connect us.

5 What connects us most strongly, however, is baseball.

6 When I visit her on weekends, my grandmother often tells me exciting stories about playing baseball back in the 1940s.

7 She must have loved the sport very much.

8 I listen to these stories over and over.

9 She always says, "Go after what you want, Sarah.

10 Don't be afraid of trying something new or challenging.

11 Don't be ashamed of failing."

12 In 1943, the All-American Girls Professional Baseball League was founded.

13 This league was created for baseball fans because many of America's young men were fighting in World War II.

14 Helen was told that there would be local tryouts right in South Bend.

15 She wondered, "What would it be like to be on a baseball team and to make it to the finals for my hometown?"

16 She imagined a large banner hanging at the baseball field which included the name Helen Baker.

17 On the day of the tryouts, all the rules were explained by an old man in a suit, who sounded very serious and unkind.

18 She thought that wearing a suit in the hot sun might have made him impatient.

19 On that day, Helen played baseball for hours with many other young women.

20 She was excited to go after her baseball dreams!

21 About a week later, Helen found a letter in the mailbox.

22 It was from people who worked for the girls' baseball league in Chicago.

23 It read that she had been invited to the league's main tryouts in Chicago!

24 As the days went by, however, Helen became worried that she might fail.

25 She also became worried about traveling alone to Chicago, which was far away from home.

26 When the day of the main tryouts came, she was too afraid to go.

27 My grandmother has spent the rest of her life regretting her decision.

28 When she watches a baseball game on TV, she often says, "I should have gone to Chicago.

29 You know, all your dreams are worth chasing, even if you catch only a few of them.

30 Never miss an opportunity."

01 (A) used to   (B) What   (C) must   02 ③
03 ④   04 ③   05 all your dreams
06 ②, ⑤
07 World War Two 또는 the Second World War
08 ④   09 (A) young men   (B) baseball fans
10 ④   11 ③   12 ④   13 ②
14 wearing a suit in the hot sun might have made him impatient
15 ③   16 ⑤   17 connect → connects

01 (A) 할머니는 식당의 '요리사였다'고 해야 하므로 used to가 적절하다. used to: 과거의 규칙적 습관이나 현재와 비교한 과거의 상태를 나타냄. would: 과거의 불규칙적 습관을 나타냄. (B) 우리를 가장 강하게 연결하는 '것'이라고 해야 하므로 선행사가 포함된 관계대명사 What이 적절하다. (C) 야구를 무척 '좋아했던 게 분명하다'고 해야 하므로 must가 적절하다. must have p.p.: ~했음에 틀림없다(과거에 대한 강한 추측), should have p.p.: ~했어야 했는데(과거 사실에 대한 후회나 유감을 나타냄.)

02 ③ 모험심이 강한, 할머니는 항상 "새로운 것이나 도전적인 것을 시도해 보기를 두려워하지 말거라."라고 말씀하시는 것으로 보아, 할머니의 성격은 '모험심이 강하다'라고 하는 것이 적절하다. ① 완고한, 고집스러운, ② 우유부단한, ④ 보수적인, ⑤ 소심한

03 'Sarah의 할머니'가 종종 과거 1940년대의 야구 경기에 관해 흥미로운 이야기를 'Sarah에게' 들려주신다. ③ common interest: 공통된 관심

04 ⓐ와 ③: ~할수록(접속사), ①: ~한 대로(접속사), ②: ~로서(전치사), ④ [보통 as ~ as ...로 형용사·부사 앞에서] ~와 같을 정도로, (as ~ as ...에서, 앞의 as가 지시부사, 뒤의 as는 접속사), ⑤ ~이므로, ~이기 때문에(접속사)

05 be worth ~ing = be worth while to 동사원형: ~할 만한 가치가 있다

06 이 글은 '본심사가 있는 날 할머니는 너무 두려워서 갈 수 없었고 남은 인생을 자신의 결정을 후회하며 보내셨으며, 종종 "절대 기회를 놓치지 마라."라고 말씀하셨다'는 내용의 글이므로, 어울리는 속담으로는 ②번 '기회를 놓치지 마라'와 ⑤번 '쇠뿔도 단김에 빼라.'가 적절하다. ① 급할수록 돌아가라. ③ 안 좋은 일은 겹쳐서 일어나기 마련이다. ④ 잘 생각해 보고 행동하라[돌다리도 두드려 보고 건너라].

07 'World War Ⅱ(제2차 세계대전)'는 World War Two 또는 the Second World War로 읽는다.

08 ⓑ와 ②: 명사적 용법, ①, ④: 부사적 용법, ③, ⑤: 형용사적 용법

09 미국의 '청년' 중 많은 수가 제2차 세계대전에 참전해 있었기 때문에 1943년, 전미 여자 프로야구 리그가 '야구 팬들'을 위해 창립되었다.

10 앞에 나오는 내용과 상반되는 내용이 뒤에 이어지므로 however가 가장 적절하다. ② 즉[말하자면], ③ 게다가, 더욱이, ⑤ 따라서, 그러므로

11 이 글은 'Helen은 리그의 본심사에 초청되었지만 심사에 떨어질까봐 걱정되기도 하고 시카고까지 혼자 여행하는 것도 걱정되어, 본심사가 있는 날이 되었을 때 너무 두려워서 갈 수 없었다.'

는 내용의 글이므로, 제목으로는 ③번 '두려움 때문에 이루지 못한 꿈'이 적절하다. unfulfilled: 이루지 못한, out of fear: 두려움 때문에, ④ What if ~?: ~면 어쩌지[~라면 어떻게 될까]?, ⑤ No way!: 절대로 안 되다, 싫다

12 Helen은 시카고까지 혼자 여행하는 것이 걱정되었는데, 시카고는 집에서 멀리 떨어진 곳이었다.

13 ⓐ in: '착의'를 나타내는 전치사, ⓑ go after: ~을 추구하다

14 might have p.p.: 과거에 대한 추측(~했을지도 모른다)

15 (B)의 Food는 주어진 글에서 말한 food를 가리키므로 제일 먼저 오고, (A)의 these stories가 (C)의 exciting stories about playing baseball back in the 1940s를 가리키므로 (C) 다음에 (A)가 와야 한다. 그러므로 (B)-(C)-(A)의 순서가 적절하다.

16 (A)와 ①, ②, ③, ④: 현재와 비교한 과거의 상태(would로 바꿔 쓸 수 없음.), ⑤ used to: 과거의 규칙적 습관(would로 바꿔 쓰면 과거의 불규칙적 습관을 나타내게 됨), call on: ~을 방문하다

17 우리를 가장 강하게 연결하는 것은 바로 '야구'라는 뜻으로 What은 단수인 The thing which를 대신한 것이기 때문에, connect를 connects로 고치는 것이 적절하다.

18 이 글은 'Sarah와 할머니를 연결하는 많은 것 가운데 하나가 요리지만 그들을 가장 강하게 연결하는 것은 야구라는 것과, 할머니께서 과거 1940년대의 야구 경기에 관한 흥미로운 이야기를 몇 번이고 반복해서 하시면서 Sarah를 격려해 주시는' 내용의 글이므로, 주제로는 ③번 'Sarah의 할머니의 야구에 대한 사랑'이 적절하다. ⑤ nursery story: 옛날 이야기

19 (A) 감각동사의 보어는 형용사를 써야 하므로, 'serious and unkind'가 적절하다. (B) 목적격 보어이므로 형용사 impatient가 적절하다. (C) 그 편지에는 그녀가 시카고에서 열리는 리그의 본심사에 초청되었다고 '적혀 있었다'고 해야 하므로 read가 적절하다. read: (~라고) 적혀[쓰여] 있다

20 'Helen이 리그의 본심사에 참가했는지는' 알 수 없다. ① An old man in a suit did. ② With many other young women. ③ People who worked for the girls' baseball league in Chicago did. ④ In Chicago.

🐱 서술형 시험대비   p.220~221

01 that → which   **02** loved

03 (A) was   (B) Sarah   **04** regretting

05 so, that, couldn't

06 must have gone → should have gone

07 (1) 심사에 떨어질까봐 걱정되었기 때문이었다.

   (2) 시카고까지 혼자 여행하는 것이 걱정되었는데,
     시카고는 집에서 멀리 떨어진 곳이었기 때문이었다.

08 What connects us most strongly

09 every weekend

10 exciting stories about playing baseball back in the 1940s

11 and he 12 had been invited

13 (A) wearing a suit (B) serious and unkind

01 관계대명사 that은 계속적 용법으로 쓸 수 없기 때문에, which로 고치는 것이 적절하다.

02 must have p.p.는 과거에 대한 강한 추측을 나타내므로 'loved'로 쓰는 것이 적절하다.

03 Sarah의 할머니는 식당의 '요리사였지만', 지금은 더 이상 요리사가 아니다. 그렇기는 하지만, 그녀는 여전히 맛있는 음식을 즐겨 만들고, 'Sarah'는 그 음식들을 무척 좋아한다.

04 spend+시간+~ing: ~하는 데 시간을 보내다

05 too ~ to ... = so ~ that 주어 can't ...: 너무 ~ 해서 …할 수 없다

06 '난 시카고에 갔어야 해.'라고 해야 하므로, must를 should로 고치는 것이 적절하다. must have p.p.: ~이었음에 틀림없다, should have p.p.: ~했어야 했는데(과거의 일에 대한 후회나 유감)

07 Helen은 '심사에 떨어질까 봐 걱정되었고' 또 '시카고까지 혼자 여행하는 것이 걱정되어', 본심사가 있는 날이 되었을 때, 그녀는 너무 두려워서 갈 수 없었다.

08 선행사가 포함된 관계대명사 What을 쓰는 것이 적절하다.

09 on weekends = every weekend: 주말마다

10 '과거 1940년대의 야구 경기에 관한 흥미로운 이야기'를 가리킨다.

11 계속적 용법의 관계대명사는 '접속사+대명사'로 바꿔 쓸 수 있다.

12 그 초청 편지에는 '그녀가 시카고에서 열리는 리그의 본심사에 초청되었다'는 사실이 적혀 있었다.

13 Helen은 뜨거운 태양 아래 '정장을 입고 있는 것'이 모든 규칙을 설명한 나이 든 남자를 짜증나게 만들었을지도 모르고, 그 결과 그는 무척 '진지하고 불친절하게' 들렸다고 생각했다.

영역별 핵심문제 p.223~227

01 decision 02 ④ 03 ③

04 (1) How come Mr. Lee always works overtime?

(2) If you want to accomplish your dream, you should go after it.

(3) Does the recipe include eggs and milk?

05 ① 06 ⑤ 07 ①

08 You're mistaken. 09 ④

10 Because she thinks a good designer should create a completely new world in a game.

11 I shouldn't have done that.

12 How come?

13 If I were you, I'd get help from a computer service center right now.

14 ② 15 ⑤ 16 ①, ③

17 with whom

18 (1) should have gone (2) can't have gone
(3) must have gone (4) shouldn't have gone
(5) might[may] have gone

19 ② 20 ④ 21 ⓐ, ⓒ, ⓔ

22 ③ 23 ③

24 Don't be afraid of trying something new or challenging.

25 (A) founded (B) wondered (C) What 26 ④

27 ①, ⑤ 28 a letter

01 주어진 관계는 동의어의 관계이다. offer: 제의, 제안 proposal: 제안, 제의 determination: 결심, 결단(력) decision: 결정, 판단

02 tryout: 심사, 테스트

03 주어진 문장에서 apply는 '~에 지원하다, ~을 신청하다'를 의미하며 이와 같은 의미로 쓰인 것은 ③번이다. ① 가는 붓으로 물감을 칠해라. ② 그 규칙은 여기에서는 적용되지 않는다. ③ 저는 영업 이사직에 지원하고자 합니다. ④ 그는 문을 열기 위해 힘을 써야 했다. ⑤ 이 규정은 당신의 경우에는 해당되지 않습니다.

04 (1) How come: 왜. How come을 이용하여 의문문을 쓸 때는 평서문의 어순임에 주의해야 한다. (2) go after: ~을 추구하다, ~을 얻기 위해 노력하다 (3) include: 포함하다

05 주어진 문장에서 rest는 '나머지'를 의미하며 이와 같은 의미로 쓰인 것은 ①번이다. ② 쉬다, ③ 휴식, ④ 기대다, ⑤ 의지하다

06 '과거에 한 것에 대해 서운함을 느끼다'는 의미로 'regret(후회하다)'이 적절하다 ① 연습하다, 훈련하다 ② 이루다, 달성[성취]하다 ③ 향상시키다, 개선하다 ④ 연결하다

07 주어진 문장은 '면접을 시작합시다.'라는 말이다. ①번 다음부터 면접에 관련된 질문이 나오고 있으므로 ①번이 가장 적절하다.

08 상대방의 말을 수정하기 위해 'That's not right[true].', 'I don't think that's right.', 'That's wrong.', 'You're mistaken.' 등의 표현을 사용한다.

09 소라는 '만화가가 되고 싶나요?'라는 질문에 '꼭 그렇지는 않습니다. 저는 게임 디자이너가 되고 싶습니다.'라고 답하고 있다.

10 소라는 '게임 디자이너에게 필요한 가장 중요한 기량이 무엇이라고 생각하나요?'라는 질문에 '상상력이라고 말씀드리겠습니다. 훌륭한 게임 디자이너는 게임 속에서 완전히 새로운 세계를 창조해야 하거든요.'라고 답하고 있다.

11 shouldn't have p.p.: 하지 말았어야 하는 일을 한 것에 대한 후회를 나타낼 때 쓸 수 있다. 앞 문장에서 말한 내용을 that으로 받아 한 단어로 처리한다.

12 How come?: 왜 그렇지?, 어쩌다 그렇게 됐니?

13 가정법 과거를 이용한다. If I were you: 내가 너라면, I

41

would를 줄여서 I'd로 축약하여 단어 수를 맞춘다.

14 'My nose is getting longer.'에 이어 'I shouldn't have told lies.'라고 하는 것이 적절하다.

15 a picture를 선행사로 하는 계속적 용법의 목적격 관계대명사 which가 와야 한다. that은 계속적 용법의 관계대명사로 쓸 수 없다.

16 ① You should have come to the meeting on time. ③ He might[may] have been in Paris when Irene went to Finland.

17 앞에 콤마(,)가 있는 관계대명사의 계속적 용법을 이용한다. 함께 달린 것이므로 전치사 with와 목적격이므로 whom을 쓴다.

18 (1) should[ought to] have p.p.: ~했어야 한다 (그런데 하지 못했다) (후회) (2) cannot have p.p.: ~했을 리가 없다 (강한 부정의 추측) (3) must have p.p.: ~했음이 틀림없다 (강한 추측) (4) should not[ought not to] have p.p.: ~하지 않았어야 했는데 (그런데 했다) (후회) (5) may[might] have p.p.: ~했을지도 모른다 (약한 추측)

19 계속적 용법의 관계대명사는 '접속사(and, but, for, though 등)+대명사'로 고쳐 쓸 수 있다. 여기서는 'though she'가 적절하다.

20 앞에 콤마(,)가 있으므로 관계대명사의 계속적 용법으로 loved의 목적어 역할을 할 수 있는 whom이 적절하다.

21 ⓑ eat → eaten ⓓ should → shouldn't ⓕ that → who

22 주어진 문장의 however에 주목한다. ③번 앞 문장의 내용과 상반되는 내용이 뒤에 이어지고 있으므로 ③번이 적절하다.

23 이 글은 'Sarah와 할머니를 연결하는 많은 것 가운데 하나가 요리지만 그들을 가장 강하게 연결하는 것은 야구라는 것과, 할머니께서 과거 1940년대의 야구 경기에 관한 흥미로운 이야기를 몇 번이고 반복해서 하시면서 Sarah를 격려해 주시는' 내용의 글이므로, 제목으로는 ③번 '야구, 우리를 가장 강하게 연결하는 것'이 적절하다.

24 -thing이나 -body로 끝나는 부정대명사는 형용사가 뒤에서 꾸며 주어야 하므로, new or challenging이 뒤에서 something을 꾸며 주는 것이 적절하다.

25 (A) 전미 여자 프로야구 리그가 '창립되었다'고 해야 하므로 founded가 적절하다. found-founded-founded: 설립하다, find-found-found: 찾다[발견하다]. (B) "야구 팀에 들어가서 고향을 위해 결승전까지 진출한다는 건 어떤 기분일까?"라며 '궁금해 했다'고 해야 하므로 wondered가 적절하다. wonder: 궁금해 하다, wander: 거닐다, 돌아다니다. (C) like의 목적에 해당하므로 의문대명사 What이 적절하다. 의문부사 How는 목적어 자리에 쓸 수 없다.

26 Helen은 야구 팀에 들어간 것이 아니라, "야구 팀에 들어가서 고향을 위해 결승전까지 진출한다는 건 어떤 기분일까?"라며 궁금해 했다.

27 ⓐ와 ①, ⑤: 동명사, ②, ③, ④: 현재분사

28 Helen이 우편함에서 발견한 '편지 한 통'을 가리킨다.

01 ②
02 (1) curious (2) regretful (3) jealous (4) relieved (5) gloomy
03 ③　　**04** What made you apply for our school?
05 various subjects　　**06** do you? → are you?
07 ④　　**08** ④　　**09** That's not quite right.
10 ④　　**11** ④　　**12** ③, ⑤
13 and it　　**14** (1) should have spent (2) shouldn't have wasted (3) should have brought　　**15** ②
16 making　　**17** ②　　**18** ③　　**19** ④
20 ④　　**21** ⑤　　**22** didn't go
23 all your dreams

01 '단체나 전체의 일부로 어떤 것을 갖다'를 나타내는 말은 include(포함하다)이다.

02 gloomy: 우울한, regretful: 후회하는, curious: 호기심 있는, jealous: 질투심이 많은, relieved: 안도하는

03 (A) 긍정문이므로 too가 적절하다. (B) because of+명사(구), because+주어+동사, (C) if는 불확실한 내용을 이끌 때 쓰이고, that은 확실한 내용을 이끌 때 쓰인다.

04 What made you ~? = Why did you ~?: 왜 ~했나요?

05 앞에서 말한 'various subjects'를 가리킨다.

06 앞에서 'I'm preparing for ~'라고 하고 있으므로 'do you'가 아닌 'are you'로 쓰는 것이 적절하다.

07 소라는 'I should have practiced more.'라고 후회하고 있다.

08 언제부터 소라가 게임 디자이너가 되고 싶었는지는 알 수 없다.

09 상대방의 말을 수정하기 위해 'That's not right[true].', 'I don't think that's right.', 'That's wrong.', 'You're mistaken.' 등의 표현을 사용한다.

10 내용상 'I shouldn't have made you wait.'라고 하는 것이 적절하다.

11 모두 관계대명사 who가 적절하지만 ④번은 선행사가 앞선 절의 일부(went on a trip to Africa)이므로 which가 적절하다.

12 ① I should have practiced more to improve my speaking skills. ② I think sending text messages might have been better. ④ It must have rained last night.

13 계속적 용법의 관계대명사는 '접속사(and, but, for, though 등)+대명사'로 고쳐 쓸 수 있다.

14 'should (not) have p.p.'가 '후회'의 의미로 쓰이지만 2인칭을 주어로 하여 '충고'하는 의미로도 쓰일 수 있다.

15 첫 번째 문장에서는 날이 더워서 '티셔츠와 반바지를' 입었어야 한다'는 'should have p.p.'가 적절하다. 두 번째 문장에서는 선행사가 Sydney로 사물이고 계속적 용법이므로 which가 적절하다.

16 enjoy는 동명사를 목적어로 취하는 동사이므로, making으로 쓰는 것이 적절하다.

42 정답 및 해설

17 (A)와 ②: 관계대명사, the thing(s) which로 바꿀 수 있음.
①과 ④: 의문대명사, ③과 ⑤: 의문형용사

18 ③ 한 걸음 한 걸음, 점차로, ⓒ와 나머지: 반복해서

19 ④번 다음 문장의 It이 주어진 문장의 a letter를 가리키는 것이므로 ④번이 적절하다.

20 이 글은 'Helen이 자신의 야구 꿈을 좇아가기 위해 선수 선발 테스트를 받고 시카고에서 열리는 리그의 본심사에 초청되는' 내용의 글이므로, 주제로는 ④번 '자신의 야구 꿈을 좇아가는 것에서부터 오는 Helen의 흥분'이 적절하다.

21 중반부의 'She was excited to go after her baseball dreams!'를 통해 'excited'를 찾을 수 있다. ① 후회하는, ② 두려운, ③ 어리둥절해 하는, ④ 실망한

22 should have p.p.는 '~했어야 한다'라는 뜻으로 과거의 일에 대한 후회나 유감을 나타내므로, '나는 시카고에 가지 않아서 유감이다.'로 고치는 것이 적절하다.

23 '모든 꿈'을 가리킨다.

서술형 실전문제 p.232~233

01 They are going to the school festival.

02 Because he got up early but it took him some time to do his hair.

03 Because she thought (that) they were stuck in a heavy traffic jam.

04 (1) This book is about Abraham Lincoln, who was the 16th President of the U.S.

(2) My grandmother's house, which was built 100 years ago, is still nice to live in.

(3) She enjoys making delicious food, from which she finds satisfaction.

05 (1) Fallen leaves are on the ground. It might[may 또는 must] have been windy.

(2) Sam looks very tired this morning. He must [또는 shouldn't] have stayed up late last night.

(3) His favorite place is his house, which is next to mine.

(4) My brother, whose major was history, is a professor of the university.

06 (1) The train may[might] have arrived at the station.

(2) He cannot have done this by himself.

(3) This smartphone, which I bought last month, has a great design.

07 and I love it so much   **08** nineteen forties

09 what she wants   **10** had been invited

11 an old man in a suit explained all the rules

12 (A) letter   (B) main tryouts

01 지호가 '학교 축제에 늦고 싶지 않은데.'라고 하고 있다.

02 '무슨 일로 늦었'는지 묻는 Amber의 질문에 지호는 '난 일찍 일어났어. 그런데 머리를 손질하느라 시간이 좀 걸렸어.'라고 답하고 있다.

03 Amber가 '우리 교통 체증에 갇혔어. 버스에서 내려서 뛰어가자.'라고 하고 있다.

04 (1) 선행사가 사람이므로 who를 이용한다. (2) 선행사가 사물이므로 which를 이용한다. (3) 선행사가 앞 절의 일부 (making delicious food)이므로 which를 이용한다. 전치사 from의 목적어로 쓰이는 것에 주의한다.

05 (1) 낙엽이 떨어져 있는 것이므로 '추측'을 나타내는 표현이 적절하다. (2) 매우 피곤해 보이는 것이므로 '단정적인 추측이나 후회'를 나타내는 표현이 적절하다. (3) 계속적 용법에는 that을 사용하지 않는다. which가 적절하다. (4) 뒤에 나오는 major(전공)를 수식해 주는 소유격 whose가 적절하다. 내 동생은 전공이 역사였는데 그 대학의 교수이다.

06 (1) may[might] have p.p.: ~했을지도 모른다 (약한 추측) (2) cannot have p.p.: ~했을 리가 없다 (강한 부정의 추측) by himself: 혼자서 (3) 선행사가 사물이므로 which를 이용한다.

07 계속적 용법의 관계대명사는 '접속사+대명사'로 바꿔 쓸 수 있고, 본문에서 which는 delicious food를 추가 설명하기 위해 쓰인 목적격 관계대명사이므로, 접속사 and와 대명사 it을 사용하여 고치는 것이 적절하다.

08 연도는 두 자씩 끊어서 읽고, 1940s(1940년대)는 복수이므로 뒷부분을 forties로 읽는 것이 적절하다.

09 Sarah의 할머니는 Sarah에게 '그녀가 원하는 것'을 이루려고 노력하라고 항상 말씀하신다.

10 본심사에 초청된 것은 편지를 읽은 것보다 앞선 시제이므로 '과거완료(had p.p.)'로, 그리고 '초청된' 것이므로 '수동태'로 쓰는 것이 적절하다.

11 'an old man in a suit'를 주어로 해서 고치는 것이 적절하다.

12 Helen은 리그의 '본심사'가 열리게 될 시카고에 있는 여자야구리그에서 일하는 사람들이 보낸 초청 '편지'를 받았다.

창의사고력 서술형 문제 p.234

|모범답안|

01 (1) 더 많은 책을 읽었어야 했다.

(2) 온라인 게임을 그렇게 많이 하지 말았어야 했다.

(3) 선생님들과 반 친구들에게 더 친절했어야 했다.

(4) 패스트푸드를 그렇게 많이 먹지 말았어야 했다.

02 (1) It must have rained last night.

(2) She may have gone out for dinner.

(3) I should have studied math harder.

03 (A) in London, England   (B) wild chimpanzees

(C) the protection of chimpanzees
(D) the Hubbard Medal

01 ②   02 ③

03 (1) imagination   (2) confident   (3) disappointed

04 You can make it!

05 She will have the exam for Mana Animation High School this Friday.

06 ④   07 She forgot to set her alarm.

08 Because she thought they were stuck in a heavy traffic jam.

09 (B) → (A) → (D) → (C)   10 ④

11 It's because she thinks it'll be a good job in the future.

12 (1) Mina got her finger burned while making coffee, which is her favorite drink. She ought to have been more careful.

   (2) Mina got her finger burned while making coffee, and it is her favorite drink. She should have been more careful.

13 ③, ⑤, ⑥   14 must have been   15 ④

16 ①

17 (1) She does not work anymore, but she still enjoys making delicious food, which I love so much.

   (2) She is my friend, Nida, who[whom] I met in Germany.

   (3) Gogh met Gauguin in Arles, which changed his life.

   (4) The rabbit shouldn't have slept during the race to beat the turtle.

   (5) Hanju must have lost his umbrella in the subway. He doesn't have it now.

18 ⑤

19 exciting stories about playing baseball back in the 1940s

20 ③   21 ②   22 ①   23 ④

24 ①   25 ②

01 '어떤 것에 대해 좋거나 충분히 중요한'을 가리키는 것은 worth(~할 가치가 있는)이다.

02 even if: 비록 ~하더라도 / 싫더라도 꼭 해야 한다.

03 imagination: 상상, 상상력, confident: 확신하는, 자신만만한, disappointed: 실망한, 낙담한

04 You can make it!: 넌 해낼 수 있어!

05 'When is the exam?'이라는 남자의 질문에 소라는 'On Friday'라고 답하고 있고 이틀 남았다고 했으므로 이번 금요일임을 알 수 있다.

06 '버스에서 내려서 뛰어가자.'라는 Amber의 말에 ④번 다음에 '차들이 다시 움직이기 시작해. 내리지 말자.'라고 하고 있으므로 '네가 잘못 생각하는 거야.'라는 주어진 글은 ④번에 들어가는 것이 가장 적절하다.

07 Amber는 '알람을 맞출걸. 내가 깜빡했어.'라고 후회하고 있다.

08 Amber는 '우리 교통 체증에 갇혔어. 버스에서 내려서 뛰어가자.'라고 하고 있다.

09 긴장했는지 질문하는 문장에 이어 (B)에서 약간이라고 답하고 (A)에서 면접을 시작하자고 하면서 지원한 이유를 묻고 (D)에서 이유를 대답하고 (C)에서 행운을 빌자, 마지막에 주어진 문장에서 감사를 표하는 순서가 자연스럽다.

10 (A)는 상대방의 말을 수정하기 위해 쓰는 표현이지만, ④번은 상대방이 맞다고 말하는 것이다.

11 G는 '왜?'라고 묻는 질문에 '그것이 미래에 좋은 직업이 될 거라고 생각하기 때문이야.'라고 하고 있다.

12 and it is her favorite drink =, which is her favorite drink. should have p.p. = ought to have p.p.: ~했어야 한다 (그런데 하지 못했다) (후회). to를 추가한다.

13 ① He is my son, who works at the amusement park. ② I got up late. I should have set my alarm. ④ One of my friends, who wants to be a teacher, is Abigail. ⑦ She also became worried about traveling alone to Chicago, which was far away from home.

14 'must have p.p. ~했음이 틀림없다'를 이용하여 '강한 추측'을 나타낸다.

15 첫 번째 빈칸에는 'should have p.p.: ~했어야 한다 (그런데 하지 못했다) (후회)'를 이용하고, 두 번째 빈칸에는 'should not have p.p.: ~하지 않았어야 했는데 (그런데 했다) (후회)'를 이용한다.

16 which는 앞 문장 전체를 선행사로 받을 수 있으므로 접속사 and와 it 대신에 쓸 수 있다.

17 (1) 관계대명사의 계속적 용법으로 that을 쓰지 않으며, 관계대명사는 접속사와 대명사의 역할을 하므로 목적어로 쓰인 it을 삭제해야 한다. (2) 선행사가 사람이고 목적격이므로 which를 who나 whom으로 고치는 것이 적절하다. (3) 관계대명사의 계속적 용법으로 that을 쓰지 않으며 앞에 나오는 절을 선행사로 받는 which가 적절하다. (4) should not[ought not to] have p.p.: ~하지 않았어야 했는데 (그런데 했다) (후회) (5) must have p.p.: ~했음이 틀림없다 (강한 추측)

18 앞에 나오는 내용과 상반되는 내용이 뒤에 이어지므로 however가 적절하다. ① 그러므로, ② 게다가, 더욱이, ③ 다시 말해서, ④ 그 결과

19 '과거 1940년대의 야구 경기에 관한 흥미로운 이야기'를 가리킨다.

20 ⓐ for baseball fans: 야구 팬들을 위해, ⓑ on: '소속'을 나타내는 전치사, be on ~: ~의 일원이다

21 (A)와 ②: '바로'라는 뜻으로 뒤의 내용을 강조하는 표현, ① (의견, 판단이) 옳은[맞는], ③ (법적, 도덕적) 권리[권한], ④ 오른쪽의, 우측의, ⑤ (도덕적으로) 옳은, 올바른

22 ⓐ와 ①: ~라고 적혀 있다, 그 표지판에는 '입장 금지'라고 적혀 있었다. ②와 ④: 읽어 주다, ③과 ⑤: (글, 기호 등을) 읽다

23 '시카고에 있는 여자 야구 리그에서 일하는 사람들'이 초청 편지를 보냈다.

24 주어진 문장의 also에 주목한다. ①번 앞 문장에 이어 또 다른 걱정을 말하는 것이므로 ①번이 적절하다.

25 should have p.p.는 '~했어야 한다'라는 뜻으로 과거의 일에 대한 후회나 유감을 나타내는 표현이므로 ②번 regretful이 적절하다. regretful: 유감스러워[애석해] 하는, 후회하는, ① 혼란스러워 하는, ③ 부끄러운, ④ 초조한, ⑤ 우울한

Keep Out

교과서
Reading

확인문제	p.244

1 T 2 F 3 T 4 F 5 T 6 F

확인문제	p.245

1 T 2 F 3 T 4 F 5 T 6 F

확인문제	p.246

1 T 2 F 3 T 4 T 5 F

확인문제	p.247

1 T 2 F 3 T 4 F 5 T 6 F

교과서 확인학습 A
p.248~251

01 Keep Out	02 used to go
03 stayed at	04 swimming, walking
05 In other words, anything special	
06 At the time of	07 had had
08 day in and day out	09 the heat
10 further and further	11 take us
12 as usual, set off	13 side by side
14 one behind the other	15 ahead
16 grew darker, formed a roof	
17 Look ahead	18 next to him
19 a tunnel	20 Keep Out
21 have a look	22 Actually
23 all of a sudden	24 moved ahead
25 left	26 entered
27 heavy	

28 grew louder and louder   29 called out

30 Keep, down   31 called after

32 leave, behind

33 thumping, like an express train

34 what's up   35 what's happened

36 where Ron had been   37 something wet

38 were closed   39 get you out

40 (I')ve broken, go and get help

41 get you out of here   42 moving away

43 in control   44 covering

45 managed to free

46 Holding, inch by inch   47 to take ages

48 look too well

49 stop, from crying out   50 two water bottles

51 go and get help

52 In reply, pressed my hands

53 raced back

54 washing some dishes

55 Thanks to her, where   56 with relief

57 Let that be a lesson   58 *Stay out of trouble*

59 safety products   60 fire fighter

교과서 확인학습 B   p.252~255

1 Keep Out

2 Every summer, my family used to go on holiday to the coast.

3 We always went to the same place and stayed at the same small guesthouse.

4 We would stay for two weeks, swimming in the sea and walking around the little town.

5 In other words, we never did anything special, and nothing ever really happened on these vacations.

6 At the time of this story I was twelve years old.

7 Most people can remember this particular summer, as it was the hottest summer England had had since records began.

8 It did not rain throughout June and July, and the sun shone day in and day out.

9 But Ron and I loved the heat and the sun.

10 Every day, we would ride our bicycles further and further away from the guesthouse.

11 One day Ron decided that we should ride our bikes along the old train tracks to see where they would take us.

12 I was happy to follow Ron, as usual, and we set off after breakfast.

13 At first, the tracks were easy to follow, and we

cycled along side by side.

14 After a while, the grass grew thicker, and we had to ride one behind the other.

15 Ron was ahead.

16 The tracks went toward the woods and it grew darker as the trees stood tall and formed a roof over the tracks.

17 Ron stopped suddenly. "Look ahead!" he shouted.

18 I stopped next to him and saw a white, wooden gateway across a black opening.

19 "It's a tunnel," I said.

20 "Yes, and it says, 'Keep Out' on the gate," replied Ron.

21 "Do you want to have a look inside?"

22 Actually, I did not want to go inside.

23 I felt a little cold all of a sudden, and I wanted to go back into the sunlight.

24 But I answered, "Sure," and moved ahead.

25 We left our bikes at the gate and climbed over.

26 We entered the cool tunnel.

27 The air inside was heavy.

28 Above our heads there was a sound that grew louder and louder.

29 "What's that?" I called out.

30 "Bats," said Ron, "Keep your head down." Then he moved on.

31 "Don't go so fast." I called after him.

32 I meant, "Don't leave me behind" but I didn't say so.

33 The next thing I heard was a loud noise right above us, a thumping sound like an express train and then a scream.

34 "Ron!" I shouted. "Ron, what's up? Can you hear me?" No reply.

35 "Speak to me, Ron. Tell me what's happened."

36 I slowly walked toward where Ron had been and found only dirt and small rocks.

37 As I reached out my hands, I felt something wet — Ron's face!

38 His eyes were closed, and he was breathing weakly.

39 "It's okay, Ron," I whispered. "I'll get you out."

40 "I think I've broken my leg. It really hurts. Just go and get help, Ben."

41 "No," I replied. "I'll get you out of here to safety first."

42 I started moving away the dirt and rocks with my hands.

43 I felt calm, and I felt in control.

44 It took a long time to clear away the earth covering Ron.

45 Finally, I managed to free his body.

46 Holding him under the arms, I pulled him backward, inch by inch, toward the tunnel entrance.

47 It seemed to take ages, but finally I was able to get Ron out of the tunnel.

48 He didn't look too well, though.

49 His face was white, and he was trying hard to stop himself from crying out from crying out.

50 I found our bikes and brought the two water bottles to Ron.

51 "Here, drink these," I said. "I'll go and get help. I'll be as quick as I can."

52 In reply, Ron simply pressed my hands.

53 I got on my bicycle and raced back along the tracks until I got to the nearest farmhouse.

54 I ran past the gate and found a woman washing some dishes in the kitchen.

55 Thanks to her, Ron was taken to the hospital, where his leg was put in a cast.

56 As soon as our parents arrived at the hospital and saw us, my mother cried with relief.

57 But all my father said was, "Let that be a lesson to you."

58 And what was the lesson? It was "*Keep out* means *Stay out of trouble*."

59 Ron is now the manager of a big company which produces helmets and other safety products.

60 And me? I am a fire fighter.

서술형 실전문제
p.256~257

01 (t)hin

02 (1) thumping (2) In other words (3) managed to
   (4) All of a sudden

03 (1) as usual (2) at first (3) As soon as

04 ⑤, There being no objection, the meeting was put off.

05 (1) would → used to (2) covered → covering
   (3) which → where (4) that → what

06 had had 07 (1) going (2) to go

08 Because it was the hottest summer England had had since records began.

09 (A) where (B) calm (C) to free

10 It took a long time to clear away the earth covering Ron.

11 a shovel → his hands

01 주어진 단어의 관계는 반의어 관계이다. entrance: 입구, exit: 출구, thick: 두꺼운, thin: 얇은

02 all of a sudden: 갑자기, thumping: 쿵쾅거리는, manage to: 간신히 ~하다, in other words: 다시 말해서, 즉

03 as usual: 여느 때처럼, at first: 처음에는, as soon as: ~하자마자

04 주절의 주어와 부사절의 주어(유도부사, 허위 주어: there)가 다르므로 부사절의 유도부사 there를 써 주어야 한다. As there was no objection, the meeting was put off.를 분사구문으로 쓴 것이다.

05 (1) used to: ~하곤 했다(과거의 규칙적이고 반복적인 동작이나 상태), would: ~하곤 했다(과거의 불규칙적 습관) (2) while 뒤에 '주어+be동사'가 생략된 문장이다. 분사구문에서 접속사 while을 남겨 두었다고 보아도 좋다. this case로 목적어가 있으므로 covering이 적절하다. (3) happen은 자동사로 which 다음의 절이 완전하므로 which를 관계부사 where로 고쳐야 한다. (4) Tell의 직접목적어와 has happened의 주어 역할을 하도록 that을 what으로 고쳐야 한다.

06 주절보다 먼저 있었던 일을 언급하므로 과거완료 (had had)로 쓰는 것이 적절하다.

07 used to는 '~하곤 했다'라는 뜻으로 과거의 규칙적이고 반복적인 동작이나 상태를 나타낸다. used to 동사원형 = be in the habit of ~ing = make it a rule to 동사원형

08 '관측 이래 영국이 겪은 가장 더운 여름이었기 때문'이었다.

09 (A) Ron이 있던 '곳'으로 걸어갔다고 해야 하므로 where가 적절하다. 관계부사 where 앞에 선행사 the place가 생략되어 있다. (B) 감각동사의 보어는 형용사로 써야 하므로 calm이 적절하다. (C) manage는 to부정사를 목적어로 취하므로 to free가 적절하다.

10 take+시간+to부정사의 순서로 쓰는 것이 적절하다.

11 Ben은 '손으로' 흙과 자갈을 치우기 시작했다. shovel: 삽

단원별 예상문제
p.258~262

01 (1) wooden (2) cast (3) thanks to
   (4) After a while (5) relief

02 ①   03 ④   04 ⑤   05 hurt

06 (1) She leaned over and whispered something in his ear.
   (2) I would often practice reading the scripts in the empty recording room.
   (3) I wanted to show that I could improve my

47

acting inch by inch.

07 (1) I'm so tired of eating at the same restaurant day in and day out.

(2) Please keep out of that room.

(3) As I reached out my hand, I felt something wet.

08 ①

09 (1) It did not rain throughout June and July, the sun shining day in and day out.

(2) It having been the hottest summer England had had since records began, most people can remember this particular summer.

(3) Ron decided that we should ride our bikes along the old train tracks to see where they would take us.

(4) I'd like to see if she can give me a hand.

10 (1) The book is a detailed piece of work covering all aspects of the subject.

(2) The two men were walking quickly, one behind the other.

(3) Ron was taken to the hospital, where[in which] his leg was put in a cast.

(4) It took her some time to realize the dangers of her situation.

11 ④　　　12 ②, ⑤　　　13 ⑤

14 the old train tracks　　15 ③　　　16 ②

17 all of a sudden

18 saw a white, wooden gateway across a black opening

19 Keep Out　20 ④　　　21 ②　　　22 ⑤

23 there, in the hospital　　24 being → be

25 *Stay out of trouble*

---

01 thanks to: ~ 덕분에, wooden: 나무로 된, 목재의, relief: 안도, 안심, after a while: 얼마 후에, cast: 석고붕대, 깁스

02 '크고 날카로운 울음이나 소음'을 의미하는 말은 'scream(비명)'이다.

03 '고통스러운 어떤 것의 제거'를 의미하는 말은 'relief(안도, 안심)'이다.

04 side by side: 나란히

05 • 나는 그가 다치지 않은 것이 감사했다. (동사) • 승객 중 심하게 다친 사람은 아무도 없었다. (형용사) • 그녀의 목소리에는 상처와 진짜 분노가 서려 있었다. (명사)

06 (1) whisper: 속삭이다, (2) would: ~하곤 했다(과거의 불규칙적 습관), (3) inch by inch: 조금씩

07 day in and day out: 매일, keep out of: ~에 들어가지 않다, reach out: (손·팔·다리 등을) 뻗다

08 ② has had → had had ③ to ache seeing → ache to see

④ to cry → from crying ⑤ other → the other

09 (1) 주절과 부사절의 주어가 다르므로 부사절의 주어를 생략하면 안 되며, 부사절의 시제가 앞서므로 완료분사구문으로 써야 한다. (2) 주절과 부사절의 주어가 다르므로 부사절의 주어를 생략하지 않은 독립분사구문으로 써야 한다. (3) 목적을 나타내는 'so that ~ can'은 to부정사를 이용하여 부사적 용법(목적)으로 바꿔 쓸 수 있다. (4) 의문사가 없는 간접의문문은 'if+주어+동사'의 형태로 써야 한다.

10 (1) work를 수식하는 현재분사가 적절하다. (2) 둘 중에서 하나는 one으로 나타내고 나머지 하나는 the other로 나타낸다. (3) where 다음의 절이 완전하므로 in을 생략하거나 where를 which로 고쳐야 한다. (4) it takes+시간+to부정사: ~하는 데 …의 시간이 걸리다

11 as와 as 사이에 be동사의 보어로 형용사가 나와야 한다. I'll be as quick as I can.

12 ⓐ와 ②, ⑤: 계속 용법, ① 경험 용법, ③ 완료 용법, ④ 결과 용법

13 매일 Ron과 글쓴이는 게스트하우스에서 '조금씩 먼 곳으로' 자전거를 타고 가곤 했다.

14 '낡은 철로'를 가리킨다.

15 ③번 다음 문장 'Ron was ahead.'에 주목한다. 주어진 문장의 'one behind the other'를 더 자세히 설명하는 것이므로 ③번이 적절하다.

16 ⓑ와 ②, ④: 부사적 용법, ①: 형용사적 용법, ③, ⑤: 명사적 용법

17 all of a sudden 갑자기

18 '색깔+재료'의 순서로 쓰는 것이 적절하다.

19 문에는 '들어가지 마시오'라고 적혀 있었다.

20 ⓐ, ⓒ, ⓓ: 글쓴이, ⓑ, ⓔ: Ron

21 위 글의 분위기로는 '긴급한'이 적절하다. ③ 축제의, 축하하는, ④ 우울한, ⑤ (지루할 정도로) 단조로운

22 'Ron에게 무슨 일이 생겼는지'는 대답할 수 없다. ① They left their bikes at the gate. ② They entered the cool tunnel. ③ There were bats above their heads. ④ Ron said it.

23 관계부사 where는 계속적 용법으로 쓰여 and there, 즉 and in the hospital의 의미이다.

24 사역동사 let 뒤에는 목적보어로 동사원형을 쓴다.

25 그들은 '들어가지 마시오'라는 말은 '곤경을 멀리하라'는 뜻이라는 것을 배웠다. stay out of trouble: '재난[곤란, 어려움, 문젯거리 등]으로부터 벗어나다'

교과서 파헤치기

Lesson 5

01 도착	02 시인	03 문학
04 (책) 한 부; 베끼다, 복사하다		05 특별한, 특정한
06 기소, 혐의	07 문학의, 문학적인	08 표현하다
09 외로움	10 어린 시절	11 자유
12 출판하다	13 희귀한	14 더, 더 멀리
15 도서관	16 정부, 정권	17 이루다, 얻다
18 졸업	19 운동	20 (문학 장르) 시
21 기념하다, 축하하다		22 전체의, 모든
23 가혹한, 혹독한	24 남아 있다, 계속 ~하다	
25 바느질하다	26 (한 편의) 시	27 대우, 처리
28 지갑	29 선사하다, 주다	30 출판, 발행
31 독립	32 동경, 갈망	33 저자
34 편집자	35 포기하다	36 서둘러
37 (도서관에서) 대출하다		38 ~로 유명하다
39 ~와 시간을 보내다		40 ~에 참가하다
41 ~을 염두에 두다	42 ~에 잘 어울리다	43 시도하다

01 harsh	02 whole	03 arrest
04 loneliness	05 arrival	06 independence
07 charge	08 poem	09 literary
10 graduation	11 editor	12 yearbook
13 present	14 achieve	15 borrow
16 celebrate	17 longing	18 movement
19 freedom	20 rare	21 remain
22 further	23 government	24 author
25 poetry	26 publish	27 sew
28 literature	29 publication	30 treatment
31 childhood	32 express	33 poet
34 recommend	35 give up	36 put up
37 take part in	38 in a hurry	39 look good on
40 have ~ in mind	41 give it a try	
42 look forward to		43 hang out with

1 whole, 전체의, 모든   2 rare, 희귀한   3 poet, 시인
4 graduation, 졸업   5 literature, 문학
6 longing, 동경, 갈망   7 recommend, 추천하다
8 hometown, 고향   9 independence, 독립
10 sew, 바느질하다   11 harsh, 가혹한, 혹독한
12 loneliness, 외로움   13 poem, (한 편의) 시
14 publication, 출판, 발행   15 editor, 편집자
16 celebrate, 기념하다, 축하하다

Listen – Listen & Answer Dialog 1

Long, no, brings / have to, a book report, recommend, to read / about / heard of, show me / New Arrivals, popular among / check, out / borrow, for seven days

Listen – Listen & Answer Dialog 2

are, doing / novel, book report / me see / borrowed / course, big fan, all, mystery books / writer, stop reading / what, has been made into / looks interesting / come out, looking forward to seeing / together

Listen More – Listen and complete

Take a seat, How would you like / taking, yearbook, cool / take / particular, mind / recommend / Look at, look good on / can't wait to see / sure, look cool

My Speaking Portfolio

to meet, real name / where you're from / from / usually, write / short story writer, have written / special / well known for, surprise endings / recommend, with, surprise ending / recommend / about / who saves her life / can't wait

Listen – Listen & Answer Dialog 1

Minjun: Hello, Ms. Seo.

Ms. Seo: Hi, Minjun. Long time no see. What brings you here?

Minjun: I have to write a book report. Can you recommend a good novel to read?

Ms. Seo: How about a mystery? There's a new Ken Kuller book, *22nd Street*.

Minjun: Oh, I've heard of him. Can you show me the book?

49

Ms. Seo: It's in the "New Arrivals" area. It's really popular among teens in Great Britain.

Minjun: Thank you for your help. Can I check it out?

Ms. Seo: Sure. You can borrow new books for seven days.

Minjun: Okay.

Sora: Hey, Minjun. What are you doing?

Minjun: I'm reading a novel for a book report.

Sora: Let me see. Oh, is this a new book by Ken Kuller?

Minjun: Yeah, I borrowed it this morning. Do you know Ken Kuller?

Sora: Of course. I'm a big fan of his. I've read all of his mystery books.

Minjun: I think he's a great writer. I can't stop reading this book.

Sora: You know what? His novel *Four Eyes* has been made into a movie.

Minjun: Yeah. I saw the movie poster. It looks interesting.

Sora: It'll come out next Thursday. I'm looking forward to seeing it!

Minjun: Maybe we can see the movie together.

Mike: Good morning, Jiho.

Jiho: Good morning.

Mike: Take a seat, please. How would you like your hair done?

Jiho: Well, I'm taking my pictures for the yearbook. So I want to look cool.

Mike: When do you take the pictures?

Jiho: This Friday at Dream & Joy Park.

Mike: Sounds good. Do you have a particular style in mind?

Jiho: No. Can you recommend one for me?

Mike: Look at this. How about this style? It'll look good on you.

Jiho: Wow, I like it. I can't wait to see how I'll look in the pictures.

Mike: I'm sure you'll look cool.

Jane: Nice to meet you, Mr. Henry. Is O. Henry your real name?

Mr. Henry: No. My real name is William Sydney Porter.

Jane: Can you tell me where you're from?

Mr. Henry: I'm from the U.S.

Jane: What do you usually write?

Mr. Henry: I'm a short story writer . I have written about 300 short stories.

Jane: Wow! You're great! What is special about your short stories?

Mr. Henry: They're well known for their surprise endings.

Jane: Can you recommend a popular story with a surprise ending?

Mr. Henry: Sure. I recommend *The Last Leaf*.

Jane: What is it about?

Mr. Henry: It's about a sick girl and an old artist who saves her life.

Jane: Oh, I want to read it. I can't wait.

본문 TEST Step 1 p.09~11

01 Poet Who Loved
02 where, in a hurry
03 Autumn fills, air
04 ready, stand, without, worry
05 To count, stars
06 Memory, one
07 Love, another
08 Loneliness, another
09 Longing, another
10 Poetry for, star
11 for another star
12 Have, read, lines
13 part of, poem, by
14 written, still remains, poems
15 was born in, near
16 As, for, school
17 sewing so, that, sewed
18 it was, that, most
19 wrote, lot, poems
20 literary magazine with, cousin
21 borrowed, poetry, copied, whole
22 have, own copy, rare
23 doctor, chose, literature, college
24 hung out, expressed, lost
25 celebrate, graduation, publish, under
26 three copies, by hand
27 given, another, presented, kept
28 advised against, because, publication
29 followed, advice, gave up
30 study further, had studied
31 in, began to, study
32 following, arrested, part, independence
33 later, arrested, same charges
34 prison after harsh treatment

35 It, few, that, achieved

36 brought, poet's, finally published

37 was given, had thought

38 ages, brightly, hearts like

본문 TEST Step 2
p.12~14

01 Poet Who   02 where, in a hurry

03 fills   04 without a worry

05 count   06 Memory

07 another   08 Loneliness

09 Longing   10 Poetry for

11 for another star

12 Have, read these lines   13 part of, by

14 was written, still remains, poems

15 was born in   16 As, for his school

17 sewing so, that, sewed   18 it was, that, most

19 wrote a lot of poems

20 a literary magazine with

21 borrowed, copied, by hand

22 to have his own copy, rare book

23 to be a doctor, chose to study literature

24 During, hung out with other young poets, where, expressed feelings, lost country

25 To celebrate his graduation, publish, under the title

26 three copies, by hand

27 was given to, another, the last one, for himself

28 advised against, because, allow, publication

29 followed, gave up

30 decided to study further, had studied before

31 began to study

32 following year, for taking part in, independence movement

33 later, arrested on the same charges

34 after harsh treatment by the police

35 It was, that, achieved independence

36 brought, to, they were finally published

37 was given, had thought of, before

38 are loved by, shine birghtly, like

본문 TEST Step 3
p.15~17

1 별을 사랑한 시인

2 계절이 지나가는 하늘에는

3 가을로 가득 차 있습니다.

4 나는 아무 걱정도 없이

5 가을 속의 별들을 다 헤일 듯합니다.

6 별 하나에 추억과

7 별 하나에 사랑과

8 별 하나에 쓸쓸함과

9 별 하나에 동경과

10 별 하나에 시와

11 별 하나에 어머니, 어머니,

12 당신은 이 시 구절을 읽어 본 적이 있는가?

13 이것은 윤동주의 시 '별 헤는 밤'의 일부이다.

14 시는 오래 전에 쓰였지만 여전히 한국이 가장 좋아하는 시 중의 하나로 남아 있다.

15 동주는 중국 연변 근처에서 1917년에 태어났다.

16 어린 소년이었을 때 그는 운동을 좋아했고, 학교의 축구 선수였다.

17 그는 또한 바느질하는 것을 무척 좋아해서 친구들의 축구 유니폼에 번호를 바느질해 주기도 했다.

18 그러나 그가 가장 사랑한 것은 문학이었다.

19 초등학교에 다닐 때 그는 많은 시를 썼다.

20 심지어 사촌 송몽규와 문학잡지를 만들기도 했다.

21 그가 중학교에 다니던 때 한번은 당대의 유명한 시인 백석의 시집을 빌려 와서 책 전체를 필사하기도 했다.

22 그는 정말로 그 희귀한 책을 한 부 갖고 싶었던 것이다.

23 그의 부모는 그가 의사가 되기를 바랐지만 동주는 서울에 있는 대학에서 문학 공부를 하기로 했다.

24 대학 시절에 그는 종종 다른 젊은 시인들과 어울려 다녔고, 고향과 잃어버린 조국에 대한 심정을 표현하는 시를 썼다.

25 졸업을 기념하여 그는 '하늘과 바람과 별과 시'라는 제목으로 자신의 시 19편을 출판하고 싶어 했다.

26 그는 책 세 부를 손으로 만들었다.

27 한 부는 가까운 친구인 정병욱에게 주었고, 또 하나는 그가 가장 좋아하는 교수에게 선물했으며, 마지막 하나는 자신이 보관했다.

28 그러나 그의 교수는 일본 정부가 출판을 허가하지 않으리라 여겨, 그의 계획에 반대하는 충고를 했다.

29 동주는 그의 충고를 따랐고 그 생각을 포기했다.

30 동주는 그의 아버지가 예전에 공부했던 나라에서 학업을 이어 가기로 했다.

31 그리하여 1942년에 동주와 그의 사촌은 일본에서 공부를 시작했다.

32 다음 해 7월 10일에 그의 사촌은 독립운동에 가담했다는 이유로 일본 경찰에게 체포되었다.

33 나흘 뒤 동주 역시 같은 혐의로 체포되었다.

34 1945년에 동주와 그의 사촌은 경찰의 가혹 행위를 당한 후 감옥에서 사망했다.

35 한국이 일본으로부터 독립을 이룬 것은 그로부터 불과 몇 달 후의 일이었다.

36 1948년에 정병욱이 동주의 시를 시인의 동생에게 가져다주었고, 마침내 그것들은 출판되었다.

37 그 책에는 시인이 수년 전에 생각해 두었던 제목이 붙었다.

38 그의 시는 모든 세대의 사랑을 받고 있고, 따라서 그것들은 가을밤 하늘의 별처럼 우리 가슴 속에 여전히 밝게 빛나고 있다.

본문 TEST Step 4·Step 5 p.18~23

1 A Poet Who Loved Stars

2 In the sky where seasons pass in a hurry

3 Autumn fills the air.

4 And ready I stand, without a worry,

5 To count all the stars there.

6 Memory for one star,

7 Love for another star,

8 Loneliness for another star,

9 Longing for another star,

10 Poetry for another star,

11 And, oh, mother, mother for another star.

12 Have you read these lines before?

13 They are part of the poem "Counting Stars at Night" by Yoon Dong-ju.

14 The poem was written a long time ago but still remains one of Korea's favorite poems.

15 Dong-ju was born in 1917 near Yanbin, China.

16 As a young boy, he loved sports, and he was a soccer player for his school.

17 He also loved sewing so much that he sewed the numbers on all his friends' soccer uniforms.

18 However, it was literature that he loved most.

19 In elementary school he wrote a lot of poems.

20 He even made a literary magazine with his cousin, Song Mong-gyu.

21 In middle school he once borrowed a poetry book by a famous poet of the time, Baek Seok, and copied the whole book by hand.

22 He really wanted to have his own copy of the rare book.

23 His parents wanted him to be a doctor, but Dong-ju chose to study literature at a college in Seoul.

24 During his college years, he often hung out with other young poets and wrote poetry where he expressed feelings about his hometown and lost country.

25 To celebrate his graduation, he wished to publish 19 of his poems under the title, *Heaven, Wind, Stars, and Poetry*.

26 He made three copies of the book by hand.

27 One was given to his close friend, Jeong Byeong-uk, another was presented to his favorite professor, and the last one was kept for himself.

28 However, his professor advised against his plan because he thought the Japanese government would not allow the publication.

29 Dong-ju followed his advice and gave up the idea.

30 Dong-ju decided to study further in the country where his father had studied before.

31 So, in 1942, Dong-ju and his cousin began to study in Japan.

32 On July 10 the following year, his cousin was arrested by the Japanese police for taking part in an independence movement.

33 Four days later, Dong-ju was also arrested on the same charges.

34 In 1945, Dong-ju and his cousin died in prison after harsh treatment by the police.

35 It was just a few months later that Korea achieved independence from Japan.

36 In 1948, Jeong Byeong-uk brought Dong-ju's poems to the poet's brother, and they were finally published.

37 The book was given the title the poet had thought of many years before.

38 His poems are loved by people of all ages, and thus they still shine brightly in our hearts like the stars in the autumn night sky.

구석구석지문 TEST Step 1 p.24

Communicate: Speak

1. look excited

2. looking forward to

3. on

4. curling match, can't wait

Before You Read

1. Last week, celebrated

2. put up, had lived, harsh times, tried to achieve

3. writers, had expressed, longing for freedom, literary works

Wrap Up READING

1. pomes, cartoons

2. different kinds of, differ in which kind they prefer

3. allow us to go beyond, where we live

4. come across, writers who lived

5. being, living, completely different place

6. In short, have never visited

구석구석지문 TEST Step 2   p.25

Communicate: Speak

1. Tom: Hi, Sora. You look excited.

2. Sora: Yeah. I'm really looking forward to this Tuesday.

3. Tom: This Tuesday? What's on Tuesday?

4. Sora: There's a big curling match. I can't wait!

Before You Read

1. Last week we celebrated August 15 in our class.

2. We put up pictures of people who had lived through harsh times and tried to achieve independence.

3. Also, there was a talk on writers who had expressed their longing for freedom in literary works.

Wrap Up READING

1. Do you enjoy plays, pomes, novels, or cartoons?

2. They are different kinds of literature, and people differ in which kind they prefer.

3. However, all of them allow us to go beyond our own small world where we live.

4. When we read literature, we come across the ideas of great writers who lived long ago.

5. We can even imagine being someone else or living in a completely different place.

6. In short, literature opens up for us new worlds that we have never visited before.

단어 TEST Step 1   p.26

01 추가적인	02 지역의	03 자랑스러운
04 기르다, 올리다	05 함께함, 동행	06 나이가 많은
07 자원봉사하다; 자원봉사자		08 진지한
09 전망, 경관	10 개체 수, 인구	11 가혹한, 냉혹한
12 지저분한	13 공유지, 공원	
14 지지하다, 부양하다		
15 꼬르륵 소리가 나다		16 실망하게 하다
17 오염시키다	18 교훈	19 꽤
20 알아채다	21 나르다	22 오염
23 소중히 여기다	24 자원	25 뱃멀미가 나는
26 인내심이 있는; 환자		27 사라지다
28 초지, 풀밭	29 풀을 뜯다	30 충전기
31 비밀	32 ~당, ~마다	33 졸리는
34 기쁨	35 몰래, 비밀리에	36 그런데
37 옛날에	38 ~을 돌보다	39 ~으로 가득 차다
40 부탁하다	41 ~의 수	42 엎친 데 덮친 격으로
43 규칙을 어기다		

단어 TEST Step 2   p.27

01 pollution	02 borrow	03 serious
04 charger	05 lesson	06 fairly
07 population	08 local	09 directly
10 per	11 cause	12 pollute
13 secret	14 patient	15 additional
16 sleepy	17 grassland	18 common
19 support	20 graze	21 lay
22 seasick	23 messy	24 disappoint
25 view	26 value	27 notice
28 growl	29 harsh	30 mind
31 proud	32 company	33 resource
34 disappear	35 in harmony	36 break a rule
37 take care of	38 in secret	39 the number of
40 be full of	41 once upon a time	
42 ask a favor	43 keep ~ in mind	

단어 TEST Step 3

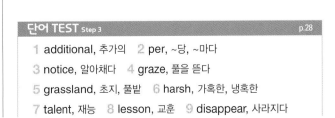

1 additional, 추가의   2 per, ~당, ~마다

3 notice, 알아채다   4 graze, 풀을 뜯다

5 grassland, 초지, 풀밭   6 harsh, 가혹한, 냉혹한

7 talent, 재능   8 lesson, 교훈   9 disappear, 사라지다

대화문 TEST Step 1　　　　　　　　　　p.29~30

Listen – Listen & Answer Dialog 1

where to volunteer / good place to volunteer / were, community center / community center / senior citizens, looking for / sounds, never taught / to do is help / advice

Listen – Listen & Answer Dialog 2

letting me volunteer / pleasure, decided to / should / lesson, taking photos, Why don't you, slow learners / there anything / patient, kind, learners / keep that in mind, By the way, do you mind if, charger, a little low / not

Listen – Listen More

on this ship / the same, seats / Do you mind if, window seat, view outside / problem / like noodles, sandwiches / If I were you, wouldn't eat, like / make, seasick / some / either, Let's, after we arrive

Speak – Talk in groups

bring / If, were, during breaks / for, advice

Speak - Talk in pairs.

mind if / at all, ahead

Wrap Up 5

What's up / called, ask you a favor / sleeping bag, Do you mind if, borrow / No

Wrap Up 6

stomach growls / have breakfast / no time to eat / If I were you, bring

대화문 TEST Step 2　　　　　　　　　　p.31~32

Listen – Listen & Answer Dialog 1

B: Jimin, have you decided where to volunteer?

G: Not yet. Do you know a good place to volunteer?

B: If I were you, I'd go to the community center.

G: The community center? What can I do there?

B: There's a smartphone class for senior citizens, and they're looking for volunteers.

G: That sounds interesting, but I've never taught anyone.

B: Don't worry. All you need to do is help the teacher there.

G: Okay. Thanks for your advice.

Listen – Listen & Answer Dialog 2

G: Thanks for letting me volunteer here, Ms. Yun.

W: It's my pleasure, Jimin. I'm glad you decided to help.

G: Well, what should I do?

W: Today's lesson is about taking photos with smartphones. Why don't you help the slow learners?

G: Okay. Is there anything I should know?

W: Yes. Please be patient and kind to the learners.

G: I'll keep that in mind. By the way, do you mind if I use Your charger? My battery is a little low.

W: Of course not. Go right ahead.

Listen – Listen More

G: Wow, it feels great to be on this ship, Dad.

M: I feel the same, Sora. Here are our seats, 20A and 20B.

G: Yeah. Do you mind if I take the window seat? I like to see the view outside.

M: No problem.

G: By the way, I want to eat something like noodles or sandwiches.

M: If I were you, I wouldn't eat anything like that.

G: Why is that?

M: They may make you seasick.

G: Oh, I see. Then, I'll have some ice cream.

M: That's not a good idea, either. Let's eat after we arrive.

Speak – Talk in groups

A: I didn't bring my science homework.

B: If I were you, I'd do it during breaks.

A: Thanks for your advice.

Speak - Talk in pairs.

A: Do you mind if I eat your sausage?

B: Not at all. Go ahead.

A: Thank you.

Wrap Up 5

W: Hi, Kevin. What's up?

B: Hi, Aunt Victoria. I called to ask you a favor.

W: What is it?

B: I need a sleeping bag for my science camp. Do you mind if I borrow yours?

W: No, not at all.

G: My stomach growls every morning. What should I do?

B: Ha ha. Do you usually have breakfast?

G: No, I have no time to eat anything at home.

B: If I were you, I'd bring some snacks.

G: That's a good idea.

본문 TEST Step 1   p.33~35

01 Story, Commons

02 Once upon, village, forest

03 villages, farmers, raised cows

04 Luckily, lay, middle, village

05 Space for Everyone

06 Let's share, commons   07 cow, enough grass

08 plenty, every cow   09 allowed to use

10 Therefore, called, commons

11 tradition, easy, enough grass

12 grass, all summer long   13 had, would be richer

14 No one, notice   15 one, broke, rule

16 another, let, graze, commons

17 thought, nobody would notice

18 filled, heart, thought, bring

19 has four children

20 were, would raise another

21 Thanks for, tip   22 few, later, close, who

23 in secret, bring, raise   24 thanked, as, told, next

25 Who, you   26 I'm new

27 is lying there   28 don't know

29 the richest farmer, village

30 other, did the same

31 secretly, while, even, without

32 thought, would, enough, additional

33 village, full, happy-looking, farmers

34 stop pushing me   35 Move over

36 This, my spot   37 need rain

38 I'm hungry   39 Me, too

40 number of, rose slowly

41 cow population grew more

42 disappear, harder, find, eat

43 To make matters worse   44 have, cow left

45 Good bye   46 happened to, commons

47 past, number, something, eat

48 However, left, because there

49 Things, harsh, villagers, died

50 remember, rule, OLNY, PER

51 At last, came back   52 able, support, per

53 village went back, rule

54 lesson, shared, value, fairly

55 villagers, tell, to, children

56 call it, Story, Commons

본문 TEST Step 2   p.36~38

01 Commons

02 Once upon a time, was, forest

03 farmers, raised cows   04 Luckily, lay

05 Space for Everyone

06 Let's share, commons   07 enough grass

08 there's plenty   09 was allowed to use

10 was called

11 By tradition, for, to, enough grass to eat

12 all summer long   13 had, would be richer

14 notice

15 one day, broke the rule   16 brought, let it graze

17 thought, nobody would notice

18 filled, thought of, would bring

19 has, children   20 were, would raise

21 Thanks for   22 later, who

23 in secret, were, would bring in, raise it

24 as he was told   25 Who

26 new   27 lying

28 don't know   29 the richest farmer

30 other, did the same

31 secretly, even more, without telling anyone

32 enough grass, additional

33 full of looking   34 stop pushing

35 over   36 spot

37 rain   38 hungry

39 Me, too   40 The number, rose

41 cow population grew

42 to disappear, harder, grass to eat

43 To make matters worse, for a long time

44 any cows left   46 happened to

47 something to eat

48 because there were too many

49 harsh   50 rule, PER FAMILY

51 At last, came back

52 was able to support only one cow

53 one-family-one-cow rule

54 lesson, are shared, for everyone to value, fairly

55 villagers, to   56 call it, Commons

55

1 공유지 이야기

2 옛날, 숲속에 작은 마을이 있었다.

3 마을 주민들은 농부였고 소를 길렀다.

4 다행히도, 마을 한 가운데에 좋은 목초지가 있었다.

5 공유지: 모두를 위한 장소

6 이장: 공유지를 함께 나누어 씁시다.

7 마을 사람 1: 내 소가 풀을 충분히 뜯을 수 있겠어.

8 마을 사람 2: 맞아, 모든 소에게 충분한 양이야.

9 모든 사람들이 목초지를 사용하도록 허락되었다.

10 그러므로 목초지는 '공유지'라고 불렸다.

11 전통에 따라 각 가정은 소가 한 마리만 있었고, 그래서 마을에 있는 소들이 충분히 먹을 풀을 찾는 것은 쉬운 일이었다.

12 공유지의 풀은 여름 내내 푸르렀다.

13 농부 1: 만약 소가 두 마리 있다면, 내가 더 부유할 텐데.

14 농부 1: 아무도 눈치 채지 못할 거야.

15 그러나 어느 날 마을 사람 하나가 규칙을 깨뜨렸다.

16 그는 또 다른 소를 가져와 공유지에서 풀을 뜯게 했다.

17 그는 아무도 그것을 눈치 채지 못할 거라고 생각했다.

18 두 번째 소가 가족에게 가져다줄 우유와 치즈를 생각하자 그의 마음은 행복감으로 충만했다.

19 농부 1: 그는 아이가 네 명이나 있어.

20 농부 1: 내가 당신이라면, 소를 한 마리 더 기르겠어요.

21 농부 2: 조언 고마워요!

22 며칠 후, 그 농부는 아이가 네 명 있는 친한 친구 집을 방문했다.

23 그는 친구를 도와주고 싶어서 몰래 그에게 말했다. "내가 당신이라면, 소를 한 마리 더 데려와 공유지에서 키우겠어요."

24 친구는 그에게 고마워했고 그다음 날 자신이 들은 대로 했다.

25 소 1: 넌 누구니?

26 소 2: 난 새로 왔어.

27 소 3: 누가 저기 누워 있는 거야?

28 소 4: 몰라.

29 농부 3: 내가 마을에서 가장 부유한 농부가 될 수 있어.

30 곧, 다른 사람들도 그렇게 했다.

31 어떤 사람들은 은밀하게 소를 한 마리 더 공유지에 데려왔고, 또 어떤 사람들은 아무에게도 말하지 않고 훨씬 많은 소를 목초지에 데려왔다.

32 그들은 추가된 소에게도 충분한 풀이 있을 것이라고 생각했다.

33 곧 마을은 행복해 보이는 농부들로 가득 찼다!

34 소 1: 이봐, 밀지 마!

35 소 2: 저기로 가!

36 소 3: 여긴 내 자리야!

37 소 1: 비가 필요해!

38 소 2: 배고파.

39 소 3: 나도.

40 처음에는 소의 수가 천천히 늘어났다.

41 그러더니 소의 개체 수는 더 빨리 증가했다.

42 공유지의 풀은 사라지기 시작했고, 소들이 먹을 풀을 찾기가 더 힘들어졌다.

43 엎친 데 덮친 격으로, 오랫동안 비가 내리지 않았다.

44 농부 1: 이제 나는 남은 소가 없어!

45 소 1: 안녕.

46 이장: 공유지에 무슨 일이 일어난 거지?

47 과거에는 비가 오지 않는 해에도 공유지에 있는 적은 수의 소들이 먹을 것을 항상 찾을 수 있었다.

48 하지만, 지금은 소가 너무 많아서 풀이 남지 않았다.

49 상황은 마을 사람들에게 가혹했다; 많은 소들이 죽었다.

50 즐겨라, 그러나 규칙을 기억해라: 가구당 오직 소 한 마리.

51 마침내 목초지가 회복되었다.

52 이제는 가구당 한 마리의 소만 감당할 수 있게 되었다.

53 마을은 '한 가구, 한 마리 소' 규칙으로 돌아갔다.

54 마을 사람들 모두는 중요한 교훈을 배웠다. 즉, 자원이 공유될 때는 모두가 그 자원을 소중히 여기고 공평하게 사용하는 것이 중요하다는 것이다.

55 이제 마을 사람들은 이 이야기를 자신들의 후손에게 들려준다.

56 그들은 이 이야기를 '공유지 이야기'라고 부른다.

1 The Story of the Commons

2 Once upon a time there was a small village in a forest.

3 The villagers were farmers and raised cows.

4 Luckily, some good grassland lay in the middle of the village.

5 The Commons: Space for Everyone

6 Head of a village: Let's share the commons.

7 Villager 1: My cow can get enough grass.

8 Villager 2: Yeah, there's plenty for every cow.

9 Everyone was allowed to use the grassland.

10 Therefore, it was called "the commons."

11 By tradition, each family only had one cow, so it was easy for each cow in the village to find enough grass to eat.

12 The grass on the commons was green all summer long.

13 Farmer 1: If I had two cows, I would be richer.

14 Farmer 1: No one will notice it.

15 But one day a villager broke the rule.

16 He brought another cow and let it graze on the commons.

17 He thought that nobody would notice it.

18 A happy feeling filled his heart when he thought of the milk and cheese that the second cow would

bring to his family.

19 Farmer 1: He has four children.

20 Farmer 1: If I were you, I would raise another cow.

21 Farmer 2: Thanks for the tip!

22 A few days later, the farmer visited a close friend who had four children.

23 He wanted to help his friend, so he told him in secret, "If I were you, I would bring in one more cow and raise it on the commons."

24 The friend thanked him and did as he was told the next day.

25 Cow 1: Who are you?

26 Cow 2: I'm new.

27 Cow 3: Who is lying there?

28 Cow 4: I don't know.

29 Farmer 3: I can be the richest farmer in this village.

30 Soon, other villagers did the same.

31 Some secretly brought one more cow to the commons, while others brought even more to the grassland without telling anyone.

32 They thought that there would be enough grass for the additional cows.

33 Soon the village was full of happy-looking farmers!

34 Cow 1: Hey, stop pushing me!

35 Cow 2: Move over!

36 Cow 3: This is my spot!

37 Cow 1: We need rain!

38 Cow 2: I'm hungry.

39 Cow 3: Me, too.

40 The number of cows rose slowly at first.

41 Then the cow population grew more quickly.

42 The grass on the commons began to disappear, and it became harder for the cows to find grass to eat.

43 To make matters worse, it did not rain for a long time.

44 Farmer 1: I don't have any cows left!

45 Cow 1: Good bye.

46 Head of a village: What happened to the commons?

47 In the past, when a dry year came, the small number of cows on the commons always found something to eat.

48 However, no grass was left now because there were too many cows.

49 Things were harsh for the villagers; many of the cows died.

50 Enjoy, but remember the rule: ONLY ONE COW PER FAMILY.

51 At last, the grass came back.

52 Now it was able to support only one cow per family.

53 The village went back to the one-family-one-cow rule.

54 The villagers all learned an important lesson: when resources are shared, it is important for everyone to value the resources and use them fairly.

55 The villagers now tell this story to their children.

56 They call it "The Story of the Commons."

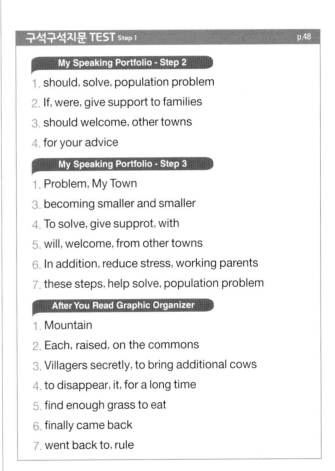

구석구석지문 TEST Step 1   p.48

My Speaking Portfolio - Step 2

1. should, solve, population problem

2. If, were, give support to families

3. should welcome, other towns

4. for your advice

My Speaking Portfolio - Step 3

1. Problem, My Town

3. becoming smaller and smaller

4. To solve, give supprot, with

5. will, welcome, from other towns

6. In addition, reduce stress, working parents

7. these steps, help solve, population problem

After You Read Graphic Organizer

1. Mountain

2. Each, raised, on the commons

3. Villagers secretly, to bring additional cows

4. to disappear, it, for a long time

5. find enough grass to eat

6. finally came back

7. went back to, rule

구석구석지문 TEST Step 2   p.49

My Speaking Portfolio - Step 2

1. A: How should I solve the population problem in my town?

2. B: If I were you, I'd give support to families with children.

3. C: I think you should welcome people from other towns.

4. A: Okay. Thank you all for your advice.

My Speaking Portfolio - Step 3

1. A Problem in My Town

2. Rareville

3. The population is becoming smaller and smaller in my town.

4. To solve this serious problem, I will give support to families with children.

5. I will also welcome people from other towns.

6. In addition, I will reduce stress for working parents.

7. I am sure that these steps will help solve the population problem in my town.

After You Read Graphic Organizer

1. Story Mountain

2. Each family raised one cow on the commons.

3. Villagers secretly started to bring additional cows.

4. The grass began to disappear, and it did not rain for a long time.

5. Many cows could not find enough grass to eat and died.

6. The grass finally came back.

7. The villagers went back to the one-family-one-cow rule.

Lesson S

단어 TEST Step 1   p.50

01 주의 깊게	02 시험	03 입다
04 ~ 없이	05 유혹적인, 솔깃한	06 고요, 적막, 침묵
07 걱정하는, 걱정스러워 하는		
08 (안내문 등을) 게시[공고]하다		09 준비가 된
10 놀랍게도	11 거의	12 전직 우체부
13 전체의, 모든	14 하지만, 그러나	15 이상한, 낯선
16 ~을 통해[관통하여]		17 전직 시장
18 마지막의	19 시장	20 화, 분노
21 초조하게	22 부끄러움	23 명령, 지시
24 문장	25 시끄러움, 소란	
26 공고문; 알아차리다		27 마음
28 따뜻한	29 특별한	
30 궁금하다, 궁금해하다		31 자리, 좌석
32 달콤한	33 사랑스러운	34 사무실
35 화나다	36 오직, 그저[단지] ~일 뿐인	
37 ~을 멀리하다	38 시험을 치대[보다]	39 잠시 동안
40 ~의 도중에, ~의 중앙에		41 매우 슬프게 하다
42 화난 기색 없이	43 가능한 한 ~한[하게]	

단어 TEST Step 2   p.51

01 mayor	02 post	03 place
04 sentence	05 silence	06 notice
07 lovely	08 language	09 ex-mayor
10 wear	11 noise	12 anger
13 back	14 special	15 nervously
16 office	17 heart	18 warm
19 however	20 strange	21 through
22 ready	23 surprisingly	24 carefully
25 exam	26 whole	27 almost
28 ex-postman	29 without	30 inviting
31 shame	32 order	33 worried
34 kindly	35 nothing but	36 be late for
37 for a while[moment]		38 get angry
39 take an exam	40 stay away from	
41 break one's heart		
42 with no sign of anger		
43 in the middle of		

1 whole, 전체의, 모든   2 anger, 화, 분노

3 silence, 고요, 적막   4 wonder, 궁금해 하다, 궁금하다

5 noise, 시끄러움, 소란   6 lovely, 사랑스러운

7 order, 명령, 지시   8 exam, 시험   9 notice, 알아차리다

10 wear, 입다   11 mayor, 시장   12 office, 사무실

13 post, (안내문 등을) 게시[공고]하다   14 strange, 낯선

15 inviting, 유혹적인, 솔깃한   16 shame, 부끄러움

01 Last Class

02 late, worried, get angry

03 take, exam, sentences, ready

04 such, along, sweet, inviting

05 staying away from, walking

06 fast as I could

07 passed, mayor's, reading, notices

08 For, had come from

09 wondered, What, now   10 ran faster

11 there was noise, laughing

12 However, everything, quiet

13 Through, walking nervously around

14 entered, middle, strange silence

15 hot with shame

16 with, anger, seat, without

17 sat down at   18 It was, that, noticed

19 wearing, only wore, special

20 something strange, whole class

21 What, sitting, so were   22 seemed so sad

23 While, wondering at, front

24 for, while, kindly, last

25 Orders, from, nothing but

26 new teacher arrives   27 last, in, to listen

28 few, broke, made, angry

29 what, posted, mayor's office

30 last, in, own language

01 Last Class

02 late for, worried, get angry

03 take an exam, sentences, ready

04 such, smelled sweet, inviting

05 staying away from, walking around

06 as fast as I could

07 As, passed, saw people reading, notices

08 had come from   09 wondered

10 faster

11 there was noise, talking, laughing

12 was quiet

13 Through, walking nervously around

14 in the middle of, strange silence

15 with shame

16 with no sign of anger, without

17 sat down at   18 It was, that, noticed

19 was wearing, he only wore on

20 something strange, whole class

21 What, to see, so were, ex-mayor, ex-postman

22 seemed, sad   23 While, wondering at

24 for a while, the last time

25 Orders, come from, nothing but German

26 arrives

27 in French, to listen carefully

28 broke, made me angry   29 what, mayor's office

30 in my own language

1 마지막 수업

2 그날 아침 나는 수업에 늦었고, Hamel 선생님이 화를 내실까 걱정되었다.

3 며칠 전에 선생님은 그날 프랑스어 문장 시험을 보겠다고 말씀하셨는데, 나는 준비가 되어 있지 않았다.

4 날씨는 무척 포근하고 사랑스러웠으며 길가의 들판에서는 달콤하고 유혹적인 향기가 났다.

5 잠깐 동안 나는 학교에 가지 않고 들판을 거닐까 생각했다.

6 하지만 나는 최대한 빨리 학교로 달려갔다.

7 시장의 집무실을 지나면서 나는 사람들이 게시판에 붙어 있는 공고문을 읽고 있는 것을 보았다.

8 지난 2년 동안 모든 나쁜 소식은 저 게시판에서 나왔다.

9 나는 "이번에는 뭐지?"라는 궁금증이 들었다.

10 나는 더욱 빨리 달렸다.

11 보통, 아침에는 학생들이 떠들고 웃는 소리로 학교가 소란스러웠다.

12 그러나 그날은 모든 것이 고요했다.

13 창문을 통해 나는 학급 친구들이 제자리에 앉아 있고 Hamel 선생님이 초조하게 교실을 돌아다니시는 것을 보았다.

14 나는 문을 열고 낯선 침묵 속으로 들어갔다.

15 부끄러워서 얼굴이 화끈거렸다!

16 놀랍게도 Hamel 선생님은 화난 기색이 전혀 없이 나를 보시고 자상하게 말씀하셨다. "Frantz야, 네 자리로 가서 앉아라. 너 없이 수업을 시작할 뻔했구나."

17 나는 내 책상으로 가서 앉았다.

18 내가 Hamel 선생님의 파란색 외투를 알아차린 것은 바로 그때였다.

19 선생님은 특별한 날에만 입는 외투를 입고 계셨다.

20 더구나 교실 전체도 무언가 이상했다.

21 나는 교실 뒤에 앉아 있는 사람들을 보고 가장 놀랐다. Hauser 할아버지가 앉아 계셨고 전직 시장님, 전직 우체부 아저씨를 비롯한 많은 사람들이 있었다.

22 그들은 모두 슬퍼 보였다.

23 내가 이 모든 것에 대해 의아해 하는 동안, Hamel 선생님이 천천히 교실 앞으로 걸어가셨다.

24 그는 잠시 생각에 잠긴 후 다정하게 말씀하셨다: "어린이 여러분, 이것이 내가 여러분을 가르치는 마지막 시간입니다.

25 Alsace와 Lorraine에 있는 학교에서는 독일어만 가르치라는 명령이 베를린에서 내려왔습니다.

26 새로운 선생님이 내일 오실 겁니다.

27 이 시간이 프랑스어로 하는 마지막 수업이니 여러분이 주의 깊게 들어 주기 바랍니다."

28 이 몇 마디는 내 마음을 아프게 하고 또 화가 나게 했다.

29 그래, 이게 바로 시장 집무실 게시판에 공고되어 있던 것이다.

30 내 모국어로 하는 마지막 수업이라니!

---

1 The Last Class

2 I was late for school that morning, and I was worried Monsieur Hamel would get angry.

3 A few days before, he had told us that we would take an exam about French sentences that day, and I was not ready.

4 It was such a warm, lovely day, and the fields along the road smelled sweet and inviting.

5 For a moment, I thought of staying away from school and walking around the fields.

6 However, I ran as fast as I could to school.

7 As I passed the mayor's office, I saw people reading the notices on the board.

8 For two years all our bad news had come from that board.

9 I wondered, "What is it now?"

10 I ran faster.

11 Usually, there was noise in the morning at school—sounds of students talking and laughing.

12 However, that day everything was quiet.

13 Through the windows I saw my classmates in their places and Monsieur Hamel walking nervously around the classroom.

14 I opened the door and entered in the middle of the strange silence.

15 My face felt hot with shame!

16 Surprisingly, Monsieur Hamel looked at me with no sign of anger and said kindly, "Go to your seat, my little Frantz; we almost began without you."

17 I sat down at my desk.

18 It was then that I noticed Monsieur Hamel's blue coat.

19 He was wearing the coat he only wore on special days.

20 Also there was something strange about the whole class.

21 What surprised me most was to see people sitting at the back of the room: old Hauser was there, and so were the ex-mayor, the ex-postman, and many others.

22 They all seemed so sad.

23 While I was wondering at all this, Monsieur Hamel walked slowly to the front.

24 He thought for a while and kindly said: "My children, this is the last time that I'll teach you.

25 Orders have come from Berlin to teach nothing but German in the schools of Alsace and Lorraine.

26 The new teacher arrives tomorrow.

27 This is the last class in French, so I want you to listen carefully."

28 Those few words broke my heart and made me angry.

29 So, this was what they had posted at the mayor's office.

30 It was the last class in my own language!

10 rainfall, 강우량 11 crop, 농작물 12 dust, 먼지
13 planet, 행성 14 disturb, 방해하다
15 volcano, 화산 16 landslide, 산사태

단어 TEST Step 1   p.63

01 먼지	02 방해하다	03 지진
04 완화하다, 줄이다	05 모래 폭풍	06 가뭄
07 영향, 효과, 결과	08 분출하다	09 농작물
10 자원	11 분출	12 파괴하다
13 발표하다, 발행하다		14 범람하다; 홍수
15 태풍	16 부피, 용적	17 경치, 풍경
18 산불	19 막다, 예방하다	20 황사
21 주의, 경고	22 화산	23 해일
24 전체의, 온	25 갑작스러운	26 위협하다
27 산사태	28 강우, 강우량	
29 ~의 위치를 찾아내다		30 근처의; 근처에
31 일어나다, 발생하다		32 재
33 가능성	34 둘러싸다	35 A를 위험하게 하다
36 ~을 이용하다	37 다치다	38 ~을 따라 이름 짓다
39 ~을 명심하다	40 ~에 영향을 미치다	
41 A가 ~하지 못하게 하다		42 ~을 …으로 내뿜다
43 ~와 조화를 이루어		

단어 TEST Step 2   p.64

01 rainfall	02 drought	03 active
04 crop	05 destroy	06 earthquake
07 disturb	08 eruption	09 relieve
10 threaten	11 tsunami	12 flood
13 occur	14 dust	15 volume
16 scenery	17 warning	18 landslide
19 effect	20 ash	21 wildfire
22 yellow dust	23 entire	24 resource
25 sandstorm	26 typhoon	27 volcano
28 sudden	29 erupt	30 prevent
31 issue	32 soil	33 circle
34 overnight	35 millions of	36 shoot ~ into …
37 get stuck in	38 name after	
39 have an effect on		40 make use of
41 put A in danger		42 in harmony with
43 on one's way back		

단어 TEST Step 3   p.65

1 eruption, 분출 2 active, 활동 중인 3 circle, 둘러싸다
4 traffic, 교통 5 earthquake, 지진 6 flat, 평평한
7 prevent, 막다, 예방하다 8 ash, 재 9 flood, 홍수

대화문 TEST Step 1   p.66~67

Listen - Listen & Answer Talk 1

hit, warning, issued, rainfall, flooding, inside, make sure, keep listening to

Listen - Listen & Answer Dialog 2

do, a favor / typhoon, bring in, outside / No, bike / take care of, dishes / typhoon / tell, to stay home

Listen - Listen More

going out / sandwiches / ride my bike / good, a favor / on your way back / problem / make sure, wear, no / Don't worry

Speak - Talk in pairs.

Wash your hands / problem / more, you don't play with the knives / keep, mind

Wrap Up 5

having a good time / cool, going / going fishing / make sure, wear a life jacket / keep, in mind

Wrap Up 6

do me a favor / Sure / on Christmas, buy, tickets / problem, tickets do you want

대화문 TEST Step 2   p.68~69

Listen - Listen & Answer Talk 1

M: Hi, this is Cha Gisang from the Weather Station. Here is today's weather. Typhoon Doni is moving north and is going to hit Jejudo tonight. A typhoon warning has been issued. There will be lots of rainfall with a high chance of flooding in some areas. Please stay inside because Typhoon Doni will come with strong winds. Also, please make sure you keep listening to our reports. Thank you.

Listen - Listen & Answer Dialog 2

M: Sora, can you do me a favor?

G: What is it, Dad?

M: A typhoon is coming tonight. Can you bring in the clothes from outside?

G: No problem. What about your bike?

M: I'll take care of it after I finish the dishes.

G: Okay. Do you want me to call Grandma and tell her about the typhoon?

M: Yes. Please tell her to stay home.

G: Okay, Dad.

Listen - Listen More

B: Jimin, are you going out?

G: Yeah. I'm going to buy some sandwiches at Choi's.

B: Are you walking there?

G: No. I'll ride my bike.

B: That's good. Can you do me a favor?

G: Sure. What is it?

B: Can you buy chocolate ice cream for me on your way back?

G: No problem.

B: Thanks. Please make sure you wear a helmet and no ear phones!

G: Don't worry about that.

Speak - Talk in pairs.

A: Can I start now?

B: Wash your hands before you start.

A: Okay. No problem.

B: One more thing. Make sure you don't play with the knives.

A: I'll keep that in mind.

Wrap Up 5

B: Hi, Mom.

W: Hi, Junho. Are you having a good time with Dad?

B: Yeah. Today we visited Dokdo.

W: That sounds cool. What are you going to do tomorrow?

B: We're going fishing on a boat.

W: Great. Please make sure you wear a life jacket.

B: Okay, Mom. I'll keep that in mind.

Wrap Up 6

W: Can you do me a favor?

B: Sure, Grandma. What is it?

W: I want to go to the Tom Dylan concert on Christmas. Can you buy some tickets for me?

B: No problem. How many tickets do you want?

W: Two tickets, please.

본문 TEST Step 1   p.70~72

01 Power, Volcanes   02 have in common
03 islands, of course
04 fact, islands, volcanic eruptions
05 powerful, so, named after
06 make, appear, destroy entire
07 Therefore, should, studied, understood
08 for sure, volcanoes there
09 According, active, above, level
10 underwater, hard to locate
11 Still, discovered, number, far
12 volcanoes, located along, circles
13 about, long, home, around
14 alone, since, lies on
15 area, most, earthquakes occur
16 Sudden, Volcano
17 Working, cornfield, something surprising
18 appeared overnight, flat cornfield
19 Residents, grow over, within
20 called, kept, stopped growing
21 may, can be found
22 been discovered, such as
23 fact, largest known, solar
24 times greater, largest volcano
25 Being, dangerous, harm, ways
26 get hurt, may lose
27 may, destoryed, be threatened
28 have serious effects on
29 shoots, preventing, reaching, disturbing
30 Deadly Volcano
31 active volcano, island, erupted
32 eruption, more than, residents
33 caused, unusually, around, following
34 What volcanoes, humans, however
35 soil, volcano, good, farming
36 Volcanoes, great tourist attraction
37 Looking, scenery, millions, tourists
38 be used, produce electricity
39 for, turns, volcanoes', into
40 ways, harmony, hopeful, found

본문 TEST Step 2   p.73~74

01 Power, Volcanoes   02 have in common
03 islands, of course
04 fact, volcanic eruptions
05 are named after

06 make big islands appear, destory

07 should be studied and understood

08 how many volcanoes there are

09 According to, about, above sea level

10 underwater, hard to locate

11 a large number of, so far

12 are located along

13 home to, active volcanoes

14 alone, since, lies on   15 where, occur

16 Sudden

17 Working, something surprising

18 appeared overnight, flat cornfield

19 grow, within

20 kept growing, stopped growing

21 can be found

22 have been discovered, such as

23 the largest known, solar system

24 100 times greater than that of

25 do harm to, in many ways

26 get hurt

27 may be destoryed, can be threatened

28 have serious effects on

29 shoots, into, preventing, from reaching, disturbing

30 Deadly Volcano

31 active volcano, erupted   32 eruption, more than

33 unusually, following year

34 What volcanoes do, not always

35 is good for   36 tourist attraction

37 Looking for, millions of   38 can be used

39 turns, into electricity

40 greater harmony with, will be found

본문 TEST Step 3   p.75~76

1 화산의 힘

2 제주도, 시칠리아, 하와이의 공통점은 무엇일까?

3 물론, 그것들은 섬이다.

4 사실, 그것들은 모두 화산 분출에 의해 형성된 섬이다.

5 화산은 매우 강력한 힘을 가지고 있어서 로마의 불의 신, 불카누스에게서 이름을 따왔다.

6 화산은 큰 섬이 생겨나게 하거나 폼페이 같은 도시 전체를 파멸시킬 수도 있다.

7 그러므로 화산은 연구되고, 이해되어야 한다.

8 세계에 얼마나 많은 화산이 있는지 누구도 정확히 알지 못한다.

9 과학자들에 따르면, 해수면 위에 대략 1,500개의 활화산이 있다.

10 더 많은 화산이 해저에 존재하는데, 그것들은 정확한 위치를 파악하기가 어렵다.

11 그럼에도 불구하고, 과학자들은 지금까지 그중 많은 수를 발견했다.

12 지구상에 있는 많은 화산들은 태평양을 둘러싸는 '불의 고리(환태평양조산대)'를 따라 위치한다.

13 그 고리는 길이가 약 40,000km에 달하며, 전 세계 활화산의 약 75%가 여기에 있다.

14 인도네시아에만 120개가 넘는 활화산이 있는데, 이 나라가 '불의 고리'에 위치하고 있기 때문이다.

15 이 고리는 또한 전 세계 지진의 대부분이 발생하는 곳이다.

16 갑작스럽게 생겨난 화산

17 1943년 어느 날 옥수수 밭에서 일을 하다가 멕시코의 농부들이 놀라운 것을 발견했다.

18 밤사이에 평평한 옥수수 밭 위로 화산이 생겨난 것이다.

19 주민들은 그 화산이 일주일이 못 되는 사이 100m 넘게 자라는 것을 지켜보았다.

20 'Paricutin(파리쿠틴)'이라고 불리는 이 화산은 계속 자라났고, 1952년에 424m로 드디어 성장을 멈추었다.

21 화산이 지구에만 존재한다고 생각할지 모른다.

22 그러나 화산은 화성이나 목성 같은 다른 행성에서도 발견되어 왔다.

23 사실 화성에 있는 Olympus Mons(올림푸스 몬스)가 태양계에서 가장 크다고 알려진 화산이다.

24 그것의 부피는 지구에서 가장 큰 화산 Mauna Loa(마우나로아)의 부피보다 약 100배 더 크다.

25 매우 강력하고 위험하기 때문에, 화산은 여러 면에서 사람들에게 해를 끼친다.

26 때로는 사람들이 다치기도 하고, 집을 잃기도 한다.

27 작물이 파괴되거나, 항공 교통이 위협받을 수도 있다.

28 화산은 또한 세계 날씨에 심각한 영향을 미치기도 한다.

29 화산 분출은 다량의 화산재와 먼지를 공중으로 내뿜어, 태양 광선의 일부가 지구에 도달하는 것을 방해하고 그리하여 정상적인 기상 패턴을 깨뜨린다.

30 목숨을 앗아 가는 화산

31 인도네시아 Sumbawa(숨바와) 섬에 위치한 활화산, Tambora(탐보라) 산이 1815년에 분출했다.

32 분출은 주민 1만 명 이상을 죽음에 이르게 했다.

33 또한 이듬해 전 세계에 비정상적으로 추운 여름을 초래했다.

34 그러나 화산이 인류에게 항상 나쁜 것만은 아니다.

35 화산 인근의 토양은 농사에 좋다.

36 화산은 또한 매우 훌륭한 관광 명소이다.

37 환상적인 경관을 찾아 매년 수백만 명의 여행객들이 제주도의 한라산, 시칠리아의 Etna(에트나) 산, 하와이의 Diamond Head(다이아몬드헤드)를 방문한다.

38 화산은 또한 전기를 생산하는 데에도 이용될 수 있다.

39 예를 들어, 아이슬란드는 적극적으로 화산의 열에너지를 전기로 바꾼다.

40 오늘날 전 세계에서 사람들이 화산과 더 조화롭게 살 방법을 연구하고 있으며, 더 많은 방법이 곧 발견될 것으로 기대하고 있다.

1 The Power of Volcanoes

2 What do Jejudo, Sicily, and Hawaii have in common?

3 They are islands, of course.

4 In fact, they are all islands made from volcanic eruptions.

5 Volcanoes are very powerful, so they are named after Vulcan, the Roman god of fire.

6 They can make big islands appear or destroy entire cities like Pompeii.

7 Therefore, they should be studied and understood.

8 Nobody knows for sure how many volcanoes there are in the world.

9 According to scientists, there are about 1,500 active volcanoes above sea level.

10 Many more are underwater, and they are hard to locate.

11 Still, scientists have discovered a large number of them so far.

12 Many of the volcanoes on Earth are located along the Ring of Fire that circles the Pacific Ocean.

13 The ring is about 40,000 kilometers long, and it is home to around 75% of the world's active volcanoes.

14 Indonesia alone has over 120 active volcanoes since the country lies on the Ring of Fire.

15 This ring is also the area where most of the world's earthquakes occur.

16 A Sudden Volcano

17 Working on a cornfield one day in 1943, farmers in Mexico found something surprising.

18 A volcano appeared overnight on a flat cornfield.

19 Residents watched the volcano grow over 100 meters tall within a week.

20 The volcano, called Paricutin, kept growing, and it finally stopped growing at 424 meters in 1952.

21 You may think volcanoes can be found only on Earth.

22 However, they have been discovered on other planets, too, such as Mars and Jupiter.

23 In fact, "Olympus Mons" on Mars is the largest known volcano in the solar system.

24 Its volume is about 100 times greater than that of Mauna Loa, the largest volcano on Earth.

25 Being very powerful and dangerous, volcanoes do harm to people in many ways.

26 Sometimes people get hurt, or they may lose their houses.

27 Crops may be destoryed, and air traffic can be threatened.

28 Volcanoes can also have serious effects on world weather.

29 A volcanic eruption shoots lots of ash and dust into the air, preventing some of the sunlight from reaching Earth and thus disturbing usual weather patterns.

30 A Deadly Volcano

31 Mt. Tambora, an active volcano on the island of Sumbawa, Indonesia, erupted in 1815.

32 The eruption killed more than 10,000 residents.

33 It also caused an unusually cold summer around the world the following year.

34 What volcanoes do is not always bad for humans, however.

35 The soil near a volcano is good for farming.

36 Volcanoes are also a great tourist attraction.

37 Looking for fantastic scenery, millions of tourists visit Mt. Halla in Jejudo, Mt. Etna in Sicily, or Diamond Head in Hawaii every year.

38 Volcanoes can be used to produce electricity, too.

39 Iceland, for example, actively turns its volcanoes' heat energy into electricity.

40 Today people around the world are studying ways to live in greater harmony with volcanoes, and they are hopeful that more ways will be found soon.

My Speaking Portfolio Step 1

1. electricity, out
2. caught on fire
3. got stuck
4. burned my finger
5. fell down, broke

After You Read Details

1. volcano, comes from
2. the world's active volcanoes are located along
3. stopped growing
4. The eruption, brought about an unusually cold summer

My Writing Portfolio

1. Perfect Storm
2. saw, last weekend

3. came out, was directed by

4. about, in the Atlantic Ocean, in danger

5. because the scenes were exciting, realistic

6. good acting of the leading actor

7. learned, natural disasters like storms, dangerous

구석구석지문 TEST Step 2　　　　　p.83

My Speaking Portfolio Step 1

1. The electricity is out.

2. The pan caught on fire.

3. I got stuck in the elevator.

4. I burned my finger in hot water.

5. I fell down the steps and broke my arm.

After You Read Details

1. The name "volcano" comes from the Roman god of fire. - Mila

2. 75% of the world's active volcanoes are located along the Ring of Fire. - James

3. The volcano Paricutin in Mexico stopped growing. - Lucy

4. The eruption of Mt. Tambora brought about an unusually cold summer in 1816. - David

My Writing Portfolio

1. The Perfect Storm

2. I saw the movie *The Perfect Storm* last weekend.

3. The movie came out in 2000, and it was directed by the German director Wolfgang Petersen.

4. It is about a big storm in the Atlantic Ocean that put a fishing boat in danger.

5. I liked the movie because the scenes were exciting and very realistic.

6. Also, I liked the good acting of the leading actor George Clooney.

7. From the movie, I learned that natural disasters like storms can be very dangerous.

Lesson 8

단어 TEST Step 1　　　　　p.84

01 이루다, 달성[성취]하다

02 확신하는, 자신만만한　03 현수막

04 심사, 테스트　05 난처한, 걱정[근심]스러운

06 침착한, 냉정한　07 수도　08 제의, 제안

09 기회　10 일생[평생]의　11 쫓다, 추적하다

12 보호　13 ~할 가치가 있는　14 완전히, 전적으로

15 짜증 난, 참지 못하는　16 연결하다

17 아주 기뻐하는　18 규칙

19 구하다, 절약하다, 저축하다　20 심각한, 진지한

21 표현하다　22 무서워하는, 겁먹은

23 기분 좋은, 즐거운　24 후회하다　25 도전적인

26 설립하다　27 상상, 상상력

28 향상시키다, 개선하다　29 수리하다

30 포함하다　31 잘못 알고 있는　32 결정, 판단

33 나머지, 휴식　34 기량, 기술　35 고장 나다

36 ~했을지도 모른다　37 ~을 다루다

38 발발[발생]하다　39 (과거에) ~이었다[했다]

40 ~을 부끄러워하다

41 ~에 지원하다, ~을 신청하다　42 ~와 시간을 보내다

43 반복해서

단어 TEST Step 2　　　　　p.85

01 confident　02 improve　03 banner

04 completely　05 include　06 lifelong

07 achieve　08 calm　09 express

10 connect　11 found　12 cheerful

13 delighted　14 chase　15 practice

16 regret　17 capital　18 tryout

19 protection　20 challenging　21 impatient

22 opportunity　23 worth　24 imagination

25 repair　26 skill　27 decision

28 save　29 scared　30 serious

31 mistaken　32 rest　33 pick

34 quite　35 go by　36 over and over

37 break down　38 must have p.p.

39 be ashamed of　40 break out

41 hang out with　42 deal with　43 apply for

1 found, 설립하다   2 connect, 연결하다   3 rest, 나머지

4 create, 만들다, 창조하다   5 read, ~라고 적혀 있다

6 opportunity, 기회   7 impatient, 참지 못하는

8 decision, 결정, 판단   9 challenging, 도전적인

10 tryout, 심사, 테스트   11 banner, 현수막

12 include, 포함하다   13 serious, 심각한, 진지한

14 league, 리그, 연맹   15 regret, 후회하다

16 worth, ~할 가치가 있는

Listen - Listen & Answer Dialog 1

What / drawing cartoons, preparing for / are, when /
On, left / How's, gojng / It, to draw what, to express,
should have practiced / worry, make it

Listen - Listen & Answer Dialog 2

to meet, do well on, drawing exam / sure, did my
best / What made, apply for / (I')ve, loved, since, little
child / cartoon artist / quite right / What, think, most
important skill / I'd say, completely

Speak - Talk in pairs.

matter / hungry, saved / Don't, share, with

Listen - Listen More

to see / I'm afraid, be late / hate to be late for /
should have set / happens a lot, tired / What made,
late / got up, it took, do my hair / We're stuck in,
traffic jam, get off / you're mistaken, stay on /
terribly

Wrap Up 6

when, grow up / with / interested in making / that's,
quite right, repair / why / Because, think

Wrap Up 7

has viruses / How / shouldn't have done / were you,
I'd get, right now

Listen - Listen & Answer Dialog 1

B: Hi, Sora. What are you doing?

G: I'm drawing cartoons. I'm preparing for the exam
for Mana Animation High School.

B: Oh, are you? When is the exam?

G: On Friday, so I only have two days left.

B: How's it going?

G: It's not easy to draw what I want to express. I
should have practiced more.

B: Don't worry! You can make it!

G: Thanks.

Listen - Listen & Answer Dialog 2

M: Nice to meet you, Sora. Did you do well on the
drawing exam?

G: I'm not sure, but I did my best.

M: Okay. Let's start the interview. What made you
apply for Mana Animation High School?

G: Well, I've really loved drawing cartoons since I was
a little child.

M: So, you want to be a cartoon artist?

G: That's not quite right. I want to be a game
designer.

M: I see. What do you think is the most important
skill a game designer needs?

G: I'd say imagination. A good designer should create
a completely new world in a game.

M: Sounds good.

Speak - Talk in pairs.

A: What's the matter?

B: I feel hungry. I should have saved food for the
winter.

A: Don't worry. I'll share my food with you.

B: Thanks.

Listen - Listen More

G: Hi, Jiho.

B: Hi, Amber. It's nice to see you on the bus.

G: Yeah, but I'm afraid we're going to be late.

B: Yeah. I hate to be late for the school festival.

G: Me, too. I should have set my alarm. I forgot.

B: I understand. That happens a lot to me when I'm
tired, too.

G: How about you? What made you late?

B: Well, I got up early. But it took me some time to
do my hair.

G: Oh, I see. We're stuck in a heavy traffic jam. We
should get off and run.

B: No, you're mistaken. The traffic is starting to
move again. Let's stay on.

G: Okay. I just hope we're not terribly late.

Wrap Up 6

B: What do you want to do when you grow up?

G: I want to work with robots.

B: Are you interested in making robots?

G: No, that's not quite right. I want to repair robots.

B: I see. But why?

G: Because I think it'll be a good job in the future.

Wrap Up 7

G: My computer has viruses.

B: How come?

G: I opened an e-mail from a stranger. I shouldn't have done that.

B: If I were you, I'd get help from a computer service center right now.

본문 TEST Step 1   p.91~92

01 GRANDMOTHER'S BASEBALL DREAMS

02 used to, cook, near

03 work anymore, delicious, which

04 one, that connect us

05 What connects, strongly, however

06 When, weekends, exciting, back

07 must have loved   08 listen to, over and

09 says, Go after what

10 afraid, something new, challenging

11 Don't, ashamed of failing

12 In, Professional, was founded

13 created, because, were fighting

14 there would, local tryouts

15 What would, like, finals

16 imagined, hanging, which included

17 explained, suit, serious, unkind

18 thought, wearing, made, impatient

19 On, for hours, other   20 excited to go after

21 About, later, found, mailbox

22 It, from, worked for

23 read, had, main tryouts

24 As, went by, worried

25 traveling, which, far away

26 tryouts, too afraid to

27 spent, rest, regretting, decision

28 watches, should have gone

29 worth chasing, even, few

30 Never miss, opportunity

본문 TEST Step 2   p.93~94

01 GRANDMOTHER'S, DREAMS

02 used to be a cook, near

03 anymore, enjoys making, which

04 one, that connect us

05 What connects, strongly, is

06 on weekends, exciting stories, back

07 must have loved

08 listen to, over and over   09 Go after what

10 afraid of, something new or challenging

11 Don't be ashamed of   12 was founded

13 was created, were fighting

14 there would be local tryouts

15 What would it be like, the finals

16 imagined, hanging, which included

17 were explained, in a suit, serious

18 wearing a suit, might have made, impatient

19 for hours, other, women   20 to go after

21 later, found a letter   22 It was from

23 It read, had been invited, league's main tryouts

24 As, went by, worried

25 worried about, which, far away from

26 main tryouts, too, to   27 has spent, regretting

28 should have gone

29 are worth chasing, even if

30 Never miss, opportunity

본문 TEST Step 3   p.95~96

1 할머니의 야구 꿈

2 우리 할머니 Helen은 Indiana주 South Bend 근처 작은 마을에 있는 식당의 요리사였다.

3 할머니는 더 이상 일을 하지 않지만 여전히 맛있는 음식을 즐겨 만드시고, 나는 그 음식들을 무척 좋아한다.

4 음식은 우리를 연결하는 많은 것 가운데 하나이다.

5 하지만 우리를 가장 강하게 연결하는 것은 바로 야구이다.

6 주말마다 할머니 댁에 가면, 할머니는 종종 과거 1940년대의 야구 경기에 관해 흥미로운 이야기를 내게 들려주신다.

7 그녀는 야구를 무척 좋아했던 게 분명하다.

8 나는 이 이야기들을 몇 번이고 듣는다.

9 그녀는 항상 "네가 원하는 것을 이루려고 노력하렴, Sarah.

10 새로운 것이나 도전적인 것을 시도해 보기를 두려워하지 말거라.

11 실패하는 것을 부끄러워하지 마라."라고 말씀하신다.

12 1943년, 전미 여자 프로야구 리그가 창립되었다.

13 미국의 청년 중 많은 사람들이 제2차 세계대전에 참전해 있었기 때문에 이 리그가 야구 팬들을 위해 만들어졌다.

14 Helen 할머니는 지역 심사가 바로 South Bend에서 있을 거라고 들었다.

15 그녀는 "야구 팀에 들어가서 고향을 위해 결승전까지 진출한다는 건 어떤 기분일까?"라며 궁금해했다.

16 그녀는 Helen Baker라는 이름이 포함된 큰 현수막이 야구장에 걸려 있는 것을 상상했다.

17 심사 당일 모든 규칙이 정장을 입은 나이 든 남자에 의해 설명되었는데, 그는 무척 진지하고 불친절하게 들렸다.

18 뜨거운 태양 아래 정장을 입고 있는 것이 그를 짜증나게 만들었을지도 모른다고 그녀는 생각했다.

19 그날, Helen 할머니는 다른 젊은 여성과 함께 몇 시간 동안 야구를 했다.

20 그녀는 자신의 야구 꿈을 좇아가게 되어 신이 났다!

21 일주일쯤 지나, Helen 할머니는 우편함에서 편지 한 통을 발견했다.

22 그것은 시카고에 있는 여자 야구리그에서 일하는 사람들이 보낸 것이었다.

23 그 편지에는 그녀가 시카고에서 열리는 리그의 본심사에 초청되었다고 적혀 있었다!

24 하지만 하루하루 갈수록, Helen 할머니는 심사에 떨어질까봐 걱정되었다.

25 그녀는 또한 시카고까지 혼자 여행하는 것이 걱정되었는데, 시카고는 집에서 멀리 떨어진 곳이었다.

26 본심사가 있는 날이 되었을 때, 그녀는 너무 두려워서 갈 수 없었다.

27 할머니는 남은 인생을 자신의 결정을 후회하며 보내셨다.

28 텔레비전에서 야구 경기를 볼 때, 그녀는 종종 "난 시카고에 갔어야 해.

29 너도 알겠지만, 모든 꿈은 추구할 가치가 있단다. 비록 일부만 이루게 되더라도 말이야.

30 절대 기회를 놓치지 마라."라고 말씀하신다.

1 MY GRANDMOTHER'S BASEBALL DREAMS

2 My grandmother Helen used to be a cook in a restaurant in a small town near South Bend, Indiana.

3 She does not work anymore, but she still enjoys making delicious food, which I love so much.

4 Food is one of the many things that connect us.

5 What connects us most strongly, however, is baseball.

6 When I visit her on weekends, my grandmother often tells me exciting stories about playing baseball back in the 1940s.

7 She must have loved the sport very much.

9 I listen to these stories over and over.

9 She always says, "Go after what you want, Sarah.

10 Don't be afraid of trying something new or challenging.

11 Don't be ashamed of failing."

12 In 1943, the All-American Girls Professional Baseball League was founded.

13 This league was created for baseball fans because many of America's young men were fighting in World War II.

14 Helen was told that there would be local tryouts right in South Bend.

15 She wondered, "What would it be like to be on a baseball team and to make it to the finals for my hometown?"

16 She imagined a large banner hanging at the baseball field which included the name Helen Baker.

17 On the day of the tryouts, all the rules were explained by an old man in a suit, who sounded very serious and unkind.

18 She thought that wearing a suit in the hot sun might have made him impatient.

19 On that day, Helen played baseball for hours with many other young women.

20 She was excited to go after her baseball dreams!

21 About a week later, Helen found a letter in the mailbox.

22 It was from people who worked for the girls' baseball league in Chicago.

23 It read that she had been invited to the league's main tryouts in Chicago!

24 As the days went by, however, Helen became worried that she might fail.

25 She also became worried about traveling alone to Chicago, which was far away from home.

26 When the day of the main tryouts came, she was too afraid to go.

27 My grandmother has spent the rest of her life regretting her decision.

28 When she watches a baseball game on TV, she often says, "I should have gone to Chicago.

29 You know, all your dreams are worth chasing, even if you catch only a few of them.

30 Never miss an opportunity."

After You Read Graphic Organizer

1. broke out
2. so much
3. was, sure of, was afraid of traveling alone
4. founded
5. joined the local tryouts
6. main tryouts

My Writing Portfolio

1. MOTHER OF CHIMPANZEES
2. was born in London, England
3. Her interest in, when she first read
4. has been studying, since her twenties
5. has, been working, protection of chimpanzees
6. received, for protecting whild animals
7. Thanks to her lifelong study, come to know
8. one of the greatest scientists

Words in Action

1. are winning, are singing a cheerful song
2. If, stays calm, catches
3. misses
4. make two runs, game continues
5. looks ashamed, nervous
6. going wild, while, look scared, worried

7. Thanks to her lifelong study, we have come to know a lot about chimpanzees.
8. Jane Goodall is one of the greatest scientists in history.

Words in Action

1. The Cheetahs are winning the game, and their fans are singing a cheerful song.
2. If Jason stays calm and catches the ball, the game ends.
3. Oh my! He misses the ball!
4. The Ducks make two runs, and the game continues.
5. Jason looks ashamed and nervous.
6. The Ducks fans are going wild, while the Cheetahs fans look scared and worried.

After You Read Graphic Organizer

1. The Second World War broke out.
2. She loved baseball so much.
3. She was not sure of her success. Also, she was afraid of traveling alone.
4. In 1943, the All-American Girls Professional Baseball League was founded.
5. She joined the local tryouts in South Bend.
6. She didn't go to the main tryouts.

My Writing Portfolio

1. JANE GOODALL, MOTHER OF CHIMPANZEES
2. Jane Goodall was born in London, England, in 1934.
3. Her interest in chimpanzees began when she first read about Tarzan.
4. She has been studying wild chimpanzees in Africa since her twenties.
5. She has also been working for the protection of chimpanzees.
6. In 1995, she received the Hubbard Medal for protecting whild animals.

14 manager, 경영자, 관리자　15 record, 기록

16 whisper, 속삭이다

단어 TEST Step 1　　　　　　　　　p.103

01 외치다, 소리[고함]치다　　02 안도, 안심

03 안전 제품　04 실제(로)는, 사실은

05 고통을 주다, 아프다　　06 교훈

07 자전거를 타다　08 ~ 내내, ~ 동안 쭉

09 흙, 먼지　10 입구, 입장　11 그러나, 그래도

12 나무로 된, 목재의　13 숨 쉬다　14 입구, 관문

15 석고붕대, 깁스　16 경영자, 관리자　17 쿵쾅거리는

18 열린 구멍, 창(窓), 구멍, 틈　19 특별한

20 ~하곤 했다 (과거의 불규칙적 습관)　21 기록

22 비명　23 두터운, 빽빽한　24 속삭이다

25 여느 때처럼　26 출발하다　27 대답으로

28 (손 · 팔 · 다리 등을) 뻗다　29 매일

30 조금씩　31 얼마 후에　32 나란히

33 ~하자마자　34 처음에는　35 다시 말해서, 즉

36 갑자기　37 간신히 ~하다　38 ~ 덕분에

39 ~하곤 했다　40 ~가 …하는 것을 막다

단어 TEST Step 2　　　　　　　　　p.104

01 wooden　02 safety product　03 would

04 cast　05 though　06 scream

07 cycle　08 dirt　09 entrance

10 throughout　11 lesson　12 manager

13 opening　14 gateway　15 particular

16 record　17 thumping　18 hurt

19 whisper　20 relief　21 shout

22 actually　23 breathe　24 thick

25 at first　26 reach out　27 inch by inch

28 stop ~ from -ing　29 thanks to

30 set off　31 after a while　32 side by side

33 day in and day out　34 in other words

35 as soon as　36 in reply　37 as usual

38 manage to　39 all of a sudden　40 used to

단어 TEST Step 3　　　　　　　　　p.105

1 breathe, 숨 쉬다　2 cycle, 자전거를 타다

3 dirt, 흙, 먼지　4 entrance, 입구

5 thick, 두터운, 빽빽한　6 scream, 비명

7 relief, 안도, 안심　8 gateway, 입구　9 flood, 홍수

10 throughout, ~ 내내, ~ 동안 쭉　11 lesson, 교훈

12 particular, 특별한　13 thumping, 쿵쾅거리는

본문 TEST Step 1　　　　　　　　　p.106~109

01 Keep Out　02 used to go, coast

03 place, stayed at, same

04 stay, swimming, walking, little

05 other words, anything, happened

06 At the time of

07 particular, as, had, since

08 throughout, shone, in, out

09 But, loved, heat, sun

10 ride, further, away from

11 decided, ride, along, take

12 as usual, set off

13 easy, follow, cycled, by

14 while, thicker, behind, other

15 was ahead

16 toward, darker, formed, roof

17 stopped suddenly, ahead, shouted

18 to, wooden, across, opening

19 a tunnel, said

20 Keep Out, gate, replied

21 have a look inside

22 Actually, not want, inside

23 little, sudden, back into

24 answered, moved ahead

25 left, gate, climbed over　26 entered, cool tunnel

27 air inside, heavy

28 Above, sound, grew louder

29 called out

30 Keep, down, move on

31 Don't, fast, called after

32 meant, leave, behind, so

33 loud, thumping, express, scream

34 shouted, up, hear, reply

35 Speak, Tell, what's happened

36 toward where, been, dirt

37 reached out, something wet

38 were closed, breathing weakly

39 whispered, get, out

40 broken, hurts, get help

41 replied, get, out, safety

42 moving away, dirt, with

43 felt calm, in control

44 took, clear away, covering

45 Finally, managed to free

46 Holding, backward, toward, entrance

47 seemed, ages, able, out   48 look too well, though

49 stop, from crying out

50 found, brought, water bottles

51 get help, quick as

52 In reply, simply pressed

53 raced back, until, nearest

54 past, gate, washing, dishes

55 Thanks, taken, put, cast

56 soon, arrived, with relief   57 Let, be, lesson

58 lesson, *out, Stay, trouble*

59 manager, produces, safety products

60 am, fire fighter

39 get you out

40 (I')ve broken, go and get help

41 get you out of here   42 moving away

43 felt calm, in control

44 clear away, covering   45 managed to free

46 Holding, inch by inch, tunnel entrance

47 to take ages, out of   48 look too well, though

49 stop, from crying out, crying out

50 two water bottles

51 go and get help, as quick as, can

52 In reply, pressed my hands

53 raced back, the nearest farmhouse

54 ran past, washing some dishes

55 Thanks to her, where, put, cast

56 As soon as, with relief   57 Let that be a lesson

58 lesson, *Stay out of trouble*

59 other safety products   60 fire fighter

01 Keep Out   02 Every, used to go

03 stayed at, guesthouse

04 stay for, swimming, walking

05 In other words, anything special

06 At the time of   07 had had

08 throughout, shone day in and day out

09 the heat

10 further and further away from

11 take us

12 to follow, as usual, set off

13 cycled along side by side

14 grew thicker, one behind the other

15 ahead

16 grew darker, formed a roof

17 Look ahead, shouted

18 next to him, black opening

19 a tunnel   20 Keep Out

21 have a look   22 Actually, go inside

23 all of a sudden, go back into

24 moved ahead   25 left, climbed over

26 entered   27 inside, heavy

28 grew louder and louder   29 called out

30 Keep, down, moved on

31 Don't go, called after   32 leave, behind

33 loud noise, thumping, like an express train, scream

34 what's up, reply   35 what's happened

36 where Ron had been

37 reached out, something wet

38 were closed, breathing weakly

1 들어가지 마시오

2 여름마다 나의 가족은 해안으로 휴가를 가곤 했다.

3 우리는 항상 같은 곳에 가서 똑같은 작은 게스트하우스에 묵었다.

4 우리는 2주 가량 머물며 바다에서 수영하고 작은 마을 주위를 돌아다니곤 했다.

5 다시 말해서, 그런 휴가에서 우리는 특별한 일을 하지 않았고 정말 아무 일도 일어나지 않았다.

6 이 이야기는 내가 12살 때 일이다.

7 관측 이래 영국이 겪은 가장 더운 여름이었기 때문에, 대부분의 사람들은 이 특별한 여름을 기억할 수 있다.

8 6월과 7월 내내 비가 오지 않았고 태양은 연일 쨍쨍했다.

9 하지만 Ron과 나는 그 더위와 태양을 사랑했다.

10 매일 우리는 게스트하우스에서 조금씩 먼 곳으로 자전거를 타고 가곤 했다.

11 어느 날, Ron은 낡은 철로가 우리를 어디로 데려다줄지 알아보려고 그 철로를 따라 자전거를 타기로 결정했다.

12 난 늘 그랬듯 Ron을 따르는 게 즐거웠고, 아침 식사 후에 우리는 출발했다.

13 처음에는 철길을 따라가는 게 어렵지 않아 우리는 나란히 자전거를 타고 갔다.

14 한참 후, 풀이 점점 우거져서 우리는 한 사람이 앞서가고 다른 사람이 뒤에서 가야 했다.

15 Ron이 앞서가고 있었다.

16 철길은 숲으로 이어졌고 나무가 높이 자라 철길 위로 지붕을 형성하며 점점 더 어두워졌다.

17 Ron이 갑자기 멈췄다. "앞을 봐!"라고 그가 외쳤다.

71

18 나는 그의 옆에 멈춰서 캄캄한 입구를 가로지르는 흰색 나무문을 보았다.

19 "터널이네." 내가 말했다.

20 "맞아. 그리고 문에 '들어가지 마시오'라고 적혀 있어." Ron이 대답했다.

21 "안을 보고 싶니?"

22 사실, 난 안으로 들어가고 싶지 않았다.

23 갑자기 나는 한기를 살짝 느꼈고 햇빛 속으로 되돌아가고 싶었다.

24 그렇지만 나는 "물론이지."라고 답하며 앞으로 움직였다.

25 우리는 문 앞에 자전거를 남겨 두고 넘어갔다.

26 우리는 서늘한 터널로 들어갔다.

27 안의 공기는 묵직했다.

28 우리 머리 위로 점점 더 커지는 소리가 났다.

29 "저게 뭐야?"라고 내가 소리쳤다.

30 "박쥐야." Ron이 말했다. "머리를 숙여." 그러고 나서 그는 계속 움직였다.

31 "너무 빨리 가지 마." 나는 그를 부르며 뒤쫓았다.

32 '나를 두고 가지 마'라고 말하고 싶었지만, 나는 그렇게 말하지 않았다.

33 그다음 내가 들은 것은 바로 앞에서 나는 큰 소음이었는데, 그것은 마치 고속열차 같은 쿵쾅거리는 소리였다. 이어서 비명이 들렸다.

34 "Ron!" 나는 외쳤다. "Ron, 무슨 일이야? 내 말 들려?" 아무 응답이 없었다.

35 "Ron, 나에게 말해 봐. 무슨 일이 생겼는지 말해 줘."

36 나는 천천히 Ron이 있던 곳으로 걸어갔고 흙과 작은 자갈만을 발견했다.

37 손을 뻗었을 때 나는 축축한 무언가를 느꼈다. Ron의 얼굴이었다!

38 그의 눈은 감겨 있었고 약하게 숨을 쉬고 있었다.

39 "괜찮아, Ron." 나는 속삭였다. "내가 꺼내 줄게."

40 "다리가 부러진 것 같아. 정말 아파. 그냥 가서 도움을 요청해, Ben."

41 "안 돼." 나는 대답했다. "우선 안전한 곳까지 여기에서 형을 꺼낼 거야."

42 나는 손으로 흙과 자갈을 치우기 시작했다.

43 나는 침착했고 내가 잘할 수 있다고 느꼈다.

44 Ron을 뒤덮은 흙을 치우는 데에 오랜 시간이 걸렸다.

45 드디어 나는 그의 몸을 자유롭게 할 수 있었다.

46 팔 밑으로 그를 안고서 그를 터널 입구 쪽으로 조금씩 뒤로 끌어당겼다.

47 오랜 시간이 걸린 듯했지만 결국 나는 Ron을 터널 밖으로 데리고 나올 수 있었다.

48 그는 별로 좋아 보이지 않았다.

49 그의 얼굴은 창백했고 울음을 터뜨리지 않으려고 몹시 애쓰고 있었다.

50 나는 우리 자전거를 찾아서 Ron에게 물병 두 개를 가져다주었다.

51 "여기, 이거 마셔." 나는 말했다. "내가 가서 도움을 구할게. 최대한 빨리 올게."

52 대답으로 Ron은 그저 내 손을 꽉 잡았다.

53 나는 자전거를 타고 왔던 철길을 따라 달려, 마침내 가장 가까운 농가에 도착했다.

54 대문을 지나 달려가 나는 부엌에서 설거지를 하고 있는 부인을 발견했다.

55 그 부인 덕분에 Ron은 병원으로 이송되었고, 병원에서 다리에 석고붕대를 했다.

56 부모님이 병원에 도착해서 우리를 보자마자, 어머니는 안도감에 울음을 터뜨리셨다.

57 하지만 아버지가 하신 말씀은 "이 일이 너희에게 교훈이 되기를 바란다."가 전부였다.

58 그래서 교훈이 무엇이었을까? 그것은 '들어가지 마시오'라는 말은 '곤경을 멀리하라'는 뜻이라는 것이다.

59 Ron은 지금 안전모와 여러 안전 제품을 생산하는 큰 회사의 관리자이다.

60 그럼 나는? 나는 소방관이다.

본문 TEST Step 4 · Step 5 p.118~125

1 Keep Out

2 Every summer, my family used to go on holiday to the coast.

3 We always went to the same place and stayed at the same small guesthouse.

4 We would stay for two weeks, swimming in the sea and walking around the little town.

5 In other words, we never did anything special, and nothing ever really happened on these vacations.

6 At the time of this story I was twelve years old.

7 Most people can remember this particular summer, as it was the hottest summer England had had since records began.

8 It did not rain throughout June and July, and the sun shone day in and day out.

9 But Ron and I loved the heat and the sun.

10 Every day, we would ride our bicycles further and further away from the guesthouse.

11 One day Ron decided that we should ride our bikes along the old train tracks to see where they would take us.

12 I was happy to follow Ron, as usual, and we set off after breakfast.

13 At first, the tracks were easy to follow, and we cycled along side by side.

14 After a while, the grass grew thicker, and we had

to ride one behind the other.

15 Ron was ahead.

16 The tracks went toward the woods and it grew darker as the trees stood tall and formed a roof over the tracks.

17 Ron stopped suddenly. "Look ahead!" he shouted.

18 I stopped next to him and saw a white, wooden gateway across a black opening.

19 "It's a tunnel," I said.

20 "Yes, and it says, 'Keep Out' on the gate," replied Ron.

21 "Do you want to have a look inside?"

22 Actually, I did not want to go inside.

23 I felt a little cold all of a sudden, and I wanted to go back into the sunlight.

24 But I answered, "Sure," and moved ahead.

25 We left our bikes at the gate and climbed over.

26 We entered the cool tunnel.

27 The air inside was heavy.

28 Above our heads there was a sound that grew louder and louder.

29 "What's that?" I called out.

30 "Bats," said Ron, "Keep your head down." Then he moved on.

31 "Don't go so fast." I called after him.

32 I meant, "Don't leave me behind" but I didn't say so.

33 The next thing I heard was a loud noise right above us, a thumping sound like an express train and then a scream.

34 "Ron!" I shouted. "Ron, what's up? Can you hear me?" No reply.

35 "Speak to me, Ron. Tell me what's happened."

36 I slowly walked toward where Ron had been and found only dirt and small rocks.

37 As I reached out my hands, I felt something wet — Ron's face!

38 His eyes were closed, and he was breathing weakly.

39 "It's okay, Ron," I whispered. "I'll get you out."

40 "I think I've broken my leg. It really hurts. Just go and get help, Ben."

41 "No," I replied. "I'll get you out of here to safety first."

42 I started moving away the dirt and rocks with my hands.

43 I felt calm, and I felt in control.

44 It took a long time to clear away the earth covering Ron.

45 Finally, I managed to free his body.

46 Holding him under the arms, I pulled him backward, inch by inch, toward the tunnel entrance.

47 It seemed to take ages, but finally I was able to get Ron out of the tunnel.

48 He didn't look too well, though.

49 His face was white, and he was trying hard to stop himself from crying out from crying out.

50 I found our bikes and brought the two water bottles to Ron.

51 "Here, drink these," I said. "I'll go and get help. I'll be as quick as I can."

52 In reply, Ron simply pressed my hands.

53 I got on my bicycle and raced back along the tracks until I got to the nearest farmhouse.

54 I ran past the gate and found a woman washing some dishes in the kitchen.

55 Thanks to her, Ron was taken to the hospital, where his leg was put in a cast.

56 As soon as our parents arrived at the hospital and saw us, my mother cried with relief.

57 But all my father said was, "Let that be a lesson to you."

58 And what was the lesson? It was "*Keep out* means *Stay out of trouble*."

59 Ron is now the manager of a big company which produces helmets and other safety products.

60 And me? I am a fire fighter.

MEMO

MEMO

MEMO

적중 100 + 특별부록

Plan B

우리학교
최신기출

천재 · 이재영 교과서를 배우는

학교 시험문제 분석 · 모음 · 해설집

전국단위 학교 시험문제 수집 및 분석
출제 빈도가 높은 문제 위주로 선별
문제 풀이에 필요한 상세한 해설

중3-2
영어

천재 · 이재영

적중 100 + 특별부록
Plan B
우리학교 최신기출

중3-2
영어

천재 · 이재영

◎ 선택형 문항의 답안은 컴퓨터용 수정 싸인펜을 사용하여 OMR 답안지에 바르게 표기하시오.
◎ 서술형 문제는 답을 답안지에 반드시 검정 볼펜으로 쓰시오.
◎ 총 28문항 100점 만점입니다. 문항별 배점은 각 문항에 표시되어 있습니다.

[전북 ○○중]

01 다음은 책이 만들어지는 과정을 기록한 것이다. 빈칸에 가장 알맞은 것은?   (4점)

Authors develop an idea for a book.
They write poems, fantasies, mysteries, and other kinds of stories. Designers and editors try their best to make a good book. The book is printed at a factory and finally _____. Copies of the book are sent to libraries and bookstores.

① published
② recommended
③ housed
④ remained
⑤ discovered

[경기 ○○중]

02 다음 중 단어의 관계가 나머지 넷과 <u>다른</u> 것은?   (3점)

① treat - treatment
② express - expression
③ literary - literature
④ graduate - graduation
⑤ publish - publication

[부산 ○○중]

03 다음 대화의 흐름상 적절하지 <u>않은</u> 것은?   (4점)

Minjun: Hello, Ms. Seo.
Ms. Seo: Hi, Minjun. Long time no see. ⓐWhat brings you here?
Minjun: I have to write a book report. ⓑCan you recommend a good novel to read?
Ms. Seo: How about a mystery? There's a new Ken Kuller book, *22nd Street*.
Minjun: Oh, I've heard of him. ⓒWhy don't you buy me the book?
Ms. Seo: It's in the "New Arrivals" area. It's really popular among teens in Great Britain.
Minjun: Thank you. ⓓCan I check it out?
Ms. Seo: Sure. ⓔYou can borrow new books for seven days.
Minjun: Okay.

① ⓐ   ② ⓑ   ③ ⓒ   ④ ⓓ   ⑤ ⓔ

[전북 ○○중]

04 다음 대화의 내용과 일치하는 것은?   (3점)

G: Hey, Minjun. What are you doing?
B: Hi, Jina. I'm reading a novel for a book report.
G: Let me see. Oh, is this a new book by Ken Kuller?
B: Yeah, I borrowed it this morning. Do you know Ken Kuller?
G: Of course. I'm a big fan of his. I've read all of his mystery books.
B: I think he's a great writer. I can't stop reading this book.
G: You know what? His novel *Four Eyes* has been made into a movie.
B: Yeah. I saw the movie poster. It looks interesting.
G: It'll come out next Thursday. I'm looking forward to seeing it!
B: Maybe we can see the movie together.

① Minjun has to write a movie review.
② Minjun borrowed the book this afternoon.
③ Minjun is a big fan of Ken Kuller.
④ Ken Kuller wrote the novel, 'Four Eyes.'
⑤ 'Four Eyes' will come out next Tuesday.

05 다음 대화의 빈칸에 가장 알맞은 것은? (4점)

G: You look excited.
B: Yeah. I'm going to the Thunder concert this Friday. I can't wait!
G: Who are you going to the concert with?
B: With my mom.
G: Does your mother like hip-hop?
B: Yes, she's into hip-hop. _____
_____

① She's looking for the new phone.
② She's really looking forward to the concert.
③ She's looking forward to getting flowers at the concert.
④ She hopes you enjoy the concert.
⑤ I'm looking forward to visiting the restaurant by the river.

06 다음 대화의 빈칸 (A)에 들어갈 말로 가장 적절한 것은? (4점)

Man: Good morning, Jiho. Take a seat, please. How would you like your hair done?
Jiho: Well, I'm taking my pictures for the yearbook. So I want to look cool.
Man: When do you take the pictures?
Jiho: This Friday at Dream & Joy Park.
Man: Sounds good. Do you have a particular style in mind?
Jiho: No. Can you recommend one for me?
Man: Look at this. (A)_____
It'll look good on you.
Jiho: Wow, I like it. I can't wait to see how I'll look in the pictures.
Man: I'm sure you'll look cool.

① I recommend you try this style.
② I don't have a particular style in mind.
③ Why don't you recommend my hair style?
④ I wonder if there's a particular style in mind.
⑤ How about taking pictures of your hair style?

[7~8] 다음 대화를 읽고 물음에 답하시오.

B: Hello, Ms. Seo.
W: Hi, Chan. Long time no see. What brings you here?
B: I have to write a book report. Can you ⓐ추천하다 a good novel to read?
W: How about a mystery? There's a new Ken Kuller book, *22nd Street*.
B: Oh, I've heard of him. Can you show me the book?
W: It's in the "New Arrivals" area. It's really popular among teens in Great Britain.
B: Thank you for your help. Can I check it out?
W: Sure. You can borrow new books for seven days.
B: Okay.

B: Boy, W: Woman

07 위 대화의 ⓐ에 해당하는 영어 표현으로 옳은 것은? (2점)

① recomend
② recomeand
③ rekomend
④ rekommend
⑤ recommend

08 위 대화의 내용과 일치하는 것은? (4점)

① Chan은 영화 리뷰를 써야 한다.
② Ms. Seo는 공포 소설을 추천했다.
③ Chan은 Ken Kuller를 들어 본 적이 있다.
④ 22nd Street은 미국 10대들에게 인기 있다.
⑤ 새 책은 6일 동안 빌려서 볼 수 있다.

09 다음 〈보기〉에서 대화의 밑줄 친 표현이 의미하는 것은? (3점)

> A: I feel a little bored. <u>Can you recommend</u>
> <u>some good music?</u>
> B: I recommend you to listen to *Dynamite*
> by BTS. I'm sure you'll like it.
> A: Thanks. I'll give it a try.

> **보기**
> ⓐ 궁금한 점 묻기　　　ⓑ 허락 구하기
> ⓒ 추천 요청하기　　　ⓓ 기대 표현하기
> ⓔ 충고하기

① ⓐ　　② ⓑ　　③ ⓒ　　④ ⓓ　　⑤ ⓔ

10 다음 중 어법상 어색한 것은? (4점)

① It was Korea that achieved independence from Japan just a few months later.

② It was from Japan that Korea achieved independence just a few months later.

③ It was independence that Korea achieved from Japan just a few months later.

④ It was just a few months later that Korea achieved independence from Japan.

⑤ It was achieved that Korea independence from Japan just a few months later.

11 다음 빈칸에 들어갈 가장 적절한 표현은? (3점)

> • Sam said he _____ to bring water.
> (Sam은 물을 가져오는 것을 잊었었다고 말했다.)

① forget　　② forgets　　③ forgot
④ forgotten　　⑤ had forgotten

12 다음 중 밑줄 친 'It ~ that …'의 쓰임이 〈보기〉와 다른 것은? (4점)

> **보기**
> • <u>It</u> was Judy <u>that</u> lost her wallet on the bus.

① <u>It</u> was Jimin <u>that</u> ate the cake.

② <u>It</u> was my grandfather <u>that</u> named me Jongsu.

③ <u>It</u> is important <u>that</u> you finish your test in time.

④ <u>It</u> was a story book <u>that</u> he bought for his sister.

⑤ <u>It</u> was in 1885 <u>that</u> Vincent van Gogh painted *The Potato Eaters*.

13 다음 문장을 어법상 옳게 고쳐 다시 쓰시오. (4점)

> 1. He asked me where I had lose my puppy.
> 2. It was two years ago which Yujin got her cat.

> **조건**
> 1. 대·소문자 구분 있음.
> 2. 철자, 구두점에 유의할 것. (마침표, 콤마, 물음표 등)
> 3. 부분 점수 있음.

→ _____

14 다음 문장에서 어법상 어색한 부분을 찾아 바르게 고쳐 쓰시오. (3점)

> • It was a bad day. I lost my umbrella that my brother bought me on my birthday.

_____ → _____

[15~16] 다음 글을 읽고 물음에 답하시오.

Dong-ju was born in 1917 near Yanbin, China. As a young boy, he loved sports, and he was a soccer player for his school. He also loved sewing so much that he sewed the numbers on all his friends' soccer uniforms. (A)[Therefore / However], it was literature that he loved most. In elementary school he wrote a lot of poems. He even made a literary magazine with his cousin, Song Mong-gyu. In middle school he once borrowed a poetry book by a famous poet of the time, Baek Seok. Also, he copied the whole book by hand (B)[whereas / because] he really wanted to have his own copy of the rare book.
Dong-ju chose to study literature at a college in Seoul (C)[although / unless] his parents wanted him to be a doctor. During his college years, he often hung out with other young poets and wrote poetry where he expressed feelings about his hometown and lost country.

15 위 글을 읽고 알 수 없는 내용은? (4점)

① the year when Dong-ju was born
② the thing Dong-ju loved most as a young boy
③ the job Dong-ju wanted to have during his college years
④ the time Dong-ju made a literary magazine with his cousin
⑤ the subjects Dong-ju represented feelings about in his poetry

16 위 글의 괄호 (A), (B), (C) 안에 들어갈 말을 나열한 것으로 옳은 것은? (4점)

	(A)	(B)	(C)
①	Therefore	whereas	unless
②	However	because	although
③	Therefore	because	although
④	However	whereas	unless
⑤	Therefore	because	unless

[17~18] 다음 글을 읽고 물음에 답하시오.

Dong-ju decided ⓐto study further in the country where his father ⓑstudied before. So, in 1942, Dong-ju and his cousin began to study in Japan. On July 10 the following year, his cousin was arrested by the Japanese police for ⓒtaking part in an independence movement. Four days later, Dong-ju ⓓwas also arrested on the same charges. In 1945, Dong-ju and his cousin died in prison after harsh treatment by the police. It ⓔ was just a few months later that Korea achieved independence from Japan.

17 위 글의 분위기로 가장 적절한 것은? (4점)

① mysterious (신비로운)
② vigorous (활기찬)
③ tragic (비극적인)
④ urgent (긴박한)
⑤ peaceful (평화로운)

18 위 글의 ⓐ~ⓔ 중 어법상 바르지 못한 것은? (3점)

① ⓐ ② ⓑ ③ ⓒ ④ ⓓ ⑤ ⓔ

19 다음 글의 밑줄 친 부분이 의미하는 것을 한글로 쓰시오. (4점)

To celebrate his graduation, he wished to publish 19 of his poetry under the title, *Heaven, Wind, Stars, and Poetry*. However, his professor advised against his plan because he thought the Japanese government would not allow the publication. Dong-ju followed his advice and gave up the idea.

→ _____

[20~21] 다음 글을 읽고 물음에 답하시오.

Dong-ju ⓐwas born in 1917 near Yanbin, China. ⓑAs a young boy, he loved sports, and he was a soccer player for his school. He also loved sewing so much that he ⓒsews the numbers on all his friend's soccer uniforms. However, it was literature ⓓthat he loved most. In elementary school he wrote a lot of poems. He even made a literary magazine ⓔwith his cousin, Song Mong-gyu. In middle school he once borrowed a poetry book by a famous poet of the time, Baek Seok, and copied the whole book by hand. He really wanted to have his own copy of the rare book.

20 위 글의 밑줄 친 ⓐ~ⓔ 중 어법상 적절하지 <u>않은</u> 것은? (3점)

① ⓐ　　② ⓑ　　③ ⓒ　　④ ⓓ　　⑤ ⓔ

21 위 글을 읽고 대답할 수 <u>없는</u> 질문은? (4점)

① What is the title of Dong-ju's poem?

② What did Dong-ju do for his friends?

③ Whose book did Dong-ju copy by hand?

④ Why did Dong-ju copy a poetry book by hand?

⑤ What did Dong-ju do with his cousin in elementary school?

[22~24] 다음 글을 읽고 물음에 답하시오.

His parents wanted him to be a doctor, but Dong-ju chose to study literature at a college in Seoul. During his college years, he often ⓐhang out with other young poets and wrote poetry ⓑ where he expressed feelings about his hometown and lost country.

To celebrate his graduation, he wished to publish 19 of his poems under the title, *Heaven, Wind, Stars, and Poetry*. He made three copies of the book by hand.

ⓒOne was given to his close friend, Jeong Byeong-uk, ⓓanother was presented to his favorite professor, and ⓔthe last one was kept for himself. However, his professor advised (A)~에 반대하여 his plan because he thought the Japanese government would not allow the publication. Dong-ju followed his advice and gave up the idea.

22 위 글의 밑줄 친 ⓐ~ⓔ 중 어법상 적절하지 <u>않은</u> 것은? (3점)

① ⓐ　　② ⓑ　　③ ⓒ　　④ ⓓ　　⑤ ⓔ

23 위 글의 내용과 일치하는 것은? (4점)

① 동주는 의사가 되고 싶어 했다.

② 동주는 서울에 있는 대학에서 국어 교육학을 전공했다.

③ 동주는 고향과 잃어버린 조국에 대한 마음을 소설 속에 담았다.

④ 시집 복사본 중 하나는 절친인 정병욱에게 있다.

⑤ 교수는 한국 정부가 출판을 허락하지 않을 것이라고 했다.

24 위 글의 (A)에 들어갈 적절한 단어를 쓰시오. (4점)

조건

반드시 a로 시작하는 한 단어로 쓸 것.

→ _____

[25~26] 다음 글을 읽고 물음에 답하시오.

His parents wanted him (A)[be / to be] a doctor, but Dong-ju chose to study literature at a college in Seoul. During his college years, he often hung out with other young poets and wrote poetry (B)[which / where] he expressed feelings about his hometown and lost country. To celebrate his graduation, he wished to publish 19 of his poems under the title, *Heaven, Wind, Stars, and Poetry*. He made three copies of the book by hand. One was given to his close friend, Jeong Byeong-uk, (C)[another / the other] was presented to his favorite professor, and the last one was kept for himself. However, his professor advised against his plan because he thought the Japanese government would not allow the publication. Dong-ju followed his advice and gave up the idea.

25 위 글의 괄호 (A), (B), (C)에 들어갈 알맞은 말은? (4점)

	(A)	(B)	(C)
①	be	which	another
②	be	where	another
③	to be	which	the other
④	to be	where	the other
⑤	to be	where	another

26 위 글의 내용과 일치하지 <u>않는</u> 것은? (3점)

① 동주는 대학 시절에 젊은 시인들과 종종 어울렸다.
② 동주는 고향과 잃어버린 조국에 관한 느낌을 표현하는 시를 썼다.
③ 동주는 자신의 책 세 부를 손으로 만들었다.
④ 대학을 졸업하기 위해서 동주는 시 19편을 출판해야 했다.
⑤ 교수는 동주의 계획에 반대하는 충고를 했다.

[27~28] 다음 글을 읽고 물음에 답하시오.

Dong-ju decided to study further in the country where his father ⓐ<u>had studied</u> before. So, in 1942, Dong-ju and his cousin began to study in Japan. On July 10 the following year, his cousin ⓑ<u>was arrested</u> by the Japanese police for taking part in an independence movement. Four days later, Dong-ju was also arrested on the same charges. In 1945, Dong-ju and his cousin died in prison after harsh treatment by the police. It was just a few months later that Korea achieved independence from Japan.

In 1948, Jeong Byeong-uk brought Dong-ju's poems to the poet's brother, and they were finally published. The book ⓒ<u>had given</u> the title the poet ⓓ<u>had thought</u> of many years before. His poems ⓔ <u>are loved</u> by people of all ages, and thus they still shine brightly in our hearts like the stars in the autumn night sky.

27 위 글을 다음과 같이 표로 정리할 때 빈칸에 들어갈 알맞은 것은? (4점)

<Dong-ju's life>	
When	What
⋮	⋮
1942	started to study in Japan
1943	_____
1945	died in prison
1948	His poetry book was published.

① arrested by the Japanese police
② loved by people of all ages in Korea
③ decided to study in a foreign country
④ wrote poems in prison with his cousin
⑤ Korea achieved independence from Japan.

28 위 글의 ⓐ~ⓔ 중 어법상 <u>어색한</u> 것은? (3점)

① ⓐ had studied　　② ⓑ was arrested
③ ⓒ had given　　④ ⓓ had thought
⑤ ⓔ are loved

◎ 선택형 문항의 답안은 컴퓨터용 수정 싸인펜을 사용
하여 OMR 답안지에 바르게 표기하시오.
◎ 서술형 문제는 답을 답안지에 반드시 검정 볼펜으
로 쓰시오.
◎ 총 28문항 100점 만점입니다. 문항별 배점은 각
문항에 표시되어 있습니다.

B: Thank you for your help. Can I check ⓔ
it out?
W: Sure. You can borrow new books for
seven days.
B: Okay.

B: Boy W: Woman

① ⓐ   ② ⓑ   ③ ⓒ   ④ ⓓ   ⑤ ⓔ

[서울 관악구 ○○중]

01 다음 중 단어의 성격이 <u>다른</u> 하나는?   (2점)

① poem   ② poet   ③ reader

④ librarian   ⑤ illustrator

[경북 ○○중]

02 다음 중 영영 풀이가 적절하지 <u>않은</u> 것은?   (4점)

① harsh: pleasant or painful

② rare: unusual, not common

③ poet: a person who writes poems

④ longing: a strong feeling of wanting
something

⑤ sew: to use a needle and thread to make or
repair clothes

[경기 ○○중]

[4~5] 다음 대화를 읽고 물음에 답하시오.

W: Good morning, Jiho.
M: Good morning.
W: Take a seat, please. How would you like your
hair done?
M: Well, I'm taking my pictures for the yearbook.
So I want to look cool. (A)
W: When do you take the pictures? (B)
M: This Friday at Dream & Joy Park.
W: Sounds good. (C)
M: No. Can you recommend one for me?
W: Look at this. How about this style? It'll look
good on you. (D)
M: Wow, I like it. I can't wait to see how I'll look
in the pictures. (E)
W: I'm sure you'll look cool.

W: Woman M: Man

[경기 ○○중]

03 다음 대화의 밑줄 친 ⓐ~ⓔ 중 가리키는 대상이 나머지 넷과
<u>다른</u> 것은?   (3점)

B: Hello, Ms. Seo.
W: Hi, Minjun. Long time no see. What
brings you here?
B: I have to write ⓐa book report. Can you
recommend a good novel to read?
W: How about a mystery? There's a new
Ken Kuller book, ⓑ*22nd Street*.
B: Oh, I've heard of him. Can you show
me the book?
W: ⓒIt's in the "New Arrivals" area. ⓓIt's
really popular among teens in Great
Britain.

04 위 대화의 마지막에 드러난 남자의 심정으로 가장 적절한 것
은?   (4점)

① confused   ② frightened

③ concerned   ④ pleased

⑤ disappointed

05 위 대화의 (A)~(E) 중 주어진 문장이 들어가기에 가장 적절한
곳은?   (3점)

Do you have a particular style in mind?

① (A)   ② (B)   ③ (C)   ④ (D)   ⑤ (E)

[6~7] Read the following dialogue and answer the questions.

Minjun: Hello, Ms. Seo.

Seo: Minjun. Long time no see. What brings you here?

Minjun: I have to write a book report. Can you recommend a good novel to read?

Seo: How about a mystery? There's a new Ken Kuller book, *22nd Street*.

Minjun: I've heard of him. Can you show me the book?

Seo: ⓐIt's in the "New Arrivals" area. It's really popular among teens in Great Britain.

Minjun: Thank you for your help. Can I check it out?

Seo: Sure. You can borrow new books for 7 days.

Cathy: Hey, Minjun. What are you doing?

Minjun: I'm reading a novel for a book report.

Cathy: Let me see. ⓑI've recently joined that book club. Oh, is this a new book by Ken Kuller?

Minjun: Yeah, I borrowed it this morning. Do you know Ken Kuller?

Cathy: Of course. ⓒI'm a big fan of his. I've read all of his mystery books.

Minjun: I think he's a great writer. I can't stop reading this book.

Cathy: You know what? ⓓHis novel *Four Eyes* has been made into a movie.

Minjun: Yeah. I saw the movie poster. It looks interesting.

Cathy: It'll come out next Thursday. ⓔI can't wait to see it!

Minjun: Maybe we can see the movie together.

06 Which of the following sentences can be inferred from the dialogue above? (4점)

① Minjun is in a bookstore with Ms. Seo.

② Minjun has visited Ms. Seo very often recently.

③ The book *22nd Street* was published a long time ago.

④ Cathy and Minjun don't agree on Ken Kuller's works.

⑤ Minjun wants to watch the movie *Four Eyes* with Cathy.

07 Which of the sentences ⓐ~ⓔ does NOT relate to the context? (3점)

① ⓐ   ② ⓑ   ③ ⓒ   ④ ⓓ   ⑤ ⓔ

08 다음 대화의 내용과 일치하는 것은? (4점)

Jiyeon: Hey, Minjun. What are you doing?

Minjun: Hi, Jiyeon. I'm reading a novel for a book report.

Jiyeon: Let me see. Oh, is this a new book by Ken Kuller?

Minjun: Yeah, I borrowed it this morning. Do you know Ken Kuller?

Jiyeon: Of course. I'm a big fan of his. I've read all of his mystery books.

Minjun: I think he's a great writer. I can't stop reading this book.

Jiyeon: You know what? His novel *Four Eyes* has been made into a movie.

Minjun: Yeah. I saw the movie poster. It looks interesting.

Jiyeon: It'll come out next Thursday. I'm looking forward to seeing it!

Minjun: Maybe we can see the movie together.

① Jiyeon borrowed a new book by Ken Kuller this morning.

② Minjun has read all of Ken Kuller's mystery books.

③ Ken Kuller is a big fan of mystery books.

④ Minjun watched the movie, *Four Eyes*.

⑤ Jiyeon can't wait to see the movie, *Four Eyes*.

09 Which of the following questions CANNOT be answered? (4점)

> Ken: Good morning, Jiho. Take a seat, please. How would you like your hair done?
> Jiho: Well, I'm taking my pictures for the yearbook. So I want to look cool.
> Ken: When do you take the pictures?
> Jiho: This Friday.
> Ken: Sounds good. Do you have a particular style in mind?
> Jiho: No. Can you recommend one for me?
> Ken: Look at this. How about this style? It'll look good on you.
> Jiho: Wow, I like it. I want to see how I'll look in the pictures.
> Ken: I'm sure you'll look cool.

① How does Jiho want to look?
② Why does Jiho take pictures?
③ Where does Jiho take pictures?
④ What does Jiho ask Ken to do?
⑤ What is the relationship between Jiho and Ken?

10 다음 밑줄 친 부분 중 문장에서의 쓰임이 <u>다른</u> 하나는? (3점)

① It was at the park <u>that</u> we met Mina.
② It was in 2014 <u>that</u> the building was built.
③ It was a wallet <u>that</u> I bought for his gift.
④ It was no surprise <u>that</u> she passed the exam.
⑤ It was my little brother <u>that</u> broke the vase.

11 다음 문장에서 her wallet을 강조하여 문장을 다시 쓰시오. (4점)

> • Judy lost her wallet on the bus.

조건

> 1. 반드시 It과 that을 사용하여 적을 것.
> 2. 철자, 대·소문자 구분, 구두점에 유의할 것. (마침표, 콤마 등)
> 3. 부분 점수 있음.

→ _____

12 다음 중 어법상 옳은 것은? (4점)

① He had already leave when I returned home.
② When I got home, the pizza party had finished.
③ When he got to school, the class already began.
④ Jake was late for school because he missed the bus.
⑤ When she came back, she found someone opened the door.

13 다음 밑줄 친 부분을 어법상 바르게 고친 것은? (4점)

① When I got home, my favorite TV show <u>ended</u>. → has ended
② <u>It was on Saturdays</u> that they take swimming lessons. → That was on Saturdays
③ Dobin forgot to bring the report that <u>he already finished</u>. → he already had finished
④ Susan had never been to Gumi before <u>she has been 16</u>. → she had been 16
⑤ <u>It was Antonio which</u> watched the accident on the street yesterday. → It was Antonio that

[14~16] 다음 글을 읽고 물음에 답하시오.

Dong-ju decided to study further in the country where his father (A)_____ before. So, in 1942, Dong-ju and his cousin began to study in Japan. On July 10 the following year, his cousin was arrested by the Japanese police for taking part in an independence movement. Four days later, Dong-ju was also arrested on the same charges. In 1945, Dong-ju and his cousin died in prison after harsh treatment by the police. Korea achieved independence from Japan (B)just a few months later.

In 1948, Jeong Byeong-uk brought Dong-ju's poems to the poet's brother, and they were finally published. The book was given the title the poet had thought of many years before. His poems are loved by people of all ages, and thus they still shine brightly in our hearts like the stars in the autumn night sky.

14 위 글의 빈칸 (A)에 가장 알맞은 동사의 형태는? (3점)

① studies
② was studying
③ had studied
④ has studied
⑤ has been studied

15 위 글의 밑줄 친 부분 (B)를 강조하여 문장으로 쓰시오. (4점)

→ _____

16 위 글의 내용과 일치하지 않는 것은? (3점)

① Dong-ju began to study in Japan in 1942.
② Dong-ju's cousin was arrested by the Japanese police for taking part in an independence movement in 1943.

③ Dong-ju was also arrested on the same charges.
④ Dong-ju died in prison after harsh treatment by the police in 1945.
⑤ The book's title was different from what Dong-ju had thought.

[17~18] 다음 글을 읽고 물음에 답하시오.

Dong-ju was born in 1917 near Yanbin, China. As a young boy, he loved sports, and he was a soccer player for his school. He also loved sewing so much that he sewed the numbers on all his friends' soccer uniforms. However, ⓐhe loved literature most. In elementary school he wrote a lot of (A)_____. He even made a literary magazine with his cousin, Song Mong-gyu. In middle school he once borrowed a (B)_____ book by a famous (C)_____ of the time, Baek Seok, and copied the whole book by hand. He really wanted to have his own copy of the rare book.

17 위 글의 빈칸 (A)~(C)에 각각 알맞은 것을 골라 바르게 짝지은 것은? (3점)

	(A)	(B)	(C)
①	poem	poetry	poet
②	poem	poet	poems
③	poems	poetry	poems
④	poem	poet	poetry
⑤	poems	poetry	poet

18 위 글에서 밑줄 친 ⓐ가 구체적으로 드러난 세 가지의 사례를 찾아 우리말로 적으시오. (5점)

→ (1) _____
　　(2) _____
　　(3) _____

[19~21] 다음 글을 읽고 물음에 답하시오.

Dong-ju's parents wanted him (A)[being / to be] a doctor, but he chose (B)[studying / to study] literature at a college in Seoul. During his college years, he often hung out with other young poets and wrote poetry where he expressed feelings about his hometown and lost country. To celebrate his graduation, he wished (C)[publishing / to publish] 19 of his poems under ⓐthe title, *Heaven, Wind, Stars, and Poetry*. He made three copies of ⓑthe book by hand. ⓒOne was given to his close friend, Jeong Byeong-uk, ⓓanother was presented to his favorite professor, and ⓔthe last one was kept for himself.

19 위 글의 괄호 (A), (B), (C) 안에서 어법에 맞는 표현으로 가장 적절한 것은? (4점)

	(A)	(B)	(C)
①	being	studying	publishing
②	being	to study	publishing
③	being	to study	to publish
④	to be	studying	to publish
⑤	to be	to study	to publish

20 위 글의 밑줄 친 ⓐ~ⓔ 중 가리키는 대상이 나머지 넷과 <u>다른</u> 것은? (2점)

① ⓐ ② ⓑ ③ ⓒ ④ ⓓ ⑤ ⓔ

21 위 글의 내용과 일치하는 것은? (4점)

① 동주는 의사가 되고 싶어 했다.
② 동주는 대학 시절에 다른 젊은 시인들을 멀리했다.
③ 동주는 대학 시절에 잃어버린 조국에 대한 시를 썼다.
④ 동주는 '하늘과 별과 바람과 시'라는 제목의 시를 썼다.
⑤ 동주는 교수님에게서 시집을 선물 받았다.

[22~23] 다음 글을 읽고 물음에 답하시오.

Dong-ju decided to study further in the country where his father ⓐhad studied before. So, in 1942, Dong-ju and his cousin began to study in Japan. On July 10 the following year, his cousin was arrested by the Japanese police for ⓑ<u>participating in</u> an independence movement. Four days later, Dong-ju was also arrested on the same charges. In 1945, Dong-ju and his cousin died in prison after harsh treatment by the police. It was just a few months later that Korea ⓒ<u>was achieved</u> independence from Japan.

In 1948, Jeong Byeong-uk brought Dong-ju's poems to the poet's brother, and they were finally published. The book was given the title ⓓ<u>that</u> the poet had thought of many years before. His poems are loved by people of all ages, and thus they still shine brightly in our hearts ⓔ<u>like</u> the stars in the autumn night sky.

22 위 글의 ⓐ~ⓔ 중 어법상 옳지 <u>않은</u> 것은? (3점)

① ⓐ ② ⓑ ③ ⓒ ④ ⓓ ⑤ ⓔ

23 위 글의 내용과 일치하는 것은? (4점)

① Dong-ju had never studied abroad in his life.
② Korea didn't gain independence until Dong-ju died.
③ His poems are still loved by people of a certain age.
④ Dong-ju wasn't arrested for the same reason why his cousin was.
⑤ A friend of Dong-ju created the title of poetry book written by Dong-ju.

Dong-ju decided to study ⓐ더 in the country ⓑw_____ his father ⓒ공부했었던 before. So, in 1942, Dong-ju and his cousin began to study in Japan. On July 10 the following year, his cousin was arrested by the Japanese police for taking part in an independence movement. Four days later, Dong-ju was also arrested on the same charges. In 1945, Dong-ju and his cousin died in prison after harsh treatment by the police. (A)It was just a few months later that Korea achieved independence from Japan.
In 1948, Jeong Byeong-uk brought Dong-ju's poems to the poet's brother, and they were finally published. The book was given the title the poet had thought of many years before. His poems are loved by people of all ages, and thus they still shine brightly in our hearts like the starts in the autumn night sky.

24 위 글의 (A)에서 강조하는 부분으로 알맞은 것은?　　(3점)

① just

② Korea

③ independence

④ just a few months later

⑤ Korea achieved independence from Japan

25 위 글의 ⓐ, ⓑ, ⓒ에 들어갈 표현을 쓰시오.　　(4점)

> 조건
> 1. ⓐ는 f로 시작하는 단어로 쓸 것.
> 2. ⓑ는 w로 시작하는 관계부사를 쓸 것.
> 3. ⓒ는 '공부했었던'을 study를 이용하여 쓸 것.

ⓐ _____　ⓑ _____　ⓒ _____

26 Why were Dong-ju and his cousin arrested by the Japanese police?　　(5점)

> 조건
> 1. 본문의 내용을 활용하여 문장으로 답을 쓸 것.
> 2. 부분 점수 있음.

→ _____

27 다음 밑줄 친 ⓐ와 ⓑ가 의미하는 것은?　　(4점)

Do you enjoy plays, poems, novels, or cartoons? ⓐThey are different kinds of literature, and people differ in which kind ⓑthey prefer. However, all of them allow us to go beyond our own small world where we live. When we read literature, we come across the ideas of great writers who lived long ago. We can even imagine being someone else or living in a completely different place. In short, literature opens up for us new worlds that we have never visited before.

	ⓐ	ⓑ
①	the ideas of great writers	writers
②	the ideas of great writers	kinds
③	our own small world	people
④	plays, poems, novels, or cartoons	kinds
⑤	plays, poems, novels, or cartoons	people

28 다음 문장에서 틀린 부분을 찾아 바르게 고쳐 문장으로 다시 쓰시오.　　(3점)

> • The last book kept for himself.

→ _____

◎ 선택형 문항의 답안은 컴퓨터용 수정 싸인펜을 사용하여 OMR 답안지에 바르게 표기하시오.
◎ 서술형 문제는 답을 답안지에 반드시 검정 볼펜으로 쓰시오.
◎ 총 26문항 100점 만점입니다. 문항별 배점은 각 문항에 표시되어 있습니다.

[부산 ○○중]

01 다음 중 밑줄 친 단어의 쓰임이 어색한 것은? (3점)

① Oops, I didn't notice you.

② Please lie the food on the table.

③ A: The water is getting thick.

　 B: Yes. People are polluting the river.

④ Some people just don't value what they have.

⑤ They should learn how to use their resources more wisely.

[전북 ○○중]

02 다음 단어의 영영 풀이가 바르지 못한 것은? (4점)

① graze: to eat something in a restaurant

② value: to think that something is important

③ lesson: something to be learned

④ common: a piece of land used jointly

⑤ notice: to become aware of something

[전북 ○○중]

03 다음 중 자연스러운 대화가 되도록 바르게 배열한 것은? (3점)

G: Wow, it feels great to be on this ship, Dad.

M: I feel the same, Sora. Here are our seats, 20A and 20B.

G: Yeah. Do you mind if I take the window seat? I like to see the view outside.

M: No problem.

(A) If I were you, I wouldn't eat anything like that.

(B) They may make you seasick.

(C) Why is that?

(D) By the way, I want to eat something like noodles or sandwiches.

G: Oh, I see. Then, I'll have some ice cream.

M: That's not a good idea, either. Let's eat after we arrive.

① (A)-(B)-(C)-(D)　　② (B)-(A)-(D)-(C)

③ (D)-(A)-(C)-(B)　　④ (D)-(B)-(C)-(A)

⑤ (C)-(A)-(B)-(D)

[경기 ○○중]

04 다음 대화의 내용과 일치하지 않는 것은? (4점)

G: Thanks for letting me volunteer here, Ms. Yun.

W: It's my pleasure, Jimin, I'm glad you decided to help.

G: Well, what should I do?

W: Today's lesson is about taking photos with smartphones. Why don't you help the slow learners?

G: Okay. Is there anything I should know?

W: Yes. Please be patient and kind to the learners.

G: I'll keep that in mind. By the way, do you mind if I use your charger? My battery is a little low.

W: Of course not. Go right ahead.

*G: Jimin, W: Ms. Yun

① Jimin will be responsible for the slow learners.

② Ms. Yun does not allow Jimin to use her charger.

③ Jimin needs patience to deal with the learners.

④ Jimin is going to help the learners use the smartphones.

⑤ Ms. Yun is pleased Jimin participated in the volunteer work.

05 다음 중 대화가 <u>어색한</u> 것은? (3점)

① A: I didn't bring my science homework.

　B: If I were you, I'd talk to the teacher.

② A: I'm too sleepy.

　B: If I were you, I'd take a nap.

③ A: I found a fly in my soup.

　B: Why don't you send the soup back and ask for a refund?

④ A: I broke my friend's umbrella.

　B: I think you should drink some cold water.

⑤ A: I have a runny nose and a sore throat.

　B: If I were you, I would wear a warm coat.

[6~7] Read the following dialogue and answer the questions.

Minsu: Jimin, have you decided where to volunteer?

Jimin: Not yet. Do you know a good place to volunteer?

Minsu: (A)_____.

Jimin: The community center? What can I do there?

Minsu: There's a smartphone class for senior citizens, and they're looking for volunteers.

Jimin: That sounds interesting, but I've never taught anyone.

Minsu: Don't worry. All you need to do is help the teacher there.

Jimin: Okay. Thanks for your advice. I will go to the community center then.

06 According to the dialogue, which of the following is correct? (4점)

① Jimin does not know how to use a smartphone.

② There is a teacher at the community center.

③ Minsu likes to teach senior citizens at the community center.

④ Jimin and Minsu will volunteer together at the community center.

⑤ Jimin had decided where to volunteer before Minsu recommended her a good place.

07 위 대화의 (A)에 들어갈 수 있는 Minsu의 advice를 조건에 맞게 서술하시오. (5점)

　조건

• 대화의 흐름에 맞게 서술할 것.

• 자원봉사를 할 장소가 드러나는 advice를 가정법 과거를 사용하여 서술할 것.

• 주어와 서술어가 나타나는 완전한 문장으로 서술할 것.

→ _____

08 다음 〈보기〉에서 대화의 밑줄 친 표현이 의미하는 것은? (3점)

A: I didn't bring my English homework.

B: <u>If I were you, I'd talk to an English teacher, Mr. Lee.</u>

A: Thanks for your advice.

　보기

ⓐ 궁금한 점 묻기　　　ⓑ 허락 구하기

ⓒ 추천 요청하기　　　ⓓ 기대 표현하기

ⓔ 충고하기

① ⓐ　　② ⓑ　　③ ⓒ　　④ ⓓ　　⑤ ⓔ

[9∼10] 다음 대화를 읽고 물음에 답하시오.

> G: Wow, it feels great to be on this ship, Dad.
> M: I feel the same, Sora. Here are our seats, 20A and 20B.
> G: Yeah. Do you mind if I take the window seat? I like to see the view outside.
> M: No problem.
> G: By the way, I want to eat something like noodles or sandwiches.
> M: If I were you, I wouldn't eat anything like that.
> G: Why is that?
> M: They may make you ⓐ_____.
> G: Oh, I see. Then, I'll have some ice cream.
> M: That's not a good idea, either. Let's eat after we arrive.
>
> *M: Dad, G: Sora

09 위 대화의 내용상 빈칸 ⓐ에 알맞은 것은? (3점)

① happy ② seasick ③ sleepy
④ angry ⑤ hungry

10 위 대화의 내용으로 알 수 <u>없는</u> 것은? (3점)

① 소라와 아빠는 배를 탔다.
② 소라는 창가 자리에 앉았다.
③ 소라는 샌드위치를 먹고 싶어 한다.
④ 소라는 아이스크림을 먹는 것을 좋아한다.
⑤ 아빠는 배에서 내려 음식을 먹자고 제안했다.

11 다음 빈칸에 공통으로 들어갈 말로 적절한 것은? (4점)

> • It is very smart _____ you to answer the question.
> • It was careless _____ her to leave her cell phone in the taxi.

① to ② of ③ by
④ at ⑤ for

12 다음 중 어법상 올바른 문장은? (4점)

① It is stupid of you to believe her.
② It will be easy for Tom passing the exam.
③ She is dangerous for her to swim in this river.
④ It was hard of my uncle to finding a good job.
⑤ It is important to students to have breakfast every day.

13 다음 중 문장 전환이 바르게 된 것은? (5점)

① As I am not you, I won't do anything.
  → If I were not you, I would do something.
② If it were sunny, we could go on a picnic.
  → As it wasn't sunny, we couldn't go on a picnic.
③ If she lived in China, she could speak Chinese.
  → As she lives in China, she can speak Chinese.
④ As I don't have enough money, I can't buy you a present.
  → If I had enough money, I could buy you a present.
⑤ If I were in Paris, I could attend my cousin's wedding.
  → As I wasn't in Paris, I can't attend my cousin's wedding.

[14～17] 다음 글을 읽고 물음에 답하시오.

(가) Once upon a time there was a small village in a forest. The villagers were farmers and raised cows. Luckily, some good grassland lay in the middle of the village.

Everyone was allowed ⓐ(use) the grassland. Therefore, it ⓑ(call) "the commons." By tradition, each family only had one cow, so (A)(각 소들이 충분한 풀을 찾는 것은 쉬운 일이었다). The grass on the commons was green all summer long.

(나) But one day a villager broke (B)the rule. He brought another cow and let it graze on the commons. He thought that nobody would notice it. A happy feeling filled his heart when he thought of the milk and cheese that the second cow would bring to his family.

A few days later, the farmer visited a close friend who had four children. He wanted to help his friend, so he told him in secret, "Why don't you bring in one more cow and raise it on the commons?" The friend thanked him and did as he was told the next day.

14 위 글의 (가)의 내용과 일치하지 <u>않는</u> 것은? (3점)

① 숲속 작은 마을의 주민들은 소를 기르는 농부였다.
② 주민들은 마을 한 가운데에 목초지를 만들었다.
③ 주민들의 각 가정에는 소가 한 마리씩 있었다.
④ 목초지의 풀은 마을의 소들이 먹기에 충분했다.
⑤ 공유지의 풀은 여름 내내 푸르렀다.

15 위 글의 ⓐ, ⓑ의 형태가 바르게 짝지어진 것은? (3점)

	ⓐ	ⓑ
①	using	called
②	to use	called
③	using	had called
④	using	was called
⑤	to use	was called

16 위 글의 밑줄 친 우리말 (A)를 아래 〈조건〉에 맞게 영어로 쓰시오. (5점)

조건

1. 10 단어로 쓸 것.
2. 주어와 동사를 포함하는 완전한 한 문장의 영어로 쓸 것.
3. 아래 어구를 반드시 포함할 것. (단, 필요시 형태를 변형하시오.)
   be, each cow, enough grass, find, it, to

→ _____

17 위 글의 (나)의 밑줄 친 (B)the rule에 해당하는 것은? (4점)

① 각 가구가 돌아가면서 공유지를 감독하는 것
② 모든 마을 사람들이 공유지를 사용할 수 있는 것
③ 한 가정에서 한 마리의 소만 공유지를 이용하는 것
④ 각 가구의 소가 공유지에서 먹을 수 있는 풀의 양을 제한하는 것
⑤ 한 마리 이상의 소를 공유지에 데려오기 위해서 다른 농부들의 동의가 있어야 하는 것

[18~20] 다음 글을 읽고 물음에 답하시오.

ⓐ~의 수는 cows rose slowly at first. Then the cow population grew more quickly. The grass on the commons began to (A)_____, and it became (B)_____ for the cows to find grass to eat. ⓑ 엎친 데 덮친 격으로, it did not rain for a long time. In the past, when a dry year came, the small number of cows on the commons always found ⓒ 먹을 것. However, no grass was left now because there were too many cows. ⓓ상황은 were harsh for the villagers; many of the cows died. ⓔ마침내, the grass came back. Now it was able to support only one cow per family. The village went back to the one-family-one-cow rule. The villagers all learned an important lesson: when resources are shared, it is important for everyone (C)_____. The villagers now tell this story to their children. They call it "The Story of the Commons."

18 위 글의 빈칸 (A), (B)에 들어갈 알맞은 말로 짝지어진 것은?
(4점)

	(A)	(B)
①	grow	easier
②	raise	harder
③	appear	harder
④	disappear	easier
⑤	disappear	harder

19 위 글의 밑줄 친 ⓐ~ⓔ의 올바른 표현이 <u>아닌</u> 것은? (3점)

① ⓐ - A number of

② ⓑ - To make matters worse

③ ⓒ - something to eat

④ ⓓ - Things

⑤ ⓔ - At last

20 위 글의 빈칸 (C)에 들어갈 말로 가장 알맞은 것은? (4점)

① to develop the resources

② to learn the environment

③ to value the resources and use them fairly

④ to protect their children from every danger

⑤ to make decisions how to raise their cows

[21~22] 다음 글을 읽고 물음에 답하시오.

A few days later, the farmer visited a close friend who had four children. He wanted to help his friend, so he told him in secret, "내가 당신이라면, 나는 소를 한 마리 더 데려와 공유지에서 키우겠어요." The friend thanked him and did as he was told the next day. Soon, other villagers did the same. Some secretly brought one more cow to the commons, while others brought even more to the grassland without telling anyone. They thought that there would be enough grass for the _____ cows. Soon the village was full of happy-looking farmers!

21 위 글의 빈칸에 가장 알맞은 것은? (4점)

① additional ② traditional

③ natural ④ national

⑤ magical

22 위 글의 우리말을 다음 어구를 사용하여 영어로 옮기시오.
(5점)

> (bring in / on the commons / and raise it / one more cow)

→ _____, _____.

[23~26] Read the passages below and answer the questions.

(가) But one day, a villager broke the rule. He brought another cow and let it graze on the commons. He thought that nobody would notice it. A happy feeling filled his heart when he thought of the milk and cheese that the second cow would bring to his family.

A few days later, the farmer visited a close friend who had four children. He wanted to help his friend, so he told him what he did in secret. "If I were you, I would bring in one more cow and raise it on the commons." The friend thanked him and did ⓐas he was told the next day.

(나) Soon, other villagers did the same. Some secretly brought one more cow to the commons, (A)[if / while] others brought even more to the grassland without telling anyone.

(B)[A number of / The number of] cows rose slowly at first. Then the cow population grew more quickly. The grass on the commons began to disappear, and it became harder for the cows to find grass to eat. To make matters worse, it did not rain for a long time. No grass was left because there were too many cows. Things were harsh for the villagers; many of the cows died.

(다) Once upon a time there was a small village in a forest. The villagers were farmers and raised cows. Luckily, some good grassland (C)[lie / lay] in the middle of the village.

Everyone was allowed to use the grassland. Therefore, it was called "the commons." By tradition each family only had one cow, so it was easy for each cow in the village to find enough grass to eat. The grass on the commons was green all summer long.

23 Which of the following is the correct order? (4점)

① (가)-(나)-(다)
② (나)-(가)-(다)
③ (나)-(다)-(가)
④ (다)-(가)-(나)
⑤ (다)-(나)-(가)

24 위 글의 밑줄 친 ⓐas he was told가 나타내는 문장을 찾아 첫 두 단어와 마지막 두 단어를 쓰시오. (4점)

→ _____

25 Which of the following is most appropriate for (A)~(C)? (4점)

	(A)	(B)	(C)
①	if	A number of	lie
②	if	The number of	lay
③	while	A number of	lie
④	while	The number of	lie
⑤	while	The number of	lay

26 위 글을 통해서 마을 사람들이 배울 수 있는 교훈으로 가장 적절한 것은? (5점)

① Be brave and face the difficulties.
② Value the shared resources and use them fairly.
③ It is common for a family to raise only one cow.
④ Do not waste the resources and protect the environment.
⑤ Nobody can use the grassland for everyone in the village.

3학년 영어 2학기 중간고사(6과) 2회

문항수 : 선택형(21문항) 서술형(6문항)   20 . . .

◎ 선택형 문항의 답안은 컴퓨터용 수정 싸인펜을 사용
하여 OMR 답안지에 바르게 표기하시오.
◎ 서술형 문제는 답을 답안지에 반드시 검정 볼펜으
로 쓰시오.
◎ 총 27문항 100점 만점입니다. 문항별 배점은 각
문항에 표시되어 있습니다.

[경북 ○○중]

01 다음 밑줄 친 단어의 쓰임이 올바르게 된 것은?   (4점)

① Have you <u>lied</u> a new carpet in the living room?
② I have never <u>sat</u> on such a comfortable chair before.
③ The vegetable prices have <u>raised</u> sharply since March.
④ Elizabeth was tired and <u>laid</u> on the floor to take a nap.
⑤ When she asked the students a difficult question, no hand was <u>risen</u>.

[경기 ○○중]

02 다음 빈칸에 공통으로 들어갈 말로 알맞은 것은?   (3점)

> • When you cross the street, _____ your hand.
> • My grandparents _____ about 200 cows on their farm.

① put   ② take   ③ rise
④ keep   ⑤ raise

[경기 ○○중]

03 다음 중 A, B의 대화가 <u>어색한</u> 것은?   (4점)

① A: Do you mind if I sit here?
   B: Not at all, you can't.
② A: Have you decided what to eat?
   B: Not yet.
③ A: What can I do there?
   B: You can help the senior citizens.
④ A: Do you know a good place to volunteer?
   B: If I were you, I'd go to the community center.
⑤ A: Thanks for letting me volunteer here, Ms. Yun.
   B: It's my pleasure.

[부산 ○○중]

04 다음 대화를 읽고 우리말 (A)를 아래 〈조건〉에 맞게 영어로 쓰시오.   (5점)

> Minjun: Jimin, have you decided where to volunteer?
> Jimin: Not yet. Do you know a good place to go?
> Minjun: (A)(내가 너라면, 지역 주민 센터에 갈 거야).
> Jimin: The community center? What can I do there?
> Minjun: There's a smartphone class for senior citizens, and they're looking for volunteers.
> Jimin: That sounds interesting, but I've never taught anyone.
> Minjun: Don't worry. All you need to do is help the teacher there.
> Jimin: Okay. Thanks for your advice.

조건
1. 10개 이상의 단어를 사용할 것.
2. 주어와 동사를 포함하는 완전한 한 문장의 영어로 쓸 것.
3. 아래 표현을 반드시 사용할 것. (단, 'I'는 두 번 사용할 것.)
   I, if, the community center, to

→ _____, _____.

[5~6] 다음 대화를 읽고 물음에 답하시오.

> G: Wow, it feels great to be on this ship, Dad.
>
> M: I feel the same, Sora. Here are our seats, 20A and 20B.
>
> G: Yeah. (A)제가 창가 자리에 앉아도 될까요? I like to see the view outside.
>
> M: No problem.
>
> G: By the way, I want to eat something like noodles or sandwiches.
>
> M: If I were you, I wouldn't eat anything like that.
>
> G: Why is that?
>
> M: That may make you seasick.
>
> G: Oh, I see. Then, I'll have some ice cream.
>
> M: That's not a good idea, either. Let's eat after we arrive.
>
> G: Sora, M: Dad

05 위 대화의 내용과 일치하지 <u>않는</u> 것은? (3점)

① 아빠와 소라의 자리는 20A, 20B이다.

② 소라는 바깥 풍경을 보고 싶어 한다.

③ 아빠는 소라가 창가 자리에 앉는 것을 거절하신다.

④ 소라는 국수나 샌드위치 같은 것을 먹고 싶어 한다.

⑤ 아빠는 소라가 먹고 싶어하는 것을 말리신다.

06 위 대화의 (A)를 〈보기〉를 참고하여 영어로 쓰시오. (3점)

> **보기**
>
> Do / mind / if / take / the window seat / I /
> you

> **조건**
>
> 1. 대 · 소문자 구분 있음.
>
> 2. 철자, 구두점에 유의할 것. (마침표, 콤마, 물음표 등)
>
> 3. 부분 점수 있음.

→ _____

07 다음 그림 속에서 남학생이 부탁한 말을 주어진 어구를 사용하여 완성하시오. (4점)

> M: _____?
>
>   (mind / if / have / an extra orange)
>
> W: Sorry, you can't. We should save the oranges for other students.
>
> M: Okay, then.

→ _____

08 다음 밑줄 친 ⓐ~ⓔ 중 대화의 흐름상 <u>어색한</u> 것은? (4점)

> G: Thanks for letting me volunteer here, Ms. Yun.
>
> W: ⓐIt's my pleasure, Jimin. I'm glad you decided to help.
>
> G: Well, what should I do?
>
> W: Today's lesson is about taking photos with smartphones. ⓑWhy don't you help the slow learners?
>
> G: Okay. ⓒIs there anything I should know?
>
> W: Yes. Please be patient and kind to the learners.
>
> G: ⓓI'll keep that in mind. By the way, do you mind if I use your charger? My battery is a little low.
>
> W: ⓔOf course. Go right ahead.

① ⓐ　　② ⓑ　　③ ⓒ　　④ ⓓ　　⑤ ⓔ

09 다음 빈칸 (A), (B)에 들어갈 말을 나열한 것으로 옳은 것은? (3점)

> G: Wow, it feels great to be on this ship, Dad.
> M: I feel the same, Sora. Here are our seats, 20A and 20B.
> G: Yeah. Do you mind if I take the window seat? I like to see the view outside.
> M: No problem.
> G: (A)_____, I want to eat something like noodles or sandwiches.
> M: If I were you, I wouldn't eat anything like that.
> G: Why is that?
> M: They may make you seasick.
> G: Oh, I see. Then, I'll have some ice cream.
> M: That's not a good idea, (B)_____. Let's eat after we arrive.

	(A)	(B)
①	By the way	either
②	However	either
③	By the way	too
④	However	too
⑤	Therefore	neither

10 다음 우리말을 영어로 바르게 옮긴 것은? (4점)

> • 그들이 그 창문을 수리하는 것은 가능하다.

① They are possible to repair the window.
② That is possible them to repair the window.
③ It is possible them to repair the window.
④ It is possible for their to repair the window.
⑤ It is possible for them to repair the window.

11 다음 우리말을 영어 문장으로 쓰시오. (5점)

> • 내가 만약 차가 있다면, 부산으로 여행을 갈 텐데.

조건
1. If와 travel을 사용하여 문장을 답안으로 작성할 것.
2. 대·소문자 구분 있음.
3. 철자, 구두점에 유의할 것. (마침표, 콤마, 물음표 등)
4. 부분 점수 있음.

→ _____

12 다음 중 어법상 옳은 것은? (4점)

① It isn't easy of me to make decisions.
② It is helpful for me to go swimming.
③ It is good to me for exercise regularly.
④ If I am a cat, I could sleep all day long.
⑤ If I were a CEO, I would working at home.

13 다음 중 어법상 바른 문장은? (4점)

① If I'll have enough time, I would take a walk.
② Is it necessary for her to rewrite the report?
③ He lost his umbrella that his mother has given him this morning.
④ It was 1776 that the U.S. gained its independence from Great Britain.
⑤ The interviewer is asking him how long he had worked for the company.

[14~16] 다음 글을 읽고 물음에 답하시오.

(A) In the past, when a dry year came, the small number of cows on the commons always found something to eat. (B) However, no grass was left now because there were too many cows. (C) Things were harsh for the villagers; many of the cows died.

(D) Now it was able to support only one cow per family. The village went back to the one-family-one-cow rule. The villagers all learned an important lesson: when resources are shared, ⓐ모두가 그 자원을 소중히 여기고 공평하게 사용하는 것이 중요하다는 것이다. The villagers now tell this story to their children. They call it "The Story of the Commons." (E)

14 위 글의 흐름으로 보아, 다음 문장이 들어갈 가장 적절한 곳은? (3점)

| At last, the grass came back. |

① (A) ② (B) ③ (C) ④ (D) ⑤ (E)

15 위 글의 ⓐ를 〈보기〉를 참고하여 영어로 쓰시오. (4점)

보기
important / value / fairly / the resources / everyone / for / it / to / is / use / them / and

→ _____

16 위 글을 읽고 대답할 수 있는 질문은? (3점)

① 몇 마리의 소가 죽었는가?
② 마을 사람들 중 누구의 소가 살아남았는가?
③ 가뭄 때에 마을 사람들은 무엇을 먹었는가?
④ 마을 사람들의 이야기에서 주인공은 누구인가?
⑤ 공유지에 소가 먹을 만한 풀이 없었던 이유는 무엇인가?

[17~18] 다음 글을 읽고 물음에 답하시오.

Soon, other villagers did the same. Some secretly brought one more cow to the commons, ⓐwhile others brought even more to the grassland without telling anyone. They thought that there would be enough grass for the additional cows. Soon the village was full of happy-looking farmers!
The number of cows rose slowly at first. Then the cow population grew more quickly. The grass on the commons began to disappear, and ⓑ_____ became harder for the cows to find grass to eat. To make matters worse, ⓑ_____ did not rain for a long time.

17 위 글의 밑줄 친 ⓐ와 의미가 같은 것은? (4점)

① She ran out while no one was looking.
② While the pasta is cooking, prepare the sauce.
③ The pills he had weakened the pain for a while.
④ While travelling, she missed the comforts of home.
⑤ Some of the studies show good results, while others do not.

18 위 글의 ⓑ에 공통으로 들어갈 단어는? (3점)

① it   ② who   ③ what
④ that   ⑤ this

[19~22] 다음 글을 읽고 물음에 답하시오.

(A) Soon, other villagers did the same. Some secretly brought one more cow to the commons, while others brought even more to the grassland without telling anyone. They thought that there would be enough grass for the additional cows. Soon the village was full of happy-looking farmers!

(B) The number of cows rose slowly at first. Then the cow _____ grew more quickly. The grass on the commons began to disappear, and to find grass to eat became harder for the cows. To make matters worse, It did not rain for a long time.

(C) In the past, when a dry year came, the small number of cows on the commons always found something to eat. However, no grass was left now because there were too many cows. Things were harsh for the villagers; many of the cows died.

(D) At last, the grass came back. Now it was able to support only one cow per family. The village went back to the one-family-one-cow rule. The villagers all learned an important lesson: when resources are shared, it is important for everyone to value the resources and use them fairly. The villagers now tell this story to their children. They call it "The Story of the Commons."

19 위 글의 (A)에 앞서 일어난 사건으로 알맞은 것은? (4점)

① 규칙 위반에 대한 법을 만듦
② 마을 목초지에 비가 내리지 않음
③ 소의 먹이가 사라져 죽기 시작함
④ 몇몇 사람들이 소를 한 마리 이상 공유지에 데려옴
⑤ 다른 마을 사람들도 공유지를 사용할 수 있게 허용함

20 위 글 (B)의 흐름상 빈칸에 들어갈 알맞은 단어는? (3점)

① population ② protection
③ pollution ④ problem
⑤ patience

21 위 글의 내용에 따라 ⓐ~ⓔ를 사건이 일어난 순서대로 알맞게 배열한 것은? (4점)

ⓐ The grass finally came back.
ⓑ Villagers secretly started to bring additional cows.
ⓒ Many cows could not find enough grass to eat and died.
ⓓ The grass began to disappear, and it did not rain for a long time.
ⓔ The villagers went back to the one-family-one-cow rule.

① ⓑ-ⓓ-ⓒ-ⓐ-ⓔ ② ⓑ-ⓓ-ⓐ-ⓔ-ⓒ
③ ⓓ-ⓐ-ⓒ-ⓔ-ⓑ ④ ⓓ-ⓐ-ⓑ-ⓒ-ⓔ
⑤ ⓔ-ⓑ-ⓐ-ⓒ-ⓓ

22 위 글의 내용에 따라 〈조건〉에 맞게 아래 질문에 대한 대답을 영어로 쓰시오. (5점)

Q. Why did many of the cows in the village die?

조건
1. Because로 시작할 것.
2. 주어와 동사를 포함하는 완전한 한 문장의 영어로 쓸 것.

→ _____

[23~24] 다음 글을 읽고 물음에 답하시오.

Once upon a time there was a small village in a forest. ⓐThe villagers were farmers and raised cows. Luckily, some good grassland lay in the middle of the village.
ⓑEveryone was allowed to use the grassland. Therefore, it was called "the commons." By tradition, each family only had one cow, ⓒso it was easy of each cow in the village to find enough grass to eat. The grass on the commons was green all summer long.
But one day a villager broke the rule. ⓓHe brought another cow and let it graze on the commons. He thought that nobody would notice it. ⓔA happy feeling filled his heart when he thought of the milk and cheese that the second cow would bring to his family.

23 위 글의 밑줄 친 ⓐ~ⓔ 중 어법상 어색한 것은?　(3점)

① ⓐ　② ⓑ　③ ⓒ　④ ⓓ　⑤ ⓔ

24 위 글의 내용과 다른 것은?　(4점)

① 작은 마을에 사는 주민들은 농부이고 소를 길렀다.
② 전통에 따르면 각 가정은 소를 여러 마리를 기를 수 있었다.
③ 마을에 있는 소들은 충분히 먹을 풀을 찾는 것은 쉬운 일이었다.
④ 공유지의 풀은 여름 내내 푸르렀다.
⑤ 마을 사람 한 명이 다른 소를 데려와 공유지에서 풀을 뜯게 했다.

25 다음 빈칸에 들어갈 말로 적절한 것은?　(3점)

I like to share my time and talents with other people. For example, each week I give two hours of my free time to senior citizens who live alone. I carry hot meals to their homes and talk with them. I enjoy their company,

and they enjoy mine. I also _____ my talents with patients at a local hospital. My friends and I get up on stage and dance for them. It is a lot of fun! I love it when the patients smile and seem to forget their worries. Sharing myself with others makes me happy.

① love　② smile　③ enjoy
④ share　⑤ dance

26 다음 빈칸에 들어갈 말로 가장 적절한 것은?　(4점)

The population is becoming smaller and smaller in my town. To solve this problem, I will give support to families with children. I will also welcome people from other towns. In addition, I will _____. I am sure that these steps will help solve the population problem in my town.

① charge more taxes on fast food
② reduce stress for working parents
③ not be more diligent for my town
④ persuade people to switch to electric cars
⑤ make students feel valued and well-treated

27 다음 글의 밑줄 친 부분 중 문맥상 낱말의 쓰임이 어색한 것은?　(3점)

Jessy started to ⓐsew clothes for fun. Making clothes by hand was ⓑhard, but she did not ⓒabandon. Before long, her friends wanted to buy her clothes because they were ⓓcommon and unique. Soon she was able to ⓔachieve popularity.

① ⓐ　② ⓑ　③ ⓒ　④ ⓓ　⑤ ⓔ

3학년 영어 2학기 중간고사(7과) 1회

문항수 : 선택형(25문항) 서술형(1문항)   20 . . .

◎ 선택형 문항의 답안은 컴퓨터용 수정 싸인펜을 사용하여 OMR 답안지에 바르게 표기하시오.

◎ 서술형 문제는 답을 답안지에 반드시 검정 볼펜으로 쓰시오.

◎ 총 26문항 100점 만점입니다. 문항별 배점은 각 문항에 표시되어 있습니다.

[서울 관악구 ○○중]

01 다음 단어의 영영 풀이가 어색한 것은?   (4점)

① chase: to run after

② overnight: during the night

③ rainfall: the amount of rain that falls

④ landslide: a sudden shaking of Earth's surface

⑤ impatient: angry because of the waiting time

[전북 ○○중]

02 다음은 자연재해 설명이다. 빈칸에 가장 알맞은 것은? (3점)

• It is very hot in summer. _____ can be dangerous to humans and animals. Public places like the Acropolis are often closed if temperatures reach 36℃.

① Heatwaves   ② Snowstorms

③ Earthquakes   ④ Floods

⑤ Tornadoes

[전북 ○○중]

[3~4] 다음 대화를 읽고 물음에 답하시오.

B: Jimin, are you going out?

G: Yeah. I'm going to buy some sandwiches at Choi's.

B: Are you walking there? (A)

G: No. I'll ride my bike. (B)

B: That's good. (C)

G: Sure. What is it, Jiho?

B: Can you buy chocolate ice cream for me on your way back? (D)

G: No problem. (E)

B: Thanks. Please make sure you wear a helmet and no earphones!

G: Don't worry about that.

03 위 대화에서 다음 문장이 들어갈 곳으로 가장 알맞은 것은? (3점)

• Can you do me a favor?

① (A)   ② (B)   ③ (C)   ④ (D)   ⑤ (E)

04 위 대화의 내용과 일치하지 않는 것은?   (4점)

① Jimin is going to ride her bike to Choi's.

② Jimin is going to buy some sandwiches for Jiho.

③ Jiho advises Jimin to wear a helmet.

④ Jimin will not use earphones while riding a bike.

⑤ Jimin is going to buy chocolate ice cream.

[서울 관악구 ○○중]

05 다음 중 대화가 자연스럽지 않은 것은?   (3점)

① A: Can you do me a favor?

   B: Sure. What is it?

② A: Vincent van Gogh was French, wasn't he?

   B: That's right. He was Dutch.

③ A: Do you mind if I use my phone?

   B: Sorry. Phones are not allowed in this zone.

④ A: Make sure you don't play with knives.

   B: I'll keep that in mind.

⑤ A: I got a bee sting. I shouldn't have touched the beehive.

   B: That's too bad. I'll go and get some medicine.

06 주어진 대화문 다음에 이어질 순서로 가장 적절한 것은? (3점)

M: Sora, can you do me a favor?

G: What is it, Dad?

M: A typhoon is coming tonight. Can you bring in the clothes from outside?

(A) I'll take care of it after I finish the dishes.

(B) Yes, I can. What about your bike?

(C) Yes. Please tell her to stay home.

(D) Then, do you want me to call Grandma and tell her about the typhoon?

M: Dad, G: Sora

① (B)-(A)-(D)-(C)　　② (B)-(D)-(A)-(C)

③ (C)-(A)-(D)-(B)　　④ (D)-(A)-(B)-(C)

⑤ (D)-(C)-(A)-(B)

[8~9] Read the following dialogue and answer the questions.

Junho: Jimin, are you going out?

Jimin: Yeah. I'm going to buy some sandwiches. I'm going to ride my bike.

Junho: That's good. (A)Can you do me a favor?

(B)

Jimin: Don't worry about that.

08 Which of the following has the same meaning with (A)? (4점)

① Can I help you?

② Can I ask you a favor?

③ Don't you need any help?

④ I would like to do you a favor.

⑤ Do you want me to do something for you?

07 다음 대화의 빈칸에 알맞은 표현을 〈보기〉에서 고르면? (4점)

보기

ⓐ It's totally my pleasure.

ⓑ I'm afraid you're mistaken.

ⓒ I should have saved food for the winter.

ⓓ Can you do me a favor?

ⓔ Make sure you don't play with the knives.

A: Can I start now?

B: Wash your hands before you start.

A: Okay. No problem.

B: One more thing. _____

A: I'll keep that in mind.

① ⓐ　　② ⓑ　　③ ⓒ　　④ ⓓ　　⑤ ⓔ

09 Which of the following is the most appropriate order for (B)? (4점)

ⓐ Thanks. Don't forget to wear a helmet and no earphones.

ⓑ Sure. What is it?

ⓒ No problem.

ⓓ Can you buy chocolate ice cream for me on your way back?

① ⓐ-ⓒ-ⓑ-ⓓ　　② ⓑ-ⓓ-ⓐ-ⓒ

③ ⓑ-ⓓ-ⓒ-ⓐ　　④ ⓓ-ⓑ-ⓐ-ⓒ

⑤ ⓓ-ⓑ-ⓒ-ⓐ

10 다음 문장 중 어법상 <u>어색한</u> 것은? (4점)

① Waiting for the bus, I saw my teacher.

② Not finishing my project, I couldn't go out and play.

③ My mom made dinner, watched a drama.

④ Foods should be kept cool.

⑤ The party will be held at 7 p.m.

11 다음 밑줄 친 부분을 분사구문으로 가장 적절하게 바꾼 것은? (5점)

① <u>As she was sick</u>, she couldn't go there.

　　→ It being sick

② He did his homework <u>while he was listening to music</u>.

　　→ listened to music

③ <u>Because I was tired</u>, I went to sleep early.

　　→ Being tired

④ <u>If you turn to the left</u>, you will find the school.

　　→ Turned to the left

⑤ <u>As it was cold outside</u>, I stayed at home all day.

　　→ Being cold outside

12 다음 중 어법상 가장 알맞은 문장은? (4점)

① The chair will deliver on Thursday.

② Your room should cleaned every day.

③ Almost all tickets can be buyed online.

④ The meeting room should be kept clean.

⑤ School rules must are followed by all students.

13 다음 ⓐ~ⓔ 중 어법상 올바른 것은? (4점)

> A Sudden Volcano
> ⓐ<u>To work</u> on a cornfield one day in 1943, farmers in Mexico found ⓑ<u>surprising something</u>. A volcano appeared overnight on a flat cornfield. Residents watched the volcano ⓒ<u>grows</u> over 100 meters tall within a week. The volcano, ⓓ<u>called</u> Paricutin, kept growing, and it finally stopped ⓔ<u>to grow</u> at 424 meters in 1952.

① ⓐ　　② ⓑ　　③ ⓒ　　④ ⓓ　　⑤ ⓔ

14 다음 빈칸에 들어갈 말로 가장 알맞은 것은? (3점)

> • _____ hungry, I couldn't walk more.

① Be　　② Being　　③ Am
④ Been　　⑤ To be

15 다음 글의 ⓐ~ⓔ 중 어법상 <u>어색한</u> 문장은? (4점)

> ⓐ<u>Walking home after school, Tom found a soccer ball in the street.</u> He kicked it, and it broke a neighbor's window. ⓑ<u>Hearing the loud noise, Mr. Lee came out and shouted angrily.</u> ⓒ<u>Knowing not what to do, Tom just tried to run away.</u> ⓓ<u>He ran as quickly as possible, thinking that Mr. Lee would not know who was responsible.</u> ⓔ<u>A few hours later, however, he went back to Mr. Lee, feeling guilty.</u>

① ⓐ　　② ⓑ　　③ ⓒ　　④ ⓓ　　⑤ ⓔ

[16~17] 다음 글을 읽고 물음에 답하시오.

What do Jejudo, Sicily, and Hawaii have in common? They are islands, of course. (A)_____, they are all islands made from volcanic eruptions. Volcanoes are very powerful, so they are named after Vulcan, the Roman god of fire. They can make big islands appear or destroy entire cities like Pompeii. (B)_____, they should be studied and understood.

Nobody knows for sure how many volcanoes there are in the world. (C)_____ scientists, there are about 1,500 active volcanoes above sea level. Many more are underwater, and they are hard to locate. Still, scientists have discovered a large number of them so far.

16 위 글의 (A)~(C)에 들어갈 말이 차례대로 짝지어진 것은?

(4점)

	(A)	(B)	(C)
①	In short	However	According to
②	In fact	Therefore	According to
③	Actually	However	Though
④	In fact	Furthermore	Since
⑤	For example	Therefore	As a result

17 위 글의 내용과 <u>다른</u> 것은?

(3점)

① 시칠리아, 하와이는 화산 분출에 의해 형성된 섬이다.

② 화산은 로마의 불의 신에게서 이름을 따왔다.

③ 화산 폭발로 폼페이 도시 전체가 파괴되었다.

④ 우리는 화산의 수를 잘 알고 있고 그 수는 약 1,500개가 있다.

⑤ 화산 위치는 잘 모르지만 지금까지 많은 수의 화산을 발견했다.

18 다음 글의 내용과 일치하는 것은?

(4점)

Hi, this is Cha Gisang from the Weather Station. Here is today's weather. Typhoon Doni is moving north and is going to hit Jejudo tonight. A typhoon warning has been issued. There will be lots of rainfall with a high chance of flooding in some areas. Please stay inside because Typhoon Doni will come with strong winds. Also, please make sure you keep listening to our reports. Thank you.

① 태풍 경보가 발효되었다.

② 태풍 도니가 북쪽에서 내려오고 있다.

③ 태풍 도니를 피해서 대피소로 가야 한다.

④ 태풍 도니는 강한 바람만 몰고 올 것이다.

⑤ 태풍 도니는 현재 제주도에 머무르고 있다.

19 주어진 문장 다음에 이어질 글의 순서로 가장 적절한 것은?

(4점)

You may think volcanoes can be found only on Earth.

(A) In fact, "Olympus Mons" on Mars is the largest known volcano in the solar system.

(B) However, they have been discovered on other planets, too, such as Mars and Jupiter.

(C) Its volume is about 100 times greater than that of Mauna Loa, the largest volcano on Earth.

① (A) - (C) - (B) ② (B) - (A) - (C)

③ (B) - (C) - (A) ④ (C) - (A) - (B)

⑤ (C) - (B) - (A)

[20~21] 다음 글을 읽고 물음에 답하시오.

What do Jejudo, Sicily, and Hawaii have ⓐ_____ common? They are islands, of course. In fact, they are all islands made ⓑ_____ volcanic eruptions. Volcanoes are very powerful, so they are named ⓒ_____ Vulcan, the Roman god of fire. They can make big islands appear or destroy entire cities like Pompeii. Therefore, they should be studied and understood.

Nobody knows for sure how many volcanoes there are in the world. According to scientists, there are about 1,500 active volcanoes ⓓ_____ sea level. Many more are underwater, and they are hard to locate. Still, scientists have discovered a large number of them so far.

20 위 글의 빈칸 ⓐ~ⓓ에 알맞은 것은? (3점)

	ⓐ	ⓑ	ⓒ	ⓓ
①	in	from	after	above
②	in	of	from	on
③	of	for	after	under
④	to	from	of	above
⑤	for	of	to	beyond

21 위 글의 내용으로 알 수 없는 것은? (4점)

① 화산의 위력
② Volcano 이름의 유래
③ 해수면 위 활화산의 수
④ 해수면 아래 화산의 수와 위치
⑤ Jejudo, Sicily, Hawaii의 공통점

[22~23] 다음 글을 읽고 물음에 답하시오.

You may think volcanoes can be found only on Earth. However, they have been (A)[discovered / covered] on other planets, too, such as Mars and Jupiter. In fact, "Olympus Mons" on Mars is the largest known volcano in the solar system. Its volume is about 100 times greater than that of Mauna Loa, the largest volcano on Earth.

Being very powerful and dangerous, volcanoes do (B)[good / harm] to people in many ways. Sometimes people get hurt, or they may lose their houses. Crops may be destroyed, and air traffic can be threatened. Volcanoes can also have serious effects on world weather. A volcanic eruption shoots lots of ash and dust into the air, stopping some of the sunlight from reaching Earth and thus (C)[disturbing / causing] usual weather patterns.

22 위 글의 괄호 (A), (B), (C) 들어갈 말을 나열한 것으로 옳은 것은? (4점)

	(A)	(B)	(C)
①	discovered	good	causing
②	discovered	harm	disturbing
③	covered	good	disturbing
④	discovered	harm	causing
⑤	covered	harm	causing

23 위 글의 내용과 일치하지 <u>않는</u> 것은? (4점)

① Volcanoes have been found in Mars and Jupiter.
② Volcanic eruptions can have serious influences on world weather.
③ Lots of ash and dust can be made by a volcanic eruption.
④ "Olympus Mons" on Mars is 100 times greater than the largest volcano on Jupiter.
⑤ There is a volcano which is the largest known in the solar system on Mars.

[24~25] 다음 글을 읽고 물음에 답하시오.

(A) ⓐBeen very powerful and dangerous, volcanoes do harm to people in many ways. Sometimes people get hurt, or they may lose their houses. Crops may be destroyed, and air traffic ⓑcan be threaten. Volcanoes can also have serious effects on world weather. A volcanic eruption shoots lots of ash and dust into the air, preventing some of the sunlight from reaching Earth and thus disturbing usual weather patterns.

(B) ⓒWhich volcanoes do is not always bad for humans, however. The soil near a volcano is good for farming. Volcanoes are also a great tourist attraction. ⓓBeing looked for fantastic scenery, millions of tourists visit Mt. Halla in Jejudo, Mt. Etna in Sicily, or Diamond Head in Hawaii every year. Volcanoes ⓔcan be used produce electricity, too. Iceland, for example, actively turns its volcanoes' heat energy into electricity. Today people around the world are studying ways to live in greater harmony with volcanoes, and they are hopeful that more ways will be found soon.

24 위 글의 (A)와 (B)의 주제로 가장 알맞은 것은? (4점)

	(A)	(B)
①	화산 폭발의 원인	세계 화산의 분포도
②	화산이 인류에게 이로운 점	화산 분출의 형태
③	화산이 인간에게 끼치는 피해	화산이 인류에게 이로운 점
④	기상 이변의 원인	화산의 생성 과정
⑤	화산과 인간의 주거와의 관계	화산과 섬 형성 관계

25 위 글의 밑줄 친 ⓐ~ⓔ는 모두 어법상 어색한 것이다. 바르게 고친 것은? (5점)

① ⓐBeen very powerful → Be very powerful
② ⓑcan be threaten → can threaten
③ ⓒWhich volcanoes do → What volcanoes do
④ ⓓBeing looked for → Looked for
⑤ ⓔcan be used produce → can be using to produce

26 다음 글을 읽고 Mr. Watson의 일기를 완성하시오. (5점)

Last Friday, Mr. Watson came back home early. When he arrived home, he cleaned the whole house. After he finished cleaning the house, he felt hungry. So he cooked dinner, watching TV. After he finished dinner, he went out to the park. He met a friend there. But he had to come back home because he did not have enough time to talk to his friend.

조건
• 글의 내용과 일치하게 서술할 것.
• 분사구문을 사용하여 일기를 완성할 것.

Last Friday, I came back home early. (A)_____, I cleaned the whole house. After cleaning the house, I had dinner. Finishing dinner, I went out to the park. I met a friend there . But (B)_____. I had to come back home.

(A): _____
(B): _____

3학년 영어 2학기 기말고사(7과) 2회

반		점수	
이름			

문항수 : 선택형(25문항) 서술형(6문항)　　20 ． ． ．

◎ 선택형 문항의 답안은 컴퓨터용 수정 싸인펜을 사용하여 OMR 답안지에 바르게 표기하시오.
◎ 서술형 문제는 답을 답안지에 반드시 검정 볼펜으로 쓰시오.
◎ 총 31문항 100점 만점입니다. 문항별 배점은 각 문항에 표시되어 있습니다.

01 다음 빈칸에 들어갈 단어가 알맞지 <u>않은</u> 것은? (3점)

- A wildfire has ⓐ_____. We cannot yet ⓑ_____ where the fire started. The city has ⓒ_____ a warning because the fire may ⓓ_____ and ⓔ_____ the residents nearby.

① ⓐ - occurred
② ⓑ - locate
③ ⓒ - issued
④ ⓓ - spread
⑤ ⓔ - protect

02 다음 중 단어의 영영 풀이가 적절하지 <u>않은</u> 것은? (4점)

① earthquake: a sudden shaking of the Earth's surface
② locate: to find the exact position of something
③ threaten: to express an intention to please
④ traffic: the movement of cars, ships, or aircraft
⑤ volcano: a mountain with a big hole at the top, through which lava is pushed up

[3~4] Read the following dialogue and answer the questions.

Dad: Sora, can you do me a favor?
Sora: What is it, Dad?
Dad: A typhoon is coming tonight. Can you bring in the clothes from outside?
Sora: Oh, I've heard that from the Weather Station. No problem. I will! What about your boxes?
Dad: I'll take care of them after I finish the dishes.
Sora: Okay. Do you want me to call Grandpa and tell him about the typhoon?
Dad: Yes. Please tell him to stay home and keep listening to weather reports.
Sora: Okay, Dad.

03 According to the dialogue, which of the following is <u>incorrect</u>? (3점)

① Dad has not finished the dishes.
② Sora knows that the typhoon is coming tonight.
③ Sora will bring in the clothes and boxes from outside.
④ Sora will call her Grandpa and tell him about the typhoon.
⑤ There are two things that Sora has to do after the conversation.

04 위 대화를 읽고 조건에 맞게 주어진 질문에 답하시오. (4점)

조건
- 대화의 내용과 일치하게 서술할 것.
- 단어 'make'를 사용하여 당부하는 문장으로 서술할 것.
- 주어와 서술어가 나타나는 완전한 문장으로 서술할 것.

Q: What two things will Sora say to her Grandpa?
"Grandpa, _____."

→ _____

05 다음 대화의 내용과 일치하지 <u>않는</u> 것은? (3점)

> B: Jimin, are you going out?
> G: Yeah. I'm going to buy some sandwiches at Choi's.
> B: Are you walking there?
> G: No. I'll ride my bike.
> B: That's good. Can you do me a favor?
> G: Sure. What is it?
> B: Can you buy chocolate ice cream for me on your way back?
> G: No problem.
> B: Thanks. Please make sure you wear a helmet and no earphones!
> G: Don't worry about that.
> *B: boy, G: girl

① The boy advises the girl to wear a helmet.
② The girl is going to buy chocolate ice cream.
③ The girl will ride her bike to go to the Choi's.
④ The girl is going out to buy some sandwiches.
⑤ The boy is asking the girl to buy him some sandwiches.

06 다음 대화의 빈칸에 알맞은 표현을 〈보기〉에서 찾으면? (2점)

> 보기
> ⓐ It's totally my pleasure.
> ⓑ I'm afraid you're mistaken.
> ⓒ I should have saved food for the winter.
> ⓓ Can you do me a favor?
> ⓔ Make sure you don't play with the knives.

> A: _____
> B: Sure. What is it?
> A: Can you feed the dog?
> B: No problem. Anything else?

① ⓐ ② ⓑ ③ ⓒ ④ ⓓ ⑤ ⓔ

07 다음 밑줄 친 (A)를 '현재분사'를 이용한 '부사구'로 바꿔 쓰시오. (4점)

> • (A)<u>Because she didn't know what to do</u>, she asked for my advice.

> 조건
> • (A)에 있는 단어만 사용할 것.
> • 5개 단어로 쓸 것.

→ _____, she asked for my advice.

08 다음 '접속사+주어+동사' 형태의 문장을 분사를 사용한 문장으로 바꾼 것 중 알맞은 것은? (4점)

① Although I was sick in bed, I did my homework.
→ Although being sick in bed, I doing my homework.

② As he lived in the country, he became very healthy.
→ Living in the country, he became very healthy.

③ A black cloud appeared and it covered the whole sky.
→ A black cloud appearing and covering the whole sky.

④ All of the people watched the sunrise while they were drinking hot coffee.
→ All of the people watched the sunrise being drinking hot coffee.

⑤ Because he doesn't have a car anymore, he has to use public transportation.
→ Doing not have a car anymore, he has to use public transportation.

09 다음 문장의 밑줄 친 부분 중 올바른 것은? (3점)

① <u>Watch</u> television, he fell asleep.

② The problem <u>should solved</u> right now.

③ I <u>can be seen</u> germs through a microscope.

④ <u>Knowing not</u> what to do, she asked for my advice.

⑤ <u>Getting up</u> late, she was late for school yesterday.

[10~12] 다음 글을 읽고 물음에 답하시오.

(A) <u>Being very powerful and dangerous</u>, volcanoes do harm to people in many ways. (B) Sometimes people get hurt, or they may lose their houses. (C) Crops may be destroyed, and air traffic can be threatened. (D) A volcanic eruption shoots lots of ash and dust into the air, preventing some of the sunlight from reaching Earth and thus disturbing usual weather patterns. (E) What volcanoes do is not always bad for humans, however.

10 위 글의 흐름으로 보아, 주어진 문장이 들어가기에 가장 적절한 곳은? (4점)

Volcanoes can also have serious effects on world weather.

① (A) ② (B) ③ (C) ④ (D) ⑤ (E)

11 위 글의 밑줄 친 부분의 의미로 가장 알맞은 것은? (2점)

① Because volcanoes are very powerful and dangerous

② Although volcanoes are very powerful and dangerous

③ After volcanoes are very powerful and dangerous

④ Though volcanoes are very powerful and dangerous

⑤ Before volcanoes are very powerful and dangerous

12 위 글의 다음에 올 내용으로 알맞은 것은? (3점)

① 화산의 피해를 줄이는 법

② 화산이 인간에게 주는 이점

③ 화산이 인간에게 끼치는 위험성

④ 화산 분출이 날씨에 미치는 영향

⑤ 화산이 주로 분포되어 있는 대륙

[13~14] 다음 글을 읽고 물음에 답하시오.

The soil near a volcano is good for farming. Volcanoes are also a great tourist attraction. ⓐ<u>Look</u> for fantastic scenery, millions of tourists visit Mt. Halla in Jejudo, Mt. Etna in Sicily, or Diamond Head in Hawaii every year. Volcanoes ⓑ<u>can use</u> to produce electricity, too. Iceland, for example, actively turns its volcanoes' heat energy ⓒ<u>from</u> electricity. Today people around the world are studying ways ⓓ<u>live</u> in greater harmony with volcanoes, and they are hopeful that more ways ⓔ<u>will be found</u> soon.

13 위 글의 ⓐ~ⓔ 중 어법상 올바른 것은? (3점)

① ⓐ ② ⓑ ③ ⓒ ④ ⓓ ⑤ ⓔ

14 위 글의 제목으로 알맞은 것은? (3점)

① The Good Things That Volcanoes Gives to People

② Iceland: Making Energy from Volcanoes

③ The Effects of Soil near Volcanoes

④ Tourist Attractions in the World

⑤ Hopeful Future with Volcanoes

[15~18] Read the following passage and answer the questions.

You may think volcanoes can be found only on Earth. ⓐHowever, they can be discovered on other planets, too, such as Mars and Jupiter. ⓑIn fact, "Olympus Mons" on Mars is the largest know volcano in the solar system. Its volume is about 100 times greater than that of Mauna Loa, the largest volcano on Earth.
(A)Being very powerful and dangerous, volcanoes do harm to people in many ways. ⓒSometimes, people hurt, or they may lost their houses. Crops may be destroyed, and air traffic can be threatened. ⓓVolcanoes can also have serious affects on world weather. A volcanic eruption shoots lots of ash and dust into the air, preventing some of the sunlight from reaching Earth and thus disturbing usual weather patterns. ⓔBut what volcanoes do are not always bad for humans, however.

15 Which of the following statements is most appropriate after reading the passage above? (4점)

① Jin: "We can find volcanoes only on Earth, Mars, and Jupiter."
② Lisa: "The volume of Mauna Loa is about 100 times smaller than that of Olympus Mons."
③ Jisu: "Volcanoes have positive effects on Earth destroying crops and threatening air traffic."
④ Rose: "A volcanic eruption can be a threat to air traffic but it does not change world weather."
⑤ Jennie: "When the usual weather pattern is changed, a volcanic eruption will prevent the sunlight from reaching Earth!"

16 Which of the underlined ⓐ~ⓔ is grammatically correct? (4점)

① ⓐ   ② ⓑ   ③ ⓒ   ④ ⓓ   ⑤ ⓔ

17 Which of the following is the most appropriate topic after the given passage? (3점)

① how to live in volcanoes
② how do volcanoes erupt?
③ the countries where you find volcanoes
④ the weather change from volcanic eruption
⑤ some good effects that volcanoes bring to humans

18 위 글의 밑줄 친 (A)를 조건에 맞게 바꿔 서술하시오. (4점)

조건
• 내용상 적절한 접속사를 사용할 것.
• 주어와 서술어가 나타나게 서술할 것.

→ _____

19 다음 글의 제목으로 가장 알맞은 것은? (2점)

Working on a cornfield one day in 1943, farmers in Mexico found something surprising. A volcano appeared overnight on a flat cornfield. Residents watched the volcano grow over 100 meters tall within a week. The volcano, called Paricutin, kept growing, and it finally stopped growing at 424 meters in 1952.

① A Deadly Volcano
② A Sudden Volcano
③ A Fantastic Volcano
④ A Powerful Volcano
⑤ A Dangerous Volcano

[20~22] 다음 글을 읽고 물음에 답하시오.

What volcanoes do is not always bad for humans, however. The soil near a volcano is good for farming. Volcanoes are also a great tourist attraction. Looking for fantastic scenery, millions of tourists visit Mt. Halla in Jejudo, Mt. Etna in Sicily, or Diamond Head in Hawaii every year. (A)(Volcanoes, to, can, used, produce, be, electricity), too. Iceland, for example, actively turns its volcanoes' heat energy into electricity. Today people around the world are studying ways to live in greater harmony with vlocanoes, and they are hopeful that more ways will be found soon.

20 위 글의 주제로 가장 적절한 것은? (3점)

① 화산을 찾아보기 어려운 이유
② 화산 분출로 인한 지형 변화
③ 화산이 끼치는 해로움
④ 화산이 주는 이로움
⑤ 화산을 연구해야 하는 이유

21 위 글의 바로 앞에 올 내용으로 가장 알맞은 것은? (3점)

① 화산 폭발의 원인
② 화산의 분포
③ 화산이 인류에게 이로운 점
④ 화산이 기후에 미치는 영향
⑤ 화산이 인류에게 끼치는 피해

22 위 글의 (A)의 단어를 다음 우리말과 일치하도록 바르게 배열해 쓰시오. (3점)

• 화산은 전기를 생산하기 위해서 이용될 수 있다.

→ _____

[23~24] 다음 글을 읽고 물음에 답하시오.

Many of the volcanoes on Earth are ⓐlocated along the Ring of Fire that ⓑcircles the Pacific Ocean. The ring is about 40,000 kilometers long, and it is home to around 75% of the world's active volcanoes. Indonesia alone has over 120 ⓒactive volcanoes since the country ⓓlays on the Ring of Fire. This ring is also the area where most of the world's earthquakes ⓔoccur.

23 위 글의 ⓐ~ⓔ 중 어휘의 쓰임으로 올바르지 않은 것은? (3점)

① ⓐ ② ⓑ ③ ⓒ ④ ⓓ ⑤ ⓔ

24 위 글의 The Ring of Fire에 관한 내용과 일치하지 않는 것은? (2점)

① 태평양을 둘러싸고 있다.
② 길이가 약 40,000km이다.
③ 전 세계 활화산의 75%가 분포해 있다.
④ 인도네시아가 이곳에 위치해 있다.
⑤ 세계에서 가장 지진이 일어나지 않는 곳이다.

25 다음 글의 ⓐ~ⓔ 중 흐름과 어울리지 않는 것은? (3점)

A wildfire has ⓐoccurred. We cannot yet ⓑlocate where the fire started. The city has ⓒissued a warning because the fire may ⓓspread and ⓔrelieve the residents nearby.

① ⓐ ② ⓑ ③ ⓒ ④ ⓓ ⑤ ⓔ

[26~29] Read the following passage and answer the questions.

What do Jejudo, Sicily, and Hawaii have in common? They are all islands, of course. In fact, ⓐthey are all islands that (A)[made / are made] from volcanic eruptions. Volcanoes are very powerful, so ⓑthey are named after Vulcan, the Roman god of fire. ⓒThey can make big islands appear or ⓓthey can destroy entire cities like Pompeii. Therefore, ⓔthey should be studied and understood.

Nobody knows for sure how many volcanoes there are in the world. According to scientists, there are about 1,500 active volcanoes above sea level. Many more are underwater, and they are hard to locate. ⓕStill, scientists have discovered a large number of them so far.

Many of the volcanoes on Earth (B)[is / are] located along the Ring of Fire that circles the Pacific Ocean. The ring is about 40,000 kilometers long, and it is home to around 75% of the would's active volcanoes. Indonesia alone has over 120 active volcanoes since the country is on the Ring of Fire. This ring is also the area (C)[which / where] most of the world's earthquakes occur.

26 위 글의 ⓐ~ⓔ 중 지칭하는 것이 다른 하나는? (2점)

① ⓐ ② ⓑ ③ ⓒ ④ ⓓ ⑤ ⓔ

27 Which of the following is most appropriate for (A)~(C)? (4점)

	(A)	(B)	(C)
①	made	is	which
②	made	are	where
③	are made	is	which
④	are made	are	which
⑤	are made	are	where

28 Which of the underlined words has the same meaning with ⓕStill? (4점)

① Dad, I'm still hungry!
② The volcano Paricutin is still growing.
③ There's still time to finish your homework.
④ The English test was hard. Still, I could get an A.
⑤ Where is James? Is he still studying in the library?

29 Why are there many active volcanoes in Indonesia? (단, 단어 lie를 사용하여 완전한 문장으로 서술하시오.) (4점)

→ Because _____.

[30~31] 다음 글을 읽고 물음에 답하시오.

ⓐBeing very powerful and dangerous, volcanoes do harm to people in many ways. Sometimes people get hurt, or they ⓑmay lose their houses. Crops ⓒmay destroy, and air traffic ⓓcan be threatened. Volcanoes can also have serious effects on world weather. A volcanic eruption shoots lots of ash and dust into the air, ⓔpreventing some of the sunlight from reaching Earth and thus disturbing usual weather patterns.

30 위 글의 ⓐ~ⓔ 중 어법상 바르지 못한 것은? (3점)

① ⓐ ② ⓑ ③ ⓒ ④ ⓓ ⑤ ⓔ

31 위 글을 다음과 같이 요약할 때 빈칸에 알맞은 말을 위 글에서 찾아 쓰시오. (4점)

Volcanoes have harmful effects on people, crops, air traffic, and _____ _____.

→ _____ _____

◎ 선택형 문항의 답안은 컴퓨터용 수정 싸인펜을 사용하여 OMR 답안지에 바르게 표기하시오.
◎ 서술형 문제는 답을 답안지에 반드시 검정 볼펜으로 쓰시오.
◎ 총 30문항 100점 만점입니다. 문항별 배점은 각 문항에 표시되어 있습니다.

[경북 ○○중]

01 다음 빈칸에 들어가기에 가장 <u>어색한</u> 단어는? (3점)

- You should be _____ of what you did wrong.
- The writer's novel is _____ reading over and over.
- The book will help you expand your _____.
- If you want to accomplish your dream, you should just _____ it.

① fail ② imagination ③ worth
④ chase ⑤ ashamed

[전북 ○○중]

02 다음 단어의 영영 풀이가 바르지 <u>못한</u> 것은? (4점)

① repeatedly: over and over
② entire: whole
③ mistaken: not wrong in your opinion or judgement
④ locate: to find the place of something
⑤ go after: to try to get something

[서울 관악구 ○○중]

[3~4] 다음 대화를 읽고 물음에 답하시오.

M: Nice to meet you, Sora. Did you do well on the drawing exam?
G: I'm not sure, but I did my best.
M: Okay. Let's start the interview. What made you apply for Mana Animation High School?
G: Well, I've really loved drawing cartoons since I was a little child.

M: So, you want to be a cartoon artist?
G: _____ I want to be a game designer.
M: I see. What do you think is the most important skill a game designer needs?
G: I'd say imagination. A good designer should create a completely new world in a game.
M: Sounds good.

03 위 대화의 빈칸에 알맞은 표현은? (3점)

① I'm afraid you can't.
② Not at all. Go ahead.
③ That's not quite right.
④ I'm happy to hear that.
⑤ You can say that again.

04 위 대화의 내용상 대답할 수 <u>없는</u> 질문은? (4점)

① What is Sora doing now?
② Which school did Sora apply for?
③ Why did Sora apply for the high school?
④ What does Sora want to be in the future?
⑤ What does Sora think is the most important skill a cartoon artist needs?

[전북 ○○중]

05 다음 대화의 빈칸에 알맞은 표현을 〈보기〉에서 찾으면? (2점)

조건
ⓐ It's totally my pleasure.
ⓑ I'm afraid you're mistaken.
ⓒ I should have saved food for the winter.
ⓓ Can you do me a favor?
ⓔ Make sure you don't play with the knives.

A: What's the matter?
B: I feel hungry. _____
A: Don't worry. I'll share my food with you.
A: Thanks.

① ⓐ ② ⓑ ③ ⓒ ④ ⓓ ⑤ ⓔ

[6~7] Read the following conversation and answer the questions.

Mr. Lee: Nice to meet you, Sora. Did you do well on the drawing exam?

Sora: I'm not sure, but I did my best.

Mr. Lee: Okay. Let's start the interview. What made you apply for Mana Animation High School?

(A)

06 Which of following is the most appropriate order for (A)? (4점)

ⓐ That's not quite right. I want to be a game designer.

ⓑ Well, I've really loved drawing cartoons since I was a little child.

ⓒ So, you want to be a cartoon artist?

ⓓ I'd say imagination. A good designer should create a completely new world in a game.

ⓔ I see. What do you think is the most important skill a game designer needs?

① ⓐ-ⓑ-ⓒ-ⓓ-ⓔ ② ⓑ-ⓒ-ⓐ-ⓔ-ⓓ

③ ⓑ-ⓒ-ⓔ-ⓐ-ⓓ ④ ⓓ-ⓐ-ⓒ-ⓑ-ⓔ

⑤ ⓓ-ⓒ-ⓑ-ⓔ-ⓐ

07 In which situation did the above conversation take place? (4점)

① an interview for entering a school

② a job interview for a game designer

③ an online call asking for a job of a cartoon artist

④ a drawing class to prepare for a college entrance exam

⑤ a meeting to have a discussion for drawing cartoons

[8~9] 다음 대화를 읽고 물음에 답하시오.

G: Hi, Jiho.

B: Hi, Amber. It is nice to see you on the bus.

(A) Yeah. I hate to be late for the school festival.

(B) Yeah, but I'm afraid we're going to be late.

(C) I understand. That happens a lot to me when I'm tired, too.

(D) Me, too. I should have set my alarm. I forgot.

G: How about you? What made you late?

B: Well, I got up early. But it took me some time to do my hair.

G: Oh, I see. We're stuck in a heavy traffic jam. We should get off and run.

B: _____ The traffic is starting to move again. Let's stay on.

G: Okay. I just hope we're not terribly late.

08 위 대화가 자연스럽도록 바르게 배열한 것은? (3점)

① (A)-(B)-(C)-(D) ② (B)-(A)-(D)-(C)

③ (D)-(A)-(C)-(B) ④ (D)-(B)-(C)-(A)

⑤ (C)-(A)-(B)-(D)

09 위 대화의 빈칸에 알맞은 것은? (3점)

① That's quite right.

② Yes, you're right.

③ No, you're mistaken.

④ That'd be great.

⑤ That makes sense.

10 다음 빈칸에 들어갈 수 있는 말은? (3점)

> A: _____
> B: I'm afraid you're mistaken.

① Vincent van Gogh was French.
② People in Brazil speak Portuguese.
③ The capital of Australia is Canberra.
④ Jindo is the third largest island in Korea.
⑤ Tomatoes were first grown in South America.

11 다음 중 어법에 맞는 문장의 개수는? (4점)

> • The meeting room should keep clean.
> • It was kind for her to give me a ride.
> • This medicine must be taken after meal.
> • Tina sat back on the sofa, close her eyes.
> • I reading comic books, I stayed home all day.
> • Having no money, I borrowed some from my older brother.

① 1개　② 2개　③ 3개　④ 4개　⑤ 5개

12 다음 두 문장의 의미가 통하도록 빈칸에 알맞은 말을 쓰시오. (4점)

> • I regret that I did not check the weather before leaving.
> → I _____ _____ _____ the weather before leaving.

> 조건
> • 본동사는 'check'를 사용할 것.
> • 3개의 단어로 쓸 것.

→ _____ _____ _____

13 Which of the following is grammatically correct? (4점)

① Hailey, that is a nurse, is on vacation now.
② Nick lost an umbrella, whom he bought yesterday.
③ The writer, whom wrote many books, lives in Canada.
④ James, who I saw on the subway, are a famous singer.
⑤ I like taking pictures of people, which is my favorite activity.

14 다음 문장이 들어갈 곳으로 가장 알맞은 것은? (3점)

> About a week later, Helen found a letter in the mailbox.

> On the day of the tryouts, all the rules were explained by an old man in a suit, who sounded very serious and unkind. (A) She thought that wearing a suit in the hot sun might have made him impatient. (B) On that day, Helen played baseball for hours with many other young women. (C) She was excited to go after her baseball dreams! (D) It was from people who worked for the girls' baseball league in Chicago. (E) It read that she had been invited to the league's main tryouts in Chicago!

① (A)　② (B)　③ (C)　④ (D)　⑤ (E)

[15~17] 다음 글을 읽고 물음에 답하시오.

[전북 ○○중]

In 1943, the All-American Girls Professional Baseball League ⓐwas founded. This league was created for baseball fans because many of America's young men were fighting in World War Ⅱ.

Helen ⓑwas told that there would be local tryouts right in South Bend. She ⓒwondered, "What would it be like to be on a baseball team and to ⓓmake it to the finals for my hometown?" She imagined a large banner ⓔsitting at the baseball field which included the name Helen Baker.

15 위 글의 밑줄 친 ⓐ~ⓔ 중 글의 흐름상 어울리지 <u>않는</u> 것은? (3점)

① ⓐ　② ⓑ　③ ⓒ　④ ⓓ　⑤ ⓔ

16 Helen의 심정으로 가장 알맞은 것은? (2점)

① excited　② uneasy　③ shocked
④ unfriendly　⑤ nervous

17 다음 질문에 대한 답을 영어로 쓰시오. (4점)

Q: Why was the girls' league created?
A: _____

→ _____

18 다음은 친구를 소개한 글이다. 밑줄 친 ⓐ~ⓔ 중 어법상 어색한 것끼리만 짝지어진 것은? (3점)

[경북 ○○중]

I'd like to introduce my friend Squidward ⓐwho ⓑwant to be an artist in the future. His favorite place is his house, ⓒthat ⓓis next to mine. He likes painting pictures very much, which ⓔis his number-one free time activity.

① ⓐ, ⓒ　　② ⓑ, ⓒ
③ ⓐ, ⓑ, ⓒ　　④ ⓐ, ⓓ, ⓔ
⑤ ⓐ, ⓑ, ⓒ, ⓓ

[전북 ○○중]

[19~20] 다음 글을 읽고 물음에 답하시오.

As the days went by, however, Helen became worried that she might fail. She also became worried about traveling alone to Chicago, which was far away from home. When the day of the main tryouts came, she was too afraid to go.

My grandmother has spent the rest of her life _____ her decision. When she watches a baseball game on TV, she often says, "<u>나는 Chicago에 갔어야 했어.</u> You know, all your dreams are worth chasing, even if you catch only a few of them. Never miss an opportunity."

19 위 글의 흐름으로 볼 때 빈칸에 가장 알맞은 것은? (3점)

① regretting　② satisfying
③ supporting　④ permitting
⑤ admitting

20 위 글의 밑줄 친 우리말을 주어진 동사를 사용하여 영어로 옮기시오. (4점)

→ _____ (go)

Lesson 8 All Your Dreams Are Worth Chasing **41**

[21~22] 다음 글을 읽고 물음에 답하시오.

My grandmother Helen used to be a cook in a restaurant in a small town near South Bend, Indiana. She does not work anymore, but she still enjoys making delicious food, (A)[which / who] I love so much. Food is one of the many things that connect us. (B)[What / Whether] connects us most strongly, however, is baseball.

When I visit her on weekends, my grandmother often tells me exciting stories about playing baseball back in the 1940s. She must have loved the sport very much. I listen to these stories over and over. She always says, "Go after (C)[what / that] you want, Sarah. Don't be afraid of trying something new or challenging. Don't be ashamed of failing."

21 위 글의 괄호 (A), (B), (C) 안에서 어법상 알맞은 말로 짝지어진 것은? (4점)

	(A)	(B)	(C)
①	which	What	what
②	who	Whether	that
③	which	What	that
④	who	Whether	what
⑤	which	Whether	that

22 위 글의 내용과 일치하지 <u>않는</u> 것은? (3점)

① Helen worked as a cook in a restaurant.

② Helen enjoys making delicious food.

③ Sarah loves her grandmother's food.

④ Helen tells Sarah exciting stories about playing baseball.

⑤ Sarah is afraid of trying something new and challenging.

[23~25] 다음 글을 읽고 물음에 답하시오.

Helen ⓐ<u>was told</u> that there would be local tryouts right in South Bend. She wondered, "What would it be like ⓑ<u>being</u> on a baseball team and to make it to the finals for my hometown?" She imagined a large banner hanging at the baseball field ⓒ<u>that</u> included the name Helen Baker.

On the day of the tryouts, all the rules were explained by an old man in a suit, ⓓ<u>which</u> sounded very serious and unkind. She thought that wearing a suit in the hot sun ⓔ<u>might have made</u> him impatient. On that day, Helen played baseball for hours with many other young women. She was (A)_____ to go after her baseball dreams!

23 위 글의 ⓐ~ⓔ에서 어법상 옳은 것끼리 짝지어진 것은? (4점)

① ⓐ, ⓓ 　　② ⓑ, ⓔ

③ ⓐ, ⓑ, ⓒ 　　④ ⓐ, ⓒ, ⓔ

⑤ ⓐ, ⓑ, ⓒ, ⓓ

24 위 글의 (A)에 들어갈 가장 적절한 말은? (2점)

① bored　　② tired　　③ excited

④ scared　　⑤ sad

25 위 글을 읽고 대답할 수 <u>없는</u> 질문은? (4점)

① Where would the local tryouts be held?

② When did Helen make it to the finals for her hometown?

③ How was the weather on the day of the tryouts?

④ Who explained all the rules on the day of the tryouts?

⑤ Who did Helen play baseball with on the day of the tryouts?

[26~27] 다음 글을 읽고 물음에 답하시오.

On the day of the tryouts, all the rules were explained by an old man in a suit, who sounded very serious and unkind. She thought that wearing a suit in the hot sun might have made him impatient. On that day, Helen played baseball for hours with many other young women. She was excited to go after her baseball dreams!

About a week later, Helen found a letter in the mailbox. It was from people who worked for the girls' baseball league in Chicago. (A)It read that she had been invited to the league's main tryouts in Chicago!

26 위 글의 (A)에 나타난 Helen의 심정으로 가장 알맞은 것은?

(3점)

① upset   ② regretful
③ excited   ④ ashamed
⑤ disappointed

27 위 글의 내용과 일치하지 <u>않는</u> 것은?   (3점)

① 심사 당일 날씨가 쌀쌀해졌다.
② 심사 당일 정장을 입은 남자가 규칙을 설명했다.
③ Helen 할머니와 다른 여성들은 몇 시간 동안 야구를 했다.
④ Helen 할머니는 야구에 대한 꿈을 추구하게 되어 신이 났다.
⑤ Helen 할머니는 시카고에서 열리는 리그의 본심사에 초청되었다.

28 다음 글의 (A)의 의도로 가장 알맞은 것은?   (3점)

My grandmother has spent the rest of her life regretting her decision. When she watches a baseball game on the TV, she often says, "(A)I should have gone to Chicago. You know, all your dreams are worth chasing, even if you catch only a few of them. Never miss an opportunity."

① 나는 시카고에 갈 수가 없었다.
② 나는 시카고에 간 것을 후회한다.
③ 나는 시카고에 가는 방법을 몰랐다.
④ 나는 시카고에 가지 않은 것을 후회한다.
⑤ 나는 시카고에 갔었다.

29 다음 글에서 어법상 <u>어색한</u> 곳은 몇 군데인가?   (4점)

My grandmother Helen used to being a cook in a restaurant in a small town near South Bend, Indiana. She does not work anymore, but she still enjoys to make delicious food, which I love so much. Food is one of the many things that connect us. What connects us most strongly, however, are baseball.

① 1군데   ② 2군데   ③ 3군데
④ 4군데   ⑤ 5군데

30 다음 글의 밑줄 친 ⓐ의 단어들을 바르게 배열할 때 6번째 오는 것은?   (3점)

When I visit her on weekends, my grandmother often tells me exciting stories about playing baseball back in the 1940s. She must have loved the sport very much. I listen to these stories over and over. She always says, "Go after what you want, Sarah. ⓐ(new, don't, afraid, trying, of, something, be)."

① new   ② afraid   ③ trying
④ of   ⑤ something

◎ 선택형 문항의 답안은 컴퓨터용 수정 싸인펜을 사용하여 OMR 답안지에 바르게 표기하시오.
◎ 서술형 문제는 답을 답안지에 반드시 검정 볼펜으로 쓰시오.
◎ 총 28문항 100점 만점입니다. 문항별 배점은 각 문항에 표시되어 있습니다.

[경북 ㅇㅇ중]

01 다음 중 영영 풀이가 바른 것은? (3점)

① chase: to run into

② opportunity: a place for doing something

③ mistaken: wrong in your opinion or judgement

④ regret: to feel happy about something that you did in the past

⑤ stuck: easy to move from one position to another

[대구 ㅇㅇ중]

02 Which of the following words does not have its English meaning? (4점)

- to join things together
- wrong in your opinion or judgement
- difficult to move from one position to another
- to feel sorry about something that you did in the past

① regret　　② mistaken　　③ stuck

④ connect　　⑤ impatient

[전북 ㅇㅇ중]

03 다음 대화를 요약할 때 빈칸에 알맞은 말을 쓰시오. (4점)

M: Nice to meet you, Sora. Did you do well on the drawing exam?
G: I'm not sure, but I did my best.
M: Okay. Let's start the interview. What made you apply for Mana Animation High School?
G: Well, I've really loved drawing cartoons since I was a little child.
M: So, you want to be a cartoon artist?
G: That's not quite right. I want to be a game designer.
M: I see. What do you think is the most important skill a game designer needs?
G: I'd say imagination. A good designer should create a completely new world in a game.
M: Sounds good.

Sora applied for Mana Animation High School.
She thinks that ＿＿＿＿ ＿＿＿＿ ＿＿＿＿ ＿＿＿＿ ＿＿＿＿ ＿＿＿＿ to be a good game designer.

→ ＿＿＿＿＿＿＿＿＿＿＿＿＿＿＿＿＿＿＿＿

[경북 ㅇㅇ중]

04 다음 대화 중 자연스럽지 못한 것은? (2점)

① A: I feel cold.
　 B: You shouldn't have worn a warm sweater.

② A: There is no cake on the table.
　 B: Minsu must have eaten it. He was near the table a few minutes ago.

③ A: I can't find my umbrella.
　 B: You may have left it in the classroom.

④ A: My bike is completely wet.
　 B: You shouldn't have left it outdoors.

⑤ A: Sam is late.
　 B: He may have taken the wrong bus.

[5~7] 다음 대화를 읽고 물음에 답하시오.

[8~9] Read the following dialogue and answer the questions.

Man: Nice to meet you, Sora. Did you do well on the drawing exam?

Sora: I'm not sure, but I did my best.

Man: Okay. Let's start the ⓐ_____. What made you apply for Mana Animation High School?

Sora: Well, I've really loved drawing cartoons since I was a little child.

Man: So, you want to be a cartoon artist?

Sora: ⓑ_____. I want to be a game designer.

Man: I see. What do you think is the most important skill a game designer needs?

Sora: I'd say imagination. A good designer should create a completely new world in a game.

Jiho: Hi, Amber. It is nice to see you on the bus.

Amber: Yeah, but I'm afraid we're going to be late.

Jiho: Yeah, I hate to be late for the school festival.

Amber: Me, too. I should have set my alarm. I forgot.

Jiho: I understand. That happens a lot to me when I'm tired, too.

Amber: How about you? What made you late?

Jiho: Well, I got up early. But it took me some time to do my hair.

Amber: Oh, I see. We're stuck in a heavy traffic jam. We should get off and run.

Jiho: No, (A)_____. The traffic is starting to move again. Let's stay on.

Amber: Okay. I just hope we're not terribly late.

05 위 대화의 내용으로 보아 빈칸 ⓐ에 가장 알맞은 말은? (2점)

① race　　② speech　　③ final match
④ interview　　⑤ audition

06 위 대화의 빈칸 ⓑ에 들어갈 가장 알맞은 말은? (3점)

① That's okay.

② Yes, I love to.

③ That's not quite right.

④ I totally agree with you.

⑤ No, I don't care about it.

07 위 대화를 읽고 빈칸 (A), (B)에 알맞은 말은? (4점)

Sora thinks (A)_____ is the most important thing to be a (B)_____.

	(A)	(B)
①	experience	cartoon artist
②	imagination	game designer
③	a good skill	game designer
④	experience	cartoon artist
⑤	a good computer	cartoon artist

08 Which of the following is most appropriate according to the dialogue? (4점)

① They have the School Sport Day today.

② Jiho wasted his time on choosing his clothes.

③ Amber regrets getting up late in the morning.

④ After the dialog, they will ride bikes to school.

⑤ There is a traffic jam because of the parade in the city.

09 Which of the following is most appropriate for (A)? (4점)

① you are mistaken

② that's very common

③ you'd better get a taxi

④ it's too good to be true

⑤ you should do your best

[전북 ○○중]

10 다음 대화의 빈칸에 알맞은 표현을 〈보기〉에서 찾으면? (3점)

> 보기
>
> ⓐ It's totally my pleasure.
> ⓑ I'm afraid you're mistaken.
> ⓒ I should have saved food for the winter.
> ⓓ Can you do me a favor?
> ⓔ Make sure you don't play with the knives.

> A: People in Brazil speak Spanish, right?
> B: _____ They
>   speak Portuguese.

① ⓐ ② ⓑ ③ ⓒ ④ ⓓ ⑤ ⓔ

[경북 ○○중]

11 다음은 겨울 개미와 베짱이의 대화이다. 빈칸에 가장 알맞은 말은? (2점)

> Ant: What's the matter, Grasshopper?
> Grasshopper: I feel hungry. _____
> Ant: Don't worry. I'll share my food with
>   you.

① I shouldn't have told lies.

② I shouldn't have touched the beehive.

③ I should have taken a nap during the race.

④ I should have saved the food for the winter.

⑤ I should have built my house with strong
   materials.

[경북 ○○중]

12 다음 중 어법상 가장 알맞은 문장은? (4점)

① You may left your wallet in your room.

② Mr. Smith must has seen the movie before.

③ I met a friend, whom I had gone to school
   with.

④ The computer, I bought last week, is a
   secondhand product.

⑤ My sister likes this book, that has many
   colorful pictures.

[대구 ○○중]

13 다음 글의 빈칸을 조건에 맞게 완성하시오. (6점)

> 조건
>
> • 글의 흐름에 맞게 서술할 것.
> • 두 문항 각각 다른 조동사를 사용할 것.
> • 문항 (A): 부정어를 사용하고 강한 부정적 추측을 나타내는 표현을 쓸 것.
> • 문항 (B): 과거 사실에 대한 강한 추측(확신)을 나타내는 표현을 쓸 것.

> (A)
> A: Jess called me yesterday that she was
>   sick and would stay at home, so she
>   didn't join our important meeting. But I
>   saw her at a mall with her friend!
> B: I think you mistook her for someone else.
>   She's always been honest. She _____
>   _____ a lie to us.
>
> (B)
> A: Where are all the foods? They were here
>   on the table. But there's nothing on it now.
>   What happened? Who is responsible?
> B: Yumi was the only one that visited this
>   room. She _____ all of them.

(A): _____

(B): _____

[14~17] 다음 글을 읽고 물음에 답하시오.

My grandmother Helen (A)used to be a cook in a restaurant in a small town ⓐnear South Bend, Indiana. She does not work anymore, but she still enjoys making delicious food, ⓑthat I love so much. Food is one of the many things ⓒthat connect us. ⓓWhat connects us most strongly, however, is baseball.

When I visit her on weekends, my grandmother often tells me exciting stories about ⓔplaying baseball back in the 1940s. (B)그녀는 그 운동을 매우 좋아했음에 틀림없다. I listen to these stories over and over. She always says, "Go after what you want, Sarah. Don't be afraid of trying something new or challenging. Don't be ashamed of failing."

14 위 글의 (A)used to와 쓰임이 같은 것은?　(4점)

① She soon became used to the work.

② I am used to making speeches in public.

③ She is used to having dinner alone.

④ The scale is used to weigh the crops.

⑤ He used to live in London.

*scale: (무게를 재는) 저울, 체중계

15 위 글의 ⓐ~ⓔ 중 어법상 바르지 못한 것은?　(3점)

① ⓐ　② ⓑ　③ ⓒ　④ ⓓ　⑤ ⓔ

16 위 글의 (B)의 우리말을 영어로 옮길 때 빈칸에 알맞은 말을 쓰시오.　(4점)

> • 그녀는 그 운동을 매우 좋아했음에 틀림없다.
>
> ──조건──
> 동사는 'love'를 사용할 것.

→ She _____ _____ _____ the sport very much.

17 위 글의 Helen 할머니에 관한 내용과 일치하지 <u>않는</u> 것은?　(3점)

① 그녀는 예전에 요리사였다.

② 그녀는 여전히 요리하는 것을 좋아한다.

③ 그녀는 필자에게 1940년대의 야구 경기에 관해 종종 이야기한다.

④ 그녀와 필자를 가장 강하게 연결하는 것은 요리이다.

⑤ 그녀는 항상 필자에게 실패하는 것을 부끄러워하지 말라고 말한다.

[18~19] 다음 글을 읽고 물음에 답하시오.

Tom showed me a picture, ⓐthat he took yesterday. Surprisingly, it was a selfie with Ken Kuller, ⓑwho is a famous detective story writer. According to Tom, he was reading Ken Kuller's book on a bench. The writer, ⓒwhich was taking a walk in the park, sat down on the bench. Tom was lucky to take a picture with him. Tom also showed me a book, ⓓwhere had Ken Kuller's autograph on it. How lucky Tom was!

18 위 글의 밑줄 친 ⓐ~ⓓ 중 어법상 <u>잘못된</u> 것은 몇 개인가?　(4점)

① 없음　② 1개　③ 2개　④ 3개　⑤ 4개

19 위 글의 내용과 일치하는 것은?　(3점)

① Ken Kuller is a photographer.

② Ken Kuller took a picture with Tom.

③ Tom was taking a walk in the park.

④ Tom met Ken Kuller in the library.

⑤ Tom has a picture with Ken Kuller's autograph.

[20~22] 다음 글을 읽고 물음에 답하시오.

About a week later, Helen found a letter in the mail box. (A) It was from people who worked for the girls' baseball league in Chicago. It read that she ⓐ_____ to the league's main tryouts in Chicago!
(B) As the days went by, however, Helen became worried that she might fail. (C) When the day of the main tryouts came, she was too afraid to go. My grandmother has spent the rest of her life regretting her decision. (D) When she watches a baseball game on TV, she often says, "I ⓑ _____ to Chicago. You know, all your dreams are worth chasing, even if you catch only a few of them. Never miss an opportunity." (E)

20 위 글의 (A)~(E) 중 주어진 문장이 들어가기에 가장 알맞은 곳은? (3점)

She also became worried about traveling alone to Chicago, which was far away from home.

① (A) ② (B) ③ (C) ④ (D) ⑤ (E)

21 위 글의 ⓐ, ⓑ에 들어갈 말로 알맞은 것은? (4점)

ⓐ	ⓑ
① has been invited	may have gone
② had invited	could have gone
③ has invited	might have gone
④ had been invited	should have gone
⑤ had been inviting	must have gone

22 위 글을 요약할 때, 빈칸에 들어갈 말로 어색한 것은? (4점)

Helen passed the local tryouts and received an ⓐ_____ to the league's main tryouts in Chicago. ⓑ_____, she did not go because of two reasons. All her life, she has regretted

her decision ⓒ_____ to the main tryouts. Helen tells her granddaughter to ⓓ_____ her dreams and ⓔ_____ an opportunity.

① ⓐ invitation ② ⓑ However
③ ⓒ not to go ④ ⓓ go after
⑤ ⓔ to miss

[23~24] 다음 글을 읽고 물음에 답하시오.

My grandmother Helen used to be a cook in a restaurant in a small town near South Bend, Indiana. ⓐ_____, but she still enjoys making delicious food, which I love so much. Food is one of the many things that connect us. What connects us most strongly, however, is baseball.
When I visit her on weekends, my grandmother tells me exciting stories about playing baseball back in the 1940s. ⓑ그녀는 스포츠를 무척 좋아했던 게 틀림이 없다. I listen to these stories over and over. She always says, "Go after what you want, Sarah. Don't be afraid of trying something new or challenging. Don't be ashamed of failing."

23 위 글의 내용으로 보아 빈칸 ⓐ에 가장 알맞은 말은? (3점)

① She is a great cook
② She is not afraid to cook
③ She doesn't like baseball anymore
④ She has been working in a restaurant
⑤ She does not work anymore as a cook

24 위 글의 밑줄 친 ⓑ의 우리말을 가장 바르게 영작한 것은? (3점)

① She is going to love the sport very much.
② She must have loved the sport very much.
③ She cannot have loved the sport very much.
④ She might have loved the sport very much.
⑤ She shouldn't have liked the sport very much.

[25~27] Read the following passage and answer the questions.

On the day of the tryouts, Helen played baseball for hours with many other young women. She was excited to go after her baseball dreams!

About a week later, Helen found a letter in the mailbox. ⓐIt was from people who were worked for the girls' baseball league in Chicago. ⓑIt reads that she had been invited to the league's main tryouts in Chicago!

As the days went by, however, Helen was worried about failure and traveling alone to Chicago, ⓒ which was far away from home. When the day of the main tryouts came, she was too afraid to go.

My grandmother ⓓhas spent the rest of her life regretted her decision. When she watches a baseball game on TV, she often says, "(A)_____ _____. You know, ⓔall your dreams are worth chase, even if you catch only a few of them. Follow your dream. (B)_____ _____."

25 Which of the following is grammatically correct? (3점)

① ⓐ   ② ⓑ   ③ ⓒ   ④ ⓓ   ⑤ ⓔ

26 Which of the following is contextually different from the passage above? (4점)

<Summary>
Helen passed the local tryouts and ⓐreceived an invitation to the league's main tryouts in Chicago. However, she did not go because ⓑ she was worried about travelling a long distance alone and ⓒafraid of succeeding in the tryouts. All her life, ⓓshe has regretted her decision not to go to the main tryouts. ⓔ Helen tells her granddaughter to go after her dreams.

① ⓐ   ② ⓑ   ③ ⓒ   ④ ⓓ   ⑤ ⓔ

27 위 글의 빈칸 (A), (B)에 알맞은 말을 각 문항의 주어진 어구를 이용하여 조건에 맞게 쓰시오. (6점)

조건
• 글의 흐름에 맞게 서술할 것.
• 각 문항의 주어진 단어를 변형 없이 모두 사용할 것.
• (A): 조동사를 사용하고 과거 사실에 대한 후회를 나타내는 표현을 쓸 것. (Chicago)
• (B): 명령문으로 쓸 것. (an opportunity, never)

(A): _____

(B): _____

28 다음 글의 괄호 (A)~(C)에 들어갈 알맞은 말로 바르게 짝지어진 것은? (4점)

In 1943, the All-American Girls Professional Baseball League (A)[had founded / was founded]. This league was created for baseball fans (B)[because of / because] many of America's young men (C)[was fought / were fighting] in World War II.

	(A)	(B)	(C)
①	had founded	because	was fought
②	was founded	because of	were fighting
③	had founded	because of	was fought
④	had founded	because of	were fighting
⑤	was founded	because	were fighting

MEMO

정답 및 해설

Lesson 5 (중간) 1회

01 ① 02 ③ 03 ③ 04 ④ 05 ② 06 ① 07 ⑤ 08 ③
09 ③ 10 ⑤ 11 ⑤ 12 ③
13 1. He asked me where I had lost my puppy.
  2. It was two years ago that Yujin got her cat.
14 bought → had bought 15 ③ 16 ② 17 ③ 18 ②
19 하늘과 바람과 별과 시라는 제목으로 시집을 출판하는 것
20 ③ 21 ① 22 ① 23 ④ 24 against 25 ⑤ 26 ④
27 ① 28 ③

01 책이 인쇄된 후에 출판이 된다. 출판된 책은 도서관이나 서점으로 보내진다. publish: 출판하다

02 모두 '동사 - 명사'의 관계인데 ③번은 '형용사 - 명사'의 관계이다.

03 뒤에서 'It's in the "New Arrivals" area. It's really popular among teens in Great Britain.'이라고 했으므로 ⓒ는 'Can you show me the book?'이 적절하다.

04 'His novel *Four Eyes* has been made into a movie.'라고 했고 His는 Ken Kuller를 가리키므로 ④번이 일치한다.

05 'look forward to+명사'는 '~을 고대하다'라는 의미이다. '콘서트를 무척 기대하고 계셔.'라는 의미의 말이 적절하다.

06 앞에서 'Can you recommend one for me?'라고 했으므로 추천해 주는 ①번이 적절하다.

07 '추천하다'는 'recommend'라고 쓴다.

08 B(Chan)가 'Oh, I've heard of him.'이라고 했으므로 ③번이 일치한다.

09 'Can you recommend ~?'라고 추천을 요청할 수 있다.

10 'It is[was] ~ that …' 강조 구문으로 동사를 강조할 수 없다.

11 말한 시점보다 잊은 시점이 앞서므로 과거완료로 나타내는 것이 적절하다.

12 ③번은 가주어이지만 <보기>와 나머지는 모두 'It ~ that …' 강조 용법으로 쓰였다.

13 1. 먼저 일어난 일을 과거완료로 써야 하며 과거완료는 'had+과거분사'의 형태이다. 2. 'It ~ that …' 강조 구문으로 강조되는 것이 two years ago이므로 which를 that으로 바꿔 써야 한다. (when으로 바꿔 쓸 수도 있음.)

14 우산을 잃어버린 시점보다 형이 사 준 것이 앞서는 시점이므로 '과거완료'로 써야 한다.

15 대학 때 동주가 갖고 싶었던 직업에 대해서는 알 수 없다.

16 (A) 앞의 내용과 상반되는 내용이 이어지므로 However (B) 이유를 나타내는 내용이 이어지므로 because (C) 앞의 내용과 상반되는 내용이 이어지므로 although가 적절하다.

17 'In 1945, Dong-ju and his cousin died in prison after harsh treatment by the police.'로 보아 ③번이 적절하다.

18 결심한 시점보다 아버님이 공부했던 시점이 앞서므로 '과거완료'로 써야 한다.

19 앞에 나온 그의 시 19편을 출판하고 싶어 한 것을 말한다.

20 과거의 일로 과거형으로 써야 하며 'sew'의 과거형은 'sewed'이다.

21 동주의 시의 제목은 알 수 없다.

22 과거의 일로 과거형으로 써야 하며 'hang'의 과거형은 'hung'이다.

23 'One was given to his close friend, Jeong Byeong-uk'이라고 했다.

24 'against'는 '~에 반대하여, ~에 거슬러, ~에 기대어서, ~을 배경으로 하여' 등의 뜻을 갖는다.

25 (A) wanted의 목적격보어로 to be (B) 이어지는 절이 완전하므로 where (C) 셋 중에서 두 번째를 가리키므로 another가 적절하다.

26 대학을 졸업하기 위해서가 아니라 졸업을 기념하여 시 19편을 출판하고 싶어 했다.

27 '다음 해 7월 10일에 그의 사촌은 독립운동에 가담했다는 이유로 일본 경찰에게 체포되었다. 나흘 뒤 동주 역시 같은 혐의로 체포되었다.'라고 했다.

28 제목이 붙여지는 것이므로 수동태 'was given'이 적절하다.

Lesson 5 (중간) 2회

01 ① 02 ① 03 ① 04 ④ 05 ③ 06 ⑤ 07 ② 08 ⑤
09 ③ 10 ④ 11 It was her wallet that Judy lost on the bus.
12 ② 13 ⑤ 14 ③
15 It was just a few months later that Korea achieved independence from Japan.
16 ⑤ 17 ⑤
18 (1) 초등학교에 다닐 때 그는 많은 시를 썼다.
  (2) 사촌 송몽규와 문학잡지를 만들었다.
  (3) 중학생일 때 당대의 유명한 시인인 백석의 시집을 빌려 와서 책 전체를 필사했다.
19 ⑤ 20 ① 21 ③ 22 ③ 23 ② 24 ④
25 ⓐ further ⓑ where ⓒ had studied
26 They took part in an independence movement. 27 ⑤
28 The last book was kept for himself.

01 ①번은 '시'라는 의미의 명사이지만 나머지는 모두 '사람'을 가리키는 명사이다.

02 harsh: unpleasant and causing pain to the body or senses

03 ⓐ는 B가 작성해야 할 '독후감'이지만 나머지는 모두 Ken Kuller의 책 '22nd Street'이다.

04 'I can't wait to see how I'll look in the pictures.'라고 했으므로 ④번이 적절하다. ① confused: 당황한; 혼란한 ② frightened: 겁먹은, 무서워하는 ③ concerned: 걱정[염려]하는 ④ pleased: 기쁜, 만족해하는 ⑤ disappointed: 실망한, 낙담한

05 (C) 다음에 'No. Can you recommend one for me?'라고 주어진 문장에 대한 답을 하고 있으므로 (C)가 적절하다.

06 'Maybe we can see the movie together.'라고 했다.

07 Ken Kuller의 책에 관한 대화에서 '최근에 독서 동아리에 가입했다.'라는 말은 어울리지 않는다.

08 Jiyeon이 'It'll come out next Thursday. I'm looking forward to seeing it!'이라고 말했다.

09 지호가 어디에서 사진을 찍는지는 알 수 없다.

10 ④번은 접속사로 진주어절을 이끌고 있지만 나머지는 'It ~ that ...' 강조 구문에 쓰인 that이다.

11 'It ~ that ...' 강조 구문에서 It was와 that 사이에 강조하려는 말을 쓰고 나머지를 that 다음에 쓴다.

12 ① leave → left ③ already began → had already begun ④ missed → had missed ⑤ opened → had opened

13 ① has ended → had ended ② That was → It is ③ already had finished → had already finished ④ had been 16 → was 16

14 결심한 시점보다 아버님이 공부했던 시점이 앞서므로 '과거완료'로 써야 한다.

15 'It ~ that ...' 강조 구문에서 It was와 that 사이에 강조하려는 'just a few months later'를 쓰고 나머지를 that 다음에 쓴다.

16 'The book was given the title the poet had thought of many years before.'라고 했다.

17 (A) a lot of가 있으므로 poems (B) poetry book: 시집 (C) poet: 시인

18 뒤에 나오는 세 가지를 쓰면 된다.

19 (A) wanted의 목적격보어로 to be (B) choose는 to부정사를 목적어로 받으므로 to study (C) wish는 to부정사를 목적어로 받으므로 to publish가 적절하다.

20 ⓐ는 시집의 제목이지만 나머지는 모두 그가 손으로 쓴 책(시집)을 가리킨다.

21 'wrote poetry where he expressed feelings about his hometown and lost country'라고 했다.

22 대한민국이 독립을 이룬 것이므로 '능동태'로 써야 한다.

23 'It was just a few months later that Korea achieved independence from Japan.'이라고 했다.

24 'It ~ that ...' 강조 구문에서 It is[was]와 that 사이에 강조하려는 부분을 쓴다.

25 ⓐ further: 더, 더 멀리 ⓑ the country를 선행사로 하는 관계부사 where ⓒ 결심한 시점보다 아버님이 공부했던 시점이 앞서므로 '과거완료'가 적절하다.

26 'his cousin was arrested by the Japanese police for taking part in an independence movement. Four days later, Dong-ju was also arrested on the same charges.'라고 했다.

27 ⓐ 앞에 나온 plays, poems, novels, or cartoons를 가리킨다. ⓑ people을 가리킨다.

28 책이 간직하는 것이 아니라 간직되는 것이므로 '수동태'로 써야 한다.

Lesson 6 (중간) 1회

01 ② **02** ① **03** ③ **04** ② **05** ④ **06** ②
07 If I were you, I would go to the community center. **08** ⑤
09 ② **10** ④ **11** ② **12** ① **13** ④ **14** ② **15** ⑤
16 it was easy for each cow to find enough grass　　**17** ③
18 ⑤ **19** ① **20** ③ **21** ①
22 If I were you, I would bring in one more cow and raise it on the commons.
23 ④ **24** If I, the commons **25** ⑤ **26** ②

01 lie: 눕다, 거짓말하다(자동사) lay: 눕히다, 두다, 놓다(타동사)

02 graze: to eat grass in a field

03 (D) 국수나 샌드위치 같은 걸 먹고 싶다고 하자 (A) 내가 너라면, 그런 것들을 먹지 않을 거라고 하자 (C) 이유를 묻고 (B) 뱃멀미하게 할 수 있기 때문이라고 답하는 순서이다.

04 'do you mind if I use your charger?'라는 질문에 'Of course not. Go right ahead.'라고 했다.

05 친구의 우산을 부러뜨렸다는 말에 '찬물을 마셔야 한다고 생각한다'는 말은 어울리지 않는다.

06 'All you need to do is help the teacher there.'라고 했다.

07 'The community center?'라고 반문하고 있으므로 가정법 과거를 사용하여 '내가 너라면, the community center에 가겠다.' 정도로 영작한다.

08 'If I were you, I'd …' 또는 'Why don't you …?'를 이용하여 충고할 수 있다.

09 배에 타고 있는 상황이므로 ②번이 적절하다.

10 'I'll have some ice cream.'이라고 했지만 좋아한다는 언급은 없다.

11 사람의 성격을 나타내는 형용사 'smart'와 'careless'가 있으므로 의미상의 주어로 'of+목적격'을 써야 한다.

12 ② passing → to pass ③ She → It ④ of → for, finding → find ⑤ to → for

13 ① not → 삭제 ② wasn't → isn't, couldn't → can't ③ lives → doesn't live, can → can't ⑤ wasn't → am not

14 'Luckily, some good grassland lay in the middle of the village.'라고 했지 '주민들은 마을 한 가운데에 목초지를 만들었다.'라는 언급은 없다.

15 ⓐ allow의 목적격보어로 to use ⓑ 불리는 것이므로 '수동태'가 적절하다.

16 가주어로 it을 쓰고, 의미상의 주어로 'for+목적격'을 쓴 후 'to부정사'로 진주어를 쓴다.

17 이어진 문장에서 'He brought another cow and let it graze on the commons.'라고 했으므로 ③번이 적절하다.

18 '소의 개체 수는 더 빨리 증가했다.'고 했으므로 (A)에는 disappear (B)에는 harder가 적절하다.

19 a number of: 많은, the number of: ~의 수

20 앞에서 '한 가구, 한 마리 소' 규칙으로 돌아가서 '목초지가 회복되었다'라고 했으므로 ③번이 적절하다.

21 앞에서 '어떤 사람들은 은밀하게 소를 한 마리 더 공유지에 데려왔고, 또 어떤 사람들은 아무에게도 말하지 않고 훨씬 많은 소를 목초지에 데려왔다.'라고 했으므로 'additional'이 적절하다.

22 가정법 과거(If+주어+동사의 과거형 ~, 주어+조동사의 과거형+동사원형 ….)를 이용하여 영작한다.

23 (다) 숲속의 작은 마을의 목초지에 대한 이야기가 시작되고 (가) But으로 (다)와 상반되는 말이 나오고 규칙을 깬 이야기가 이어지며 (나)에서 규칙을 깬 결과가 이어지는 것이 자연스럽다.

24 ⓐ는 '그가 들은 대로'라는 의미로 앞에서 그가 들은 'If I were you, I would bring in one more cow and raise it on the commons.'를 의미한다.

25 (A) '~인 데 반해'라는 의미의 '대조'를 나타내는 접속사 while (B) 주어로 쓰였으므로 The number of(~의 수), A number of: 많은 (C) 과거시제로 서술하고 있으므로 lie(놓여 있다)의 과거형 lay가 적절하다.

26 각 가정마다 소 한 마리씩을 키워야 하지만 그 규칙을 깨뜨린 결과 많은 소들이 죽었으므로 ②번이 적절하다.

Lesson 6 (중간)

01 ② **02** ⑤ **03** ①
04 If I were you, I'd go to the community center. **05** ③
06 Do you mind if I take the window seat?
07 Do you mind if I have an extra orange? **08** ⑤ **09** ①
10 ⑤ **11** If I had a car, I would travel to Busan. **12** ②
13 ② **14** ④
15 it is important for everyone to value the resources and use them fairly
16 ⑤ **17** ⑤ **18** ① **19** ④ **20** ① **21** ①
22 Because many cows could not find enough grass to eat.
23 ③ **24** ② **25** ④ **26** ② **27** ④

01 ① lied → laid ③ raised → risen ④ laid → lay ⑤ risen → raised

02 your hand와 about 200 cows라는 목적어가 있으므로 타동사 raise(~을 위로 올리다, ~을 기르다, ~을 사육하다)가 적절하다.

03 'Do you mind ~?'라고 물었으므로 'Not at all'은 '긍정'의 답이다. 이어서 'you can't'라고 하는 것은 어색하다.

04 if를 이용하여 가정법 과거(If+주어+동사의 과거형 ~, 주어+조동사의 과거형+동사원형 ….)로 쓴다.

05 소라가 '창가 자리에 앉아도 괜찮을까요?'라는 질문에 'No problem.'이라고 했다.

06 'Do you mind if ~?'로 허락을 구하는 말을 할 수 있다.

07 '다른 학생들을 위해 남겨 두어야 한다'라는 답으로 보아 하나 더 먹어도 되는지 묻는 말을 if와 mind를 이용하여 'Do you mind if ~?'로 쓴다.

08 'Do you mind ~?'라고 물었으므로 'Of course.'는 '부정'의 대답이다. 이어서 'Go right ahead.'라고 하는 것은 어색하다.

09 (A) 화제를 전환하고 있으므로 By the way (B) 부정문이므로 either가 적절하다.

10 가주어로 it을 쓰고, 의미상의 주어로 'for+목적격'을 쓴 후 'to부정사'로 진주어를 쓴다.

11 가정법 과거(If+주어+동사의 과거형 ~, 주어+조동사의 과거형+동사원형 ….)를 이용하여 대·소문자, 철자, 구두점 등에 유의하여 영작한다.

12 ① of → for ③ to me for → for me to ④ am → were[was] ⑤ working → work

13 ① I'll have → I had ③ has → had ④ 1776 → in 1776 ⑤ is → was

14 (D) 뒤에서 'Now it was able to support only one cow per family.'라고 주어진 문장의 결과가 이어지므로 (D)가 적절하다.

15 가주어로 it을 쓰고, 의미상의 주어로 'for+목적격'을 쓴 후 'to부

정사'로 진주어를 쓴다.

16 'However, no grass was left now because there were too many cows.'라고 했다.

17 ⓐ와 ⑤: ~인데 반해 ①, ②, ④: ~하는 동안 ③ 잠시

18 첫 번째 빈칸에는 가주어 it, 두 번째 빈칸에는 비인칭주어 it이 들어가야 한다.

19 'did the same'으로 보아 이어서 언급한 '소를 한 마리 이상 공유지에 데려온 것'이 적절하다.

20 "소의 '개체 수'는 더 빨리 증가했다"라고 하는 것이 적절하다.

21 ⓑ 소를 더 데려오기 시작함 ⓓ 풀이 사라지기 시작함 ⓒ 많은 소들이 죽음 ⓐ 목초지가 회복됨 ⓔ '한 가구, 한 마리 소' 규칙으로 돌아감

22 많은 소들은 먹을 충분한 풀을 찾을 수 없었기 때문에 죽었다.

23 사람의 성격을 나타내는 형용사가 쓰인 것이 아니므로 의미상의 주어를 'of+목적격'이 아닌 'for+목적격'으로 쓴다.

24 'By tradition, each family only had one cow'라고 했다.

25 마지막에 'Sharing myself with others makes me happy.'라고 했으므로 'share'가 적절하다.

26 마을의 인구 문제 해결책을 제시하고 있으므로 ②번이 적절하다.

27 손으로 의상을 제작하는 것이므로 ⓓ의 common은 uncommon으로 고치는 것이 적절하다.

Lesson 7 (기말) 【1회】

01 ④	02 ①	03 ③	04 ②	05 ②	06 ①	07 ⑤	08 ②
09 ③	10 ③	11 ③	12 ④	13 ④	14 ②	15 ③	16 ②
17 ④	18 ①	19 ②	20 ①	21 ④	22 ②	23 ④	24 ③
25 ③

26 (A) Arriving home
    (B) Not having enough time to talk to my friend

01 earthquake: a sudden shaking of Earth's surface

02 더위와 관련된 것으로 heatwaves(열파, 장기간의 혹서)가 적절하다.

03 (C) 다음에서 'Sure. What is it, Jiho?'라고 주어진 문장에 답하며 무엇인지 묻고 있으므로 (C)가 적절하다.

04 Jimin이가 'I'm going to buy some sandwiches at Choi's.'라고 했다.

05 고흐가 프랑스 사람이 아니냐는 질문에 맞다고 하고서 네덜란드 사람이라고 하는 것은 어색하다.

06 바깥에서 옷가지들을 들여와 주겠느냐는 아빠의 부탁에 (B) 그러겠다며 자전거는 어떻게 할지 묻자 (A) 아빠가 처리하겠다고 답하고 (D) 할머니께 전화해서 태풍에 관해 말씀드릴지 묻자 (C) 그러

07 'I'll keep that in mind.'는 '명심하겠다'라는 뜻으로 어떤 '당부'를 받았을 때 그에 대한 답으로 쓰는 말이므로 ⓔ가 적절하다.

08 'Can you do me a favor?'는 부탁하는 말로 'Can I ask you a favor?'로 바꿔 쓸 수 있다.

09 부탁 좀 들어주겠느냐는 말에 이어 ⓑ에서 알았다며 무엇인지 묻고 ⓓ에서 '오는 길에 초콜릿 아이스크림 좀 사다 줄 수 있는지' 묻자 ⓒ에서 문제없다고 답하고 ⓐ에서 고맙다며 헬멧을 꼭 쓰고, 이어폰은 안 된다고 하자 마지막 문장에서 걱정하지 말라는 응답으로 끝나는 순서가 자연스럽다.

10 접속사 없이 두 개의 동사가 나올 수 없으므로 watched를 watching으로 하여 분사구문으로 바꿔야 한다.

11 ① It being sick → Being sick ② listened → listening ④ Turned → Turning ⑤ Being → It being

12 ① deliver → be delivered ② cleaned → be cleaned ③ buyed → bought ⑤ are → be

13 ⓐ To work → Working
    ⓑ surprising something → something surprising
    ⓒ grows → grow[growing]
    ⓔ to grow → growing

14 접속사 없이 두 개의 동사가 나올 수 없으므로 Being을 이용하여 분사구문으로 쓴다.

15 분사구문의 부정은 not이나 never를 분사 앞에 붙인다. ⓒ의 'Knowing not'을 'Not knowing'으로 고쳐야 한다.

16 (A) 앞에서 한 말에 대해 자세한 내용을 덧붙일 때 쓰는 In fact (B) 결과를 이끄는 Therefore (C) According to: ~에 따르면

17 'Nobody knows for sure how many volcanoes there are in the world.'라고 했다.

18 'A typhoon warning has been issued.'라고 했다.

19 '화산이 지구에만 존재한다고 생각할지 모른다.'라는 주어진 문장에 이어 (B) However로 상반되는 내용이 이어지고 (A) In fact로 앞에서 한 말에 대해 자세한 내용을 덧붙이고 (C)의 Its가 (A)의 Olympus Mons를 가리키므로 마지막에 이어지는 순서가 적절하다.

20 ⓐ have ~ in common: 공통적으로 가지다
    ⓑ made from: ~로부터 만들어진
    ⓒ name after: ~을 따서 이름 짓다
    ⓓ above sea level: 해수면 위에

21 'Many more are underwater, and they are hard to locate.'라고 했다.

22 (A) 발견된 것이므로 discovered (B) 이어지는 내용으로 보아 해를 끼치는 것이므로 harm (C) 정상적인 기상 패턴을 깨트리는 것으로 disturbing이 적절하다.

23 '"Olympus Mons" on Mars is the largest known volcano in the solar system.'이라고 했다.

24 (A)는 화산이 인간에게 끼치는 피해에 대해 언급하고 있고 (B)는 화산이 인류에게 이로운 점에 대해 언급하고 있다.

25 ⓐ Be → Being ⓑ threaten → be threatened
ⓓ Looked → Looking ⓔ using → used

26 (A) 'When he arrived home'을 분사구문으로 고치면 'Arriving home'이다. (B) 'because he did not have enough time to talk to his friend'를 분사구문으로 고치면 'Not having enough time to talk to my friend'이다. 주어가 I이므로 그에 맞게 쓰는 것에 유의한다.

Lesson 7 (기말)

```
01 ⑤  02 ③  03 ③
04 make sure to stay home and keep listening to weather
   reports
05 ⑤  06 ④  07 Not knowing what to do    08 ②  09 ⑤
10 ④  11 ①  12 ②  13 ⑤  14 ①  15 ②  16 ①  17 ⑤
18 Because volcanoes are very powerful and dangerous,
19 ②  20 ④  21 ⑤
22 Volcanoes can be used to produce electricity    23 ④
24 ⑤  25 ⑤  26 ①  27 ⑤  28 ④
29 Indonesia lies on the Ring of Fire    30 ③
31 world weather
```

01 산불이 발생하여 주민들을 'protect'하는 것이 아니라 'threaten' 할지도 모른다고 하는 것이 적절하다.

02 threaten: to express an intention to harm

03 소라가 'What about your boxes?'라고 묻자 아빠가 'I'll take care of them after I finish the dishes.'라고 했다.

04 'make sure'를 써서 당부하는 말을 할 수 있다. 아빠가 'Please tell him to stay home and keep listening to weather reports.'라고 했으므로 그 두 가지를 make sure 다음에 to부정사를 이용하여 쓴다.

05 B가 'Can you buy chocolate ice cream for me on your way back?'라고 했다.

06 무엇인지 묻자 부탁을 했으므로 처음 질문은 부탁을 들어 줄 수 있는지 묻는 ⓓ가 적절하다.

07 분사구문의 부정은 not이나 never를 분사 앞에 붙이므로 'Because she'를 삭제한 후 'didn't know'를 'Not knowing'으로 쓴다.

08 ① doing → did ③ appearing and → appeared,

④ being → 삭제 ⑤ Doing not have → Not having

09 ① Watch → Watching ② solved → be solved
③ be seen → see ④ Knowing not → Not knowing

10 (D) 다음에 화산이 날씨에 끼치는 영향에 대해 언급하고 있으므로 '화산이 날씨에 영향을 끼친다'는 주어진 문장은 (D)에 들어가는 것이 적절하다.

11 문맥상 '이유'를 나타낸다고 보는 것이 적절하다.

12 마지막에 '그러나 화산이 인류에게 항상 나쁜 것만은 아니다.'라고 했으므로 '화산이 인간에게 주는 이점'이 이어질 것이다.

13 ⓐ Look → Looking ⓑ use → be used ⓒ from → into
ⓓ live → to live

14 '화산이 사람들에게 주는 좋은 것들'에 대해 언급하고 있다.

15 'Its volume is about 100 times greater than that of Mauna Loa, the largest volcano on Earth.'라고 했다.

16 ⓑ know → known ⓒ hurt → get hurt, lost → lose
ⓓ affects → effects ⓔ But → 삭제, are → is

17 마지막에 '그러나 화산이 인류에게 항상 나쁜 것만은 아니다.'라고 했으므로 '화산이 인간에게 가져다주는 좋은 영향들'이 이어질 것이다.

18 문맥상 '이유'에 해당하므로 접속사 Because를 쓰고 주어로는 volcanoes, 서술어로는 are를 쓴다.

19 하룻밤 사이에 화산이 생긴 것이므로 ②번이 적절하다.

20 화산이 주는 여러 가지 이점에 대해 기술하고 있다.

21 'What volcanoes do is not always bad for humans, however.'로 보아 '화산이 끼치는 해로움'에 대한 내용이 나왔을 것임을 유추할 수 있다.

22 주어진 단어만 배열하여 영작하면 'Volcanoes can be used to produce electricity'이다.

23 자동사이므로 'lies'가 되어야 한다.

24 'This ring is also the area where most of the world's earthquakes occur.'라고 했다.

25 'relieve'는 '경감하다, 안도케 하다' 등의 뜻이므로 'threaten' 정도로 고치는 것이 적절하다.

26 ⓐ는 'Jejudo, Sicily, and Hawaii'를 가리키지만 나머지는 모두 'volcanoes'를 가리킨다.

27 (A) 섬이 만들어지는 것이므로 수동태 are made (B) Many of the volcanoes가 주어이므로 are (C) 이어지는 관계사절이 완전하므로 관계부사 where가 적절하다.

28 ⓕ와 ④: 그럼에도 불구하고. ①, ②, ③, ⑤: 아직도, 여전히

29 'since the country is on the Ring of Fire.'라고 했으므로 is 대신에 lies를 쓴다.

30 작물이 파괴되는 것이므로 'may be destroyed'가 되어야 한다.

31 'Volcanoes can also have serious effects on world weather.'라고 했다.

01 ① **02** ③ **03** ③ **04** ⑤ **05** ③ **06** ② **07** ① **08** ②

09 ③ **10** ① **11** ② **12** should have checked **13** ⑤

14 ④ **15** ⑤ **16** ①

17 Because many of America's young men were fighting in World War II.

18 ② **19** ① **20** I should have gone to Chicago. **21** ①

22 ⑤ **23** ④ **24** ③ **25** ② **26** ③ **27** ① **28** ④ **29** ③

30 ⑤

01 순서대로 • ashamed • worth • imagination • chase가 들어간다.

02 mistaken: wrong in your opinion or judgement

03 'you want to be a cartoon artist?'라는 질문에 'I want to be a game designer.'라고 답했으므로 ③번이 적절하다.

04 게임 디자이너의 중요한 기량에 대한 언급은 했지만 만화가의 중요한 기량에 대한 언급은 없다.

05 'should have+p.p.'를 이용해 '후회'를 표현할 수 있다.

06 ⓑ 지원한 이유에 대해 답하자 ⓒ 만화가가 되고 싶은지 묻고 ⓐ 꼭 그렇지는 않다며 게임 디자이너가 되고 싶다고 답하자 ⓔ 게임 디자이너에게 필요한 기량이 무엇인지 묻고 ⓓ 상상력이라고 답하는 순서이다.

07 마나 애니메이션 고등학교에 지원한 이유 등을 묻고 답하고 있으므로 ①번이 적절하다.

08 버스에서 보니 반갑다는 말에 이어 (B) 맞다며 늦을 것 같다고 하자 (A) 그렇다며 학교 축제에 늦고 싶지 않다고 하고 (D) 자기도 그렇다며 알람을 맞춰야 했는데 깜빡했다고 하자 (C) 이해한다며 자기도 피곤할 때 그런 일이 많이 일어난다고 하는 순서이다.

09 내려서 뛰어가자는 제안에 '차들이 다시 움직이기 시작해. 내리지 말자.'라고 했으므로 ③번이 적절하다.

10 '네가 잘못 생각하는 거야.'라고 했으므로 ①번이 적절하다.

11 순서대로 • keep → be kept • for → of • 맞음 • close → closing • I reading → Reading • 맞음

12 'should have+p.p.'를 이용해 '후회'를 표현할 수 있다. regret: ~을 후회하다

13 ① that → who ② whom → which ③ whom → who ④ are → is

14 (D) 다음의 It이 가리키는 것이 주어진 문장의 a letter이므로 (D)가 적절하다.

15 현수막이 야구장에 '걸려 있는(hanging)' 것을 상상했다고 하는 것이 적절하다.

16 야구 팀에 들어가서 결승전까지 진출하고', '이름이 포함된 큰 현수막이 걸려 있는 것을 상상하는' 것으로 보아 ①번이 적절하다.

17 'This league was created for baseball fans because many of America's young men were fighting in World War II.'라고 했다.

18 ⓑ want → wants ⓒ that → which

19 '나는 Chicago에 갔어야 했어.'라는 것으로 보아 ①번이 적절하다.

20 'should have+p.p.'를 이용해 '후회'를 표현할 수 있다.

21 (A) food가 선행사이므로 which (B) connects와 is의 주어 역할을 할 수 있는 What (C) after와 want의 목적어 역할을 할 수 있는 what이 적절하다.

22 Helen이 Sarah에게 'Don't be afraid of trying something new or challenging.'이라고 충고한 것이다.

23 ⓑ being → to be ⓓ which → who

24 자신의 야구 꿈을 좇아가게 되었으므로 ③번이 적절하다.

25 언제 Helen이 고향을 위해 결승전에 진출했는지는 답할 수 없다.

26 그녀가 시카고에서 열리는 리그의 본심사에 초청되었다고 적혀 있었으므로 ③번이 적절하다.

27 'She thought that wearing a suit in the hot sun might have made him impatient.'라고 했다.

28 should have+p.p.: ~했어야 했는데 (하지 않았다)

29 being → be, to make → making, are → is

30 주어진 단어들을 배열하여 영작하면 'Don't be afraid of trying something new.'이다.

01 ③ **02** ⑤ **03** imagination is the most important skill

04 ① **05** ④ **06** ③ **07** ② **08** ③ **09** ① **10** ② **11** ④

12 ③ **13** (A) cannot have told (B) must have eaten **14** ⑤

15 ② **16** must have loved **17** ④ **18** ⑥ **19** ② **20** ③

21 ④ **22** ⑤ **23** ⑤ **24** ② **25** ③ **26** ③

27 (A) I should have gone to Chicago.
(B) Never miss an opportunity.

28 ⑤

01 ① chase: to run after
② opportunity: a chance to do something
④ regret: to feel sorry about something that you did in the past
⑤ stuck: difficult to move from one position to another

02 순서대로 • connect • mistaken • stuck • regret이다.

03 'What do you think is the most important skill a game designer needs?'라는 질문에 'I'd say imagination.'이라고

답했으므로 imagination is the most important skill이 적절
하다.

04 춥다는 말에 '따뜻한 스웨터를 입지 말았어야 했다'고 하는 것은
어색하다.

05 마나 애니메이션 고등학교에 지원한 이유 등을 묻고 답하고 있으므
로 interview(면접)가 적절하다.

06 'you want to be a cartoon artist?'라는 질문에 'I want to be
a game designer.'라고 답했으므로 ③번이 적절하다.

07 'What do you think is the most important skill a game
designer needs?'라는 질문에 'I'd say imagination.'이라고
답했으므로 'imagination'과 'game designer'가 적절하다.

08 'I should have set my alarm. I forgot.'이라고 후회하고 있으
므로 ③번이 적절하다.

09 내려서 뛰어가자는 제안에 '차들이 다시 움직이기 시작해. 내리지
말자.'라고 했으므로 ①번이 적절하다.

10 브라질 사람들이 스페인어를 한다고 하자 포르투갈어를 쓴다고 답
했으므로 ②번이 적절하다.

11 'should have+p.p.'를 이용해 '후회'를 표현할 수 있다. 먹을 것
과 관련해서 ④번이 적절하다.

12 ① left → leave ② has → have
④ I bought → which I bought ⑤ that → which

13 (A) 강한 부정적 추측은 'cannot have+p.p.'를 쓴다.
(B) 과거 사실에 대한 강한 추측은 'must have+p.p.'를 쓴다.

14 (A)와 ⑤: (과거에) ~이었다[했다] ①, ②, ③: 익숙해지다 ④ 사용
되다

15 계속적 용법이므로 'that'이 아니라 'which'를 써야 한다.

16 과거 사실에 대한 강한 추측은 'must have+p.p.'를 쓴다.

17 'What connects us most strongly, however, is baseball.'
이라고 했다.

18 ⓐ that → which ⓒ which → who ⓓ where → which

19 'Tom was lucky to take a picture with him.'이라고 했다.

20 (C) 앞의 걱정에 이어 주어진 문장의 also로 걱정이 이어지는 것
이 자연스러우므로 (C)가 적절하다.

21 ⓐ 초대받은 것으로 '수동태' ⓑ 후회하는 표현으로 'should
have gone'이 적절하다.

22 'Never miss an opportunity.'라고 했으므로 ⓔ에는 'not to
miss'가 적절하다.

23 'used to be a cook'이라고 했으므로 ⑤번이 적절하다.

24 과거 사실에 대한 강한 추측은 'must have+p.p.'를 쓴다.

25 ⓐ were → 삭제 ⓑ reads → read
ⓓ regretted → regretting ⓔ chase → chasing

26 'Helen was worried about failure'라고 했다.

27 (A) 'should have+p.p.'를 이용해 '후회'를 표현한다. (B) 명령

문의 부정은 'don't'나 'never'를 문장 앞에 붙인다.

28 (A) 전미여자프로야구리그가 창립된 것이므로 '수동태' (B) '절'
이 이어지고 있으므로 because (C) 미국의 청년 중 많은 수가 제2
차 세계대전에 참전 중이었으므로 were fighting이 적절하다.

MEMO

MEMO

MEMO